P9-BZC-655

D0015045

The Rorschach: A Comprehensive System, in two volumes
  by John E. Exner

Theory and Practice in Behavior Therapy
  by Aubrey J. Yates

Principles of Psychotherapy
  by Irving B. Weiner

Psychoactive Drugs and Social Judgment: Theory and Research
  edited by Kenneth Hammond and C. R. B. Joyce

Clinical Methods in Psychology
  edited by Irving B. Weiner

Human Resources for Troubled Children
  by Werner I. Halpern and Stanley Kissel

Hyperactivity
  by Dorothea M. Ross and Sheila A. Ross

Heroin Addiction: Theory, Research and Treatment
  by Jerome J. Platt and Christina Labate

Children's Rights and the Mental Health Profession
  edited by Gerald P. Koocher

The Role of the Father in Child Development
  edited by Michael E. Lamb

Handbook of Behavioral Assessment
  edited by Anthony R. Ciminero, Karen S. Calhoun, and Henry E. Adams

Counseling and Psychotherapy: A Behavioral Approach
  by E. Lakin Phillips

Dimensions of Personality
  edited by Harvey London and John E. Exner, Jr.

The Mental Health Industry: A Cultural Phenomenon
  by Peter A. Magaro, Robert Gripp, David McDowell, and Ivan W. Miller III

Nonverbal Communication: The State of the Art
  by Robert G. Harper, Arthur N. Wiens, and Joseph D. Matarazzo

Alcoholism and Treatment
  by David J. Armor, J. Michael Polich, and Harriet B. Stambul

A Biodevelopmental Approach to Clinical Child Psychology: Cognitive Controls and Cognitive Control Theory
  by Sebastiano Santostefano

Handbook of Infant Development
  edited by Joy D. Osofsky

Understanding the Rape Victim: A Synthesis of Research Findings
  by Sedelle Katz and Mary Ann Mazur

Childhood Pathology and Later Adjustment: The Question of Prediction
  by Loretta K. Cass and Carolyn B. Thomas

Intelligent Testing with the WISC-R
  by Alan S. Kaufman

Adaptation in Schizophrenia: The Theory of Segmental Set
  by David Shakow

Psychotherapy: An Eclectic Approach
  by Sol L. Garfield

Handbook of Minimal Brain Dysfunctions
  edited by Herbert E. Rie and Ellen D. Rie

Handbook of Behavioral Interventions: A Clinical Guide
  edited by Alan Goldstein and Edna B. Foa

Art Psychotherapy
  by Harriet Wadeson

Handbook of Adolescent Psychology
  edited by Joseph Adelson

Psychotherapy Supervision: Theory, Research and Practice
  edited by Allen K. Hess

Continued on back

IN TRIBUTE TO

Anna E. Mullet

BY

Goshen College

ex Libris
Good Library
Goshen College

MOTHERS, GRANDMOTHERS, AND DAUGHTERS

About the Authors

BERTRAM J. COHLER received his Ph.D. in Social Relations from Harvard University in 1967, and received post doctoral training in social science and mental health at Harvard. Currently William Rainey Harper associate Professor of Social Sciences at the University of Chicago, Dr. Cohler is also an advanced candidate at the Institute for Psychoanalysis in Chicago. Author of numerous papers and book chapters, he is also co-author, with Dr. Henry Grunebaum and others, of MENTALLY ILL MOTHERS AND THEIR CHILDREN. A fellow of the Society for Personality Assessment, the American Orthopsychiatric Association, and the Gerontological Society, Dr. Cohler is also a consultant to a number of community mental health centers.

Associate Clinical Professor of Psychiatry at Harvard Medical School, and a member of the Group for the Advancement of Psychiatry, HENRY U. GRUNEBAUM received his M.D. from Harvard Medical School in 1952 and has served on its faculty since 1960. A fellow of the American Psychiatric Association, Dr. Grunebaum has co-authored a number of books, including CONTEMPORARY MARRIAGE: STRUCTURE, DYNAMICS, AND THERAPY and serves on the board of editors of *Family Process*. He is also Director of Family Studies at the Cambridge Hospital, Cambridge, Massachusetts.

14470/

HQ
1064
.U5
C 523

MOTHERS, GRANDMOTHERS, AND DAUGHTERS

PERSONALITY AND CHILDCARE IN THREE-GENERATION FAMILIES

BERTRAM J. COHLER
The University of Chicago

HENRY U. GRUNEBAUM
The Cambridge Hospital
Harvard Medical School

With the Assistance of
DONNA MORAN ROBBINS

A WILEY-INTERSCIENCE PUBLICATION

JOHN WILEY & SONS, New York • Chichester • Brisbane • Toronto

BIP `86`

GOSHEN COLLEGE LIBRARY
GOSHEN, INDIANA

Copyright © 1981 by John Wiley & Sons, Inc.

All rights reserved. Published simultaneously in Canada.

Reproduction or translation of any part of this work
beyond that permitted by Sections 107 or 108 of the
1976 United States Copyright Act without the permission
of the copyright owner is unlawful. Requests for
permission or further information should be addressed to
the Permissions Department, John Wiley & Sons, Inc.

Library of Congress Cataloging in Publication Data:

Cohler, Bertram J
  Mothers, grandmothers, and daughters

  (Wiley series on personality processes)
  "A Wiley-Interscience publication."
  Includes bibliographical references and index.
    1. Aged women—United States—Family relation-
ships. 2. Middle aged women—United States—
Family relationships. 3. Mothers and daughters.
4. Conflict of generations. 5. Socialization.
I. Grunebaum, Henry, 1926-   joint author.
II. Robbins, Donna Moran. III. Title.
HQ1064.U5C523   306.8'7   80-17979
ISBN 0-471-05900-5

Printed in the United States of America

10 9 8 7 6 5 4 3 2 1

24.95

B+7

soc/a bowman

9/16/81

For
Anne and Judy,
who have helped us to understand
interdependence in adult life,
with love.

Series Preface

This series of books is addressed to behavioral scientists interested in the nature of human personality. Its scope should prove pertinent to personality theorists and researchers as well as to clinicians concerned with applying an understanding of personality processes to the amelioration of emotional difficulties in living. To this end, the series provides a scholarly integration of theoretical formulations, empirical data, and practical recommendations.

Six major aspects of studying and learning about human personality can be designated: personality theory, personality structure and dynamics, personality development, personality assessment, personality change, and personality adjustment. In exploring these aspects of personality, the books in the series discuss a number of distinct but related subject areas: the nature and implications of various theories of personality; personality characteristics that account for consistencies and variations in human behavior; the emergence of personality processes in children and adolescents; the use of interviewing and testing procedures to evaluate individual differences in personality; efforts to modify personality styles through psychotherapy, counseling, behavior, therapy, and other methods of influence; and patterns of abnormal personality functioning that impair individual competence.

IRVING B. WEINER

University of Denver
Denver, Colorado

Acknowledgments

Without the participation and involvement of the mothers, grandmothers, and their families, the study presented in this book would never have been possible. During the study, several of the mothers and grandmothers provided additional information in the forms of letters and diaries that added a special, personal quality to the narrative. The hospitality of the families taking part in this study made possible a depth of understanding that would otherwise have been absent. Naturally, to preserve the anonymity of each of these families, names and places all have been disguised.

A number of our colleagues and students provided detailed comments that were of great help in preparing this book. Merilyn Salomon, Scott Geyer, Judy Wilen, and Paula Gorlitz are among the many present and former students who commented on drafts of this book. Professor Fred Lighthall of the University of Chicago was helpful in suggesting revisions for several chapters. Professor Bernice Neugarten of the University of Chicago read all the chapters in draft form, and gave generously of her time in order to improve both the content of the study and also the manner in which it has been presented. Drs. Justin L. Weiss, Eliott G. Mishler, David H. Gallant, and Carol R. Hartman served as important sources of inspiration and help throughout our work. Wise colleagues and good friends, we are delighted to acknowledge their help. We wish to take note of Judy Grunebaum's important contributions to this book, in particular, her perceptive understanding of the high level of psychological integration required to perform the tasks of mothering in an effective way. Mrs. Donna Moran Robbins helped interview family members including the entire set of formal follow-up interviews. Her sensitive and informed interviews helped make this study possible. Appreciation is due our editor Mrs. Judith Sensibar, who worked with us to present an extensive body of research findings and professional experiences in nontechnical form without sacrificing accuracy or content. She further contributed many helpful suggestions regarding the dynamics of intergenerational relations among the families described in this book. The help of Judy Wilen and Betty Storz in reading galleys and page proofs is also gratefully acknowledged. Parts of this book have been used over the past few years in the course Self, Culture and Society in the College of the University of Chicago. Without the education provided by this course for both students and staff, the interdisciplinary spirit of inquiry reflected in this book would never have been possible. Discussions with Professors Ralph Nicholas, John MacAloon, Michael Schudson, Susanne Hoeber Rudolph, Donald Levine, and Peter Homans have been particularly helpful in clarifying a number of problems raised as a result of teaching the material in this book.

Parts of Chapter 2 originally appeared in the *Merrill-Palmer Quarterly*. We wish to thank the editor and publisher for permission to reprint this material. The study was assisted by grant MH-13946 from the National Institute of Mental Health and by grants from the Social Sciences Division Research Committee of the University of Chicago.

BERTRAM J. COHLER
HENRY U. GRUNEBAUM

Chicago
Boston
September 1980

Contents

Unless psychical processes were continued from one generation to another, if each generation were obliged to acquire its attitude to life anew, there would be no progress in this field and next to no development. This gives rise to two further questions: How much can we attribute to psychical continuity in the sequences of generations? and what are the ways and means employed by one generation in order to hand on its mental states to the next one?

SIGMUND FREUD, Totem and Taboo

MOTHERS, GRANDMOTHERS,
AND DAUGHTERS

Introduction

During the past two decades, there has been a dramatic shift in understanding the place of the urban family within contemporary society. Rather than seeing the family as vulnerable, its functions usurped by other social institutions, there has been increased awareness of the continuing significance of the multigeneration family for socialization of its members across the life cycle. There have been several quantitative studies demonstrating the extent of contact and support of family members across generations, but there have been few studies of the modified extended family that focus on the psychological significance of such contact and support for the continued adult development of these family members. Among these adult relationships, that between the mother of young children and her own mother is perhaps the most complex. This book is an effort toward understanding this relationship; it also provides a study of this relationship as it affects the mother's care of her own children. On the basis of a quantitative study of intergenerational relations, also included in this book, four multigeneration Italian American families were selected for more intensive study.

The quantitative study made it possible to select women living with their mothers or apart from them and with more or less adaptive attitudes regarding a dimension of socialization that concerns a mother's capacity to see her child as a separate or individuated person. The four mothers and grandmothers selected for this more intensive study represented each of the four cells of this design: living apart-adaptive attitudes regarding closeness, living apart-maladaptive attitudes regarding closeness, living together-adaptive attitudes regarding closeness, living together-maladaptive attitudes regarding closeness.

Once the mothers were selected for study, and both they and their own mothers had agreed to participate, members of each generation were interviewed over a number of weeks and were given several paper-and-pencil and semistructured or "projective" techniques. In several of the families, grandfathers and fathers were also interviewed, and parents and children were observed together. This book reports on the findings from this naturalistic study of the three generations in these four families and was begun with the intent of showing that it is useful to investigate human behavior in ways which preserve the complex quality of this behavior, while simultaneously permitting cross-case comparisons and the development of generalizations on the basis of observed findings. In our investigation, we have relied on concepts and methods from several related disciplines within the behavioral sciences, including psychology, sociology, anthropology, and psychoanalysis, in order to better understand the meaning of complex behavior as it is located in a particular time and place.

1

This approach to the study of intergenerational relations is unique in behavioral science investigation. The literature thus far consists of a few pioneering studies of the family as a unit (best exemplified by Hess and Handel's (1959) study of *Family Worlds*) and of multigenerational families studied retrospectively (Parker's 1972 volume *A Mingled Yarn*). This book is among the first to combine intergenerational with cross-case comparisons, providing detailed studies of members of more than one generation within the family.

CONTRASTING APPROACHES TO THE STUDY OF PERSONALITY

Using a case-study approach, we have taken a controversial position within the behavioral sciences regarding the extent to which the case study can provide us with valid information regarding human behavior. In part, this controversy stems from the abuse of the case-study method in journal articles that substitute the "clinical" vignette for discussion based on a more extensive presentation of findings regarding observed consistencies in the behavior of persons said to share a common psychiatric syndrome. However, the greater part of this controversy arises from what we believe to be a misunderstanding of what constitutes a "fact" in the study of personality.

There was little systematic study of personality processes until just prior to World War II, when Allport (1937) published his textbook presenting a unified point of view on personality, supported by available findings from the application of a natural science approach, using methods of generalization and inference, to the study of observed consistencies among persons. These consistencies were believed to be linked by particular structures or processes within the person that could be observed or measured and, as a result, demonstrated to exist.

In the decades following World War II, the empirical study of personality emerged as a major area of psychological investigation. Influenced both by psychoanalytic and learning theory formulations and, more recently, by existential and social psychological formulations, a large literature has developed in which the attempt is to demonstrate statistical relationships between observed responses said to measure a construct derived from theories of personality and either other test responses or actual behavior. Using the logic of construct validity (Cronbach and Meehl, 1955), both the test and the theory are said to be validated if the predicted relationship is found. This leads to a "bootstraps" psychology of personality based on the "logic of explanation" (Sherwood, 1969), generalizing from findings to theory.

Such systematic empirical investigation appears to have added relatively little to understanding personality processes across the life cycle in the context of differing life circumstances (Neugarten, 1977; Fiske, 1978). Measures of the relationship between test behavior and either other test responses or actual behavior have consistently been reported to account for about 10% of the common variance. Even in those instances where such findings have been demonstrated to be nonrandom or significant at an accepted probability level, these statistically significant relationships provide little information about the manner in which persons interpret their experiences. More recently, in an attempt to improve the magnitude of such relationships between test responses and both other tests and actions, multivariate procedures have been used that move beyond previous univariate statistical analyses. Such procedures as factor analysis and multiple regression have added little to increased understanding of complex personality processes.[1]

Such premature application of quantitative procedures has led an increasing number of behavioral scientists to become disillusioned with our progress in understanding human behavior. As social scientists become ever more abstracted from the data and preoccupied with problems of method, they tend to lose sight of the goal of their efforts: that of understanding human behavior. This has led to the kind of scientific fragmentation that Swift described in *Gulliver's Travels*. In the mythical kingdom of Laputa, the inhabitants, who prided themselves on their scientific learning, were "so abstracted and involved in speculation" that they were incapable of making a wearable suit of clothes or a habitable dwelling. Preoccupation with method led these mythical scientists to lose sight of the essential purpose of science: to provide reasonable and workable methods for dealing with real life events.

As a result of the limits of the empirical study of personality in realizing its initial promise, there have been several recent stinging critiques of this area of study. Mischel (1973, 1977), relying on Rotter's (1954) formulation of social learning, has suggested that environmental contingencies are the major determinant of actions: consistency is a function primarily of the nature of particular contingencies of reinforcement rather than of any enduring motivational dispositions. Fiske (1974, 1978) has suggested that the very ratings made of personality dispositions are greatly influenced by intraobserver qualities; little empirical generalization regarding underlying personality dispositions is possible when such observer characteristics account for such a significant amount of the variance. Fiske notes, in addition, that concept and measure have been shown to have a very tenuous relationship in the study of personality and suggests that this area of psychology may be in a prescientific stage. Further, he believes that we may have approached the limits of this study of personality as pursued by presently accepted methods. Shweder (1975), basing his position on the importance of cultural determinants of thought, has shown that cultural constructions of personality account for much of what has been assumed to be "individual differences." Implicitly recognizing both Mischel's stress on the importance of the situation or context as a determinant of action and Fiske's emphasis on the characteristics of the observer as important determinants of codes and scores in the psychology of personality,

[1]It has been assumed that many of the problems involved in generalizability in the study of personality are a result of grouping together persons who are not sufficiently alike on other factors beside the one being studied, leading to large "within group" variation. The statistical study of the single case (Allport, 1962; Davidson and Costello, 1969) has been viewed as a means of preserving natural science modes of inquiry, while avoiding the problems involved in studies of groups of persons. Such statistical studies of the single case still fail to consider the assumption that natural science modes of inquiry may not be most appropriate for the study of lives and that some new approach may be required.

Shweder's critique of personality research points to the importance of understanding the cultural context in which the observer works and questions the utility of present modes for understanding individual differences.

Such recent critiques are consistent with earlier comments by philosophers of science such as Von Mises (1951), who observed that the search for laws of personality may be a valuable goal of our inquiry in the social sciences, but that there is insufficient understanding of the person to realize the degree of generalizability which investigators working in this area have sought. Nagel (1961), reviewing assumptions involved in the study of the person, notes that much of what is supposed to represent "laws" of human behavior, based on empirical evidence, is seriously limited by the impact of such factors as cultural and historical variation among the groups being studied.

Particularly important, in the empirical approach to the study of personality using a logic of explanation, has been the assumption of "reliability" of observation in which holistic events are transformed into units that can be demonstrated to have been tabulated in the same way by more than one observer. According to Hempel (1960), such operationism serves to render a theory more amenable to empirical test, providing a means for connecting observation and theory. However, operationism supposes the capacity for studying multiple dependent facts that are not yet available in the study of lives.

It is believed that operationism forces private concepts to become public. Reliability, as understood in the behavioral sciences, is evidence of the extent to which a particular concept is public or teachable. The transformation process in which naturalistic events become quantified scores permits not only the empirical test of the theory, but also evidence regarding the degree to which others are able to make this translation from theory to observation, to construct, to data, and to replicate the results of any particular study. Typically, this process is achieved through the development of a "coding manual" that makes public the implicit assumptions about the theory. Such a manual is also supposed to contain information regarding the "raw" observations that are claimed to be theoretically relevant.

If the process of operationism is viewed in terms of this issue of specifying the means by which inferences are made from theory to data, then it can be seen that the larger problem of inference is not one that is limited to the behavioral sciences, but, as Holt (1961) has shown, is a problem that is intrinsic in all scholarly work where the internal consistency of theory and data must always be demonstrated. Nagel (1961) has made essentially the same point when discussing the logical foundations of historical inquiry. Internal consistency or coherence becomes the major criterion for determination of the validity of an interpretation of data; that interpretation is judged most successful which provides the most complete account and which is most capable of integrating additional data into the formulation. (In the present instance, the reader is provided with interview and projective test data, as a way of both judging the adequacy of the interpretations provided and permitting the reader to form some independent judgments concerning what family members are like as persons.)

Rather than relying solely on inference from a set of data-points to a hypothesized underlying construct, where the very validity of such constructs in the study of personality has been called into question by critics of this field, the scope of inquiry might be enlarged to include both the study of such inferences or "facts," as well as the interpretations that link these facts into a larger narrative, so that internal consistency itself becomes a part of the "fact." This historical approach (Collingwood, 1946; Gardiner, 1959) has recently been applied to the discipline of psychoanalysis (Novey, 1968; McGuire, 1971), as well as to dynamic personality research itself (Wyatt, 1962, 1963; Wyatt and Wilcox, 1959), and is a step toward meeting the criticisms of both Shweder and Fiske, as well as consistent with the emphasis placed by Holt on internal consistency as a criterion of analysis in the study of personality.

This emphasis on internal consistency as the criterion for validity in judging the adequacy of the narrative has been referred to by Sherwood (1969) as the "logic of narrative," as contrasted with the "logic of explanation," which involves generalization from observation to inference according to a natural science mode of inquiry. Sherwood suggests that quite often we confuse description with explanation, since these terms are understood in the natural sciences. It is particularly in the realm of case history reports that this confusion most often arises. As Sherwood observes:

Psychoanalytic explanations begin with an individual case history, and the real job of explanation occurs through ordering the mass of biographical material and attempting to organize it into a coherent whole. This is accomplished by constructing some sort of narrative account containing as much of the material as possible. (p. 231)

The adequacy of this narrative is assessed in terms of its internal consistency; the internal consistency is assessed both in terms of generally accepted theoretical propositions within psychoanalysis and in terms of the general criteria in our culture for a successful narrative. That is, to be adequate, the interpretation must be consistent, coherent, and comprehensive (Wyatt and Wilcox, 1959; Holt, 1961; Wyatt, 1962, 1963; Sherwood, 1969; Ricoeur, 1970, 1977).

This narrative approach to the study of lives is appropriate precisely because of the fact that, as Ricoeur (1977) has noted, the concept of a coherent narrative is a central tenet of Western thought, as represented in the "story" or epic. Since the time of the classical poem cycles, we have expected that texts or stories must have some narrative intelligibility which the competent reader can interpret or understand. This criterion applies equally to stories, historical interpretations, and scientific treatises. As Ricoeur observes:

Narrative intelligibility implies something more than the subject accountability of one's own life-story. It comes to terms with the general condition of acceptability that we apply when we read any story, be it historical or fictional . . . a story has to be "followable" and, in this sense, "self-explanatory." (p. 869)

Successive revisions are sometimes required in order that all the elements of the test may finally be integrated into an overall interpretation which will make greatest "sense" of the work as a whole.

The use of case-study or life-history material, when presented in detail and judged according to the logic of narrative rather than that of explanation, may provide a workable and valuable addition to empirical methods. However, precisely because social context is important in the study of lives, some normative information is helpful in understanding actions of particular persons.

The method of dimensional analysis used in this book permits selection of families on other than an anecdotal basis and preserves important elements of the context in which relations between generations are studied, combining the empirical and narrative approaches. Both of the dimensions used in the selection of families for study—joint versus separate residence and scores on a measure of the mother's attitudes toward attainment of appropriate closeness with the child—assume this normative context, while preserving that uniqueness of the individual which is possible only in the study of the single case.

OUTLINE OF THE PRESENT BOOK

The case studies presented in this book represent an effort at understanding the modified extended Italian American family in contemporary urban American society. These studies represent contemporary social history and yet speak to our own time in describing how mothers and their own mothers participate in a continuing relationship. However, this study also considers the issue of intergenerational continuity more broadly understood and provides a contribution to our understanding of socialization across several generations. The first chapter places the subject of our study, that of intergenerational continuity, in the context of other work in the study of socialization across the life cycle and describes the major psychological and sociocultural concepts used in the study of the four families discussed in this book.

Chapter 2 provides the background for this study of intergenerational continuity and reviews the findings of our earlier quantitative investigation. This second chapter also describes the means by which the four families were selected for intensive study, the cultural background of the families, and the methods used in collecting comparable data on them. We believe that an understanding of the means by which these four families were chosen is important in placing the case studies in the context of other work in the area of intergenerational relations.

Chapters 3 through 6 describe the individual families and characterize in depth the personality of mother and grandmother, and the mother's and grandmother's attitudes toward childcare, and the extent and quality of present contact between the two generations. In the case of each chapter, there is first a description of the physical environment in which the grandmother lives, followed by a description of her personality and life history and her retrospective account of her experiences in rearing her daughter. This account is followed by a description of the physical environment in which the daughter lives (in those families where mother and grandmother live apart), followed by a description of the mother's personality and life history. Maternal personality is related to childrearing attitudes and practices, and the mother's childcare practices are discussed in terms of her typical daily round. Finally, there is a discussion of the mother's relationship with her mother, including the nature and extent of contacts between the two generations and the reactions of both mother and grandmother to these contacts.

Having described and presented data on each family, we then take this data from the four families and, in Chapter 7, integrate these case studies around several conceptual issues we believe to underline family structure and process. This conceptual framework permits cross-case comparison and leads to several additional questions to be investigated in subsequent research. Chapter 8 considers these four families in terms of their common ethnic heritage. A summary of the cultural background of Italian American families in Italy and the United States is followed by a discussion of these four families in terms of their particular ethnic heritage. Chapter 9 summarizes the findings from this study.

SOME CHARACTERISTICS OF THIS STUDY

At the outset, it is important to alert the reader to some of the problems presented by this study. First, the present report is based on the study of only four families, a small number of such families on the basis of which to make any conclusions about the relationship between adult women, mothers of young children, and their own mothers. Were the literature replete with such case studies, a report based on the intensive study of a few families over time would be superfluous, but this is not the case. Much can be learned from the study of a few families selected on the basis of a theoretically defined criteria in an area where there is so little information.

The women whose lives are described in this study may not be completely representative of adult women in this society, for each of the mothers and grandmothers volunteered for the study and was willing to spend countless hours with the investigators talking about her life. In most of the families, husbands and children also were willing to be interviewed. These family members cared enough about each other to talk with each other and to participate together in the study. These family members were articulate about their lives—and also very self-reflective.

The lives of these family members have been studied from the perspective of contemporary social science theory and research as informed by psychoanalysis. It should be recognized at the outset that this framework for study is alien to the ways in which these persons understand their own lives, particularly among the members of the grandparental generation, nearly all of whom are from a culture very different from that which has produced the concepts and methods of social science investigation. There is a danger that the framework used for studying lives distorts these lives in ways which make them less real and less active. In particular, social science investigation is better able to document sources of psychopathology than of resilience and competence. Sources of personal distress are more clearly represented than sources of strength and personal courage. Most troublesome of all is how adult relationships are portrayed. Most reports on adult lives are based on the assumption that it is particularly good in this culture to be "independent," "autonomous," and "differentiated" from others. Most psychological terms for describing relationships are based on this implicit value judgment. Such a value on independence in adult relationships represented in contemporary formulations of adult lives is in marked contrast with the interdependent manner in which adults actually get along with each other as described in Chapter 1. Interdependence refers to the fact of high rates of interaction across generations and accompanying exchanges of resources and services that take place across the generations in American society. This interdependence contributes to the maintenance of the multigeneration family as a "unity of interacting personalities" (Burgess, 1926). In contrast, "dependence" refers to a psychological characteristic in which, particularly among women during the first half of the life cycle, there is a psychological representation of one's own mother as a source of soothing and support. This psychological representation is the result of a particular mode of socialization from earliest childhood in which, while little boys are encouraged to become instrumental and independent, little girls are encouraged to maintain an undifferentiated tie with their mothers. This distinction between the concepts of dependence and interdependence within the family suggests that it is necessary to rethink the value placed on independence and autonomy in adult relationships, both within social science investigation and clinical work with adults and their families.

Psychological studies inevitably focus attention on problems and failures in development; even the language used to describe adults suffers from this bias. There is an implicit belief that adults should be other than they inevitably are and that they should be "mature" in ways they are not. Over the six years that these families have participated in this study, the investigators have come to appreciate the strengths these persons have shown in times of adversity and stress and the extent to which family members genuinely care for each other. The language of social science is all too restrictive in being able to characterize these strengths; a study such as this is lacking in some critical areas: it comes too much from the head and too little from the heart.

Finally, it should be noted that this is a study carried out by two men, although with the help of several informal consultants, many of them women, who have been able to correct some initial sources of bias. A study of this sort conducted by others, particularly women, might have reached different conclusions, perhaps with greater wisdom and compassion. It is important that men and women in this society come to understand each other better, and the present study is one small effort in that regard.

CHAPTER 1

Psychosocial Perspectives on Intergenerational Relations

For social life to continue for more than one generation, it is essential that society not only provide for the maintenance of its members, but also provide for the continuity of social life across generations (Simmel, 1898; Mannheim, 1952). This continuity is made possible as a result of socialization, the process by which persons are taught, and by which they learn, aspects of social structure and culture, including values and norms, as well as enduring personality and cognitive dispositions. Socialization takes place within and across generations and is typically reciprocal, involving both "forward" socialization from agent (parent) to novice (offspring) and "reverse" socialization from novice to agent (Hagestad, 1974; Lerner and Spanier, 1978b). Adult offspring help to socialize their parents into new conceptions of the parental role appropriate for the offspring's new status as adults and may also help socialize their parents into such new adult roles as that of grandparent (Rosow, 1967). Such forward and reverse socialization affects both individual family members and also the family as an intergenerational unit (Mortimer and Simmons, 1978).

SOCIALIZATION AND INTERGENERATIONAL CONTINUITY

From the perspective of the life cycle, the earliest and most significant socialization takes place within the context of the nuclear family (Sewell, 1963; Whiting et al., 1963; Brim, 1966). Maternal care of the infant represents the first opportunity for transmitting culture to the next generation. As a result of subtle variations in attachment and nurturance, parental control of motility and both bowel and bladder, culturally defined restrictions on the availability of family members as sexual partners, and the active teaching of survival skills, young chidren are provided with rather complete mental guides to their culture (Whiting and Child, 1953). These guides include preferred modes of relating to others, acceptable means for attaining gratification of basic needs, schemata for conceiving of self and others, and structures for processing cognitions. Such early childhood socialization is possible largely as a result of young children's dependence on their parents, who can withhold their love and support when the children fail to conform to their socialization (Sears, Maccoby, and Levin, 1957). This mode of socializa-

9

tion has been termed "effect dependency" by Jones and Gerard (1967), for the children's ties to the caretakers motivate performance in accordance with a specified standard by using the children's need for love or care as a resource that can be withheld until the desirable behavior is elicited.

Effect dependency may be differentiated from "information dependency" or reliance on others for information about the world about one. This second mode of socialization may be observed both in forward socialization of the younger generation across the life cycle, as well as in reverse socialization. Writing from a psychoanalytic perspective, Parens and Saul (1971) draw a similar distinction between "libidinal," "effect," or "affectional" dependence and "ego-developmental" or "informational" dependence. While informational or ego-developmental dependence contributes to the child's developing mastery of reality, libidinal or affective dependence represents the child's need for emotional support, protection, and care.

As the child moves out beyond the family into school and other community settings, the diffuse pattern of attachment and solidarity maintained between parent and child since infancy is continued not only in the enduring relationship between parent and child, but also in such other roles as that of student and, later, worker. Further, the fusion between informational and affectional dependence continues, both in relation to parents and in other settings beyond the family. Throughout the life cycle, parents remain an important source of forward socialization into such new roles as spouse and parent. The parents' role as socialization agents into adulthood is reinforced by the continued provision of financial assistance and emotional support for their adult offspring (Sussman, 1953, 1959, 1965; Hill 1970). Later, the same issue of dependency is apparent in the reliance of the younger generation on the older during such successive phases of the family life cycle as the advent of parenthood and the launching of the third generation into adolescence and young adulthood.

There is a paradox in contemporary society where, on the one hand, it is believed that adults will strive to become both psychologically and economically autonomous and self-reliant, while, on the other, findings from systematic investigations of family life show that dependence across the generations is the typical mode of intergenerational relations, including the interdependence of the very old parents on their middle-aged offspring (Shanas and Streib, 1965).

In an early statement of this problem of dependency, S. Freud (1905a) observed:

One of the most significant, but also one of the most painful, physical achievements of the pubertal period [is] detachment from parental authority, a process that alone makes possible the opposition, which is so important for the progress of civilization, between the new generation and the old. At every stage in the course of development through which all human beings ought by rights to pass, a certain number are held back; so there are some who have never gotten over their parents' authority and have withdrawn their affection from them very incompletely or not at all. (p. 227)

However, observation of the course of human development across adulthood shows that conflict regarding dependency is characteristic of most adults to such an extent that it may be questioned whether this conflict is not an essential fact of human experience, never resolved, and managed in a more or less adaptive manner at particular critical points in the life cycle, depending on the nature of the transition event itself, the nature and extent of stressful, eruptive life events, and the nature of strains perceived in such major life roles as those of parent, spouse, and worker.

Writing about attachment from a life-span perspective, Bowlby (1969) notes the great degree of individual variation that exists in maintaining such ties to others; he also notes that for most adults, attachments based on anaclitic or dependent ties continue to exist in adulthood and old age, with such ties extended even to institutions such as the college or university, generally referred to as the "alma mater," which in Latin may be translated as fostering or caring mother. The paradox is that such dependency is readily acknowledged to exist; yet our model of life-span development is one that emphasizes a developmental line from dependency to self-reliance (A. Freud, 1965; Lichtenberg, 1975).

The concept of dependency is one frequently used in the socialization literature, generally with a critical overtone when referring to adult development. For example, in discussing intergenerational relations among adults, Goldfarb (1965) distinguishes between what he terms "type-one socialization," which "produces" rationally nondependent adults able to distinguish between the need for information contributing to further ego development and emotional refueling such as is characteristic of affectional dependence, and "type-two socialization," which produces adults who are dependent and who maintain ambivalent, symbiotic relationships with others, even if masked by a showy pseudoindependence.

In commenting on this dependent personality type Goldfarb observes:

> The dependently socialized person searches for aid and, even more obviously, for emotional support, for praise, and for external proofs of worth and ability. He appreciates praise for effort as much as praise for achievement. At times he is even more interested in effort than achievement, because actual achievement, although praised and approved, might threaten his dependent status . . . because the behavior of a dependent person is contingent upon another's supportive personal attributes, it can be recognized that the dependent person has made of what was once—in childhood—a means to the end of achieving social and personal value, an end in itself. (1965, p. 26)

According to Goldfarb, the dependent person, the product of type-two socialization, spends much of his or her time and effort searching for emotional refueling as a response to feelings of helplessness. The need for affectional dependence becomes a central motive in the person's life, leading to the use of information dependence as a way of initiating and perpetuating dependency relationships that were appropriate during childhood, but are considered to be inappropriate among adults in our culture. In commenting on this extensive reliance in our society on affectional dependence among adults, Goldfarb makes this conclusion:

> The belief that the majority of persons is independent and self-reliant is probably unwarranted. The preponderance of our population appears to be socialized as dependent. This socialization is economical, it can be quick, and it affords a maximum of personal suggestibility and malleability. . . . The preponderant number of families in our society appear to

come into existence and to be held together on the basis of relatively nonaffectionate, that is to say, dominance-submission governed dependent relationships. . . . Families with dependent relationships tend to perpetuate themselves in this manner, and families with non-dependent relationships are prone to develop dependent personalities in their children under economic stress. (pp. 38, 43)

If most adults in our society are dependent, then such dependence may be normative, and we must reconsider the entire question of the significance for individual adjustment of this continuing affectional dependence across the life cycle, including the development of affectional dependence from earliest childhood.[1]

In the past decade, the work of Mahler and her colleagues has emerged as the most representative formulation of the development of that psychological disposition which results in the dependency seen among adults (Mahler and La Perriere, 1965; Mahler, 1972a, 1972b; Mahler, Pine, and Bergman, 1975; Panel, 1972b, 1972c). A child analyst with impressive clinical acumen, Mahler's first work concerned the syndrome of the symbiotic psychosis, which was observed occasionally in young children. Accordingly, the young child is unable to differentiate between self and other, shows a marked arrest in intellectual and emotional development and a gross deficiency in reality testing, and uses little speech beyond the echolalic repetition of questions posed by others. Believed to be a step forward in development beyond the autistic psychosis described by Kanner (1944), Bettelheim (1967), and others, it is a psychotic disorder of childhood with a particularly malignant prognosis.

Beginning with the description of this syndrome, Mahler and her colleagues explored its antecedents, focusing particularly on the contribution of the very early relationship between mother and child (Mahler, 1968). As a result of this earlier research, Mahler and her colleagues subsequently studied the development of the mother-infant relationship in well families more intensively and eventually formulated a process in which the baby appeared to "hatch" out of a symbiotic stage and to gain increased psychic autonomy as a result of the ability to create a representation of self as psychologically separate from mother.

According to the results of careful longitudinal observation, based on groups of both normal and psychotic young children and their mothers, it would appear that the critical period for the development of a sense of separateness is from about 5 to 30 months (after the resolution of the first or primary narcissism phase), with a series of subphases delineated in this phase of the development of separation-

[1]This Western pattern is in striking contrast to traditional Japanese society where, as several observers have reported, it is expected that adults will permit themselves to become dependent on others and permit others to become dependent on them (Vogel and Vogel, 1961; Doi, 1962, 1963, 1967; Caudill and Frost, 1974). In the Japanese family, closeness between family members is emphasized to such an extent that members of several generations may sleep together in one common room, even where alternative arrangements are possible (Caudill and Plath, 1969). However, the expression of the wish to remain dependent on another causes such discomfort in American families that, as Boszormenyi-Nagy and Spark (1973) observe, helping family members to accept their dependency wishes and encouraging them to acknowledge and strengthen nascent patterns of interdependence within the family is perhaps the central issue in family therapy.

individuation. The first or differentiation subphase (about 5 to 9 months) is viewed as a hatching phase during which the child begins to differentiate self from mother and to develop from the original mother-child symbiosis to a more reciprocal relationship. The second or practicing subphase (about 9 to 15 months) is marked by the child's attempts to explore the world about him or her. With the development of crawling and, later, walking, the infant is able to move away from the mother, practice these newly acquired locomotor skills, and actively explore the environment. The very fact of physical separateness which the child experiences helps him to recognize that mother and he can be separate, but also that mother can be absent and apart from him. This realization engenders a third or rapprochement subphase (15 to 24 months) during which the child both ventures out into the world and, at the same time, needs to return to the security of his mother's arms. The vulnerability the child feels is well illustrated by the darting away and shadowing the child shows from about 15 to 17 months as he moves away from mother, hoping that she will follow him and once more hold him, as well as by the fear that many children of this age show when their mother is physically out of their sight.

The rapprochement crisis reaches its peak during the period of about 18 to 24 months, during which time the child shows marked anxiety when apart from his mother, together with increasingly sophisticated and determined efforts at preserving the exclusivity of the mother-child relationship. This crisis, in turn, leads to the consolidation of individuality and emotional object constancy by about the end of the second year of life, when the child is able to perceive his mother as a separate person in the time and space world and yet is able to maintain an enduring representation of the mother's functions as part of his increasing capacity for inner regulation. At about this time, the child shows both an increased ability to maintain intrapsychic awareness of the separation between mother and self and also an acquisition of a distinct individuality or firm sense of self. Although understood as separate and parallel lines of development, Mahler and her colleagues generally regard separation and individuation as a part of a unitary process that, optimally, leads to a sense of self as separate and differentiated from others and as having relatively complete psychic autonomy (Angel, 1972).

When a mother cannot permit much individuation and needs to have her child bound to her in a continuing symbiotic relationship, the child's own ego development becomes impaired, leading to the development of severe psychopathology. When a mother permits somewhat greater differentiation, but still infantalizes the child, the child develops excessively demanding behavior, expects indulgence of every whim, and shows problems in controlling his temper. This phenomenon was first described by D. Levy (1943) in his studies on maternal overprotection.

In her own work, Mahler has described the process of separation-individuation both as it pertains to disturbed children and their parents (Mahler, 1952, 1958, 1968) and in 1972a the "normal" process of development (Mahler, 1963, 1965, 1972a, 1972b; Pine and Furer, 1963; Panel, 1972a; Mahler, Pine, and Bergman, 1975). However, the generality of this developmental process has been widely recognized, even beyond the developing mother-child relationship itself, and there have been several important applications of this concept of intrapsychic differentiation in studies of older children, adolescents, and adults that are implicit in the work of Stierlin (1974) and Boszormenyi-Nagy (1973). Such studies suggest that the paradigm of separation-individuation may be useful in considering problems of dependency and separation throughout the life cycle.[2] As Mahler comments, in one of her few explicit references to this problem of separation-individuation during adulthood:

> One could regard the entire life-cycle as constituting a more or less successful process of distancing from and introjection of the lost symbiotic mother, an eternal longing for the actual or fantasied "ideal state of self," with the latter standing for a symbiotic fusion with the "all good" symbiotic mother, who was at one time part of the self in a blissful state of well being. (1972a, p. 338)

In particular, the development from infantile to mature dependency is a lifelong process as Mahler explains here:

> For the more or less normal adult, the experience of being both fully "in" and at the same time basically separate from the "world out there" is among the givens of life that are taken for granted. Consciousness of self and absorption without awareness of self are the two polarities between which we move, with varying ease and with varying degrees of alternation or simultaneity. This too is the result of a slowly unfolding process ... in relation to (a) one's own body, and (b) the principal representative of the world, as the infant experiences it, namely the primary love object. *As is the case with any intrapsychic process, this one reverberates throughout the life-cycle. (p. 333)*

A similar view has been adopted by Fairbairn (1941, 1951) in his discussion of "mature dependence," by Balint (1965), and especially by A. Freud (1965) in her discussion of the developmental line of dependence/self-reliance.

The paradigm used by Mahler and other object relations theorists, including Kernberg (1976), assumes a developmental course beginning with autism, in which the child is alone and can only hallucinate satisfaction, and continuing through the child's increasing capacity to associate satisfaction delivered by the mother in the course of caretaking with her presence, which gradually leads to the development of the capacity for person permanence and satisfaction of needs in an interpersonal context. The child's emerging "love affair with the world" (Mahler, Pine, and Bergman, 1975) alternates with the need to reassure himself of his mother's presence until the establishment of what Mahler, Pine, and Berg-

---

[2]Although we have stressed the extent to which there is continuity across the life cycle in dealing with the issue of separation-individuation, we must also recognize that this approach emphasizes continuities in socialization rather than possible discontinuities. Further, we must not assume that the meaning of separation and the desire for reunification with the lost person are necessarily the same for the two year old searching for his mother whom he has lost sight of while absorbed in play and for the middle-aged mother whose own mother has recently died. As Neugarten (1972) has cautioned, changes in the context in which this issue appears are such that there may be little direct continuity in reactions to the issue of separation from childhood through adulthood and middle and old age.

man term "libidinal object constancy" (p. 111), when the intrapsychic representation of the mother replaces the need for her physical presence.

In contrast to Mahler's emphasis on the process of attachment and individuation, Kohut (1977) and his colleagues (Ornstein, 1978; Kohut and Wolf, 1978; Tolpin and Kohut, 1979) have proposed an alternative view of development as one in which, when viewed from the infant's perspective, mother and child exist as a single entity. The mother exists as a tension-regulating mechanism that is not experienced by the child as apart from the child himself. The developmental task is much more one of differentiating self from mother than of first making and then dissolving an attachment to mother. Based in part on Winnicott's earlier (1960) concept of the transition from the early childhood experience of a fusion or merger of the mother-child dyad to the experience of "living with mother," these psychologists of the self suggest that the mother's function in helping the infant to regulate tensions is perceived by the child as coming from within the self and that this function continues to exist across the life cycle as a "self-object," more or less continually available as a source of soothing in times of crisis.

From the perspective of psychology of the self, the extent of this separation between self and perceived other as a tension-regulating function is only relative. Those persons who have had "good enough" mothering—meaning that a reasonably empathic mother has been able to help the infant to deal with inner tensions—will, in time, develop a relatively strong sense of self and will be able to modulate those later ambitions and ideals that are the successors of such early tension states (Winnicott, 1960). Those persons with a less clearly defined sense of self are relatively less able to modulate such tensions in the absence of another reasonably empathic person who can function to regulate such adult tensions and who continues to be perceived as a self-object or aspect of self. On the other hand, each of us relies on such self-objects at times of crisis in our life, including such normative transitions as the advent of parenthood.

SOCIALIZATION, IDENTIFICATION, AND IDENTITY

The developing use of attributes of the other as a part of one's own ability to regulate tension presumes that these self-object attributes have become a part of the self through internalization, as a result of which perceived characteristics of the other have become elements of one's enduring subjective or private world (Schafer, 1968, 1976; Stierlin, 1973). Because of this process of internalization, it is also possible to form stable identifications with another, where "identifications" refer to those internalizations that contribute to regulatory or adaptational interactions with the environment (S. Freud, 1923, 1938a, 1938b; Hendrick, 1951; Heimann, 1952; S. Isaacs, 1952; Klein, 1952b; Rapaport, 1957; Bibring et al., 1961; Sandler and Rosenblatt, 1962; Pollock, 1964; Kernberg, 1966; Schafer, 1968; Meissner, 1972, 1979). The continuing relationship between mother and daughter across the life cycle not only supports early formed identifications, but also fosters changes in the manner in which these identifications are used in resolving subsequent conflicts encountered in adulthood.

It should be noted that although identifications are viewed in the present instance as representations of significant persons which function in the attempt to resolve conflict and promote adaptation, such identifications may be more or less successful in promoting this adaptation across the life cycle. Some identifications functioned successfully in early childhood, but are no longer appropriate in the search for more flexible and adaptative resolutions of conflicts encountered in adulthood.

Several other aspects of this definition of identification should be noted. First, identifications may be accompanied by more or less positive or negative affect and may be more or less ego syntonic. Especially in the case of defensive identifications, reliance on identification may evoke only slightly less pain than would obtain if this defense were not available.

Second, just as is true of all mental representations, identifications may bear a greater or lesser resemblance to those real life persons, the perceptions of which make up the internal world. Similarly, the identification may represent the more or less observable actions of particular real life persons. Frequently, identifications develop from some perception of another that is not among the most outstanding characteristics of the other. They do not have to be within awareness: in contrast to sheer imitation, which requires a willfull or volitional act, identifications may remain largely preconscious and not directly accessible to awareness (Greenson, 1954b).

Third, it should be noted that this is a definition of identification which is based on function rather than process. That is, identifications are labeled as such according to their role in providing for adaptation rather than according to the degree of structural change in the ego which they foster or according to the degree to which they reflect a differentiation of self from object. Just as Schafer's (1968) definition of internalization avoids the necessity of distinguishing between internal representations that do and do not contribute to the structural development of the ego, similarly, this definition of identification avoids the necessity of distinguishing between internalized objects that do and do not contribute to self-other differentiation.

From the perspective of the study presented in this book, a woman's identification with her mother provides her with a means for adapting to adult psychosocial conflicts, including those engendered by the developmental task of caring for young children. Based on her lifelong intimate contact with her mother, and supported by continuing contact between the generations, the adult daughter has internalized many of the mechanisms used by her own mother in resolving psychosocial conflicts. Defenses such as denial, projection, withdrawal into fantasy or isolation are largely learned through socialization and, subsequently, become a part of the daughter's psychological repertoire for dealing with reality.

While other sources of identification are also used by the daughter, including her father, other family members, and favorite teachers, identifications transmitted from mother to daughter are among the most salient for the daughter herself, especially when she is confronted with the task of rearing children. As one mother observed, in discussing the influence of her own mother on her response to childcare:

There are times when I sound just like my mother . . . it's like I was a child again, and I can hear my mother yelling at Betsy and myself, and then going cold and ignoring us when we didn't do what she wanted. I find myself doing the same things with Billy and Susan, though I try and stop myself . . . but, it's just like with my mother, when I get angry with people, and can't let them know it, it's like all my feelings freeze up inside me, and I sort of close up inside myself . . . and get that hard, sort of icy tone in my throat, and know that my mother is there inside me.

Some support for this theoretical position is found in case reports of the simultaneous psychoanalysis of mother and daughter (K. Levy, 1960; Sprince, 1962), as well as in studies of the transmission of psychological themes across the generations of modified extended families in contemporary society (Rosenzweig and Isham, 1947; S. Fisher and Mendell, 1956; Mendell and S. Fisher, 1956, 1958; Cleveland and Longaker, 1957; Hatch and Hatch, 1962; Borke, 1963, 1967; Mendell, Cleveland, and S. Fisher, 1968; Zelen, 1971; Parker, 1972). Each of these reports has been based on the study of a single family; with the exception of the studies by Borke, Cleveland and Longaker, and Parker, these reports have been based primarily on the reports of projective test data that demonstrate continuity in psychological themes across the generations.

Many of these studies do not contain sufficient data to permit detailed observations of family process. However, they have provided some evidence of the use of identifications across two or more generations, as demonstrated by the striking parallels found in the projective test data of family members. For example, Fisher and Mendell were able to show that concern with the issues of exhibitionism, cleanliness, and control of violent emotions was present in the projective test protocols of grandparents, parents, and children in one particular family. In a similar way, research both by Lidz, Fleck, and Cornelison (1965) and by Wynne and M. Singer 1963a, 1963b; M. Singer and Wynne, 1965a, 1965b) has demonstrated that family members show communality in styles of sharing attention and responding to external stimuli.

In the present study, we are concerned primarily with the intergenerational transmission of these psychological themes, as represented by the content of a woman's identification with her own mother. We believe that this identification, enhanced and enlivened by the continuing relationship between the two generations, represents the most significant of the factors which influence the mother's adaptation to the developmental task of caring for young children.

Identification and Identity

The internalization of attributes of another that fosters adaptation has important implications for the developing sense of self, as well as for the developing sense of connection between self and surround, which Erikson (1958, 1959, 1963, 1968) has termed "identity." In contrast with identification, identity represents a psychosocial rather than an intrapsychic attribute, reflecting the perceived continuity between self and others. As Erikson (1963) notes, identity represents the consolidation of all previously established identifications with enduring wishes and needs, as well as with performance in relevant adult social roles.

As described by Erikson, identity is but one of eight developmental tasks of the life cycle, the outcome of which is critical for the manner in which subsequent phases of the life cycle are understood and the manner in which the nuclear developmental issues or tasks associated with each subsequent issue are to be resolved. This concept of developmental task or issue is based on the epigenetic formulation of development first described in psychoanalysis in terms of psychosexual maturation (S. Freud, 1905a; Abraham, 1924) and extended by Erikson to include psychosocial as well as libidinal phases of development. In discussing this epigenetic concept of development, Bibring (1959) has described these tasks of the life cycle as "turning points," the outcome of which can lead to increased ability to resolve subsequent issues or crises in development or, if not resolved, to impairment in the ability to resolve later developmental tasks or issues.

The issue of identity arises in late adolescence and was formulated on the basis of Erikson's work with young people who showed personal "diffusion" and estrangement not characteristic of usual psychiatric syndromes, including schizophrenia and the borderline personality disorders. Since the ability to achieve continuity between the past, present, and future depends on the capacity for making abstractions, termed by Piaget (1954) as "formal operations," it is understandable that this issue would not appear before adolescence and the development of formal operations. However, there are clearly precursors of this issue throughout the life cycle in the manner in which such developmentally relevant crises as those concerning trust, autonomy, initiative, and industry are resolved, together with successors of this identity conflict in the resolution of such later developmental tasks or challenges of the life cycle as mutuality and generativity.

Erikson views identity as an issue or crisis leading to a variety of outcomes. On the one hand, the resolution of this crisis, as is true of all such issues across the life cycle, necessarily involves some experience of conflict and personal discomfort that fosters further development. "Foreclosure" or the failure to reconsider personal and psychosocial identity is believed to be as serious a failure to resolve this issue as prolonged diffusion in which the person is unable to settle on any identity or to make any lasting commitments.

The successful resolution of this identity crisis leads to an enduring sense of place in the cycle of generations and in the life cycle. As Erikson notes, it is far more than a sense of "Who am I?" It is a sense of a sameness and continuity, both for oneself and as a part of a larger entity, including family and community. The alternative to this positive identity is either a diffused identity or a negative identity, so well expressed by Martin Luther in Erikson's (1958) psychobiography, "I am not it."

Not only is identity the crucible in which earlier socialization issues are transformed in order that a sense of continuity with the past and future is provided, but also as a result of this struggle the capacity is forged for the later achievement of intimacy, so critical for marriage, as well as generativity, the psychosocial issue central to realization of the parental role. Indeed, of all developmental tasks across the life cycle, parenthood is perhaps the most salient for the ultimate resolution not only of preadult issues, but also of identity itself, for parenthood uniquely recapitulates the parent's own childhood and adolescence and also anticipates the offspring's own future development to adulthood. In discussing parenthood as a developmental phase, Benedek (1973) observes:

> Not only corresponding with and as a result of the physiologic symbiosis of pregnancy and the oral phase of development, but in each "critical" period the child revives in the parent his related developmental conflicts. This brings about either pathologic manifestations in the parent, or by resolution of the conflict, it achieves a new level of integration in the parent. (1973, p. 385)

Each of these phases in the socialization of the next generation rekindles the parent's own unresolved conflicts about similar issues in her own development (Behrens, 1954) and also has critical implications for the parent's own continuing identification with her own parents and for the maintenance of identity within the family and across generations.

For the mother, optimal resolution of the identity conflict fosters perceptions of prior life experiences as a relevant preparation for her adaptation to the maternal role; the mother's reservoir of previous positive life experiences and relationships provides her with the sustenance necessary to develop a mutually satisfying and reciprocal relationship with her young child. Becoming and being a mother are viewed as congruent both with previous experiences and with hopes and wishes for the future. If a woman has not been able to place motherhood within the context of family and generation, motherhood may further intensify unresolved identity conflicts. Viewing childcare as a repetition of the manner in which she herself was reared, a woman may assume a negative identity, including a determination to rear her own children in a different manner from that in which her mother had reared her. Alternatively, a mother may not be able to settle on any consistent manner of resolving the developmental tasks associated with childcare; identity diffusion may result from the fact that her own mother had also experienced difficulty placing herself in the context of a family tradition, now expressed in the mother's own conflict in establishing her identity as a mother, or may result from her fear of becoming a mother and assuming this role for herself. Identity diffusion may be transmitted across successive generations within the family and may be expressed as a particularly pronounced psychopathology associated with mothering (Grunebaum et al., 1975).

While the present and past combine in both mother and father to shape their present responses to the continuing relationship with their own children, the mother's generally greater immersion in the minute details of childcare (Rebelsky and Hanks, 1971) means that the immediacy of childcare presents her with a particularly large number of issues and evokes particularly complex and, frequently, confusing responses. A mother responds to the day-to-day strains involved in parenthood largely on the basis of her identification with her own mother and is both helped and, often, burdened by the failure to comfortably resolve issues of identity and continuity with the most important figure in her own life.

PSYCHOLOGICAL DIFFERENTIATION AND GENDER IDENTITY: DYNAMICS OF THE MOTHER-DAUGHTER BOND

It is interesting to note that, in Mahler, Pine, and Bergman's (1975) discussion of the response of boys and girls to the rapprochement subphase it is reported that little girls show less interest than little boys in exploring the environment apart from mother (1975, p. 214) and also show less enjoyment in exploration, characterized by a more "low-keyed" attitude.[3] The explanation provided by Mahler, Pine, and Bergman for the low-keyed attitude and fear of exploration is that the little girl is already becoming aware of her lack of a penis and is beginning to accept her role as a little girl. While Mahler's preference for an object-instinctual explanation may be questioned, the phenomenon she notes is of critical importance in understanding the relationship between women and their mothers in our society. Already during the second year of life, a pattern is beginning to emerge that will shape the future of the relationship between adult women and their own mothers. In contrast with the little boy, who is already beginning autonomous exploration of the environment that, in time, will lead to relatively greater psychological differentiation, the little girl is beginning to show the pattern of continued closeness to her mother in which issues of dependency and attachment on an anaclitic mode and continued lack of separateness become the basis for the subsequent adult relationship between women across three and even four generations within the American modified extended family.

The origin of the continuing and frequently ambivalent relationship between mothers and their own mothers is found in the very structure of childrearing itself in Western society. In what is perhaps the most important contribution to the study of socialization to date, T. Parsons (1955) has described the very different dilemmas faced by young boys and young girls in their early emotional development. Beginning with the fact that parenthood organizes perceptions of appropriate sex-role behavior in quite different ways for men and women, Parsons suggested that the role of the woman within the family is essentially an expressive one, with the mother the family member primarily responsible for nurturance and emotional support. In contrast with the mother, who provides succor and care, the

---

[3]It is interesting to speculate whether this "low-keyed" attitude that Mahler finds more typically among girls and which Chodorow (1978) reinterprets in terms of socialization into a feminine gender identification is the developmental precursor of the proclivity to a depressed mood reported in a variety of studies to be characteristic of women in contemporary society (Gove and Tudor, 1972; Radloff, 1975; Richman, 1976; Campbell, Converse, and Rodgers, 1976; Ripley, 1977; Weissman and Klerman, 1977; Weissman and Meyers, 1978; G. Brown and Harris, 1978; Rosenfeld, 1980). While this depression is particularly pronounced among the mothers of young children, even among working women, there is a markedly lowered mood in contrast with that among men counterparts.

husband-father enacts the instrumental role, and is responsible for the provision of income and other tangible support that the mother and children depend on.

Formulations of the development of interpersonal relations from infancy, including those of psychoanalysis (Winnicott, 1960, 1963), cognitive psychology (Piaget, 1954; Decarie, 1965; Basch, 1977), and sociology (T. Parsons, 1955), all concur in viewing the infant's developing relationship with the mother as a "dyadic" and anaclitic one, marked by an exclusivity so well expressed in Middlemore's (1941) concept, "the nursing couple". From the baby's perspective, among both boys and girls, the mother is the sole person in the baby's life. However, beginning with the second year of life and the attainment of the preoperative period of cognitive development, there is increased ability to differentiate between self and others and also to differentiate between these others (Mahler, Pine, and Bergman, 1975; Basch, 1977). As a result of this increasing person differentiation, the child develops the capacity for forming triadic relationships. It is with the development of the capacity for a triadic relationship that the developmental course begins to diverge for boys and for girls, both in terms of the resolution of the Oedipus complex, as well as in terms of subsequent patterns of closeness with the mother.

Parsons notes that the developmental task facing the three-to-five-year-old boy is more complex and leads to greater strain than that facing the girl of the same age. The boy must undergo a double emancipation, for he is forced to recognize the generational difference between children and parents, and, at the same time, he must shift his gender identity from mother to father. This shift means renouncing his previous affection for his mother as a source of satisfaction for combined nurturant-erotic wishes. Solidarity is now expected with his father, who is also a threatening person for him; the young boy is forced over time to deal with this threatening person without recourse to the safety and support provided by his mother.

The situation with the little girl is precisely the opposite of that with the little boy. While the boy is forced to renounce his dependency on his mother, the little girl is encouraged to retain this dependence. The adoption of a gender identity like that of her mother fosters this dependence, for it increases the congruence in interests and life-style between mother and daughter. While the son must work hard at learning to become a man like his father and must renounce passive wishes earlier learned in his relationship with his mother, the little girl is encouraged to become ever more like the original anaclitic object in her life.

Since women in our society are expected to be housekeepers and kinkeepers, even in those families in which mothers have full-time employment, the nature of the woman's domestic role supports this continuing dependency across successive generations of women. Komarovsky (1950, 1956) suggests that socialization into dependency begins in early childhood and notes that while parents and other family members encourage independence from the family among boys they encourage dependence on the family among girls. Boys are provided with greater incentive for activities that are independent of the family and are permitted greater privacy in personal affairs. Girls are encouraged to run errands and to help other family members and are more likely than boys to be pressured into attending family rituals. Komarovsky suggests that this childhood socialization is functional in training boys and girls in their respective sex roles:

> The role of the provider, on the one hand, and of the homemaker on the other, call for different attitudes and skills. Competitiveness, independence, dominance, aggressiveness are all traits felt to be needed by the future head of the family. Although the girl can train for her adult role and rehearse it within the home, the boy prepares for *his* outside the home, by taking a "paper route" or a summer job away from home . . . the greater sheltering of the girl has, as unintended by-products, further consequences for kinship roles which are not perceived. (1950, p. 512)

This greater sheltering of the girl within the home, while it provides socialization into the "domestic" role, may also impair the young woman's ability to develop a more independent life outside the family and to adapt successfully to her role as wife and mother within her own "family of procreation." While women may attempt to use the instrumental skills they were taught during childhood, both the asymmetry of the American kinship system and socialization into the dependent-expressive role within the family makes it more difficult for women than for men to relinquish their ties to their own parental family.

The result of this early socialization is the creation of a dependency between little girls and their mothers that is reinforced by the domestic tasks women are supposed to share together. Always at her mother's side, the little girl is neither expected nor encouraged to become independent of her mother or the immediate family in the manner expected of the little boy. Chodorow (1978) observes that the mother of the girl is available to her in a way that the father is not available to the little boy. The intense personal relationship that develops from this early identification reinforces the primary or anaclitic mother-child tie. At the same time, as M. Johnson (1975) observes, while little boys are specifically taught to be men, little girls are not explicitly taught to be women. To the extent that there is such specific sex-role learning, as Chodorow (1978) notes, it is in terms of the parental (maternal) role rather than the feminine role:

> Girls' identification processes, then, are more continuously embedded in and mediated by their ongoing relationship with their mother. They develop through and stress particularistic and affective relationships to others. A boy's identification processes are not likely to be so embedded in or mediated by a real affective relation to his father. (p. 176)

While socialization into masculinity involves inherently a socialization into separateness, outside the home and beyond the family, denying the importance of the earlier relationship with the mother, the little girl's socialization emphasizes these relationships.[4] The paradox is that the little girl is expected to achieve a sense of

---

[4]In the account by Rudolph and Rudolph (1978) of a classical extended family in North India, the young nobleman Amar Singh, whose diaries form the basis of the account, is closely tied to his family, while apparently individuated. He lives within certain constraints, while feeling free to come and go, and uses the variety of older men within the family as the building blocks for his own identity. The variety of such models gives the young nobleman a freedom not found in the nuclear family. The same conclusions would probably apply to extended families in the West for men; the question is

differentiation and separateness from her mother, and yet her early socialization prevents her from achieving this sense of separateness.

Writing from the perspective of cross-cultural studies of sex roles and parenthood, Gutmann (1975) has suggested that the very advent of parenthood has a unique impact on the organization of sex roles in the life cycle. According to this perspective, the necessity for the care of dependent offspring invokes a sense of chronic emergency among both mothers and fathers that leads to the organization of sex-role performance along particularly stereotyped lines. Fathers become instrumental in providing for the family's economic welfare, earning a living, and providing the necessities of life, while mothers become important in providing childcare and emotional support. The result of this parental imperative is that children learn the sex roles of men and women from their parents at that time when mothers act most clearly like women and fathers act most clearly like men. The biosocial fact of the parental imperative acts as the background against which the child's own sex-role socialization takes place and contributes to the learning by little boys of a differentiated role within the family and by little girls of a nondifferentiated and dependent role.

The impact of early socialization, including the very different outcome of the process of separation and individuation for little boys and girls, is gradually but powerfully realized with time. During the period of middle childhood, girls are already more compliant in school and less exploratory in their interaction with the environment than boys of the same age. But it is with adolescence, and the second phase of separation-individuation (Blos, 1967), that this difference becomes apparent. To a much greater extent than girls, adolescent boys are expected to leave home and to "strike out" on their own.

The continuing interdependence between adolescent daughters and their mothers is further affected by the fluidity of the adolescent's own conflicting wishes to grow up and to remain a child. The fluidity of ego processes in adolescence, the frequent regression to forms of behavior more characteristic of childhood, and the paradoxical wish to be both a child and an adult at the same time intensify the conflict the adolescent feels in the search for an identity that places both family and generation into perspective. The result is the encouragement of a kind of closeness and lack of separateness between young women and their mothers that is not present in the relationship between young men and their fathers. As Chodorow describes this relationship between the young woman and her mother:

A daughter acts as if she is and feels herself unconsciously one with her mother . . . daughters are apt still to feel dependent on and attached to their mother . . . the issue is not individuation in its infantile sense: most girls can act in the world according to the reality principle, know cognitively that they are differentiated. In relation to their mother, however (and similarly, the mother in relation to her daughters), they experience themselves as overly attached, unindividuated and without boundaries. (1978, pp. 136-137)

still of the nature of patterns of identification and resolution of problems of identity among women in these families, either in North India or in Europe and the United States (Kakar, 1978).

The continuing contact and need for informational dependence which is mixed with affectional dependence further support a continuing lack of differentiation between mother and daughter across the life cycle. Chodorow notes that the expectations of others, both men and women, all of whom have been mothered, mean that the woman is always responded to in a less differentiated manner, enhancing the increased relational orientation of girls and women, as contrasted with the more instrumental orientation of boys and men (Parsons, 1955; Maccoby, 1966; McClelland, 1965).

Most important of all, the continuing contact between adult women and their own mothers, further enhanced by adult socialization into the parental role, supports a degree of closeness that has important psychological consequences for each generation. The relationship between adult women and their own mothers is perhaps the most complex and emotionally charged of all the relationships within the family. The intense concern with this relationship is shown by the popular success of such recent discussions of the mother-daughter relationship as those of Neisser (1973) and Hammer (1975), as well as Freeman's (1979) autobiography and, in particular, Friday's (1977) revealing best-seller, *My Mother/Myself*. These latter two books describe in particularly graphic terms the lack of separateness adult women show in their continuing relationship with their own mothers and document the extent to which this closeness may remain a source of distress and discomfort for each generation.

The lack of separateness between mothers and their adult daughters is further supported by continued shared kin-keeping obligations within the larger family unit (Firth, Hubert, and Forge, 1970), by increasing role complementarity as the daughter becomes a mother, and by the socialization the mother provides for her adult daughter as the daughter becomes a mother herself. Increased role complementarity means that increased communication and sharing between the two generations of mothers is possible as they find increasing areas of common interest. On the other hand, such complementarity further emphasizes for the daughter the ways in which she is like her own mother and may, in the case of a woman who has not resolved the earlier identity crisis, lead to a negative identity.

As the daughter looks to her own mother for socialization into the developing parental role, it is increasingly difficult to separate informational aspects of the dependence of the daughter on her mother from affective aspects, including expectation of support and emotional supplies. In our own study of this continuing adult relationship between mothers and their own mothers we found that contact between the two generations is quite frequent, with mothers and grandmothers each reporting numerous contacts daily by telephone or in person. While many of these contacts, generally initiated by the mother, ostensibly concern requests for homemaking advice or information about childcare, such requests disguise the daughter's wish for soothing and support from her mother as she struggles to fulfill her responsibilities as wife and mother.

Finally, it should be noted that this continuing closeness between the generations has implications not only for the daughter's adult psychological development, but also for that of her own older mother. While there has been renewed appreciation over the past few years of the extent to which personality can change across adulthood (L. Yarrow and M. Yarrow, 1964), much of the emphasis in recent accounts has been on the transition from young to middle adulthood (Sheehey, 1976; Levinson, 1977; Vaillant, 1977).

The relationship between adult women and their own mothers leads to consideration of the next of the important transitions across the life cycle: that of the transition from middle to old age (Cumming and Henry, 1961; Neugarten, 1973). It should be noted that many of the grandmothers in the study reported in this book are already in their sixties and beginning the process of dealing with their own mortality. The expectations these women's daughters have for support and care may interfere with the older women's struggles to deal with issues regarding their own aging and with their attempts to deal successfully with the transition from middle to old age (Kalish and Knudtson, 1976). Interestingly, in a recent report by Cohler and Lieberman (1979), the extent of family social ties among a group of older women was actually inversely related to measures of positive morale and adjustment. While the role of grandmother has often been viewed in stereotyped and idealized ways, aspects of this role may be a source of discomfort rather than of satisfaction for older women.

Personal Adjustment and the Mother-Daughter Relationship

While childrearing and culture combine to foster a relationship between two and three generations of women within the family who feel a sense of closeness and lack of individuation not generally found among men and their fathers, this continuing closeness is not necessarily a source of psychic pain. Indeed, much of the confusion surrounding the study of the relationship between mothers and their adult daughters is a result of the fact that this relationship is too often viewed in terms of some ideal of individuation and autonomy which differs in significant ways from the reality of family life in contemporary society. Closeness is too often misunderstood as signifying conflict, and "invisible loyalties" across generations are too often overlooked, even in family treatment.

If closeness between mother and daughter is not itself a sign of conflict in adjustment for either generation, it should be noted that much of the psychic conflict women experience is related to their struggle to achieve some resolution of the closeness they perceive between mother and self (and also between daughter and self). The question is not whether any observed lack of differentiation is an indication of pathology in the family system, but rather whether it is an indication of the nature of the success of the adaptation each generation has made to the continuing closeness of mother and daughter. Issues such as the nature of the daughter's identification with her mother, the extent to which she has resolved the identity conflict of late adolescence, and the degree of comfort shown in her continued use of her mother as a self-object available for soothing at times of inner pain and tension (Kobut, 1977) all serve as evidence of the extent to which the daughter has been able to adapt to the continuing interdependence which characterizes the relationship between adult women and their own mothers.

While the precursors of the daughter's adult relationship with her mother can be seen even during middle childhood, it is during adolescence that the first evaluation is possible of the manner in which the adult relationship between the generations will be negotiated, including the extent of success or failure in achieving a comfortable continuity across generations. Having been socialized into a dependent role as mother's helper, the adolescent daughter is now expected to go out into the world, find a spouse, and establish a new family, at the same time preserving the original tie between mother and daughter. Much of the strain the daughter feels is a result of the very ambiguity of her mission. She is expected to find a spouse who will not interfere in the closeness between mother and daughter, and yet she is expected to become economically independent of her parents. It is interesting to note, as J. Fischer and A. Fischer (1963) have suggested, that a modal pattern in American society is for the young couple to settle in the community of the wife's parents in a kind of matrilocal residence pattern.

For the mother, the relationship with her adolescent daughter is frequently a strained one. From her perspective, just as her daughter is becoming a woman and sexually active, she herself may be experiencing menopause and also diminishing sexual activity and satisfaction. Much of the concern mothers express about the sexuality of their daughters is actually a projective identification of the mothers' own wishes and fears (Klein, 1937). As Anthony (1970) observes, this unfortunate timing of the mother's menopause only increases her envy of her daughter and may lead the mother to overcontrol her daughter's activities outside the house.

Where conflict regarding separation and individuation has been prevalent throughout the daughter's childhood socialization, the conflict between mother and daughter regarding this second individuation of adolescence (Blos, 1967) may be so pervasive that they become involved in a folie à deux (Anthony, 1971), sharing common psychiatric symptoms and describing common delusions and hallucinations. Similar dynamics have been shown to exist in the development of anorexia nervosa in which, as a result of basic confusion regarding bodily signals because of the daughter's difficulty in her perception of herself as separate from her mother, the adolescent girl loses her appetite and becomes emaciated (Ehrensing and Weitzman, 1970; Palazzoli, 1970, 1971; Bruch, 1973, Cohler, 1977).

While attainment of young adult status may mark the resolution of the adolescent identity crisis and lead to increased independence, the intrapsychic conflict regarding separation continues into adulthood. For the middle-class family, there are more often institutional supports that facilitate interpersonal autonomy. Typically, entrance into college follows almost directly after graduation from high school and represents a clear break with adolescence. Although parents may maintain their young adult offspring's room for occasional visits home, there is a gradual decrease in such visits during the college years as the young person makes new friends and develops a more autonomous life. Murphey et al. (1963) have reported that the parents of college students more capable of such autonomous relationships were themselves better able to differentiate between their own needs and those of their children and had succeeded to a greater extent than parents of nonautonomous young adults in fostering independence appropriate to the young adult's own needs. Unfortunately, this report does not discuss parent-child relations separately for late adolescent boys and girls.

Within working-class families, there is often no such institutional support as college in fostering independence. Particularly in the case of young adult daughters, it is common for the daughter to live at home while working and preparing for marriage. Studies of family relations among working-class young adults and their parents show that fully 40% of young adults and their spouses share their parents' home for some period of time following marriage. Ultimately, most couples do establish a separate household, and, even if this new household is just down the street, there is at least some recognition given to the belief that the young adult couple should have a separate life. The extent to which this separation can be negotiated in a manner satisfying for both the parental and the young adult generation depends on the life experiences of the parents and of the young people themselves.

In a series of studies, Stierlin (1974) and his colleagues (Stierlin, Levi, and Savard, 1971; Stierlin and Ravenscroft, 1972; Stierlin, Levi, and Savard, 1973) have described the process by which young adults and their own middle-aged parents negotiate this issue of individuation. Stierlin views the developmental task of separation and individuation during late adolescence and early adulthood as that of establishing mature relations between the generations: successful resolution of this task is contrasted with uncompleted or immature outcomes. An immature resolution leads either to centripetal separation in which the young person views the world as dangerous and as less able than the parental family to satisfy basic needs or to a centrifugal separation in which the young person is pushed out of the family by virtue of the lack of commitment among family members regarding the stability of the family unit itself.

According to Stierlin and Ravenscroft (1972), the centripetal pattern of separation has the effect of binding the young person to the family. The young person, in turn, becomes overly dependent on his or her parents who, while continuing to infantalize their young adult child, also feel resentful about the limitations that the continuing relationship places on their autonomy. Feelings of ambivalence and guilt characterize both generations in this separation pattern. The centrifugal separation pattern involves either ''delegation,'' sending the young person out into the world, while fostering a feeling of obligation to the family, or ''expulsion,'' sending the young person out into the world at a fixed time, largely to relieve intrafamilial conflicts regarding available emotional and/or financial resources.

Delegation, as a separation pattern, may lead to particularly intense conflict between young adults and their families. A young person who is serving as a delegate of the parental family feels a conflict between commitment to parents and commitment to spouse, as well as a conflict between commitment to own parents and to in-laws. To the extent that parents send a young person out as a delegate of their own needs, hoping to achieve ''vicarious gratification'' through the offspring, the young adult fails to achieve autonomy and remains a family captive (Giovacchini, 1970; Shapiro, 1972).

Continued conflict between young adults and their own parents regarding the issue of separation-individuation may be a result of the ambivalent feelings of members in each generation regarding this issue. Nowhere is this perspective better demonstrated than in Sampson, Messinger, and Towne's (1964) analysis of extended interview data from 17 mothers hospitalized for mental illness during the first years after childbirth. These authors distinguish between what they term a "crisis of separation" and a "crisis of identification." One group of six women, characterized as showing this crisis of separation, moved away from their parental home when they got married, but were unable to deal with this separation or with subsequent life-event stress. During the first years after marriage, whenever there was a problem, particularly in their relationships with their husbands, these women would return home to seek their own mothers' help. However, after they each had a child, they were no longer able to return home as freely as before and, unable to function on their own, developed psychiatric symptoms.

Women showing this crisis of separation require the constant "emotional refueling" described by Pine and Furer (1963) as a part of the separation-individuation phase of development. Unable to sustain affection over time, and feeling depleted as a result of the demands imposed on them from having to care for a baby, these women need to return home frequently to obtain security from their own mothers and to forestall fears of emotional starvation. These women are bound to their own mothers in a centripetal relationship that creates much ambivalence within each generation. The daughter both needs her mother's care and yet also feels guilty about her requests for care. The middle-aged mother needs to have her daughter return home at frequent intervals and even encourages her to return. However, after the daughter returns home, the mother becomes angry with the magnitude of the daughter's requests for care and frightened both at the prospect of the daughter's continued dependence and the severity of the limitations the daughter shows in being able to deal with problems such as those in her marriage.

A similar pattern has been described by Abrahams and Varon (1953) in their study of mentally ill women and their own mothers participating in a therapeutic group, as well as by Lyketsos (1959) in his description of the relationship between women hospitalized for schizophrenia and their mothers and Dell and Applebaum (1977) in their study of single mothers. These three accounts also emphasize the psychological significance for the family of the continued symbiosis between mother and daughter. Since the need for continued emotional sustenance is not considered appropriate for women in contemporary society, the dependent woman is likely to be confused and disappointed by the response of her own mother, who may encourage the daughter's dependence as a result of her conflict in achieving differentiation from her own mother, but who is also afraid that she will lose her autonomy if she gives in to her daughter's dependency needs.

The husband is also perplexed by his wife's need to maintain a symbiotic tie with her own mother and expresses disappointment at his wife's inability to cope with the demands imposed by the adult roles of wife and mother. In addition, the husband of such a dependent woman feels envy and frustration regarding his wife's relationship with her own mother, which is given greater priority than that of husband and wife and so completely satisfies the wife's desire for intimacy. While this crisis of separation has been described in detail among families where a young adult woman has been hospitalized for mental illness, as we see later, the crisis of separation can also be observed among women in the community who have not developed psychiatric impairment.

In contrast to the group of six women who showed crises of separation, Sampson, Messinger, and Towne (1964) also described a second group of women who showed what was termed a "crisis of identification," understood in the terms of the present discussion as a crisis of identity. This group of patients characteristically perceived their own mothers as providing little satisfaction of affectional dependence from childhood to the present and particularly felt that their own mothers resented the sacrifices they had previously made in caring for young children.

As these young women had become parents, and had observed that their own reactions to childcare were similar to those of their own mothers, they had become increasingly fearful that they would experience the same life outcomes, including feelings of pervasive dissatisfaction with their roles as housewives, wives, and mothers. The response of these women to the developmental task of childcare is similar to that of psychiatric patients showing the "anniversary reaction" described by Hilgard (1953, 1959; Hilgard and Fisk, 1960). According to Hilgard, some patients develop psychiatric symptoms in response to the perception of a parallel between events taking place in the patient's life and the recollection of stressful life events among persons close to the patient herself. Typically, it is the perception of events parallel in time or date that evoke the anniversary reaction, but even the perception of a similarity between actual events in a patient's own life and those recurring in the life of close friends or relatives has been shown to foster the development of psychological distress.

These patients developed psychiatric symptoms as their responses to, or defenses against, perceptions of similarities in their own lives or those of close relatives or friends. Similarly, women showing a crisis of identification developed psychiatric impairments in response to painful memories of the conflict their own mothers had experienced at similar phases in the life cycle. As Sampson, Messinger, and Towne comment, in discussing this crisis of identification:

[These] wives experienced difficulties . . . primarily in the establishment of an appropriate female identity which would promote and sustain intimate heterosexual relations and feminine role performance. These difficulties seemed to be associated not with leaving mother (as was the case with the separation crisis) but with being mother, or at least some aspect of their internalized mother image . . . childbearing and childrearing pressed for the synthesis of identifications with the young mother's own mother. (1964, pp. 65-66)

For some of these women, assumption of a "negative identity" had seemed like a possible alternative to becoming like their own mothers. Such women had attempted to perform the roles of housewives, wives, and mothers in a manner opposite to that of their own mothers. If their own mothers were meticulous housekeepers, they neglected housekeeping chores; if their own mothers were overly strict, they became overly permissive as parents. However, for these women autonomy of action was still largely lacking, since they had adapted all their decisions about housekeeping or childcare from their own mothers. All too often, the negative identity fails to achieve its purpose, and the woman finds herself experiencing the very crisis of identification she had hoped to avoid.

LaBarre, Jessner, and Ussery (1960) and Clarke (1967) observe that continued close contact between a woman and her mother can further intensify this crisis of identification. However, as Rappaport (1958) notes, the grandmother does not have to be physically present to intensify this crisis of identification. It may also occur through the transmission of family legends or myth about what the grandmother was like. Such fantasies may motivate behavior even in the physical absence of the model.

While there has been some clinical study of the crisis of identification among mentally ill women (Gottheil, Paredes, and Exline, 1968), there has been much less study of this crisis of indentification among women in the community. Bibring (1959; Bibring et al., 1961) notes that this conflict was among the most frequent sources of disturbance among the pregnant women studied by her group prior to first delivery. Stolz (1967) reports that a majority of the mothers in her interview study of women in the community have spontaneously commented on their mothers' continuing influence on their childrearing attitudes and practices and that these women report that this continuing maternal influence causes them considerable psychological discomfort, a finding confirmed by us and discussed in greater detail in this book. However, Stolz makes little more than passing reference to this problem. I. Harris (1959) also comments on the importance of a woman's identity as a maternal woman, derived from that of her own mother, as a factor determining her adaptation to the maternal role.

SOCIAL-PSYCHOLOGICAL PERSPECTIVES ON INTERGENERATIONAL RELATIONS: KINSHIP ASYMMETRY AND PATTERNS OF CONTACT AMONG AMERICAN FAMILIES

As a result of the very structure of childcare in contemporary American society, women are early socialized by their own mothers into the same dependent and expressive role within the family as they themselves have been taught by their own mothers. Women appear not to attain the same degree of psychological differentiation from their own mothers as is found between men and their fathers. Indeed, as Chodorow argues, women are not specifically socialized into a feminine role, but into a role as potential mother in which the continuing closeness of mother and daughter is maintained and extended. This "reproduction of mothering" (Chodorow, 1978) is supported by the very frequency and intensity of the contact maintained by mothers and their own mothers across adulthood.[5]

Increasing complementarity of the roles of adult mother and daughter—together with the daughter's expectation of information about housekeeping and childcare, which acts as a medium for the solicitation of affectional dependence, and the frequent and often emotionally charged contact resulting from shared obligations within the larger family unit as kinkeeper—further maintains the closeness between mother and daughter present since childhood. However, of perhaps greatest importance is the fact that in contrast to popular conceptions of family life in contemporary society there is considerably greater contact across generations and greater mutual interdependence than is often recognized, and this very interdependence fosters and supports early socialization, which forms the basis for a nondifferentiated subjective understanding of the relationship between mother and self.

Findings from sociological studies of the family across social strata and within diverse subcultures show that the modal family arrangement in American society is that of a modified extended family in which, while not necessarily sharing a common household, family members live close to each other and exchange both tangible resources and help and assistance (Uzoka, 1979). Litwak defines the term "modified extended family" thus:

Between the nuclear and the extended family structure is the modified extended family structure which consists of a coalition of nuclear families in a state of partial dependence. Such partial dependence means that nuclear family members exchange significant services with each other, thus differing from the isolated nuclear family, as well as retaining considerable autonomy (that is, not bound economically or geographically), therefore differing from the classical extended family. (1965, p. 291)

Adams' (1970) review supports Litwak's definition and shows that this modified extended or expanded family is the characteristic family type in contemporary urban American society across families differing both in social status and region of the country.

It is part of the American romance with our rural past to believe that urbanization resulted in the destruction of a tightly knit extended family. Available evidence suggests that this form of family organization never existed in American society (Demos, 1970), and it is likely that this form of family organization has never even existed in Europe, at least since the Renaissance (Laslett and Wall,

---

[5]In addition to Chodorow's analysis of the means by which girls are socialized into continuing closeness across the life cycle, leading to the reproduction of mothering rather than to the development of femininity, she also argues that this identity as mother rather than as woman is necessarily an adverse influence leading to impaired adjustment. She believes that the means for correcting this socialization and consequent perpetuation of the mother-daughter symbiosis is for fathers to participate equally in childcare. However, as Gutmann (1975) has noted, parenthood as a biosocial event crystallizes sex roles along traditional lines, with the husband-father as instrumental leader in the family and the wife-mother as expressive leader. This biosocial event is even prior to the socialization of the next generation and suggests that such a radical feminist solution is not possible in contemporary society. While recognizing the impact on women of their roles as wives and mothers (see footnote 3 in this chapter), the problem is less with the ways in which roles are assigned than with the failure to develop institutions to support women as they manage their responsibilities as wives and mothers (Houston-Stein and Higgins-Trenk, 1978).

1972; P. Laslett, 1977). As Seward (1978) has shown in his study of the American family across the nineteenth century, vertical or horizontal extension was characteristic of less than 10% of the families. However, during this time the size of the household was reduced, for the practice of taking in boarders, employees, and other nonrelatives largely disappeared in American society. Also, during this period the family stayed remarkably constant in terms of such factors as the number of broken families and number of children per family.

Critics of urbanization such as Park, Burgess, and McKenzie (1925) and Wirth (1938) had maintained that the diversity of city life tends to dissolve primary bond groups such as those of the family. While fostering the individuality which makes possible greater freedom to innovate, both Wirth and Park, Burgess, and McKenzie believed that such creativity was only possible when persons were freed from the constraints imposed by such traditional roles as those among members of the family. Other social theorists (T. Parsons, 1949) have suggested that the emphasis on geographic and social mobility in American society is incompatible with the preservation of extended family ties. However, as Haller (1961) notes, the very heterogeneity and diversity of the city makes possible a variety of occupational choices not available in the small town. It is not necessary to leave the city in order for the young married couple to find suitable employment. Indeed, as we see later, among both working- and middle-class families, the economic "connections" established by the parental generation make it less difficult for the younger generation to find work. It is not uncommon for a young man's father or father-in-law to obtain employment for him either in the same company or in the same kind of work as that which he himself does.

Historical studies of the American family (Furstenberg, 1966; Greenfield, 1967; Hareven and Langenbach, 1978; Kanter, 1978; Seward, 1978) and studies of present-day families by Litwak (1960a, 1960b), as well as those by Reiss (1962), Leichter and Mitchell (1967), Adams (1968), Shanas (1961a, 1961b, 1968), Troll and Smith (1976), Bane (1976), and Uzoka (1979), all show that urban life actually helps to draw the family together. Greater population density makes it possible for several generations of the same modified extended family to live in geographic proximity. Mass transit and the automobile make it possible for family members to visit together frequently, and the telephone permits easy communication at any hour of day or night. Indeed, it is interesting to note that in Shanas' (1968, 1979) report of contact between members of urban families, fully 62% of older persons in her survey reported living within walking distance of at least one daughter or son.

Patterns of Intergenerational Contact

Research regarding relations between the generations in American society leads to two particularly important conclusions: (1) There is a greater degree of shared agreement in attitudes and values among working-class than among middle-class families (Sussman, 1960; Rosenberg, 1970; Anspach and Rosenberg, 1972; M. Fried, 1973; Rubin, 1976). (2) The single most important source of intrafamily agreement is the mother-daughter tie, which is particularly strong within working-class families (Glick, 1957; Komarovsky, 1962; Aldous, 1967; Troll, Miller, and Atchley, 1979).

Findings supporting these conclusions come from studies of kinship and social organization within working- and middle-class communities in England and the United States. Young and Wilmott (1957), describing family life in a London housing project, report that 55% of the women interviewed had talked with their own mothers in the past day, as contrasted with 31% of the men who had talked with their fathers in this period of time. In a subsequent report of family life in a London suburb (Wilmott and Young, 1960), it was reported that women in this suburb maintained more frequent contact than their husbands with parents on either side of the family, but parents were somewhat less frequently seen than among urban families, largely because the generations lived farther apart and transportation was more difficult to arrange.

Furthermore, both in working-class London and in the suburbs, should the need arise for an older woman to live with her children, either through death of a husband or illness within a family, these older parents tended predominately to join the household of their daughter rather than that of their son. As one older respondent observed:

> My daughter-in-law is a wonderful girl . . . but her ways are not my ways. If you are cooking something . . . you can't seem to get on with your daughter-in-law's methods. It's different with your own daughter—her way is more like your own way. (Wilmott and Young, 1960, p. 69).

Findings reported by Kerr (1958) and by Townsend (1957) suggest that the youngest daughter is especially likely to keep in touch with her parental family and in particular with her mother. In many families it is expected that the youngest daughter either will not marry at all or that she will live sufficiently close to her own mother to maintain frequent contact and provide help during illness.

Comparison of these English results with those reported for a California suburb suggests that the extent of intergenerational continuity may be even greater within the American community. This community surveyed by Young and Geertz (1961) was largely middle class and generally comparable in social background characteristics with the London suburb. Women in both suburban communities visited with their own mothers less than was true for the London housing project, but California women saw their mothers with somewhat greater frequency than women in the London suburb. In each community, more than 40% of the women interviewed had some daily contact with their own parents, primarily their mother, either by telephone or in person. In each community, less than a quarter of the respondents had contact with their own parents less often than once a month.

The California findings are particularly interesting, since the stereotyped picture of California is of an area with a high degree of geographic mobility, where young adults have infrequent contact with their own parents. Indeed, results of several studies regarding mobility and kinship in American society show that geographic and occupational mobility have a less disruptive influence on relations with one's own parental family than had been previously believed (Litwak, 1960a, 1960b; Haller, 1961; Reiss, 1962; Adams, 1968). As Adams comments, in reviewing a decade of research on kin relations in American families:

> In short, then, proximity, not separation, is the rule, with actual geographic isolation from kin being characteristic of only a small portion of the population. It is the professional and managerial families of the upper-middle-class who are most likely to be separated from their kin, and these are more often proximate than distant. (1970, p. 578)

Other findings are similar to those reported for the California community. On the basis of a probability sample of U.S. households, Shanas (1961b, 1968, 1979) reports that nearly 8 out of 10 older persons in the United States with children had seen at least one child within the week preceding the survey. Frequency of contact was somewhat greater between working-class parents and their young adult offspring than between middle-class parents and their offspring. However, across all social strata, parents were more likely to have visited with an adult daughter than with a son.

Similar results, based on intensive interviews with a group of working-class wives in a northeastern United States community, have been reported by Komarovsky (1962), who notes in addition that frequency of contact is greatest between these working-class women and their own mothers during the first seven years of marriage, declining somewhat in the succeeding years. Since women regard their own mothers as the first and most important source of childrearing information, it is probable that the presence of young children in the family provides a focal point of communication during the first years after the daughter's marriage and further strengthens the role convergence, which, as Adams (1968) notes, is fostered by the daughter's marriage and assumption of the maternal role. Furthermore, regarding the quality of the mother-daughter tie between the generations, more than 60% of the daughters report close and harmonious relationships with their mothers, with somewhat less harmonious relations reported between daughters and their fathers, particularly when both generations are from the lowest social stratum. Similar results were reported for husbands, with these men maintaining closer relations with their mothers than their fathers, except within the group of men with less than high school education, where relations with both parents were likely to be less harmonious than among husbands with greater education.

A third study that bears out the findings of both the California and northeastern studies, as well as the national sample findings, has been reported by Adams (1968), based on a group of young adults and their parents in the South. Once more, when considering the category of face-to-face contact, women were found to have more frequent contact with their parental families than was true among their husbands and the husbands' parental families. This contact with one's own parental family was greater among working-class families than among middle-class families, and geographic mobility had little effect on the frequency of contact. Indeed, Adams reports that, at least in the case of the husband's family, there was a curvilinear relationship, with visits more likely when husband's parental family lived in the same community or more than 100 miles away than when husband's family lived at some intermediate distance.

Consistent with the findings of Litwak (1960a) regarding families in upper New York State and those of Bott (1971) regarding families in England, Adams' study shows that occupational mobility has little effect on the extent of generational continuity. The only group of persons having decreased contact with their own parents were downwardly mobile women. Overall, more than 50% of both husbands and wives had contact with their respective families at least weekly, with a larger number of husbands having their own family living in geographic proximity than has typically been reported.

It is interesting to note that when evaluating the degree of affection women feel toward their own mothers, a greater proportion of middle- than working-class women reported close affectional bonds, a finding consistent with results reported by Firth, Hubert, and Forge (1970) among urban English families. In contrast with most other studies, Adams also reports little difference in the degree of intergenerational value consensus among the families in his study, considering either social status or social mobility. Another interesting point is that neither expressed feelings of closeness nor value consensus is associated with the extent of contact; Adams finds little relationship between feelings toward parents and the amount of actual contact with them.

Although adult offspring and their own parents in modified extended families typically live apart, as we see subsequently, it is not uncommon for the generations to share a common residence or even a common household, particularly during the period just after marriage when the young couple has not achieved economic self-sufficiency or later in the family life cycle when the parents of the adult offspring are no longer able to live alone (Streib and Thompson, 1960; H. Smith, 1965). Nor is it uncommon for parents, adult offspring, and the unmarried children of the adult offspring to live together in a three-generation residence or household even when economic self-sufficiency is not an issue (Koller, 1954).

Typically, such living arrangements are asymmetrical, and the three-generation family is comprised of the parents of the daughter rather than the son. Indeed, Sweetser (1963) reports that 60% of young couples living with either set of parents choose to live with the wife's parents. Leichter and Mitchell (1967) report that 93% of the women in their study of extended Jewish families in New York had lived with their own mothers at some time since marriage and that 54% of these women still lived no farther away from their own mother than the same building. This finding is consistent with results reported by Smith, Britton, and Britton (1958) that 75% of the young couples in two Pennsylvania communities studied by his research group had shared a common residence with their own parents for some period of time since marriage.

Literature reviewed by Sweetser (1966) shows that in contemporary American and Western European society, when parents and their adult offspring share a common residence or establish a common household, it is almost always with the wife's parents. This pattern is also consistent with observations by J. Fischer and A. Fischer (1963), based on an ethnographic study of a New England community, that the normative pattern was for adult children to live as near as possible to the wife's parents. Even in the case where, as a result of the husband's work, the young couple was forced to move to another community, it was considered desirable to move back to the community of the wife's parents as soon as such a move could be arranged.

Psychosocial Origins of Kinship Asymmetry in American Society

Findings such as those from the studies we have reviewed show that within contemporary American society the generations are much less isolated than has often been claimed for the nuclear family as a structural unit (T. Parsons, 1949; Ogburn, 1953) and that individual families of the parental and grandparental generations are linked through the continuing relationship between adult daughters and their own mothers. While most striking among working-class families, it is clear that, across social strata, women maintain greater contact than men with their own parental family. This conclusion obtains even when considering factors such as occupational and geographic mobility and region of country (E. Fried and Stern, 1948; Reiss, 1962; Komarovsky, 1962; L. Robins and Tomanec, 1962; Sweetser, 1963, 1964; Aldous and Hill, 1965; Hagstrom and Hadden, 1965; Bernardo, 1967; Leichter and Mitchell, 1967; Farber, 1971). Such asymmetry, emphasizing the importance of relations with the wife's parental family, in spite of the supposed bilaterality of kinship, naturally affects both patterns of visiting and the decision regarding which family the young couple will share a household with when the two generations do live together. In the studies of Wilmott and Young (1957, 1960), as well as in studies of American families, a majority of cases in which parents and children share a common residence are those in which mothers come to live with their daughters or in which daughters and their husbands and children come to live with the wife's mother (Sweetser, 1963, 1964, 1966).

Two reasons have generally been advanced in explaining the greater tendency to share a household with the wife's parents than with the husband's parents. First, there is likely to be greater conflict between a woman and her in-laws than between a woman and her own parents. Having lived together for so many years, mothers and daughters typically have reached some compromise regarding desirable ways of keeping house and rearing children, issues that would have to be negotiated from scratch if the residence or household were to be shared with the husband's parents.

Second, as Komarovsky (1950, 1956, 1962) and L. Robins and Tomanec (1962) have shown, the culture itself intensifies the continuing dependence of a woman on her own family during adulthood, with daughters expected to be more available than sons for family errands, for fulfilling kinship obligations, and for serving as kinkeepers. As Young and Geertz conclude, on the basis of their cross-national survey:

In all industrial countries, because of the similarities in their occupational structures, the tie between mothers and daughters is more strongly stressed than that between mothers and sons or between fathers and either sons or daughters, the strength or significance of the tie varying for social groups such as class. If we are right, daughters and mothers are the organizers of the wider family and the repositories of information about it, and form the central nerves of the loose but still highly important kinship network which is characteristic of modern society. (1961, p. 133)

This continuing attachment of women to their own parental families means that additional conflict is engendered between women and their husbands' parental families, for women continually choose to spend holidays with their own parental families and place kinship obligations to their own families above obligations to their husbands' families. Wallin (1954) and Gray and Smith (1960) both report that among young couples living some distance away from their parents, wives were more homesick for their own parents than husbands were for their parents. Stryker (1955) also reports that women are more attached than men to their own parental families.

The pattern of a woman's continued dependence on her own parental family for advice and assistance during the time she is caring for young children is particularly striking within working-class families (Glick, 1957; Komarovsky, 1962). This finding is of importance in this book, for most of the families we discuss have working-class origins. M. Fried (1973), in discussing this greater dependence of working-class women on their own parental families, suggests that working-class persons generally value comfort and pleasure in interpersonal relationships to a greater extent than middle-class persons; enjoyment of interpersonal closeness is more important than technical mastery, an observation consistent with findings reported by Rainwater, Coleman, and Handel (1959) and Rainwater and Handel (1964), in their study of working-class wives, as well as by Aldous (1967) on the basis of results of a survey study of three-generation families.

Support for this position, which suggests that working-class families are more conformist and dependent, is also found in several recent studies of working-class "culture" (Dyer, 1956; Miller and Riessman, 1961; Rubin, 1976). This literature is well summarized by Paterson (1964) who observes:

> The working class family tends to be a family of limited social activity and experience which emphasizes personal . . . bases of status and social identity . . . they tend to prize the present, the known, the personal. They avoid the competitive, the impersonal, and the uncertain. They tend to indulge rather than invest—they are overly preoccupied with the stability of basic human relationships and they are in large measure "other directed." (p. 78)

An explanation for this more conformist, dependent orientation toward the world found among working-class persons has been provided by Kohn (1969), who notes that the critical factor is not social status as such, but the degree of responsibility and judgment required by the job held by most working-class persons. While middle-class occupations typically demand reliance on internal standards of excellence and call for professional competence in which decisions are made on the basis of judgment rather than specific directives, working-class occupations typically demand harmony among fellow workers, conformity to externally determined standards for performance of the job, dependence on the leadership of others, and the capacity to follow orders in an exact manner. The same skills required on the job are carried into the home and govern both interpersonal relations within the family and parental socialization practices.

The Mother-Grandmother Relationship

Particularly within working-class families, mothers of young children are likely to maintain close ties with their own mothers. As Bott (1971) has noted, social relations within working-class families are typically arranged in such a way that husbands and wives lead quite separate lives. While the husband's free hours are often spent away from home, typically with friends from work, the wife's social contacts are oriented primarily toward members of her own extended family. As the wife's life situation comes increasingly to resemble that of her own mother after she had had children, leading to greater convergence of attitudes and values, and increased role colleagueship (Hagestad, 1974), the bond between the mother of young children and her own middle-aged mother is further strengthened.

At the same time the relationship between mother and grandmother becomes close, the development of such closeness is accompanied by some ambivalence for both parties. In part, this ambivalence may be due to the middle-aged mother's attempt to dominate her daughter's life. Apple (1956) reports that, across cultures, to the extent that grandparents have recognized authority over their adult children, they have less friendly relations with them. Within our own society, findings reported by Sussman (1954) and Boyd (1969) suggest that the best relationship between the two generations is that in which the grandparental generation is willing to provide help and assistance, while recognizing the need of the young adult generation for autonomy and independence.

In the literature, it is this issue of autonomy and control that is viewed as the major source of intergenerational conflict (Abrahams and Varon, 1953; Vollmer, 1937; Rheingold, 1964; Ackerman and Franklin, 1965). However, as we see later, such conflict regarding autonomy is much less often the major source of intergenerational conflict than has been recognized in previous studies of intergenerational relations. A much more important source of conflict is the feeling among members of the grandparental generation that their young adult offspring expect advice and assistance which they are unwilling to provide and the feeling of young adult offspring that their need for help and advice is rebuffed by their parents.

Following the "launching" of adult children into marriage and career, parents enter the postparental phase of the life cycle, a time when they have decreased responsibility for the care of dependent children (Hill and Rodgers, 1964). While the departure of adult children leaves an "empty nest," engendering some feelings of loss in the parents, research on this phase of the life cycle suggests that middle-aged parents also enjoy the greater freedom the empty nest makes possible. Deutscher (1964) reports that 79% of the women in his study found the postparental phase of the life cycle to be "better" than preceding phases, with greater freedom from responsibilities and less need to restrict expression of one's own personality as a result of the expectation that parents should serve as good role models for their own young children. Neugarten (1970) reports that for many women this phase of the life cycle may provide even greater satisfaction than preceding ones. Similar results have been reported in the studies of Spence and Lonner (1971), Wood and Robertson (1970, 1976), Lowenthal and Chiriboga (1972), and Robertson (1977).

Because of their reluctance to accept once more the obligations and responsibilities associated with parenthood, as we have already suggested, many middle-aged mothers feel ambivalent about responding to their daughter's continued requests for advice and assistance in caring for their young children. Albrecht (1954b) reports that only 19% of the grandmothers in her study assumed anything more than occasional babysitting responsibility. E. Fried and Stern (1948) report that women over age 50 show less conflict with their own mothers than was true for younger mothers. While this diminishing conflict may stem from the adult daughter's increased maturity, it is more likely that women over 50 had successfully launched their own children and no longer needed to rely on their own mothers for help and advice regarding childcare.

Consistent with this view that the adult daughter's expectations of help and assistance from her own mother regarding childcare represent a major problem in relations between the two generations, Neugarten and Weinstein (1964) report that in the one-third of their group of middle-class grandparents who felt discomfort with their role the major issue was that of being asked to assume continuing responsibility for childcare. Describing styles of grandparenthood largely in terms of such responsibility for childcare, together with the extent of contact with grandchildren, Neugarten and Weinstein report that, with age, grandparents become increasingly formal, believing to an even greater extent that parenting should be left to the parental generation and that grandparents should not be expected to provide regular childcare.

While Blood and Wolfe (1960) report that the shift from the role of mother to grandmother is often accompanied by feelings of tension and anxiety, findings from the studies we have discussed suggest that this anxiety may be due less to the fact that transition to grandparenthood is an unmistakable sign of one's own aging, as suggested by Deutsch (1945), than to the ambivalence the grandmother experiences in trying to maintain close ties with her own young adult daughter, while resisting the demands that the daughter makes for her mother's advice and assistance during the years when the daughter is caring for her own young children.

This view of the grandmother's response to her role as grandparent is quite discrepant from the stereotype of the grandmother as an intrusive "busybody" who is perpetually hurt by her daughter's refusal to accept the help she offers and who delights in every minute she can spend with her grandchildren. On the other hand, it is a view consistent with other studies of middle-aged and older women (Neugarten and Associates, 1964) suggesting that as persons grow older they become more concerned with their own internal life and with the task of coming to terms with aging and death. Such greater concern with self takes time and effort, and demands for help and advice regarding the young adult daughter's own life may be experienced by middle-aged mothers as particularly burdensome.

From the young adult daughter's perspective, the expectation of greater self-reliance may seem quite unreasonable. Particularly within working-class families, this young woman has, since childhood, been socialized into a dependent role. Increased role convergence further strengthens the bond between the generations. However, following the birth of the first child, the young mother experiences great disappointment. Within our society, it is expected that childcare is primarily the mother's own responsibility. While the mother's own mother may stay with her daughter and help out during the first weeks after the baby is born, it is expected that she will only stay for a few weeks.[6]

Although they respect this norm, many mothers report that their own anxiety is so great, particularly after the birth of their first child, that they feel compelled to call on their own mothers for advice and help. These mothers may feel sadness and helplessness when their own mothers return home, leaving them alone to care for another totally dependent person. At a time in a woman's own life when she feels most in need of help, a high degree of independence and self-reliance is expected of her.

Should the daughter object to her mother's demand that she be more independent or should she ignore the mother's stated wish not to assume greater responsibility for the grandchild's care, serious conflict may arise between the generations. In such a situation the middle-aged mother may either withdraw from her previously close relationship with her daughter or, as a result of her own ambivalent feelings, attempt both to provide the nurturant care her daughter seeks and then, feeling pressured and resentful, suddenly become angry and explosive in her criticism of her daughter. The daughter, in her turn, may become frustrated, disappointed, confused, and angry over her mother's unpredictable responses to her request for help and assistance.

CONCLUSION

The nature of the forward socialization observed among mothers and daughters in contemporary society, together with asymmetrical living arrangements that foster continued contact and exchange of both emotional and economic resources across generations, leads to lifelong interdependence among the several generations. This poses both unique opportunities and unique problems for women in each

---

[6]This emphasis on self-reliance among mothers of young children has sometimes been mistaken to mean that the mother is isolated from extended family ties in ways which are not true among families in traditional societies. As we have seen in this chapter, it is not so much that the mother is isolated from her extended family as it is expected that she will not depend on her own mother's help and assistance for extended periods of time. Even where, as is quite usual, mother and grandmother live in geographic proximity, it is still the case that the mother is expected to provide the care for her own children.

generation. While there is opportunity for mutual interdependence and support in the fulfillment of demanding responsibilities as kinkeeper, housewife, wife, and mother, the very nature of the socialization process—which supports the maintenance into adulthood of the close and undifferentiated relationship of early childhood—frequently leads to crises of separation and identity.

The advent of parenthood is a pivotal point in the life cycle. Not only does this time recapitulate all previous socialization, as earlier issues are experienced anew in caring for the next generation, but also it creates an imperative toward sex-role performance along the most traditional lines from the perspective of the socialization of this next generation. The sense of chronic emergency created by the need to provide for the care of relatively dependent offspring leads both mother and father to enact their roles in the most traditional manner: the husband-father provides economic support and the mother provides nurturant care as the parent with the greatest day-to-care responsibility for childcare, even among those families, now modal for our society, in which the wife-mother also works at least part time to support the family.

For the parental couple, parenthood reinforces earlier learned sex roles in their own families during childhood and adolescence. Each parent comes to parenthood with an understanding of the manner in which the parental role is to be enacted. For the father, relatively less central to childcare, parenthood largely involves provision of economic support and emotional support for the wife and mother in her struggle to discharge her domestic responsibilities. There can be little question that conflicting expectations of the woman as parent and wife represent a source of severe role strain in present-day urban society; indeed, the extent of lowered morale and psychological symptoms, found to be far greater among women than among men, attest to the impact of this role strain on adjustment. It is also the case that there are few institutional supports to help a woman negotiate this role strain; the result is that the mother of young children, maximally taxed in her ability to fulfill the multiple responsibilities expected of her, turns to her own mother as the most readily available resource for help and support.

The ready ability of the daughter to seek help from her mother is a result of the very different manner in which men and women are socialized into their sex roles from earliest childhood. While the little boy is faced with the problem of shifting his gender identity from mother to father and adapting to increased involvement in the world outside the home, in which he is self-reliant and largely separate from the parental family, the little girl is able to maintain her gender identity with the same parent who was the source of earlier satisfaction of dependency needs. As a result, the little girl experiences little of the psychological differentiation from her mother that is possible for the little boy and maintains this relative lack of differentiation across the life cycle, always tied to her mother by subsequent experiences which reinforce this early lack of psychological differentiation. The little girl's socialization into dependency is reinforced by the expectation that she will continue to maintain this dependency throughout adolescence and adulthood. The continuing adult relationship between a woman and her own mother further encourages such dependency, for not only is the girl dependent on her mother in learning her role as kinkeeper and housekeeper, but also her mother remains the primary source of information on childcare, which, for most women, remains a central task until middle age when children leave the family to start their own marital families. The daughter's requests for information serve to disguise her request for her mother's comfort and support as she attempts to fulfill her role as wife and mother. A vehicle is thus provided for the continued gratification of dependency needs and for the maintenance of a lack of separateness across the generations.

Since a lack of separateness between adult women and their own mothers is characteristic of relations between the generations in contemporary society, it is necessary to rethink the entire question of the meaning of this enduring closeness for the members of each generation of women. The psychological significance clearly varies with the nature of the life experiences of each generation. The question is not that of determining why some women are dependent on their own mothers, while others are not, but of the meaning of this dependence for each generation. While some women in each generation are able to deal adaptively with this closeness and lack of psychological separateness, others are not able to deal with it, so that the continuing contact and closeness become a source of conflict. Such conflict appears to be expressed through two principal modalities: a fear of any kind of separation from mother and a fear of becoming like (merged with) mother. These crises of separation and identity can be seen in a large number of present-day families, but have been phrased principally in terms of the meaning of the relationship for the mother herself, with less attention paid to the consequences of this enduring closeness for the mother's own mother.

Finally, it should be noted that the very pattern of living arrangements in contemporary urban society fosters intergenerational dependence. Rather than destroying the close-knit intergenerational unit, urban life actually supports continuing close relationships across the generations. The diversity of available employment and the existence of a variety of contacts among members of the larger family unit itself combine to prevent the necessity of moving in order to find work. The telephone and the ease of transportation over relatively short distances together facilitate frequent contact with other family members that, in turn, permits realization of dependency needs, often in the guise of seeking information.

This book discusses the impact of socialization into dependency and the lack of separateness characteristic of relations among women across generations in contemporary urban American society and examines a variety of psychological solutions to this dilemma among families in which the generations of women differ in the extent of contact (living together and apart) and in the extent of comfort the second generation shows with the undifferentiated relationship between self and mother. As a result it is possible to study in greater detail the manner in which members of each generation resolve conflicts associated with the lack of separateness, as well as the impact of this lack of separateness on the manner in which the woman in the second generation cares for her own young children in the third generation.

CHAPTER 2

Intergenerational Relations and Childcare Attitudes

A woman's own mother is generally the first and most important influence in her own psychosocial development toward becoming a mother herself. Childhood experiences within a woman's own parental family largely determine both how much satisfaction she will be able to obtain in later relationships, as well as the degree of comfort she will be able to feel in a continuing close relationship with her own mother, and the extent to which she can feel that she is an effective and competent woman and mother herself (Erikson, 1959; Bibring, 1959; Bibring et al., 1961; Benedek, 1959, 1970). Experiences during adulthood play an important part in a woman's continuing psychosocial development across the life cycle. At the same time, these adult experiences continually interact with a woman's character as a whole, so that continuity is maintained across the life cycle.

Motherhood represents a particular challenge to a woman's sense of identity; for, as Benedek (1959) has so well noted, the developmental issues involved in caring for young children call forth relevant unresolved conflicts in her own preadult development. Continuing contact between the young adult daughter, now a mother herself, and her own mother, together with the adult daughter's lack of feelings of separateness from her mother, and increased role complementarity resulting from her assumption of the maternal role all determine her tendency to look to her own mother for help and support and also the conflict related to this request for help, as she assumes a role for which she has had little preparation, but which, together with that of housewife, will take up more than 75% of her time (Lopata, 1971). As a result, personal discomfort resulting from the developmental conflicts evoked in the mother by childcare are intensified by the continuing, often ambivalent, relationship between the mother of young children and her own mother. Such conflict, in turn, is likely to be transmitted to the third generation, leading to the perpetuation of family conflict across generations (Hess and Handel, 1959; Parker, 1972).

During childcare, the mother's first task is that of learning to understand and meet the baby's needs and then one of fostering a more reciprocal social relationship—well portrayed in the smiling play between mothers and their six month old infants. During the second year of the baby's life, the relevant developmental task for both mother and child is that of fostering in the child some sense of differentiation and individuation within the context of this reciprocal relationship, recognizing that this is a more relative sense of separateness among girls than among boys. This formulation of the developmental sequence across the first years of life, together with the implications of this development for the mother's own continued successful adaptation to motherhood, has been clearly described by Sander (1964, 1969, 1975) and provides the conceptual basis for the Maternal Attitude Scale (MAS), a self-report questionnaire developed by Cohler, Weiss, and Grunebaum (1970; Cohler et al., 1976, 1980,) for measuring mothers' attitudes toward these phases or issues in the developing mother-child relationship (the MAS is described later in this chapter).

MATERNAL PERSONALITY AND CHILDCARE

In this book, attitudes toward childcare are viewed as one aspect of maternal personality that, in turn, directly affects the child's socialization. Following McClelland (1951), "attitudes" are viewed as that component of personality which orders or schematizes the interpersonal world and serves as a guide to action with regard to specific interpersonal interactions. As Smith, Bruner, and White (1956), Katz and Stotland (1959), and Sarnoff (1960) all show, attitudes foster evaluation of events in terms of one's own needs and concerns, reflecting both present and past life experiences. In the context of her relationship with her child, a mother's childcare attitudes influence her appraisal of transactions between her child and herself and determine the range of responses possible regarding particular actions on the child's part.

One relevant evaluation a mother makes regarding her child's development is that of the child's competence in dealing with the environment. Mothers differ in the extent to which they regard infants and young children as competent to maintain interpersonal mutuality and to explore and order the world about them (R. White, 1963), just as mothers differ in the extent to which they believe that children's needs and intents may be differentiated from their own needs (D. Levy, 1943; Mahler, 1968). Mothers also differ in the extent that they can recognize and accept the ambiguities and complexities involved in rearing children in contemporary urban society (Minturn and Lambert, 1964).

Empirical support for this view of the mother's developing relationship with her child and the implications for the mother's adaptation has been provided by comparative studies of the childcare attitudes of mentally ill and well mothers, where mental illness is regarded as an indication that a woman has been largely unable to resolve the developmental tasks associated with the care of young children (Cohler, Weiss, and Grunebaum, 1970; Cohler, 1975; Cohler et al., 1976, 1980). These studies have shown that compared with mentally ill mothers, well mothers express more adaptive attitudes regarding the formation of a reciprocal relationship with the baby, believe to a greater extent in the importance of differentiating between their own needs and those of the baby, and express greater capacity for resolving ambivalent feelings regarding childcare. At the same time, these well women expressed less adaptive attitudes than mentally ill women regarding their ability to recognize and meet the baby's physical needs. As long as the baby is a passive being who demands only physical care, mentally ill mothers feel able to provide nurturant care. Only when the baby demands a more complex relationship in which the mother must be able to take the role of the other and to develop reciprocity with the child does the mentally ill mother feel unable to master this developmental task.

INTERGENERATIONAL RELATIONS AND ATTITUDES TOWARD CHILDCARE

Epigenetic formulations of personality development suggest that there is a "critical period" early in the child's life during which the subsequent capacity for mature relationships is largely determined. The form of the infant's tie to the caretaker and the degree of the caretaker's capacity to meet both physiological and emotional needs influence the child's ability to differentiate himself or herself from the caretaker and to take the first tentative steps away from the caretaker in order to explore and master the external environment. The pattern of this first experience, in turn, influences the child's subsequent ability to develop patterns of autonomous behavior that lead to feelings of effectance regarding both the intrapersonal and interpersonal environment.

In a study of conflict in psychosocial development as measured by responses to picture thematic stimuli, Cohler (1975) has reported that young adult mothers hospitalized for mental illness showed greater conflict than well mothers regarding the capacity for interpersonal relations. Well mothers, while showing no greater conflict regarding autonomy versus perception of coercive control by another, did show that this issue in psychosocial development was a greater source of concern for them. While the mentally ill mothers were concerned with developing satisfying relationships primarily with their own mothers, well women were particularly concerned about establishing more autonomous relationships with their own mothers. Furthermore, within the group of well mothers, those women who continued to share a household or residence with their own mothers appeared to experience greater ambivalence about issues of dependence and separation than women living apart. While the large majority lived within easy driving distance of their own mothers and maintained close and frequent communication, a minority of these women still lived within the same dwelling as their own mothers. Since there was no difference in the proportion whose mothers were widows among these two groups of mothers living together and apart, it appeared that the decision to share a common dwelling was based on some factor other than sheer economic necessity.

Within the group of women living with their mothers, two arrangements were possible. There was a low proportion of grandmothers who were widows; there were no cases in which the grandmother had joined the mother and her family in the younger woman's residence. Rather, in every instance, the mother and her family had returned home to her own parents' residence. Among those families in

GOSHEN COLLEGE LIBRARY
GOSHEN INDIANA

which the grandmother was a widow, the mother and her family shared a household with the grandmother in the grandmother's longtime residence.

However, the more typical situation was that in which the mother and her family rented or were given an apartment in the house owned by the mother's parents. Either the house was partitioned into two side-by-side residences, each with a separate entryway or the apartment was located on the second floor of a two-family house. In the latter case, the parental and grandparental generations usually shared a common stairway that led to a common foyer. Of course, in the latter case, interaction between the two generations was particularly frequent since family members were required to share a common entrance.

Prior research regarding childcare attitudes, and the comparative study of psychosocial development among mentally ill and well mothers, led to the study of the childcare attitudes of mothers and their own mothers, specifically in regard to the relationship between the living arrangements of the two generations and childcare attitudes. It was hypothesized that both mothers and grandmothers who shared residence would believe to a greater extent than mothers and grandmothers living apart that a mother cannot differentiate her own needs from those of her children. That is, the same close and undifferentiated relationship shown in the continued shared living arrangements of mother and grandmother would be reflected in the attitudes of the two generations regarding that childcare issue most closely related to the issue of separation and individuation (Mahler, Pine, and Bergman, 1975).

While there have been several previously published reports of the childcare attitudes of the two generations, most such reports do not differentiate between one's own mother and mother-in-law and consider only those childcare attitudes that refer to the issue of authoritarian control. In the first of these published reports, Staples and Smith (1954) report a significant relationship between mothers and their own mothers on a scale of authoritarian-democratic attitudes toward control of the child's expression of autonomy. These authors report less of a difference between the attitudes of the two generations when they live apart than when they share a common residence. Kell and Aldous (1960) report a significant relationship between the attitudes of the two generations regarding discipline, but not regarding the display of affection, and do not consider the question of the living arrangements of the two generations.

Using groups of upper-middle-class mothers and their teenaged daughters, Woods, Glavin, and Kettle (1960) reported little congruence across the generations regarding attitudes toward such childcare issues as weaning, modesty training, and modification of the child's expression of dependency and aggression needs. The daughters were found to be more indulgent and permissive than their own mothers, a finding consistent with those of other studies (McGahey and Sporakowski, 1972), although neither generation was indulgent regarding the child's expression of parent-directed aggression. Woods, Glavin, and Kettle interpret their findings as showing a "generation gap" with regard to childcare attitudes. A study of the childcare attitudes of Japanese and Japanese American women (Kitano, 1964) also suggests that the attitudes of the same generation across cultures were more highly associated than different generations within the same culture.

These studies raise more questions than they answer. Most are based only on groups of upper-middle-class women, and, where differences are found between the childcare attitudes of the two generations, these studies do not consider the greater degree of formal education of the daughters that may account for generational differences independent of other effects. At least two studies (Woods, Glavin, and Kettle, 1960; McGahey and Sporakowski, 1972) compared mothers with daughters who were in college and did not yet have children of their own. Attitudes are situationally specific, and there is little reason to believe that attitudes of mothers can be compared with those of college students who do not yet have children of their own.

The investigation reported in this chapter was begun to obtain comparative quantitative data regarding the personality and childcare attitudes of mothers and grandmothers living together or apart and also to obtain a baseline for subsequent case studies of mothers and grandmothers. It was hoped that the combination of nomothetic and idiographic approaches would provide a more powerful method for understanding intergenerational continuity and its impact on childcare attitudes and practices than could be obtained using either approach independently.

THE QUANTITATIVE STUDY: MEASURING THE CHILDCARE ATTITUDES OF MOTHERS AND THEIR OWN MOTHERS[1]

Method of Study

The sample consisted of 90 mother-grandmother pairs, in each of which the mother had at least one child below age five. These mother-grandmother pairs were recruited through newspaper advertisements. As Cohler, Woolsey, Weiss, and Grunebaum (1968) have noted, mothers recruited in such a manner do not display notable psychopathology and seem, at least in terms of their Minnesota Multiphasic Personality Inventory (MMPI) profiles, to be similar to other normal samples such as that described by Gloye and Zimmerman (1967).

All participants were administered the Maternal Attitude Scale (MAS), a 233-item Likert-type instrument developed to measure attitudes regarding several issues with which a mother is confronted sequentially in the care of her infant or young child. (Appendix D) Items for this instrument were based largely on Sander's (1964, 1969) formulation of the developing mother-child relationship. The MAS yields standardized scores based on 5 orthogonal or independent second-order factors derived from a principal components analysis of a set of 13 such

---

[1]Material in this section and Tables 1 through 7 are based on material previously reported in the *Merrill-Palmer Quarterly of Behavior and Development*, 1971.

"issue" scales, in addition to a number of empirically derived scales (Cohler, Weiss, and Grunebaum, 1970).[2] The original scales were developed in several pretest studies involving more than 700 mothers from all social strata.

Each factor refers to a particular developmental issue in the early mother-child relationship. Clearly, both the child's own development and the mother's continued effectiveness and satisfaction in adapting to the maternal role are shaped by the extent to which these developmental issues have been resolved in an appropriate manner. As suggested previously, a woman's attitudes toward childcare permit her to appraise or interpret transactions between her child and herself. To the extent that her appraisal and interpretations are congruent with the needs and intentions of the child, her attitudes are more adaptive for the resolution of the particular issue or issues being negotiated between mother and child at any given point in the child's development. In sum, a mother's attitudes regarding each of these issues measured by the MAS may be viewed as more or less adaptive to the extent that they either facilitate or impair the resolution of a particular issue being negotiated by mother and child. Table 1 provides a brief summary of adaptive and maladaptive attitudes reflected by each of these five factors.

In addition to the administration of the MAS, subjects completed a Family Information Form that provided data concerning the education of the respondent and her husband, the household composition, distance between the residence of mother and grandmother, and frequency of contact between mother and grandmother. The social class of mothers and grandmothers was coded according to Hollingshead's "two factor" index with seven-point scales used for coding one's own education and the husband's occupation (Myers and Bean, 1968). It should be noted that a low score on this index indicates high educational and occupational status. The respondent's age was coded according to a nine-point scale.

The age of the mothers ranged from 20 to 40, with a mean of approximately 24½ years. The level of educational attainment of the mothers ranged from postcollege work to less than 4 years of high school, with a mean of approximately 12½ years of schooling; the number of children in the household ranged from 1 to 8, with a median of 2 children in the household. The age of the grandmothers ranged from 51 to 75 years, with a median age of 58. The level of educational attainment of the grandmothers ranged from college graduate to less than 8 years of grammar school, with a median of 10 years of schooling. These grandmothers reported having as many as 10 children, with a median of 3 children in their own families.

Following the collection of data from the mother-grandmother pairs, mothers were individually matched with mothers from a much larger sample who had completed the MAS, but who had not volunteered with their own mothers. Matching was based on the following criteria: own education, husband's occupa-

---

[2]Copies of the *Manual for the Maternal Attitude Scale* are available, without charge, from the authors.

Table 1. Schematic Description of Childrearing-Attitude Factors—Maternal Attitude Scale[a]

Factor	Adaptive Attitude	Maladaptive Attitude
I. Appropriate versus inappropriate control of Child's aggression[b]	Intent of aggressive impulse should be recognized, but it is important to modulate expression of aggression by providing alternate channels	Overly restrictive attitudes or, less commonly, overly permissive
II. Encouragement versus discouragement of reciprocity[b]	Babies can communicate with their mothers, and mothers should encourage development of a reciprocal relationship between mother and child	Babies cannot communicate with their mothers and are unable to develop a reciprocal social relationship or to respond to appropriate cues from their mothers
III. Appropriate versus inappropriate closeness with the child	A mother can enjoy and care for a baby without sacrificing herself, without becoming overly binding or overly protective, and without yielding to the baby's demand for an exclusive relationship (Mahler, Pine and Bergman, 1975)	Pregnancy, delivery, and childcare are seen as burdensome, depleting, and destructive of self; vacillation between the wish to be the sole caretaker and perpetuate the mother-infant symbiosis and the wish to relegate all aspects of childcare to others, a pattern similar to that described by D. Levy (1943) as the "overprotective mother"
IV. Acceptance versus denial of emotional complexity in childcare	Acceptance of ambivalent feelings about childcare, of some feeling of inadequacy as a mother, and of uncertainty regarding some aspects of childcare without loss of self-esteem	Denial of any concerns or doubts regarding childcare and of inadequacy in the maternal role, together with highly conventional and stereotyped beliefs and the feeling that mothers require little childcare assistance from others
V. Feeling of competence versus lack of competence in perceiving and meeting the baby's needs	Mothers can understand the infant's physical needs and meet them adequately	Babies are unable to let others know what their physical needs are, and mothers find it very difficult to understand and meet these needs

[a]Factor scores are expressed in standardized form based on a larger normative sample, with mean = 0.000 and standard deviation = ±1.000.

[b]Scores on the first two factors have been reflected so that a positive score indicates more adaptive attitudes.

tion, own age, number of children, and religious preference (Catholic vs. non Catholic). Each of these variables, with the exception of age, had demonstrated a significant relationship with maternal attitudes in previous research (Cohler, Weiss, and Grunebaum, 1970). In addition, no woman from this larger normative sample was used whose own mother was no longer alive or who visited with her own mother less often than once a year.[3]

Table 2 indicates the precision of the matching procedure based on age, education, husband's occupation, number of children, and religion (Catholic vs. non-Catholic). In general, these matched samples of mothers and their peers were drawn primarily from the blue-collar or working-class strata, and both samples represent the range of education, parity, age, husband's occupational level, and geographic mobility as prior research with the MAS. Only 88 of the 90 mothers were successfully matched with peers. Two women had husbands whose occupational levels could not be determined and were dropped from the sample.

Table 2. Comparison of Mother and Peer Samples on Background Variables Used in Matching

Variable	Mothers[a]		Peers[a]		t test[b]	p
	Mean	SD	Mean	SD		
Own age[c]	2.744	0.996	2.920	0.985	1.181	n.s.
Own education[d]	3.114	1.011	3.193	0.920	0.546	n.s.
Husband's occupation[d]	3.759	1.917	3.557	1.831	0.712	n.s.
Number of children	2.063	1.330	2.352	1.605	1.301	n.s.
Percent Catholic	47%		47%		—	n.s.

[a]$N = 88$ for each group.

[b]t test for independent samples, d. f. = 174.

[c]Mothers' ages range from 20 to 40 and were coded according to a 9 point scale. The obtained means are equivalent to an age of approximately 24½ years for both groups.

[d]Mother's own education and husband's occupation were coded according to a 7 point scale; a higher score indicates fewer years of education (the obtained means are equivalent to about 12½ years for both groups) and a lower-ranked occupation.

Information was also obtained from the women in these two samples regarding the frequency of contact with their own mothers and regarding their major sources of information regarding childrearing. Among the mothers, 86% reported that they visited with their own mothers at least once a week, as contrasted with 69% of their peers. This difference is statistically significant ($x^2 = 5.395$, d.f. $= 1, p$ $<.03$). That is, although both groups of women visited their own mothers quite frequently, mothers who volunteered together with their own mothers visited them much more frequently. Furthermore, 30% of the mothers studied indicated

[3]This selection of women reporting more frequent contact with their own mothers may have selectively eliminated women from the study who maintained total independence and may have therefore affected the distribution of scores on precisely those measures of interest to the study. However, only four mothers were eliminated on the basis of lack of contact less often than once a year, and the scores of each of these women were within one standard deviation (SD) from the mean score of the mother group on the MAS factor of appropriate closeness.

that their own mothers served as their primary source of childrearing information, as contrasted with 16% of their peers. This difference is also statistically significant ($x^2 = 4.16$, d.f. $= 1$, $p < .05$).

All participants were paid for their participation in the study (three dollars each for mother and grandmother), but only after all data had been received from both mother and grandmother. For each pair, the individual who had responded to the advertisement (generally the mother) was responsible for encouraging the other to return the materials. Most of the data were obtained at two group sessions; some grandmothers had difficulty completing the materials in the time allowed and were permitted to finish them at home.

Results and Discussion

When studying the childcare attitudes of mothers and their own mothers, one important question concerns the relationship between a mother's childcare attitudes and those of her own mother. However, it is also important to determine the extent to which there have been generational shifts in attitudes toward childrearing.

Intergenerational Relationships.   The relationship between the childcare attitudes of mothers and their own mothers is shown in Table 3.

Table 3.   Intercorrelations of Mothers' and Grandmothers'[a] Childcare Attitudes

		Grandmother Attitudes				
MAS Factors		I	II	III	IV	V
Mother Attitudes	I. Appropriate control	.370**	.078	−.145	−.080	−.034
	II. Encouragement of reciprocity	.126	.306**	−.079	.037	−.173
	III. Appropriate closeness	−.024	−.156	.156	−.005	.166
	IV. Acceptance of emotional complexity	−.231*	−.168	.090	.186	−.116
	V. Competence in meeting baby's needs	.035	.040	.104	−.071	.295**

[a]N = 88 mother-grandmother pairs.
*$p < .05$.
**$p < .01$.

Significant positive intergenerational relationships were found for three of the five factors: appropriate control, encouragement of reciprocity, and competence in meeting the baby's needs. Feelings of being able to channel the child's expression of angry feelings, of being able to respond to the baby's demand for a social relationship, and of feeling competent to interpret the baby's cues regarding physical needs are all related to the attitudes one's mother has regarding these issues. On the other hand, maternal attitudes toward self-sacrifice for the baby and differentiating a mother's needs from those of a child, together with attitudes reflecting the expression of more ambivalent feelings regarding childcare, are less closely related to the attitudes of one's own mother.

It is important to note that for four of the five MAS factors, the intergenerational correlations on the same factor were higher than those obtained by correlating different factors. As Campbell and Fiske (1959) have noted, interpretation of evidence for convergent-discriminant validity from a matrix of intercorrelations can be supported only if the off-diagonal correlations are lower than those on the diagonal.

Intergenerational Differences. To determine a change in childrearing attitudes from the grandmother's generation to the mother's generation, difference scores were calculated for each MAS factor in each mother-grandmother pair (see Table 4). Using the *t* test for matched pairs, significant differences were found between the grandmother and mother generations. Grandmothers showed significantly less adaptive attitudes than mothers regarding the MAS factors of appropriate control, encouragement of reciprocity, and appropriate closeness. However, grandmothers showed more adaptive attitudes than mothers regarding one factor: competence in meeting the baby's needs. There were no intergenerational differences regarding the factor of acceptance of emotional complexity.

Table 4. Comparison of Childrearing Attitudes of Grandmothers and Mothers

Factor	Statistic	Grand-mothers[a]	Mothers[a]	t test[b]	p
I. Appropriate control	Mean	−0.314	0.568		
	SD	1.175	1.078	6.531	.001
II. Encouragement of reciprocity	Mean	−0.382	−0.011		
	SD	0.805	0.909	3.430	.001
III. Appropriate closeness	Mean	−0.596	−0.258		
	SD	1.051	0.885	5.503	.01
IV. Acceptance of emotional complexity	Mean	−0.831	−0.586		
	SD	1.320	1.233	1.411	n.s.
V. Competence in meeting baby's needs	Mean	0.724	0.240		
	SD	0.067	0.741	5.618	.001

[a]N = 88 for each group.
[b]t test for matched pairs, d. f. = 87.

Differences between the two generations regarding attitudes toward the control of aggressive feelings and behavior are consistent with the findings of virtually every study of childrearing attitudes and practices (Wolfenstein, 1953; Staples and Smith, 1954; Bronfenbrenner, 1958a; Miller and Swanson, 1958; Kell and Aldous, 1960). Books and popular magazine articles on this subject have had an important influence on the attitudes of both middle- and working-class mothers in the present generation.

It is not surprising that mothers believe more strongly than grandmothers in the importance of fostering mother-child reciprocity. This increased emphasis on the importance of reciprocity in the mother-child relationship is consistent with recent trends in ego psychology in which the baby is viewed as active, striving, and capable of initiating changes in his or her environment (R. White, 1963). Recent research in child development suggests that infants are capable of a more differentiated relationship earlier in life than was formerly recognized (Wolff, 1963; Stern, 1977). Furthermore, in contrast to older parents' manuals that specifically criticized mothers who played with their babies or provided much stimulation (Wolfenstein, 1953), more recent discussions have stressed the importance for the baby's development of the mother's fostering a reciprocal relationship. However, as Senn (1957) has pointed out, both the nature of the problems investigated and also the interpretation of the findings of child development research are related to shifts in the value system of the society itself, such as increased emphasis on interpersonal relationships and togetherness. The attitudes of mothers seem to reflect this more recent focus on interpersonal relationships and concern with the development of closeness and reciprocity.

To understand why grandmothers have more adaptive attitudes than mothers regarding the factor of competence in meeting the baby's needs, it is important to recall that this factor depends heavily on attitudes toward the preference for breast-feeding rather than bottle-feeding, and demand rather than scheduled feeding, together with attitudes indicating that one can understand the baby's cues regarding his or her physical needs. Several studies (Bronfenbrenner, 1958a; Caldwell, 1964; Miller and Swanson, 1958; Stendler, 1950; Wolfenstein, 1953) have demonstrated that there have been rather dramatic shifts in attitudes toward these aspects of childcare since World War II. This has been shown to be especially true among working-class mothers. Bronfenbrenner (1958a) notes in his survey that as many as 82% of the women interviewed in 1932 reported a preference for breast-feeding rather than bottle-feeding. Thirty years later, Sears, Maccoby, and Levin (1957) reported only 39% of the women in their interview study expressed a preference for breast-feeding when replying to a paper-and-pencil multiple choice questionnaire. Fischer and Fischer (1963) report that about 38% of the women in their ethnographic study expressed a preference for breast-feeding. Even considering differences due to the manner in which mothers were surveyed, it would appear that fewer mothers prefer breast-feeding than was true a generation ago.

Similar findings were obtained regarding the preference for demand rather than scheduled feeding. Bronfenbrenner reports that only 23% of the mothers in the 1932 interview study used scheduled feeding. Sears, Maccoby, and Levin (1957) note that 71% of the mothers in their later study used scheduled feeding. Clearly, the grandmothers in the present study expressed attitudes more similar to those of the past generation than the present generation regarding the perception and care of the baby's physical needs.

Finally, it should be noted that mothers expressed more adaptive attitudes than grandmothers regarding the factor of appropriate closeness. The grandmothers in the present study regard childrearing as especially demanding on the mother herself and believe that it is particularly difficult for a mother to differentiate her own needs from those of her children. While expressing more adaptive attitudes than their mothers, these mothers, as a group, showed less adaptive attitudes than either hospitalized or nonhospitalized mothers (Cohler et al., 1976). The problem these mothers experience in resolving this issue becomes even more apparent when contrasting their attitudes with those of the matched peer control group.

Intragenerational Differences.   We have found that the attitudes of mothers differ in important respects from those of grandmothers. However, these mothers volunteered for the study, together with their own mothers, and had more frequent contact with them than was true of their peers who also volunteered for the study, but without the additional requirement of their own mothers' participation. For this reason, it is necessary to contrast mothers' attitudes both with those of the grandmother generation and also with those of other mothers in their own generation. Difference scores were calculated for each of the five MAS factors between mothers and their matched peers (see Table 5). Using the t test for matched pairs, several significant intragenerational differences were found.

Table 5.   Comparison of Childrearing Attitudes of Mothers and Peers

Factor	Statistic	Mothers[a]	Peers[a]	t test[b]	p
I. Appropriate control	Mean	0.568	−0.005		
	SD	1.078	1.027	4.075	.001
II. Encouragement of reciprocity	Mean	−0.011	0.117		
	SD	0.909	0.804	1.014	n.s.
III. Appropriate closeness	Mean	−0.258	0.172		
	SD	0.885	0.844	3.500	.001
IV. Acceptance of emotional complexity	Mean	−0.586	−0.066		
	SD	1.233	0.894	3.541	.001
V. Competence in meeting baby's needs	Mean	0.240	0.078		
	SD	0.741	0.923	1.309	n.s.

[a]N = 88 for each group.
[b]t test for matched pairs, d. f. = 87.

Mothers indicate more adaptive attitudes than their peers regarding the MAS factor on appropriate control, although their peers show more adaptive attitudes regarding the factors of appropriate closeness and acceptance of emotional complexity. No significant intragenerational differences were found for the factors of encouragement of reciprocity or competence in meeting the baby's needs.

Comparison of intergenerational and intragenerational differences regarding the MAS factor of appropriate control shows that mothers' attitudes are significantly more adaptive than either those of grandmothers or those of peers. In this instance, mothers may be especially accepting or permissive in the area of control of the child's aggression, even for their own generation. If this is the case, then the magnitude of Staples and Smith's (1954) and Kell and Aldous' (1960) findings regarding the less controlling attitudes of mothers, compared with grandmothers, may also have been due to the restriction of the sample of women volunteering with their own mothers.

While mothers showed more adaptive attitudes than peers regarding the MAS factor of appropriate control, they showed less adaptive attitudes concerning appropriate closeness and acceptance of emotional complexity. These findings are consistent with the mothers in this study having more frequent contact with their own mothers than peers and relying more often on their mothers as their major source of childrearing information.

Mothers who bring their own mothers to participate in a psychological study appear to be especially dependent on their own mothers and may have unusual difficulty in differentiating their own needs from those of their own mothers. The attitudes of these mothers suggest that they are a rather compliant, dependent, and conventional group of women who have particular difficulty in separating from their own mothers and achieving autonomy. While these women express less concern than their peers about feeling able to provide appropriate control of their children's expression of angry feelings, they also feel less able than their peers to take independent action, and they express more conventional and stereotyped attitudes regarding childcare.[4]

Age Differences within Each Generation.   These findings regarding differences between the childcare attitudes of mothers and their own mothers raise the question of whether such differences may be accounted for by age alone or whether there is some more fundamental shift in childcare attitudes within our culture. To answer this question, each generation was divided into two separate age groups. The group of mothers was divided into those younger than 30 and those older than 30, and the grandmother generation was divided into those younger than 60 and those older than 60. While there were no differences in the mother's childcare attitudes as a function of age, several striking differences were found in the childcare attitudes of older and younger grandmothers. These results are shown in Table 6.

Older grandmothers show particularly maladaptive attitudes regarding the factors of appropriate control and appropriate closeness. On the other hand, the older grandmothers indicate more adaptive attitudes than the younger grandmothers regarding the factor of acceptance of emotional complexity. No differences were found on the other two factors. These older grandmothers experience ambivalent feelings regarding the care of young children. They also believe that mothers should establish close and binding relationships with their children, that mothers should be expected to make enormous self-sacrifices for the sake of maintaining this close and protective relationship, and that mothers should keep a tight rein

---

[4]This interpretation of the childcare attitudes of the mothers in the present study is consistent with their scores on a sentence completion test derived from Loevinger's formulation of moral and interpersonal development (Loevinger, 1966, 1968; Loevinger, Wessler, and Redmore, 1970). A disproportionately high percentage of these women were classified as "conformist," the fourth of seven developmental phases. Loevinger notes that such women, while capable of genuine reciprocity, may be characterized especially by "their preoccupation with reputation, status, appearance, and adjustment. References to inner feelings are typically stereotyped, banal, and often moralistic" (1966, p. 199).

Table 6.   Comparison of Background Variables and Childcare Attitudes of Younger and Older Grandmothers

Variable	Statistic	Younger Grandmothers[a]	Older Grandmothers[b]	t test	p
Background					
Husband's occupation	Mean	4.019	4.091		
	SD	1.578	1.571	0.179	n.s.
Wife's education[c]	Mean	4.217	4.609		
	SD	1.066	1.234	1.209	n.s.
Attitudes					
I. Appropriate control	Mean	−0.175	−0.698		
	SD	1.246	0.983	1.781	.07
II. Encouragement of reciprocity	Mean	−0.373	0.396		
	SD	0.746	0.874	0.120	n.s.
III. Appropriate closeness	Mean	−0.382	−1.050		
	SD	0.971	1.288	2.481	.01
IV. Acceptance of emotional complexity	Mean	−0.611	−1.497		
	SD	1.138	1.659	2.687	.009
V. Competence in meeting baby's need's	Mean	0.721	0.814		
	SD	0.615	0.592	0.611	n.s.

[a]$N = 52$.
[b]$N = 53$.
[c]The obtained means are equivalent to approximately 10 years of education for both groups.

over the child's expression of his or her own impulses. In sum, these older grandmothers deny the possibility of more subtle feelings regarding childcare and view children's hostility as potentially destructive and therefore necessary to control at any cost.

Joint versus Separate Residence.   When contrasted with their peers, the pattern of attitudes expressed by the mothers in the study presented in this book suggests that they are more compliant and dependent and have had greater difficulty achieving autonomy from their own mothers. It was expected that this difficulty would be accentuated when considering the attitudes of mothers who share a residence with their own mothers.

Mothers were classified as sharing a common residence with their own mothers only if, at the time of the study, they were living in the same residence. Information regarding residence patterns was available for 89 of the 90 mother-grandmother pairs. Only 17 women (19%) were currently residing with their own mothers, although 30 women (32%) indicated that they had lived with their own mothers at some point following marriage. Neither mothers nor grandmothers sharing a common residence or living apart could be differentiated according to their husband's occupational level, their own educational attainment, or their age. (T tests for the significance of the differences between these variables for either generation living together or apart was less than 1.26, d.f. $= 85$). It should, however, be noted that while the absence of the grandfather from the household was not associated with the pattern of joint versus separate residence, there was a tendency ($x^2=3.14$, p <.09, 1. d.f.) for mothers whose husbands were absent from the home through death or divorce to share a common residence with their own mothers. The decision to share a common residence or live apart cannot simply be explained on the basis of demographic or economic factors such as social class for either generation.

Table 7 indicates that only one MAS factor, appropriate closeness, differentiated mothers living together with their mothers from mothers living apart. This same factor also differentiated grandmothers living with their daughters from grandmothers maintaining a separate residence. It is striking that for both generations the same factor differentiates between women within each generation living together or apart. On each of the other four factors mothers living together with their own mothers indicated less adaptive attitudes than mothers living apart. Using the sign test for small samples, this pattern is significantly different from that which would be expected by chance alone (p =.03). No such consistent pattern was found in the case of grandmothers living together or apart. It should also be noted that among mothers and grandmothers who lived apart there was no relationship between the distance the mother lived from the grandmother and any one of the five MAS factors.

These findings show that mothers and grandmothers who share a common residence do have less adaptive attitudes regarding the establishment of appropriate closeness than do mothers and grandmothers living apart. Furthermore, the one MAS factor which most closely approximates the attitude measure used by Staples and Smith (1954), that dealing primarily with control of the child's aggressive impulses, was not found to be related to residence patterns in either generation. It is somewhat difficult, however, to interpret these findings as discrepant from Staples and Smith, since the present scale is not interchangeable with theirs and since they included both mothers and mothers-in-law in the grandmother generation without distinguishing between their responses.

Since the essential difference between mothers and grandmothers living together or apart is related to the ways in which problems of closeness and separation have been resolved, it is not surprising that both mothers and grandmothers sharing a common residence express less adaptive attitudes regarding this issue than mothers and grandmothers living apart. We have already suggested in Chapter 1 that the issue of separation is a critical one among mothers and their daughters in comtemporary society. However, there is likely to be some variation in the extent to which women within the two generations experience discomfort in maintaining continuing closeness and in resolving conflicts associated with this issue.

The findings from this study suggest that the degree of continuing contact represented by joint residence is associated with heightened concern with the issue of psychological closeness among members of each generation. However, these findings do not suggest that conflict regarding this issue is necessarily causal in the decision to maintain a joint residence. As we see later in studying individual families, the reasons for sharing a common residence are numerous. It is more likely that this decision to live together intensifies preexisting conflict between

Table 7. Comparison of Childcare Attitudes Among Mothers and Grandmothers Living Together and Apart

MAS Factor	Statistic	Grandmothers		Mothers		Grandmothers: Together versus apart t test
		Together[a]	Apart[b]	Together[a]	Apart[b]	
I. Appropriate control	Mean	-0.481	-0.370	0.310	0.588	0.361
	SD	0.883	1.160	1.158	1.055	
II. Encouragement of reciprocity	Mean	-0.406	-0.413	-0.252	0.043	0.037
	SD	0.607	0.823	0.915	0.902	
III. Appropriate closeness	Mean	-1.136	-0.498	-0.744	-0.143	2.334*
	SD	1.002	1.019	0.801	0.866	
IV. Acceptance of emotional complexity	Mean	-0.933	-0.802	-0.877	-0.520	0.360
	SD	1.149	1.368	1.536	1.152	
V. Competence in meeting baby's needs	Mean	0.639	0.725	0.223	0.251	0.533
	SD	0.450	0.634	0.738	0.755	

[a] N = 17.
[b] N = 79.
*p < .05.
**p < .01.

mothers and daughters regarding attainment of a sense of separateness. Such conflict, also reflected in attitudes concerning the resolution of this issue among mothers and their young children, is then transmitted to the third generation, as seen in the belief, more prevalent among these mothers living together with their own mothers, that attainment of psychic autonomy is not of much importance in the child's development during the first years of life.

Among those families in which mothers and their own mothers live together, it may be hypothesized that there is a greater degree of conflict, vacillation, and ambiguity, both in the relationship between mother and grandmother and in the relationship of each with the child than among those families where mothers and grandmothers live apart. Furthermore, the fact that mothers sharing a joint residence with their own mothers are somewhat more likely to have had marital conflicts suggests either greater difficulty in separating from their own mothers and establishing an independent life or that such a joint residential pattern intensifies conflict between husband and wife in the second generation. If, as seems likely, both the mother of young children and her own mother have had particular difficulty separating from each other, neither one is in an optimal position to reach an adaptive resolution of this issue. The mother is likely to feel inadequate, to be sensitive to criticism, and to deal with these feelings sometimes by pulling the baby to herself and sometimes by relinquishing total responsibility for the baby's care to the grandmother. The grandmother may feel that her daughter is inadequate as a mother and may also vacillate between the wish to take over and resentment of the daughter's demand that she do so.

Preliminary review of these findings regarding mother-grandmother pairs living together and apart suggested that intensive clinical study of mother-grandmother pairs would be required to determine the validity of this interpretation regarding the impact of common residence on intergenerational relations. At the same time, such a clinical study would also permit a more careful examination of the role of the mother's identification with her own mother in mediating her present relationship both with her own mother and with her children.

THE CASE STUDIES: SELECTION OF FAMILIES FOR INTENSIVE STUDY

In the past several years, there has been considerable controversy regarding the usefulness of the intensive case study as a research tool in the behavioral sciences. Much of the ill-repute into which this method has fallen arises from the way in which it is used in clinical psychiatry. However, it also arises from the ways in which cases have been selected for study.

As originally used by Freud, the case study provided a basic resource for learning psychoanalytic theory and therapy. Sufficient data were always available for the readers to form their own understandings of the case and then to compare their interpretations with that provided by Freud. These types of case studies continue as a major way for learning about psychoanalysis. However, as used in contemporary clinical psychiatry and psychology, the case study often consists of little more than an abbreviated vignette lacking data sufficient for readers to understand the source of the author's interpretation. These brief excerpts generally leave the readers frustrated and dissatisfied. However, there have been several exemplary contemporary studies, including Evan's (1954) study of three men; Barron's (1955) case study of a "residual"; Murray's (1955) study of an American Icarus; Smith, Bruner, and White's (1956) study of the formation of political opinions; Hess and Handel's (1959) studies of the social worlds of five American families; Keniston's (1960) study of an American Ishmael, a portrait of alienated youth; R. White's (1966) *Lives in Progress;* and Wessman and Ricks' (1966) study of mood and personality.

These cases of nonpsychiatric subjects were all selected to represent some ideal type defined either in conceptual or empirical terms. While information about group differences can be of great use in the behavioral sciences, idiographic research can illustrate the ways in which these traits are organized in the unique individual. The study of randomly selected subjects leads to the loss of interpretative power in case study investigations. If the individual selected for study has been defined as particularly representative of the group from which he is selected, the study of his personality and experiences may provide greater understanding about the meaning of these group differences, as well as providing additional information for subsequent empirical investigation. At the same time, it is important to specify the criteria by which a particular case is selected for study. Indeed, the reports of Hess and Handel (1959) and Senn and Hartford (1968), the only detailed published case studies of families, suffer from precisely this problem. While both studies propose dimensions according to which families can be described, neither study selects families for intensive study that represent the typologies they so carefully describe.

In this book, the technique of dimensional sampling (Arnold, 1970) was used. A purposive sample was selected using a systematic framework for sampling based on the MAS scale of appropriate closeness. This approach is followed implicitly in such classic personality research as that of Adorno et al. (1950) in their studies of the authoritarian personality and by Couch and Keniston (1960) in their studies of response styles and acquiescence. Arbitrary selection of cases for intensive study is prevented by relying on a preconceived theoretical framework and systematic selection of cases, based on a measure of that theory, according to some specified criterion.

In this book, mother-grandmother pairs were carefully selected to represent the theoretical frameworks being studied: (1) closeness-separation, which measures an important aspect of psychic closeness discussed in Chapter 1 as a central determinant of the relationship between adult women and their mothers, and (2) joint versus separate residence. Residence patterns were determined from demographic information available for each family. Particular mother-grandmother pairs were first selected according to the mother's score on the MAS factor of appropriate closeness. This MAS factor was selected as a dimension for ordering the case studies because it represented the issue of closeness-separation, already dicussed in Chapter 1 as one of the most important issues in understanding the relationship between adult women and their own mothers. It was assumed that less adaptative attitudes regarding appropriate closeness between mother and child reflected a similar conflict between self and one's own mother and that this continuing conflict regarding closeness and separation is associated both with the decision to live together or apart and with the impact of those living arrangements on the personality development and adjustment of members of each generation.

The scores of all mothers in the sample on this factor were first transformed into ranks. Then the mothers with the 10 highest- and the 10 lowest-ranking scores were selected from the total sample (a high score on this factor indicates more adaptive attitudes and a low score indicates less adaptive attitudes). The scores of each of these 20 mothers exceeded the mean for the total sample by an SD of ±1.50 or greater. Finally, names were drawn at random from among the 10 highest and 10 lowest-ranking scores until there were 4 mother-grandmother pairs corresponding to the 4 cells of the design for the study as shown in Table 8.

Each of these four mothers was telephoned and asked if she would be willing to participate in the study. Permission was also sought to contact her own mother who was also asked if she would participate. Each of these four mother-grandmother pairs agreed enthusiastically to participate in this additional study; both mothers and grandmothers had enjoyed participating in the initial project and looked forward to contributing to the additional study. All four mothers selected for the study were of Italian descent and had been reared as Catholics. Each of these women had married a Catholic man from either an Italian or an Irish family. Mr. Russo was from a second-generation Italian family, while Mr. Murphy and Mr. McGorty were from Irish families. Mr. Czaja's family included Hungarian ethnic traditions on his father's side and both Irish and German ethnic traditions on his mother's side. It is particularly interesting to note that the husbands in those families living with the wife's mother do not necessarily earn less income than husbands in families living apart. This supports the finding of the quantitative study that the decision to live with the wife's mother is based on factors other than sheer economic necessity. The grandmothers are nearly as well matched on the relevant background characteristics as the mothers. All four are of about the same age and are of Italian Catholic descent; three of the four have husbands who are still alive. These three husbands are all laborers or skilled workmen.

Measures Used in the Case Studies

All grandmothers and mothers had previously completed both the MAS and a social background form as a part of the quantitative study. For the case studies, several projective tests were administered. In this order, the eight women were asked to draw a picture of a whole person, a person of the opposite sex, and a baby, and then to describe the personality of each person they had drawn (Weiss, Grunebaum, and Schell, 1964). Each was also administered the standard Rorschach following the procedure described by Rapaport, Gill, and Schafer (1968). Finally, each woman was asked to respond to a number of pictures from

Table 8. Design for Intensive Case Study of Mother-Grandmother Pairs

	Mother and Grandmother Live Apart	
	Mother	Grandmother
Appropriate Closeness (More Adaptive Attitudes)		
Name:	Mrs. McGorty	Mrs. Limpari
Own lineage:	Italian	Italian
Husband's lineage:	Irish	Italian
Own age:	38	59
Own education:	Law school graduate	Elementary school
Husband's occupation:	Postal clerk	Construction foreman
Number children:	3	4
Own religion:	Catholic	Catholic
Inappropriate Closeness (Less Adaptive Attitudes)		
Name:	Mrs. Russo	Mrs. Scardoni
Own lineage:	Italian	Italian
Husband's lineage:	Italian	Italian
Own age:	27	53
Own education:	High school graduate	Elementary school
Husband's occupation:	Laborer	Laborer
Number children:	1	2
Own religion:	Catholic	Catholic

Table 8. Continued

		Mother and Grandmother Share Residence	
		Mother	Grandmother
Appropriate Closeness			
(More Adaptive Attitudes)	Name:	Mrs. Czaja	Mrs. Giorgio
	Own lineage:	Italian	Italian
	Husband's lineage:	Hungarian-Irish	Italian
	Own age:	31	64
	Own education:	College graduate	High school graduate
	Husband's occupation:	College art professor	Physician (deceased)
	Number children:	1 (and currently pregnant)	5
	Own religion:	Catholic	Catholic
Inappropriate Closeness			
(Less Adaptive Attitudes)	Name:	Mrs. Murphy	Mrs. Pescatore
	Own lineage:	Italian	Italian
	Husband's lineage:	Italian Irish	Italian
	Own age:	28	53
	Own education:	Some college	Grammar school
	Husband's occupation:	Drama teacher	Machinist
	Number children:	3	3
	Own religion:	Catholic	Catholic

63

the standard Thematic Apperception Test (TAT) series (Murray, 1943) and the pictures used by Cohler (1975) for the Interpersonal Apperception Technique (IAT) series. The sequence of adminstration of these pictures is indicated in Table 9.

Mothers were also asked to complete the Minnesota Multiphasic Personality Inventory MMPI. Since this paper-and-pencil test can be particularly exhausting for older persons to complete, this request was not made of the grandmothers.

Following this first session, respondents were also interviewed on their childcare practices and attitudes, family cultural traditions, and problems in relating to

Table 9.   Thematic/Interpersonal Apperception Test Picture Descriptions[a]

TAT	1	A young boy is comtemplating a violin which rests on a table in front of him.
IAT	M1	A younger woman is standing up and talking with an older woman who is seated at a table on which there are two coffee cups.
IAT	H4	A young woman is seated on a sofa talking with a young man.
IAT	Si3	A young woman is looking straight ahead as another young woman wearing a coat and carrying a handbag is about to go out the door.
IAT	F2	A young woman is seated in a chair and an older man is standing behind her holding a letter.
IAT	B5	A young woman is seated on a park bench in the city and is watching a young boy playing with a ball.
IAT	Se8	A young woman stands holding a cat and looking out the window.
IAT	Fam	Living room scene: a woman has her hand on a little boy's shoulder, a baby girl is seated on the floor, and a man is standing to the side.
IAT	Tel[b]	A woman is standing with a telephone receiver in her hand.
IAT	G6	A woman is washing dishes and in the background a little girl is seated at a table.
IAT	Se7	A woman in a raincoat is walking down the street. A path leads to the house portrayed in the background.
IAT	W9	Two women are engaged in conversation, one with her hand on her hip and the other with her arms crossed.
TAT	2	Country scene: In the foreground is a young woman with books in her hand; in the background a man is working in the fields and an older woman is looking on.
TAT	6GF	A young woman sitting on the edge of a sofa looks back over her shoulder at an older man with a pipe in his mouth who seems to be addressing her.
TAT	7GF	An older woman is sitting on a sofa close beside a girl, speaking or reading to her. The girl, who holds a doll in her lap, is looking away.
TAT	10	A young woman's head against a man's shoulder.
TAT	12F	The portrait of a young woman. A weird old woman with a shawl over her head is grimacing in the background.
TAT	13MF	A young man is standing with downcast head buried in his arm. Behind him is the figure of a woman lying in bed.
TAT	15	A gaunt man with clenched hands is standing among gravestones.
TAT	18GF	A woman has her hands squeezed around the throat of another woman whom she appears to be pushing backward across the banister of a stairway.

[a]TAT descriptions are quoted directly from Murray's (1943) Manual. IAT descriptions are by B. Cohler (pictures used with the IAT are shown in Appendix A).

[b]The description for Tel, and picture © by Daniel Fishman, Ph. D. and reproduced by permission.

other members of the family (see appendices B and C).[5] Grandmothers were asked questions about their relationships with their sons-in-law and their own mothers, when still alive, and their other daughters. The design of the semistructured interview follows quite closely that described by Hoffman and Sigel and these authors' colleagues at the Merrill-Palmer Institute (Hoffman, 1954; I. Sigel, Hoffman, Dreyer, and Torgoff, 1954, 1957). This interview focuses on a typical day, and the respondent is asked to describe everything that happened during the previous day or the most recent day that was viewed as typical and to report everything that took place during that day from awakening until bedtime.

The only probes used in this interview were those required to be certain that every moment of the day had been accounted for or those required to obtain the necessary details about some incident being described (i.e., "Can you tell me more about that?"). As Hoffman (1954) notes, the requirement that a person account in minute detail for the events of the previous day means that she becomes more involved in the situation and loses much of her self-consciousness. Furthermore, probing for exact details helps to fragment the event and thus divests it of some of the emotional impact it would possess if viewed as a whole.

Following the collection of these measures, the investigators reviewed the information collected and noted additional information that it would be desirable to have. Family members were then reinterviewed over a period of several additional days. During this more informal interview, an attempt was made to talk with the husbands in the first and second generations and with any children in the family who might be at home at the time of the interview, which was usually arranged for the late afternoon. As a result, it was possible to supplement the systematically collected information with additional observations regarding life in these families. Such information, gathered in the respondents' homes, provides a wealth of detail about the course of family life that is so often missing from information collected in laboratory settings.

[5]There has been a good deal of methodological criticism of interviews aimed at obtaining retrospective accounts of childrearing (Wenar, 1961; Mednick and Schaeffer, 1963; Robbins, 1963; Yarrow, Campbell, and Burton, 1968). Since the study presented in this book is concerned with present and not with past practices, many of these problems could be avoided. In addition, since the repondents provided their own accounts, many of the problems were avoided that arise when standard questions are used. Participants frequently complain that they have never made observations regarding the behaviors under investigation. Such problems in rapport are avoided by permitting participants to provide their own accounts of their childrearing attitudes and practices. Having previously used the more structured format characteristic of the studies of Sears, Maccoby, and Levin (1957) and Miller and Swanson (1958) in earlier studies of hospitalized and nonhospitalized mothers, we were impressed with the greater richness of the data provided by the "typical day" format.

CHAPTER 3

Mrs. Limpari and Mrs. McGorty: The Effects of Fostering Separateness in a Three-Generation Family

LIVING APART-ADAPTIVE ATTITUDES

Among Bethany's many ethnic neighborhoods, the Italian district of Tower Point is the most intact and closely knit. Small shops line narrow streets down which grocerymen wheel cartons of dried fish and kegs of olives and nuts. Families out for the day's shopping pull carts piled high with groceries and dry goods. Old apartment houses are interspersed with shops and their occupants sit on the front stoop, conversing with each other and gesturing as they talk. It is not uncommon for two- and three-generation families to live together in one building. Nor is it unusual for whole villages to settle in adjoining buildings, continuing rivalries and friendships first begun in Europe. Migration from Tower Point is quite uncommon, and, even when people hold jobs in distant parts of the city, they continue to live in Tower Point.

To understand Mrs. Limpari and her family, it is necessary to place them in the appropriate cultural perspective. First, it should be noted that the Limparis, as is true of almost all Tower Point families, come from southern Italy. Most such families migrated to this country shortly before the turn of the century. Typically, one member of the immigrating family is still alive and provides strong continuity with the traditions of the Old Country. However, in contrast with the descriptions of Child (1943) and Campisi (1948), the second-generation family in Tower Point maintains strong European traditions. The emphasis on tradition is largely a result of the fact that these second-generation residents live in a homogeneous neighborhood in which the residents know each other far better than is the case in most urban neighborhoods. Different blocks represent different villages, each of which preserves its own customs.

Gans (1962) provides a fairly accurate picture of second-generation Italian American families, such as those living in Tower Point. In contrast to earlier studies, Gans stresses the nondemocratic family organization and nonmobile orientation of these second-generation families. Considerable in-group solidarity has been retained, and the emphasis on family rituals is stressed to almost the same

66

degree as in the first-generation family. Even more striking, the third generation preserves these family ties, and it is common for married sons and daughters to reside near their own parents. Migration to the suburbs is uncommon and is even discouraged among several families.

Within the family, clear distinctions are made between the duties and obligations of men and women, and the sexes have few shared tasks in common. The segregated role relationship, described by Bott (1971), is most typical of these second-generation families. The husband and wife have their own friendship networks, and each has differentiated and specialized roles within the household. Gans suggests that husbands are more likely to bring their men friends into the home during leisure hours than was true in Italy; however, this has not been true of Tower Point families we have studied. Typically, the husband leaves the house after dinner and plays cards with his men friends either in the Lodge or in a local coffee house.

Children are desired and enjoyed, but they are expected to conform to the wishes of adults. Girls are expected to help their mothers from the time they reach their teens, and, if their mothers work outside the home, they may even take over household duties before this time. Boys are not expected to help in household chores and are encouraged to find their own friends in the neighborhood. When discipline is required, it is usually the mother's task to administer it, and Tower Point second-generation families typically pay little attention to their children's reactions to their mothers' demands.

In sum, Tower Point second-generation families differ from second-generation families in less tightly knit communities by preserving, to a greater extent, the traditions and patterns of family organization emphasized by their immigrant parents. Indeed, the influence of the community on family organization is so strong that we have observed a number of third-generation families who still retain these traditional patterns of family life.

MRS. LIMPARI: CHILDREN SHOULD MAKE THEIR OWN LIVES

At first, it would appear that Mrs. Limpari, Mrs. McGorty's mother, is a very typical Tower Point resident. Together with her husband and one unmarried son, Mrs. Limpari lives in a small third floor apartment in a building on a quiet, narrow street that is removed from commercial traffic. There is no nameplate on the mailbox for the postman knows every resident of the building by his or her first name. Mrs. Limpari's married son and his family live in the adjoining building, and the two families cross back and forth using the fire escape that they share in common. Indeed, all the neighbors are close friends and chat with each other across fire escapes or up and down the stairs. Mrs. Limpari is especially active in numerous Tower Point civic organizations and is responsible for one of the major saint's days, holidays celebrating the patron saints of the towns in southern Italy from which members of the community have come.

Although Mrs. Limpari is one of the more actively involved and respected members of the community, she has many beliefs and aspirations that differ from those of typical Tower Point residents. For instance, while she always attends Sunday Mass, Mrs. Limpari also enjoys visiting various Protestant churches and has a strong interest in Yoga. While she is reported by her family to be a superb cook and seamstress, she has, in addition, held a full-time factory job for many years. While she has only a grammar school education, she believes very strongly in the importance of higher education, and two of her four children hold advanced degrees from local universities. While she maintains strong ties with her own parents and friends with whom she grew up, she believes that children should make their own way in the world and should live wherever they choose to live. In contrast with many Tower Point residents, she has encouraged her children to leave the area and has been especially disappointed that three of her four children have returned to Tower Point to live or are planning to do so. How, then, do we explain such inconsistencies in this remarkable woman?

Born in Tower Point of Italian immigrants, Mrs. Limpari has spent nearly all her 57 years within the district's boundaries and seldom ventures from the confines of the community, except to baby-sit for her daughter. She is the eldest of five children born to a common laborer. Mrs. Limpari's father died when she was 10, and Mrs. Limpari, the only girl, was forced to assume responsibility for the care of her younger brothers. Since she was the only daughter, she was expected to help her mother keep house. In addition, when her mother went off to work, she was given the full responsibility of caring for the household. Mrs. Limpari's mother appears to have been a stern, unhappy woman who struggled continually to make ends meet. As a result of her father's early death, Mrs. Limpari was forced to give up any aspirations for the future and was required to lead a very regimented life. She comments:

> Well she was quite strict . . . (since) my father died when I was 10 . . . she felt that she had to discipline us more than another family that had a mother and father for the children . . . and we were restricted in a lot of things, for instance going out nights. I wanted to take a night course in high school, 'cause I just went to the eighth grade . . . and ah . . . a social worker from the welfare department wanted my mother to send me and my mother said "No," she says, "what will people think," she says, "if she has no father that's why she goes out and never come . . . you know, she'll come home late."

The restrictive manner in which her mother reared her caused a good deal of conflict for Mrs. Limpari. On the one hand, she felt quite keenly her obligation to the family and the responsibility of helping her mother care for her younger brothers. On the other hand, she desired greater autonomy and a chance to make something of her own life. A story Mrs. Limpari tells about Cohler IAT picture Si3 (a picture of a young woman looking straight ahead as another young woman wearing a coat and carrying a handbag is about to go out the door) illustrates this desire for autonomy:

> This reminds me of me and my mother . . . she was a very domineering woman and if . . . I had friends of my own, she sort of resented them, she wanted above all, to be a part

of my life and I guess this time I got her mad, she walked out of the house and I'm pretty mad about it 'cause I don't . . . I want things of my own, I want to have secrets, not exactly secrets, but things I don't have to divulge, you want to keep to yourself, even if they're silly or . . . trivial things you don't want to . . . without having your mother knowing everything that's going on and I was her whole life or her family is her whole life and she's a selfish person; in the future I'd probably ignore her, which I did, because I felt like I'd had enough of her.

Similarly, in response to the Loevinger sentence completion stem "Whenever she was with her mother," Mrs. Limpari indicates that "she would rather be with her friends." The same data are apparent in the story she tells to Murray TAT picture 7GF, a picture of a woman reading to a little girl.

The woman's reading to her daughter, but her mind is far away . . . I think she's past the stage of playing with dolls . . . she seems to have other things on her mind, whether her friends . . . she wants to go out and play and her mother is trying to make her interested in staying home . . . in having her stay home with her . . . I think her . . . the whole . . . the mother's whole life is all more or less encompassed around the daughter . . . and it would be that way later on too unless the daughter decides to make her way to college . . . or another life far away from the mother . . . the feeling here is that she doesn't want to stay where she is . . . the mother is still treating her as a younger child.

From the intensity of the affect with which this story is told, it would appear to be the story of a child still very much involved in the struggle for autonomy from her own mother. It is striking when one recalls that this story is told by a 59-year-old grandmother for whom the basic conflict to which the story refers is one that happened more than 50 years ago. Both Gans (1962) and Lolli, Serianni, and Luzzatto-Fegiz (1958) suggest that the ability to recollect feelings connected with events in the distant past is characteristic of south Italian culture. Suffice it to say that conflict regarding autonomy from her own mother is still salient for Mrs. Limpari, and her own feelings regarding this struggle have never been fully resolved. Thus, in completing a sentence stem "When she thought of her mother . . . she felt guilty". As the only girl in the family, it was appropriate that she and her mother would develop a special kind of closeness. However, Mrs. Limpari seems to have had difficulty resolving her own feelings about this closeness. While she was able to take effective steps to resolve her feeling that she had no life of her own, she was less able to deal with the feelings of guilt that accompanied her striving for greater autonomy.

While a part of the guilt Mrs. Limpari feels toward her mother is related to this struggle for autonomy, this guilt is also related to her competitive struggle with her mother for her father's love and affection. Recall that Mrs. Limpari's father died when she was 10. In completing the sentence stem "My father . . .," she notes, "he died when I was only a child and I missed him a long, long time." According to her recollections, her father was a stern man, but a good provider for the family. Relevant in this connection is Mrs. Limpari's story to a picture (IAT F2) showing a young woman seated in a chair and an older man standing behind her and holding a letter:

Well this is a woman who married an older man and he seems to be quite concerned about her and she's happy in the role of having an older man for her husband . . . and he seems to cater to her needs and wants . . . and is more concerned about her than a younger fellow would be . . . that's the present . . . past . . . what made her marry an older man . . . maybe she adored her father, thought the father . . . had the father image . . . now this is me again . . .

This story suggests that Mrs. Limpari was quite attached to her father. In fact, she attempted to marry a man who showed those same attributes that she admired in her father: self-reliance, stern manner, an ability to provide for the family, and a desire to lead the family. Mrs. Limpari's competitive involvement with her mother may have led to feelings of guilt, but also to the wish to marry a man like her father.

Mrs. Limpari met the man she eventually married when she was 16 while attending the marriage of mutual friends. After a three-and-a-half-year courtship, which Mrs. Limpari says is a bit longer than that typical of the community, the couple was married in a church service. Following the wedding, the couple returned to live next door to Mrs. Limpari's mother and her three younger brothers.

Mrs. Limpari's description of the marriage closely resembles marriages Bott (1971) has described among members of closely knit kinship networks. In this segregated role pattern, both the husband and the wife have separate interests and friendship patterns and maintain a clear division of labor within the home. Mr. Limpari was clearly the boss and dictated his wife's actions. Mrs. Limpari describes their relationship as formal and controlled. She believes that most men regard women as "silly fools" and that the worst thing about being a woman is "having to obey one's husband when a woman knows she is right." For example, her husband insists that she be home each night by 9:00, and this prevents her from seeing her women friends. Indeed, she says that for the first several years they were married, she had no friends at all and seldom saw anyone beside her husband and her family. She says, "I still . . . more or less stay home and get home early . . . that's the way he wants it and I feel he's the boss."

While he had attended only three years of elementary school, Mr. Limpari was a skillful construction welder and soon rose to the rank of foreman. Considered quite successful in his work, he has retired within the past year and has found it somewhat difficult to use his time in a way that provides satisfaction. Mrs. Limpari sees her husband as extremely stern, but also as dependable, responsible, and intelligent:

He is very severe . . . he isn't a smiling kind of person or a happy person . . . he's a very strict person, the kind of person who's definitely in charge.

However, in contrast with her description of her father, she views her husband as more directly concerned with his own welfare and his own comforts:

He's an honest man . . . but where money is concerned, he's a little selfish, his personal comfort and interests come first for him . . . before the children's or anybody's, but he's a hardworking man, so I suppose he deserves it and he's always supported the family and he's got a good sense of values.

There has been particular conflict between the two of them regarding Mr. Limpari's card playing, which is his favorite hobby and which takes him away from the family several nights a week. Mrs. Limpari has very mixed feelings about her husband's card playing, for, while she is frequently left at home at night and must also bear the costs of his financial losses at cards, she is also at this time free from her husband's careful surveillance.

Mr. Limpari's major concession to his wife has been to allow her to work. Particularly during World War II, when the children were all in school, financial resources within the family were strained. Construction jobs were quite scarce, and there was little employment in defense industries in the area. Mrs. Limpari determined to work, as had her mother before her, to supplement the family income. Mr. Limpari was opposed to his wife taking a job, but, when he saw that she could manage both the household and her job at a clothing firm around the corner, he permitted her to continue working.

Mrs. Limpari stresses the importance of the job for her; she says that it gave her a sense of autonomy and independence she had not previously had. The role of wife and mother was somewhat threatening to Mrs. Limpari, for this role demanded that she be passive and deferent. One solution to this conflict was to flee into activity—to seek a job and become part of the work world for a part of each day. Otherwise, as she observed in her story to IAT Card G6 (a picture of a woman washing dishes, while in the background a little girl sits at a table), ''If a woman does not stay bright and alert, she can no longer be a good wife and mother.'' At the same time, Mrs. Limpari was concerned about the care of the children and only worked when suitable baby-sitting arrangements were available. It should be noted that Mrs. Limpari's insistence on working is inconsistent with the pattern of the segregated marital relationship, where the husband performs the executive or instrumental tasks (such as work) and the wife performs the role of housewife and mother. Mrs. Limpari's decision to work engendered conflict both because of her own personality and that of her husband and also because of the necessary structural change in this pattern of segregated family organization.

Mrs. Limpari's description of her marriage suggests that the same struggle for her own autonomy which she experienced with her mother has continued with her husband. Her marriage has only partially helped her in her goal of achieving greater freedom. At the same time, her decision to remain near her own mother indicates the degree of conflict she has experienced regarding the attainment of autonomy from her family. Mrs. Limpari has a strong sense of moral obligation and a strong sense of responsibility. The active involvement she has with charities is one reflection of this sense of obligation; similarly, she continues to visit her aged mother several times a week in spite of other pressing obligations. This sense of responsibility and obligation seems to have interfered with her ability to achieve real happiness.

Throughout the interview and test material, there is a sense of wistfulness, as if there are times when she wishes things had turned out differently. In response to the sentence stem ''Raising a family,'' Mrs. Limpari replies that it ''is rewarding like anything else if you find satisfaction.'' In response to the sentence stem ''Sometimes she wished that,'' Mrs. Limpari replies, ''things were different.'' In response to a picture showing a woman holding a telephone receiver (IAT Tel), Mrs. Limpari comments:

> This woman . . . was disrupted in her work. She has a lot of work to do to get the kids off to school and doesn't have too much time to talk on the phone . . . some people talk half an hour with little to say . . . it's all in a day's work . . . she's probably thinking that, you know, she's late planning a meal for supper tonight for the family. That's the future . . . a housewife has no future, it's one thing after another, the kids go by, and then you wonder . . .

Even more striking is a story she tells to a picture (IAT H4) of a young woman seated on a sofa talking to a young man:

> Well, I see this person as an older woman . . . the man is trying to encourage her in some way, and she seems as though she needs help . . . I guess mental help . . . but I guess he won't do any good. The man has done all he can and now he'll give up and just think of his own . . . of what he wants for himself. She couldn't stand the world as it is, probably has children . . . too many children and responsibilities and feels tied down. It isn't the life . . . the life that she had dreamed of when she was younger.

Mrs. Limpari's story to this picture is especially significant, since most persons perceive the woman as a good deal younger. When she says, ''I see this person as an older woman,'' she is indicating quite clearly that she is going to restructure the picture in accordance with her own feelings. The picture of the marriage one obtains from this picture is consistent with other data, and yet there is also some evidence that Mr. Limpari is seen as able to understand his wife's concerns. Unable to help her to achieve more for herself, he withdrew in favor of his own interests. The result is that Mrs. Limpari feels some dissatisfaction looking back over her life, but was never able to free herself of her deep feelings of obligation. Almost certainly, the fact that she was the only daughter in a family with several brothers as well as the oldest child in her own family contributed to this sense of responsibility and also contributed to the feeling that men enjoyed special advantages not available to women.

Mrs. Limpari's conflict with her mother regarding the attainment of autonomy, as well as her competition with her mother for her father's affection, has had an effect on her self-esteem and feelings about being a woman. In part, she envies the masculine assertive role, although she also indicates some relief that she is not burdened by such responsibilities. This conflict is quite clearly described in her response to Card III of the Rorschach, typically seen as two figures in action. Mrs. Limpari provides the following response:

> They seem to be two persons . . . maybe men . . . they seem to be carrying something between them. Then I look at it again, it could be women. (E: What about them made it look like men?) 'Cause they seem to be carrying a weight and a man would carry a weight more than woman. (E: And if it were women, what about it would make it look like women?) Well, it seems to have the outline of a bosom . . . and heels on the shoes.

What is striking about Mrs. Limpari's response is not simply that she chooses to identify the figures as being of the opposite sex, but that she is unable to decide if the figures are those of men or women. She appears unable to resolve for herself whether she wants to be a man and carry the weight of the world on her shoulders or to be a woman who is nurturant and feminine.

It is this conflict between striving and self-assertion on the one hand and passivity and submission on the other that makes Mrs. Limpari such an unusual woman for the community in which she lives. It is not enough merely to be a woman, for there is something that a woman misses; this is clearly reflected in her wistfulness. On the other hand, she is glad she is free of the major responsibilities that confront men.

Mrs. Limpari has found three ways of dealing with her conflict between activity and passivity. One was to marry a man who was clearly dominant and assertive and willing to accept the masculine role. The second was to try to live out her own unfulfilled aspirations through her children. The third was to accept a full-time factory job. Mr. Limpari is, according to the accounts of other family members, a man who is comfortable with his masculinity and who has been able to provide leadership within the family. Within limits, Mrs. Limpari attained some autonomy; she was able to arrange her life so that she could work, even though it meant confronting her husband. At the same time, she and her husband reached a common agreement that her work would come second to her role as wife and mother.

While Mrs. Limpari's relationship with her husband appears to be a source of support in dealing with this conflict regarding her striving for activity, it is primarily through her children that she has worked out this conflict. Mrs. Limpari thinks she has devoted considerable effort to insuring that her children, particularly her two girls, had the kind of freedom she was denied.

The Limpari's have four children. The eldest, a daughter, 38 years old, was born after they had been married for about two years. This daughter, Mrs. McGorty, is married and lives in a Bethany suburb. A second daughter, five years younger than Mrs. McGorty, is married and lives in California. A son, two years younger than the younger daughter, is unmarried and is living at home, while working as a high school teacher. The youngest son, two years younger than his brother, is married and lives in the adjoining apartment building that is connected to the Limpari's apartment by a common fire escape.

It is clear that Mrs. Limpari's feelings about the manner in which her mother reared her has had considerable influence on the manner in which she has reared her own children. Mrs. Limpari places primary emphasis on teaching children independence, responsibility, and self-control, while also recognizing that each of her children has a distinct personality and unique needs.

Interestingly, based on a discriminant function analysis of the responses of grandmothers, mothers, and peers to the MAS, Mrs. Limpari's childcare attitudes resemble those of the mother generation more closely than those of her own generation. Based on the discriminant functions, the probability that her attitudes are those of a mother is 51%. This only confirms our impression that Mrs. Limpari's values are in many ways atypical of the grandmother generation.

Based on her responses to the MAS, Mrs. Limpari's attitudes can be described as follows: she believes that mothers should keep a tight rein on their children's expression of anger and that infants are not capable of meaningful social interchange with their mothers. On the other hand, she believes quite strongly that the child should develop as a separate person and achieve autonomy from his or her family. It is in this belief that a child should grow as a separate person that her attitudes are most strikingly divergent from those of other grandmothers. Mrs. Limpari expresses difficulty in accepting her own complex or ambivalent feelings about childrearing. Finally, she says that she knows what a baby wants when he or she cries and knows how to read a baby's cues regarding his or her needs.

Additional information regarding Mrs. Limpari's childcare attitudes and practices based on interview data is consistent with her responses to the paper-and-pencil measure. She was quite insistent about the value of demand feeding. As she commented, "When they cry, you want to give them a bottle so that they don't cry and so that they are quiet." She also commented that mothers in her generation were far more willing to feed children when they cried than was true of mothers in the current generation. Mrs. Limpari's attitudes in this respect are consistent with her responses to the MAS.

Mrs. Limpari toilet trained her children quite early. This was achieved by capitalizing on the regularity of their bowel movements rather than through any direct pressure or use of physical punishment. In describing the toilet training, she notes the following:

> I'd make sure they had regular bowel movements and . . . especially if it was warm in summer, I could put them in panties instead of diapers . . . I trained them very early . . . at three months . . . by six months I knew just when they had to have . . . you know, get them ready 'cause I used to wash clothes on a scrubbing board by hand and I made sure that I didn't have more than one child for whom I had to . . . wash dirty panties.

The same belief she expressed in her responses to the MAS regarding the importance of encouraging the child to grow up as a separate person is also evident in her comments during the interviews. While not believing in excessive indulgence, she believes it is important to recognize and allow for a child's preferences. For example, in describing how she prepared meals for her family, she comments:

> I made one dish and that was on the table, and . . . if they didn't like it . . . I knew that they didn't like it and I tried not to fix things they didn't like . . . you can't get them to eat things they don't like . . . you try to fix things that they do like . . . but I didn't tell them, like mothers do nowadays . . . do you want some of this, do you want some of that . . . I didn't give them a choice . . . except for small things . . . you should be able to decide what to give them and do it one way, it will be easier on you and easier on them, they sit down and eat, if they don't like it, they eat less, and if they like it, they eat more of it, or they fill up with bread and butter or something.

Elsewhere, in comparing her own daughter, Mrs. McGorty, with her other children, Mrs. Limpari states:

> Yes, I think every child of mine was/is a little different. Some I could be more stern with and some of them I had to go a little easier or they would rebel . . .

Clearly, she believes that the child's own temperament should be respected, but she also believes that mothers should preserve their own dignity and not yield entirely to their children's demands.

Mrs. Limpari's description regarding the development of autonomy and self-reliance are particularly striking:

> I encouraged them all to work. I think it's important that they can feel they can make their own way . . . that they can work and earn a decent living.

Mrs. Limpari took a firm stand toward her husband regarding Mrs. McGorty's education, and, even though he felt it inappropriate for a woman to have a college education, Mrs. Limpari supported what she believed were her daughter's rights. She also encouraged her children to explore their community, and, even though she sometimes worried about the possibility that they might get hurt, she encouraged them to take part in athletic activities. Mr. Limpari did not approve of these activities. He believed that the world was full of dangers and that his children would be injured if they ventured beyond Tower Point or rode on the public transportation. Mrs. Limpari notes:

> I had a husband who was very, very strict and ah . . . I would go as far as I, you know, thought that I could get away with, even with him . . . in other words, they were held back a little more than my children's children since there is no accounting to their husband.

On several occasions, Mrs. Limpari purchased play equipment for the children, even though Mr. Limpari had forbidden them to have such equipment. Sometimes, when Mr. Limpari discovered this equipment, he insisted that it be returned. However, more often, once the equipment had been purchased, nothing further was said.

Mrs. Limpari felt that either complete freedom or complete control were equally destructive for children. In comparing her own childrearing practices with those of her eldest daughter whom she believes is too permissive with her children, she notes the following:

> I feel that children shouldn't absorb all these things at once, like ice-skating, going to see certain shows . . . I think they're too young to take all this in at once, because if you've seen everything, if you went every place, what is there left for you to do, and how much can children absorb at once. Parents today push their children too fast in this respect.

Once more, Mrs. Limpari indicates awareness of the child's age-appropriate needs. The description she gives of her childrearing attitudes and practices is notable in several respects. First, she recognizes that each child is a unique person with his or her own interests and needs. Second, she believes in fostering a sense of self-reliance and autonomy. While she showed considerable involvement in her children's care, this involvement did not appear to conflict with her own needs and interests. There was little feeling of self-sacrifice or of any necessity for having to choose between what she wanted for herself and what was best for her children. Rather, she recognized that she, too, had needs such as preserving her own autonomy and that some compromise must be struck between her needs and those of her children.

It is important to note that Mrs. Limpari's beliefs, as measured by our paper-and-pencil questionnaire, are quite consistent with her own report of the ways in which she reared her children. The emphasis she placed on the encouragement of the child's development as a separate person reflects her attitudes in the MAS, which, as we have already noted, were quite deviant from those of other members of her own generation. However, as was true of other mothers of her own generation, she believed that she could recognize her children's needs as infants and could meet those needs without inner conflict. Indeed, like other mothers in her generation, she minimizes the possibility that mothers have complex and ambivalent feelings regarding childrearing; as she herself observes, "I generally knew what was the best thing to do and I did it." She also maintains that it was easier to rear children when her children were young and feels that if she were in her daughter's position, it would be much more difficult to know the best thing to do.

Mrs. Limpari was able to achieve many of her goals through her children. The desire she had for mastery and independence, for bettering her own station in life, and for breaking away from the restrictive environment of her own family were at least partially fulfilled through marriage and parenthood. In particular, our discussion of Mrs. Limpari's conflict between activity and passivity provides us with an understanding of why she believes in the importance of recognizing a child's own needs and encouraging his or her development of a strong sense of separateness and autonomy. Although she had experienced conflict in this regard, she was determined that her children would not have to struggle with this issue.

While her emphasis on fostering a sense of separateness and self-reliance may have contributed to her children's success in the community, Mrs. Limpari's determination to resolve this conflict through her children has had the opposite effect of perpetuating the conflict in the next generation. As we see in our subsequent discussion, the issue of closeness and separation is one of the paramount issues in the family and one with which all four children continue to struggle. This is most clearly seen in her relationship with her eldest daughter, Mrs. McGorty who, like Mrs. Limpari, is the eldest daughter.

Mrs. Limpari was quite concerned that her eldest daughter succeed where she did not. Simultaneously, she was aware of and bothered by the possibility that her daughter would achieve more than had been possible for her. In part, Mrs. Limpari has dealt with her own competitive feelings through her vicarious enjoyment of her daughter's professional success. However, some residual competitive feelings remain. She describes an image on Card VIII of the Rorschach as a "fat woman like me climbing the hill with her child: It looks to me like she seems to be chasing the child, the child is getting away from her. The child's climbing the hill higher . . . she has to keep up with her child." Mrs. Limpari's feelings of pleasure in her daughter's achievements, combined with some feelings of compe- tition, have become even more complex since Mrs. McGorty has apparently re- jected the active professional role her mother helped her to attain and, rather, has devoted her efforts to returning to Tower Point and becoming once more a part of that special community she so much misses in the suburbs.

MRS. McGORTY: IT WOULD BE NICE TO BE HOME AGAIN

South Tuxton is a typical middle-class suburb, located about 25 minutes away by car from Tower Point. Single-family dwellings occupy large lots and large maple trees line the quiet streets. Mrs. McGorty, her husband, and three daughters live in an older house in what they regard as the less well-to-do section of the commu- nity. Her husband, a civil service clerk, works long hours to provide for his fami- ly, and Mrs. McGorty has also worked to help make ends meet.

While she likes the large house and the spacious backyard, Mrs. McGorty fre- quently comments unfavorably on how quiet and lonely the neighborhood is com- pared with Tower Point:

> I don't know many people out here . . . if I'm out with my children and some of the neighbors come out, but . . . ah, they don't come out very much, that's why I don't like to . . . I don't like this neighborhood; I like Tower Point because people are out and they're friendly but . . . I don't know what these women do with their children; they never bring them out for airings or anything, I don't understand it . . .

At the time of the study, she and her husband were seriously considering moving back to Tower Point. This prospective move, and the feelings that accompany it, reflects the ambivalent relationship between Mrs. McGorty and her mother. Both women have struggled with the same dilemma concerning closeness and separa- tion, although they have resolved their difficulties with their mothers in quite opposite ways.

Mother and daughter mirror each other's physical appearance. Both are stocky and large-boned women, attractive and yet not conforming to traditional notions of femininity. Weight control is but one of many concerns mother and daughter share. Since both are known as excellent cooks of south Italian specialties, they have found it difficult to deal with this problem. In response to the sentence completion stem "My mother and I . . .," Mrs. McGorty indicates that they are both good cooks and fat mothers. Mrs. Limpari notes that her daughter is over- weight and wishes she would diet occasionally, but also comments that she has never been able to resolve her weight problem and doubts that her daughter will. Mrs. McGorty comments that "fat mothers have fat children" and says that like her mother she will go right on eating, but always trying to reduce. She sighs when she says that they continue to "cluck sympathetically" with each other, all the while continuing to gain weight.

Mrs. McGorty and her mother have an unusually close but complex relation- ship. Like her mother before her, Mrs. Limpari expected her daughter to help in the care of her younger brothers and sisters, but, even more important, when her daughter reached the eighth grade, Mrs. Limpari began work outside the home. It is interesting to note that her own mother had also begun working when Mrs. Limpari was in the eighth grade. According to Mrs. Limpari's account, it was her daughter's suggestion:

Of course, Frances was the oldest . . . and she understood so that, when she was 14, and there wasn't enough to go around, she says, "Ma, why don't you get yourself a job and I'll take care of the children for you." She was very understanding, being the oldest. I suppose I confided in her and she saw that what went on in the house . . . the responsibility then for caring for the others was hers . . . she was 14 and going to the Classical School.

Mrs. McGorty certainly seems to have anticipated her mother's own wishes in this regard. The job Mrs. Limpari had, together with her numerous civic commitments, meant that she seldom arrived home from work until dinner time. Thus, Mrs. Limpari expected that Mrs. McGorty, her daughter, would manage her younger brothers and sister, together with the housework and cooking, just as she herself had done when she was her daughter's age:

Well, I guess her being the oldest she had a little more . . . knowing of what went on in the home and the house . . . and she took all the responsibility of taking care of them [the younger children] and . . . I gave her chores to do every week, they were hers, where she had to take care of the children, and she had to, you know, dishes and things, she had responsibility, I didn't have no problem with them . . . that's where it was easy. I didn't have to tell her things. She knew they were hers to do because I was working and she had responsibilities of her own . . . and what I made went for them.

Mrs. McGorty was a dutiful daughter who took her responsibilities seriously. However, Mrs. Limpari felt it was not sufficient that her daughter keep house and go to school. She also expected that, especially during the summers, Mrs. McGorty should work and help support herself through school. As Mrs. Limpari herself notes, she placed considerable pressure on her daughter to take a job:

I happened to get laid off one summer when she was about 16 . . . it was about 100° that day, so I says, "You go out and get a job," and ah . . . which I think I made a mistake but anyway I felt that where I had worked for her she had to be on her own so I says, "You got to go out and look anyway." So she wanted a job in a factory here she was all dressed up with gloves like she was going to some office or something and then it was a factory job so the boss looked at her and said, "Are you sure you want to work in a factory?" "Yes," she said, "I want a job." So he says, okay, and she stands up all day hemming curtains in her fancy dress and she come home red as a lobster and says, "Are you happy now, Ma?" . . . I says to tell me what she did. "At 100° I was bolting curtains," and then I felt guilty that I was pushing her too much. So I says, "Well, you don't have to work tomorrow," and she never did, but got an office job . . . and then for a while as a salesgirl and I felt she had to do *something*. I says, "Take your time, you don't have to work in a factory, but you got to go out and work." Maybe I was wrong in insisting on that but I believed that since I was doing it for them, they had to help too.

From this account we can see that Mrs. Limpari expected her eldest daughter to be responsible and self-reliant. Just as she had kept house while her mother worked and just as she had begun working when she had turned 16, she expected her own daughter to act in a similar way. There was, however, one crucial difference between the demands imposed by Mrs. Limpari and those imposed by her own mother. Mrs. Limpari's own mother had prevented her from attaining a sense of autonomy and separateness, and Mrs. Limpari set about to insure that her daughter would be an active, autonomous, and separate person. But just like her own mother, Mrs. Limpari attempted to work out her unresolved conflicts through her daughter.

Perhaps because this insistence on Mrs. McGorty's self-reliance arose from Mrs. Limpari's own needs rather than from those of her daughter, her daughter has not fulfilled her mother's expectations. While she has become an active and self-reliant person, she has devoted her professional skills to trying to become closer to her mother in a way Mrs. Limpari will accept. For Mrs. McGorty the conflict is not between a desire for self-reliance in the face of her mother's demand for control, but rather the desire for closeness in the face of her mother's demand that she be independent. For example, Mrs. McGorty continues to wish that her mother would do more to help her with the house and children.

She notes in completing the sentence stem "A good mother . . . is always there to comfort her children, no matter what their age.'' This wish of Mrs. McGorty's to lean on her mother and receive her support is well illustrated by her story to IAT picture Si3 (a picture of two women, one of whom has on a coat and is going out a door, while the other stares straight ahead):

> That's a housewife who's taking care of her children and ah, this is grandma that's just come in the door and she's looking for the grandchildren, and they're all here, they're going to race up to her, ah . . . she wasn't expecting grandma's visit this particular day, and ah, grandma's smiling . . . and the children are going to race up to her and she's going to play with them for a while and give them a treat and, meanwhile, allow this woman, her daughter, a few extra minutes to do something that she wanted to do in the house without the children interfering and then grandma's going to give her an extra treat by cooking dinner.

Mrs. McGorty wishes that her mother would help her with her work and lighten her burden. The discussion she gives of a typical day in the household, as well as her discussion of her relationship with her mother, is replete with comments that she hopes her mother will come to her assistance.

The literature on child training and personality development demonstrates that dependency needs may be increased in children by a mother's failure to meet these needs rather than by their too frequent gratification (Sears, Maccoby, and Levin, 1957). Mrs. McGorty's mother may have too often demanded that her daughter strike out on her own without sufficient recognition of her desire for support and attention. At the same time, while Mrs. McGorty does indicate some concern with this issue of dependency, she feels that her basic needs have been met. She does not feel empty or deprived. This is nicely demonstrated in a story she tells to IAT picture Se7 (a picture of a woman in a raincoat walking down the street):

It's a cold Sunday and this girl . . . is not married. She goes to school, and dinner is over and the family's all stretched out reading the newspaper. The dishes are done and she's just decided it's a nice day to take a walk so she bundles up and she just walks around the neighborhood and there's not a soul around and it's very peaceful, and she'll go home eventually and they'll . . . she'll be nice and tingly from the outside and they'll all sit and have a cup of coffee and a piece of cake together.

This story indicated that Mrs. McGorty feels basic satisfaction and contentment and is sure that she will not be disappointed. Mrs McGorty is an optimist rather than a pessimist. While she depends on others for support she does not doubt that this help will be forthcoming.

Fortunately, Mrs. McGorty was a good student in school and education became the route through which Mrs. Limpari could consciously encourage this active mastery and separateness in her daughter. During seventh grade, one of Mrs. McGorty's classmates had told her about Bethany Classical School, a public high school offering the same traditional curriculum usually found only in elite New England preparatory schools. For some reason that Mrs. McGorty claims not to be able to understand, this conversation put an idea into her head which she could not dismiss. Mrs. Limpari was, as might be expected, delighted with the idea that her eldest daughter wished a high school education and, further, had secret hopes that her daughter might go on to college.

Mrs. McGorty began eighth grade at a new and much more difficult school than the one she had previously attended. It is interesting to note that at a time when Mrs. Limpari was consciously fostering separateness and independence in her daughter by urging her to get a high school education and to attend college, she simultaneously created barriers to achieving this separateness by giving her daughter responsibility for the care of her younger siblings, just as her own mother had required of her. The effect of this latter move is reflected in Mrs. McGorty's comment about her high school days. Mrs. McGorty feels that she was not an especially good student in high school. She says that she was more interested in extracurricular activities than in her schoolwork. Since she had such a major responsibility for her family's welfare, there was little opportunity for her to see her friends after school and thus these extracurricular activities where she could be a child rather than a surrogate mother took on added significance for her.

Although her mother believed in fostering a sense of separateness in her daughter, together with positive self-esteem as a woman, Mrs. McGorty's father was quite controlling and restrictive. Her father was particularly concerned about the possible dangers that could befall his family once they ventured beyond their courtyard. As Mrs. McGorty observes:

My father was one who was always worried that ah . . . something physically might happen to you . . . . I couldn't have roller skates because you might fall and get hurt, you couldn't have a bike for the same reason, you couldn't go out on the streetcar because some bad man might molest you.

Mr. Limpari also maintained very traditional views regarding his daughter's social life. She was expected to be home before dark on those rare occasions when she was not needed at home and later on in high school when she began to date she was expected to be home before 9:30. Mrs. McGorty never challenged her father in this respect, although her younger sister did rebel against these rules. While Mrs. McGorty makes some references to other aspects of her struggle for autonomy from her father, this struggle lacks the intensity of her younger sister's rebellion.

It is possible that Mrs. McGorty found her father's restrictive attitudes and actions a welcome compiment to her mother's insistent demands that she excel in the world outside as well as within the family. There is also a teasing aspect to Mrs. McGorty's negotiations with her father regarding issues such as dating. While he set firm limits, the bargaining process itself provided a source of positive interaction. As she comments in recollecting this process of negotiation:

Of course, in many respects my father was completely flexible . . . I'm probably going to be just as strict as my father because ah . . . when my children are out, the two oldest ones, I should be with them . . . and I'm the one who will wait up and worry just as my father did . . . but of course, there were some things which he would not allow me which are not dangerous . . . these things I will allow my children, but I give them lessons so that they will be proficient.

Mrs. McGorty remembers her father primarily through what he would not allow her to do. It was in this way that he could show he cared for her. In replying to the sentence completion stem "My father . . .," Mrs. McGorty replies that he "was a stern old-fashioned Italian I hated while I was growing up but whom I adore now." It is interesting to note that both her mother and father viewed the world outside the home as somewhat dangerous. However, her mother's solution was to encourage active mastery of danger, while her father's solution was to avoid such dangers. Mrs. McGorty has internalized both parent's views. She worries in the same manner as her father, but relies primarily on her mother's solutions that, of course, are also supported by the middle-class milieu in which she lives.

In spite of what Mrs. McGorty describes as an undistinguished high school career, she went on to both college and law school. Several factors must have contributed to this decision, with her mother's aspirations for her eldest daughter being foremost among them. There is somewhat less evidence that Mrs. McGorty wished these things for herself. However, we have noted that Mrs. McGorty was dutiful and compliant; perhaps a part of her decision stemmed from her attempts to please her mother and receive her attention. Then, too, Mrs McGorty was somewhat suggestible. The decision she made to go to Classical School had been sparked by the decision of a girl friend, and it was largely as a result of her conversations with her college-bound classmates at Classical that she decided to go to college.

While Mrs. McGorty's father resisted the idea, he was pleased that his daughter was attending an academically excellent high school and obtaining good marks. Simultaneously, Mr. Limpari worried that Mrs. McGorty's younger brothers would not have intellectual talents and aspirations, thus proving inferior. But since both parents wanted to see their children get ahead, it seemed the wisest thing to send Mrs. McGorty on for further education. There remained, however, the unspoken feeling, on Mr. Limpari's part, that it was too bad the eldest child was not a boy.

Mrs. McGorty enrolled in a large private university in the Bethany area and worked toward a baccalaureate degree, supported by savings, scholarships, and the money her mother had saved during her many years of work as a stitcher. Mrs. McGorty attended a college in the area because she had no desire to go away from home, and the expenses involved if she had attended a college in another city would also have been higher. Mrs. McGorty also insists that her mother would not have allowed her to go far away from home. However, her mother gives no indication that this was the case and, indeed, welcomed the thought that Mrs. McGorty's younger sister was moving to California. The issues of separation and closeness are prominent in this family, and Mrs. McGorty's feeling that she should stay in Bethany was prompted as much by her own desire to remain close by her mother as by what she believed was her mother's feeling that she ought to stay in Bethany.

It is difficult to determine exactly how much Mrs. McGorty was involved in her studies or exactly how much she wanted a career. While she made excellent grades, she reports that the work was not especially interesting and that "education is fun only until children come along." There is little indication that education was important to her beyond the possibility it offered her of pleasing her mother by satisfying her mother's own aspirations.

Mrs. McGorty practiced law for six years after graduating from law school, although she herself makes little reference to her career. She does note that it was much more difficult for a woman than for a man to attain success in practice and that she must have looked awfully young to her clients. During this period Mrs. McGorty also met and married her first husband, a man who is described as having little control over his feelings and a heavy drinking problem; this marriage lasted only a few months. Afterward Mrs. McGorty returned to her law practice.

Two years after her divorce, Mrs. McGorty met and married her second husband and quit her law practice. She notes that it was not difficult to give up her work and that she never enjoyed her profession. Mrs. Limpari was unhappy that her daughter had given up her profession for good after she married, and, more than she being unhappy, she was mystified at the ease with which her daughter made her decision.

Mr. McGorty is described by his wife as tall and strong, not handsome, but good looking, and, most important, a family man. He left school during high school and began to work as a clerk for the government; there is no indication that he ever aspired to higher education. He is a hardworking man who leaves for his job before 8:00 in the morning and does not return until after dark. While at home, he devotes his time to his wife and three daughters and is described by his wife as good around the house. Just as Mrs. McGorty's parents had established a segregated role relationship, the McGorty's relationship is quite typical of joint role relationship as described by Bott (1971). All aspects of childcare are shared by husband and wife when both are home, and weekends are spent doing errands as a family and working around the home. The couple has a small circle of mutual friends, and Mr. McGorty seldom goes out without his wife.

Mr. McGorty was born and reared in one of Bethany's largest Irish neighborhoods. There was little contact between Mr. McGorty's and their own parents, and his family spent little time together. It is clear from the accounts of Mrs. Limpari and Mrs. McGorty that Mr. McGorty thoroughly enjoys the opportunity to participate in the activities of their extended family. Mrs. Limpari was scarcely overjoyed when she heard that Mrs. McGorty was planning to marry her second husband. As she says:

> One reason why I wanted to give them an education was that they would meet people of their level or higher than them, which didn't happen, that was one of my ambitions when I sent them to school . . . that when they marry they'll marry you know, another bracket than me.

While she acknowledges that she has never said anything to Mrs. McGorty, the fact that Mr. McGorty had not gone on to college, rather than any disparity in ethnic background, was most disturbing to her.

Mr. and Mrs. McGorty seem well suited as husband and wife. A fairly quiet and nonassertive man, Mr. McGorty finds little to dispute about with his more dominant, assertive, and expressive wife. As Mrs. McGorty comments, in describing their relationship:

> He's an easy-going kind of fellow, and we get along very well because ah . . . I think I'm a dominant personality and he is very easy going and thinks that I am wonderful and that everything I do is right . . . of course, he's only a high school graduate and ah . . . but he approves of college in a nebulous sort of way.

Like his wife's father, Mr. McGorty has some reservations about the importance of education and status, but, as long as there is no requirement that he become involved, he is willing to let his wife assert her will. However, unlike Mrs. McGorty's father, Mr. McGorty is not at all restrictive or controlling and allows his wife and daughters to do as they wish. Thus, it appears that Mrs. McGorty is the more active and assertive partner in the marriage. Mr. McGorty has expressed little interest in the two projects that most directly involve the family's financial resources and Mrs. McGorty's time: the children's education at exclusive private schools, and Mrs. McGorty's business involvement with the apartment house construction project in Tower Point.

Because Mr. McGorty is not an active or assertive man he is able to accept Mrs. McGorty's dominance, and the assertive role she has does not appear to be a source of marital conflict. He is quite comfortable with his passive role. Furthermore, it should be recalled that although Mrs. McGorty is an active and assertive woman, she also requires considerable support and attention from others. Mr. McGorty appears willing to provide this support; in fact, he enjoys helping his wife with the children and working around the house. He is not only able to accept Mrs. McGorty's dominance, but also her dependency. One of the main reasons Mrs. McGorty was attracted to her husband may have been this apparent ability of his to support her desire to be dominant and assertive, while conversely supporting her desire to be passive and dependent.

In spite of Mrs. Limpari's attempt to instill a sense of mastery and self-esteem as a woman in her daughter, or perhaps because of her effort in this regard, Mrs. McGorty shares both her mother's conflict in relation to her definition of her sex role and her mother's concern with her self-image, a conflict expressed by Mrs. McGorty in terms of her feeling that she must choose between motherhood and career. Like her mother, Mrs. McGorty expresses some confusion regarding her sex-role identity and seems uncertain whether she would rather be a man or a woman. In describing her drawing of a woman, she comments that "the only way I can distinguish my male drawing from my female drawing is to draw the woman with long hair." This is the only characteristic she uses in her drawing for distinguishing between men and women. On the Rorschach, when describing a percept on Card III, typically seen as two human figures in action, she comments: "At first I thought that they were men, but now I think that they're women." Mrs. McGorty's response to this card is especially interesting, since she gives almost the same response her mother gave and articulates her response in almost the same way. In the case of both Mrs. Limpari and Mrs. McGorty, what is revealing is not that the figures seen in action are men rather than women, but that neither generation is able to settle on the sex of the figure. Similarly, on Card V of the Rorschach, she sees "Pan, that half animal, half man, halfcow." Mrs. McGorty's percept shifts from man to animal to man to a female animal.

Just as the two generations have struggled over the attainment of an appropriate identity and with the reconciliation of conflicting wishes between activity and passivity, they have also struggled with their feelings of inadequacy as women. We have already noted the concern of each of these women regarding her attractiveness as a woman. Mrs. McGorty sums up this dissatisfaction with her body when she completes the stem, "A woman's body . . . is not the most beautiful thing in the world as the advertising men would have you believe by their over-exposure of it." We have already seen that both Mrs. Limpari and Mrs. McGorty are concerned with their weight and that neither feels she is able to resolve this problem; neither mother nor daughter feels entirely comfortable with either her figure or her womanliness. For example, Mrs. McGorty tells the following story to IAT picture H4 (a picture of a man and woman sitting on a sofa talking):

This girl reminds me of somebody that I know, so I shall tell you a story about her . . . they're married, and they're sitting in a doctor's office . . . they have a little girl five years old . . . and she doesn't seem to be able to get pregnant so they have gone to see the doctor for examinations and so forth . . . the doctor is able to clear everything up without too much complication . . . and she gets pregnant and has a baby . . . they're a little bit apprehensive and concerned but I know behind the door, the doctor has the answer.

This story shows that Mrs. McGorty has some doubts about her ability to succeed in that one uniquely feminine function: bearing a child. However, this story has a hopeful side as well. The heroine in this story has at least been able to have one child. Further, this child is a girl. Finally, it should be noted that the doctor feels he can help the woman and man portrayed in this story. We may infer that if the heroine has indeed been able to have one child, then she does show some ability to respond in a feminine way. Furthermore, the fact that the child's sex is a girl suggests that being feminine, while conflictful, is not totally disvalued. If a woman feels feminine enough to care for a daughter, then she feels that she has something as a woman she can offer her daughter. Finally, the fact that the situation may be resolved suggests that while Mrs. McGorty may be conflicted about being feminine, she has by no means abdicated the feminine role, nor has she given up the possibility of resolving this conflict for herself.

The options available to Mrs. McGorty in dealing with her conflicting feelings regarding her sex role and self-image differ somewhat from those available to her mother just as the character of the two women differs and as they have handled their marriages in different ways. Certainly, Mrs. McGorty does not wish to rely on her husband to assume a clearly masculine and dominant role within the family. Nor is it clear that Mrs. McGorty could permit herself to defer to such masculine leadership. Mrs. McGorty's first husband was a very insecure and troubled man who depended on her for guidance. Her second husband is a man of considerably less education than his wife and with few aspirations. It would appear that Mrs. McGorty selected a husband who would be more passive and permit her to be more assertive.

Her legal training does not, as such, provide an option for Mrs. McGorty, although the skills she learned in law school have been of use to her. She indicates that she never derived much satisfaction from her professional work and notes that she felt especially inadequate when compared with her masculine colleagues. It is probable that the necessity for taking a direct and competitive role with her male colleagues was quite threatening for her. Furthermore, legal practice demanded that Mrs. McGorty renounce her feminine interests, and, while she was conflicted about her role as a woman, she did not intend to abandon her role as a woman. Mrs. McGorty has put her taining to use in the construction of a waterfront apartment complex, a business project she shares with her mother. This project has many meanings for Mrs. McGorty: it provides a suitable reason for moving back to Tower Point and closer to her mother and helps her to channel her aspirations and assertiveness, while at the same time not requiring her to forego her feminine role. In addition, this project allows Mrs. McGorty to use her identification with her father in a particularly constructive way. Just as her father's work has been that of the supervision of construction, Mrs. McGorty is planning a building project in which she will have a direct supervisory role in the building, a prospect to which she particularly looks forward.

The extent that this construction project occupies Mrs. McGorty's attention is apparent at several points in her projective test and interview material, but is nowhere more clearly seen than in the following story told to IAT Card B5 (a picture of a woman sitting on a park bench, while a little boy plays with a ball):

> A mother and her little boy out in the park . . . she's watching him but her mind has wandered and she is thinking . . . she has other interests . . . I see myself in her . . . I'm busy at the moment and my mind is seething and churning with ah . . . talks with the architect and the lawyers, and the bank mortgage and the design of the building . . . and right now we have a problem with the design . . . ah, about how to make two apartments out of one because of a fire egress problem . . . her eyes are vacant because her mind is thinking about these problems, meanwhile, she is watching the baby.

From this story it may be inferred that Mrs. McGorty finds it difficult to find much satisfaction from the maternal role; while she is doing what is expected of her, her real interest is in the construction project.

For Mrs. Limpari, an important way of dealing with her mixed feelings about herself as a woman was to try to rear her eldest daughter differently from the way in which she herself had been reared. This concern with doing things differently is much less evident in Mrs. McGorty who supports her own mother's childrearing attitudes and practices more than most mothers. On the other hand, the nurturant component of mothering provides Mrs. McGorty with less satisfaction, as we have seen in the story of the woman sitting on the park bench. Mrs. McGorty places a premium on activity and mastery in childcare. The fact that she has three children and still feels conflicted about her own femininity suggests that childrearing is particularly challenging for her.

Just as Mrs. Limpari's childrearing attitudes were more typical of the mother generation than her own grandmother generation, Mrs. McGorty's attitudes are more typical of those of the control group of peers who volunteered without their own mothers than of the women who volunteered with their mothers. This is particularly true of her score on the MAS factor of appropriate closeness, on the basis of which she was selected for intensive clinical study. Mrs. McGorty not only believes that mothers should establish an appropriate distance between mother and child, but also that mothers should foster social responsiveness and a sense of mastery over the environment in the young child. On the other hand, she denies the complexity of mothers' feelings about childcare and indicates less recognition of her own mixed feelings than is true for the majority of mothers in our prior studies (Cohler, Weiss and Grunebaum, 1970; Grunebaum et al., 1977). She believes that she can understand and meet an infant's physical needs and believes that mothers should rechannel a child's aggressive feelings in a socially appropriate direction.

Mrs. McGorty's eldest daughter, eight years old at the time of this study, was born two years after her marriage to Mr. McGorty. A second daughter, six years old, was born one year later and a third daughter, three years old, was born two years after that. As we have said, Mrs. McGorty has very high educational aspirations for her children and spends considerable effort in providing the best possible education for them; she notes that "education is the most important thing, starting at a very early age." One daughter attends first grade in an exclusive private school located in another suburb; another daughter attends a nationally renown Montessori nondenominational nursery school whose clientele is drawn from the ranks of the city's intellectual leadership.

Mrs. McGorty manages this private education because of scholarship aid for her eldest daughter and because she serves as the bus driver for her daughter's nursery school in exchange for a tuition rebate. Mrs. McGorty says she is not an educational snob. However, since she and her family live in what she describes as a deteriorating area with poor school facilities and since she believes that the teachers in public school are more concerned with keeping children quiet than with helping them to learn, she wants all her children to have a private education. While she is sensitive to the status difference between her family and the families of the other children in the school, she believes that until children are in the upper elementary grades they are not even aware of such status differentials.

To fulfill her dual role of mother and bus driver, it is necessary for her to arise early in the morning. Fortunately, since Mr. McGorty enjoys helping around the house he is up first, usually around 5:30, at which time he walks the dog and gives the youngest daughter her morning bath. Mrs. McGorty then arises and tends to getting her two older daughters dressed for school. After Mrs. McGorty has prepared a big breakfast for her husband and a ligher breakfast for her children, the baby-sitter arrives to care for the youngest daughter. Since Mrs. McGorty regards the baby-sitter as a close friend, she has only a little discomfort at leaving her daughter with her at frequent intervals during the morning.

Sometimes, around 7:45, Mrs. McGorty bundles her two older daughters into the family's Volkswagen microbus and begins her rounds. First, she drives to one suburb to leave her oldest daughter at her school. Since her daughter arrives before school opens in the morning, Mrs. McGorty has made an arrangement with the teacher to meet her daughter at school each morning; her daughter looks forward to this time during the day when she can be alone with her teacher. Mrs. McGorty then drives to another suburb where she begins her rounds of picking up her other daughter's schoolmates. She is responsible for being sure that all her charges are well enough to attend school for the day and must wait until each child has been cleared by the school nurse.

The part of the day Mrs. McGorty most looks forward to is the period in the morning after she returns home from school. The baby-sitter is a woman of about her mother's age whose own children are grown. In describing this woman, who is both neighbor and confidant, Mrs. McGorty comments:

She is an elderly woman who is more like a grandmother . . . she has been through all my pregnancies and she's known the children ever since they were infants and she's very fond of them. Even when she doesn't baby-sit we see her everyday. She loves Italian cooking and usually stays for lunch . . . she's like part of the family.

Mrs. McGorty usually has coffee and talks over her problems with her baby-sitter. In view of her feelings regarding her mother and her wish to have more attention and support from her mother, it is not surprising that this close relation-ship with her baby-sitter is so important for Mrs. McGorty. It is also a sign of the extent to which she is able to resolve this conflict that she has found an older woman with whom she can get along as mother and daughter and yet in an appropriate way.

After her morning chat with her babysitter, Mrs. McGorty has what she calls an "educational program" with her youngest daughter. This program consists primarily of teaching her daughter a more extensive vocabulary and teaching her how to count. It is important to note, however, that this period of educational activity in the morning is regarded as a serious time and not merely as a time for her to be alone with her daughter or to play with her. Indeed, there are few times in the day when Mrs. McGorty can allow herself to be with her children without being involved with them in some highly structured activity.

Mrs. McGorty does not believe that women should work while their children are growing up and even feels somewhat guilty about the time she spends driving the school bus. Since she is out a good deal during the morning, she tries to arrange her youngest daughter's nap for the time when she is returning the chil-dren home from nursery school. The babysitter returns at this time and, as Mrs. McGorty notes, frequently stays for lunch. Mrs. McGorty also does her house-hold chores during the baby's nap; if the baby does not nap early enough, then her chores do not get done.

While Mrs. McGorty generally returns home after discharging her last passen-ger, on some days she must also pick up her oldest daughter at school. However, by 12:00, her chores as an educator are over, and she assumes her chores as a homemaker. She enjoys cooking and keeps a large recipe file of special dishes. She particularly enjoys cooking Italian specialties and works very hard to provide the same large meals for which her mother is famous. It is so uncommon for children to eat American food that her oldest daughter finds the food in the school cafeteria strange and unpalatable.

Mrs. McGorty feels quite isolated in the suburbs and finds it difficult to make friends with her non-Italian neighbors. Generally, she spends her afternoons in the backyard if the weather is nice or inside if the weather is bad. If she and her children stay inside, Mrs. McGorty helps her children learn to read and write. She does not encourage her children to play games, preferring that they take up more quiet educational activities. What particularly annoys her about caring for her children is just standing around watching them play; she feels that this is a waste of time. She would like to meet other mothers and have her children play with other children, but says that the other mothers in the neighborhood have not reciprocated. She wonders what these women do with their time.

Household chores and errands are less important activities in Mrs. McGorty's day than is true for other women in our study, with the exception of Mrs. Czaja. Mrs. McGorty well summarizes her feelings about housework in this comment:

The little bit of housework that I do doesn't bother me at all because ah . . . I ignore it . . . I have too many things to do that are important to me. . .

Mrs. McGorty describes one occasion when she felt guilty about the fact that the house was not dusted and the floors were not waxed. So she spent the day cleaning. However, when her husband came home from work, rather than being pleased, he was distressed because the house looked so changed. He said he missed the chaos and that he was used to the way the house looked, because that had been the way his house had looked when he was growing up. Following this incident, Mrs. McGorty observes, she has spent less time cleaning.

Mrs. McGorty's response to housekeeping chores is quite similar to that of her mother, Mrs. Limpari, who commented on the subject in this manner:

I'm a haphazard housekeeper, I just ah . . . when I feel like it . . . when I see everything in a mess, then I go around and get it done and I whip up a storm but other than that . . . I think that there's other things to do. I can't see myself keeping an immaculate house and depriving myself of things that I would like to do, 'cause the years are slipping by and I like time to myself.

The attitudes of mother and daughter, in this respect, parallel each other quite closely. They feel that there are too many other things to do beside cleaning house, and neither is very troubled by disarray or lack of order.

Mrs. McGorty feels that her daughters are still too young to be given responsibility for household chores. In contrast to her mother she is not even certain it is good to require such responsibility from them. She says she can remember, from the time she was growing up, the amount of responsibility she had for cooking, cleaning, and washing, as well as for the care of her younger brothers and sister. She feels quite strongly that this responsibility limited her own opportunities for making friends and does not want this to happen to her own children. What she is not aware of is how it may have limited her ability to develop independence from her mother.

The two oldest daughters are given considerable freedom in the neighborhood as long as they do not cross any major streets. Since her oldest and middle daughters differ in age by only 19 months, she would like to see them become friends and to learn to play together. One of the problems is that her oldest daughter is among the youngest children in the neighborhood and has had such a difficult time being accepted by them that it is even more difficult for her to include her younger sister in her activities.

Since she and her husband frequently have friends or relatives over in the evening, Mrs. McGorty tries to spend a part of the afternoon baking. Sometimes, when the weather is nice, she takes the children to the zoo, the beach, or the harbor to watch the boats. In contrast to standing around and watching her children play, she does not feel that these outings are a waste of time. She enjoys relaxing away from the house and enjoys teaching the children about the world.

According to Mrs. McGorty, her husband always comes home from work smiling and cheerful. She describes him then as content and relaxed. She feels that his arrival marks the high point in her day. After changing his clothes, he helps get the children ready for bed and draws pictures with them until dinner is ready. Mrs. McGorty has been trying to teach the children table manners. For example, she insists that no one start before she has served the food and is ready to sit down. In general, she uses child-centered techniques in influencing her children's manners:

> If they take giant mouthfuls or talk while chewing, I just look and say their name, and I put my finger up and they know what I'm talking about, yeah, I don't like to yell and I don't believe in arguing for you can do things discreetly.

According to her description, her children are all good eaters, and while she encourages them to take taste portions, there does not seem to be any problem in getting them to eat. It is clear that food plays an important role in family transactions: most major decisions are made around the dinner table, and both Mr. McGorty and the children look forward to the special dishes that Mrs. McGorty has prepared for them.

Just as the dinner hour is an enjoyable time in the household, bedtime is also relaxed. Starting with the youngest girl, both parents spend time talking with the children and reading to them. Mrs. McGorty refers to this time in the evening, before bedtime, as "cuddle time," and it is during this time that the parents listen to each of their children and find out what, if anything, is troubling them. If the children wish a glass of water, they are free to get up and get it, but, according to Mrs. McGorty's descriptions, the children go to bed quite easily at night.

In the evening, after the children are in bed, Mrs. McGorty washes clothes, while her husband washes the dishes and helps tidy up the house. Several evenings a week their friends come over to play cards. While she and her husband frequently entertain at their house, they are much less likely to go over to their friends' houses. Mrs. McGorty says that they go out only a few times a year, and at these times, her neighbor who baby-sits for her during the morning comes over to baby-sit.

This description of a typical day in the McGorty household is consistent with Mrs. McGorty's personality, including her expressed childrearing attitudes. She finds it boring and a waste of time to watch her children in the yard, but is greatly involved in their education. Indeed, she spends considerable time and energy in providing the best educational experiences for all three of her daughters, whether driving the school bus for her middle child's school or devising a program of instruction for her youngest daughter. Mrs. McGorty's day is highly organized, and as we have already seen, she dislikes passively sitting while her children play. Most of the activities that she plans are quite structured and businesslike. It is interesting to note that even the period just before bedtime has been given a name and has been carefully established in the daily schedule. While Mrs. McGorty shows considerable warmth toward her daughters, she does not feel comfortable unless she is involved in a structural activity.

Mrs. McGorty's insistence on providing highly organized activities for her daughters and, particularly, her involvement in her children's education have numerous determinants. While she certainly values education, her concern that her children receive the best possible education stems as much from her own conflicts as from her interest in providing for her children. Foremost among the reasons for this concern with her daughters' education is her fear of her own passivity. Rather than become a mother who sits and watches her children or who simply tends to do housework, she actively strives to provide her children with an education. This is well documented in her story to IAT Card G6 (a picture of a woman washing dishes, while a little girl sits at a table in the background):

This woman is using her time that she's washing the dishes to teach her little girl phonics and the little girl takes to it . . . I never can figure out why either because she's bright or loves the attention and she's learning them well and her mother's proud of her and herself and the little girl is proud because children love to learn and the woman feels she is accomplishing at being a good mother by ah . . . doing the dishes, doing her work, and making her child brighter and enjoys doing it because she's creating, and the little girl turns out to be quite bright.

The woman in this story is unable even to wash the dishes without involving her daughter in some educational program. It is important to note that the mother in this picture is proud both of the little girl and of herself as well. Mrs. McGorty equates success in mothering with success in rearing bright children. Mrs. McGorty's daughters' educational attainments are important to her not only because an emphasis on education offers her a way out of the passive feminine role as housekeeper, but also because her daughters' intelligence and educational attainments serve as a direct reflection of her adequacy as a woman. For Mrs. McGorty, a defective woman is a woman who does not have intelligent children.

It will be recalled that in her previous story about the woman having difficulty in bearing her second child, the age of the first child, a girl, was given as about five. It is at about this age that a little girl is most directly concerned with learning about her role as a woman and with her own feminine adequacy. Erikson (1963) documents this concern quite well in his discussion of the configurations of children's play. Furthermore, two of Mrs. McGorty's three daughters are in the midst of resolving this developmental crisis. For a woman who feels herself to be especially inadequate as a woman, this must be a very threatening time in her own life. This is one reason why the extent of her involvement in her business arrangement has so greatly increased in the past two years. Since she feels somewhat inadequate as a woman and since she feels some lack of competence in preparing her daughters to be women, it is much less threatening and much easier for her to prepare them for scholastic achievement, an area she has so successfully mastered.

THE TWO GENERATIONS TOGETHER: PATTERNS OF COMMUNICATION AND INTERGENERATIONAL VISITING

Although Mrs. McGorty and her mother live only a short distance apart, they seldom see each other during the week. Mrs. McGorty explains that her mother works during the day and that their mutually busy schedules make it difficult for them to find times to visit together. However, over the weekend, Mrs. McGorty and her family come in town to Tower Point to do their week's marketing, and they often have lunch with Mrs. Limpari on these Saturday shopping trips. However, during the week, Mrs. McGorty and her mother talk with each other at least daily by telephone, with Mrs. McGorty most often calling her mother.

Both the calls and the weekend shopping trips, together with conflict regarding Mrs. Limpari's availability as a baby-sitter, represent sources of tension between the two generations. Mrs. Limpari complains that the telephone calls are made at a time of the day convenient for her daughter, but not for her:

I talk with my daughter about four o'clock, just when I've gotten home, and I'm trying to prepare supper . . . as soon as she knows I'm home . . . that's her best hour to call but it isn't mine. I'm right in the middle of, you know, my busy time, but it's all right for her to call.

These are not the comments of a woman who looks forward eagerly to hearing from her daughter; she wishes Mrs. McGorty would call less often and at a more convenient time.

Mrs. Limpari's mixed feelings about her daughter's attempts to maintain closeness are seen not only in her feelings about her daughter's telephone calls, but also in her feelings about the visits Mrs. McGorty and her family pay to Tower Point each Saturday. Because of the family preference for Italian food, very little shopping is done in their own neighborhood. For Mrs. McGorty, the most important part of the time is the opportunity to visit with her parents and to enjoy the special lunch that Mrs. Limpari fixes for the family. In describing these visits, Mrs. McGorty comments:

My mother's got a great house, there's always something, something different, a great delicacy; she's a terrific cook and ah, much more so than I, she's always got some little goody there.

While the McGorty family is quite enthusiastic about these visits, Mrs. Limpari is somewhat less so. Although she makes a special effort to prepare foods that she knows the McGortys like, she also complains about the confusion that it causes in the household:

I used to enjoy cooking because everything I cooked he had never heard of it or never saw it, and I was happy I could surprise them so . . . but then, now I get pooped and my son and husband began to complain . . . and they like to come here and eat, even their children go 'let's go to grandma's and eat' but my husband and my son asked me to discourage them . . . so actually I have been discouraging them a little bit 'cause I have to, you know, they have their own home and their own . . . they can't very well barge in you know.

These Saturday visits cause additional problems because Mrs. McGorty's brother, who lives at home, uses his free time on Saturday to make extra money tutoring students. It is impossible to tutor, he says, when my sister and her family are there. Mrs. Limpari says that there is an additional problem in that Mrs. McGorty feels her parents' apartment belongs to her as well and that her brother resents this attitude. In spite of Mrs. Limpari's mixed feelings about these Saturday visits, she goes to extra effort to prepare special dishes for her daughter's family.

Babysitting is a third area of tension between Mrs. Limpari and Mrs. McGorty. As is true of other grandmothers in the study presented in this book, Mrs. Limpari values her own freedom and autonomy. She notes that with her children grown up she has greater time for the things she enjoys doing and likes being able to make plans without having to consider her children's needs. She knows that her daughter would like to bring her children in to have her mother care for them while Mrs. McGorty and her husband go out for the evening, but she does not welcome this possibility:

I told her, once in a while it's all right . . . if it's a special party and they will be out late. But not as a usual thing . . . I told her, I don't think she likes it, but I told her 'look, I have things of my own to do, and I can't help you out all the time.' I tried to explain to her that grandmothers get tired, too . . . I think she didn't like what I said to her.

Mrs. McGorty is concerned that her children do not see their grandmother often enough. She recalls how her own grandmother lived just around the corner from her the entire time she was growing up and feels that her own children will not have this chance to get to know their grandmother. In addition to the importance she attaches to intergenerational continuity, she also wishes that her mother would live closer to her and would be more available for help with housework. If she and her mother lived closer to each other, then her mother could more frequently prepare meals for her. Mrs. Limpari does not share her daughter's enthusiasm for living closer together or for babysitting more often. Mrs. Limpari says she dislikes babysitting and expects the children to be in bed before she arrives. In describing her feelings about not wanting to live any closer to her daughter than she does, Mrs. Limpari comments:

I would like to see them a little more often than I do, especially the children, but I think far away is good, you don't get in each other's hair . . . otherwise I probably would be interfering . . . ah . . . she has to bring up the children in the way she sees fit . . . I'm an outspoken woman and if we were too close I'd probably ah . . . say something that I don't have no business in saying.

It is interesting to note that this conflict between Mrs. Limpari and Mrs. McGorty regarding the issue of separation and closeness is shared by Mrs. Limpari's other children. She tells a story about the time, just after her son and daughter-in-law were married, when they had moved out to a suburb and then complained that Mrs. Limpari never visited them. In commenting on this incident, Mrs. Limpari says:

I told them that 'I'm sorry, but I can't help you. I have my clubs and other activities and I can't go out every night.' I told them I could only come like on a special occasion, baby baptized or the baby's sick . . . I have things of my own to do here.

When her other daughter told her that she planned on moving far away after she got married, Mrs. Limpari says that her response to this was "beautiful." It should be noted that Mrs. Limpari is aware of Mrs. McGorty's feelings. Several times over the past few years, Mrs. Limpari and Mrs. McGorty have tried to talk about this issue of Mrs. McGorty's reliance on her mother and Mrs. Limpari's determination to preserve her own autonomy. As Mrs. Limpari comments:

Before she had children . . . I never went to see her, 'cause that's what she wanted and she says, "Now don't make it a habit of coming down here," which I never did unless I was invited so . . . after they were married they would come here and have dinner but, in other words, if I'm not invited, I don't go. And I think that keeps a happy relation and often times she's been saying that I've neglected her . . . well, actually I have . . . I have my own responsibilities, I . . . and I can't be going every place with them; I have to devote a little time for myself too . . . ah, I am not like a devoted grandmother, but I think she'd like to see more of me, because I could give her a helping hand.

This conflict regarding separation and autonomy leads to differences in the perceptions of the two generations regarding what has actually happened in the past. For example, Mrs. McGorty says that her mother expected her to live at home while attending college, although her mother insists that she told her daughter she could live anywhere she liked. Mrs. McGorty says that her mother expected her married son and daughter-in-law to move in next door to her, while her mother expresses surprise that they decided to return to Tower Point. Mrs. McGorty says that her mother is unhappy that her sister has moved to California, although her mother says she is delighted that her daughter has moved away. Mrs. Limpari hopes that her children will find their own way, but they hope that they can all live together in Tower Point. For Mrs. McGorty, a move back to Tower Point means that she can have more of her mother's attention and support.

Unfortunately, it is not as easy for Mrs. McGorty to return to Tower Point as it was for her brothers. The aspirations she has for her children make it difficult for her to move back to Tower Point. On the other hand, the desire she has for maternal support and for a greater sense of community serve as factors encouraging such a move. Mrs. McGorty has resolved this issue in a unique manner. She is building a condominium apartment complex and plans to move into one of the apartments herself and then to sell the rest. The origins of this project are difficult to trace. Apparently, Mrs. Limpari suggested the idea. Together with a neighbor, she had owned a valuable piece of waterfront property for many years. Mrs. Limpari recollects that some five or six years ago, her daughter became quite depressed living in the suburbs:

She didn't have too many friends and . . . you know that she's an attorney and yet all she does is to take care of babies and couldn't go out and financially not even have a baby-sitter and these things depressed her a lot, so I told her well, if she was . . . you know, she had always wanted to come down to Tower Point where the people are more sociable and more pleasant 'cause you know everybody . . . I says, I'll give you that piece of land, you buy off my partner, you can build a house there, and that seemed to perk her right up.

Both Mrs. Limpari's motives for making this offer and Mrs. McGorty's motives for accepting the offer were quite complex. Mrs. Limpari saw this business venture as a way of helping her daughter out and as a way of making it possible for her daughter to return to Tower Point under what she perceives as the right circumstances. Simultaneously, she was ambivalent about the fact that Mrs. McGorty even wished to return to Tower Point and was disappointed that her daughter had not made greater use of her skills in other ways. Thus, having made the original offer, she says she declined to give further help; it was up to Mrs. McGorty to make the plan a reality. Mrs. Limpari did not offer further assistance, saying she lacked any knowledge of real estate and construction.

As previously indicated, this construction project has several complex meanings for Mrs. McGorty as well, in terms of her relationship with her parents. We discussed the role of this project in helping her to deal with her own feelings of passivity. In addition, this project provides Mrs. McGorty with a way of returning to Tower Point and yet of maintaining her social position in the community. It also provides her with a way of using her training and abilities in the service of something she wants for herself. As she says:

I am very eager to go back to Tower Point because it's where I was born and brought up and I just love it there.

What is so ironic about the project, from her mother's point of view, is that the skills she had struggled so hard to help her daughter attain to prepare her to go out into the world beyond Tower Point have become precisely the same skills Mrs. McGorty is using to be able to return to Tower Point.

The condominium project documents in clear detail both the kind of relationship Mrs. McGorty and her mother have established and the manner in which each has perceived this relationship in terms of her own developmentally salient conflicts. As a result of her conflict with her own mother, Mrs. Limpari attempted to insure that her daughter would be freed of the constraints she felt. Indeed, in an attempt to resolve her own conflict, she went almost to the other extreme and in some ways actually discouraged Mrs. McGorty from retaining close ties with the family. Mrs. McGorty's response was to articulate a greater desire for her mother's help and attention than Mrs. Limpari would acknowldege or accept. The result of this conflict, enacted across several generations, is that Mrs. McGorty feels that grown daughters should remain with their mothers and live close by, even if they have to make some sacrifices to do so. Thus, in replying to a question about how she would feel if her daughters wanted to go off to college, Mrs. McGorty remarks:

This is a bugaboo (laughs). I want my family around me . . . I probably will be flexible about it but . . . I don't think they do as well when they go away to school. I think they have too many outside influences which is another reason I'd like to keep them at home . . . I want them with me until they get married, and then I want them living next door.

There is a controlling aspect of this wish. In a story told to a picture portraying the profiles of an older and a younger woman (TAT 12F), Mrs. McGorty says:

This is an old woman, and this is her unmarried daughter who is in her 40's so that there is little likelihood that she will ever marry and she lavishes a great deal of affection on her mother but is probably resentful that she isn't married. Her mother has other married children and she wants her daughter to be married because she knows she'll be happier married, yet she's ah . . . selfish enough to want to keep her with her as a single girl because she knows that she will take care of her and, although she sometimes tells the girl to go out and make friends and have a good time, yet if the girl does anything and does make plans to go out, the old woman suddenly becomes sick or . . . said something that will keep the girl at home with her. The girl, to all outward appearances, is happy because she does have someone to care for, which is essential, and the old woman is very happy, of course, because she's being cared for, which ah . . . nowadays many old people are relegated to homes and they'll go on this way, living this way until the old woman dies and she dies happy and then the girl will just have herself and I don't know if she'll be able to fill the void left by her mother.

These data are even more striking since Mrs. McGorty was originally selected as a subject for the study on the basis of her adaptive attitudes regarding the issue of closeness-separation. It would seem that although Mrs. McGorty believes in attaining proper distance between mothers and their younger children, these attitudes shift as children grow up. While she believes that young children should have contact with persons other than their mothers and that mothers should feel able to tend to their own needs without feelings of self-sacrifice, even though their children may fuss when left with a babysitter, she also believes that adults have a responsibility toward their parents which must be met. Because Mrs. McGorty believes so strongly in the importance of daughters helping their mothers, she is particularly puzzled by her mother's response to her bid for greater closeness.

It should be noted that Mrs. Limpari, too, has mixed feelings regarding this issue of separation and closeness. While Mrs. Limpari's attitudes regarding this issue were particularly adaptive for the grandmother generation as a whole, her attitudes were not as adaptive as those of the mother generation. Likely, her children have acted on another aspect of her attitudes than the one she consciously expresses to them: that of emphasizing the lack of separateness of parent and child. In this regard, it is interesting to note that three of her four children have either returned to live in the neighborhood or are planning to do so.

While it may appear that Mrs. Limpari's values differ from those of her daughter, there are also striking similarities across the two generations. For example, Mrs. McGorty is working just as hard to see that her children obtain the best possible education as her mother had worked to insure her own education. While it may be true that Mrs. McGorty's husband is not as opposed to her goal as her father was to her mother's, nevertheless, he is by no means enthusiastic about this concern with education. Mrs. Limpari believes that she is becoming ever closer to her daughter as time goes by:

Things are better now that my daughter is married and has children. I think I'm closer to her. Maybe because I could . . . because I am helping her and she realizes that I am helping her, you know, and I'm pretty fair. I don't know why, I just feel this closeness.

On the other hand, Mrs. Limpari also worries about what her daughter thinks of her:

I know that she does a lot of comparing me with other women . . . different women . . . mothers . . . and I think I come out pretty high with her. I think I do anyway.

Mrs. McGorty also acknowledges that she and her mother have grown closer now that she is married and has a family of her own. While she gives no overalll evaluation of her present relationship with her mother, she would like to be even closer to her than she is and would like to have her mother's assistance with her housework, childcare, and chores. In sum, she would like to have more of her mother's attention and support, as she goes about the task of rearing her own children.

Mrs. McGorty sees her mother as a woman who is conflicted about her own femininity and who has difficulty maintaining her self-esteem. (Mrs. McGorty's admiration of her mother's cooking and her emulation of her culinary skills is an exception to her evaluation of her mother's adequacy as a woman.) Throughout this discussion, we have shown that Mrs. McGorty experiences essentially the same psychosocial conflict as her mother. While she relies on her own profession- al skills and her concern for her children's education, avenues not open to her mother, a similar flight from passivity into activity can be observed in each gen- eration. Recall that Mrs. Limpari comments in her story to IAT picture G6 (a picture of a woman washing dishes, while in the background a little girl sits at a table) that as long as the woman stays bright and alert she will be able to fulfill the homemaker role. For Mrs. McGorty, this picture also evokes fear of passivi- ty. Just as was true for her mother, her solution to the woman's dilemma is to devise some sort of activity. By being active and competent in the world outside the family (a solution Mrs. Limpari also sought through her work), as well as by helping her daughters to attain self-esteem by means of intellectual competence, a modality she herself had relied on, Mrs. McGorty has reached a solution for her conflicting feelings about herself as a woman.

Mrs. McGorty's identification with her mother's technique for resolving her own conflicting feelings about her femininity has led to a reasonably good adapta- tion. While she is fairly dependent on her mother and wishes she felt more confi- dent, Mrs. McGorty obtains considerabie satisfaction from her life. She has a marriage that is stable and gratifying, and she is pleased with the way her daugh- ters are growing up. She is a spontaneous woman and capable of feeling both sadness and joy without periods of either despondency or elation.

At age 38, Mrs. McGorty is a rather practical and sensible woman who believes in dealing actively with the world and who feels little sympathy with those who are unwilling to struggle to better their life. Although she looks forward to a closer relationship with her mother than seems possible at the present time, it is probable that with her eventual return to Tower Point (and as her mother grows older and is no longer so insistent on her own autonomy) Mrs. McGorty may realize her wish for a closer relationship.

CONCLUSION

Mrs. McGorty and her mother were selected for more detailed study precisely because of Mrs. McGorty's adaptive attitudes regarding the resolution of the MAS issue of appropriate versus inappropriate closeness toward the child. More careful study of the personality of each of these women and of the relationship they have with each other indicates that Mrs. McGorty's expressed attitudes are determined by a variety of factors, including the kind of relationship Mrs. Limpari had with her mother, her mother's determination to work this conflict through with her own daughter, Mrs. McGorty's own childhood experiences, her subsequent educational and professional career, her marriage, and her relationship with her children.

We have seen that, according to her own account, Mrs. McGorty believes quite strongly in fostering a sense of separateness in her own daughters, does not feel that childrearing imposes undue sacrifices, and does not feel that childcare is depleting. What her attitudes will be toward her grown daughters is difficult to predict. A great deal will depend on the nature of her relationship with her own mother during the next few years and the extent that she is able to resolve her own residual conflicts regarding her feelings of dependency and lowered sense of self-esteem as a woman.

CHAPTER 4

Mrs. Scardoni and Mrs. Russo: The Transmission of Family Symbiosis Across Three Generations

LIVING APART—LESS ADAPTIVE ATTITUDES

Winterfield is a fairly typical "outlying" community, further removed from the city than a suburb but clearly not the country. It was built during the engineering boom in the early fifties when highly specialized research and development firms dealing in nuclear and space engineering were constructed in previously unincorporated areas. These firms are now interspersed with traditional commercial and industrial areas and small housing developments that often are lost among the large industrial concerns surrounding them.

Mrs. Scardoni's neighborhood is typical of this residential isolation. Unless one makes a quick turn, just beyond the warehouselike discount store, with its garish neon lights, it is easy to miss the crooked, unpaved street leading into the cul-de-sac where some fortune hungry developer scattered gray clapboard houses among the boulder-strewn and uneven terrain so characteristic of the New England countryside.

A woman who has moved frequently, ever since childhood, Mrs. Scardoni is socially isolated and culturally uprooted. The move she made to Winterfield seven years ago was but one in a long series of previously unsuccessful moves in search of a cultural and personal identity. Although she has lived in Winterfield for several years, Mrs. Scardoni has still to settle on any favorite drug, notion, or grocery store. This is only one indication of her difficulty in adapting to her new community and in becoming a part of it. Uncertain how to get from one part of the community to another, she makes long lists of errands she cannot complete.

Isolated and apart, and unable to put down roots where she might become part of a well-established community, Mrs. Scardoni rejects and feels rejected by her Italian American Catholic heritage. Instead, she relies almost exclusively on her children for her own sense of personal adequacy and identity, just as they, in turn, use her as a measure of their own identity. The importance of family ties for the identity of individual family members is apparent from the living arrangements of the second generation. Located in a nearby community, Mrs. Scardoni's son and his family and her daughter and her family share a duplex frame house and depend, almost exclusively, on each other and their mother for companionship and baby-sitting.

Many factors contribute to personality formation: genetic predisposition, early life experiences, later experiences both at home and in school, and such adult experiences as marriage, work, and parenthood. Environment also has an important impact on personality throughout the life cycle and may foster certain needs or attitudes, while it inhibits others (G. Stern, 1970). In contrast to Mrs. Limpari (discussed in Chapter 3), who thrives in the close-knit community of Tower Point, Mrs. Scardoni would experience Tower Point as intrusive and annoying. To some extent, this problem arises for Mrs. Giorgio in Somerset (to be discussed later): she would prefer greater privacy and less contact with her neighbors than her neighbors believe desirable. On the other hand, Mrs. McGorty (in Chapter 3) would prefer less privacy than other South Tuxton residents believe desirable.

Clearly, where people choose to live is determined by many factors, only one of which is proximity to work. Other important factors include the extent to which basic values and attitudes are consistent with those of prospective neighbors. For members of the Italian American community, there are a variety of communities in the greater Bethany area to live. Indeed, geographic mobility among members of this ethnic group parallels that of the entire area, which can be viewed as a giant wheel with a hub or center and spokes radiating out toward the edge. At the hub are the city's leading educational and cultural institutions, the business district, and the tightly knit core Italian American community of Tower Point. Most first- and second-generation Italian American families choose to live in Tower Point. Values are shared and there is little sense of normlessness: personal and cultural identity is intact.

Transportation from the hub along the spokes of the wheel is quite good, and many second- and third-generation families have moved from Tower Point to suburban communities. While there is less of an emphasis on community cohesion and cooperation in these suburban communities, there is still a clear sense of what may be expected from one's neighbors, and cultural traditions are fairly well preserved. Transportation from the central city or from these suburban communities to more distant areas like Winterfield is much less satisfactory, and residents of outlying areas are cut off from many of the cultural events shared by residents of the central city and the near suburbs.

Overall disregard for planning and transience of the residents combines with the lack of transportation to create an environment of normlessness in these socially and culturally unstable outlying areas. Identity becomes diffuse, and, while a good deal of personal freedom and privacy is possible, such privacy is obtained at the cost of a sense of direct social participation. Identity diffusion is characteristic both of individual residents and the community itself.

MRS. SCARDONI: IT'S HARD TO KNOW WHAT A FAMILY IS

With an insistent look on her face, Mrs. Scardoni urges the visitor to accompany her on a "tour" of her living room, which, she says, expresses both her family's and her interests. She points out the antique chair she acquired in New Kaneville, the handcrafted imitation antique table she purchased at a garage sale in Thompsonville, and the tottering brass candlestick she bought in Havensport. These three articles reassure Mrs. Scardoni that she can have a place in the American heritage. By adopting this heritage, she hopes to find a set of values that will help her to define who and what she is. Given her status as a marginal member of her religious and ethnic community, together with her residence in a new and still undefined community, Mrs. Scardoni relies on this historical tradition and on her own children to provide a sense of personal and historical identity.

The antiques prominently displayed in her living room and the chintz sofa, matching chairs, and love seat, together with the colonial external appearance of the house, which includes an American eagle over the door, would suggest that Mrs. Scardoni had achieved an identity with the Protestant New England gentry whose cultural stability she so much envies. These symbols of colonial American culture are even more striking when compared with the traditional religious symbols that adorn the houses of other Italian American grandparents in this study. Once inside Mrs. Scardoni's house, framed needlepoints praising God and country substitute for the crucifixes and religious paintings found in the halls of other families in this study. Inside, the Madonna and Child have been discarded by Mrs. Scardoni for porcelain figurines of seventeenth-century English aristocracy.

The substitution of New England culture for the Italian American culture of her own family is evidence of the extent to which Mrs. Scardoni has rejected her cultural heritage. However, considering both her parents' attitudes toward their Italian American heritage and her early history of physical and emotional neglect, it is clear why Mrs. Scardoni rejects her heritage and why it is so important to have the tangible evidence of cultural continuity and bourgeois stability.

A heavy-set, stolid woman in her early fifties, her black hair streaked with gray, only her soft brown eyes reflect her early life of turmoil and hardship. Mrs. Scardoni's father was an invalid, and her mother ran an unsuccessful boarding-house and restaurant for a living. With seven other children already in this first-generation Italian immigrant family, Mrs. Scardoni's birth was hardly welcomed or even noticed. According to family legend, her mother was already back at work by the evening of her birth. Mrs. Scardoni consoles herself by thinking that her three younger brothers and sisters suffered even greater hardship and turmoil.

With 11 children in the family, a constant influx of new boarders who would stay for only a few weeks before moving on, and frequent visits by members of both of her parents' extended families, it was difficult for Mrs. Scardoni to know who was a member of her own immediate family. This confusion about family membership is one major source of her confusion about her own identity. Furthermore, with 11 children and only sporadic income, resources were always very scarce. Mrs. Scardoni can remember many times, throughout her childhood, when she went to bed hungry because there was not enough food for everyone in the family.

It was a rule that her father and his family had the first priority when there was not enough food to go around. Mrs. Scardoni remembers times when she and her brothers and sisters would look on with her mother, while her father and grandmother ate whatever scraps remained after the restaurant had closed. Since her mother did not wish to make trouble within the family, she would seldom complain and would chastise the children when they complained about how hungry they were.

The lasting effects of such childhood deprivation are reflected in Mrs. Scardoni's responses to the Rorschach blots. In response to Card IV she says:

> This looks like a cow, something like a cow, and it's hard to tell whether it has . . . can give any milk . . . looks like the pulls, what you call them, are dried up . . . cow won't . . . can't give any milk. . . at least I think that's a cow . . . of course it could also be an ape . . . but I'm not sure now what it is . . . it could be something else but I'm not sure what.

Here, Mrs. Scardoni shows her concern about the ability to receive nourishment. Milk is one of the prime symbols in our culture for good maternal care: a cow with dried-up udders provides little nourishment. Mrs. Scardoni first observes that the cow "won't" give milk, but such a refusal to provide nourishment creates too much anxiety, and she rephrases her response by maintaining that the cow "can't" give milk. The possibility that her mother willfully deprived her is unthinkable, although, as we see subsequently, Mrs. Scardoni harbors considerable resentment and guilt toward her mother.

The most important part of the response is contained in the last few lines, where Mrs. Scardoni concludes that if the "cow won't" or "can't give any milk" then it might not be a cow. Stated in other terms, Mrs. Scardoni recognizes that the basis of a good sense of identity is to be found in the child's first experiences in receiving basic maternal care. Erikson, in discussing the origins of the sense of identity, makes this observation:

> As the newborn infant is separated from his symbiosis with the mother's body, his inborn and more or less coordinated ability to take in by mouth meets the mother's more or less coordinated ability and intention to feed him and to welcome him . . . What would we consider to be the earliest and most undifferentiated "sense of identity"? I would suggest that it arises out of the encounter of maternal person and small infant, an encounter which is one of mutual trustworthiness and mutual recognition. This, in all its infantile simplicity, is the first experience of what in later reoccurrences in love and admiration can only be called a sense of 'hallowed presence,' and the need for which remains basic in man. (1968, pp. 97, 105)

The child first learns who she is through the experience of receiving basic care, and, as a result of getting what she needs, she is able to define herself in terms of her mother. Lack of such basic care leads to a feeling of uncertainty about who and what one is. For Mrs. Scardoni, the origin of her conflict regarding her own identity, so well reflected in her uncertainty about whether the inkblot is that of a cow or an ape, derives from her feelings of lack of maternal care, supported by a family environment in which a large number of relatives came and went at unpredictable times. In addition, the extreme disorganization within this impoverished family meant that the usual intrafamilial roles were not performed. Erikson also notes the following:

It is already in his earliest encounters that the human infant meets up with the principal modalities of his culture. The simplest and easiest modality is *to get*, not in the sense of 'go and get' but in that of receiving and accepting what is given . . . The groping and unstable newborn's organism learns this modality only as he learns to regulate his readiness to 'get' with the methods of a mother who, in turn, will permit him to coordinate his means of getting what is given, and in learning to get somebody to do for him what he wishes to have done, the baby also develops the necessary groundwork 'to get to be' the giver—that is, to identify with her and eventually become a giving person. (1968, p. 99)

As Mrs. Scardoni's own experiences show, early deprivation affects one's ability to give and to establish mutuality with others. Her feelings of deprivation lead not only to a diffusion of identity, but also to withdrawal from relationships, since they only intensify her sense of emotional and physical starvation. This theme emerges quite clearly in Mrs. Scardoni's story to picture TAT 13MF in which "a young man is standing with downcast head buried in his arm. Behind him is the figure of a woman lying in bed":

Now this . . . this picture looks like, maybe he had come in unexpected and found her dead . . . he doesn't look like a doctor . . . he was surprised to see her in that condition . . . maybe she was murdered or maybe. . .yes, she died of an illness. . .he came in and found her in that condition. . .she must have had a bad sickness. . .ah, it was malnutrition, something that she had nothing to eat, she had not been able to find. . .he did not. . .could not. . .no one would help her to get anything to eat, and she became more and more hungry and finally died. . .feelings of hunger there at the end, hurt more and more, till finally she died and now he feels sorry for himself. . .for her. . .(E: What was his relationship to her?) They were. . .boy, ah, boy and girl. . .how you say, going out planning to get married, engaged, ah. . .married.

It is not unusual to view this picture as a scene of violence. Indeed, a majority of women in Eron's (1953) normative study perceived this scene as one of violence, typically as one in which a man attacked a woman. However, it is most unusual to see this as a scene in which a woman is dying of starvation and malnutrition. Given her history of deprivation throughout childhood and into adulthood, it is not surprising that anxiety concerning starvation would continue throughout her life. Following Erikson's interpretation of the effects of physical and emotional starvation, it makes sense to assume that Mrs. Scardoni was unable to teach others to care for her. That is, she had never learned to be a good "getter." This problem is clearly portrayed in her story when she indicates that the man could not provide for the woman or help her to get much needed supplies. The heroine of her story could not turn to her boyfriend, or, indeed, any one, for sustenance. In reality, while she can depend on her children for certain kinds of help, Mrs. Scardoni's conflicts in being able to establish mutuality preclude the possibility of forming intimate, satisfying, and mature relationships.

Mrs. Scardoni's earliest experiences contributed to her uncertainty about who she was; cultural and social factors also contributed to her identity diffusion. Neither of her parents had any connection with the church, and none of the children were christened. Mrs. Scardoni's mother, in particular, was quite cynical and viewed the Catholic church as organized robbery of the poor and underprivileged. With so many children, a husband with both physical and mental illness, and the responsibility of providing for this family, Mrs. Scardoni had neither the time nor the inclination to attend Mass, and used to tell her children that it was a waste of time and that "you can't eat by going to Church." Since the church is the focus of much of the social life of the Italian American community, by not attending church, family members were further isolated from the surrounding community. As she looks back on her childhood, Mrs. Scardoni regrets not having been able to take first communion and wear the traditional white dress that symbolizes becoming a "daughter" of the church (A. Parsons, 1969a).

Isolated from others and living in a fragmented household, Mrs. Scardoni had relatively few resources within her family that might foster a sense of identity. Indeed, she has some difficulty in being able to understand of what a family actually consists or in knowing how to define family boundaries. Mrs. Scardoni's confusion is apparent in her response to the Rorschach blots (I. 1, IV. 1, V.1) where she equates quite disparate objects as members of the same "family":

I.1 I don't know if that looks like a bat or a butterfly. I don't know, a butterfly and a moth, they're about the same as a family. . .what belongs together in a family, are a butterfly and a bat related. . .

IV. 1 It looks more like an ape type of family. Gorilla and ape, you know, a family type. I wonder if they are related as a family. It's hard to know what a family is. . .

V. 1 It could be that butterfly or moth family again. Maybe the butterfly and the moth are both part of the same family.

Mrs. Scardoni's early life was characterized by deprivation and chaotic disorganization. In addition, it was punctuated by frequent periods of unpredictable terror. Mrs. Scardoni's father was, as she recalls, a man who never cared much for work and who drank heavily. Her parents quarreled frequently about her father's laziness and his refusal to provide for the family. On several occasions, when he physically threatened her mother, he was committed to a state hospital. In addition, her father's mother decided to move in with the family when Mrs. Scardoni was in grade school and set about to make trouble between her parents on those rare occasions when everything was peaceful. As Mrs. Scardoni observes, in recalling her childhood:

Of course, we didn't have a good life ourselves at home because everything was always disturbed like, ah. . .my father abused my mother in different ways, he used to have long hands, like to hit, and my grandmother used to hit, too, and they'd both hit my mother, and there were lots of tears and it was always like frightened like in the house, you know, the home was like that you didn't know what to expect and that made it difficult and we'd all begin to cry and then they would all turn on us and we'd run and hide.

The picture Mrs. Scardoni presents of her early life is one of constant terror in which the children lived in fear of the future and the random punishment that might be handed out. This feeling of terror was further increased by her parents' socialization practices and, in particular, by their mode of fostering bladder and bowel control. All the children were expected to be able to use the toilet by the time they were a year and a half old, and accidents were followed by severe beatings and the application of enemas, which further emphasized the message that impulse control could be achieved by forces outside one's own will. As Mrs. Scardoni observes:

My mother. . .we just had to submit. . .she had no time to bother with such things. She would just call my father. . .he was. . .it was he. . .would beat the hell out of us. . .you quickly learned not to fight back for it was no use. One time, my younger sister was beat so bad after she messed that they almost had to take her to the hospital.

Mrs. Scardoni is the only one of the four grandmothers in this study to remember such details of her toilet training. Clearly, the toilet training she received was intensely harsh, and its effects are visible in her adult personality. The preoccupation she has with her bowels and the anatomical region she refers to as her "backside" is revealed in her responses to the Rorschach, as well as in her current medical complaints.

For example, on Card VI of the Rorschach, she provides the following response:

This could be. . .this looks like your backside, back where you sit.

On inquiry about this response, she adds:

It's just the way it looks by your backside (She gets out of the chair and points to her buttocks). . .it just looks like cheek-to-cheek. . .

Similar responses are found on cards II and VII. Mrs. Scardoni seeks frequent medical consultations because she is chronically constipated and relies heavily on suppositories and enemas. Furthermore, in her discussions about herself and her feelings, she continually refers to herself as an "old fart." Thus she views herself in her entirety literally as feces. She notes, for example, in talking about her place in the birth order, that "those of us who were at the tail-end of the family were treated like we were shit." She also observes, in speaking of herself, that she is not sure why anyone would want to study her, because, as she says, "I'm just an old fart, an old shit, and why waste your time with that." To the extent that Mrs. Scardoni has achieved any self-definition, it is a negative identity, as a leftover or waste product at the end of the family.

Her parents, by forcing enemas into her, deprived Mrs. Scardoni of the experience of developing impulse control by herself. The effect of this intrusive and brutal method of bowel control was to make Mrs. Scardoni fear she might lose control of her impulses. She states this fear as "I might let myself go, like my father, and become an alcoholic." Several of her picture thematic stories refer to people who have become mentally ill or who have had a nervous breakdown as a result of drinking. However, she does not or cannot allow herself the pleasure of discarding impulse control. Instead, she does precisely the opposite and prides herself in her ability to deny all her pleasure-seeking impulses. She tells, with pride, how she can walk through a grocery store and buy only what she needs and how, while starving herself, she was able to prepare steak dinners for her daughter who had serious eating problems throughout childhood and adolescence.

The demand for self-control became even more important when, during seventh grade, Mrs. Scardoni was forced to leave school and help in the family restaurant. Since her father was ill and unable to work, the children were forced to leave school and begin work as soon as they were legally old enough to do so. Largely for this reason, none of Mrs. Scardoni's brothers or sisters have gone beyond grammar school in their education, and each feels resentful about having to work to support family members; rivalry between them has been intense and continuous.

While working in the restaurant and waiting on customers, Mrs. Scardoni herself was frequently on the edge of starvation, for, as we have noted, there was little food left over for the family. The only way she could survive was for Mrs. Scardoni to steal scraps left by customers, and, when her mother found her doing so, she was severely beaten.

Mrs. Scardoni hoped that working with her mother in the restaurant would at least provide her with a way of getting the maternal care she felt she had missed in infancy. However, except for discipline, her mother was too busy to attend to her daughter, and Mrs. Scardoni was expected to get along by herself. In addition, her mother was adamant that Mrs. Scardoni should not receive any advantages from working in the restaurant and that her father and grandmother had the highest priority for any food that was left over. Eventually, Mrs. Scardoni and her mother became bitter enemies, and they would scream and quarrel with each other in front of customers. Mrs. Scardoni attempted to find excuses for not working, only to be beaten by her father or mother. Ultimately, she was only able to resolve this bizarre situation by running away from home, marrying at an early age, and establishing her own household.

In spite of this earlier conflict between mother and daughter, Mrs. Scardoni remained very much involved with her mother throughout her adult life, until her mother's death four years ago. The very ambivalent feelings she has about her mother are revealed in her responses to Loevinger sentence completion stems:

If my mother. . . only didn't hate me so much.

My mother and I . . . she fought with me too much.

When my mother spanked me . . . it was because I was too spoiled.

Whenever she was with her mother . . . she felt very sad.

When she thought of her mother . . . I feel very sorry for myself.

Mrs. Scardoni's first reaction to her mother is that of a persecutory figure. This first response is then reworked so that it is she who deserves her mother's verbal criticism and physical abuse. Finally, she acknowledges her sadness at not having been able to obtain the care she sought from her mother.

It is not surprising that her mother's death four years ago had a profound effect on Mrs. Scardoni, for, given the intensity of her hatred for her mother, it is not surprising that she should view herself as the cause of her mother's death. This conflict is well portrayed in Mrs. Scardoni's story to TAT Card 12F in the Murray picture thematic series, described as ''the portrait of a young woman. A weird old woman with a shawl over her head is grimacing in the background'':

This here looks like a ghost or might be a you know, like a memory that she's got in the past, maybe she didn't treat her mother right or something and it's coming back in memory and the mother's in back there like . . . like an older woman. Now her conscience kind of bothers her. Maybe she didn't treat her mother right one way or the other, something is here cause she's thinking what to do with her one way or the other. (E: How didn't she treat her mother right?) Well maybe she. . . 'cause her mother got old or something and she didn't . . . maybe like to have her mother around or something or she and her mother had fights all the time . . . maybe she's sorry she had those fights. Looks like she is . . . like she's got a shadow of her mother, whatever this could be, grandmother, but it looks like her mother in back here . . . things she didn't do right maybe and she's appearing in back of her or something to warn her one way or the other, yeah, that's what it looks like. Oh, it's going to be a sad future for her, something that she didn't do right for/by her mother, looks like.

This story starts with the perception that it was she who injured her mother and who now feels guilty about what she did to her. There is even some attempt to distance the conflict by suggesting that it is her grandmother, and not her mother, who is the focus of the conflict. Ultimately, this conflict has become an intrapsychic conflict in which her mother has become a part of herself.

As Mrs. Scardoni sees herself, she is but a shadow of her own mother, and the ambivalent feelings she has about her mother continue to the present. Just as her mother lived and died an unhappy woman who was never able to realize her goals, Mrs. Scardoni has the same pessimistic view of the future. Twelve of her 20 thematic apperceptive stories have unfortunate endings, and, even in the 3 stories in which the long-term outcome is seen as favorable, there are losses in the present or financial reversals that have to be mourned. To the extent that she has made her conflict with her mother a part of her own personality and to the extent that she identified with this aspect of her mother's personality, she feels unable to rise above her own misfortunes.

From her mother's relationship with her father, Mrs. Scardoni learned that ''men abuse women and treat them like slaves.'' We have described the terror Mrs. Scardoni felt when she watched her father hit her mother. She explains her father's proneness to violence by saying it was due to his mother's pernicious influence. She cites the following as typical of her grandmother's behavior: when the grandmother came to visit the family from New York, where she lived, she would tell her son stories that enraged him about his wife's misbehavior and sexual provocativeness. In addition to her feeling that her father was mean, strict, and unreasonable, Mrs. Scardoni noted, with real sadness, that there had been little love in her family when she was growing up. This feeling of sadness and of being overwhelmed is vividly presented in her description of the little baby she had drawn:

(E: And the baby, can you tell me about him?) Her . . . it's a little girl, sort of looks like a little Chinese girl . . . sort of Chinese you know, don't you think? And, he's unhappy . . . she's unhappy, an unhappy child, with all this going on, all this war, a little Chinese child, wandering, alone and helpless. A little Chinese boy, ah, girl lost with all this war that's going on.

Like the Chinese child she describes, she felt alone, unhappy, and helpless as a little girl with the constant strife in her own house.

This conflict within Mrs. Scardoni's family has only intensified her fantasies of the "Ideal Father." This fantasied father is nicely portrayed in her story to one of the cards (IAT F2 rev) in the Cohler picture thematic series in which "a young woman is seated in a chair and an older man is standing behind her holding a letter":

Well, he looks like an older person here, you know. Something he's holding in his hand. That could be a letter that she received that the father didn't like and he just warned her that some letter she received wasn't nice and she doesn't like it so he must be giving her hell or threatening to kill her or beat her or something . . . looks like he's mad and he's talking to the daughter or whatever (long pause) . . . that's what I think he's thinking, ah . . . (long pause while S. picks up and studies the picture) . . . you know, that he's saying here, you . . . it looks like a letter, it could be a sad letter, it could be news of death or something, you know, because he's holding the letter or something, maybe looks like comfort, he wants to comfort her or something one way or the other, you know. It could be two different things (E: Which is the better story do you think?) Well, I think the letter could be good news that's come because there, he's trying to convince her one way or the other . . . he looks like a mature man there, yeah, that's about all I can think of (E: And the outcome?) Well, in the future, it looks like she'll be brought up in a good home, 'cause I can see it, you know, it won't be a bad life, cause you can see the nice home, the nice back lawn of the home, the nice furniture (S. voice trails off) . . . It looks a little sad at the moment but the future . . . she'll establish, come out of it now, you know what I mean.

This is a very confused story. Mrs. Scardoni develops two quite different themes, neither of which she resolves. The long pause is her story's pivotal point; here she switches from describing the reality of her own life, where her father continually threatened to beat her, to her fantasied father who would be kind and understanding and who would be able to comfort his daughter in her sadness. The extent to which she lives in this fantasy is seen by her elaboration of the story to include the family's house and a large back lawn that is not even in the picture. Again, in the future, as contrasted with the past, she will be brought up in a "nice" home and have a "nice" life.

When one considers Mrs. Scardoni's emotionally and physically deprived childhood, her terrifying memories of the intense fury that raged through the household, and the family's self-imposed isolation from their community, it is not surprising that Mrs. Scardoni should be so uncertain about her identity. Nor is it surprising that Mrs. Scardoni should be so preoccupied by what it means to be a woman and so uncertain whether she even wants to be a woman. Just as with her mother, the relationship she had with her father was stormy and violent; she continually witnessed her father and his family abusing her mother, and when she did escape this abuse, it was into a marriage not unlike that of her parents.

Mrs. Scardoni's preoccupation with her sex-role identity is well illustrated in her responses to Rorschach blots such as to Card III.1:

This looks like a heart, I don't know now if it looks like a heart . . . but, to me, have this got . . . has this the men, too, and women, like I see in this card . . . Gee, this is kind of difficult here now, I wouldn't think now, you know, what really confuses me is knowing whether they are men or women.

Similar responses to cards VI and IX of the Rorschach underline the salience of this conflict for Mrs. Scardoni. One of the questions that most concerns her is what differentiates the internal and external anatomy of men from that of women. On card VI.2 of the Rorschach blots she muses:

(Inquiry) (E: And the woman's insides?) It ah . . . well it's got two little, I don't know if it's got two little . . . I don't know if it's got two little inside organs or your . . . the . . . the lungs/part of the lungs part of a . . . could be a man you know . . . I wonder what makes a man's lungs different from a woman's lungs.

Similarly, on card IX.1, she observes:

This here looks like the insides of a woman or a man or something the way it's spread like either the man's or the woman's insides . . . could either be the man's or the woman's organs. (Inquiry) (E: What kind of an organ might it be?) Well, the man's ah . . . ah men/ah, the man himself, you know, maybe the wrong man. Do you know about the man's insides? The tubes down around the stomach, could be a man's stomach, could be a woman's stomach. Do you know if a man's stomach and a woman's stomach look alike?

Mrs. Scardoni's fantasy life centers around the issue of sex and reproduction. From a total of 16 Rorschach responses, 9, or 56%, were explicit sex and sex-anatomy responses. Most of these responses were generated from her own anxiety and showed little adherence to the form of the blots, indicating the extent to which her conflict regarding the issue of sexuality impairs Mrs. Scardoni's ability to accurately appraise reality. Fourteen of the 16 Rorschach responses, or 88%, would be considered by Holt (1977) to represent extreme primary process imagery (Level I).

Several other factors, in addition to earlier life experiences, also contribute to Mrs. Scardoni's anxiety regarding sexuality and reproduction. First, Mrs. Scardoni has just completed menopause, which was particularly uncomfortable for her. At the same time, she has been trying to develop a relationship with her second husband that is both interpersonally and sexually satisfying for her. She is particularly concerned about her ability to satisfy her husband, since one of the reasons he left his first wife was because of sexual incompatibility.

Mrs. Scardoni's preoccupation with her sexual and reproductive functioning is manifest not only in fantasy, but also in her daily life, for she spends much time and energy worrying about her body and complains of frequent but vague oches and pains. She also spends a good deal of time seeking medical advice and is a frequent visitor at the outpatient department of the community hospital. In describing her contacts with her physician, she observes:

> I wake up in the morning terrified, afraid that I am falling apart . . . that I have some disease and I call my doctor. He says that it is nerves and that I worry too much about my health but I . . . many mornings I wake up feeling sickly, sometimes with an upset stomach, or stomachache. Joe hates to miss work on account of how I am feeling so I have to get myself to the doctor. Maybe I need your kind of doctors (laughs). I don't think my doctor wants to see me again. I have been asking around about changing doctors. It's one of the big problems in my life.

These hypochondriacal fears can be understood as an expression of Mrs. Scardoni's fear about her adequacy as a woman. This is documented in her response to Card II.2 of the Rorschach:

> Two kidneys or a lung or something . . . it could be one you know like, the lungs are there. More like lungs, I . . . I don't know. But it looks more to me like . . . ah . . . a woman like she's have . . . you know a private . . . anyway I don't know how I want to say it a little more . . . let it sound better, I don't know the way it looks like the opening or something, you know. She's having a period I think . . . yeah, it looks like she's having a menstruation or . . . maybe she's ready to deliver . . . yes, she's ready to deliver . . . it could be ready for her . . . ah, looks like she's dying, ah ready to deliver the way it looks to me, she could be delivering or she could be dying. They're both the same. That's the way it looks to me.

Mrs. Scardoni views even normal menstruation as life-threatening, and childbirth is also associated with a fatal outcome.

Mrs. Scardoni grew up with little sense of self, enormous insecurity, feelings of resentment and mistrust of others, and uncertainty regarding who and what she was. Unable to establish meaningful emotional contact with her mother, subjected to frequent beatings by both her parents, and forced to leave school in the seventh grade to work, it is little wonder that she ran away from home at age 17 and married a distant relative whom she had met briefly at a christening. The precise quality of the pressure to marry is well portrayed in the response she gives to picture IAT Se7 in the Cohler series in which "a woman in a raincoat is walking down the street. A path leads to the house portrayed in the background":

> This looks like a teenager, you know . . . going away from home or something or going to . . . this looks like a teenager . . . she's sad, going out of the house sad or something, some disturbance there somewhere in the house, she must have a bad . . . you know, like a not good home, and she's walking out of the house now, downhearted like you know maybe there's not a good background of a home or something and she's walking away a little disturbed, as I picture her. (E: And the outcome?) Well, she's thinking ahead of her future maybe good or maybe bad if she's on the loose by herself, you know. If they start off at a young age like this, they always end up with a bad future. I mean to say, it won't look good if she wants to leave the home, looks like she's just walking, walking away from home, some disturbance in the back . . . some disturbance in her home.

The man Mrs. Scardoni married was her first suitor. Mrs. Scardoni's father discouraged relationships outside the family and became especially enraged if young men paid attention to his girls. He would, in Mrs. Scardoni's words, "turn the house upside down in his anger." As adolescents, the children were always expected to be home before dark and were not permitted out after that time, a factor that further increased the family's social isolation.

Fearing her father's anger Mrs. Scardoni denied herself a period of courtship. However, she was determined to find some way of leaving home. So after a very short correspondence and two formal meetings in the Scardoni's parlor, she accepted her fiance's marriage proposal. Then, when her father refused to give his permission, she eloped in the middle of the night. Like the teenager in her story, she left home and ran away from a disturbance of major proportions. Also, like the teenager in her story, she was well aware of the risks involved and of the inherent danger of marrying a man who was almost a stranger. However, given the pressure to leave home and the impossibility of having any time before marriage in which to get to know her fiance, she felt she had to take the chance and hope that she had made the right decision.

Perhaps it was her own experience that elicited Mrs. Scardoni's observation that "if they start at a young age like this, they always end up with a bad future." Mrs. Scardoni had two children within the first two years of her marriage, and, shortly after their second child was born, her husband became mentally ill and was hospitalized. Within the first days of his hospitalization, he managed to hang himself in the seclusion room to which he had been confined because of his disruptive behavior. Thus, at age 19, Mrs. Scardoni was left penniless, with two children, and no husband. Terrified of her parents, she was unwilling to return home and decided to remain on her own by going "on relief." As she observed, since there was high unemployment in the Bethany area, where she lived, it was not thought at that time disgraceful to be on relief.

Mrs. Scardoni's pessimism is well illustrated by the story she tells to Card IAT H4 in which "a young woman is seated on a sofa talking with a young man":

This looks like a husband and wife I could gather . . . could be girlfriend and boyfriend, you don't know, you know I don't know . . . let's see, talk it over, looks like they're both discussing, you know, try to . . . talk to talking over, which, you know, between themselves, doesn't look a ha . . . you know, pleasant . . . they don't look too pleasant here. Things don't agree as they're talking, something that they're discussing you know . . . that's all, I gather . . . talking about maybe financial things, some way, they can't get together . . . not really talking to each other. (E: And the future?) It's not going to be a nice future. Looks like they're going to be alone, not together . . . it don't look like a good future there . . . real trouble . . . maybe he'll murder her.

In this story, difficulties in communication ultimately lead to violence, an experience Mrs. Scardoni so often witnessed during her own childhood.

In spite of the unhappiness and fear her own father caused her in childhood and adolescence, Mrs. Scardoni married a man with many of her father's problems, including alcoholism and serious difficulties controlling his own violent urges, who committed suicide many years ago while her children were still very young. In her picture thematic stories, the theme of close relationships between men and women resulting in violence is quite pronounced; the only possible outcome of relationships between men and women is violence leading to murder.

Given her view of heterosexual relationships—and considering that Mrs. Scardoni reared her children herself and was widowed for more than 25 years—it is most remarkable that she remarried just 7 years ago. She met her second husband through her daughter's husband's family. However, the circumstances of this meeting are an embarrassment in the family and have caused an estrangement between Mrs. Scardoni and her son-in-law's family. Mrs. Scardoni's second husband left his own wife to marry her, and, while the church was willing to sanction Mrs. Scardoni's remarriage, the fact that she was marrying a divorcee was, of course, against church doctrine. When Mrs. Scardoni persisted in marrying, she was excommunicated and, as a result, was even further isolated from her religious and cultural heritage.

In contrast to her description of her first husband, which is one of bitterness, Mrs. Scardoni has attained a much more balanced view of her second husband. As she comments, in describing her drawing of a man whom she acknowledges with some surprise, he looks a good deal like her husband:

> He looks a little excited, like you know, ah, like he wants to say something exciting . . . he also wants to test . . . like test his rights . . . an impatient man . . . easily excited.

This description is consistent with the description she provides in talking more directly about her and her second husband's relationship:

> He is a good man . . . he's a hardworking man but see, they're Italians and they got old fashioned ideas, you know, what I mean is that he wouldn't abuse me, but sometimes there's a little misunderstanding . . . he's a hard man to understand . . . and to please. He has always told me 'I don't know, I don't have a lot of patience.' He wants to win, he's got to be right. He can be pretty mean at times . . . stubborn . . . he'll put on his coat, take the car, and go. That's it, that's the only way he can get mad, he's not the kind to argue back with you . . . if there's a misunderstanding, maybe I want to go some place and he won't take me, he'll just put on his coat and take off, which is better than with my first husband, where he used to drink and then abuse me; the argument stops and he comes in different. I still don't understand him.

Thus, while Mrs. Scardoni's second husband is like her father and first husband in being impetuous and lacking control of his anger, when he is aroused, he withdraws into his own world and flees rather than entering into direct combat with her.

Occupation? A steady worker, and concerned about his wife, Mr. Scardoni has provided her with companionship and support. However, the issue of Mr. Scardoni's own first marriage still comes between them, and Mrs. Scardoni is worried that perhaps it was not right for him to leave his first wife. One of the major issues in Mr. Scardoni's first marriage was that his wife would not let him have enough freedom to visit with his friends. Particularly on Friday and Saturday nights, Mr. Scardoni likes to drive back to Tower Point in the Bethany area and visit with his old friends, many of whom he has known since they were boys together in Italy. Mrs. Scardoni insists that she is not suspicious of his activities:

A wife can't be with them all the time or on their tail all the time . . . I don't think that it is right to haunt your husband.

Typically, when he goes to Tower Point to visit with his friends, Mr. Scardoni drives his wife to her daughter's house, where Mrs. Scardoni spends the evening. Sometimes, on weekends, the couple goes shopping together; Mrs. Scardoni likes her husband's advice before she buys a new dress. In the summer, Mr. Scardoni spends much of his spare time in the evenings and on weekends gardening or watching sporting events on television. When they sit down together to talk, it is mainly about bills that have to be paid or other such details of running the household. While the Scardonis spend a good deal of time together—watching television, working in the garden, or shopping—they seldom discuss such difficult topics as their past lives or their feelings about each other. While in some ways Mrs. Scardoni would like to share more of past life with her husband, she notes that when they do talk about such intimate subjects, they find themselves frequently talking past each other and end up misunderstanding each other. In discussing this problem, Mrs. Scardoni provided the following observation that clearly portrays the trouble she and her husband have understanding each other:

Yeah, well at times I was trying to ah, you know, like explain to him little things like if I have a conversation with my husband and I'm telling him something, he always seems to understand the opposite, which I'm not saying it that way, you know, I say to him Pete you're putting words in your own mouth because it's not that way, and he takes . . . misunderstands like you're saying it to him in a different way . . . and that used to cause us arguments.

While she admits that communication between them is difficult, Mrs. Scardoni recognizes her own contribution to their problem. This is demonstrated by her story to picture TAT 6GF in which "a young woman sitting on the edge of a sofa looks back over her shoulder at an older man with a pipe in his mouth who seems to be addressing her":

Well, this is a conversation between husband and wife . . . looks like he must be telling her some happy news, 'cause he looks kinda pleasant here . . . there . . . Well, he's telling her some news and the way she was, she looks happy, and the way she doesn't . . . it looks like it disturbed her in some way, whatever he's telling her. Some news that she didn't like that stunned her that he's trying to tell his wife. And she can't accept it whatever he's trying to tell her . . . looks like, he's content about it but she's amazed to hear what he's telling her . . . He's trying to explain it to her but she couldn't accept whatever he's telling her because she's astonished and she looks a little excited to think whatever he's telling her. And there's going to be a little disagreement there because she didn't really listen to what he had to say there.

In this story, the husband returns home with good news, and his wife's reaction is one of displeasure, as if she cannot permit her husband to have any good fortune. Just as in her description of her relationship with her husband, the couple in this picture is unable to communicate. The wife cannot listen to the husband or respond to him in a way congruent with his expectations. Of course, the outcome of this situation is a disagreement between them in a way consistent with Mrs.

Scardoni's description of her relationship with her husband. It is interesting to note that in this story it is the wife who does not listen well to her husband and who does not respond in the appropriate manner. It is in this way that Mrs. Scardoni acknowledges that she contributes to her marital difficulties. Of course, given her fear of men and her anger at both her father and her first husband, it is understandable that she should have little desire to support her husband. Nonetheless, she appears to have some realization of her motives.

Mrs. Scardoni had lived many years by herself and was bitter about her suffering at the hands of her father and her first husband, so it was difficult for Mrs. Scardoni to adjust to having a husband once more. However, while she sometimes finds that she becomes resentful when she thinks of the years when she lived in poverty struggling to rear her two children by herself, she enjoys the companionship her second marriage provides and hopes that intimacy can develop over time. Although she is clearly quite worried about her adequacy as a sexual partner and is unhappy that her husband is so temperamental, she has also become more philosophical about relations between the sexes and observes that "anyway, life is just not a bed of roses."

Freedom from financial hardship is a relatively new experience for Mrs. Scardoni, since she has lived in poverty for most of her life. Until her son finished high school and began contributing to the family income, she supplemented a meager pension and welfare income by working as a cleaning woman. Until her remarriage, Mrs. Scardoni's son continued to support her and his sister some two years after his own marriage.

Although she succeeded in rearing her children alone, this effort has left Mrs. Scardoni feeling bitter and resentful of the demands her children made on her. This resentment is most clearly expressed in her story to Card IAT M1 in which "a younger woman is standing up and talking with an older woman who is seated at a table on which there are two coffee cups":

> This looks like mother and daughter, I gather, and the mother is disappointed over his [sic] daughter's unbehavior and she doesn't want to discuss it . . . it's like a not happy meeting between the mother and the teenage daughter . . . things don't seem to click here, and, uh, the mother is thinking about how hard it has been to raise her daughter by herself, without a husband, for this looks like a broken home; there's no father around. It's pretty hard for a mother to do everything, and pretty tough to raise children and do it all by yourself, and it looks like this mother is resentful, pretty angry about it and feeling "here she wants to go out again, and what about me, what . . . when does anyone think of me . . . who takes me out" and she's thinking of all she can't have because she has to do it all herself . . . how it's been more than five years since she had a new winter coat and wondering how she's gonna make it through this winter . . . she just feels mad, defeated, alone. (E: And the outcome?) There ain't no outcome, gee, the future don't look too . . . at all good, you know, when you have to handle a situation like this, with a broken home.

The fact that Mrs. Scardoni had to be both mother and father may account for the slip she makes in the second line where she notes that the mother is disappointed over "his" daughter's behavior, and the fact that she had to set limits, typically the father's role with teenage children in our culture, brought back to her those feelings of desertion and anger she so well describes in this clearly autobiographical story.

This resentment is also clearly reflected in Mrs. Scardoni's childcare attitudes. In her attitudes toward the issue of authoritarian control, Mrs. Scardoni ranks second to Mrs. Giorgio whose attitudes were the most authoritarian of the four grandmothers and are discussed in Chapter 5. Mrs. Scardoni does not believe that children should be permitted to express their angry feelings, even in a socially modulated form, and values the control of angry feelings at any cost. Considering her childhood experience and the frequent eruptions within her family that resulted in severe beatings and in overpowering fear among the children, it is not surprising that Mrs. Scardoni should value highly the overcontrol of aggressive feelings and should view it as difficult to express such feelings in a socially modulated form.

Typical of women in the grandmother generation, Mrs. Scardoni does not believe that young children can communicate socially with their mothers or that their mothers can achieve mutuality with them. Regarding the issue of appropriate closeness, Mrs. Scardoni shows the least adaptive attitudes of the four grandmothers. She views childrearing as an exhausting experience, beginning with childbirth, which, as Mrs. Scardoni's Rorschach responses so clearly show, is seen as threatening to a woman's very life. Children are seen by her as competitors for precious supplies, and the care of young children robs a mother of these supplies.

As is true of most other grandmothers and mothers in this study, Mrs. Scardoni cannot face her own ambivalent feelings about having children. Because of her concern about her own impulse control, she cannot recognize the intensity of her anger and resentment toward her children. Regarding the issue of competence in meeting the baby's needs, Mrs. Scardoni's attitudes reflect her belief that she can understand a baby's needs, although her attitudes on this issue are not as adaptive as is found for most other grandmothers.

Overall, Mrs. Scardoni's attitudes are more typical of mothers than of grandmothers. The discriminant function analysis reveals that the chances are 86 in 100 that Mrs. Scardoni is a member of the mother generation. This finding is largely accounted for by feelings of depletion, reflected by her extreme score on the issue of appropriate closeness, and her somewhat hesitant stance regarding the issue of competence in meeting the baby's needs. Mrs. Scardoni's profile on the MAS most resembles that of Mrs. Giorgio, a grandmother whose attitudes also more closely related to those of the mother than the grandmother generation. Both of these grandmothers are particularly resentful of the demands placed on them by the task of caring for children, a feeling more characteristic of the mother generation.

Goaded by unpleasant memories of her own childhood, Mrs. Scardoni was determined to rear her two children differently from how she had been reared. Reflecting on the differences between the ways in which her mother had reared her and the ways in which she reared her own children, Mrs. Scardoni recalled her constant feelings of terror during her own childhood, together with the feeling that adults' needs were more important than those of children. In addition, the obedience expected from the children was inhuman in its extremity. Mrs. Scardoni and her sisters and brothers were expected to be grateful for whatever scraps of food they received and were expected to do all the heavy work around the house. She was hardly old enough to walk when she was given a scrub brush and told to wash the floors. As she observed: "I never had a chance to be a child, and, and until recently, I have never had a chance to enjoy life at all. It was all hard work and sacrifice."

Largely as a result of these childhood experiences, Mrs. Scardoni was determined not to be punitive and to put her children's needs ahead of her own. In fact, she gave them so much that not only did she feel depleted, but also, they may have become spoiled. As she observed:

My daughter doesn't have the same problems I had because she had . . . how do you say . . . good experiences as a girl . . . she was . . . may have even been a little bit spoiled . . . she had everything when she was at home, she had a car, everything she wanted, best of clothes, and I never took anything from her, but always gave to her, gave the very best I could afford . . . she worked in the bank, didn't have to work in a factory like when I was a girl, to slave away in the heat like I did . . . when it came to meals, I used to please her. She'd say "Mom, please make this," and she'd bring her girl friends down to supper . . . even though it meant there was not enough for me; oh, I didn't get too intimate with her, and she was supposed to behave; she couldn't just go out and be wild with every boy she met and I think I did a good job and she's happy and not haunted in the way I was.

These comments are consistent with Mrs. Scardoni's responses to the MAS. Once more, sacrifice for her children emerges as a salient theme. In her determination to rear her children differently from how she had been reared, Mrs. Scardoni allowed her daughter to bring her girl friends home to dinner, even though it meant that she went without dinner. At the same time, she did not believe in becoming "intimate" with her daughter or in developing true closeness or reciprocity.

This conscious attempt of Mrs. Scardoni's to rear her children differently from how she had been reared also affected her children's personalities and, as we see subsequently, actually fostered the transmission to the next generation of many of those problems that she had tried so hard to avoid. For example, Mrs. Scardoni's children clearly perceived her negative feelings about sacrificing for them. They, in turn, view their parental roles in terms of the self-sacrifice expected of them. In addition, Mrs. Scardoni's anger at self-sacrifice engendered resentment that made communication between herself and her children difficult. Her decisions about how to rear her children were based partially on feelings she did not fully understand. This can be clearly seen in her story to picture IAT B5 in which "a young woman is seated on a park bench in the city and is watching a young boy playing with a ball":

This looks like a boy and a mo . . . you know, a mother, with a boy. And he's playing with something, I don't know, it could be a ball there. She's sitting down, like an angry type. She don't look too, you know, happy about something there, or maybe was the boy's doing which, whatever he's got in his hand or something. And she's thinking what are you going to do with that ball . . . she don't like it. She's just watching to see what he's going to do with that ball, which way he's going to throw it, and she's not happy about it, you know, cause . . . he's got . . . ah . . . she don't want him to play with the ball which he shouldn't have . . . I think balls are dangerous for children, very dangerous . . . They chase after them and they can get killed one way or the other with them. There are so many dangerous things that can happen to children, like drowning, being killed by cars, why they can even get killed in bed.

What Mrs. Scardoni describes in this picture is her fear that she will enact her own aggression toward her children and kill them. Mrs. Scardoni's anger and resentment were intensified because she was the sole caretaker of the children. Her thematic apperceptive data contain numerous references to women having difficulty rearing their children without husbands and expressions of sympathy for women who have been left with enormous responsibility. Unable to admit her hostility toward her children, Mrs. Scardoni externalizes it and views the dangers as environmental rather than within herself. This is the classic dynamic described by D. Levy (1943) in his discussion of maternal over-protection, and it helps to explain Mrs. Scardoni's extremely maladaptive attitude regarding the issue of appropriate closeness.

Unable to accept or consciously recognize her own hostility, Mrs. Scardoni acted in the opposite manner and tried to keep her children close to her, fearing that if she could not see them, some danger might overcome them. The more she discouraged distance by performing acts of self-sacrifice in an attempt to keep her children close by her, the more angry she became and the more she needed to keep her children with her to prove to herself that her wishes had not actually succeeded in harming them.

This conflict is evoked anew by the presence of two grandchildren; Mrs. Scardoni calls her daughter several times each day to be sure that her granddaughter is all right. She worries continually about what her granddaughter might do, as seen in her discussion about offering childrearing advice to her daughter. When asked how she gives childrearing advice to her daughter, Mrs. Scardoni responded:

I have to tell her little things to watch out for . . . she isn't nearly careful enough, like her daughter, at the beginning . . . she is a child who is likely to be hurt by anything . . . she'd pick up anything she saw and then choke on it . . . I tried to tell my daughter that it wasn't safe to allow a child to crawl around the house . . . when I go there, I tell her, "don't keep all those dangerous things around the house . . ." everything around the house is dangerous . . . that her daughter could pick one of those things up and choke on it . . . choke to death . . . everything has to be high on a shelf . . . it would be a disaster or something, and I tell her sometimes, when you go out, watch out, it's not safe outside . . . watch you don't snap the door on her fingers, and which way the wind is blowing, so that nothing gets in her eyes . . . oh, there are so many things to warn her about!

This issue of maternal overprotection and inappropriate closeness, stemming from the inability to accept feelings of hostility, emerges as a major theme across the generations of this modified extended family.

Reflecting on her children's early years and their lives as adults, Mrs. Scardoni feels she has done a fairly good job of rearing her children. She observes that both seem to have happy marriages and settled lives. Of equal importance, neither has any debts. In explaining why she was such a successful mother, she points to three specific aspects of her childrearing philosophy. First, she did not believe in letting the children go hungry. As she says:

Even if I was worried about where the next meal was coming from, I wouldn't talk about it with them. When they was small, I always had nourishing food. I made most of my own pasta, and even if there was nothing else, there was pasta and sauce.

Recalling her own feelings of deprivation, Mrs. Scardoni acknowledged that her memories of her own childhood directly affected her attitudes toward food.

Second, Mrs. Scardoni's attitudes toward her children's toilet training were also affected by her memories of her own childhood. In talking about what she says to her daughter regarding training her little girl, Mrs. Scardoni comments:

I tell my daughter, "When you take and toilet train 'em, never frighten them or give them a beating, 'cause that's the worst thing you could ever do . . ." of course, I know that because of when I was a girl and my parents used to beat us all the time if we didn't go when they said we did . . . or they would force a suppository . . . that only frightens . . . it frightened us . . . it would frighten them the same way . . . and then they hold it all back and they will not go . . . and that gives them a tense feeling . . . and I don't believe in . . . a mother to frighten them and let them be frightened because if they did make a mistake once or twice, you know, you have to expect plenty more yet.

As a result of the severe method in which toilet training had been carried out in her own parental family, Mrs. Scardoni consciously determined to be more permissive with her own children and not to subject them to the same harshness that had characterized her own childhood.

While permissive about toilet training, Mrs. Scardoni was somewhat more restrictive about modesty training. She says she does not like to see little children going around without clothes on, since she believes that children become too easily aroused. She observes that "they become too sexy while still too young, and that ain't right." Considering the intensity of her conflicts regarding sexuality, it is not surprising that Mrs. Scardoni should believe in fostering greater external control in this area of childrearing.

Third, Mrs. Scardoni's girlhood memories were also an important factor in her decision to allow her teenage daughter considerable freedom from parental restrictions. Even as a girl, she had determined that if she ever had a daughter, she would not be as restrictive as her own parents. Her daughter was permitted to come and go as she pleased and, often, she would be out with her girl friends until after midnight. While Mrs. Scardoni acknowledges concern about what the neighbors might have thought, she insists that she had complete confidence in her daughter and never harbored any suspicions about her activities.

Comparing her two children, both as children and adults, Mrs. Scardoni feels that her son was much easier to rear than her daughter. She describes her son as a warm and emotional man, stating that even as a boy he enjoyed staying around the house with his mother. Later, in high school, when her son had a part-time job, he took pride in helping his mother pay the household bills. He spent his free hours doing chores around the house and watching television. He is responsible, frugal, and, in Mrs. Scardoni's opinion, a good husband and father.

While Mrs. Scardoni's daughter also enjoyed staying at home and helping her mother, in contrast to her brother, she has always had greater difficulty expressing her feelings and is seen by other family members as reserved and detached. However, while Mrs. Scardoni's son sees his sister, whom he is older than, as "a bit cold," Mrs. Scardoni defends her daughter and explains that she is a bit shy. However, she sees her daughter as less responsible and more self-centered than her son.

To a greater extent than is true of the other grandmothers in this study, Mrs. Scardoni consciously determined to rear her children differently from the way in which she was reared. Feeling deprived, unclear about her own identity, uncertain of her own self-worth, and still reliving her own terrorized childhood, Mrs. Scardoni struggled to gain a perspective on her feelings which would insure that her own children would have a happier childhood. This determination to break with the past only intensifies her identity conflict, for, unlike other grandmothers in this study, Mrs. Scardoni could not look to her own childhood for guidance in rearing her children and had to consciously reject her family traditions. While Mrs. Scardoni's parents had contact with their extended families, these contacts left each generation bitter and frustrated. In a similar way, Mrs. Scardoni and her sisters and brothers do not get along at all well and, even as adults, continually fight.

In her mid-fifties, alienated from her family and from her religious and cultural background, leading a marginal life in a marginal community, Mrs. Scardoni exists largely for her children and grandchildren who represent a future that may be better than the past. Mrs. Scardoni's greatest wish is that her children and grandchildren will finally be able to set down firm roots in the rocky New England soil and become recognized members of some cultural tradition. She is less concerned that they be a part of the Italian American heritage than that they be a part of some heritage and that, as a result of this achievement, she can finally find an identity for herself.

MRS. RUSSO: BUT I CAN'T GET AWAY FROM MY MOTHER

The most striking characteristic of Dorset is its grayness. The gray of the pavement meets the gray of the houses, and the gray of the houses meets the gray of the wintry New England sky. Not only is Dorset gray, but also almost oppressively uniform and stolid. Frame houses, with overhanging eaves, have been built to withstand the gales that blow in off the New England coast. Uniform and impassive, Dorset offers a drab sameness that is, at the same time, both reassuring and overpowering. Dorset residents are from the same social class and share the same cultural and religious background. They are clear about what makes for proper human conduct and tolerate little deviance from the clearly established norms. The neighborhood gossip system is both effective and particularly intolerant of human frailties.

For a woman like Mrs. Russo, the daughter of Mrs. Scardoni, who grew up largely in isolation from her culture, and who was denied a clear cultural identity, such definitive statements about how community members should lead their lives are very reassuring. As she observes, "In our community, people know what is expected of them and they are very good about following the usual ways of doing things." Further, in one of her picture thematic stories she adds:

the situation will probably resolve itself; now, why did I say that they have children . . . maybe they don't even have any children, but then everyone in my neighborhood has children . . . they're all pretty much like me.

Mrs. Russo gains a great deal of security from living in a community where her life is so much like that of her neighbors. In describing people, she makes statements like "he's a regular sort of guy," "she's an old fashioned, solid woman," and "she's a popular girl, really one of the crowd." Fitting in and being accepted are very important for Mrs. Russo, just as it is important that her house be like other houses in the neighborhood. Even the living room furniture she has is a copy of furniture she has seen in her neighbors' houses.

While she is a careful observer of the life-style of her neighborhood, Mrs. Russo actually has very little to do with her neighbors. Her brother, who is older than she, Mr. Butoni, and his family live on the other side of the two-family duplex, and his family and her frequent contacts with her mother provide all the social life that she desires. She does enjoy pushing her two-year-old daughter down to the square in her stroller and derives a sense of security and belonging just from knowing that other residents of her neighborhood share her values and that they lead their lives in very much the same way.

Mrs. Russo's continuing emotional involvement with her mother is both a source of support as well as a source of considerable discomfort and strain. Neither Mrs. Scardoni nor Mrs. Russo can tolerate any disagreement or disharmony, for neither mother nor daughter can admit to her own mixed feelings. On the one hand, Mrs. Russo is very dependent on her mother for help with even the most minute aspects of her life, such as recipes for supper or advice on her problems with her daughter or her husband. On the other hand, she is afraid that her mother will forget about her if she does not maintain continual contact. Burdened by her mother's demand that she and her brother provide Mrs. Scardoni with the identity that she had never achieved for herself and unable to derive any sense of security or satisfaction from this relationship, Mrs. Russo feels frustrated, resentful, and then guilty. Finally, she becomes so distraught that she can only continue to function by swallowing large doses of the several "tranquilizers" that her family doctor has prescribed for her.

It is important for Mrs. Russo to maintain a sense of security and equanimity; she is a "worrier." She worries about whether her husband will arrive home at the right time in the afternoon, whether her mother will come to visit her and at what time. She worries whether she will get her housework done each day and whether her daughter will fight about eating what is served her. Unless, each day, the same routine is observed, she becomes anxious and believes she will collapse under the strain.

Shouldering the burden of these concerns and anxieties is an exhausting task for Mrs. Russo and, at age 27, her face is already lined and drawn. A thin woman, with dark curly hair and nervous, darting eyes, she perpetually wears her hair in curlers, as if forever waiting in anticipation of an occasion sufficiently important for her to appear with a fresh hairdo. Although she compulsively reads the sale advertisements in the newspaper each day, she is afraid to go shopping in the unfamiliar and potentially dangerous areas outside her neighborhood and ends up wearing the same four or five wash dresses, day after day, summer and winter.

More than any other woman in this study, Mrs. Russo's life is marked by an absence of joy or pleasure and by a determination to hold to routines that she herself admits leave her feeling "nervous and tired." As Mrs. Russo observes:

I have a system and if anyone . . . if I interrupt this system, I'm gone for the day. I have to do clothes at a certain time; I have to have my table set at a certain time; everybody makes fun of me, but if I don't keep to my schedule I get so nervous that I have to call my doctor for more tranquilizers.

Even the fact that her neighbors admire the efficiency with which she carries out her daily routine gives her little satisfaction, and she gains scant pleasure from the carefully planned and scheduled life she has created for herself.

According to Mrs. Scardoni, Mrs. Russo has not always been such a worrier:

When she was a girl, she used to have better coloring to her face, she didn't look so frail and delicate. Before she wasn't all skin and bones, but now she has trouble standing on her own feet and doing her housework. I . . . we all try to tell her to take it easier, not to be so hard on herself and on the go so much . . . she pushes herself to the limit but, of course, she doesn't listen to us.

Mrs. Scardoni recognizes that Mrs. Russo has difficulties but that she sees these difficulties as beginning only recently. However, according to Mrs. Russo, her problems began during childhood. For example, she makes this observation:

I've always been thin and we . . . I . . . my mother has always worried about my weight and encouraged me to eat more and not to be so skinny. My sister-in-law says the same thing to me now . . . they all say I should eat more and put on weight, but I . . . quite frankly, I don't like to eat . . . I don't get much pleasure out of it, and if I didn't have other mouths to feed, I guess I would never eat.

In understanding the origins of Mrs. Russo's eating problem, it is particularly important to already have some familiarity with her mother's life experiences and character, as has been provided earlier in this chapter. We know that Mrs. Scardoni was determined to provide for her children in a way she had not been provided for during her own childhood. However, the husband she chose meant that as a mother, Mrs. Scardoni experienced much the same poverty as she had during her own childhood. As a result, what she provided for her children she gave with a sense of sacrifice that, in turn, inspired feelings of guilt and resentment. For example, Mrs. Scardoni often went hungry to be sure that her children had enough. As Mrs. Scardoni's daughter comments:

> I always had what I wanted, I mean, I don't know how . . . where she got it, you know, rob from Peter to pay Paul, but she . . . my mother was always generous with my brother and myself . . . to whatever she had . . . and sometimes she went hungry for our sake and, ah, she didn't want us to know it, but of course we knew it, and she wouldn't eat. Later I became a finicky eater, and had trouble eating . . . she would take me down to the drugstore; she knew the druggist, and I was told to drink milk, and, ah, my mother . . . later on she was always telling me to gain weight and, whatever I wanted to eat, if I felt like eating steak at 12 o'clock at night, my mother would make it for me or, if we were sleeping, she would wake me up and ask me, did I want any macaroni? Then the next day, it would turn out that she ate the old bread crusts.

Thus, in spite of Mrs. Scardoni's expressed desire to provide good care, with undoubtedly good intentions, the realities of her poverty engendered considerable conflict regarding this issue of nurturance. At least in our culture, milk is symbolic of nurturance itself, and it is interesting to note that the pleasurable activity of feeding was turned into a routine prescription by these trips to the druggist. Then, afraid that her daughter might starve and worried about how well her daughter was eating, Mrs. Scardoni would awaken her in the night to be sure she had enough to eat. This concern perhaps explains Mrs. Scardoni's score on the attitude factor of competence meeting a baby's needs, for she was, in fact, much less certain than other grandmothers that she could meet a baby's physical needs. Her memories of her own deprived childhood, her impoverished economic situation, and her guilt regarding her hostility toward her children for depriving her of food were all related to her decision to wake her daughter to see if she needed something more to eat.

There is a striking parallel between Mrs. Scardoni's own childhood experiences with impulse control and her insistence on waking her daughter to be sure that her daughter had had enough to eat. By subjecting her to harsh bowel control in childhood, Mrs. Scardoni's parents had taught her both that she was not capable of assuming control over her own impulses and also that internal cues of need states are not to be trusted. In waking her daughter in the night, Mrs. Scardoni imparted the same message to her own daughter. Even as a child, Mrs. Russo was taught that she could not trust her own inner cues regarding whether she was hungry, for Mrs. Scardoni could not allow her daughter to tell her whether or when she was hungry. As we see as this discussion progresses, this early socialization played an important role in Mrs. Russo's later development of a psychogenic eating disorder.

This basic conflict regarding nurturant care has had a significant impact on Mrs. Russo's character, as well as on her childrearing attitudes and practices.

Mrs. Russo's preoccupation with eating and food is evident throughout the psychological material. Her first comment, on drawing a woman, was to observe "she looks matronly . . . looks as though she's well fed." On the sentence completion test, in the answer to the stem "What gets me in trouble . . .," she writes that it "is my mouth." In spite of her mother's conscious intentions, Mrs. Russo never felt filled up. This feeling is well documented in her response to Card X.4 of the Rorschach, where she says:

"These look like little bugs. Eating, attacking some little things coming out from behind a bush . . . (E: And the bugs, what made them look like that?) The most important part is huge mouths, hungrily destroying, they're all eating . . . destroying each other, the thing there, the bugs coming out of the bush."

This somewhat vague and confused response suggests that for Mrs. Russo eating is equivalent to attacking and destroying. Furthermore, it is not clear in this response whether she allies herself with the passive victim or the active attacker. Considering Mrs. Russo's observation about all the other mouths she has to feed, this response suggests that she allies herself with both the greedy creatures who eat and thereby destroy the provider of care and also with the caretaker who, through the greed of others, is devoured. As a daughter, Mrs. Russo feels greedy and wishes to attack and destroy. Simultaneously, she feels devoured and overwhelmed by her mother's overprotectiveness. As a mother she also feels devoured and overwhelmed by her own daughter's demands for care.

This Rorschach response shows that Mrs. Russo felt her intense needs were greater than could be met by her mother and, furthermore, that she could only receive sufficient nourishment for herself at the cost of her mother's destruction. Such destruction would, in turn, have the effect of further denying her the care she needed, so that, as a young child, Mrs. Russo was left feeling guilty over the intensity of her needs and their effect on her mother, and also resentful that she couldn't have what she wished from her mother. This conflict has been formulated in more precise theoretical terms by the English psychoanalyst Melanie Klein, who says:

Greed and the defenses against it play a significant part at this stage (of depressive anxiety), for the anxiety of losing irretrievably the loved and indispensable object tends to increase greed. Greed, however, is felt to be uncontrollable and destructive and to endanger the loved external and internal objects. The ego therefore increasingly inhibits instinctual desires and this may lead to severe difficulties in the infant's enjoying or accepting food and later to serious inhibitions in establishing both affectionate and erotic relations. (Klein, 1952c, p. 212)

According to Klein, the young child accepts the possibility of only total gratification, while harboring destructive wishes against her caretaker because she cannot possibly provide such complete satisfaction. However, the realization of destructive wishes also means the loss of any future succorance and care so that reparation is necessary. This realization leads to feelings of guilt and the urge to preserve and repair relations with the mothering person, together with abandonment of the wish for total gratification. If the greed and accompanying destructive wishes are sufficiently intense and the feelings of guilt sufficiently strong, the only way that the relation with the mothering person can be maintained is to renounce all desire for food. Feelings of greed then lead to their opposite, and impulses are viewed as destructive and are denied, leading to a constriction of impulse life and continuing feelings of guilt.

Klein's observations are consistent with Mrs. Scardoni's attitude towards her daughter's care. Clearly, with a mother who had hoped to provide nurturance, but resented the intensity of her daughter's needs, Mrs. Russo was encouraged as an infant to perceive herself as greedy. Mrs. Russo's search for perfection in her role as daughter, housekeeper, and mother is but a reflection of her attempt at reparation through a search for a more perfect self that would be less greedy and more acceptable to her mother. The sense of sadness Mrs. Russo expresses is intensified by her feeling that she is unable to attain the perfection necessary to receive good care. Indeed, Mrs. Russo's adult character well reflects this lifelong struggle with the developmental tasks posed by the depressive phase of socioemotional development as described by Klein.

This struggle emerges quite clearly in Mrs. Russo's story to the picture (IAT M1) in which "a younger woman is standing up and talking with an older woman who is seated at a table on which there are two coffee cups":

They look like very sad people to me. . .one looks like the mother, and the daughter over here. . .something. . .sometime. . .something went terribly wrong for one of them . . . and they look like something happened to one of them . . . the daughter's trying to get her mother's ideas about some problem . . . maybe a problem with her girl and her mother don't seem interested in helping . . . looks sad . . . lost in her own world. Maybe the daughter don't like the coffee, the breakfast, it's not as good as she remembered, as she hoped it would be or not what she wanted her mother to make for her. It all looks sad . . . very sad, like maybe the mother is very depressed and the daughter is sad, too . . . she don't feel the mother gave her enough or how to get the mother's attention.

Better than any theoretical statement, this story conveys the feeling that Mrs. Scardoni's care was not satisfying enough for her daughter. Mrs. Russo begins her story by noting that something had gone terribly wrong for one of the characters, obviously the daughter. In view of Mrs. Russo's own concern about her ability to care for her daughter, it is interesting that her heroine in this story seeks her mother's advice regarding this same issue.

The mother in this story is lost in her own thoughts, obviously a reflection of the fact that during her childhood Mrs. Russo's own mother was preoccupied with her troubles to such an extent that she felt left out. Indeed, the mother in this story does not have the energy to offer advice or even to listen to her daughter. The daughter feels that the mother's care is not satisfactory, and, at this point, the problem becomes related to food itself rather than merely to such symbols in adult life as advice. The breakfast is not satisfying, and the daughter feels in despair because she doesn't know how to get the kind of nurturance she wants.

Presumably, if Mrs. Scardoni felt it necessary to wake her daughter in the middle of the night to see if she were hungry, she must have felt incapable of understanding or meeting her daughter's needs. At the same time, her concern about her daughter's health was one concrete way of expressing care and concern. Mrs. Russo seems to have recognized her mother's concern about her body as an attempt to provide nurturant care; Mrs. Russo's psychosomatic symptoms may be viewed as an attempt to regain this attention. Her reliance on tranquilizers may be important for much the same reason. The one time that Mrs. Scardoni really attempted to feed her daughter was at the drugstore. Tranquilizers, as a prescription, recapture these memories of the drugstore and also have a soothing or calming effect, much like maternal care itself.

We have suggested that Mrs. Scardoni could not acknowledge her resentment of the maternal role and that she expressed her feelings in the opposite manner, in the form of maternal overprotection. She could not allow herself to be parted from her daughter, for fear of what might happen to her. The family's social isolation further intensified this mother-daughter bind. As Mrs. Scardoni observes, in recalling Mrs. Russo's infancy:

> I couldn't think of leaving her at home . . . of course, there was no one I could ask, since my brothers and sisters and I didn't talk to each other, but I was afraid of what might happen to the children if I left them alone, and we . . . were broke, so we couldn't have a babysitter.

For these reasons, the normal mother-child symbiosis was perpetuated long past the point in the child's development where such a lack of differentiation is normative (Mahler, 1968). Indeed, Mrs. Scardoni and her daughter never achieved the phase of individuation in which Mrs. Russo could attain effective autonomy from her mother. Anthony (1971), in describing the effects of such a prolonged symbiosis, observes that

> When the mother attempts to sustain the symbiosis by ignoring the existence of developing barriers or indulging herself in undue penetration and merging, a pathological prolongation and intensification of symbiosis may result . . . Maternal fantasies of merging with the child are strengthened by the child's reciprocal wish to fuse with the mother. The symptomatic developments in symbiosis—overprotection, oversolicitude, dominance, the wish to keep the child passive and dependent and the tendency to treat him as an extension of herself—all help to blur the demarcation between the maternal and self images within the child. His fear of separation and his desire to maintain or regain the original mother-child closed unit may grow so strong that he abandons any attempt to build up an enduring and consistent self-concept. His psychic organization remains undifferentiated, unstructured, and unorganized. (pp. 270–271)

Anthony describes the dynamics established during Mrs. Russo's childhood. Mrs. Russo grew up resentful of any attempts on her mother's part to separate from her, angry that she was so dependent on her mother, and disappointed that she felt so unfulfilled when with her mother. Mrs. Russo's concern with the theme of separation emerges in her story to the picture (IAT Si3) in which "a young woman is looking straight ahead as another young woman wearing a coat and carrying a handbag is about to go out the door'':

> Ah, this looks like a daughter . . . with her mother . . . the mother looks like she's leaving to go home . . . to go back to her house or something, and the daughter seems sort of sad . . . very sad and hurt. The daughter feels alone and helpless . . . maybe . . . she wanted her mother to stay with her longer but the mother says that she has . . . that she wants to go home. But the daughter looks sad and the mother looks like she's you know . . . leaving her daughter and going home somewhere. The mother looks, feels happy, maybe even glad to be going . . . it's probably the end of the day and the mother has to go home to take care of *her* family.

Mrs. Russo's reliance on her mother and her resentment of the fact that her mother leaves her to take care of her husband are stated clearly in this story. It is interesting to note that after she had told this story, she asked the investigator if she could get a cup of coffee, or whether he could find her one. This request provides evidence both of Mrs. Russo's dependence on her mother for supplies and her concern that these supplies may not be able to satisfy her.

Feeling resentful about what she does not get and guilty about her greed, it is not surprising that the issue of food and eating has continued as a major theme in Mrs. Russo's life: she is hungry and yet cannot admit to her appetite. She worries about her weight and tries to keep herself as skinny as possible, noting that she does not want to become plump like her mother. At one point, in response to the sentence completion stem "My main problem is," Mrs. Russo responds that it is "my weight. I am worried about getting too fat." Consistent with this worry, Mrs. Russo is what she describes as a "picky" eater who enjoys neither cooking nor eating:

> Sometimes, just thinking of food makes me sick. I have never been interested in cooking; my husband understands this, and often helps out when he comes home by helping with supper. My mother gives me things to finish up at home, but even then, I just pick at my food, which makes my husband angry. My mother and I also fight about this when we have dinner on Sunday. I just never seem to have an appetite. I guess it is nerves, but if I let myself go, I'd probably become a pig . . . you know, eat like a pig and become real fat.

Mrs. Russo also endorsed in the criterion direction every item on the MMPI dealing with either upper or lower gastrointestinal distress.

This conflict regarding food and eating has been described in the psychiatric literature as the syndrome of anorexia nervosa or, literally, nervous loss of appetite. Sours (1969) in reviewing the literature notes that this syndrome develops primarily in young women and in families where issues of definition of identity and domination and control are central issues. Bruch (1973), in discussing the dynamics of families with anorexic offspring, notes that the anorexic girl's problem in recognizing that she is hungry arises from the fact that she never learned from her own mother to recognize her own bodily cues and sensations; this issue was, as we have already seen, of central importance in Mrs. Russo's own childhood. Bruch also observes that the mother of an anorexic girl also shows difficulty in recognizing when she is hungry, a problem of particular importance in Mrs. Scardoni's childhood, when, in view of the uncertainty that she would be fed, denial of hunger was particularly adaptive. Ehrensing and Weitzman (1970) note that subsequently, in adolescence and young adulthood:

> The mother's narcissistic involvement and imperviousness to her daughter's real needs prevent the development of a *satisfactory* mother-daughter symbiosis; this, with continuing maternal deprivation, makes successful separation-individuation impossible. The daughter proceeds through latency with a hungry yearning for mothering, a poor sense of self, and minimal self-esteem . . . entering adolescence, with its necessary psychic restructuring for the achievement of the "second individuation process of adolescence" and, threatened by the loss of family dependencies, she develops the clinical picture of anorexia nervosa with . . . the intense craving for the primitive feeding experience of the mother [and] compliance with the mother's wish that the girl not take sustenance from her and grow up and leave her. (pp. 207–208)

A similar formulation is provided by Palazzoli (1970) who also notes that in girls whose mothers are overcontrolling, the refusal to eat or disinterest in eating represents some attempt to gain the control of oneself and one's impulses that had been surrendered to the mother.

Clinical studies suggest that conflicts regarding eating can be traced to the relationship between mother and daughter during infancy, childhood, and adolescence (Cohler, 1977). A woman who shows this hunger disturbance in young adulthood is likely to have had a mother who could not differentiate between her own needs and those of her daughter and who was unable to encourage her daughter to become a separate and independent person. The daughter both wishes to comply with her mother's desire to continue the symbiosis and yet is also resentful of her mother's continued intrapsychic domination. This formulation is substantiated by a story Mrs. Russo tells to one of the pictures (TAT 12F) that shows "the portrait of a young woman. A weird old woman with a shawl over her head is grimacing in the background:"

> Oh boy (long pause) . . . this looks like my . . . a mother and daughter . . . but it looks like the mother just won't let go of her . . . she's sort of a . . . evil sort of person that can't . . . just won't let go of her daughter . . . and she looks like she's going to get her way . . . and the daughter . . . is very sad and lost . . . the mother looks like she's very calculating and shrewd . . . or kind of shrewd . . . she's thinking . . . the daughter is thinking about . . . the mother is always at her about her eating or something . . . about her body, her health, her life . . . and the mother looks like she's going to get her way, she's going to succeed, and there's nothing the daughter can do . . . and the daughter is trying to figure something out in her mind . . . but it's not going to work out for her . . . she'd like to leave, to get away from her, to get out from that . . . but I don't think she'll . . . that she's going to be able to, not going to make it, even though she's had it. (E: What led up to this scene?) Probably, she was always under her mother's care and . . . dependent too much on her mother, then it got too much but she wouldn't . . . couldn't break away from her . . . maybe because of the way she feels, how guilty she feels about leaving her, and how afraid of being out on her own, yet in a way she wants to, she wants to get out but she wants to stay, and in the end, in the future, I don't think she'll be able to get out . . . she

can never get away from her mother . . . her mother . . . her memories . . . how she feels . . . it haunts her, always, forever.

Clearly, Mrs. Russo had difficulty maintaining any distance from this picture; she even starts with a reference to her own mother before putting the story in the perspective of the third person. This powerful story is replete with references to the mixed feelings the heroine feels toward her mother. On the one hand, she wants to stay and be taken care of by her, but, on the other, she longs to be free. Ultimately, as she recognizes, it is impossible to be free of her mother, because she continues to live inside of her, and these memories continue to determine her life, or, as she says, they continue to "haunt" her. Of course, what haunts her is not her mother as she actually is, but some mental representation or image of her mother.

The fact that the heroine of this story can differentiate between being haunted by real persons and being haunted by images indicates once more that Mrs. Russo has essentially resolved the conflict regarding the earliest issue of socioemotional development in which persons are split into their good and bad attributes. Mrs. Russo sees her mother as a whole person, but she both desires to be cared for by her mother and, terrified of the smothering closeness this dependency engenders, strives to be free and autonomous. However, Mrs. Russo's guilt over her own anger, and her need to make constant reparation, prevents her from being able to break away and establish her own life.

Perhaps the intensity of the mother-daughter symbiosis could have been reduced if Mrs. Russo had had a father. However, as she noted, her father played little role in her life, since he died while she was an infant and she did not have a stepfather until she was grown and almost married. The extent to which her father was a void in her life is shown by the fact that the only one of the 36 sentence completion stems she could not answer was the one starting with "My father. . ."

Mrs. Russo's sense that her stepfather has little to offer her is intensified by the actuality of a daughter by his previous marriage of whom he is quite fond. Mrs. Russo does visit with her stepfather when the family gathers for Sunday dinner at her mother's house, but she feels they have little to say to each other. Of course, the fact that her mother married a divorced man is a source of some embarrassment for Mrs. Russo, since her Catholic neighbors in Dorset disapprove of remarriage when a man has left his previous wife.

Mrs. Russo's recollection of her childhood years is unusually incomplete. Mrs. Russo notes that she has always had a hard time remembering her childhood, beyond her mother's continual worrying about her health, but adds that she knows she was not very happy. She remembers that they moved around a good deal and that her mother had worked hard to keep the family together, sacrificing everything for the sake of the children. Not a terribly good student, Mrs. Russo was diligent and conscientious, but not very interested in her work.

Just as is true of many girls who later have difficulty separating from their mothers, early adolescence proved to be the happiest time of Mrs. Russo's life. Mrs. Scardoni vividly remembered her own adolescence and, although she worried a great deal, she was determined that her daughter would have more freedom than she had experienced during her own adolescence. There were several years when Mrs. Russo was permitted to come and go as she pleased. Recalling these years, she observes:

> When I was much younger and single at home, I mean I had all the freedom I wanted; my mother never questioned me. I guess it was because of how things were when she was a girl and she wanted life to turn out better for me. There had to be some reason to it because sometimes the stories I told were so fantastic, she had to be crazy to believe them, but she always trusted me, and I knew how far I could push her. I did certain things I knew I could get away with, like coming in late, and I was sure that she was concerned but that she wouldn't say anything.

During this time, Mrs. Russo could pretend that she was on her own, while still having the security of home: experimentation with separation was safe because it was not yet real. Weekends were spent at parties, where, often, there was heavy petting, and Mrs. Russo would return home after midnight, a time that shocked the neighbors. She admits to having enjoyed being able to shock them in this way. Then, when she was 17, these years of freedom came to an end. Mrs. Russo remembers quite clearly how this came about. She was in her senior year of high school, and faced with the problem of deciding what she would do after high school. A girl friend had talked with her about moving to the city and attending secretarial school. After talking to her friend about this plan, she gradually and painfully realized that she could not bring herself to move out of the house and leave her mother. Describing the inner torment that led to this decision, Mrs. Russo comments:

> One night I woke up in a cold sweat. I had some sort of a nightmare . . . something about my mother being sick and my catching it from her . . . whatever it was . . . all of a sudden I began to worry whether there was something wrong with me, whether I had some sort of a disease in my stomach, and I began to go to the doctor and got more and more nervous. Of course, I couldn't eat at this time at all. I completely lost my appetite, and my ma, she would make me pasta and even steak, and I knew she couldn't afford steak, and I'd say, "But ma, I'm not hungry; I can't imagine eating," and she'd say, "You're going to waste away, come eat," and I'd try but then I'd get a nervous thing . . . an upset stomach, and feel like I was going to throw it up, and we'd quarrel, and then I'd run to my room.

This vignette describes the onset of Mrs. Russo's pattern of nervousness in the presence of food that has continued to the present. At the prospect of separating from her mother and beginning life on her own, as much as she wanted in some ways to do so, Mrs. Russo's guilt and her need for reparation became so strong that she was unable to move out on her own, just as earlier, her mother had been unable to separate from her or to foster a sense of appropriate closeness between them.

What Mrs. Russo really was afraid of "catching" from her mother was the need to perpetuate the mother-daughter symbiosis that, as we see subsequently, continues to be a problem as she rears her own daughter. That Mrs. Russo would be unable to separate from her mother could be predicted from the following story she tells to picture TAT 2, described as "a country scene: in the foreground is a young woman with books in her hand; in the background a man is working in the fields and an older woman is looking on":

> Oh, I don't know what to make of this . . . this looks like (sighs) a mother . . . maybe a son, the daughter here, too . . . doesn't like where she is or doesn't like that life or (long pause) . . . she is sad but she ends up staying, there's no other place to go, there's no other place for her, where she really belongs, and she wants to, but she can't get away from the farm, from her mother. She just looks like she is sad about where she is . . . the atmosphere of where she is, and wants to get away but can't go.

Once more we see the mixed feelings Mrs. Russo has about her mother and their relationship. While there were some ways in which she would have liked to have been on her own, she derived a sense of security from being with her mother and was afraid of what might happen to both of them if she were to move away from her.

Mrs. Russo decided to remain home, rather than going off to the city with her girl friend. During the remainder of Mrs. Russo's senior year, she received poor grades, and was often sick and missed important classes or examinations. At about this time, she began to take tranquilizers for her "nerves" and found that with these pills she could manage her life with less distress. Eating was less of a chore for her, and, while she was still "picky" about her food, there were times when she could manage enough of an appetite to eat. Following high school, she decided to study hairdressing and, each morning, took the bus into the city to learn this trade. However, being a hairdresser required her to be on her feet for several hours at a time, and Mrs. Russo soon found that she lacked the stamina to do this. While she still sets her mother and sister-in-law's hair, she failed to complete her apprenticeship and thus to earn a living and to become more independent of her mother.

Mrs. Russo's life was further complicated by two events that occurred just as she was finishing her training in hairstyling. Her doctor discovered what at first he believed might be a tumor in her back. Exploratory surgery was performed at once and a benign lump was removed. However, this experience was painful and frightening for both mother and daughter, and Mrs. Russo was left bedridden for several months.

Her daughter's illness evoked considerable guilt in Mrs. Scardoni, and she became quite depressed. Just as her doctor was about to decide she should be hospitalized for her depression, Mrs. Scardoni met the man who was to become her present husband at a party given by her son-in-law's parents. The two became fast friends, and it was not long before he proposed marriage to her. The couple was married in a quiet civil ceremony attended only by Mrs. Scardoni's daughter, son, and daughter-in-law. After a traditional honeymoon at Niagara Falls, the couple moved into their present home in Winterfield.

For Mrs. Russo, this was a particularly difficult time. Still recovering from her surgery, she managed to work part time in a beauty shop. While she had a room in her mother's new house, transportation between home and work was difficult. In addition she felt that there was no place for her in her mother's new life. It was about this time that Mrs. Russo first thought of marriage herself. She had known her future husband since high school, for they had been part of the same crowd, but before he proposed to her she had never thought seriously about marrying him.

Considering her guilt about leaving her mother, it is likely that if her mother had not remarried, Mrs. Russo herself might never have been able to consider this step. Actually, Mrs. Scardoni was opposed to the marriage, and, as a result of several bitter quarrels between Mrs. Russo and her mother, the couple broke up for almost a year. As Mrs. Scardoni said, in recalling her feelings at that time:

I said to her "You've got everything, so why should you go into that. You've got a home here, and now a father as well as a mother and someone to look after you and care for you," and Bob . . . at that time he didn't have any work, and used to hang out on the corner all the time. I never thought he'd amount to anything. Of course, she'd known him a long time, but we never expected it would amount to anything.

At the end of the year, Mr. Russo came back once more to seek his prospective in-laws' permission to get married. One outstanding issue at that time concerned his inability to support his fiancée, since he had such an unstable work history. Most recently, he had tried working as an apprentice butcher, but, after he accidently cut off one of his fingers, he had not been able to return to work. Mr. Scardoni agreed to find work for him with a construction company where he had some influence. Mr. Russo proved himself to be a reliable worker, driving one of the trucks used to haul sand and gravel for making concrete, and, after he joined the union and gained job security, the Scardonis agreed to the marriage. Throughout their courtship, and in the years since, both Mr. and Mrs. Russo have relied on the Scardonis for both advice and friendship. Compliant and conforming, they have adopted a lifestyle that is quite passive and dependent, even for families in this study. They have continued the tradition of the closely knit and socially isolated family and depend on Mrs. Russo's parents and her brother for help in times of crisis.

In view of the support he has looked for and received from his in-laws, it is not surprising that Mr. Russo gets along very badly with his own family, with whom he has only sporadic contact. Like other husbands in this study, Mr. Russo had one important reason for marrying into the Scardoni family: to find the warmth and affection he had not received in his own family. Mrs. Scardoni and Mrs. Russo agree that Mr. Russo's mother is "a cold woman, lacking in affection."

Because of her belief in the importance of family ties, Mrs. Russo has made a real effort to get along with her in-laws. She calls her mother-in-law with some regularity—and even occasionally sacrifices one of the Russos' Sundays with her parents to have dinner with her husband's parents. However, such gatherings inevitably turn out badly, and she finds herself becoming involved in quarrels with her mother-in-law regarding the way she is rearing her daughter. Mrs. Russo's in-laws feel that she is too protective and cautious, and, while they like to see their granddaughter looking pretty in her starched white dress, they also like to be able to indulge her and allow her to get messy if she wishes in order to have a good time.

Mrs. Russo is particularly surprised that her husband has little contact with his own brother and sisters, for she and her brother are very close and, for the past several years, have shared the same two-family duplex house. The two families began sharing this house when, shortly after the Russos moved to Dorset, Mr. Butoni and his wife were expecting another child and needed more room for their growing family. Mrs. Russo invited them to move, and they accepted. At the present time, the two families are planning on purchasing the house and remaining together for the foreseeable future.

At first, Mr. Russo was unhappy with these arrangements and felt particularly competitive with his brother-in-law, Mr. Butoni, who was professionally successful at a time when Mr. Russo was just getting started. In addition, Mr. Russo's brother-in-law and his wife kept visiting all the time and borrowing food and supplies. In discussing this problem, Mrs. Russo commented:

> Me and my brother were always very close, and my husband sort of resents it and its come to be that, if my brother is coming over, of course not that he meant it, but he'd say, "Oh, your brother is coming over; make sure you sneak that over on me and do that," and then he'd make me tense and then, ah, one time, I just out and told him, I says, Bob, ah, that's my brother . . . I said, and I've always been close to him and, ah . . . my brother can come up here 24 hours a day and you've got to stop fussin' about it. I could see his point, tho, 'cause his family wasn't like this, and he wasn't used to this kind of closeness that we had in our family . . . and we settled this at the beginning, right at the start, and it seemed like he wouldn't get over it, but he accepts it now.

As Mr. Russo has become a permanent part of the family, as he has experienced greater satisfaction and financial reward from his work, and as he has grown increasingly distant from his family, he has grown closer to his brother-in-law and more tolerant of the frequent visiting between the two households.

Perhaps because he was a boy and, therefore, his mother did not see so much of her own personality mirrored in him, Mrs. Russo's brother escaped much of the conflict that developed and continues between Mrs. Scardoni and her daughter. He has remained very close to his mother and very much more a part of the immediate family than is true for brothers and sisters in the other three families in this study. Mr. Butoni is able to talk to his mother in a way that is impossible for Mrs. Russo. For example, as was true of his sister, Mr. Butoni was quite critical of Mrs. Scardoni's remarriage and told his mother that Mr. Scardoni was too hard a man to understand for her to marry. He also criticized his prospective stepfather for leaving his first wife. In addition to this direct expression of feelings, Mr. Bùtoni has found some ritualized ways of expressing his hostility and resentment toward his mother. As Mrs. Russo observes:

> My brother and my mother are very close, but in a special sort of way that I've never seen with other families. Joe and my mother have this thing that they do whenever they meet. He lunges at her like he was going to kill her, and gets her in a headlock and makes these grimaces with her, and then he . . . they begin to laugh, and he grabs her and hugs and kisses her.

As is true of his sister, Mr. Butoni is quite dependent on his mother and maintains a close relationship with her. Indeed, both Mrs. Russo and her mother see him as warmer and more spontaneous than his sister in his relationship to Mrs. Scardoni. Mr. Butoni's directness, together with his skill in expressing his true feelings in ways that do not disrupt his relationship with his mother, permits him to achieve greater perspective on this relationship, while, at the same time, continuing what he readily admits is an important and satisfying relationship.

Some of Mrs. Russo's greater reserve in her relationships with other family members is tempered by her husband's warmth. As is true of other husbands, in this intergenerational study, Mr. Russo enjoys the closeness of his wife's family and in his relationship with his mother-in-law finds much of what he missed with his own mother.

Since their marriage, Mr. Russo has become increasingly docile and dependent on his wife, relying on her for leadership in such matters as making out the household budget and paying the bills. He willingly surrenders his paycheck to his wife each Thursday evening, who, in turn, cashes the check at the supermarket on Friday when she does her weekly marketing. She pays all household bills by money order at the same time that she cashes her husband's check and, after taking whatever is needed for personal and household expenses during the coming week, returns whatever is left to her husband for his own personal expenses.

In other respects as well, Mr. Russo is a dutiful, attentive, compliant, and understanding husband. For example, he is willing to do whatever is needed when he comes home from work in the afternoon to help his wife finish her chores. As Mrs. Russo comments:

> He couldn't do more fo me than he does, ah . . . he does everything . . . he'll do, for example, if I say, will you give her [their daughter] a bath while I do this, or do the windows Saturday, he'll do anything you know; he's very good like that and he'll always help me; like if a friend is up or something, he'll make sure all the ashtrays are cleaned and he'll clean up you know after or else he makes himself something, you know, and then cleans up afterwards; he don't leave nothing for me to pick up you know; he's good like that . . . I really couldn't ask for anything more . . .

Mr. Russo is also very concerned with his wife's health and welfare. Last year, when he felt that her winter coat was not warm enough, he managed to save enough money each week to buy his wife a new coat and matching handbag for Christmas. In recalling this incident, Mrs. Russo commented:

It was so beautiful. I was so surprised and delighted. I could never have purchased that myself in a million years.

Because Mrs. Russo had no father while she was growing up, she has depended solely on her mother for guidance on how husbands and wives are supposed to get along. Given her mother's memories of *her* father and her first husband, it is not surprising that she has emphasized the importance of having the woman in control of the relationship. Perhaps because she does exercise so much control, Mrs. Russo worries that her husband may not really be happy at home, is guilty about how much she asks him to do around the house, and is even suspicious of his apparent contentment at puttering around the house or visiting with her parents. For example, she tells the following story to picture TAT 13MF in which "a young man is standing with downcast head buried in his arm. Behind him is the figure of a woman lying in bed:"

This looks like a man . . . whom cheated on his wife . . . and he looks kinda sorry for it . . . he looks like he got regrets, whatever happened, but he's gonna do it again because he can't stand his home . . . his wife is after him all the time to do one thing or the other and she doesn't give him much happiness. Not happy at home . . . found some girl but he regrets it now but then he thinks about how his wife runs him and he'll probably end up doing it with another woman . . . he don't have a happy home life and wanted to go out with another woman.

Her fear of her husband's possible infidelity is an issue of considerable concern to Mrs. Russo. The reality is that neither she nor her husband has ever had sexual relations with anyone else.

In spite of his wife's concern about this issue, Mr. Russo is clearly satisfied with his marriage. Like other husbands in this study, he married his wife not only for herself, but also for her family, and he has received the support and guidance from the Scardonis that has made it possible for him to better structure his own life. Having had a chaotic childhood, and a relatively unsuccessful high school record, he now has a stable and well-paying job and a family that relies on him and on which he can rely. Mr. Russo is willing and eager to be accepted by his in-laws and is happy with his decision to spend his free time with them rather than becoming involved in activities such as social clubs or sports that would involve him more in the larger community. Having been willing to wait for nine years while his prospective wife decided whether or not to marry, he is satisfied that the wait was well worthwhile.

A cautious couple who believe in deliberating together each new decision in their marriage, the Russos had decided not to have children during the first years after marriage. They were, therefore, unhappy to learn, shortly after their second wedding anniversary, that Mrs. Russo was pregnant. As Mrs. Russo observes:

I had no idea I was pregnant. It was a surprise when my doctor told me that was why I was feeling sick. After that, I was scared . . . I didn't feel ready to be a mother and had a hard time managing the day . . . doing what I had to do at that time. It was a very difficult time for me and my husband.

Like many working-class Catholic women of her generation, while Mrs. Russo seldom attends Mass and while she is quite ambivalent about her attitudes toward the church, she does not feel comfortable about using artificial birth control methods and either practices the rhythm method or, more typically, complete abstinence. She acknowledges that her feelings about her religious heritage have made it difficult for her to select more reliable methods and, from the outset, recognized that "an accident might happen."

As the time grew closer to when the baby was expected, Mrs. Russo became increasingly concerned about whether she would die during childbirth and whether the baby would be born "normal." She was preoccupied with the fear that the baby would be malformed and that "its heart might be beating too fast" and called her doctor almost daily during the last weeks of her pregnancy. Many of Mrs. Russo's worries about her child's health and safety have continued to the present time. These fears are motivated, as were her own mother's fears for her health, by the fact that her feelings of resentment toward her daughter cannot be consciously acknowledged and are reversed so that just as during pregnancy she was worried about whether she would have a healthy baby, these feelings are now expressed as concern about her baby's development.

In her feelings about motherhood, and also in her expressed childcare attitudes, Mrs. Russo's attitudes more closely resemble those of her mother than any other mother-grandmother pair in this study. Just as was true for her mother, her own mixed feelings about the maternal role are accurately reflected in her responses to the MAS. Considering the first issue, appropriate control of the child's aggression, only Mrs. Murphy of the four mothers in the present study, shows less adaptive attitudes regarding this issue. As was true for Mrs. Murphy, Mrs. Russo does not believe that mothers can control their children's aggressive feelings, short of punitive measures, and believes that mothers are often overwhelmed by their children's anger. Mothers with scores as extreme as that of Mrs. Russo typically conceive of only extreme solutions to this issue — either severe restrictiveness or complete permissiveness. The latter is espoused on the grounds that since the child's aggression cannot be modified, there is no reason to try. The only solution therefore is to wait the child out until this childhood stage has come to an end. The former position is taken on the grounds that if a child's aggressive impulses are so overwhelming and dangerous then these impulses must be completely suppressed. In neither case do the mothers think it possible to permit their children to express anger in some modulated form.

Mrs. Russo's attitudes regarding the second factor on the MAS, discouragement of reciprocity, are consistent with those of other working-class women (Tulkin and Cohler, 1973). Mrs. Russo does not believe that mothers can communicate with their babies or that mutuality between mother and infant is even possible. The score she receives on the fifth issue, meeting a baby's physical needs, indicates that she believes that infants are incapable of any kind of social interaction and that she cannot determine or meet a baby's physical needs.

Especially useful in understanding the relationship between Mrs. Russo's character and her childrearing attitudes and practices are her scores on the third and fourth issues of the MAS, appropriate closeness, and denial of childrearing concerns. Mrs. Russo ranks second among the four mothers in this study in the degree of conflict she expresses concerning appropriate closeness. The attitudes she has regarding this issue served as a major factor in her selection for this intensive study.

Conflict over separating from her child is one of the most pronounced characteristics of Mrs. Russo's childcare practices and leaves her feeling depleted and exhausted. Mrs. Russo's feeling regarding this issue of appropriate closeness is expressed in the story she tells to picture IAT Se7 in which "a woman in a raincoat is walking down the street. A path leads to the house portrayed in the background:"

> She's just . . . going for a nice long walk . . . in the fresh air . . . just to relax and walk, and think alone . . . just in order to be free . . . for a while . . . maybe to think things out, those everyday things that go on in the house . . . she's got to get alone by herself ... she's married, has a kid that gets her down . . . feels like she has nothing . . . no time for herself . . . daughter takes it all . . . tired, longs for a vacation, and for someone else to chase her kid around all day, do the dishes, wash . . . she'll grow old before her time.

This story depicts the bleak prospect of days of drudgery and housework that provide little satisfaction and leave Mrs. Russo feeling weary and unsatisfied.

Mrs. Russo regards her maternal role as inherently not satisfying and as demanding only work and sacrifice. Paradoxically, Mrs. Russo is unable to admit to these feelings in any conscious way. On the fourth MAS factor, Mrs. Russo's score was more than four standard deviations above the mean for the mother generation as a whole and was the most deviant score in the larger sample of more than 90 mothers. Mrs. Russo's extreme denial, even in fantasy, of her anxiety about childcare is most dramatically reflected in her story to picture IAT B5 in which "a young woman is seated on a park bench in the city and is watching a young boy playing with a ball:"

> This looks like a mother who is watching her young son with complete delight and fascination. She is thinking about what a wonderful child he is, and how easy he is to raise. She feels certain that he will grow up strong and happy and that he will be secure and remain close to his mother and father. It is just an ideal scene of a mother and her delightful child. (E: And the outcome?) Oh, it will turn out just as she had hoped, they are a close family and everything comes out fine, just fine.

This story contains a positive ending and many superlative adjectives, both of which are absent from Mrs. Russo's other stories. Of course, Mrs. Russo also expresses concern with closeness. Thus, for the story's heroine, an ideal family is one in which the symbiosis between mother and child is maintained. In contrast with her own life, in this story everything turns out well, and mother and child are comfortable and contented.

Considering Mrs. Russo's response to the MAS, her profile is quite representative of other members of the mother generation. The probability that her profile is that of a mother rather than those of a grandmother is 81%, a figure suggesting that she expresses, in a more extreme form, the attitude of most members of the mother generation. This attitude may be expressed as "childcare is a tiring burden but it is difficult to fully recognize or admit to resentment of the maternal role." Mrs. Scardoni and her daughter share the common perception of childcare as an exhausting and inherently unsatisfying task. Her mother's attitude serves to strengthen Mrs. Russo's belief that childcare is incompatible with a mother having any kind of independent existence.

Having felt so keenly her own mother's mixed feelings regarding the maternal role, and knowing of her mother's feelings of resentment, guilt, and self-sacrifice, it is not surprising that Mrs. Russo perceived the maternal role as so unrewarding. At the same time, she did see some benefits from becoming a mother and, especially, the mother of a girl. As she observed:

> There were some good things about having a baby. All the girls in the neighborhood had babies, so we would be able to fit in better with what other people were doing. I hoped I would have a regular little girl, a cute and cuddly little girl, and kept thinking about an ideal little girl, a sort of Shirley Temple kind of baby.

Having a Shirley Temple baby meant being able to have a perfect child and one who would be a positive reflection on her mother's own femininity and competence, for not every mother can have such a perfect baby.

Becoming a mother meant the possibility of fitting in better with the neighbors, a goal that would get her mother's approval. Given Mrs. Russo's concern about becoming a part of her social surrounding, it is understandable that she should see motherhood as a way of realizing her goal. In fitting with her environment, she would please her mother, who is concerned about attainment of identity within the community. Also, the baby would serve as yet another link between Mrs. Russo and her own mother. Having a baby would mean that she could call her mother and seek advice concerning childcare and thus sustain her mother's interest in being with her and could invite her back for visits.

Even before the baby, Charlotte, was born she had become a part of the family and had become a repository of complex hopes, fears, and expectations. She also became heir, as the third generation, to the conflicts regarding identity, conformity, and dependency that had already been transmitted from Mrs. Scardoni to her daughter.

It is not surprising that although her daughter is only two and a half, Mrs. Russo and Charlotte have already developed a complex and conflicted relationship in which Mrs. Russo feels defeated and overwhelmed by the intensity of her daughter's needs for care and in which her daughter, having experienced her mother's feelings of exhaustion and guilt, feels uncontrolled and unfulfilled. Indeed, Charlotte's waking day is spent in combat with her mother, a struggle which leaves both mother and daughter completely depleted and which is intensified by the fact that mother and daughter are socially isolated and spend most of the day together, without contact with other children or adults.

With her daughter, Mrs. Russo has recreated the same symbiosis that exists between herself and her own mother. Mother and daughter are hardly ever apart during Charlotte's waking hours, for Mrs. Russo cannot leave Charlotte with a babysitter. As she comments:

> Oh, of course, we've never done that. I couldn't stand to leave her with a sitter. I think I'd worry all the time about how she was, afraid she wasn't being well taken care of. One time, I had to leave her with my mother and while I was gone she bumped her head. I'd be sure that something terrible was happening to her and get so worried, I'd have to turn around and come home again.

These feelings about babysitting are consistent with Mrs. Russo's childcare attitudes and demonstrate, once more, the consistency between attitudes and action. Mrs. Russo's comments about babysitting also demonstrate more powerfully than any theoretical analysis the mechanism of maternal overprotection and its origins in maternal hostility toward the child. It is ironic, considering Mrs. Russo's unrecognized hostility toward childrearing, that her overprotectiveness was the source of a serious and near fatal illness when Charlotte was seven months old. Since Charlotte's birth, Mrs. Russo had failed to take her back for routine monthly checkups. In part, as she herself observed, she was afraid the doctor would say she was a bad mother who starved her baby. But more interestingly, she stated that she was afraid the doctor would drop the baby, since she had once read an account in a Sunday supplement about a doctor who dropped and killed a baby during a routine pediatric examination.

At about the time Charlotte was seven months old, she began to have prolonged crying fits. Mrs. Russo assumed that these fits were because she left Charlotte alone with her mother, while she went out and did her mother's errands. Charlotte's crying convinced Mrs. Russo more than ever that she should never leave her baby, even for a minute. As Mrs. Scardoni recounts events subsequent to these crying fits:

> I began to get a little excited because I knew that she couldn't be crying just because her mother stepped out for a few minutes. It looked more like she had a hurt, but when I pointed this out to my daughter, she said, "Ma, you're making too much of this. I take good care of her and would know if she had a hurt." I insisted that we had to take her to a doctor and my daughter got excited and said, no, that she would never go, and the next day, when she was still crying so bad, I said that we had to go, that she should go be looked at in the hospital, and they found at the hospital, when we finally got there, that she had a lump on the side of her stomach, and we all got upset, because, of course, she [Mrs. Russo] had herself been operated on once because of a lump, so they operated on her immediately, at once, but it was a hernia that was choking off the blood supply, and she was all right after that. At the time, we were all scared and she wouldn't let her out of her sight or be operated on, and the doctor had to put her in the hospital, too, and give her some strong medicine for her nerves; she was that upset about being separated from her baby.

Clearly, separation from Charlotte is an impossible task for her mother and one that generates powerful anxiety. Mrs. Russo ovserves that the neighborhood children frequently come over to borrow sugar, coffee, milk, or something else that their mothers may need. She acknowledges that it is only a short distance, but comments that she could never feel comfortable about even letting Charlotte go next door to her sister-in-law's house to run an errand, since, as she comments, "I'd be terribly afraid something would happen to her; I'd never trust her alone."

Given the fact that Mrs. Russo feels unable to control her daughter's aggressive impulses, does not believe that she can have a real relationship with her daughter, denies her childrearing concerns, and expresses some feelings of helplessness at being able to determine a baby's physical needs, the daily round is bound to be one that is fraught with anxiety and which leaves both mother and daughter confused and exhausted. Typically, Mr. Russo rises first and leaves for work by about 6:30. Mrs. Russo stays in bed. As she explains, the day is so difficult for her that she prefers to sleep as late as possible. She is usually awake by 8:30 and, as she begins to putter around the kitchen and get the coffee going, Charlotte hears her and joins her in the kitchen.

The first contact in the morning between mother and daughter sets the mood for the rest of the day. Mrs. Russo establishes her daughter in the high chair with a glass of juice and turns on the television, prepared to begin her housework. At this point, Charlotte has her first temper tantrum of the day:

> She screams, yells, she doesn't want the juice, she don't want the cereal, she don't want this . . . she don't want that . . . it's ah . . . I have a problem with her eating anyways, like I have to really, ah . . . in other words, I give her everything she could possibly hold in her high chair . . . in order for her to eat, 'cause where I have such a tough time, you know, for her eating. Then, she insists . . . she's got to be holding something while she eats, and then she wants to get down, and then she begins to scream and I scream back at her and then I get to feeling terrible that already early in the morning we've had a fight . . . I've always had a problem with her eating, she never wanted to eat for me, and if there was something to keep her amused, she'd eat all her breakfast, her fruit or cereal. And then I get frantic, absolutely frantic, and worry that she's not getting enough, you know what I mean, that she's not healthy enough, and I worry a lot about that and have taken her to the doctor and he keeps assuring me that she's in good health and I'm sure that this worry is a part of why I get so frantic about her eating.

Already, at the age of two and a half, Charlotte reflects the same conflict around food and eating that is central to both her mother's and grandmother's personalities.

Given Mrs. Russo's feelings of greed and her defenses against recognition of intense needs, it would be expected that she would have difficulty in allowing her daughter to enjoy and gain satisfaction from eating. She complains that Charlotte is a "picky" eater in much the same way that her mother complained about her own childhood behavior regarding food. Consistent with her expressed childrearing attitudes, Mrs. Russo feels unable to determine what her daughter would like to eat and readily admits that she cannot tell when Charlotte is really hungry. Just as she runs her own daily schedule by the clock, Charlotte is put into her high chair at a specific time, whether or not she is hungry, and, when she refuses to eat, Mrs. Russo first overwhelms her with choices and then cannot decide what Charlotte's preference is.

Mrs. Russo notes that she is a messy cook and that she detests cooking and preparing meals. Of course, Mrs. Russo's unrecognized hostility toward her daughter also plays a part in the development of this conflict regarding eating. Feeling angry and resentful about her maternal role, Mrs. Russo experiences hostility toward Charlotte for forcing her to cook and plan meals. Just as was true of her mother, who used to take Mrs. Russo down to the drugstore to be sure that she had had enough milk, Mrs. Russo now takes her daughter to the doctor and tries to force food down her to be sure she's had enough to eat and will not starve. This worry is an expression of the opposite wish, which is that her daughter will starve to death and thus free her from the burdens of having to care for a baby, so that, instead, she can receive this care for herself.

The conflict between Mrs. Russo and her daughter is further intensified by the fact that Mrs. Russo has been trying to toilet train her daughter. After an unsuccessful attempt to feed Charlotte, Mrs. Russo takes her to the bathroom to sit on the toilet. Charlotte complains that she is unable to make a "b.m." and runs out of the bathroom. This frustrates Mrs. Russo who is trying to begin her daily chores, and there is a brief squabble before Mrs. Russo finally gives up and puts a diaper on her daughter.

One of the ways Mrs. Russo's conflict regarding impulse control is most clearly expressed is in her overconcern with the cleanliness of the bathroom. She cleans the bathroom several times each day, and, while she insists that it remain spotless, she is never able to clean it to her own standards. As she comments:

I just hate to do the bathroom, because no matter how much I clean, it never looks clean; no matter how much I work on it, I am never satisfied with the way it looks. I have to clean the sink every day, sometimes two or three times and every evening when my husband gets done with his bath, I clean out the tub, and then again when I am through . . . on Friday the floor gets waxed, and sometimes my husband . . . when I get too nervous, my husband will help me with it, especially the toilet bowl, I just can't do that . . . for some reason I can't bring myself to clean it out.

Developmentally, the socialization issue of toilet training is associated with the issues of impulse control and, in particular, control of aggression. Since Mrs. Russo is unable to accept or acknowledge her anger and is highly overcontrolled, it is understandable that in this area, as well as that of eating, her own conflicts determine how she resolves this issue with her daughter. In Mrs. Russo's rigid and almost ritualistic activity of cleaning the bathroom, we see the symbolic expression of this conflict regarding impulse control. In her desire to maintain a spotlessly clean bathroom, Mrs. Russo expresses her desire to maintain perfect control over her anger, a task that becomes increasingly difficult for her as the day goes on.

While Mrs. Russo admits that her housework should be finished in about half an hour, her desire for perfection means that it takes far longer. Each day she dusts every piece of furniture in the house and "does" the bathroom. In addition to these chores, there are specific major housecleaning tasks to be performed on specific days of the week: Monday and Tuesday are heavy wash days, Wednesday is reserved for waxing the floors, Thursday for defrosting the icebox, cleaning the stove, and washing the kitchen walls, and Friday for "stripping" the whole house, washing the floors, and vacuuming the curtains so that the house will be neat for the weekend. Just as she becomes increasingly frantic each hour of the day about finishing her day's work, each day of the week she becomes increasingly frantic about completing her week's work on schedule. As she observes:

Everyone makes fun of me; my sister-in-law says 'I never saw anyone like you.' I have/I have a system and if I . . . if anything interrupts my system, I'm gone for the day, like I have to do my clothes by a certain time, I have to have my table set by a certain time, everybody makes fun of me . . . if everything isn't done by like say all those rooms by 9:30, I get/work myself up/see, I'm very, ah, I'm very much a perfectionist, and I have to have everything done right, done just so and, while I'm drinking coffee I'm in there, in the bathroom, cleaning the bathroom, and then I'll run out and take a sip, but very rarely do I stop, I can't stop unless there is someone who comes to see me and, as the day goes on it gets worse and I just can't get everything done so I stop and take a tranquilizer and that helps for a while, till it all builds up again and I get frantic all over again.

Running her life on such a tight schedule is important to Mrs. Russo for much the same reason that it is important for her to clean the bathroom. Both activities permit her to use external supports as a means of controlling impulses that are frightening and unaccaptable and provide a sense of inner order. In addition, this concern with perfection, evident in so many aspects of Mrs. Russo's character, expresses her desire to conquer her greed and appear worthwhile and acceptable to her mother who herself is much concerned with Mrs. Russo's skill as a wife, housekeeper, and mother.

On those infrequent occasions when she is lucky enough to have finished her housework by 12:00, Mrs. Russo dresses her daughter and herself, puts Charlotte in her stroller, and walks down to the square to tend to her errands. Doing errands is the one pleasurable part of her day, and she notes that she enjoys buying things for the house. At the same time, these trips to the square are a mixed blessing, for, according to Mrs. Russo, Charlotte behaves very badly in stores and has earned a reputation as a local "Dennis the Menace."

She is so awful that I have to carefully plan in advance what I'm going to do, so, like the night before, I check off what I have to take and what I have to do down in the square the next day . . . but even as carefully as I plan, she drives me crazy. In the stores, she grabs everything . . . for example, there's a certain store down there and she goes right in, right on the shelf, grabs her potato chips or her things, whatever she wants and when we're out of there, by the time we've been in several different stores, by the time we get home, there's ten pounds of cookies and I've got to stop in every single store and buy her something to keep her quiet, ah, and it's murder, just murder shopping with her . . . like when we're in the checkout line at the grocery store and you know how they have cigarettes, and she's pulling out the cigarettes, ringing the cash register, she, one day she took a bite right out of the, out of a cucumber that someone was buying and I was so embarrassed, and now the whole square knows me so that I am thinking of not even going down there anymore because I keep coming with her and she's very loud and calls me Pat instead of Ma and she'll go, ''Pat, where are you, Pat'' (Charlotte's made–up name for her mother) inside the grocery store as she runs up and down down the aisles. And when I go down there, down to the square alone, they all ask me, ''Where's Charlotte, where's Charlotte?'' And I say, ''Please, she's home with her aunt, or her father, day . . . ah, today,'' and when I'm coming home with her I say to myself, ''I'm another nut,'' I get a frightful headache, my nerves are all shot, yet still I keep going down there with her.

Of course, once more, Mrs. Russo's intense and unacceptable feelings of hostility toward her daughter prevent her from taking any firm stance regarding this misbehavior.

If Mrs. Russo arrives at the square around lunchtime, her favorite way of breaking up the day is to eat lunch in the Chinese retaurant. This restaurant holds a special allure for Mrs. Russo and, even though her daughter screams and fights throughout lunch, Mrs. Russo gains some satisfaction from her meal. On rare occasions, she eats with her sister-in-law or a good friend from high school days who lives nearby. More often, she eats by herself, since, as she says, her daughter is so awful that she is ashamed to have her friends or family see her.

Mrs. Russo could not be specific about what it was that made the Chinese restaurant special for her. She did note that there were several other restaurants in the square, but that eating anywhere but the Chinese restaurant made her feel nauseous. She did mention that the portions served in the Chinese restaurant were enormous, so that there was never any worry about running out. Mrs. Russo's favorite dish is a kind of chop suey that has an especially thick gravy and soft vegetables, not unlike baby food. Chop suey is the one dish her daughter will eat without complaining or fighting, a fact that well illustrates the extent to which her own conflict around food has been learned from her mother.

If Mrs. Russo and her daughter remain at home during the morning, lunch goes in much the same way as breakfast. Eventually, Mrs. Russo becomes so distraught that she leaves Charlotte alone to finish her lunch, while she continues with her housework. She recognizes that Charlotte becomes quite upset when she has to eat alone, but also notes that she becomes frantic about whether her daughter is getting enough to eat. After lunch, Mrs. Russo attempts to find a few minutes for herself, so that she can watch her favorite soap opera. However, according to her account of the day, she almost never succeeds; Charlotte refuses to nap or even to spend a few quiet minutes playing by herself. Mrs. Russo recounts her problem of finding some time for herself during the day as follows:

She don't leave me alone for a minute, see I, she's . . . always around me, she has to be every place like . . . now, when I watch my television, she has a room in there, where she plays . . . can play . . . but it's like a psycho room it's everything . . . there is everything you can possibly think of in there, but she won't play in there, whatever she has in there, she has to take it out to the kitchen, or she has to follow me, or stand in front of my television and tell me about it, and if she doesn't see me, she says, ''Ma, where are you? Where are you.'' Or she shouts at me so I can't hear the television. I don't know what it is to go to the bathroom since . . . since she's been born alone, and this is the truth, while I'm sitting down, she's looking in my face.

The only time during the day when Charlotte and her mother see other people is at about 3:00 when her sister-in-law often comes over with her one-year-old daughter. However, several problems are connected with this visit. First, Mrs. Russo is busy at about this time getting supper ready, for her husband comes home at about 4:30 and likes to have supper when he arrives. Second, according to her mother, Charlotte is quite fresh and bossy with her little cousin, and, when this cousin comes upstairs, Charlotte attempts to imitate her mother's behavior towards her, which Mrs. Russo finds particularly embarassing:

> First she goes crazy with the sponge, cleaning everything in sight, and telling my niece not to get finger marks on the wall, and wiping up after her, and then there are some straw flowers that my niece likes to . . . that my niece grabs, and the minute my niece comes up, my daughter will get the flowers and put them on the television and say, "No, don't touch these" or, if she touches an ashtray, my daughter will scream at her like "leave it alone," or "don't touch it." And every thing that I do to her, she does to my little niece.

Charlotte has clearly internalized at least some of her mother's controls, and, just as in her resistance to eating and toilet training, she has begun to express her conflicts in ways similar to those of her mother. This behavior causes considerable conflict for both Mrs. Russo and her sister-in-law, who complains that Charlotte is so controlling and fastidious that it is unpleasant to come over for a visit.

Generally, it is impossible for Mrs. Russo to have visitors in the afternoon because, as she says:

> I don't have company . . . she's just here and running around and how can I entertain anyone because I have to look at her all the time, you know, if she sees me talking to somebody else, ah . . . she has to be the center of attention and I can't find anyone that I trust to be with her when I'm out, because she's so hard to manage . . . I can't even get a babysitter, I couldn't leave her with anybody so I take care of her all the time.

This observation is consistent with Mrs. Russo's score on the third factor of the MAS, that of inappropriate closeness and, once more, reflects her feelings of self-sacrifice and exhaustion, which intensify her resentment toward her daughter. Charlotte has succeeded in binding her mother exclusively to herself, and this bind both increases their social isolation and further intensifies the conflict between them. Finally, by the time the afternoon is over, Mrs. Russo is, as she describes it, "ready for the ash heap."

Mrs. Russo recognizes that she brings a good deal of the trouble on herself because she finds it so difficult to say no to Charlotte. However, what she fails to grasp is the fact that her feelings of resentment and frustration are intensified because she sees her daughter becoming increasingly like her. Many of the situations that arise during the day are especially difficult for her to resolve because they evoke such strong feelings in Mrs. Russo herself. This is seen in her reaction to Charlotte's treatment of her little cousin. Another such incident concerns the parakeet that Mrs. Russo has had for several years. Each afternoon at the appointed time, she changes the paper and gives the bird fresh water and food. Charlotte insists on imitating her mother's behavior and always ends up spilling the bird seed all over the floor. What worries Mrs. Russo about this is that Charlotte acts toward the bird in the way that she herself acts toward Charlotte:

> She sticks the food in the cage and yells at the bird to eat, and tells it how worried she is that it won't eat and will get sick. Then she tells the bird that it is hard on her nerves, and then she begins to scream at it. The water spills out and the bird begins to fly around and knock out the bird seed all over the floor. I have to clean up the mess but the worst part is that I feel terrible . . . I wonder if I really sound like that when I am getting her to eat.

Finally, when Mrs. Russo feels that she can not take another minute, it is about 4:30 and her husband comes home to rescue her. A placid and easy-going man, he arrives home from work in a good mood and plays with Charlotte, while his wife finishes making dinner. Since she hates to cook, Mrs. Russo puts off fixing the dinner as long as possible. Then, since Charlotte is so demanding of her time, she is inevitably late in serving dinner. Typically, everything is ready by about 5:00, and Mr. Russo washes and helps his daughter to get ready for supper, after which the family sits down together for the first time during the day. Mr. Russo tries to take over the task of feeding his daughter during supper, but his wife is very critical of the way he feeds her, so that she finally maneuvers herself into the position where she is in control. Charlotte begins to complain and throw her food, after which her mother tries to "bribe" her in order to get her to eat by offering her ice cream or fruit cocktail if she finishes her main course.

Mrs. Russo becomes increasingly upset and concerned that Charlotte has not had enough to eat. In her anxiety, she begins to plead and beg Charlotte to finish. Charlotte, sensing that she has the upper hand, begins to throw her plate and cup down to the floor, at which point Mr. Russo intervenes by assuring his wife that Charlotte will not starve and that she has had enough to eat.

Father and daughter go off into the living room to play or to watch the television, while Mrs. Russo clears the table and puts the dirty dishes into the dishwasher. They used to watch Charlotte's favorite television program as a way of helping her to relax in the evening, but, since Charlotte has broken the ultrahigh frequency receiver, this is no longer possible. Mr. Russo helps her to color or put a puzzle together, while Mrs. Russo runs her bath and sets out her night clothes. Typically, Mr. Russo bathes Charlotte and gets her into pajamas.

On weekends and holidays, Mr. Russo spends a good deal of time with his daughter. He and Charlotte go on short trips together to the zoo or the playground, while Mrs. Russo finishes her housework. He also helps his wife around the house when he is home in the evening, recognizing that this helps make Mrs. Russo less frantic about keeping on schedule. As she observes:

> He's very good about helping me out. On the weekend, he entertains Charlotte and does the heavy work around the house. Like, he will do all the windows and blinds when I ask him to. Even sometimes at night, if I am too tired, he'll do the dishes because he knows that if everything isn't finished by 6:30, I'll fall to the floor of nervous exhaustion and worry. I guess he knows that I can't take too much of it and he tries to help me along.

Perhaps because both mother and daughter have become exhausted by the daily round, bedtime is generally less of a problem than the rest of the day. Charlotte is typically ready for bed by 6:00, at which time Mrs. Russo puts her to bed. Mrs. Russo gives her cookies and a glass of milk and kisses her, after which she turns out the light and shuts the door. Charlotte has not been in the habit of coming back out after she is in bed, but she often awakens with a nightmare at about 9:30 or 10:00, an indication of the intensity of her own inner conflict, at which time Mrs. Russo gets her up and gives her another glass of milk.

Mrs. Russo describes herself as delirious with joy when Charlotte has finally gone to bed for the night:

I lay down on the floor and roll around; I can't believe it I am so gone with joy that she is in bed for the night.

In contrast with other mothers in this study, Mrs. Russo makes little attempt to arrange her daily schedule to have time for herself. Even her favorite luncheon at the Chinese restaurant in the square has to be managed around Charlotte, whose behavior is continually challenging and frustrating. Only after her daughter is asleep for the night can she allow time for herself, for, at such times, since her husband is willing to babysit, Mrs. Russo can think of her own needs without feeling guilty. Mrs. Russo's favorite activity, in the early evening, is to walk down to the square by herself to buy a newspaper. On the way home, Mrs. Russo may stop by to talk with her brother and sister-in-law or may stop over at the house of her one girl friend who is also a distant relative. Less often, she and her husband watch television together in the evening. Mr. Russo enjoys the television, especially sporting events, but he does not particularly enjoy visiting with Mrs. Russo's brother and sister-in-law, so he remains at home and baby-sits while his wife goes visiting.

When she returns home, Mrs. Russo finishes any household chores she has not been able to complete during the day and makes her husband's lunch for the next day. Finally, she cleans the bathroom and bathes. The Russos retire early, since her husband is up by about 6:00. Bedtime is a difficult time of the day for her, since Mrs. Russo is very frightened of sexual realtions, which, she acknowledges, is a point of conflict between her husband and herself. As many years as they have known each other, they have not been able to find mutual sexual satisfaction, and Mr. Russo, while finding his wife attractive, is generally compliant with her wish to avoid coitus.

This description of Mrs. Russo's attempts to survive the day with her daughter demonstrates the power of childhood socialization as a means for the transmission of personality conflicts across the generations. As a result of her suppressed hostility, Mrs. Russo shows an exaggerated concern with her daughter's eating. Reassuring advice from her pediatrician cannot ease this concern, because her fear that her daughter might become sick stems from her unrecognized and unacceptable wish that Charlotte might become sick, just as her own mother, in turn, had worried about Mrs. Russo's eating as a child. Given her refusal to eat, it is likely that as an adult Charlotte will show conflicts around eating and feelings of greed and entitlement similar to those of her mother.

Because of her own difficulty in expressing aggression in a modulated form, Mrs. Russo is unable to take a firm stand with her daughter. Thus her child is largely lacking adequate inner control: Charlotte does whatever she pleases. Like the proverbial comic strip character, Dennis the Menace, Charlotte has already acquired a reputation for destroying property and refusing to do as she is asked. Struggles of this nature are quite common among children of two-and-a-half, especially when their parents are attempting to toilet train them. However, Mrs. Russo's uncertainty about her own inner controls and her need to rigidly control her feelings means she is bringing her child up in such a way as to lead to serious difficulties regarding the issue of inner control in her daughter's own life.

THE TWO GENERATIONS TOGETHER: THE IMPACT OF FAMILY SYMBIOSIS ON DAILY LIFE

While Mrs. Russo receives more help from her husband than any other mother in this study, with the exception of Mr. Czaja (discussed later in Chapter 5), most of her time during the week is spent alone with her daughter. Almost all other social contact is with members of her family. Unfortunately, rather than providing her with some relief from the intensity of her relationship with her daughter, these contacts, particularly those with her mother, only increase the intensity of the three-generation symbiosis.

Of the four families comprising this study, Mrs. Scardoni and Mrs. Russo are most in agreement about what they want from their relationship and also maintain the closest bond. It will be recalled that Mrs. McGorty (discussed in Chapter 3), would like to return to Tower Point more often, but that her mother is much involved in her own activities and regards her daughter's visits as intrusions. A similar problem occurs between Mrs. Giorgio and Mrs. Czaja. While more isolated than Mrs. Limpari (Mrs. McGorty's mother), Mrs. Giorgio has activities during the day that are satisfying to her. On the other hand, Mrs. Czaja has other satisfactions than housework and childcare, and, while she continues to search for a way to become closer to her mother, and more comfortably dependent on her, this does not prevent her from obtaining some satisfaction from their relationship. Mrs. Murphy and Mrs. Pescatore in Chapter 6 are caught in a relationship that is satisfying for neither, and, while Mrs. Murphy finds security in living with her mother, such security is obtained at the cost of her own autonomy, and she continually encounters her mother's intrusiveness.

Mrs. Scardoni and Mrs. Russo are both determined to continue and extend their relationship, and, since neither mother nor daughter has any interests outside of her domestic duties, there are no competing interests or gratifications. Mrs. Scardoni lacks Mrs. Limpari's community involvement or Mrs. Giorgio's pleasure in autonomous self-fulfilling activities. Since Mrs. Russo's goals in life mirror those of her mother, she does not experience the conflict with her mother that is true of Mrs. Murphy, whose life-style is not one of which her mother approves.

Typically, it is Mrs. Russo who makes the first contact with her mother each day. She always calls her mother after she has fought with Charlotte about toilet training, and, since she calls each morning at about the same time, Mrs. Scardoni knows by the time and the number of rings that it is her daughter.

After the telephone has rung three times, since calls from Winterfield to Dorset cost less than calls from Dorset to Winterfield, Mrs. Scardoni returns the call. This telephone arrangement was worked out after much discussion between mother and daughter. When Mrs. Russo was first married, her mother called her first all the time. Mrs. Scardoni began to feel hurt that she was always the one to make the first call and took up this issue with her daughter:

> I said to her, for God's sake, I've got to call you all the time, call me first sometimes, you know, when we call each other. And she said, "But Ma, I'm busy, with the baby, so you have to understand,"and it seemed like a little thing, really, but I felt that she should call me first sometimes, so we talked some more about it . . . and like I said, she was a bit snappy at first, but I said to her, "You got a baby too; someday, when she's grown, someday you're gonna feel bad too."She hollered and I hollered and she hung up the phone. About five minutes later, she called back, she calls me back and says, "Ma, I'm sorry. I never knew you was hurt about it." Ever since then, we do the way I told you.

This incident is quite typical of the way in which Mrs. Scardoni and her daughter resolve disagreements. For both mother and daughter, the investment in continuing the relationship is too great to allow simple disagreements to disrupt it.

When Mrs. Russo reaches her mother, she discusses Charlotte's activities of the morning and seeks her mother's advice about her problems with Charlotte. As Mrs. Scardoni observes, Mrs. Russo feels better after being able to complain about how regimented her life is and how burdened she is by housework. Mrs. Russo then tells her mother about her brother and his family and any gossip that she had heard while visiting with the Butonis the previous evening. She then discusses her menu for the day with her mother and gets her mother's advice on the best way of preparing whatever dish she has selected for supper. Mrs. Russo may call her mother later on in the day, if she finished the chores in time or if it is too cold or too wet to walk down to the square.

Mother and daughter also visit together two or three times each week. In addition, Mrs. Scardoni also visits with her daughter most Saturday evenings, for Mr. Scardoni can drop her off on his way into Tower Point. If, as is typically the case, Mrs. Butoni is also at home on Saturday evenings, Mrs. Russo may agree to set her mother's and sister-in-law's hair. Since she has been doing their hair for the past several years, she knows just how they like it and enjoys pleasing them.

During the week, Mrs. Russo typically visits with her mother at least once in Winterfield, where they run their errands and tend to their marketing. Since Mrs. Russo so dislikes cooking, Mrs. Scardoni typically prepares and freezes pasta for her daughter to take back home with her. Much less frequently, Mrs. Scardoni is able to get into town during the week. Usually, she does not call in advance, for

Mrs. Russo's schedule is as regular as clockwork, and, should she be in the square running errands, Mrs. Scardoni visits with Mrs. Butoni until her daughter returns.

Since she detests food so much, it is paradoxical that food and food-related activities are clearly the focus of Mrs. Russo's visits to Winterfield. On the day that Mrs. Russo has selected to visit with her mother, Mr. Russo leaves the car for her. Mrs. Russo and Mrs. Scardoni do their shopping together, and this is particularly important for Mrs. Scardoni, who has no other way of getting around in a suburban area with little public transportation. Mrs. Scardoni discusses the fine points of cooking with her daughter, and, together they select Mrs. Russo's groceries. These shopping trips are also a source of some conflict between mother and daughter; Mrs. Scardoni continues to criticize her daughter's weight and encourages her to eat more nourishing and filling foods. Since Charlotte is so badly behaved in stores, her behavior is often a source of embarrassment for her grandmother. On the other hand, Mrs. Scardoni herself has so many mixed feelings about setting limits that she finds it difficult to say anything about her granddaughter's behavior.

When they return home from shopping, Mrs. Scardoni feeds her daughter and granddaughter lunch or a snack. Often, Mrs. Scardoni will cook enough that Mrs. Russo is able to take home the leftovers for her husband's supper. In that way, she does not have to do as much cooking.

The Sunday gatherings at the Scardonis are particularly important occasions for this modified extended family. Typically, Mrs. Russo, her husband, and Charlotte drive out with her brother and his family. Mrs. Russo's sister-in-law is the only member of the family who goes regularly to church, and the others wait for her return from the 11:00 Mass before setting out for Winterfield, a trip that usually takes 20 to 30 minutes.

During these Sunday get-togethers, much of the family business is discussed. Since Mrs. Russo's brother dislikes talking over the telephone, Mr. Butoni typically spends time alone with his mother talking over the week's events and getting her opinion on current issues in his own life. Mrs. Scardoni notes that Mr. Butoni is much more willing than Mrs. Russo to talk over intimate matters:

Some mothers, they don't seem to care about their children when they grow up, but go off and don't seem to care anymore . . . they're not affectionate with their children anymore but, well, I am very affectionate with my children, like, when my boy comes on Sundays, now, he's over thirty years old, but I grab him, kiss him, and he hugs me, and gives me a punch, and we wrestle and play around with each other, but I can't do that with my daughter; she's more reserved, not cold, but she doesn't like getting intimate with me. She loves you but she won't show it like my boy will. She and I spend a lot of time together, and she talks to me about her baby and her house but there are some things that my boy will ask me about that my girl won't.

As is true more generally in her relationship with her mother, these trips to Winterfield are a mixed blessing for Mrs. Russo. On the one hand, Mrs. Russo wants very much to be a child again, free from her responsibilities as wife and mother. She is resentful of her mother's remarriage and of the fact that her mother has a life apart from her, a husband, and a household in which she has no permanent residence. On the other hand, Mrs. Russo feels caught in her relationship with her mother and powerless to act on her own. Being so dependent means that she cannot act on her own and that she is compelled by inner needs to act in a way that will gain her mother's attention and praise. She is especially concerned that her mother regard her as a good wife and mother and asks continually if her mother approves of her housekeeping.

The most painful part of these visits to Winterfield, either during the week or on Sundays and holidays, is the inevitable separation at the end of the visit. As Mrs. Russo notes:

I usually feel a bit sad when we leave at the end of the day. Even though we sometimes fight, especially about my eating and the way I watch over my daughter, it is nice to have some help and to have someone else do the work.

This observation is, of course, consistent with Mrs. Russo's story to picture IAT Si3 showing a young woman looking straight ahead as another young woman wearing a coat and carrying a handbag is about to go out the door. As Mrs. Russo says, in describing the feelings of the young woman who remains behind in this story: "She wanted her [mother] to stay longer." Consistent with this feeling of longing, Mrs. Russo discusses her feeling at returning once more to her parents' home:

Of course, I didn't live there very long before I was married because they moved in just a short time before, but I always had my own room with my things. Now that I'm married, it's not my house anymore, I mean, it's my house, but when I'm there . . . sometimes I am sad because I can't stay there and have to go home again. I still can do what I want there, but it's not the same as when I lived there, you know, it doesn't feel like my house anymore. My mother treats me the same, but I feel like a guest . . . sometimes I go up to my old room and, of course, all my old stuff is there. I sit on my bed and think about the days before I was married, and about all I have to do now, and about the burdens of running the house, doing the house, my errands, bills, and taking care of Charlotte. Then it seems all like it's too much, and sometimes I begin to cry (tears come to Mrs. Russo's eyes as she talks about this) but then I wipe my eyes and try not to let anyone see and feel sad as I walk downstairs. (E: Does Charlotte ever come up there?) No, I wouldn't feel right about it. It was . . . that was my life before I got married and I go up there when I want to think about the old days. I guess I shouldn't because it makes me feel so sad, but sometimes I can't help it . . . help myself.

Although mother and daughter see each other several days each week and although the Russos and the Scardonis spend most Sundays and holidays together, both Mrs. Scardoni and Mrs. Russo would like to live even closer together than they do. They might even share a common residence, were it not for the tension between Mrs. Russo and Mr. Scardoni, together with Mr. Scardoni's desire for privacy. As a matter of fact, it is largely because of her respect for her husband's wishes that Mrs. Scardoni lives as far away from her daughter and son as she does. She comments, in discussing this problem of living so far away from her daughter:

Sometimes, yeah, I do get a little lonely because I'd like to be near . . . to live closer to her than I do. Of course, my husband says, 'I'll be glad to drive you down,' but, so often he is unable to do so. Again, I'm not too good about buses, and you have to change so many times. I worry about the fact that if I lived closer to her, I'd interfere the way my own grandmother did when I was growing up . . . and she might resent me being there. Still, I'm . . . it's a little disappointing that I don't live closer to her.

Mrs. Scardoni believes that if she did live closer to Mrs. Russo, she'd be sufficiently aware of the problems involved not to interfere in Mrs. Russo's family and also notes that since her son and his family already live next door to Mrs. Russo and her family, relationships could not become much more complex than they already are.

Just as is true of her mother, Mrs. Russo sees only advantages in being able to have her mother live closer to her than she does:

Oh, I do . . . I wish that she lived closer than she does. If I had to do an errand, she could look after Charlotte. More important, I enjoy having my mother around, and she is a great help to me. It seems like, when she is here, I can sit down and relax; she'll start doing things to be of help. And, of course, she can help prepare meals and I learn about cooking from watching her.

For Mrs. Russo, the ideal solution would be for her mother to live next door. That way, she would not be an intimate part of the household, but would be near enough to provide help.

Mrs. Scardoni is less worried than other grandmothers in this study about being burdened by a close relationship with her daughter. Of course, since mother and daughter have maintained the symbiosis throughout Mrs. Russo's life, they have never really been emotionally separated from each other. In addition, since Mrs. Scardoni reared her children by herself, she never had the help of a husband or an extended family during the years that the children were growing up.

While her relationship with her husband is important to her, most of Mrs. Scardoni's energy is devoted to thinking about her children and grandchildren, and she continually worries about what might be happening to them. Mrs. Scardoni's overprotectiveness extends to her grandchildren, and, sometimes, from a "premonition" that some terrible thing has just happened to one of her grandchildren, she will call her daughter or her daughter-in-law to be sure that everything is all right.

As we have already seen in the present study, for many modified extended families, the issue of babysitting is one that is a major source of conflict between mother and grandmother. Mothers imagine that their own mothers have plenty of time free to help and are hurt and angry when they refuse this help. Grandmothers are often irritated that their daughters have such complete disregard of their own private lives. The conflict between Mrs. Limpari and Mrs. McGorty and between Mrs. Giorgio and Mrs. Czaja is typical of this intergenerational conflict. The conflict between Mrs. Scardoni and Mrs. Russo regarding this issue is of a very different nature. Rather than feeling angry that her daughter imposes on her, Mrs. Scardoni is hurt that her daughter does not ask her more often to baby-sit for her. She recognizes the trouble that her daughter has in being able to separate from her own daughter, but also regards it as a comment on her own ability to care for children that she has never been asked:

My daughter is not one to ask me to baby-sit for her. I'm even ashamed to say that since she had the baby, and the baby is over two-and-a-half now, she never took advantage of saying to me, "Ma, please come down and baby-sit,"and I used to wait by the phone for her to ask. Of course, I know that it's one of her problems, that she's afraid to be apart from her daughter for even a few hours, and the daughter won't stay without her mother; I've told her that I think she should teach her to stay without her; that is one of the things children have to learn, but she doesn't pay no attention to it.

This criticism is in striking contrast to that of other grandmothers who become annoyed at requests to baby-sit. Mrs. Scardoni has even encouraged Mrs. Russo to bring Charlotte over while she runs errands, but Mrs. Russo is afraid to let her mother sit, justifying this refusal on the fact that her mother is not very patient with little children and that since Charlotte has seldom had a sitter, she would become confused and would refuse to stay without her mother.

The issue of babysitting is one of only two areas of disagreement between mother and grandmother regarding how Mrs. Russo is rearing her daughter. Not surprisingly, the other major source of conflict concerns Charlotte's eating habits. Mrs. Scardoni feels that Mrs. Russo is far too permissive in allowing Charlotte to eat whatever and whenever she pleases and in allowing Charlotte to walk around with food. Mrs. Scardoni sees this as typical of what is wrong with the younger generation:

This younger generation, they are really spoiling their children, and when they grow up, they get even worse and worse; that's why it's from the best families that these kids get into the most trouble. Now you take my daughter and her friends, their children couldn't have enough stuff; if they cry about something they're eating, they give 'em something else. My daughter is always fussing about Charlotte's eating, and always hovering over her and fixing her something else if she don't like what she's got. If she cries while she's eating, she's got to play with her boat to put a spoon in her mouth.

While Mrs. Scardoni readily admits to her own anxiety about whether her daughter had had enough to eat, she feels it is better to deal with that as a medical problem, feeding children as if food were medicine rather than "giving in" and spoiling them.

Mrs. Russo becomes almost frantic when her mother criticizes the way she tries to get her daughter to eat. Anxious about whether Charlotte is getting enough to eat, her mother's comments about how Charlotte is being spoiled bring tears to Mrs. Russo's eyes. As she commented, in recounting a recent incident between her mother and herself concerning Charlotte's eating:

We were at my mother's house, a week ago Sunday, and, ah, Charlotte wanted her own way, so, when we sat down to eat, she wanted raviolis, then she didn't want it, and pushed the dish away, and I could feel myself becoming tense, and she began screaming, and I brought her into the other room so that we could both calm down and, in my mind, I was going through what I would have to do to get her to eat, and becoming panicked at the thought of the struggle to get her to eat, wondering what she . . . what I could get her to eat, and seeing her not eating and crying, and Ma began calling me from the table, about how she should eat, and had I called the doctor about it, and how I should come back to the table and then she came in and started telling me about how I didn't bear down enough on her eating, and I started . . . I just broke down and began sobbing . . . about how worried I was about her, and I guess . . . I screamed at her, "Ma, please leave me alone, please get out," and the baby began crying, too, and she . . . we never ate lunch at all. Later in the afternoon, Ma made us custard and then things got better.

Mrs. Russo sees the conflict between them regarding the way she feeds Charlotte as due to her mother's "old-fashioned" ideas about rearing children.

The issue of control and autonomy is important in this modified extended family. Mrs. Scardoni enjoys and encourages her daughter's dependency and since she leads an isolated life with few interests other than her family and her house, she needs to continue this intense relationship with her daughter. Mrs. Russo both seeks the dependency her mother offers and, at the same time, is worried that she might yield to her own wish, give up her autonomy and become a child once more.

Remaining socially isolated, attempting to conform to an environment that seems as foreign and unsatisfying as their own childhood environment, each of these women is haunted by her past and by a wish for the nurturance she feels she never received. For Mrs. Scardoni, who grew up in a fragmented and disrupted family, this conflict is expressed primarily in terms of her desire to make herself a part of the culture and to find an acceptable identity. For Mrs. Russo, the conflict is expressed primarily in terms of proving herself worthy to receive her mother's care by being a successful housewife.

Although Charlotte is only a toddler, her fate appears already to be determined. She is as tightly bound to her mother as her mother was to her own mother and demonstrates the same concern about food and nurturant care as her mother and grandmother. Charlotte, too, is likely to grow up feeling greedy, unsatisfied, and guilty about her own destructive wishes. The continuing close relationship between grandmother, mother, and daughter provides for particularly effective communication of this family theme across the generations.

CONCLUSION

As a result of the closeness between the grandparental and parental generations of this modified extended family, an unusually stable pattern of mutual support and help has developed across two generations with remarkably similar interests and life-styles. Mr. Russo owes his job to his father-in-law, who works for an allied company in the building trades. Mrs. Russo sees herself as very much like her own mother and derives considerable satisfaction and security from being like her own mother. She calls her mother over the telephone several times a day and visits with her several times a week, when she and her mother do errands and exchange ideas about housekeeping and cooking.

Mrs. Russo keeps her mother company and is her mother's best friend and closest confidante. In the same way, Mrs. Scardoni is the most important person in her daughter's life and provides Mrs. Russo with an important source of emotional support. A further indication of the similarity in attitudes and values of mother and grandmother is that there was less difference between their childrearing attitudes than between those of any of the other three mother-grandmother pairs in the present intensive study of women with close and continuing relationships with their own mothers.

Change itself is frightening for both mother and grandmother, and it is important that their relationship remain static and stable. Change means disruption, the experience of painful and unpleasant feelings, and the possibility that they might become different, grow apart, and lose each other. Change has been a source of much anxiety for both mother and daughter, and, while stability has been achieved at the cost of inner growth, at least it serves to bind anxiety. For Mrs. Scardoni, being apart from her daughter means that harm may come to Mrs. Russo or her granddaughter. Frequent contact, in person or by telephone, becomes an important source of reassurance. The cost for Mrs. Scardoni has been great, but she has had such a difficult and unsettling life that stability and lack of change are of the greatest importance.

The cost of such stability and congruence has been even greater for Mrs. Russo who is a very constricted and colorless person, unable to tolerate any but the most limited range of feelings. Mrs. Russo's life consists of a round of chores that must be accomplished if she is to continue to have her mother's admiration and support; most of her waking hours are spent on tasks that provide little sense of personal achievement. Even her fantasy life has become stereotyped and mundane. A perfectionist, Mrs. Russo is controlled by unrecognized and unacceptable wishes and fears that are too frightening to acknowledge. At times when these feelings erupt in an attack of anxiety, in an attempt to regain her emotional equilibrium, she takes one or another of the tranquilizers her doctor has prescribed.

These periods of anxiety are one of the few signs of the precariousness of Mrs. Russo's adaptation. Since she has few interests, outside her all-consuming interest in preserving her relationship with her mother, Mrs. Russo has few other sources of personal satisfaction and little energy for any other interests or activities. This also means that she lacks the "safety valves" which are provided by Mrs. McGorty's interest in her housing project, Mrs. Murphy's interest in the world of the theater, or Mrs. Czaja's interest in the arts.

Particularly as contrasted with Mrs. Murphy, the other mother expressing maladaptive attitudes regarding the issue of appropriate closeness, Mrs. Russo's adjustment seems brittle and precarious. Mrs. Murphy is somewhat more able to express her feelings of resentment and, particularly, to acknowledge her mixed feelings about sharing a residence with her mother and remaining as emotionally close to her as she is. For Mrs. Russo, it is only possible to achieve a satisfactory adaptation when there is perfect control and order in her day; in the event that some unexpected event arises to throw her off her schedule, Mrs. Russo becomes anxious and confused.

Continuing close relationships between mothers and their own mothers have a variety of meaning for both generations, as well as for the family as a whole, and the observed congruence in life-style, values, and attitudes may be motivated by unique and complex factors. In the case of Mrs. Scardoni and Mrs. Russo, intergenerational similarities serve to reassure both grandmother and mother that their own hostile wishes have not actually been realized. Especially for Mrs. Russo, this closeness itself is achieved only with considerable effort and at the sacrifice of a whole range of feelings and experiences that are avoided because they are too threatening.

Rebelliousness, a "generation gap," and the determination to do things in the opposite way from one's parents require great effort and often serve to decrease rather than increase one's chances of obtaining satisfaction from life. In the same way, closeness and a high degree of congruence in attitudes and values may also be achieved at a cost that is perhaps too high and which also detracts from the possibility of a satisfying life. In both instances, actions are determined not only by the desire to have a better and more meaningful life, but also, as in Mrs. Russo's case, to avoid recognition of painful feelings and thus to avoid anxiety. It is for this reason that closeness can be exhausting.

Chapter 5

Mrs. Giorgio and Mrs. Czaja:
The Meaning of Autonomy
in a Three-Generation Household

LIVING TOGETHER–MORE ADAPTIVE ATTITUDES

Somerset is a working-class suburb that spreads to the north and east of down-town Bethany. Two-story frame houses in this somber and colorless community are built close together and of identical design, along narrow, treeless streets. The Somerset custom of not using street signs or house numbers strengthens one's initial impression of unbroken and monotonous rows of ungainly wooden boxes. Typically, two families share a residence, having separate entrances and occupy-ing either separate floors or separate halves of the same house.

Mrs. Giorgio, the grandmother, and her daughter, Mrs. Czaja, live in a corner house, distinguished from those on either side by a larger yard and a gabled roof. Mother and daughter, who was six months pregnant at the time of the study, share this rambling corner house, together with Mrs. Czaja's husband and Peter, the couple's three-and-one-half year-old son. Mrs. Giorgio owns this house and has papered it in the same faded flowered wallpaper as the houses of her neigh-bors. Mrs. Giorgio's living room furniture dates back to the early thirties, but her kitchen contains both modern and near antique appliances. In the past two years, during which Mrs. Czaja returned to her childhood home, there have been two striking changes in the external appearance of the Giorgio residence that clearly distinguish it from other houses on the block. Mrs. Czaja's family's fire-engine red sports car is now parked in the driveway and from the second-floor windows fly boldy patterned Scandinavian curtains Mrs. Czaja made for their son's bed-room. Mr. Czaja is an artist, and his wife helps him with printmaking. When he is not teaching at a local college, he is in his studio working on a canvas or printing lithographs, with sounds of classical music wafting through the house. This emphasis on art and music and the color the Czajas have brought to this drab neighborhood are in striking contrast with the gray conformity that marks this working-class community.

It is not clear how it was first decided that Mrs. Czaja, her husband, and their son would return to live with her mother. The explanation offered by the Czajas was that it was not safe for Mrs. Giorgio to live by herself. At the time, several women in the area had been attacked by a prowler who was said to have murdered an elderly widow down the street. Understandably, this event had terrified Mrs. Giorgio who had lost her own husband a short time before and now lived all by herself in the big house. At any rate, Mr. Czaja, an artist and college teacher, was bored with teaching in a nearby state and was concerned for the well-being of his mother-in-law, of whom he is quite fond. The family originally came for a short visit, which has extended into a two-year sojourn.

When they first arrived, the Czajas planned to rent a house near Mrs. Giorgio as Mr. Czaja needed lots of space for his press and printmaking equipment and a room light enough to use as a studio. Since they found nothing suitable, they solved their spatial dilemma by moving in with Mrs. Giorgio. Although originally they had come only to visit, they arranged to move their possessions, and, after the family had settled into their new quarters, Mr. Czaja had little difficulty arranging for a part-time teaching job in a nearby college to supplement his meager earnings as an artist. Two years later the Czajas are still living with Mrs. Giorgio, and, while they have made plans to move to a neighboring state where Mr. Czaja has been offered a faculty position at a well-known college, the move has been postponed for yet one more year.

Mrs. Giorgio and Mrs. Czaja were selected as participants for the present study because they shared a joint household and because Mrs. Czaja expressed adaptive attitudes on the MAS issue of appropriate closeness. In view of these criteria for selection, it is interesting to note that the decision to live together has been viewed by both generations as only a temporary arrangement. It is also interesting that like Mrs. Limpari, (discussed in Chapter 3), Mrs. Giorgio values her independence. It may well be that daughters who express more appropriate attitudes regarding this childcare issue have mothers who themselves have emphasized their own separate needs and interests to a greater extent. In examining this hypothesis, we must first consider Mrs. Giorgio's own personality and then determine the impact of her personality on her daughter's personality and childcare practices.

MRS. GIORGIO: "I'M VERY INDEPENDENT"

Among the four grandmothers in this study, Mrs. Giorgio is easily the most cosmopolitan. A 64-year-old, distinguished looking widow, Mrs. Giorgio is less in conflict with changing social conditions and innovative technology than is true of other grandmothers in the study. During the five years since the death of her husband, a well-respected physician in the Somerset community, Mrs. Giorgio has logged more air miles than many a business executive. She has little hesitation about catching an airplane, often on a whim, to go to visit her daughter in California or her son who is studying medicine in northern Italy.

For the same reasons that she enjoys being able to travel to faraway places on a moment's notice, Mrs. Giorgio does not enjoy having close friendships within her own community. She has very few acquaintances and does not enjoy visiting with neighbors. Instead, she spends a large part of her day either volunteering in the hospital where her husband was formerly on the staff, going window-shopping downtown, or just doing housework and watching television. Mrs. Giorgio values what she calls her "freedom" to come and go as she pleases, although this freedom is constrained by numerous fears, such as her reluctance to accept dinner invitations for fear both that she will commit herself to a time that may, ultimately, interfere in other plans she has made or that she will have to reciprocate and further constrain her schedule. As we see later, this same insistence on having her freedom creates tension between herself and her daughter who seeks a close and companionable relationship with her.

Mrs. Giorgio's reluctance to form close social relationships has its roots in her own childhood experiences. Economically, her childhood was the easiest of the four mothers in this study. Indeed, Mrs. Giorgio's father had accumulated some money even prior to his immigration to the United States. His wife, from a family of high social standing in her community, also had some money. An enterprising man, Mrs. Giorgio's father was soon able to go into business for himself and established a soft-drink bottling concession in another state, where Mrs. Giorgio, the third child and first girl, was born. Her father and two brothers ran the bottling concession, while she, her mother, and two sisters, managed the office (in all, Mrs. Giorgio had two brothers and two sisters). Her father was sufficiently affluent to afford several trips to Europe. These excursions were a source of pleasure for the whole family, and Mrs. Giorgio has particularly fond memories of the boat trips and of the family's adventures in Italy and elsewhere.

The family was very close knit and went everywhere together, largely excluding outsiders. Since the dinner conversation throughout Mrs. Giorgio's childhood and adolescence concerned the family business almost exclusively, visitors were not permitted. Furthermore, since everyone in the family had some role in the business, dinner provided the only opportunity during the day for the family to assemble. Mrs. Giorgio recalls feeling that family discussions were confidential. It was expected that she and her brothers and sisters would not discuss these dinnertime conversations with their friends. She remembers the exclusive quality of these dinner conversations and the pervasive sense that some outsider (alien) was trying to steal family secrets. As she notes:

> We never liked to ah, visit strange people, in other words, friends, not too many friends we had, we always stuck with aunts and uncles and in-laws; we didn't have too many friends that are in and out; if we had them they were just casual friends, but it's not like some people they really have friends that come in and out . . . . my family was very closed because of, again, about the business and we had a lot of calls and things like that, and we had a lot of discussions in the family that we couldn't let everyone hear about them; we didn't let them hear them so we more or less stayed together.

At least in her recollections of her childhood, Mrs. Giorgio describes a family that clearly distinguished the physical from the interpersonal world. For this family the former was friendly, while the latter was dangerous and hostile.

In contrast to the Murphy and Pescatore (discussed in Chapter 6) families who had always restricted both their physical and interpersonal worlds to the immediate neighborhood, Mrs. Giorgio's family traveled the world over. If the physical environment was benign, the interpersonal environment was viewed with great suspicion. Mrs. Giorgio's perception of her family's overwhelming mistrust of others' motives has had a lasting effect on her own character. Mrs. Giorgio views personal relationships with great suspicion and lives in fear of attack from others. Nowhere is this more evident than in her comments about her daily routine:

> I don't like to visit; I like to talk on the phone rather than visit one home from another . . . I don't like to barge in on anybody if they don't expect me . . . if they invite me over, I make an excuse say, well, I have something to do . . . funny, people, huh . . . of course, when my husband was alive, he was a doctor and we just couldn't have people coming into our house all the time because it, uh, we just had to tend to business and calls coming in that were personal and we couldn't make other people hear them, so it never was an in and out neighborly thing.

She goes on to comment that in the years following her husband's death, there has been little change in this pattern. As she observed, after 30 years, people get used to not coming over.

The suspicion with which Mrs. Giorgio regards others is clearly seen in her response to the Rorschach blots. Indeed, Mrs. Giorgio's first response to the testing situation was to take the blot and turn it over, reading the fine print on the back that describes copyright information and place of publication. Frequently during the test Mrs. Giorgio would stop and ask for information concerning who made the blots and what their purpose was in making such blots. The percepts she offered further attest to her suspiciousness. The response she gave to Card X.8, a colorful and loosely organized blot, provides a detailed demonstration of her suspiciousness:

> This is like two prehistorian/prehistoric men, you know the one that have ah . . . those weird looking men, with the . . . with the antennas that . . . on their heads . . . (E: What about the prehistorian men make them look like that?) They were, they had those weird eyes that we see sometimes when we . . . see pictures of them in those ah . . . antennas on their heads. Or the ones like from Mars that they say or that they show us in some of the pictures.

This large, usual detail on Card X is frequently seen as a bug, and, somewhat less often, subjects attribute some affect to these creatures. From the outset, it was clear that this blot troubled Mrs. Giorgio. She looked at the card for fully two minutes before providing a response. She then used an idiosyncratic word, "prehistorian," as she attempted to deal with the threat she felt to her own security. Such idiosyncratic words reveal the breakthrough of more developmentally primitive and less reality-oriented modes of perception into secondary process thought (Rapaport, Gill, and Schafer, 1968). Mrs. Giorgio then tried unsuccessfully to distance and, consequently, neutralize the percept: it takes place in prehistoric times.

The prehistoric men are endowed with "antennas" and have "weird eyes." Antennas serve an important purpose for persons who are suspicious about the motives of others, since they provide a means of apparently superior sensation, allowing one the greatest possible sensitivity to danger. There is experimental evidence to support this suggestion that eyes have a special meaning when viewed in the Rorschach blots (Dubrin, 1962). Eyes are most frequently seen on the Rorschach by persons who are suspicious of others and represent both the symbol of being under the surveillance of another and concurrently, as was true of antennas, a means for perceiving possible attack. Finally, she attempts to justify this percept in terms of what the "experts" have said about men from Mars. Here, once more, Mrs. Giorgio retreats into more clearly paranoid thinking. Since there are no photographs of men from Mars, Mrs. Giorgio can only justify her percept on the basis of some distortion of reality, indicating once more how threatening this stimulus must be for her.

This response to the Rorschach blots shows that Mrs. Giorgio's stance in interpersonal relationships is one of suspiciousness and that she feels she must be continually alert for possible dangers. The nature of the danger she fears is suggested by responses such as the following, to the Rorschach blots:

"Its like ah . . . insects carrying a sac in the back that he uses for protection in case he has a fight with somebody else, when he's attacked."

"This looks like two birds fighting, or two birds looking at each other. There's no bill but they're just looking like they're pecking."

In the first of these responses, Mrs. Giorgio describes an insect with a weapon that can be used in case of attack; in the second, she begins by describing two birds fighting with each other. This direct aggression becomes so frightening for her that she undoes the aggressive response: first, she says that the birds have no bills and then observes that "they're just looking like they're pecking." The active aggressive response is then changed into a passive and motionless one. At several points in the material, Mrs. Giorgio indicates discomfort with feelings of anger and, typically, deals with these feelings by either reversing the feeling from hate and anger to love or by removing the affect altogether and transforming the response into a motionless and static description, such as in the Rorschach response just described.

The fear of attack and suspiciousness Mrs. Giorgio feels was, in part, stimulated by her family's view of the interpersonal world outside the family as suspect and poised for attack. Mrs. Giorgio internalized the family secrets concerning their business. These secrets then became a part of her own person that was vulnerable and accessible to attack. Since relationships with others were portrayed as dangerous, she had little desire to form close relationships. As we have previously stated, Mrs. Giorgio's family actively discouraged extrafamilial relationships. Mrs. Giorgio adopted this attitude and continued it during her married life. While she enjoys activities she can do alone, she still shuns close relationships.

This hostile orientation toward interpersonal relationships is well portrayed in Mrs. Giorgio's story to picture IAT Si3 that shows a young woman looking straight ahead as another young woman wearing a coat and carrying a handbag is about to go out the door:

What weird pictures, you don't know what to do, you don't know who's who here, in any of them . . . this is two girls, it seems one is leaving and the other one is . . . very /is in very deep thought about something . . . the other one doesn't care too much, she has quite a decision of something to think about, she don't know what to do, she'll be glad when the girl goes out, she can probably do a little bit more deep thinking herself without no interruption, might be a decision of her life. I don't know how it's going to come out . . . she looks quite determined and she's got a determined face. She'll probably come out with a decision that she can do by herself, and it'll come out pretty good . . .

Mrs. Giorgio's description of the setting makes it clear that the two women have little to do with each other. Indeed, the heroine in this picture is so completely self-absorbed that she hardly acknowledges the existence of the other, beyond wishing that the other girl would leave so that the heroine could be by herself. This story well describes Mrs. Giorgio's own preference to be alone: isolated, safe, and unbothered.

Clearly, Mrs. Giorgio is a woman who values autonomy. Indeed, she is driven by pressing inner conflicts to seek such autonomy. This form of adaptation to intrapsychic and interpersonal conflicts is consistent with that Shapiro (1965) has termed the "paranoid style." As Shapiro notes, in speaking of the search for autonomy among persons demonstrating this paranoid style:

Paranoid mobilization implies radical constriction and narrowing of those areas of normal life that are essentially involuntary and virtual elimination of the capacity for abandonment along with the subjection of behavior to rigid directedness . . . this formal mode represents a pathology of autonomy.

In the paranoid person . . . every aspect and component of normal autonomous functioning appears in rigid, distorted and, in general, hypertrophied form; all action is purposeful, directed toward an aim [for example, a defensive aim] with an intensity close to what is normally reserved for an emergency.

This mode of functioning, pervaded by tension, certainly does not represent a greater degree of the normal person's autonomy. It reflects, rather, an exceedingly frail autonomy, in that, because it is so frail, it can be maintained only in this remarkably rigid and exaggerated form. While the normal person feels not only competent, but also free to exercise his own will and, in that sense as well, self-directing, in charge of his own life, and master of himself, the paranoid person is continuously occupied and concerned with the threat of being subjected to some external control or some external infringement of his will. (p. 80)

In using the term "paranoid" for this style of habitual adjustment to internal needs and the demands of the social environment, Shapiro attempts to relate a stable form of adjustment to a set of symptoms most often observed in extreme forms of psychopathology. Persons with a paranoid style may show the same conflicts and defenses as do paranoid patients; however such persons do not show the gross symptoms of the disturbance.

A particular style represents a mode of expressing conflicts in contemporary adult forms, whose origins are to be found in preadult life experiences: what was, at one time, a conflict in earlier life becomes, in adulthood, an integral part of one's thoughts, feelings, and actions. This is not to say that subsequent experiences, throughout adulthood, cannot alter such early learned styles or that new styles are not learned in adulthood, but only that styles which emerge from earlier experiences have a particularly significant effect on later life. For this reason it is important to consider Mrs. Giorgio's childhood in greater detail in order to understand the manner in which her unique experiences contributed to the exaggerated sense of autonomy she expresses.

Although her childhood was not lacking in material comforts, Mrs. Giorgio was often lonely. Mrs. Giorgio's brothers were much older than she and were preoccupied with the business. Mrs. Giorgio notes that she spent her early childhood years in much the same way as would be true of an only child. On the other hand, she was permitted very little independence, and she was allowed out only when the entire family went somewhere together. As a girl, she spent a lot of time with her grandmother who took care of the house while her mother worked. Mrs. Giorgio remembers these times as being especially lonely. This is well portrayed in Mrs. Giorgio's response to TAT Card 7GF in which "an older woman is sitting on a sofa close beside a girl, speaking or reading to her. The girl, who holds a doll in her lap, is looking away":

This is a grandmother, . . . uh, mother reading a story to her daughter and the daughter . . . granddaughter . . . is listening but thinking of something else. It might be a fairy tale and she imagines that she's a . . . that princess and someday will be as . . . ah . . . important as that princess or as that princess and will be wanted. The grandmother . . . mother's just a nice woman reading to her daughter. . . . or it could be a governess . . . I don't know, it looks more like a mother. She's gonna use her imagination and will be very successful . . . the little girl.

In this story one can observe Mrs. Giorgio's feeling of being unwanted and her solution of escape into fantasy to gain the attention that was not available in reality. Mrs. Giorgio's inability to decide if the little girl was being read to by the grandmother, the mother, or even the governess is consistent with her recollection that her mother was seldom around when she was a girl and that she received most of her care from her grandmother, a woman whom she also remembers as distant and physically incapacitated during much of Mrs. Giorgio's childhood.

According to Mrs. Giorgio, her family was concerned with making money and with status. The family's status in the community was a subject of almost constant discussion among her parents, and it is not surprising that this preoccupation with social status became an important concern for Mrs. Giorgio as well. Stories based on the theme of social position occur in 10 of Mrs. Giorgio's 20 picture thematic stories. In these stories, Mrs. Giorgio makes frequent reference to the heroine being from the middle class, being upwardly aspiring, being from a "good" family, or being from Yankee stock. However, the most revealing of these stories is the one she tells to TAT Card 2 in which there is a "country scene: in the foreground is a young woman with books in her hand; in the background a man is working in the fields and an older woman is looking on":

This is a very nice picture, there's a farmer toiling and the mother is expecting . . . the girl . . . looks like their daughter and she says, 'I don't want to be a part of all this when I get older,' and she looks like a smart and intelligent girl . . . and she feels that this is not for the way she's going to live, she's going to better herself. . . although she probably likes the . . . being free of all the contentment of having the world around you know, the farm . . . she still doesn't like the idea of having a manual laborer or a farmer as a father, or a husband as a farmer. Rather, she's a very characteristic strong face with strong hands . . . and I imagine she's got a very strong face with strong hands . . . she's gonna be smart and not get stuck like her mother. . .in the same work as her mother.

This picture shows Mrs. Giorgio's interest in upward mobility. While her family's business provided a good living, she felt that it afforded her little prestige in the community, just as the father's occupation as a farmer in her story afforded little status for the heroine. It should also be noted that, in view of Mrs. Giorgio's fear of attack, to be in an inferior social position would increase her feelings of insecurity and vulnerability. This fear of persecution intensified her concern with social status. Just as was true of the heroine in her story, Mrs. Giorgio left her family in her early twenties and moved in with a cousin in Bethany who "knew a host of eligible young men."

Reared by her grandmother, in a family where her mother returned to work shortly after her birth, Mrs. Giorgio appears never to have formed very intense ties with either parent. Rather, her parents were viewed as a part of the larger extended family. Feeling abandoned and neglected and believing that her parents would only pay attention to her if she could be reborn as a princess, she defended herself against inevitable disappointment by believing that her relationships with either parent were of little importance to her. Perhaps it was for this reason that it was relatively easy for Mrs. Giorgio to leave her own family and move to Bethany to begin a new life, a move that takes on added significance when it is recalled that more than 85% of the grandmothers in the larger study from which Mrs. Giorgio was selected were born within 25 miles of their present residence. Mrs. Giorgio recalls little discomfort at the prospect of leaving her family and beginning a new life in a different community from that in which she had grown up. She observed that this move was somewhat easy for her, since her family had traveled so extensively from the time that she was a little girl.

As was true of both Mrs. Limpari and Mrs. Pescatore, Mrs. Giorgio met her future husband at a wedding. At the time, she was 29, a relatively late age at which to be married among women in her social class, and he was 33. As she observed in recalling her courtship, they were both persons with enough experience to know their own minds. Given her own personality, Mrs. Giorgio's husband proved an ideal mate. A promising young physician in the Italian community, Mr. Giorgio came from a highly respected family. Marriage to a physician from a good family would fulfill Mrs. Giorgio's own status needs. In addition, Mrs. Giorgio's mother was chronically ill and needed constant care. Her marriage provided an excuse for continuing to avoid significant interpersonal contacts: she was needed at home by her sick mother-in-law who required intensive care.

It is likely that Mrs. Giorgio's feelings about her grandmother also played some part in her willingness to marry her husband and care for his ailing mother. This situation undoubtedly stirred up her own memories of the kind of care her grandmother had given to her as a child, for her grandmother was the only family member to whom Mrs. Giorgio ever referred in her discussions about her childhood and is the only person who is directly acknowledged in the picture thematic data as having taken care of her as a child. The possibility of taking care of her husband's mother may have also provided the possibility of reparation and resolution of guilt feelings concerning her grandmother who had been so important to her in her youth. In addition, her husband needed a secretary-assistant in his medical practice, and Mrs. Giorgio soon became involved in this work. To better assist him, Mrs. Giorgio enrolled in secretarial school and later derived considerable satisfaction from her professional expertise.

The couple purchased the corner house in Somerset and remodeled the downstairs into a small office and waiting room. After her mother-in-law died, Mrs. Giorgio frequently accompanied her husband on house calls and kept track of the medical literature for him. As Mrs. Giorgio observed, this work provided yet another excuse for avoiding close relationships outside the family, as well as providing her with an additional source of status in the community.

Although Mrs. Giorgio talked at some length about her husband's work and the satisfactions she gained from helping him with it, she found it very difficult to describe him or to talk in detail about their relationship, as seen in her comments after drawing a man in the draw-a-person technique. When asked to describe what kind of a person he was, she replied that the man was "just an image of a man . . . I wouldn't know what he was like." Elsewhere, she observed that her husband was a short, stocky man who was kind and intelligent.

Dr. Giorgio was a hardworking physician who, according to his wife, seldom considered his patients' ability to pay and was concerned, above all else, with relieving human suffering. The doctor's preoccupation with medicine left little time for his family, an arrangement that suited Mrs. Giorgio, but which was difficult for the children. The conflict between work and family was described by Mrs. Giorgio when she was asked what interests and activities she shared with her husband:

(E: What kinds of things did you and your husband like to do together?) He never had much time. Only once in many years did we go out to a show together . . . ah, we had a beach house in Cape Ann and we'd go there sometimes although I would take the kids and he would come out when he could. Sometimes, when he made calls, I would go with him, I'd drive . . . help him drive, and ah, that's it, that's all we ever did together. He had no hobbies or things that he did to relax. Very few doctors have hobbies; I wish he did, to/to have his escape . . . he was all wound up in his profession and any time he got, ah time he would read about what was going on and ah, medical books, medical . . . ah, journals, all that, so all he ever did for rest was to read. Every minute counted.

Dr. Giorgio was so busy with his practice that he was seldom home. Mrs. Giorgio notes that this was particularly a problem for Mrs. Czaja's older brother, as seen in a part of the story she told to Card IAT Fam that shows "a living room scene: a woman has her hand on a little boy's shoulder, a baby girl is seated on the floor, and a man is standing to the side":

This boy's gonna go on a fishing trip with his dad . . . and the outcome, I don't know what the outcome will be here . . . probably taking him on a small trip and the boy . . . the man looks a bit bewildered; he don't know whether to go or not . . . except that the mother's pushing the little boy with the father so he can get the father . . . masculine friendliness that the chi/a boy should have and be with his father more. . .

Mrs. Giorgio believed that her husband should have some direct contact with the children and felt that it was her responsibility to be sure that he spent time with them. She was quite dependent on her husband's opinions regarding childcare, especially since, as she observed, he knew so much about child health and nutrition. Indeed, Mrs. Giorgio was the only grandmother in the larger sample of 90 who indicated that her husband rather than her mother had been the most important source of childrearing information.

According to Mrs. Giorgio, her husband's most frequent criticism of her childcare practices was that she was too willing to go along with what the children wanted. For example, when Mrs. Czaja's older brother decided that he wanted to become a doctor, Mrs. Giorgio arranged for him to get a job in a local hospital in order that he might determine, in advance, if he would enjoy a career in medicine. Dr. Giorgio was very critical of this plan and was especially concerned that his son might begin an affair with a nurse and lose interest in his studies. So, at her husband's insistence, Mrs. Giorgio arranged instead for her son to get work with a relative in the construction business, although only on the condition that her son not engage in day labor, a job she regarded as demeaning. Dr. Giorgio accused her of shielding her son too much from the world and of encouraging indolence. He insisted that she not spoil her son so much and that she take a stronger stand as a disciplinarian with all her children.

In other respects, Mrs. Giorgio and her husband had a distant but mutually convenient relationship and one in which there was little friction. Mrs. Giorgio observed that while she was very liberal in her religious views and not greatly interested in the church her husband was ultraconservative. While he had attended public schools, he had attended a Catholic college and, in his youth, had been very much involved in church activities. Mrs. Giorgio said that throughout his life the event her husband remembered with greatest pleasure was the time when, as an altar boy, he had participated in a Mass said by the archbishop. When his children were ready for college, he had wanted them to attend a local and relatively unknown Catholic college. Since each of the girls had done well in school, each was offered scholarships at one or another of the five nationally known universities in the greater Boston area. Mrs. Giorgio, with her concern for social status, wanted her girls to attend these prominent centers of higher education. Mrs. Giorgio's husband, much more traditional, and much more concerned with preservation of moral standards and social standing in the community than with quality of education, strongly wished for his children to have a Catholic education.

The Giorgios had five children over a period of 10 years. The eldest, a boy, sought to follow in his father's footsteps as a physician. However, since his grades were not much above average, he was not admitted to an American medical school and is presently completing his studies at a medical school in northern Italy. Mrs. Czaja, the second child, is a year younger than her brother, and her next youngest sister was born the following year. A nursery school teacher married to an engineer, she lives within a few minutes' drive from her mother in a neighboring community. A third daughter, born three years after Mrs. Czaja, lives in California with her husband, who is completing his medical education at a leading American university. The fourth and youngest daughter married a mechanic and lives in the Boston area. Mrs. Giorgio has a conflicted relationship with her next to youngest daughter, although she does maintain that when next she visits the West Coast, she is going to try to smooth things out.

While the discriminant function analysis of the maternal attitude data shows that Mrs. Giorgio's expressed childcare attitudes are most typical of the mother generation (the probability that Mrs. Giorgio's scores belong to the mother generation is .93, while the probability that her scores belong to the grandmother generation is .07), the differences between Mrs. Giorgio's attitudes and those of the other three grandmothers are not quite as great as these figures might suggest. Typical of the grandmother generation, Mrs. Giorgio does not believe children should be permitted to express their angry feelings or that mothers should attempt to modulate these feelings in some socially appropriate form. Her scores on the factors of encouragement of reciprocity, acceptance of emotional complexity in childcare, or competence in perceiving the baby's needs are not significantly different from those of other grandmothers.

However, unlike these other women in her own generation, Mrs. Giorgio expresses more adaptive attitudes than they do regarding the factor of appropriate closeness with the child. While Mrs. Giorgio's score on this factor is somewhat less adaptive than that of the typical woman in the mother generation, she differs from other grandmothers primarily because of her belief that mothers should not make burdensome sacrifices for the baby and that mothers should not permit babies to form exclusive and binding relationships with their mothers.

These childrearing attitudes are consistent with our previous discussion of Mrs. Giorgio's personality. Given her habitual adjustment to intrapsychic and situational conflicts of overemphasizing her own autonomy while fearing control by others, it is understandable that she should believe so strongly in discouraging the child's anger and aggression. It is precisely because she fears the superior power others might gain over her that she expresses such an exaggerated concern with autonomy. At the same time, because she so highly values autonomy, it is understandable that she would not value a symbiotic relationship with a baby and would seek to preserve her own separateness in such a relationship. In view of what we know about her personality, it is not difficult to understand Mrs. Giorgio's disdain of what she views as "the spoiling" of modern children:

> I didn't have time to give them individual attention . . . I just had the meal for them and there it was, and they went along with it because I couldn't fuss over it with them. I was quite busy with the telephone because of having to help my husband and having to take

care of a family. Nowadays they spoil their children, like my daughter; if the little one doesn't like what she cooked, she cooks something else. I think that's spoiling them. I said to my children look, you don't want it, look at it, don't eat it, I don't care. Mostly they ate it but if they didn't it was up to them because I didn't have the time for special attention. That's what they want anyway. They just want your help and attention, and I'm very independent and I think that they should be, too.

This comment is very typical of Mrs. Giorgio's views on childcare. She never attempted to force-feed a child who would not eat or to argue about the matter. Her attitude was that she provided a wholesome meal and it was up to the children to decide whether they were going to eat. If they did, it was for the best, but if they chose not to eat, it was not her problem. Such decisions were left up to the children: this issue was handled with efficiency, even if not with a great deal of warmth.

In other respects as well, Mrs. Giorgio was determined, efficient, and somewhat aloof in her care of the children. Mrs. Giorgio's reliance on her husband's childrearing advice is consistent with this objective orientation. His advice tended to be precise and medically oriented. Childcare was routinized and consistent for all the children. This is seen most clearly in Mrs. Giorgio's description of the means by which the children were weaned from bottle to cup:

None of the children was especially easier than the others and . . . all together, we had to give them attention at the same rate, and they were a bit whiny once in a while . . . but nothing too different; they were all trained at one year when they had no more bottles; after that one year of their birthday, we had just no more bottles. No more bottles, that was it. They all had two or three nights of fussing but after that they were all right.

Much the same policy was pursued when, at the age of one and a half, the children were toilet trained. Mrs. Giorgio expected little difficulty and there was, in fact, very little fussing on the part of any of her five children.

All five children attended a parochial grammar and high school in the neighborhood that had a reputation for academic excellence. Since Mrs. Giorgio spent so much of the day helping her husband, she had little contact with the childrens' activities after school. They were required to be very quiet all afternoon and evening, since their father's office was in the house. For a part of the time when the children were growing up, the Giorgios had a housekeeper who cleaned the house, looked after the children when they came home from school, and started the dinner. Very little was expected from the children regarding household chores. Most of the cleaning was tended to by the housekeeper or by a woman employed for that purpose, for Mrs. Giorgio had a strong aversion to household chores. Since her family had always had household help, she had never learned the variety of skills necessary in caring for the house. She also notes that she regarded housekeeping as ''not one of the things that a doctor's wife would be expected to do.'' Once again, it is important to note how Mrs. Giorgio's concern with social status affects the manner in which she understood her role as wife and mother.

It was also expected that the children would look out for each other and that the two oldest children, Mrs. Czaja and her brother, would care for the younger children. Since her brother was seldom at home, Mrs. Czaja was in the position of the oldest child, responsible for looking out after her younger sisters. Mrs. Giorgio speaks with pride of how independent the children were and of how well they looked out for each other. She herself has few reservations about her lack of involvement in childcare and is concerned primarily about how well she was able to organize the household so that she could help her husband with his practice.

Recognizing Mrs. Giorgio's discomfort with physical or emotional closeness and her tendency to avoid intimate relationships, it is understandable that she does not see herself as a very nurturant woman. Mrs. Giorgio's lack of emotional involvement in childcare is well demonstrated in the following story she tells to picture IAT B5 in which "a young woman is seated on a park bench in the city and is watching a young boy play with a ball":

This is a babysitter taking care of a child, observing the child; she doesn't got too much on her mind because she's just taking care of the child, to occupy her time and to make some money. She's not interested in the child, doesn't look it anyway, and she's just there watching him. She's just marking time. . . . (E: How is the boy feeling?) Just playing. . . boy's looking at the ball, playing, and she doesn't give him any encouragement, how to do it, what it is, why it is, and she doesn't do that because she just doesn't care; it's just a job, a way to make some extra money.

From the outset, Mrs. Giorgio structures the story so that there is no relationship between the woman and the boy. She is just a babysitter. Then, as if she has not made this sufficiently clear, she makes certain that the examiner understands the babysitter has no feelings for the boy; she is only sitting to find some way of using her time and of making some extra money.

While it is possible that a woman could baby-sit and still enjoy her work, Mrs. Giorgio makes it clear that the babysitter in her story does not enjoy her work. In fact, she is so uninvolved in her work that she pays little attention to the boy and makes no effort to encourage him in his exploration of the ball. Other stories in the thematic apperception series have essentially the same theme: women gain little satisfaction from childcare and have little interest in it. The sole concern they have is to get through the day.

Mrs. Giorgio did not receive much satisfaction from her role as mother. While she was responsible, she did not feel very nurturant. Consistent with this negative orientation toward parenthood, Mrs. Giorgio placed a high value on separateness and autonomy. She was concerned that her children should mind her instructions, but she regarded them as separate persons, with their own interests. Once again, this is well demonstrated in Mrs. Giorgio's story to the first picture thematic card (TAT 1) that shows "a young boy contemplating a violin which rests on a table in front of him":

What the boy is thinking? I don't know, I always regarded what my children thought as their matter . . . I guess he's looking at the violin, this boy, and wondering if he's going to be a good musician . . . and he might not like the music at all, just looking at it . . . makes him wonder . . . whether he should do that or not. (E: What's going to happen in the future?) He's just thinking . . . no one knows what the future will bring for a child . . . it depends on what kind of a father and mother he has, whether they try and push him in music, which they shouldn't do, or whether they let him alone and make him do his own thinking, which is a difficult thing to do but which is right for a child. If he has any musical characteristics, he might continue and like his music . . . he don't know what to do himself . . . but he's looking at it in a very deep sense . . . if he's got an environment of musical . . . that would help him to decide what to do.

This was the first picture shown to Mrs. Giorgio, and, consistent with the usual practice in administering picture thematic materials, she was asked to tell a story with a beginning, middle, and end and in which she told what had happened in the past, what was happening now, how the characters were thinking and feeling, and what the outcome would be. In view of these instructions, it is interesting to note that she begins by denying that she could know what the boy was thinking or feeling and by asserting that it was not her business to know what he was thinking about.

The first picture is an important one in assessing a subject's attitudes toward the task and, more generally, in determining her attitudes toward autonomy. Consistent with other data regarding Mrs. Giorgio, her "metamessage" to the interviewer is that her thoughts are really none of the interviewer's business. Here again she shows the concern with her own autonomy that we have previously discussed. She is somewhat more sensitive to the examiner's possible intrusions in her own private thoughts than many subjects in our research.

Even beyond her suspiciousness and her reluctance to share her own views with the examiner, Mrs. Giorgio's story to this picture differs from that of the typical grandmother telling a story to this picture. Most women indicate either that the boy will have to practice until his parents say he is finished or that the boy does not want to practice and either goes out to play ball or is eventually permitted to do so. Mrs. Giorgio makes it clear that such a decision is entirely up to the boy himself. There is an air of touchiness in Mrs. Giorgio's story as if she is on guard lest the examiner challenge this mode of resolving the boy's dilemma. Mrs. Giorgio makes it clear that it is up to the boy himself to resolve the situation, and, although his environment can provide support in making the decision to practice, the final decision is that of the boy's; this emphasis on freedom of both thought and action is very marked, even when contrasted with the stories of other women in the mother generation, but particularly when contrasted with those of other grandmothers.

While Mrs. Giorgio has had little difficulty creating an atmosphere in the family that fosters autonomy, this has been achieved at some cost, both in terms of her own satisfactions, as well as in terms of her children's socioemotional development. Believing as strongly as she does that each person should lead his or her own life, unencumbered by relationships that make emotional demands, she simultaneously feels isolated and alienated from others and sees her life as purposeless. As she herself says: "Nothing seems to make any difference to me, and there are mornings when I wonder why I should even bother to get out of bed."

This feeling of sadness is also demonstrated in a story she tells to picture TAT 15 in the Murray series in which "a gaunt man with clenched hands is standing among gravestones":

This is a lonely old man standing in front of the graves and realizing that soon he'll be down there too, soon he'll be under the ground also . . . he's a lonely old man who never married; he just comes to the cemetery to see all of these and he realizes that soon he'll be able to be a part of them to . . . to be a part of something; he's a lonely old man who feels that his . . . he doesn't really feel that . . . that he's a part of anything, his life has just, has just always . . . just gone . . . he's just lived his life apart from others . . . the outcome will be that he'll continue coming here and thinking about these graves and the time when he can join them and be in one, too.

The depressed mood in this story is obvious. It is possible that, missing her husband, Mrs. Giorgio has thoughts about death and possible reunion with him. However, these feelings of sadness are superimposed over a more basic feeling of alienation and meaninglessness that is a consequence of the distance Mrs. Giorgio has maintained from others throughout her life. She describes her hero in this story as a man who never married and who is lonely. Even more important, he is a man who never felt a part of anything. Evidence of the importance to Mrs. Giorgio of this statement can be seen in the way in which she stumbles over her words while trying to convey this feeling of alienation. Such stumbling provides the most impressive support for the hypothesis that she feels isolated, for it signals that she feels sadness of such an intensity that it momentarily disrupts her organized thought.

If the effect of Mrs. Giorgio's exaggerated sense of autonomy in her own life has been a sense of meaningless and continual anxiety, the cost for her children has also been great. While her husband tried to find some time to be with the children and, in particular, with Mrs. Czaja's older brother, childcare was primarily Mrs. Giorgio's responsibility, a task she frequently delegated to the housekeeper and to Mrs. Czaja. The fact that her children live as far away as California and Europe attest to the success that Mrs. Giorgio had in instilling a sense of autonomy in her children. All her children went through college, reflecting both Mrs. Giorgio's status concerns and her husband's investment in intellectual and scientific subjects. Mrs. Czaja's older brother, however, has not had a terribly easy or successful academic career. While he began his college studies at his father's alma mater, he failed to compete successfully with his classmates and withdrew after two years to attend a college with less intellectual pressure. After graduation, he applied to the same medical school his father had attended, and, although he was once more admitted to his father's alma mater, he was still unable to do the work and failed after the first year. At this point, the father suggested that he try a foreign medical school, since foreign schools were much easier to enter and complete; such a school would offer the only chance for him to become a doctor.

Mrs. Giorgio was terribly upset when her son failed to complete the medical school his father had attended. She regarded her son's failure as a reflection on her own standing in the community, but was never able to convey her sense of disappointment to her son. She was also disappointed with the decisions made by two of her daughters regarding college plans and, characteristically, was unable to discuss her feelings with her daughters. In each case, college scholarships were offered by non-Catholic universities in the area. In her characteristic way, Mrs. Giorgio refused to provide any guidance in this matter, especially in the case of the older of these two girls. When her daughters then turned to her husband for guidance, she felt hurt and confused, especially when each daughter chose Catholic colleges over scholarships to prestigious non-Catholic colleges.

Particular problems arose regarding the older of these two girls who had done very well in college and who was asked to continue with graduate studies. The university she attended was more than half Jewish, including both students and faculty. When, during her graduate studies, she became engaged to a Jew from New York, Mrs. Giorgio refused to have anything further to do with her. Since her fiancé had been accepted by a medical school in California, Mrs. Giorgio's daughter had wanted to be married at home and then to leave with her husband for the West Coast. Unfortunately, her father died just at this time, and the wedding plans had to be postponed. Her fiancé moved to California to begin school, and she remained in Somerset to be with her mother during the months following her father's death. Without her husband to intervene between Mrs. Giorgio and her daughter, their differences became increasingly serious. Finally, the daughter eloped. Since her marriage, she has not returned home, but, after the first few difficult months, mother and daughter made up, and, in fact, Mrs. Giorgio has been to California several times since her daughter's marriage.

According to both Mrs. Giorgio and Mrs. Czaja, this marriage has not been very successful, and there has been frequent conflict between husband and wife. According to Mrs. Giorgio, differences in religious and cultural traditions are too great for this marriage to have much chance of success. Several months prior to the study, Mrs. Giorgio, not having heard from her daughter for several weeks, was worried that her daughter and her husband had separated and made a spur-of-the-moment decision to fly out to California to be of help:

When she met me at the airport, we both broke into tears. I said, you have picked a very hard road, I'm very sorry for you. I think they've had a hard time all along. The reason why they're on the verge of breaking up is because he is a person who presses down on you all the time and puts you down all the time . . . because of the difference in religion, of course she doesn't go to church anymore, and I think that this is their way of putting you down . . . and I said, well don't . . . mental cruelty is very, very hard, don't stand for it, I said you don't have to stand for it. You're raised differently, and she says, what do you mean raised different and I says you know what I mean . . . I said you should never let him step on you; you should have taken his foot and put it in his mouth. He thinks he's smart and he's not; he's such an ugly person, and very much of a slob but this girl was very immaculate, very prim and proper, and he'd go on and put on a shirt not ironed and overalls no matter when and sneakers. Those kind of people rebel, and he, when I was there last, they had just gotten back together; those kind of people just rebel, and at that time he had to stay up for exams and he did and wasn't very nice to me or her. I am amazed at the way those students live. . .

Mrs. Giorgio is certain that her daughter will get a divorce, but feels badly about the poor relationship between her daughter, herself, and her daughter's husband. In commenting on this same event, Mrs. Czaja observed that her sister had been caught between her mother's conflicting values. On the one hand, she had wanted her children to make their own decisions without parental pressure, while, on the other, she believed equally strongly that her daughters should marry appropriately. While not actually prejudiced, Mrs. Giorgio found it difficult to understand her daughter's husband and his totally different ethnic background. Needless to say, she was relieved that both Mrs. Czaja and her youngest sister had married within traditions she could at least understand.

Problems also arose with another of Mrs. Czaja's sisters who, Mrs. Giorgio felt, was marrying a boy who was of lower social status. This boy had only a high school education and, while Catholic, worked as a mechanic. Again, rather than becoming involved in this daughter's choice of a husband, Mrs. Giorgio sent her "financial adviser" to talk with her daughter. He reported that it was too late and that her daughter had already made plans to marry. Mrs. Giorgio says that she feels very hurt by this, but feels that there was very little she could do about it. Relations are much more cordial with a third daughter who teaches nursery school and is married to an engineer. This daughter has just returned to the Boston area from California, where her husband had worked on a space program. She describes this daughter as "very solid," a girl who knows exactly what she wants and how to get it. Because she is more conventional in her values and interests than the other children, Mrs. Giorgio finds it particularly easy to get along with this daughter.

A conservative and diffident woman, Mrs. Giorgio has offered guidance to her children on a take-it-or-leave-it basis. When her daughters become confused by this attitude and turn elsewhere for support, Mrs. Giorgio feels hurt and misunderstood. This feeling leads both to increased feelings of vulnerability and to a tendency to withdraw lest she be hurt further. This is seen most clearly in her refusal to talk with her daughters at times when she feels her own wishes have not been seriously enough considered. It is interesting to note that the most serious problems have arisen with the two youngest daughters, and it may be that Mrs. Giorgio had become particularly remote from her children by the time her last two daughters were born; she complained several times about the amount of work involved in caring for five children. Feeling overwhelmed by the burdens of parenthood, it is likely that she withdrew even more and that her withdrawal had an impact on the capacity of these two daughters for close and mutually satisfying relationships.

While it is difficult to substantiate such inferences regarding the impact of Mrs. Giorgio's own personality on her other daughters' character development, the data permit a more detailed study of her impact on Mrs. Czaja's personality and childcare attitudes. Given Mrs. Giorgio's preoccupation with maintaining her own independence and sense of separateness, her daughter's return to share her household has increased the stress she feels in her life, particularly since her daughter continues to search for the maternal care she felt was missing in her own childhood.

MRS. CZAJA: WE CAME HOME TO PROTECT MY MOTHER

Even to the most casual observer, it is obvious that Mrs. Czaja is an atypical Dorset resident. A woman of many talents, Mrs. Czaja makes most of her clothes and sometimes even prints the fabric from which she fashions her garments. Mrs. Czaja's patterns are the bold, colorful swirls and stripes first made fashionable by the Scandinavian imports. Indeed, even Mrs. Czaja's raincoat is fashioned from such colorful material. Of average height and weight, her colorful costumes look especially bright when set off against her coal black hair and flashing, bright, brown eyes. The colors also offer a sharp contrast to the rather colorless and unstylish clothes of her neighbors.

Being unusual is very important for Mrs. Czaja, and this emphasis pervades her entire expressive style. She completes the sentence stem "A woman should always be" with:

> . . . a slight mystery. She should keep her children guessing as to what next she is going to do. Even if it means cooking a different menu or dressing "mod." Becoming to her husband, yet always looking for a different look or feeling.

This preoccupation with being unique is of interest in its own right: it is important to understand the meaning for Mrs. Czaja of being different and to observe the effects of this concern on the manner in which she cares for her three-and-a-half-year-old son. However, another facet of this concern is equally important. Given Mrs. Czaja's artistic interests and her fascination with the avant garde, one might well expect that she would feel most at home in an area like New York's Greenwich Village or Boston's Back Bay or other communities inhabited largely by students and artists. Instead, she chose to return to Dorset to live with her mother, a decision only partially explained by her concern with her mother's welfare.

Mrs. Czaja has maintained a close tie with her mother and is very concerned with "family." This is seen in the response she gives to the sentence completion stem "Raising a family. . .," which was that it "is a bond or union which is complete with the help of mother, father, and *relatives*"[italics added]. As Mrs. Czaja views the ideal family, a family is only complete when all three generations are present. She sees little contradiction between her emphasis on being unconventional in most aspects of her life and returning home to live with her mother in the highly conventional working-class community of Somerset.

According to both Mrs. Giorgio's and Mrs. Czaja's accounts, Mrs. Czaja has always been fascinated with the novel and mysterious. Mrs. Czaja notes that she has always seen herself as "a bohemian, and perhaps even a freak." Mrs. Giorgio recalls how, as a child, Mrs. Czaja was fascinated by the occult and supernatural; there was a time when Mrs. Czaja was very much involved with astrology. Mrs. Giorgio also comments on how difficult it was for Mrs. Czaja to play games the way other children played them. She preferred to make up her own games or, if she played with others, to invent new rules. In view of this difficulty in doing things the conventional way, it is not surprising to learn that Mrs. Czaja had great difficulty in the parochial school and that she found it a burden to have to follow "Sister's" advice. While she was greatly attracted to the mystical elements of the church, she found the demands for obedience difficult to accept.

Since her mother was seldom at home and since the housekeeper made few demands on the children, there was little conflict at home regarding discipline. The one source of difficulty between Mrs. Czaja and her mother during her childhood, a problem that has continued to the present time, concerns Mrs. Czaja's "sloppiness." Mrs. Giorgio complained that throughout her childhood her daughter was sloppy and unkempt. In contrast to her sisters, all of whom were very tidy, Mrs. Czaja kept her possessions in complete disarray. In fact, Mrs. Giorgio used to refer to Mrs. Czaja's room as the "city dump," and the family was always surprised when Mrs. Czaja could find the thing in her room that she was looking for. Unable to explain why Mrs. Czaja differed so greatly from her younger sisters in this regard, Mrs. Giorgio finally concluded that there was something about being the second child which made it difficult to be tidy.

When Mrs. Czaja was little, her mother used to help her straighten her room and her clothes; when she began going to high school, Mrs. Giorgio refused to help Mrs. Czaja keep her possessions in order and began to nag her about the way she cared for her things. Throughout high school, this issue was a constant source of conflict between mother and daughter. Later, when Mrs. Czaja was married, Mrs. Giorgio tried once more to help her daughter run an "organized" household, but, according to Mrs. Giorgio, it was "a hopeless situation." Now that the two generations live together once more, there is renewed conflict regarding this issue. In fact, this is the only source of current overt conflict that was acknowledged by either mother or daughter.

The disagreement between Mrs. Giorgio and Mrs. Czaja regarding how Mrs. Czaja kept her belongings did have some adaptive aspects. First, the issue of Mrs. Czaja's "disorganization" provided a point of contact between mother and daughter: this conflict regarding Mrs. Czaja's care of her possessions is the only issue described by either mother or daughter during Mrs. Czaja's childhood in which they were both involved. Furthermore, in a family in which the ways the children were alike were emphasized and in which her mother had little time for children, being disorderly provided Mrs. Czaja with an identity, even if a "negative" one (Greenson, 1954a; Erikson, 1967). Mrs. Czaja's emphasis on being unique and unconventional may have the same origins: by adopting such unusual modes of dress and action, she could at least attain an identity as a separate and unique person and, hopefully, win her mother's attention.

While Mrs. Czaja's mode of dress clearly separates her from other Somerset housewives, her definition of self is much less clearly delineated than one might expect from her physical appearance. Mrs. Czaja sees herself as "nothing spectacular" and "unappealing." Indeed, both Mrs. Czaja's idiosyncratic language and her striking external appearance may, in part, be an attempt to overcome a deep sense of insecurity concerning her own identity. The projective test data support this hypothesis. Percepts such as the following are typical of Mrs. Czaja's responses to the Rorschach (VIII. 1 and VIII. 4):

> These look like some sort of rodents (?) They have those round heads and those . . . what do you call them . . . they look like that big fat rodent that's in South America, with the round heads, big gloopy heads and just there.

> These look like frogs. (E: What about them makes them look like frogs?) They're just blubby like frogs are blubby . . . they just sit there, too. They're bumpy . . . they don't have any legs and they just sit there.

The two most notable features of these responses are the failure to define body boundaries and the demonstration of great passivity. The creatures just sit there or are placed there; indeed, the frogs do not even have any legs with which to move.

The passivity and lack of innervation reflected in these Rorschach responses are seen elsewhere in the data. For example, Mrs. Czaja tells the following story to picture IAT Se7 in which "a woman in a raincoat is walking down the street. A path leads to the house portrayed in the background":

> This is probably, you know, a younger girl and she's just walking home. I don't think that this is her house, she doesn't seem to be turning in and she's just walking along and she's thinking about it . . . ah, daydreaming . . . really daydreaming. In fact, she is daydreaming so much that she's going to walk right into that puddle . . . mostly about studying and things like that . . . she's doing a term paper and has to go to the library and she's wondering how she can get . . . wishing someone would come along just then and give her a ride . . . she certainly doesn't look like she's bubbling over with emotion.

This story describes a passive and somewhat withdrawn orientation: the girl is so much lost in fantasy that she will walk right through the puddle. This is followed by the wish that someone would appear magically to give her a ride to the library. Unable to complete the story, Mrs. Czaja notes only that the heroine is not bubbling over with emotion, a comment which can only be regarded as critical, since Mrs. Czaja herself places so much importance in presenting a cheerful and colorful appearance.

Although she stresses the variety of her activities and the intensity of her involvement in what she does, Mrs. Czaja maintains a negative self-image and feels she has not realized her own potential. This is perhaps best symbolized by her observation, in response to the whole blot on Card V that "it's a butterfly . . . not really very beautiful . . . and it doesn't have its wings really out . . . really out full." Elsewhere, in the picture thematic data, she tells a story about a girl who was rejected from college, and, although the father reassures the heroine in this story and tells her that college is not everything, Mrs. Czaja observes about her heroine that "she's dejected and feels miserable, everything was probably just going along, and then she had this slip . . . and they're very, very concerned."

Other stories concern women who are too "fat and ugly" and who need to diet and women who feel that life is too much a chore.

Mrs. Czaja obtains a T-score of 76 on the MMPI Mania scale, which is more than 2½ standard score units above the mean for women. An analysis of the several subscales that comprise this scale indicates that the greatest number of items scored in the criterion direction concerns feelings of exaggerated self-importance and grandiosity. Once more we find evidence that Mrs. Czaja's emphasis on being different and "mod" represents an attempt to deal with deep-seated feelings of inadequacy.

While Mrs. Czaja's sense of inadequacy stems from many different experiences during both childhood and adulthood, the basic source lies in her perception of herself as a child whose mother ignored her. One sees, in her overt behavior, little evidence of such deprivation other than her habit of biting her lower lip when concentrating on a task like remembering and repeating a series of numbers but at a less conscious level, it is clear that she longs for what she feels she missed as an infant and resents her mother for having deprived her. Thus, older needs recur in the present situation and returning home to live with her mother represents both a renewed attempt to gain what she feels she missed as a child and an attempt to receive the support she feels she needs to succeed as wife and mother.

Strong evidence of Mrs. Czaja's feelings of deprivation appears in her sequence of responses to Rorschach Card II. 2:

1. This guy got kissed passionately . . . with lipstick (Mrs. C. smacks her lips together and makes a sucking sound to demonstrate).

2. Can I say what else it is? It's two dogs holding up the bone.

3. Here are some more mouths . . . these two look like faces . . . Guess that's all.

1. (E: Now the first thing you saw was———) Lipstick marks . . . you see a girl . . . a girl . . . girl with lipstick you know . . . all that blocked together . . . smootched [sic] together, it's just . . . indiscriminate kissing. (E: What about the lipstick makes it look like that?) What do you mean, lipstick makes it look like its . . . because it's splurshed [sic] and splobbed [sic] it's not, you know, like commercials, it's not exactly . . . tho, it's red.

2. (E: And the two dogs holding a bone. What about them makes them look like that?) Right here, there . . . they look like they're holding up a bone, you know, face to face. . . .

3. (E: And the two mouths, the two faces?) They just have mouths . . . marks for mouths and eyes; they have marks for them, too, way up in the top, they just set the faces up in the top way up there in the top.

1. (E: Can you tell me where you saw the kissing?) That place up here that looks like a lip mark . . . you know the shape of a lip (Mrs. C. draws around her

lip with her finger and then interrupts the test to ask if she might have a cup of tea. The E. indicates that they'll take a break after the inkblots are completed.)

2. (E: And the dogs?) See these little guys with the mouths, eyes, and ears. They're cute little guys, cute and cuddly . . . and that, it doesn't look too much like a bone, but what else would they . . . would dogs eat . . . you know, my favorite, their favorite would be a T-bone, you know, a steak, a T-bone steak, a T-bone steak bone. It really looks like a T-bone, see, like a T-bone steak there.

3. (E: And the mouths?) Right here, they have eyes, mouths, mouths, eyes, and eyebrows.

Mrs. Czaja's preoccupation with mouths and with oral activities is quite apparent. Although her first response is more closely associated with mature, heterosexual functioning, she then regresses to a more primitive level. That is, in her first response, the mouth is used both for mutually pleasurable activity and as a means for establishing interpersonal contact. But, in the regressed second response, the mouth is used only for receiving food. Finally, in the third response, her entire focus is the mouth, as a face. Thus, she has replaced all other senses with an enormous orifice.

Inquiry is made after each Rorschach response, and the location inquiry follows the inquiry for determinants. Mrs. Czaja became aware of her own consciously perceived need for nurturance when she asked the examiner to feed her. Postponement of her request served to intensify her preoccupation with food and nourishment, as seen in her perseverative activity concerning the T-bone steak (Atkinson and McClelland, 1948; McClelland and Atkinson, 1948). Formal regression in thought processes is seen in Mrs. Czaja's inability to articulate the third response. The reference to the "cute little guys" in the second response is consistent with Mrs. Czaja's performance throughout the test: her thought processes show considerable immaturity, and her modes of perceiving the world are essentially very childlike. As her childlike world view is only partially concealed by her apparently sophisticated interest in contemporary fashions and designs in dress and art, so her external appearance of vitality and activity belies her passivity, feelings of inadequacy, and desire to be fed and cared for on a more primitive and childlike level.

Unable to receive the mothering she wants so desperately, Mrs. Czaja experiences rage she cannot express or even admit to herself. Were she to do so, it might drive her mother even further away. On a more adult level, she contains her rage, because to express it would be inconsistent with her image of herself as a woman who has returned home to proffer care and nurturance to her elderly, widowed mother. This rage surfaces in Mrs. Czaja's one story about death that was told to Card IAT M1 in the picture thematic materials which, in almost all women, elicits stories about compatible mother-daughter relationships. This picture is one in which "a younger woman is standing up and talking with an older woman who is seated at a table on which there are two coffee cups":

(Long pause) . . . the . . . beginning is that they've received some depres . . . depressing news, something very, very disappointing, I don't know exactly what it is, but the older one is very bitter and the young one just sat there and there's no end . . . no solution to it . . . just time will take care of it. (E: Do you have any idea what the depressing news might be about?) Mm . . . (chews her lip) maybe a death, yes, I think it's about a death, a close relative, one of the members of the family . . . perhaps of the older woman. Perhaps she feels like she had some part in it, you know, feels guilty about what has happened . . . she doesn't, they don't, neither one of them say . . . can say anything, because there is nothing to say . . . they're both alone.

In contrast with Mrs. Czaja's other stories, this story has a very serious tone. That she is troubled by the picture is clear from the pause, longer than for the other stories, between the time she was presented with the card and the beginning of her story. Grandmothers are very important for Mrs. Czaja. Indeed, one of the reasons she gives for coming back to live with her mother is that, in this way, her son, Peter, will have had the experience of knowing a grandmother well.

It is interesting to note, in this context, that Mrs. Czaja's own mother was reared by her grandmother. By making the relative who died into the grandmother, Mrs. Czaja gives her story an ambiguous meaning. Either the person who died was her mother's grandmother—the woman Mrs. Giorgio viewed as her mother—or else Peter's grandmother, Mrs. Czaja's own mother. The ambiguity is further heightened by the fact that the "she" who feels guilty in the story is left unspecified and could refer equally to the older or the younger woman. If it referred to the younger woman, it could be an expression of Mrs. Czaja's own guilt. Mrs. Czaja's expressed hostility becomes particularly complex when we recognize that the death wish is expressed either toward her own mother or the woman that her mother viewed as *her* mother.

Mrs. Czaja's hostility toward her mother is intensified by the fact that it is *she* who is supposed to be caring for her mother and not her mother who is supposed to be caring for her. Considering her desire to receive rather than to give care and to be passive rather than active, it is understandable that she might wish that somehow the situation could be reversed and that she could be the recipient rather than the provider of this succor. This wish appears again (see discussion of Rorschach) in the story Mrs. Czaja tells to the well-known card in the Murray thematic apperceptive series (TAT 18GF) in which "a woman has her hand squeezed around the throat of another woman whom she appears to be pushing backwards across the banister of a stairway":

It's about two old spinsters who live together and . . . they've been living together for years and years and . . . this is the one that's been taken ill and goes out to work everyday and this poor little one . . . this woman's the one that stayed home and took care of the house and she . . . she doesn't . . . realize now that she's never going to go out again because she's so ill and that she will have to go out into the outside world see . . . so it's just a reversal; she goes out again and she stays at home . . . she feels . . . just feels sick about it, I mean she . . . but she knows that she's just going to have to face the truth that she's going to have to take care of her, and she's going to have to stay home, so she goes out to get a part-time job and supplements the income and she stays home and it's just the reverse. She doesn't feel too badly, I mean, she's sick; she feels that this is the best thing for her and she thinks that eventually she'll be better . . . maybe she'll be better . . . maybe they'll both go out together and take care of each other.

It is interesting that this picture, which shows an overt aggressive act (one woman strangling another), is seen by Mrs. Czaja as a nurturant scene in which hostility is denied. At the same time, strong feelings are evoked by the picture, for the story is somewhat disorganized. In this story, mere oral passivity is replaced by the depiction of two partners, active and passive, who, in the course of the story, first exchange and then share roles. In this story, Mrs. Czaja expresses the wish that she, the active one, who has to go out into the world, might become incapacitated so that her mother would have to take care of her. Mrs. Czaja's wish for care is intensified by her mother's strong belief that her children should become autonomous and able to manage their lives with little advice or support. It is not chance that this story was told to a picture that frequently elicits stories about angry mothers and daughters.

Mrs. Czaja herself has internalized her mother's feelings about the value of autonomy, but uses them as a way of gaining her mother's attention. How she does this is illustrated by her response to Card TAT 2 in which there is "a country scene: in the foreground is a young woman with books in her hand; in the background a man is working in the fields and an older woman is looking on":

This is about a farm family . . . this girl's not the daughter; I think she's more or less the younger sister, and this is the wife, and this is the husband and they probably want more . . . they probably want to work harder so that their child will . . . not their child, their sister because she's going to have a baby so probably the baby, they probably want the baby to have a better life, they're sending her to school and the wife has her work clothes on, the girl is dressed up to go to school; she'll do good, become a teacher or nurse and raise, she'll raise . . . she'll probably stay on the farm, but she'll be you know, a help to the family. (E: What are these people thinking, feeling?) Well . . . he's just thinking . . . he thinks it's hard work, 'cause it's his farm, and (sigh) she's just have . . . having a period of relaxation before she begins . . . starts her day's work, just sitting and meditating about that she can do and she's just going to school so that she can become a better person and come home and be . . . helping her mother.

This fragmented story describes the ambivalent feelings of a girl who wishes to stay home and help her mother, but who, largely because of her family's status strivings, is going out to learn to become a teacher or nurse. The heroine of this story accepts her parents' status strivings as legitimate, but, while she partially accepts these strivings, her basic concern is with finding a way of staying on the farm. By acquiring some skill, she can return home to be of even greater help to her family, thereby satisfying their status needs, as well as her own dependency needs.

Mrs. Czaja's own life parallels this story of the girl who returned to the farm. As a child, she was always a good student and enjoyed being helpful to the sisters at the parochial school she attended. Throughout her childhood, perhaps partly because her father was a physician, Mrs. Czaja wished to be a veterinarian. Toward this end she spent all her free time caring for a menagerie of sick birds, dogs, cats, and other small animals. Mrs. Czaja's mother, pleased that she showed such definite interests, arranged for her to help at a well-known animal dispensary in a neighboring community. Mrs. Czaja worked as a nurse's aid at this animal hospital during her first two years of high school, but afterward, since she appeared to be a "tomboy," she was sent to a parochial finishing school in Pennsylvania.

Mrs. Czaja was not party to her mother's or parents' decision to send her to finishing school. Mrs. Czaja's mother had heard from some of the sisters at her daughter's parochial school that Mrs. Czaja was a bit restless and rebellious and not sufficiently ladylike. The sisters asked Mrs. Giorgio if her daughter was receiving sufficient parental guidance and if parental standards of discipline were made clear to her daughter. Mrs. Giorgio, unwilling to make an issue of Mrs. Czaja's conduct at school, decided that the solution would be for her to go away to school where she would learn good manners and would become friendly with other girls from the appropriate social background. Mrs. Czaja's father thought this a wise decision, for, in this way, Mrs. Czaja would be sure to get a good Catholic education. Mrs. Czaja recalls hating every minute of boarding school. While she managed to graduate, she fought with the sisters about every rule and openly resented the fact that she had been forced to leave home. Although Mrs. Giorgio had hoped that Mrs. Czaja would become more "organized" at boarding school, the more the sisters pressured her into being tidy, the angrier she became.

After completing high school, Mrs. Czaja returned home to attend a local college. While she was still somewhat interested in science, she decided at that time to become a teacher. Although she was now able to live at home, she found college life so uninspiring that she dropped out after a year and a half and took a job as a waitress. During the next few years, Mrs. Czaja became what she herself calls the "black sheep of the family." According to her, she led a very bohemian life that climaxed in her moving out of her parents' house and renting an apartment with two other girls. What is particularly interesting about Mrs. Czaja's account of these two years is how miserable she felt while living this bohemian life. It was not her parents' opposition that made her miserable. Never, at any time, did her mother challenge her new life-style. Just the contrary, the source of her unhappiness was Mrs. Czaja's unfulfilled wish that her mother would intervene and, in this way, prove that she cared for her. Mrs. Czaja also felt very guilty about what she was doing. Indeed, after her father became ill, she viewed his illness as a retaliation from Heaven for her sinful conduct and left her job and apartment to move back home and help nurse her father through his last illness.

Mrs. Czaja views her father's illness as the event that caused the "greatest" change in her life. For the first time, she was needed and welcomed at home for the help she could provide, and, for the first time, she was valued not just for her service, but for herself. Even though her mother did not show her any special attention, the fact that she could contribute to the household brought her great satisfaction. During this time she returned to school and graduated with a teaching certificate so that she could earn some extra money by teaching and help out during this period of difficulty. Just as was the case with the heroine of her story, Mrs. Czaja returned home and became an important part of the family.

Mrs. Giorgio views the years Mrs. Czaja spent as a member of the "beat" generation prior to her father's death as entirely consistent with her stubborn and somewhat disorganized personality. She observes that Mrs. Czaja just had to "get it all out of her system," but notes that there were some benefits from this experience, since it was during her time as a bohemian that she met her husband. As Mrs. Czaja describes this meeting:

I had been going out with someone that everybody liked immensely, even my friends, and these two other friends of mine kept saying, you've got to meet this guy who's in Europe you know, and I said oh lookit, I've met enough of your friends and gotten into enough trouble already and I don't want to meet anymore and then . . . I just didn't want to meet him but they said, he's coming home from Europe today and we're going to have a big party and you have to come. So, I was going to bring this boy I was going out with and they said no, not to bring him because he was going to be there and (laughs) my husband showed up not with one girl but with two girls, to be, you know. I said, look, this is ridiculous, and I was hollering at him; this is really funny because he's got a birthmark, it's a red mark, it runs all over his ear and it really looks like a strange mark if you don't know what it is and I said, like, what is with this boy with two girls, not one, and he was engaged to a girl in California . . . and I said what are they trying to get me involved with so ah, I had nothing further to do with him, in fact I drove to his apartment with his two girl friends that night and came home and called my friend and blasted her the next day . . . but then one night I had gone over to her place, she had a wild apartment with all sorts of strange people, and it was at the time of the strangler [the Boston Strangler], so I had parked the car down the street and he insisted that I let him walk me to my car and, I guess we couldn't get the car out so he got the car out for me and then insisted that we shouldn't go home right away, and then . . . (trails off into reverie).

The relationship, begun in this manner, continued for several years prior to getting married when he was 24 and his wife was 21. During this time, Mrs. Czaja returned to live at home and completed her college studies. Mrs. Czaja's husband, a man with his own family difficulties, became an accepted part of her family and, especially during the difficult months after her father's death, was very important to Mrs. Giorgio in helping her to make the transition to widowhood.

According to Mrs. Czaja, her husband's family is one in which everyone feels alone and misunderstood. His father's family is Hungarian and his mother's family is German. While both sides of his family are devout Catholics, they do not believe in celebrating holidays or other important family events and lead an emotionally impoverished life. Her husband's mother died during his childhood, leaving her husband and his younger brother very much on their own. Almost immediately after her husband's mother's death, her husband's father married a woman somewhat younger than he. According to other family members, her husband's father had been seeing this woman during his wife's last illness. The family was very upset, since they felt he should wait until a respectable period of time had passed before getting remarried. Mr. Czaja cannot recall when it was that his father remarried, but believes that it was about three months after his mother died. Other members of the family think only a few weeks had passed. At any rate, it was such a short period of time that it caused a good deal of hard feeling that has not yet subsided.

Prior to his remarriage, Mr. Czaja's father had been a successful contractor. However, after his first wife's death, and his remarriage, there was a pathological shift in his character that was obvious to everyone in his family. Always an impulsive and distant man, Mr. Czaja's father now became totally introverted and began to drink heavily; his alcoholism made him unable to work, since a part of his job involved operating dangerous contruction machinery. As a result, Mr. Czaja's father was forced to give up this work, and his family was faced with a severe economic crisis. The solution was for both boys to go to work. For Mr. Czaja, this meant postponing plans for a career as an artist. Mr. Czaja was able to get a job in a distantly related field as a draftsman. Even though he had not yet completed high school, Mr. Czaja's artistic talents were obvious to his prospective employer.

During his high school days, Mr. Czaja's father and stepmother quarreled continually and finally separated. After some time they were divorced and then decided to remarry. Mr. Czaja's father began work as an assembly line worker, but his performance on the job was so poor that he was subsequently fired. He became belligerent and an alcoholic, and, finally, his wife was forced to commit him to the state hospital. During the past several years, Mr. Czaja's father has been committed several times, and, when at home, he is frequently violent and abusive to the rest of the family. This has caused a good deal of difficulty for Mrs. Czaja, and, after several painful visits, she refused to go back.

As was true of both Mr. McGorty (Chapter 3) and Mr. Murphy (Chapter 6), the greater closeness and emphasis on traditions of the Italian American family was a positive factor in Mr. Czaja's decision to get married. For each of these three men, coming from cultural traditions and family backgrounds emphasizing alienation from society and interpersonal distance, marriage represented the acquisition of a family and a cultural tradition that provided for closeness. It is also interesting to note that some clearly recognizable psychopathology was found in the nuclear families of the two men who, together with their wives, now share a household with their mothers-in-law. For Mr. Murphy and Mr. Czaja, sharing a household with their mothers-in-law provided them, at least in the beginning, with an experience they felt they had missed in their own parental families. Indeed, in the case of the Czajas, Mr. Czaja was at least as interested as his wife in moving back to Somerset to be with his mother-in-law. Mr. Czaja's mother-in-law has been teaching him Italian, and he has become quite fluent. Mrs. Czaja says that, at the time of their marriage, her husband did not know how to celebrate a holiday, but that he has gained a great deal of satisfaction from participating in saints' days, as well as birthdays. Neither was recognized in his own family.

Mrs. Giorgio reports that she has enjoyed teaching her son-in-law to speak Italian and understands the importance for him of her family's traditions; while she knows Mr. Czaja works hard and while she appreciates the ability he has to provide a comfortable life for her daughter, she also feels that Mrs. Czaja married beneath her social class and laments the fact that Mr. Czaja's father was only a "common laborer." She feels that his background will have a lasting effect on her daughter and their family. As she comments:

His are very, very frugal people; where he comes from, his family is not inclined to be like we were. They were/they didn't know . . . didn't know what a business was . . . what it means to be in business and to have a more comfortable life. Now he is a very smart boy, but the background of him is a very thrifty kind . . . a small amount of money means a lot to him because his people never had any money at all . . . they were very common sort of people . . . thrifty, not kind . . . in kind like a Yankee thrift, stingy thrift is what it is . . . was; very stingy, 'cause they're so afraid, and that's what my daughter doesn't see. When our father was alive he would take out . . . if we had three children, bring three things, ah three toys or three everything, and ah, this husband of hers is not that way. He doesn't want to spoil his children, he says, but I think it's because he doesn't want to spend the money. There's nothing I can do. I don't interfere because that's their business but . . . I am glad he is part of the family, but I had hoped that . . . she would marry a boy like the ones we introduced her to.

According to Mrs. Giorgio, she has never voiced her reservations to her daughter or son-in-law, and, while her sole disagreement with him concerns his failure to mow the lawn at what she considers the appropriate intervals, Mrs. Giorgio's concern about Mr. Czaja's background and his fears of economic insecurity are very much on her mind. Her hope is that through her continued relationship with her son-in-law, she may be able to influence his views in a manner more compatible with those of her own family.

While Mr. Czaja is often home, he has relatively little contact with his family, since he spends much of his time down in the basement working at his potter's wheel or upstairs in his studio, working on a sculpture. Mrs. Czaja worries that her husband works too hard and encourages him to spend more time relaxing. She also helps him with the mechanical and secretarial aspects of his work. For example, when he finishes a sculpture, Mrs. Czaja helps him wrap it and, in the case of out-of-town shows, is responsible for taking packages to the post office. She greatly values this time, for it gives her a chance to become involved with her husband's work. Being able to help wrap the final product means that she can spend some time with her husband in a way that contributes to his work.

As an extension of her interest in her husband and his work, Mrs. Czaja has enrolled in an adult education sculpture class. While her own work is, according to her description, "quite primitive," she tried, through learning more about her husband's work, to have more to do with him. In the past, Mrs. Czaja's husband was also much involved in bicycle racing, and, at that time, Mrs. Czaja used to go with him to the track and would read all the bicycle magazines in order to be able to converse with him about his hobby.

We see a parallel here between Mrs. Czaja and her mother. Just as her own mother had become closer to her father by participating in his work, Mrs. Czaja has attempted to become closer to her husband by becoming involved in his interests and helping him in his work. But, in spite of this effort, and, while she sees her husband as a "decent and regular guy, fond of the family and all that sort of thing," she feels that she has missed something in her relationship and that the closeness for which she searches has not been attained. This is shown in her story to picture IAT H4 in which "a young woman is seated on a sofa talking with a young man":

This . . . they're just sitting down and they're talking . . . just talking . . . then they find out they have nothing to say, so they . . . they just part. He looks like he's married but she doesn't look like it because she doesn't have a wedding band on, so I don't know. It's one of those little tricky situations . . . I can't seem to make up a story about this. They both look like duds, so I don't know where they could get together. She doesn't look like she's a very happy person, and neither does he, so I don't know, maybe they just found each other because they're both very unhappy and duddish . . . they . . . I don't think he's thinking of anything; they don't even have a picture in that picture frame. (E: And the outcome?) They're gonna part 'cause it's just a useless situation, I mean, you know that, mmm . . . she'll go on a diet or something, get a bit moody and then be alright.

What is striking in this story is the absence of any significant contact between these two persons. The fact that Mrs. Czaja says that she cannot make up a story shows that this is an extremely anxiety-provoking picture for her. Finally, she is able to admit that the heroine is not a very happy person and that the couple cannot get along together. Of course, recalling Mrs. Czaja's concern with "mod" and exciting experiences, the fact that the two persons in her story are duds is a serious indictment. Finally, unable to become involved in each other, they part.

It is also interesting that Mrs. Czaja does not place the blame for this inability to get along on the other person. The heroine's solution for the problem is to go on a diet; there is something within her such that if she could attain a better self-image she might attract a man with whom she might form a more satisfying relationship. Only after directing against herself the anger she feels toward the man and disparaging herself is the heroine of the story finally able to resolve the situation.

Mrs. Czaja tells similar stories to other pictures showing a man and woman together. In each case, the theme of the story is that of a man and a woman who have nothing to say to each other and who either part or decide on some mundane activity such as going to the movies to fill up time. In each such story, the feeling is one of emptiness and sadness.

Being drab, colorless, and unexciting is the one thing Mrs. Czaja most fears, for it symbolizes the idea that she might lose her own separate identity and that she will be overlooked. In addition, Mrs. Czaja's search for the exotic protects her from feelings of inner emptiness and depression that, if recognized, would lead to even greater internal discomfort. Just as her colorful curtains symbolize her denial of the colorlessness of the bleak Somerset neighborhood, Mrs. Czaja's exotic speech and dress represent her denial of her own feelings of emptiness and sadness. We have suggested that Mrs. Czaja feels that her mother deprived her of basic care as an infant. She interprets this deprivation as a sign that she was not worthy of attention. She now hopes that if she is sufficiently attractive and interesting she will capture her mother's attention. Thus, it is apparent that Mrs. Czaja's interest in appearing flamboyant and exciting has its roots in her childhood. That this interest has adaptive aspects may be seen in Mrs. Czaja's skill in making her own colorful and stylish clothes. Mrs. Czaja's interest in her husband's art may also have its roots in this need to be exciting and interesting.

While this interest in being mysterious helps to make life more exciting for her, Mrs. Czaja's fear of her own inner emptiness drives her to strive for uniqueness in ways that also lead to internal discomfort. At such times she becomes confused and depressed. Her search for being different and mysterious forces her into an extreme way of talking and acting that becomes exhausting. Perhaps it is for this reason that Mrs. Czaja continually complains of being tired. While she attributes this feeling to her household responsibilities, it may well be that she is unable to maintain the facade she presents without considerable effort.

The effect of Mrs. Giorgio's insistence on autonomy, while denying emotional warmth, has been severalfold. On the one hand, her daughter feels she was abandoned and deserted as a child and unworthy of receiving the attention for which she searched. On the other hand, Mrs. Czaja, too, believes in fostering separateness, but primarily because she perceives this as a way of winning her mother's approval and thus as a way of receiving maternal care. She cannot recapture what she never had. Mrs. Czaja values autonomy and separateness less because of their potential benefit for the next generation than because of the possibility that is then offered to her to get something more for herself from her own mother in the present.

Mrs. Czaja's belief in permitting autonomy in childrearing can be observed in her description of her childcare practices. Her basic attitude toward autonomy is particularly well documented in her story to Card TAT 1 in which "a young boy is contemplating a violin which rests on a table in front of him":

> Well he has to take violin lessons . . . and . . . he doesn't want to . . . so his mother says o.k. go on, play basketball or baseball. That's it. He had wanted to go out and play but he couldn't because he had to practice the violin and then his mother let him play. (E: What's he thinking about there?) Mad . . . kind of sad . . . not really crazy about it . . . not about playing the violin. He would rather be outside, so his mother said o.k. go on out and play.

This story departs, in an important way, from the story mothers typically tell regarding this picture, which is that the boy is forced to play the violin and his own wishes are not respected. In those instances in which the subjects tell stories where the mother relents and allows the boy to go out and play ball, it is typically in return for the boy's agreement to come back later and practice.

This story is one in which the boy does not want to play the violin and is permitted to go outside. Elsewhere, Mrs. Czaja says that she does not believe in forcing kids to eat or to do things simply because their parents want them to. Not surprising in this regard, Mrs. Czaja's score on the MAS of encouragement of autonomy was more than 2 standard deviations from the mean for the mother generation.

Mrs. Czaja was selected as a participant for the present study on the basis of her adaptive attitudes regarding the factor of appropriate closeness. It is not surprising that her attitudes regarding this issue are quite discrepant from the mean score for the mother generation and that she strongly believes that childrens' needs should be separated from those of their mothers. Mrs. Czaja also believes strongly in encouraging mother-child reciprocity and that infants give definite cues of their physical needs which mothers can learn to interpret. Finally, with regard to the factor of admitting to concerns regarding childrearing, Mrs. Czaja indicates somewhat greater reliance than other mothers in the present study on denial of childrearing anxieties. Mrs. Czaja's attitudes toward these childrearing issues, together with some of the factors that underlie these attitudes, are reflected in the following story she tells to picture IAT Fam in which there is "a living room scene: a woman has her hand on a little boy's shoulder, a baby girl is seated on the floor, and a man is standing to the side":

This little guy is going to go to camp right here . . . that's why he has his suitcase, and his father's going to drive him up to camp, but no/probably not camp, because they're all bundled up too much . . . maybe it's you know like . . . one of those winter weekends that, you know, fall weekends that they have with . . . must be a cub scout . . . and I don't know, the father doesn't seem to be too . . . he wants him to go but yet he doesn't want him to go, but the mother wants him to experience the outside world . . . so he goes . . . and he's gonna leave his little sister behind with her bunny. The father's a bit of a quim [sic] 'bout letting him go, because he thinks he's too young . . . ah . . . the grand . . . the mother said, this mother's very brave . . . she's going to be hard . . . she will want him to go . . . let him go . . . pat him on the back and send him out.

The mother in this story actively encourages the child to leave home and face the world on his own. First, she suggests that it is camp, but then Mrs. Czaja revises the story. Perhaps it is too difficult for her to admit to her desire to send the child away for such a long period of time, especially considering the fact that her son is only three and a half. That he is too young to go is seen by the father's observation in this regard.

Mrs. Czaja is made anxious by her wish to send the child out into the world, as can be readily observed by her use of an idiosyncratic word in discussing the father's opposition to the plan. She then makes an interesting slip and begins to refer to the grandmother. We know that Mrs. Czaja is not always clear in the way in which she uses this kinship term. However, one way she does use this term is in referring to her own mother in terms of her mother's relationship with her son. Presumably, the grandmother wants him to go to camp. However, even more likely, this slip may reflect Mrs. Czaja's own unconscious wish to have her mother all to herself and not to have to share her mother with her son. When the conflict becomes too great, Mrs. Czaja begins to deny her wish by noting that it is a sacrifice on the mother's part to have to separate herself from the child. However, with a pat on the back, she is able to send him out into the world and, one suspects, without a great deal of difficulty.

Perhaps it is because she is still so concerned with remedying deficiencies in her own childhood that Mrs. Czaja struggles with the issue of how she can care for her own needs within the confines of her roles as housewife and mother.

Some clue regarding both the intensity of her needs and the manner in which she has managed to resolve this conflict can be seen in her story to pictures IAT G6 rev in the Cohler series in which "a woman is washing dishes and in the background a little girl is seated at a table":

This poor thing thinks she is a drudge . . . she's just doing the dishes and she thinks she's the drudge of the year, doing the dishes, and the little girl's probably singing in the corner, happy, with the dishes . . . it must be after dinner or after breakfast, no, after breakfast, and she's thinking about what she has to plan for the day and what she has to do and she's just sort of thinking what a drudge she must be, and of how she hates housework. She does the dishes, which she hates, and finishes it and tries to have a good time . . . goes out. The little girl, 'cause her coat's there and her pocketbook and all . . . and the little girl's ready to go out and they'll probably shop, and maybe buy the mother a new dress and a . . . good lunch . . . they'll both have a good lunch, 'cause she's too tired to make lunch and do the dishes and wants someone else to do the work . . . make the lunch.

For Mrs. Czaja, doing housework detracts from one's ability to be interesting and colorful and leads to feelings of being a "drudge," which is just about the worst insult that Mrs. Czaja can imagine. Mrs. Czaja's distaste for doing housework is clearly reflected in this story, but, in contrast to many other women who have an equally strong distaste for housework, the heroine in Mrs. Czaja's story does not suffer. She finishes her task and goes out to have a good time.

At the same time, Mrs. Czaja's wish for "oral" supplies, a wish apparent in her response to the Rorschach, is also seen clearly in this story. The mother and daughter go out and get supplies for the mother: they buy her a new dress, and, because the mother wishes, for a change, to be fed, rather than having to feed others, they go out to lunch. That Mrs. Czaja does feel at least some conflict between her own needs and those of her children is shown by the fact that, in the story Mrs. Czaja tells, her heroine first mentions that she is going to buy herself lunch. There is a pause while Mrs. Czaja mentally reworks her story and, only after this pause, can she tell the story in such a way that the child's needs are also provided for.

While Mrs. Czaja's wish for succorance is seen quite clearly in this story, the fact that she can meet her needs within the context of her role as housewife and mother provides greater understanding of the reason why she showed adaptive attitudes regarding the MAS factor of appropriate closeness. In her daily routine, as well as in her picture thematic stories, Mrs. Czaja believes in tending both to her own needs and those of her child. She has not given up the hope of getting something for herself, and she believes that this is possible within the context of the maternal role. Since she is able to get the things for herself that she seeks, she is able to avoid some of the feelings of guilt, resentment, and self-sacrifice characteristic of women with less adaptive attitudes regarding this childcare issue.

Compared with the other mothers in the study, Mrs. Czaja has greater support available, both from her husband and from her mother. Since she and her mother keep house together, her mother has accepted some household responsibilities, somewhat reducing Mrs. Czaja's burden in caring for the house. In addition, since her husband has classes at irregular hours and spends a good part of the day at home, he is also willing to provide occasional babysitting or help with heavy housecleaning such as waxing the floors. While her mother would prefer not to have any babysitting chores during the day, she is willing, on special occasions, to take care of Peter, while Mrs. Czaja attends her printmaking class or takes care of her own personal errands.

The day in the Czaja household begins at a later hour than is the case in families where the husband/father must leave for work outside the home. In the morning, Peter usually comes into his parents' bedroom at about 8:00 and tugs at his mother until she is awakened. Peter and his mother then tiptoe out of the bedroom and allow Mr. Czaja an extra hour or so of sleep. Since her husband enjoys working late at night, Mrs. Czaja is willing to begin her daily round and to make his breakfast when he wakes up.

Since Mrs. Czaja finds it particularly distasteful to wash dishes, her attempts to avoid this task begin with breakfast. What she hopes is that her husband or mother will do the dishes for her. Having settled Peter in front of his favorite morning television program, she puts a load of laundry in the machine and settles down to talk with some of her friends over the telephone. After her husband awakens and she has prepared his breakfast, she vacuums, dusts, and occasionally washes the bathroom floor. Mrs. Czaja's mother would prefer that she do the bathroom everyday, but Mrs. Czaja attempts to avoid this chore and to clean it only once a week.

As the morning passes, Mrs. Czaja becomes increasingly resentful of her many household chores. Typically, sometime during the middle of the morning, she decides that she has done enough work and that she does not intend to waste her life doing housework. She says to herself that she will let the rest of the work go and do it later, gets Peter and herself dressed, and goes outside. Mrs. Czaja also admits to the resentment that she feels because her husband does not do more during the day to help her around the house. She says that when they were first married and her husband was still a student, he used to do more housework. Now that he is a professional and his free time is scarce, he is less willing to help her with the housework.

Getting Peter dressed always involves some sort of battle between them, but, once he is dressed, he enjoys being able to go outside for a walk. Mrs. Czaja observes about the walk:

We'll go out in the yard and ah . . . just sit down or he'll ride his little car; he has one of those crazy pedal cars or he'll play in the sand, and I try and always take a magazine out with me and if we go for a walk, I usually try to incorporate something for myself in the walk, so it's not just for walking, I'll go shopping or something like that.

This description of the morning outing suggests that Mrs. Czaja feels some competition between her own needs and those of her child. She finds it difficult to care for him simply because of his needs, but must be sure that there is something for herself as well. Mrs. Czaja's pregnancy has increased her feeling that childcare is a contest for supplies between mother and child. While she may have this view, once she is outside, Mrs. Czaja manages to care both for her own and for Peter's needs. Rather than feeling guilty or angry, she sets about to care for herself, while she is also caring for Peter. In this way, just as in her housework, she manages to avoid feeling either extreme self-pity or resentment toward Peter.

When Mr. Czaja is home, the family eats together. Mrs. Czaja's mother joins them when she is also at home. It is Mrs. Czaja's responsibility to prepare the lunch. Typically, she prepares soup for her mother, her husband, and herself and a hot dog or hamburger for Peter. Lunch is served on paper plates, unless Mr. Czaja volunteers to do the dishes and puts out the china. She is greatly relieved when her husband helps her out in this way.

Mrs. Czaja sees a difference between cooking and cleaning up: while she hates doing the dishes, she does not mind cooking. She takes frequent tastes of the meals she prepares, and, while she worries a bit about her weight, she enjoys sampling her cooking. She is able to provide some supplies for herself while she is cooking, but no such pleasures are afforded by washing the dishes. Rather, washing dishes evokes resentment that her own wish for care has not been provided, as seen in her story about the mother who does the dishes and then goes off with her daughter to get something for herself. When her husband or mother offer to do the dishes for her, Mrs. Czaja experiences a certain pleasure which suggests that her more basic needs can in some ways be satisfied by receiving help with activities especially difficult for her.

After lunch, Mrs. Czaja coaxes Peter to nap. At the age of three and a half, he resists taking naps, and, most afternoons, there is some struggle before he is finally in bed. Mrs. Czaja uses the resulting free time to relax. Mrs. Czaja's favorite form of relaxation is what she calls "transcendental meditation," which means that she sits and stares at some household object, while trying to relax each part of her body. She says that her husband and mother do not understand her meditation, which she first read about in a popular magazine, but she finds the "bliss" it offers to be very helpful in making the day easier for her.

Following her half-hour meditation period, Mrs. Czaja irons or reads. Nowhere in her narrative is there any mention of watching the television, except for the children's program that her son watches in the morning. When asked about this she reported that she found television uninteresting and preferred to read (preferably recent novels or science fiction).

In contrast to doing dishes or cleaning the house, Mrs. Czaja finds ironing a rather pleasant chore. Sometimes she reads while she irons, while at other times she reflects on her life and Peter's development. Not burdened by responsibilities at this time, she is free to indulge in her own fantasies. Sometimes while she is ironing, she gets an idea for a new print or for a new way of sewing a dress for herself.

On those days when Peter absolutely refuses to nap, Mrs. Czaja schedules a trip to the supermarket. She notes that the great advantage of going at that time is that Peter enjoys sitting in the basket and has some chance to rest. Peter particularly likes feeling and examining the fruits and vegetables, and Mrs. Czaja says she thinks he may have some of his father's artistic talents; according to his mother, he is especially interested in studying the various textures and colors. The supermarket has a coffee bar, and, typically, Mrs. Czaja indulges herself with a fresh doughnut and buys Peter an ice-cream cone before heading for the checkout counter.

Mrs. Czaja attempts to avoid other household errands durng the week, partially because Peter has become so "awful" in the car. Because she cannot control his behavior when she is driving she deals with laundries or other businesses that will pick up and deliver.

Later in the afternoon, when Peter has finished napping, he and Mrs. Czaja walk over to a neighbor's house. While neither of Mrs. Czaja's two closest friends lives in Somerset, she does enjoy visiting with two or three of her neighbors with whom she grew up. One neighbor is caring for her sick grandmother, and Mrs. Czaja makes a special point of visiting her as often as possible. Once more, we have a chance to observe the importance Mrs. Czaja places on the extended family and of maintaining close contact with older relatives. She speaks highly of her neighbor's concern for her grandmother and feels that this is an important part of a family's responsibilities.

Especially in the wintertime, the children in the neighborhood come over to visit Peter, because he has a somewhat larger house and a greater variety of toys. Mrs. Czaja spreads a large sheet of paper on the kitchen floor and encourages the children to finger paint or to use the tempra colors her husband has prepared for Peter and his friends. Mrs. Czaja notes with relief that her husband has agreed to wash the floor after these painting sessions. If he is home, he often comes into the kitchen to help Peter and his friends with their painting and is clearly pleased that his son enjoys this kind of play. Just as her husband enjoys painting with Peter, Mrs. Czaja enjoys reading to him. While she cannot understand why he likes to have the same story read over and over again, she is willing to do so. Sometimes, in the afternoon, Mrs. Czaja takes Peter to the library and selects books for each of them.

Before she became pregnant again, she also enjoyed wrestling with Peter and enjoyed walking with him down to the variety store and purchasing bags of potato chips for each of them to eat. Because she now has to watch her salt intake, she is unable to eat potato chips and since she cannot resist sharing his chips with him, she has solved her problem by not purchasing them and finding Peter some other snack he will accept. By finding activities like buying treats at the variety store with Peter, Mrs. Czaja is able to meet her child's needs, while simultaneously providing for her own strong oral needs.

If her husband has been out teaching in the afternoon, he often comes home quite cross. Mr. Czaja feels that his current students are not very interesting and are difficult to motivate. Mrs. Czaja would prefer that he "let off steam" rather than grumble all the time, but wishes for his sake that his teaching would provide him with more satisfaction.

Typically, after he has complained about the day, Mr. Czaja heads for the basement to get started with his printing. Peter joins him at this time and rides around on his tricycle, while his father works, providing Mrs. Czaja with additional time for herself. At such times she prefers to meditate once more, after which she begins preparing dinner. If his father is not home, Peter goes out to play with some of the neighbor children, so that Mrs. Czaja can generally count on this time for herself during the afternoon.

The task of making dinner typically falls on Mrs. Czaja, since her mother does not return from her volunteer work until around dinnertime. Mrs. Czaja notes that her mother has never been interested in cooking. With the exception of a few pasta dishes, her mother had always left the cooking to the housekeeper during the time that she and her brother and sisters were children. Since her father's death, her mother has experienced several periods of depression that have intensified Mrs. Giorgio's lack of interest in cooking. Sometimes, prior to leaving for the afternoon, Mrs. Giorgio prepares ravioli or noodles for spaghetti. In this case, Mrs. Czaja has only to turn on the stove.

When Mrs. Giorgio comes home, the family sits down together for dinner. Mrs. Giorgio says grace for the family and then they begin. Peter has few food fads. In the rare instance in which he refuses to eat, one of his parents assures him that race drivers especially like that food. Peter knows of his father's interest in racing and is already a willing companion for the occasional races that his father attends. While he eats a wide range of food, Peter is very finicky about new foods. Peter's parents never force him to eat what he does not want to eat. This sometimes annoys his grandmother, but Mrs. Giorgio believes that it is her daughter's responsibility to rear her children, and she very much avoids interfering in matters regarding Peter's upbringing.

Mr. Czaja and his mother-in-law often have their Italian lesson during dinner. So Peter has already learned a few Italian phrases. Less often, Mr. Czaja will discuss his classes at the college or some work he is in the middle of. Mr. Czaja looks forward to having dinner with his mother-in-law, as does his wife, and there is little discomfort created by the fact that the three generations eat dinner together. There is, however, some tension following dinner. Mrs. Giorgio brings her own plate to the sink and washes it, but refuses to take any responsibility for other dishes. Knowing his wife dislikes washing dishes, Mr. Czaja typically clears the table and puts the dishes in the dishwasher, while his wife gets Peter ready for bed.

On warm summer evenings, the Czajas may venture out with Peter after supper for a treat to the frozen custard stand. In the winter, Mr. Czaja retires to his study after the dishes are done, and Peter usually joins him there, while his father paints. Shortly before bedtime, Peter comes down to the kitchen, has some cereal, goes to the bathroom, has his last drink of water, and heads for bed. Since he has a continuing, but not serious, upper respiratory problem, Peter's mother gives him his medicine. She then arranges his stuffed animals at the appropriate place on his bed. Often, his teddy bear and his pig, his two favorite animals, are lost somewhere else around the house. At such times, mother, father, and grandmother join in the hunt for the missing animals. Peter then says goodnight to his grandmother and father and is put into bed by his mother. Before climbing into bed, he is expected to say his prayers.

Except for those occasional nights when his father or mother goes out in the evening, Peter puts up little fuss at bedtime. Sometimes he asks for another glass of water or juice or has to go to the bathroom. However, he is relatively quiet at bedtime. Since he still sleeps in a crib, he does not get out of bed after he has been put in for the night, and Mrs. Czaja acknowledges that there may be more conflict at bedtime when he has a bed of his own. As he is believed to be a very sound sleeper, Peter's parents have been reluctant to buy him a bed, fearing he may fall from it while he is asleep.

Once a week, Mrs. Czaja goes out to her printmaking class. At such times, her husband listens for Peter, although, if Mrs. Giorgio is still up, she is also willing to do so. Once or twice a week both Mr. and Mrs. Czaja go out to visit with friends or see a new movie. At such times, Mrs. Giorgio is willing to baby-sit, although, on a few occasions, she has told her daughter or son-in-law that she is tired and planning on retiring early. At such times, the Czajas ask a teenage girl in the neighborhood to baby-sit. It is clear to both generations that Mrs. Giorgio is not obligated to baby-sit and that she does so strictly as a favor. The Czajas are expected to approach her anew on each such occasion when they would like her to listen for Peter. The only problem with Mrs. Giorgio as a babysitter is that she is not very firm, and, on several occasions, the Czajas have come home from a late party to find Peter up and watching television with his grandmother.

If the Czajas are both home during the evening, Mr. Czaja usually works. If he is involved in getting some pictures ready for framing, Mrs. Czaja may help him. Typically, if he is painting or making prints, she prefers to read or look at a magazine in the living room, while her mother watches television. Less often she may watch a program with her mother, generally only when her mother asks her to do so.

Mrs. Giorgio generally retires to her room quite early. Mr. Czaja does not emerge from his studio until after both his mother-in-law and wife have already gone to bed. He takes the dishes from the dishwasher and may, on some occasions, do a little housework to clean up some particularly disagreeable mess. According to Mrs. Czaja, he is always willing to do this small part of the housework with only mimimal grumbling. Some nights, if he feels particularly inspired, he may work half the night. At such times, he is allowed to sleep as late in the morning as he likes. While she wishes that Mr. Czaja would not push himself so hard, the fact that his hours are so irregular does not disturb her. Rather, his somewhat flexible hours, together with his unconventional occupation, are consistent with her own value on being unconventional.

THE TWO GENERATIONS TOGETHER: DIVISION OF RESPONSIBILITY IN A THREE-GENERATION HOUSEHOLD

This determination to get something for herself was an important factor in Mrs. Czaja's decision to return to Somerset. While her determination is an asset in helping her to fulfill her roles of mother and housewife with somewhat greater ease, it is less clear that she has actually achieved her goal of developing a comfortably interdependent relationship with her mother.

In contrast with Mrs. Murphy and Mrs. Pescatore who live in apartments on separate floors of a three-story frame house, Mrs. Giorgio and Mrs. Czaja share both a common residence and a common household. Mrs. Giorgio's occasional resentment of Mrs. Czaja's sloppy habits has even greater impact, since the house belongs to Mrs. Giorgio. From one perspective, Mrs. Czaja and her family may be considered to be guests in her mother's house, and they must take into account Mrs. Giorgio's understandable concern that her belongings should be well cared for. As previously noted, the conflict between Mrs. Czaja and Mrs. Giorgio regarding Mrs. Czaja's disorganized living habits is rooted in her childhood. This conflict assumes an ironic cast when one learns that the Czajas sleep in the same room that Mrs. Czaja slept in as a child.

Mrs. Giorgio has tried to maintain a separate life, even though she shares a common household with her daughter's family. A self-reliant woman, she believes in managing her own life and preserving the autonomy that, as we have already seen, is a central aspect of her personality. As she answers when questioned whether there is anything that Mrs. Czaja does to be of help to her:

> I don't want . . . don't need her help. I get along pretty well what I can do. I wouldn't ask for her help though, I'm very independent. If I do need help with something, I would rather not do it than have to ask for her help.

That she does indeed maintain a separate life is documented by the fact that it was possible to describe Mrs. Giorgio's daily routine with hardly any mention of her daughter's presence in the household.

Mrs. Giorgio's first action of the day typifies the extent and the way in which she preserves her separateness. She goes into the kitchen to get her coffee, says good morning to the Czajas, and goes into the dining room to drink her coffee and watch the news on the television. Sometimes, she watches "Captain Kangaroo," a children's program, with Peter, while Mrs. Czaja begins her morning telephoning. According to both the mother and daughter, at this point in the day, there is little contact between them. Sometimes, Mrs. Giorgio goes back to her own room to watch other morning television programs, while Mrs. Czaja tends to her chores. Before going upstairs, Mrs. Giorgio makes a point of washing her own coffee cup. This gesture is particularly annoying to Mrs. Czaja who feels that her mother should be of greater help than she is around her own house. Mrs. Giorgio, on her side, feels that by washing only her own cup, she has made it clear to Mrs. Czaja that this aspect of the housekeeping is primarily Mrs. Czaja's responsibility, especially since most of the dirty dishes belong to the Czajas.

If Mrs. Czaja has not begun her vacuuming by midmorning or has not started in the bathroom, Mrs. Giorgio becomes irritated with her daughter's laziness and sloppiness and does these chores herself. As Mrs. Giorgio comments about her daughter's "sloppiness":

She doesn't have no/no system; that's the only disagreement; she's very disorganized . . . that's the only thing I have about her; she's very kind, very considerate, but she's not organized and does things as she wants to but I feel that if you have a routine, it's easier, but she can't think that way, like . . . sometimes she piles all the clothes up at once and she just does the washing and ah when it piles till she has no more left . . . and she does a washing, and, ah, I don't like that, so I tell her, say why don't you do a little bit at a time, then you won't have so much to do and . . . she doesn't want anyone to help her either . . . I say why don't you let me do it and she smiles and looks like she's about to agree and then says, no, I'll do it myself, so she does it, so I say from here on out let her do it the way she wants to, and I can't do anything about it because this is the way she wants it and her husband goes along with it and I am no one to say anymore because I'm only the mother now, second place, you're not, no more first place, so I says well, if her husband's happy, I'm happy. Let her be a slob, who cares.

Mrs. Czaja's response to this criticism is to let her mother vent her feelings without necessarily changing her ways of doing the housework:

She wants to get everything all done and everything and I never do anything, and you know I usually put things off till the last minute and she gets very disturbed about this and like . . . sometimes I won't make the beds before 10:30 and things like that and she is kind of disturbed about those things; most of this disagreement between us concerns the house . . . I just think that housework is drudgery and she thinks it's essential. So we usually have a good fight, screaming, and ah . . . I'll end up doing it in my time and she'll just grumble about it a little while and she'll say, "I don't know what I'm going to do with you" and that's it. I don't like to be sloppy, which sometimes does occur, but I don't think that the housework is that essential.

After she has finished her housework and her morning's television watching, Mrs. Giorgio dresses and goes shopping or to her volunteer job at the hospital. Whenever possible, she makes a point of getting out of the house before lunch. She feels that the Czajas should have time by themselves during the day, and, since Mr. Czaja is frequently at home for lunch, she leaves them alone for this meal. In addition, Mrs. Giorgio is very conscious of her weight and feels that if she stays home she will eat more than she should. Mrs. Giorgio prefers to window-shop early in the afternoon, stopping at a cafeteria for a dish of yogurt. However, if Mrs. Czaja has to go out in the afternoon, her mother may return home to baby-sit. Mrs. Czaja has particularly soft teeth that require constant dental attention. Mrs. Giorgio will baby-sit while Mrs. Czaja goes to the dentist. At such times, she may prepare an Italian dish like ravioli for dinner. After dinner, overt conflict between mother and daughter again centers on dishwashing. Mrs. Giorgio admits that there is some conflict about doing the dinner dishes and agrees with her daughter that the easiest compromise is for her son-in-law to do them. Sometimes, however, especially when her son-in-law is trying to finish a painting, Mrs. Giorgio will do the dishes for several nights in a row. Typically, after about a week of doing the dishes, Mrs. Giorgio's own resentment becomes such that she asks her son-in-law to resume doing the dishes.

Mrs. Giorgio makes a point of coming into Peter's room before he says his prayers and, on occasion, reads him a story. After she has said goodnight to Peter and his parents, she returns to her own room to watch television and get ready for bed. Mrs. Giorgio says that her daughter's requests that she baby-sit are sometimes quite annoying. If she is tired, she has little difficulty refusing to baby-sit, especially since there are several teenage girls in the neighborhood. But if she is not planning on going to bed early, she may even encourage the Czajas to go out for the evening and allow her to baby-sit. She concurs with her daughter's observation that she is too lenient as a babysitter, but offers the excuses that her grandson does not look tired and is engrossed in the television program, so that he refuses to go back to bed.

While Mrs. Giorgio enjoys her grandson's companionship, she does not see eye-to-eye with her daughter on how he is to be reared. When the issue is the simple one of giving advice regarding the treatment of an ailment, Mrs. Giorgio is perfectly willing to make suggestions:

> Well illnesses, then we all help then; we give him the medicine; she takes the tempera-ture; she knows all that because we brought . . . we've been brought up that, you see, it's not that difficult, we automatically take the temperature and put them (the children) in a cool place, wash them down; that's automatically done here because that's what we're used to doing. She gets a little panicky; I say, take it easy; it's not too bad you know confirming and quieting her down because she's inclined to be a little bit nervous. For the rest, there are many ways in which I disagree on how she is raising him but I feel it's not my business to comment.

Even though she herself is lenient with Peter ("that after all is a grandmother's right"), Mrs. Giorgio criticizes her daughter for being much too lenient with him:

> He's spoiled, but she's only got one . . . he does a lot of times what he wants to do and the mother goes along with it because it's her only child right now she asks him what he wants for dinner, which I think is wrong, but it's her child . . . they try to understand children more today than we did, and try to please them more, because when I had three in three years, I just couldn't do a lot of individual attention. I had the meal and it was there and they went along with it because I couldn't fuss too much. I was busy with the telephone, with the work, and couldn't give them the individual attention that she does with her own. Sometimes he talks back and sometimes he shouts at her and she says don't do that, but if I had when my children did that, I'd give them a little crack in their back and that's it, and I'd say you don't answer back but she don't tell him that and so she lets him get away with everything, but I could never tell her that.

In spite of Mrs. Giorgio's insistence that her daughter is not aware of her feelings about the way in which she is rearing her son, Mrs. Czaja is completely cognizant of her mother's feelings:

> With Peter it's very hard because I'm very easy-going and she was always a very strict mother and this really bothers her a lot; like, if he spills cereal all over the floor, I usually

let him do it and just let him get the cereal out and play with it, fill his trucks with it, but this really disturbs her and he'll take all the cans out and roll them across the floor and she can't stand cereal on the floor, I think, more than anything else. It's not that he's doing anything wrong; I just think that this is the kind of thing that really bothers her. I think that my mother was much stricter because she had five of us so that we were more in order. I think . . . my mother had help all the time . . . I do spank him, but even though she complains that I am not strict enough with him, I don't think even she was as strict with us when we were little as much as when we were more grown up and I don't know how I'm going to face that situation because I haven't arrived at it yet.

While Mrs. Giorgio does not object to her daughter and son-in-law's return to Somerset to share her household, neither is she overjoyed by their return. Mrs. Giorgio's daughter's moving in has intensified her need to exhibit her separateness and independence, because she fears that her daughter may have returned to live with her because she felt that her mother could not care for herself. Even the most casual mention of this possibility evokes Mrs. Giorgio's anger. Mrs. Giorgio herself notes she is well able to get around and is by no means, senile or unable to manage her own affairs. She comments:

After my husband died, there was a time when I was quite sad. I guess everyone must have worried about it at the time. I never stop thinking about him . . . but, I have found other things to do. I like to run my own life and not have to worry about when I am expected home or whether I have to give up my own plans in order to sit . . . I am happy to do so when it is convenient for me.

Mrs. Giorgio's greatest fear is that her daughter and son-in-law will become permanent residents. Mrs. Giorgio says that she would rather go to an old people's home than to have to give up her privacy in her own home. She is anxious for her son-in-law to begin the job he has been offered at a college in a neighboring state. The Czajas would then be close enough by to come down to Somerset for occasional holidays, but far enough away not to invade on her privacy.

In explaining why they moved in with Mrs. Giorgio, Mr. and Mrs. Czaja give different reasons. Mrs. Czaja says her husband was not really happy with his teaching and that he worried about his mother-in-law's safety in such a large house at a time when a prowler was terrorizing the area. Mr. Czaja insists that it was not he who wanted to move back to Somerset, but rather his wife who worried about her mother living all by herself. That her sister and her sister's husband had returned to the area just at the time that she herself was considering returning did not deter Mrs. Czaja from her decision.

Several levels of reasons can be advanced for Mrs. Czaja's desire to live again with her mother. Mrs. Czaja believes that rearing a family is "a bond or union that is completed with the help of mother, father, and relatives" and that she is "a woman, wife, and daughter." Only the first two of these three aspects of her conception of herself could be realized as long as she was living apart from her mother. In addition, she strongly missed her contact with her own grandparents as a child and hoped that her children would be able to have the important contract with grandparents she had missed. Of greatest importance was Mrs. Czaja's desire to receive the maternal care she felt she had missed as a child. With her brother and sisters grown up and no longer living at home, there would be a new chance to make up for her childhood. In a way, Mrs. Czaja was living out the prophecy of her own picture thematic story about the woman who grew up, went through school, became a teacher, and returned to be a help to her family. In sum, Mrs. Czaja was strongly motivated to find an excuse for returning home to share a household with her mother.

Mrs. Czaja's husband was equally motivated to find the family he felt he had never had as a child. That he has achieved his goal is apparent, for he says he has never been happier than he is now that he and his family have moved into his mother-in-law's home in Somerset. Mr. Czaja has room to spread out his many prints and to prepare for future shows. The basement provides an ideal place for the printing process he uses. Mrs. Czaja is equally pleased with the arrangements and feels that she is closer to her mother than ever before. While she complains about the manner in which her mother indulges Peter, the way she talks about this pampering suggests that she receives a certain vicarious nurturance through having her mother take care of her son. Since Mrs. Czaja's second pregnancy, her mother has been spending more time helping her and Mrs. Czaja feels that her mother's house is the best possible place to spend the first difficult weeks after the baby is born. She looks forward to having her mother care for her during this time.

Only Mrs. Giorgio is less than happy with the present arrangement that she feels is an intrusion on her own life. Mrs. Giorgio also finds the emotional strain of living with her daughter exhausting. Mrs. Czaja has internalized her mother's feelings of deprivation and of not having received sufficient care as a child. In trying to understand why her mother did not respond to her need for care, she has come to see herself as a woman of little consequence. Mrs. Czaja's identification with her mother's own childhood feelings of deprivation and lack of care leads her to redouble her efforts to be appealing and attractive, with the hope of arousing her mother's interest in her. Rather than avoiding relationships, as is true of her mother, Mrs. Czaja attempts to be sufficiently unique and appealing that others will notice and respond to her overtures. The primary target of this effort to be appealing, Mrs. Czaja's mother, is at best an elusive one. Mrs. Giorgio does admire her daughter's sense of style and her artistic talents. However, the more Mrs. Czaja attempts to interest her mother in a relationship that would finally lead to some childlike care for herself, the more Mrs. Giorgio flees from the very prospect of such a relationship and the harder Mrs. Czaja must then work to interest her mother. Such a struggle can only leave mother and daughter feeling depleted and exhausted.

At this point, it is difficult to determine how the impasse between Mrs. Giorgio and the Czajas will be resolved. Mrs. Giorgio hopes that the Czajas will be sufficiently attracted by the teaching position Mr. Czaja has been offered that they will soon move away. Mrs. Czaja, while acknowledging that the present living arrangements are only temporary, continues to postpone the date when they will be moving to Mr. Czaja's new job. What Mrs. Czaja did not consider in her story about the girl who returns to the farm after becoming a teacher is that while she can show her appreciation by coming back to help out, her mother may not welcome this help.

CONCLUSION

We have seen, in the present study, that both Mrs. Limpari (Chapter 3) and Mrs. Giorgio view their daughters' proffered help as a means by which their daughters can control their mothers' lives. Rather than enjoying the help and attention their daughters wish to bestow on them, these grandmothers make considerable effort to avoid such help. It is probable that each of these grandmothers is aware of the motive underlying this desire to be of greater help, for each of the two daughters, Mrs. McGorty (Chapter 3) and Mrs. Czaja, seeks to have her unfulfilled dependency needs met through a continuing close relationship with her own mother. Given both the strength of the daughters' needs, and the nature of their own mothers' personalities, disappointment and frustration are likely to be the only result for both generations.

It is perhaps an irony that in those two families in which daughters express adaptive attitudes toward the issue of separateness, they continue, as adults, to seek a closer and more emotionally satisfying relationship with their own mothers. In each instance, as a result of prior life experiences, and from quite different motives, the mother resists the idea of such a relationship and insists on remaining separate. Mrs. Limpari, because she has been reared in a restrictive home, believed that her daughter should be permitted the autonomy she herself had been unable to realize. Mrs. Giorgio, because she had been reared in a home where the outside world has viewed with suspicion and because of her isolated childhood which impaired her capacity for closeness, spent much of her energy fleeing from relationships which would require that she further compromise her own "autonomy." In each case, these mothers reared daughters who, while they believe that children should be separate, nevertheless still long for a closeness with their own mothers which is impossible to realize.

Each of these daughters has used her talents to bring about the reunion she seeks. Mrs. McGorty has used her legal skills to design a condominium project that will permit her to come home to Tower Point and to share a residence with her mother. Mrs. Czaja has used her artistic abilities to create a kind of uniqueness so striking that even her mother is forced to admire her style. Sears, Maccoby, and Levin (1957) first observed that mothers who trained their children more strictly in independence had children who were, in fact, more dependent. In an analogous way, in the present instance, daughters of mothers who were socialized into being separate and self-reliant express the belief that their children should be reared in a similar way. At a less conscious level, these daughters still search for the attention and care they felt they never received from their own mothers.

It is also worth noting that the one family in which the daughter shows adaptive attitudes regarding the issue of separateness, and in which the two generations have actually joined forces to create a common household, is a household in which the arrangement is perceived as only temporary. In contrast to Mrs. Murphy and Mrs. Pescatore (Chapter 6) whose relationship is so complex that it is impossible to separate the needs of each from the other, Mrs. Giorgio and Mrs. Czaja are clearly separate persons with very different needs. While the tension of living is greater in the Pescatore-Murphy household, there is, as well, a sense of permanency there that is not apparent in the Giorgio-Czaja household.

To understand the impact of a woman's mother on her own present childcare attitudes and practices, it is necessary to understand the woman's perception of her mother as well as to understand her mother's own needs, values, and beliefs. It is the combination of the personalities of mother and daughter, as well as their continuing relationship, that, together, will influence the daughter's childcare attitudes and practices.

CHAPTER 6

Mrs. Pescatore and Mrs. Murphy: Intergenerational Conflict in a Two-Family Dwelling

LIVING TOGETHER–LESS ADAPTIVE ATTITUDES

Woodland Park is a nondescript working-class community, shoved between the inner city and the more opulent and spacious suburbs. The Pescatore and Murphy families occupy two stories of a dull gray three-family frame house on one of the town's main streets. The front hallway is decorated in aging, flowered wallpaper that contrasts sharply with the freshly varnished floors. Above the table where the mail is left, there is an ornate crucifix, originally hung in that spot by Mrs. Pescatore when her family moved into the house, shortly after emigrating from Italy when she was in her teens. After her marriage, Mrs. Pescatore was given the first floor, where she has lived ever since with her husband and three children. Following her father's death, Mrs. Pescatore's mother decided to enter a nursing home. Since the second floor was vacant at the time of the marriage of Mrs. Pescatore's eldest child of three children and only daughter, Mrs. Pescatore invited her daughter to live on the second floor in exchange for a nominal rent. For the past six years, this daughter, Mrs. Murphy, her husband, and their three young children have lived in the second-floor apartment.

It should be emphasized that Woodland Park is not a suburb, defined as a well-manicured and parklike area with homes well spaced apart and surrounded by trees and shrubs. While there is much the same emphasis on privacy, with backyards the focus of family activities, and little contact between neighbors, Woodland Park is a very unpretentious working-class neighborhood on the fringe of a highly industrialized area specializing in the manufacture of heavy equipment. Factory smokestacks can be seen from most Woodland Park homes, and factory employees, together with tradesmen and a few salesmen, comprise the Pescatore's neighbors. The Pescatores and Murphys know few of their neighbors, and, as Mrs. Pescatore has tersely observed: "We have our own life, and they have theirs." As a matter of fact, these two families scarcely know the family that rents out the third floor of their own house. For members of both generations of this family, the focus of attention is on the relationship between family members and, in particular, the complex and conflicted relationship between Mrs. Pescatore and Mrs. Murphy.

199

MRS. PESCATORE: LIFE IS A HEAVY BURDEN

The term "generation gap" has become fashionable in social science writing over the past few years. While the term has been much misused, the problem to which it refers is very real. Middle-aged adults, in particular, feel very acutely the difference between codes of acceptable behavior that were current during their own youth and early adulthood and present-day statements of acceptable behavior. Mrs. Pescatore is such an adult: modern life has gone too fast for her and she is bewildered by what she reads in the papers and sees on television. In her conversation, she talks continually about "old-fashioned" people who possessed simple virtues and knew instinctively the correct modes of behavior. It is not simply that she believes things were better in the old days but that she believes she could tell young people a thing or two about how they should behave. Furthermore, she takes these changes very personally; she feels burdened by them because she thinks they threaten her very existence.

That Mrs. Pescatore feels bewildered and persecuted by contemporary existence is not immediately apparent. Mrs. Pescatore presents a solid physical appearance. A stocky woman in her early fifties, she has curly gray hair and intense black eyes. Mrs. Pescatore's house appears compulsively neat and well organized. Mrs. Pescatore takes pride in her newly redecorated kitchen that overlooks the backyard and beyond to a thicket of dense underbrush.

Beside the romantic religious pictures decorating each room, there is a different photograph of Mrs. Pescatore's oldest son who had just returned from duty with the marines in Vietnam and is planning to finish his college studies in engineering, while the younger boy has decided not to attend college and lives with three other young men in an apartment in the city. Mrs. Pescatore shakes her head when asked if her boys have any romantic inclinations and complains that she does not think she will live long enough to see them get married. She says she worries, particularly about the youngest boy whom she believes is "up to no good." She complains that his two roommates are much too wild and is sure tht they have been "into mischief," by which she means that they have been drinking and spending their paychecks on women.

Mrs. Murphy tells her mother not to worry so much, but Mrs. Pescatore will not be comforted, for she feels that her daughter is too identified with the new generation to understand the seriousness of her youngest boy's situation. Besides, Mrs. Pescatore worries about Mrs. Murphy and the kind of marriage and life that she has. She is especailly concerned that Mrs. Murphy's husband is so often away on business. In sum, she is a woman beset by worry about the present and fear of the future. Mrs. Pescatore's worry manifests itself in her stated fears about her grown children.

We have suggested that Mrs. Pescatore is a worrier; she is deeply involved in her children's lives, even to the point of being intrusive. It is not that she wants to burden her children with the responsibility of visiting her, for she leads a busy life; Mrs. Pescatore's concerns center around the fact that she feels her children are unable to manage without her continual support. While the two boys have moved out the house, indicating a kind of independence, her daughter feels more need for this support. This need involves Mrs. Murphy in a complex and uncomfortable relationship with her mother that is ultimately unsatisfying for both mother and daughter. It is this relationship, its determinants, and its effects on Mrs. Murphy's marriage and childrearing practices that must concern us in the present instances.

Mrs. Pescatore was born in a small town in southern Italy. The fifth of 10 children, Mrs. Pescatore early learned to shift for herself. Even after moving to the States, life was arduous. Mrs. Pescatore's father earned very little as a laborer, although he spent long hours away from home at his work. Mrs. Pescatore remembers that by age 7 she was expected to make the beds, sweep, and do the dishes. By age 12, she was already working as a farmhand and was expected to bring in a respectable income each week. Misbehavior was absolutely not tolerated in Mrs. Pescatore's family. Mrs. Pescatore's mother often resorted to physical pusishment, using the nearest available kitchen tool to give the offending child a serious beating. Nonetheless, her childhood was not totally punishment and drudgery. Then, as now, a favorite family leisure activity was a backyard picnic. Weekends were a time of particular enjoyment, since each child was allowed to take 10 cents from his or her weekly earnings to go to the picture show. The movie followed a big noon meal where the family sat down together for the only time all week. Since the family could not afford a car, excursions to the beach or zoo were made by public transport. But since the family was so large and the carfare was so expensive, relative to the total family income, such special trips became vacations in themselves. Mrs. Pescatore's parents were very strict. On weekdays, when she was in school, until she was 16, Mrs. Pescatore was supposed to be in the house by 8:00 and in bed with the lights off by 8:30. Dating was totally out of the question and Mrs. Pescatore says that she was not allowed to go with "a fellow" until she was 21. She notes that her parents were more strict with her older brothers and sisters than they were with her.

With so many children in the family, neither her mother nor father was very available to Mrs. Pescatore as a child. The data indicates that Mrs. Pescadore has very vague and disconnected images of her parents. Since Mrs. Pescatore's parents did not give her the opportunity to form an intense relationship with either of them at any point of her childhood, she has never developed the ability to form more than shallow relationships with anyone. This aspect of Mrs. Pescatore's personality is apparent in her response to the Sentence Completion test, where, if a stem refers to a particular person such as mother, father, or husband, she is either unable to complete the stem or else supplies a stereotyped answer. Examples of this pattern include the stem "My mother and I . . ." to which she replied, "are good friends," and "Whenever she was with her mother, she . . . " to which she replied "would make her happy."

When the situation does not permit a stereotyped response, as in the TAT, Mrs. Pescadore's stories about mothers and daughters show little connection between the generations. While there is some vague hint of mother-daughter conflict, the stories refer largely to the daughter's desire to escape from the situation, a desire never fully realized. For example, in response to TAT Card 2 (Country scene: in the foreground is a young woman with books in her hand; in the background a man is working in the fields and an older woman is looking on), Mrs. Pescadore tells the following story:

> Oh . . . this looks like it might be out in the fields . . . girl's probably not happy being on the farm . . . maybe she's thinking she's got to leave it . . . and then again she's thinking . . . looking it over how nice . . . but she doesn't look too hap . . . too, she, she looks as if she's thinking, in a thinking mood . . . going off to school . . . probably doesn't care to stay home . . . I don't think anyone is speaking . . . she's just thinking, I think, about it . . . (long pause. E: What's going to happen?) Mm . . . she may leave it or else she may continue with it; I really don't know.

In this story, Mrs. Pescadore avoids any discussion of the relationships between the three major persons in the picture: the young girl with the books in her arms, the man plowing the fields, and the pregnant woman leaning against the tree. It is clear that home offers the heroine of this story little satisfaction, but then there is also little pressure to seek any alternative. No one is speaking here, and no one is interacting. Nothing is happening; the situation is completely static.

Another story that reflects Mrs. Pescatore's relative lack of involvement in relationships is told to another mother-daughter card, TAT 7GF (an older woman is sitting on a sofa close beside a girl, speaking or reading to her. The girl, who holds a doll in her lap, is looking away). This card is particulary interesting in view of the fact that most subjects identify not with the motherly woman who is reading the story, but with the little girl to whom the story is being read (Cohler, 1975). Mrs. Pescatore tells the following story to this card.

> Oh now this, ah . . . looks like a mother and ah/could be/could be mother and daughter . . . she looks like she's reading her a story or something . . . the little girl doesn't look too interested though, whatever she's reading to her . . . seems to be far off . . . (long pause) . . . She can't be very old; she still has a doll in her arms, but she doesn't seem to be interested in what she's tell/reading to her. I don't think she could care less I think (laughs) in what she's saying . . . the story seems to me in what she's reading . . . and then again . . . it could be a mother, could be a nursemaid, but the mother's just reading on there it seems . . . and what's going to happen . . . when she gets through reading the story the little girl isn't going to care anyway, I think.

The little girl in this picture obviously finds little satisfaction in the care her mother gives her. The mother, in turn, does not provide individualized care for the child, but is largely oblivious of the child's desires. The child then responds to the mother's indifferent care with her own indifference. Neither of these two persons is at all involved in the situation and neither has any impact on the other.

These stories suggest, as do the responses to the Sentence Completion test, that Mrs. Pescatore received little in the way of individualized care from her mother and that, while her physical needs may have been met, Mrs. Pescatore felt little emotional connection with others in the family.

When Mrs. Pescatore's mother did give her attention, it was generally to discipline her. Her mother was a temperamental woman who had little time or patience for misbehavior. As Mrs. Pescatore notes, in discussing her relationship with her mother:

Well, if I did anything wrong regardless, she wouldn't even wait for an explanantion; she would just give you a good beating and that was that. She wouldn't wait for my father to come home; she'd use anything she had around the house, a wooden spoon, a spatula and she would run and take after you. I remember one time a library card came and a book was way overdue; well she wouldn't ask for a reason why you didn't get back to the library; when you came home at night you just got it with whatever she had, and it really hurt.

Both the facts that she received very little from her mother in the way of tenderness and approving attention and that attention often came in the negative form of serious beatings help explain some of the origins of Mrs. Pescatore's anxiety and insecurity. There is even less evidence that Mrs. Pescatore's father had a positive impact on her character development. In the entire series of projective tests there is not one mention of a figure who could represent the father. Nor is there any evidence of involvement with any other person, either in fantasy or reality. Mrs. Pescatore's detachment and isolation from others is nowhere better shown than in her story to IAT picture Se8 (A young woman stands holding a cat and looking out the window):

This woman has got a cat; she might be an animal lover. She's maybe staring out of the window and might be lonely . . . she's holding that cat as if she really loved it but her eyes look sad. I don't know, maybe she's a lonely woman; she's alone and she just loves the animals and maybe she doesn't like people . . . in the future she'll stay with her animals.

A variety of stories have been told to this picture by mothers and grandmothers. A frequent theme is that of a woman holding a cat and either waiting for her family to come home for a meal or watching some scene taking place outside. While there is often a tone of wistfulness in the stories told to this picture, there is seldom such isolation from others. Indeed, there is some question of whether Mrs. Pescatore can even relate to animals, as seen in her comment about the story's heroine that "she's holding that cat as if she really loved it." There is not even certainty that she loves animals.

Finally, it is important to note that Mrs. Pescatore could provide only 14 Rorschach responses, all of which were ordinary and unimaginative. Of the 14, only 1 made reference to human beings. On Card III, she saw the blot as two people: "And then, it could be a . . . people, the way they've got them . . . yet if they stand up straight, they'd seem like they could be people." This is the most impoverished and unelaborated form in which the popular human movement response could be given, and, while there is some attempt to impart action to the blot, it barely qualifies as a popular human movement response. These data are consistent with our previous observations concerning Mrs. Pescatore's lack of involvement in relationships.

The church, more than human relationships, plays the most important role in Mrs. Pescatore's life. Indeed, it was through the church that she made perhaps the most meaningful relationship in her life, for it is through the church that she met her husband. Mrs. Pescatore's family always went to Mass together on Sunday morning and sat together in the same row for more than 15 years. Both her mother and father were very devout, and Mrs. Pescatore early adopted their ardent devotion to the church. Mrs. Pescatore's fiancé's family was also devout, and the two families had a good deal of contact through church functions. Since her family and her husband's family were well acquainted, it was considered proper that he court her. The couple was married when they were 23. Mrs. Pescatore says the wedding service she and her husband had was the most memorable event in her life. She saved her wedding gown for her daughter's marriage, and tears come to her eyes when she describes walking down the aisle on her father's arm. She views her husband as honest, diligent, and sincere, but also as set in his ways and very stubborn.

Mr. Pescatore has worked the 4:00 to 12:00 shift at the industrial plant where he has been employed as a machinist since he first began work at age 17. Only after his three children had grown up did he acquire sufficient seniority to be able to work the day shift. Since he had to travel some distance to and from work, he was generally not home until well after midnight. He slept late in the morning, so that by the time he arose, the children had already left for school. Since work began at 4:00, he was often gone before the children had returned from school. The only time he saw his children was on the weekend.

In contrast with Mr. Limpari (Chapter 3) who regarded it as his right to play cards with his friends and who was seldom at home, Mr. Pescatore seldom went out on those nights when he was not working. Mrs. Pescatore notes that they lived so far away from friends and relatives that an evening out required considerable advance planning. For the first years of their marriage, she and her husband could not even afford a car, further limiting the possibility of social contact. Mrs. Pescatore describes her husband as a man who preferred to stay at home and putter around the yard on the weekend or to watch television. The only real hobby he ever had was that of poultry farming for a few years after their marriage. Mr. Pescatore's use of his leisure time is consistent both with the family's insistence on social and physical distance from others and with the family's reliance on privacy.

In contrast to Mrs. Limpari who goes shopping either alone or with her son, Mrs. Pescatore goes shopping with her husband. The Pescatores also go visiting with their friends two or three times a month. The closest friend they have is Mrs. Pescatore's cousin; since the time she was a little girl, Mrs. Pescatore has visited her cousin's family on Cape Cod each summer. During the winter, for over 30 years, she has visited with this cousin each Wednesday and Saturday evening. The cousin's winter home is in another suburb, about 30 minutes by car from the Pescatores. Visiting takes place either in Woodland Park or, more often, at the cousin's house. The Pescatores drive into the city on few occasions, and they are even less likely to visit or shop in Tower Point.

On the basis of their marital relationship, visiting patterns, and common interests, Bott (1971) would classify the Pescatores as a couple showing a "joint conjugal role-relationship.'' Between husband and wife, most tasks are done in common, and there are few duties around the house assigned solely on the basis of the sex role. Furthermore, most visiting is done jointly by husband and wife, and the couple have few separate commitments beside these joint interests in which they are both involved. This pattern is somewhat unusual among second-generation Italian American families such as the Pescatores. It is also unusual, since the Pescatores have a fairly tightly structured kinship network.

It is difficult to obtain a clear picture of the changes that have taken place in Mrs. Pescatore's relationship with her husband from the time the children were growing up to the present. Mrs. Pescatore notes that when the children were younger, Mr. Pescatore helped out more around the house than at present. At that time he did the dishes, cleaned the house, and worked on the lawn. The discipline was largely up to Mrs. Pescatore, since Mr. Pescatore had little contact with his children. Mr. Pescatore always agreed with his wife's childrearing practices, but then he had very little idea what they were, since he was either asleep or at work when the children were home. According to Mrs. Pescatore, they spent little time discussing the children's future and preferred to take each day as it came. Mrs. Pescatore says her husband did feel that education was very important and that the children should go to college. Interestingly enough, in view of the minor role he played in his children's upbringing, Mr. Pescatore's major complaint at the present time is that his children do not spend enough time at home or pay sufficient attention to his wife or himself.

Even though Mr. Pescatore spends most of his spare time at home, he and his wife have little contact with each other. Mrs. Pescatore has observed that she and her husband have been together for so long that they have little to say to each other. Typically, Mr. Pescatore comes home complaining of being tired, and, after an early supper, he reads or watches television for a few hours until he falls asleep in his chair. Mrs. Pescatore, on the other hand, complains that she has difficulty falling asleep and putters around long after her husband has retired for the night. Sometimes she runs a load of wash through the machine or cleans her kitchen. At other times, she may visit with her daughter or talk with her over the telephone.

Mrs. Pescatore's difficulties in feeling close to others also play a part in the creation of distance between her husband and herself. This is illustrated by her story to Card 10 of the standard TAT series (a young woman's head against a man's shoulder):

Now how's this . . . oh, I don't know what this is . . . is that part of a person or . . . I don't know what that is . . . it looks like a person up against something . . . oh, I don't know (deep sigh) . . . 'cept with her eyes shut . . . I can't figure that . . . could be a person . . . woman, with her eyes shut, up against something I don't know . . . like a wall or an obstacle.

It is significant that this picture creates such difficulty for Mrs. Pescatore. As with other relationships in her life, Mrs. Pescatore's inability to sustain closeness means that any demand for a relationship is perceived as an obstacle. Elsewhere, in telling stories that involve a man and a woman, the couple is either involved in some problem neither member of which is able to resolve or a man is attacking a woman. In each case, the fault is entirely that of the man, and the woman has no part in the conflict. These stories, as was true of Mrs. Pescatore's other stories, have a very static quality, and one has no sense that she even wants to find a resolution to situations. In these stories, as in other stories she tells, the statement "she could care less" comes up over and over.

Mrs. Pescatore is an anxious and confused woman, unable to derive satisfaction from relationships, unable to find much pleasure in her own pursuits, and bewildered by changes she vaguely perceives in the world about her. Mrs. Pescatore's present adaptation is also affected by her extreme difficulty in achieving clear communication with others. In a series of reports, Wynne and M. Singer (1963a, 1963b) and M. Singer and Wynne (1965a, 1965b, 1966) have shown that parents of young adult schizophrenics are particularly liable to communicate with their offspring in ways that blur and obscure reality. One such communication problem described by Wynne and M. Singer (1966) is a "closure" problem in which the listener does not know whether he or she has been invited to share the other's communication or whether speaker and listener have, in fact, been sharing a common focus of attention.

This closure problem, believed to be particularly significant in the development of psychopathology in offspring, can be observed in the projective testing situation, which is a communication setting where one person must share her focus of attention with another. To the extent that a subject is unable to share her focus of attention with another, we may assume that the same communication problem arises in the family, such as when one person asks another a direct question.

Mrs. Pescatore's Rorschach protocol is replete with such examples of closure problems and, particularly, those in which responses are given in the negative form. This form misdirects the communication and denies to the listener the certainty that there has been a communication. Some examples of this negative response from Mrs. Pescatore's record include these:

Card I: Can't be a bat. Well, maybe it's a bat.

Card III: Can't be a monkey . . . animal . . . No it couldn't be a monkey.

Card V: Can't be an animal split in half.

A communication problem of the intensity demonstrated by Mrs. Pescatore impairs her capacity to share her feelings with others. Thus, it is not surprising that Mrs. Pescatore fails to understand changes in the social order and fails also to communicate her concerns to others. Nor is it surprising to learn, as Mrs. Murphy informed us, that the youngest boy was hospitalized a few years ago for a nervous disorder she said was diagnosed as "some kind of schizophrenia."

In her mid-fifties, Mrs. Pescatore feels distant, isolated, and confused and experiences difficulty communicating with others or experiencing meaningful relationships. She is worried, insecure, and moody and reacts to others in a quarrelsome and challenging manner. This means that she cannot allow others to help her and reacts to requests for help from her family with the feeling that they are too demanding. The only human relationships that give her security are those over which she has complete control. Thus, she constantly attempts to manipulate those tenuous relationships she does have, especially those with her children. She explains her actions by saying that she wants to be sure her children are safe from what she believes to be the dangers of the modern world. In actuality, this concern is generated not so much out of an interest in her children's welfare as it is from her view of her children merely as extensions of herself.

Mrs. Pescatore has a very stereotyped working-class Catholic value system. The attitudes she has regarding the male and female roles are also in keeping with her background; it is the woman's job to rear her children and the man's job to bring home the income. She claims that her husband never directly helped with childcare, although he did some work around the house, and that she would not expect that he should do so. She noted with pride that her husband never spent any of his weekly paycheck before giving his earnings to her. He is not, she insists, the kind of man who would spend his earnings on drink.

A religious Catholic, Mrs. Pescatore performs all necessary obligations to the church, but her participation seems to offer her less of a sense of spiritual satisfaction than in the past. She says this is due, in part, to the many changes that have taken place in the church, such as alterations in the liturgy and in obligations; she criticizes those within the church who have prompted such liberalization and especially objects to changes in the Mass that permit so much English to be spoken. While readily admitting that she did not understand the Latin, she says simply that it is better that the Mass be said in Latin.

In her childrearing attitudes, Mrs. Pescatore was among the most conforming of the grandmothers. Indeed, based on her response to MAS, there was a 92% probability that she would be placed in the grandmother group. Mrs. Pescatore believes very strongly that children's expressions of aggressive feelings should be curbed, although her score on this attitude factor of the MAS ranks third among the four grandmothers. She also believes that mothers cannot achieve reciprocity with their children and that infants are unable to form social relationships. In this attitude she ranks second among the four grandmothers.

As expected from the very fact that she and her daughter share a common residence, Mrs. Pescatore does not believe that children should be permitted to live an independent existence apart from their parents. She believes that such separation is bad for the child and that, even though it may impose burdens on the mother herself, she should not be allowed to develop any separate interests apart from childcare. In this attitude, Mrs. Pescatore scored third among the four mothers, although her score is almost identical with that of two other grandmothers. Only one of the four grandmothers (Mrs. Scardoni) shows a greater denial of concerns relating to childrearing than Mrs. Pescatore. This would be expected in light of her generally stereotyped attitudes and values. Only one of the four grandmothers believes less than Mrs. Pescatore that she is unable to meet the baby's physical needs. It is striking that Mrs. Pescatore, while endorsing such conformist attitudes, can admit that she feels so unable to care for babies or to recognize and meet their primitive physical needs. We can characterize Mrs. Pescatore's childcare attitudes as remarkably typical for her own generation, with the exception of the lack of confidence she feels in caring for the physical needs of babies. Most characteristic of her attitudes, however, is her belief that it is harmful for the child to express his or her own feelings or to achieve either emotional or physical distance from the mother.

Mrs. Pescatore's impairment in forming close relationships is demonstrated once again when she says that babies cannot form reciprocal social relationships with their mothers, as well as when she says she cannot understand the babies' needs. Her belief in the importance of a close and binding relationship between mother and baby can be understood in terms of the fact that she thinks of children primarily as extensions of their mothers' own basic emotional needs.

Looking back on the way she reared her own children, Mrs. Pescatore says she thinks she was easy on them compared to what she should have been. She is very critical of all three of her children who, she says, are lazy and do not appreciate the value of hard work. Discussions of the ways she reared her children inevitably led to memories about how she had been reared. In discussing her own childhood, she commented:

> I worked all the time, from morning to night, baby-sat, worked, did chores at home, had to scrub clothes; my life as a youngster was more working than anything but in those days I felt it was a pressure, so I didn't make my own daughter do this kind of work because I had had to do it and I wanted her to do it, no . . . I just took my life more serious because it was all work.

We see here that Mrs. Pescatore in some ways wanted her daughter to suffer, just as she had suffered, but was unable to carry through in these ways. The slip Mrs. Pescatore makes concerning how she wanted her daughter to do this work demonstrates her own ambivalence. She feels that her lack of demandingness led to character faults in her children, but also recognizes that she and her husband were far better off financially than her own parents had been.

In other respects, too, Mrs. Pescatore was far more democratic with her children than her parents had been with her. She noted that when her parents had had company, the children had been fed earlier and were either sent to bed or were expected to wait in another room. In contrast to this more formal style, on the few occasions that Mrs. Pescatore and her husband had dinner guests, Mrs. Murphy and her brothers were always invited to eat with them. When Mrs. Pescatore was young, she was never allowed out at night or even late in the afternoon; however, when Mrs. Murphy was in high school, she was permitted an occasional evening movie or soda with friends. When Mrs. Pescatore was young, if she did not do as her mother told her to do, she could expect severe punishment. Things were quite different between Mrs. Pescatore and her daughter:

> My daughter, when she had to do dishes, she would do them when she was ready, so, since I couldn't wait, I'd do them myself; you know, I would say, "Do the dishes" and

later on, she'd say, "go lay down and read a book. I'll do them sometime," until she was ready, and then I'd get up myself and do them. If this had happened to me when I was a girl, I would have been beaten with the closest thing around.

Mrs. Pescatore reports that her daughter was the easiest of her three children to rear. She was a compliant youngster in elementary school and high school, went to church, and never got into trouble. From both Mrs. Pescatore's account and that of her daughter, there have always been incessant quarrels between them about Mrs. Murphy's weight. That this battle between mother and daughter still rages is clear from Mrs. Pescator's comment:

I didn't think she would stay as heavy as she has. I thought that as she grew older she would be more sensitive to that; I didn't think that she would get to be so big as she is, even bigger after she had her children. I thought that it would bother her some, and I particularly get after her for being neat . . . all the time, you know, I'd say why did she grow up to be like that . . .

Beside her physical appearance, Mrs. Pescatore had little concern with what her daughter would do, except that she hoped her daughter would marry a man with a "9 to 5 job."

In Mrs. Pescatore's comments about her daughter's childhood, as elsewhere, what emerges is a picture of a distant, constricted, conformist, and emotionally impoverished woman, more concerned with order and routine than with spontaneity or involvement. Mrs. Pescatore's main concern about her children is that they should act in accordance with her own wishes. A woman with difficulty in establishing meaningful relationships or communicating effectively with others, her intrusive childrearing practices seem to have been largely in the service of her own inner conflicts, including her anxiety about changes in the world around her that she could not comprehend.

MRS. MURPHY: THERE'S NO GLAMOUR, BUT THERE'S SECURITY IN WOODLAND PARK

"When I gave my address to the man who sold us our furniture, I still couldn't believe that I had decided to move back home." With these words, Mrs. Murphy began her description of how it had happened that six years ago she began living upstairs from her mother. Certainly, she had not intended for things to work out in that way when she left secretarial school in her hometown and headed for Bohemian theater life in New York, 10 years ago.

Mrs. Murphy and another girl took the train down to New York and settled in a furnished room near the theater district. They began making the rounds in search of bit parts in some promising play. They were not surprised at being unable to find jobs. Looking back on that more carefree time, Mrs. Murphy admits that she did not really believe they would be hired. One night, several months after arriving in New York, while having supper in a restaurant frequented by lesser notables in the theater, she met an old friend from Bethany who had numerous contacts. This friend, a young man, introduced her to another young man from Bethany, also involved in the theater and also new to New York, who was looking for companionship. Following a year's courtship, the Murphys were married. Both husband and wife agreed that they should make their home in the Bethany area and that Mr. Murphy would commute to his work in New York. Besides being involved with the technical aspects of the theater, Mr. Murphy was also teaching drama courses in several New England colleges. Thus, from the beginning of their marriage, Mr. Murphy has often been absent from home.

Money was very scarce for the Murphys, and, when Mrs. Murphy's mother offered the second floor apartment for $40 a month, just enough to offset taxes and electricity, it seemed like an attractive possibility. In addition, as was true of Mr. McGorty (Chapter 3), Mr. Murphy felt there was little warmth in his own Irish family and looked forward to the greater expressiveness of his wife's family. The Murphy's apartment is quite spacious: there are three large bedrooms that open off a long hall, a living room, a large kitchen, and a sun parlor which catches the late afternoon sun most of the year. The two boys, William, age five, and Ralph, age three, share one bedroom. Barbara, age four, has a room to herself. The children may also use the sun porch as a playroom. Mr. and Mrs. Murphy use the other room both as a bedroom and as a study. Mr. Murphy has a desk and shelves for his books and papers. Mrs. Murphy has a special display case in which she keeps her prized collection of glass and ceramic swans.

Mrs. Murphy maintains that the savings afforded by her mother's offer was the most important reason for moving into her mother's house. She did acknowledge that she was worried about how things would go when her husband was away, but, at the time, believed that they would be moving into their own place within a few months. Mrs. Murphy's husband had the possibility of making more money working with a resident theater company in Bethany, and it looked like his weekly commuting to New York was strictly a temporary arrangement. Several years later, the Murphys are still living in the same gray house on Bridge Street, and, while Mrs. Murphy insists that she is on the verge of looking for a new apartment, perhaps even in another state, the comments she makes do not convey any feeling of conviction. It is important to determine what factors were important in the decision Mrs. Murphy made to move back home and then to understand why she still feels so unable to move. To resolve these questions, it is essential that we know more about Mrs. Murphy's own personality and life experiences, including her marriage and her feelings about childrearing.

The most striking aspect of Mrs. Murphy's physical appearance is her intense dark eyes and her matronly figure at age 28. Like so many other mothers in the study, time has been harsh with Mrs. Murphy, and it is safe to predict that when she reaches middle age, she will show the characteristic physical proportions of the grandmother generation.

Many women in the mother generation fear what they themselves see as a growing congruence with their own mothers' physical appearance, personality, and lifestyle as their own children grow up. Mrs. Murphy is less concerned with the prospect of becoming like her own mother than she is with the conflict she feels between a life of glamour and excitement as represented by her husband and the world of theater and a life of stability and security sharing her mother's home in Woodland Park. What troubles Mrs. Murphy is that she feels she has the worst of each possible alternative. She says that if she could relive her life she would prefer to start again in New York and further explore the world before settling for Woodland Park.

Mrs. Murphy's brief experience in New York stands in sharp contrast with her childhood in Woodland Park. The only girl, and the oldest of the three Pescatore children, Mrs. Murphy was born three years after her parent's marriage. At the time of her birth, Mr. Pescatore was just establishing himself in his work. Mrs. Murphy was the only child for five more years, until her brother was born. Another brother was born the following year. Mrs. Murphy describes her childhood as simple and uneventful. Mrs. Murphy's mother saw her as an obedient and conscientious youngster, a bit more stubborn than her brothers, but reasonable in her requests for autonomy. As a teenager Mrs. Murphy seldom went out on dates. Mrs. Murphy's mother notes that even at that time she was quite heavy and appeared almost matronly. Mrs. Murphy never attempted to stay out late with her friends and was a faithful churchgoer. At one point, she complained about how plain and routine her childhood had been, and noted almost wistfully, "but then there's little glamour in Woodland Park."

Mrs. Murphy says that her parents provided a very stable environment when she was growing up. However, as she talked about her childhood, it became clear that Mrs. Pescatore had left her children little room for flexibility or for deviance from clearly established modes of behavior. Mrs. Murphy notes, in talking about her childhood:

My mother was a stickler about clothes. She thought everything should match. We had no choice about what to wear because she kept all our clothes and only gave them to us at the appropriate time.

She goes on to comment:

The household was always run on a strict schedule and everything was done just so by a certain time. She's extremely precise, and everything has to be just so or has to be in a certain spot . . . all her clothes have to be lying down just so. If there was a wrinkle in my dress, she would find fault for it.

Without ever using the word, Mrs. Murphy describes a woman who was extremely overcontrolling. Even Mrs. Pescatore's husband was run according to a schedule. According to Mrs. Murphy, the reason her father preferred the evening shift at work was so that he could be out of the household as much as possible; she says that he was unable to fit into the regime. Mrs. Murphy also believes that it was because of her mother's continual advice that her father gave up raising poultry, for it was easier not to have such a hobby than to have to continually listen to his wife's criticism.

Mrs. Murphy did not find her mother's care to be very satisfying or very relevant to her own needs. Rather, she perceived her mother's almost intrusive interest in her activities as arising from her mother's own personality. That is, her mother's concern that her clothes match and that her room be spotlessly neat did not originate from her mother's concern with Mrs. Murphy as a person. Furthermore, since her mother's overprotection prevented her from learning about the world around her, such smothering concern was viewed as essentially destructive. This emerges quite clearly in the following story, told to TAT picture 7GF (An older woman is sitting on a sofa close beside a girl, speaking or reading to her. The girl, who holds a doll in her lap, is looking away):

This is a very lonely little girl . . . it's a lonely Sunday afternoon, the girl is left alone with her governess again. She has been sheltered, doesn't know about life . . . and she's waiting for the Sunday to go by. I think Sunday night means that Mommy and Daddy come home from wherever they've been for the weekend, and that it will mean one hour's pleasure for them . . . her life will go on like this until she's more mature and can find her own interests but that basically it will leave scars on her, that when she will get married, she will make sure that she's always with her children.

Since her brothers were so much younger than she, Mrs. Murphy must mave felt like an only child for much of her early childhood. It is interesting to note that although her mother never left the house she felt that her mother was seldom available to her. The girl in the story complains about being sheltered from the world just as Mrs. Murphy complains about this same overprotection in describing her own childhood. Mrs. Murphy's solution to the problem posed by her own mother's overprotective care is, however, to repeat her mother's pattern and remain continually with the children, although perhaps more able to meet the children's needs as separate persons. From Mrs. Murphy's story, it is reasonable to conclude that the separation problem seems to have been continued into the next generation. This is also clearly reflected in Mrs. Murphy's observation that the poor mothering the girl in the story received would leave lifelong psychic scars.

Having felt that she had received so little from her mother besides lifelong psychic scars, it would be expected that Mrs. Murphy would turn to her father to obtain what she had not been able to receive from her mother. In fact, even though he was so often absent, Mrs. Murphy had complex and mixed feelings about her father. She was fascinated with his hobby of raising poultry, and some of Mrs. Murphy's most positive childhood memories are of watching her father collect eggs for the family's breakfast. However, her feelings about her father's hobby and her wish to receive nurturance from him were complicated by her wish to take her mother's place with him.

Mrs. Murphy's wish to be cared for by her father, together with the anxiety evoked by this wish, is found in Card V of the Rorschach, the popular "recovery" card, where most subjects, even when they have had a difficult time providing responses of an acceptable form level, are able to provide the response of a bat or a butterfly. Mrs. Murphy's first response to this card, and a response impulsively offered, is "it looks like a chicken when you've cracked it open, extended it open." Mrs. Murphy continued with a justification of her response in terms of her own experiences: "My father was in the poultry business . . ."

We must explain why Mrs. Murphy offered this response of such a poor form level. It shows us that the intensity of Mrs. Murphy's wish to be cared for by her father evokes such strong feelings that her capacity to test reality is impaired, and she offers a response that is a poor match with the blot. Mrs. Murphy elsewhere commented on how angry she was that her mother had forced her father to give up his favorite hobby. She also maintains that her parents had a poor marriage with frequent quarreling. What is important here is not the accuracy of Mrs. Murphy's belief, but rather the strength of her feeling that her mother controlled her father. Mrs. Murphy was both angered and frightened by these feelings about her parents' relationship. In the first place, when Mrs. Murphy's mother no longer allowed her father his hobby, she was both denying Mrs. Murphy nurturance and was also preventing her father from nurturing her. However, in addition to denying to Mrs. Murphy the possibility of receiving nurturance from her father, the poultry incident also confirmed Mrs. Murphy's feeling that her mother did not respect her father and that she could be a better wife for him than her mother. To some extent, Mrs. Murphy's wishes were quite usual for a daughter; a girl first learns to be a woman by receiving and by responding to her father's affection.

This wish for her father's affection is quite clearly seen in the first Rorschach blot, where Mrs. Murphy gives the response of a bat or vampire, but acknowledges that this response refers to the large center detail that is typically seen as a woman. She then says that "both the vampire and the bat take the form of a woman" and goes on to describe the vampire-woman as a figure behind the curtains who is pulling the drapes apart in response to a request.

Just as it is likely that, in her fantasy, it is her father who is pulling apart the drapes, it is also likely that it is she who is the vampire-seductress. Mrs. Murphy's fantasy self-image of the beautiful and seductive siren contrasts sharply with the reality of her present life as an overweight housewife.

Mrs. Murphy's search for glamour is really a search for her father and an expression of her wish to replace her mother as her father's wife, certainly a role that must have seemed very exciting for her. Unable to obtain the beauty and glitter for which she searches, and unable to relinquish her wish for her father's affections, Mrs. Murphy experiences both frustration and anxiety.

Because Mrs. Murphy perceived the possibility of receiving such affection from her father as dangerous and likely to bring about angry retaliation, she developed strict internal controls over expression of affection toward her father and, in time, came to feel that her impulses were sinful and bad. Indeed, she felt so guilty regarding these impulses that she needed to seek repentance. This is illustrated by the following story told to IAT picture Se7 (A woman in a raincoat is walking down the street. A path leads to a house portrayed in the background.):

This is a fall day and ah, this girl has reached a decision which is that she's going into a convent. She has come from a nice family and has graduated from high school; she has worked in business school for a couple of years; she doesn't like it that much . . . she has gone through life a very happy girl but has found, ah, felt some inner . . . something inner inside her and she wants to join the convent . . . she has already told her boyfriends that she is going in . . . Her end will be that she will join the convent and that she will be very good whether in the missionary field or in straight teaching . . . and at last she will feel happy, safe and content.

The fact that the girl in the picture has also gone through business school is an indication of the extent to which Mrs. Murphy identifies with the heroine. It is interesting to note that the heroine has not told her mother that she is joining the convent. Rather, she has told her boyfriends. Thus, she juxtaposes the convent that is asexual and forgiving of sins with boyfriends who represent sexuality. In the convent she will be safe, perhaps both from her own wishes ("she felt something inner inside her") and also from her mother's retaliation, and then will be happy. The convent offers both protection from her mother's probable retaliation for her erotic fantasies and also the care afforded to the sisters by the mother superior; the heroine (Mrs. Murphy) is able to obtain both the security and care she feels has been missing in her own life.

For Mrs. Murphy, sexuality is connected with glamour, badness, evil, and lack of control, while asexuality and even childcare are connected with the mundane, stereotyped, and boring. This is reflected in Mrs. Murphy's self-concept. On the other hand, Mrs. Murphy views herself as an average woman, with the "basic schooling," who has married and reared children, joined the Parent-Teacher Association (PTA), does a lot of work for the church, has average views on life, and has accepted her life for what it is. This is the part of Mrs. Murphy that is attracted to Woodland Park, even without its glamour. Mrs. Murphy's dissatisfaction with this way of life stems from the fact that it lacks glamour, sexuality, or the possibility of pleasure: her work with the church and the PTA and her housework are responsibilities without satisfaction.

In such a drab workaday world, even if there is little glamour, there is at least the possibility of some feminine adornment. Mrs. Murphy is attracted to such typical stereotyped feminine adornments as necklaces, fur coats, poodles, and attractive hats. It is interesting to note that Mrs. Murphy is very proud of her extensive collection of glass swans that she began in junior high school. While she does not remember how or why she first began collecting swans, she did talk about her memories of the rowboats decorated like swans that were available for rental in the big pond in the Public Gardens. Such adornment, while it may lighten Mrs. Murphy's burden, does not compensate for a marriage that, as we see subsequently, offers little satisfaction, and a daily routine which is so lacking in pleasure.

Mrs. Murphy's preferred mode of resolving inner conflict is to take flight (at least in fantasy) from uncomfortable situations, a solution she also showed when, while in secreterial school, she became dissatisfied with her life and took off on a whim for New York. For example, on Card V of the Rorschach, only after providing two other responses, those of "the Massachusetts eagle with wings extended'' and "a reindeer in flight," was she finally able to offer the popular bat response. However, even the bat response was that of a bat in flight.

Faced with a conflict between life in Woodland Park that is safe, but lacks excitement or color, and the alternative of life as a seductive siren, which in Mrs. Murphy's fantasies might lead to her mother's retaliation and her own destruction, Mrs. Murphy has settled for the former. She has tried to deal with this conflict and to find some of the excitement and sexuality for which she searches by marrying a theatrical producer. However, since Mrs. Murphy's real interest is in her father and since her husband is himself an unhappy and frustrated man who expresses little desire for an intimate relationship with his wife, she has gained neither the glamour nor the security she had sought in her marriage to Mr. Murphy. Woodland Park has become a place of safety in a troubled world.

Mr. Murphy's present difficulties are understandable in the light of his own prior life experiences. His mother and father are both Irish Catholics and people Mrs. Murphy describes as quite rigid and unemotional. Mr. Murphy's father has been an alcoholic for many years. Throughout his early childhood, his father was in and out of mental hospitals. Mrs. Murphy's mother-in-law has also had numerous health problems, both imagined and real, that have added to the atmosphere of depression which hangs over her husband's family. In this context, Mrs. Murphy notes that her husband never had any security while he was growing up. She believes that, for this reason, he feels little need for either emotional or financial security. She notes that arguments between her husband and herself almost inevitably finish with his statement that he did not even know where his next meal was coming from when he was growing up, so he does not know why his wife and children, who are clearly so much better off than that, should worry about security. She also recognizes that in some ways her husband has adopted his father's attitudes toward family responsibilities. When she becomes angry at him, she tells her husband that he is just as self-centered and unreliable as his father. According to Mrs. Murphy, her husband has never denied this statement.

Mr. Murphy and his mother have always been especially close. Mrs. Murphy believes that since her husband was an only child, mother and son were thrown together during his father's many hospitalizations. Mrs. Murphy notes that her husband has never been able to break away from his mother. She still gives him spending money and allows him to use her charge account at a downtown department store. The continuing closeness between her husband and his mother is especially difficult for Mrs. Murphy to accept, since this relationship parallels so closely her relationship with her own mother. For example, just as she feels her own mother is unwilling to make small but necessary accommodations for her grandchildren, Mrs. Murphy's mother-in-law is unwilling to put her bric-a-brac away when the children come for a visit. When the children begin to touch these objects, Mrs. Murphy's mother-in-law becomes upset and begins to criticize her daughter-in-law for not having better "control" over her children's behavior. Then, when Mrs. Murphy complains to her husband about how her mother-in-law criticizes her and makes visits so unpleasant, Mr. Murphy becomes angry and takes his mother's side against his wife. Such quarrels lead Mrs. Murphy to feel that there is no one to take her side and that her husband is so closely tied to his mother's apron strings that he is unable to see her own dilemma or to provide her with any emotional support.

Mrs. Murphy's conflicts with her mother-in-law, and her disappointment that her husband does not support her or take her side in these quarrels, is but one example of her frustration and disappointment with her marriage. On recalling her first acquaintance with her prospective husband, she says she had mixed feelings about him. For example, she observes:

> At first I really didn't like him. In fact, when I first met him, I really hated him. I told him he was a phony, ah . . . he's a very handsome man, a very striking appearance . . . He was very charming . . .

Mr. Murphy's charm, together with his work with the Broadway theater, offered excitement and glamour. On the other hand, the fact that his work was primarily with the technical aspects of the theater meant that his work would provide greater security than was possible in acting. Marriage offered both the excitement and the security that are so important for Mrs. Murphy. Reflecting on these early expectations, Mrs. Murphy observes that life with her husband has not been very exciting, but, on the contrary, "nerve-wracking." Because his life is taken up with the theater, Mr. Murphy has little emotional energy left over for his wife and family. Mrs. Murphy's description of what her husband does on those rare evenings when he is at home illustrates this point nicely. Mrs. Murphy notes that when he comes in the door:

> If there are any calls, he goes over the calls. That's the first thing. He might kiss me if he thinks of it. Maybe he has a cup of tea. And then we discuss anything that ah/ I might be in bed but he makes me get up, make tea for him; he sits up till one every night watching the late talk shows, or he does a lot of paperwork that he hasn't gotten to, or makes up a class schedule because he teaches three days a week and spends three days each week in New York. And nine out of ten times he's in a bad mood. He has had a trying day, and is aggravated, the majority of the time. I feel well it's too bad if you're tired, this is the life that you've chosen. You also have your wife and children.

Mrs. Murphy's account bristles with resentment toward her husband. Mr. Murphy spends almost half of each week in New York, and it appears to her that he spends more time on the airplane than at home. When he is home, he spends his time frantically making telephone calls, lining up actors for future shows and planning forthcoming television programs. When he is in town, he often fails to call her at home during the day, an oversight Mrs. Murphy especially resents. Mrs. Murphy hardly welcomes her husband's occasional nights at home. Often, she is already in bed by the time he arrives. She complains that he forces her to get out of bed and make tea for him. Again, she complains that "he might kiss me if he thinks of it." Sexual relations have been unsatisfactory for several years; Mrs. Murphy feels that he is very critical of her body, and she is angered by the many comments he has made about how much weight she has gained. She noted, in this regard, that she has gained more weight with each child, but said that given her husband's attitude toward her she has had little incentive to lose weight.

Nowhere do Mrs. Murphy's feelings about her relationship with her husband emerge so clearly as in a story she tells in response to TAT picture Tel (A woman is standing with a telephone receiver in her hand):

This woman has just had a very hard day, she has cleaned her house . . . from top to bottom . . . she has probably baked a nice cake and a roast beef for supper and now, about ten minutes to six her husband has just called and says that he's not coming home for supper and will be very late. She is just furious; in fact she's at the point where she could just tear her hair out . . . She worked very hard and she's thinking right now, "Oh, if I had to do it over again, I'd never do it." Ah, I think she'll calm down; sure, she'll hang the phone up, probably throw something on the floor, we'll say that, and go into the kitchen and put everything away. An hour will pass and she'll still be mad and may call a girl friend or somebody to come over and they'll go out to a show . . . the next day, when her husband does come home that night or she'll probably be asleep that night when he comes in, and the next morning there will be a bit of an argument, about why didn't he call sooner before she started the meal or else she may just be spiteful and give it to him, the same meal, the same thing the next night. I think that she's trying to teach him a lesson to use the great old phone, and it only costs a dime and, ah, I think that if she had to do it over again, I don't think she would, I think she'd say no.

Mrs. Murphy feels a smoldering anger that is never quite able to surface, but which does appear in the projective materials, such as the following Rorschach response:

Could be half a plane, it's going this way and that where the wings and tail parts were. Looks like the plane was chopped off and the piece in front of the two motors, maybe the propeller's missing. As it goes to a crash, it is trailing clouds of smoke.

Mrs. Murphy mentions her husband's frequent airplane trips often during the interviews, almost always in the context of his lack of interest in his family. The airplane has become the symbol both of her husband's absences and also of her anger and resentment toward him; there are times when Mrs. Murphy becomes so angry and bitter that she wishes his airplane would crash. However, such wishes are invariably accompanied by much guilt and anxiety, leaving her feeling depressed and pessimistic. This anxiety is evident, in the Rorschach response, in the cloud of smoke that trails behind the airplane as it crashes. Such use of the shading on the blot is almost always an indicator of anxiety regarding the content of the response (Rapaport, Gill, and Schafer, 1968).

Mrs. Murphy's compulsive attitude toward her house work and about being constantly with her children serve as a substitute for confrontation with her husband. When her husband does come home, Mrs. Murphy derives little satisfaction from being with him and feels that she is just his maid. The attempts Mrs. Murphy makes to gain her husband's affection are rebuffed for he quickly tires of conversation and turns to his work. Mr. Murphy goes to bed and rises long after his wife. When he arises, she provides his breakfast and goes on with her housework. When Mr. Murphy is home, the couple occasionally goes out. However, from Mrs. Murphy's account, most of these evenings are spent in a semi-darkened theater, where her husband is producing some play and where she is virtually alone.

Despite these disappointments, perhaps because of the aura of distant places and famous persons, Mrs. Murphy is still willing to save the marriage. She believes her marriage is no worse than her mother's marriage that she claims was beset by many of the same difficulties she herself has experienced: her father, too, was seldom at home, or, if he was home, he was generally asleep when other family members were awake. As Mrs. Murphy says in response to a picture thematic story . . . "In this day and age, where every six marriages out of ten marriages go down the drain, the daughter will stick it out the way her mother stuck it out with her father." Mrs. Murphy also feels that if she herself were thinner and thus sexually attractive, then she might be better able to arouse her husband's interest in her. She is somewhat suspicious about her husband's activities in New York. Mrs. Murphy's mother is convinced Mr. Murphy is up to no good. Nonetheless, the daughter, after stating her anxiety, quickly assures herself that such fears are nonsense. Nonetheless, Mrs. Murphy's mother's frequent talk about Mr. Murphy's possible infidelities disturbs her, and leads to many quarrels between the two women. Mrs. Pescatore is unable to understand why her son-in-law should be away three days of seven and why his hours should be so irregular and so late. A woman who thinks relationships should be conducted according to her own somewhat stereotyped beliefs, she finds the Murphy's life-style confusing and believes that it foreshadows even more serious difficulty. For Mrs. Pescatore, it is important that a man work regular hours and bring home a paycheck. Mrs. Pescatore's dissatisfaction with her son-in-law's vocation, hours, and salary, together with Mrs. Murphy's own concerns, has led to a very explosive situation in this extended family. Mrs. Pescatore's comments are difficult for Mrs. Murphy to handle precisely because these comments are so consistent with Mrs. Murphy's own fears.

In marrying and attempting to escape her childhood's stereotyped world, Mrs. Murphy has tried to find a more colorful and unique existence. Simultaneously, she has tried to maintain the security derived from living with her mother. In the final analysis, security with her mother is the dominating value. Mrs. Murphy does not feel she could build a new life outside Woodland Park. This conflict between excitement and security is more clearly described in one of her picture thematic stories (TAT Card 2), where Mrs. Murphy describes the two women in the scene as sisters. They represent the two different aspects of Mrs. Murphy's personality. One part of her would like to lead the commonplace existence of her mother and marry a steady provider like a farmer. The other part of her searches for stimulation and thrills in the world of business or the theater. In the end, tradition wins over innovation, and the other sister returns home and marries the local schoolteacher. This solution, in itself, suggests an interesting compromise. The schoolteacher is presumably more intellectual and innovative than the sister's farming husband. So, within the framework of the traditional pattern, the other sister had found some room for a less common-place life.

Just as in the story, the real Mrs. Murphy wanted both a different and more stimulating life and also the commonplace existence of her mother's family. After a brief trip to the city, she, too, married a local boy who, like herself, had gone off in search of excitement. Like her also, he still considered himself a member of the community (he did agree, with little hesitation, to return to the old gray house on Bridge Street). However, as was indicated in the story, such a compro-mise is not very satisfying. Just as hard work is better than brains, so, too, a reliable husband with a steady job and regular hours is to be preferred to a hus-band who is frequently away from home and so emotionally distant when he is home.

Like her mother, Mrs. Murphy finds it difficult to maintain a meaningful rela-tionship with her husband or with others. This is reflected in her response to the third card on the Rorschach, a card that usually elicits the strongest human move-ment responses in the whole series of 10 cards. While she was able to provide a human movement response, Mrs. Murphy changed the dancing people into Mick-ey and Minnie Mouse. Then she provided a response involving the shading of the card, an indication, as previously noted, that a person is experiencing strong anxiety.

Following the X-ray response, Mrs. Murphy then disregarded the popular human movement response on this third card and included a part of the typically seen moving figures into two people on a seesaw. The people were sitting on the ends and were rocking back and forth. This seesaw response may well character-ize the vascillation Mrs. Murphy experiences in relationships. The relationship is never well balanced and fails to develop in meaningful ways. Again, she de-scribes, on Card VI, "two people sitting back to back": distance is put between the two persons, and they are not directly involved.

Of the five human movement responses Mrs. Murphy provides on the Ror-schach, one is transformed into cartoon characters, one into a distanced and un-balanced relationship, and one into people for whom the relationship is one of distance. A fourth response is that of very stylized formal ballet dancers. The fifth human movement response is in striking contrast with the other four: on Card IX, she sees two nude people kneeling or praying. Several things are inter-esting about this response. When she tries to use both the shape and the color of the blot to fashion her response, the effort fails and the percept she offers is not reality adaptive and is of poor form. This failure to fashion a response that is reality adaptive shows the difficulty Mrs. Murphy encounters in bringing appro-priate feelings to a relationship. The only response in which persons are not in-volved in formal or distant transactions is one where they are involved in a sensual and possibly sexual relationship.

While, in part, Mrs. Murphy longs for such a profound and close sexual rela-tionship, this longing is counterbalanced by a fear of close relationships which requires that other persons be kept at a distance. Perhaps this is another reason why Mrs. Murphy's relationship with her husband is at all satisfying. He has little to do with her, except in a very formal way relating to his work. Given some impairment in her own capacity for closeness, the equilibrium between husband and wife may be better than would at first appear.

Mrs. Murphy's value system also indicates that her chief allegiance is to Woodland Park, even though she has assumed some of the values of the more liberal theatrical community in which her husband works. Mrs. Murphy notes, for example, that her views on race relationships differ from the views of most other persons in Woodland Park. She maintains that intermarriage is perfectly all right and even to be encouraged, while simultaneously maintaining a stereotyped view of black men's sexual prowess. Once again, she shows her characteristic fascination and fear of life outside the confines of Woodland Park.

In other ways as well, Mrs. Murphy demonstrates that she is a typical Woodland Park resident. She, too, values privacy and distance from others. She comments with considerable feeling about the fact that her children play with a youngster of whom she disapproves and notes that "my children are better off playing in the backyard than out with the other children." She shows a preference for distance from her neighbors and notes that while she has several friends in other suburbs, she knows relatively few neighbors. The value she places on privacy and on distance from others is in striking contrast with Mrs. McGorty who felt isolated in a similar suburb and who was looking forward to moving back to the city, where the sense of neighborhood was much stronger. Mrs. Murphy chose to live in Woodland Park, and this move was supported by her husband. It was not only Mrs. Murphy's relationship with her mother that dictated such a move. Her own character structure is compatible with the dominant value system of Woodland Park.

Mrs. Murphy's childrearing attitudes are no more typical of her own generation than they are of her mother's generation. On the basis of her expressed childrearing attitudes, it would be impossible to predict which generation she belongs to. Unlike other mothers in her own generation, Mrs. Murphy believes in maintaining firm control over a child's aggressive impulses, perhaps a reflection of her struggles to contain her own angry feelings toward her husband, mother, and mother-in-law. In fact, Mrs. Murphy's score on the relevant MAS factor was more than 2 standard deviations different from that of the three other mothers; Mrs. Murphy ranked first among the mother generation in believing that the child's aggressive impulses should be firmly checked.

In her attitudes toward reciprocity, Mrs. Murphy ranked third among the four mothers. Since she herself has a difficult time establishing meaningful social relationships, it is not surprising that she doubts that young children can form social relationships. Of the four mothers, Mrs. Murphy also shows the least adaptive attitudes regarding the achievement of appropriate closeness with the infant. She believes that children are simply an extension of their mothers' needs and discourages her own children's attempts to develop separate identities.

While she may feel unable to modify the child's expression of aggression, unable to foster the development of mother-child reciprocity, and unable to encourage the development of a sense of separateness in the child, Mrs. Murphy ranks first among the four mothers in her willingness to express uncertainty regarding the correct ways of rearing a child: she is most able to express her own ambivalence regarding childcare and is most able to express her feelings of being burdened as a mother. Consistent with her other childrearing attitudes, Mrs. Murphy ranks first among the four mothers in the belief that she cannot understand or meet a baby's physical needs.

Mrs. Murphy's responses on the MAS more closely approximate those of mothers hospitalized for an emotional disturbance following childbirth (Cohler, Weiss, and Grunebaum, 1970; Cohler et al., 1976, 1980) than any of the other mothers in this study. The overall picture which emerges is that of a woman preoccupied with issues of separation and closeness, who feels insecure as a mother, who resents the maternal role, and who, perhaps in reacting to the hostility she feels toward her children, binds them to her in a way reminiscent of the parents D. Levy (1943) has described in his work on maternal overprotection. Both Mrs. Murphy's perception of the maternal role, as demonstrated in the picture thematic materials, and her description of her own childrearing practices are consistent with her childrearing attitudes.

It was especially unfortunate that Mrs. Murphy's first child was born just 10 months after the couple was married. William, the oldest boy was followed 10 months later by Barbara and 14 months after that by Ralph. Mrs. Murphy preferred boys to girls, but also describes, in idealized terms, the kind of boy she would like to have. Following her drawing of a baby boy, she offered the following explanation:

Probably is an average, all-American, all I think of is a little boy who likes to get into dirt. Probably has a sister and a brother. Very happy home. Likes sports, likes football, baseball, swimming, what can he do, he's a little tiny b/you know, say maybe two or three years old, so he's just starting out. Likes crayons. Likes books. Likes to be read to. Full of life, runs, jumps. Probably listens to the vocabulary his parents are saying. And he's just a cute little boy.

Mrs. Murphy's description of the typical little boy indicates that she values a child who is well behaved, self-reliant, and oriented toward achievement and success. Mrs. Murphy herself exerts considerable pressure in this direction: her four-year-old daughter attends a very strict Montessori school. Despite this concern with success, Mrs. Murphy has a hard time relinquishing her children, and they have little opportunity for self-initiated activity.

This sense of closeness is enhanced by Mrs. Murphy's feelings of loneliness. It is not unusual for her to stay in her house and yard with her children for a week at a time, while her husband is in New York. This sense of closeness is enhanced by the resemblance of her own and her children's interests: William, her oldest boy, has a collection of more than 400 glass and ceramic animals. This collection is very similar, as Mrs. Murphy herself notes, to her own swan collection.

The sense of binding togetherness between mother and children can be quite clearly seen as Mrs. Murphy describes a typical day in her household. She begins by commenting that the children arise at 5:45, William first, then Ralph, and then Barbara. They are all up by 6:10. As stated, it might appear that this is a factual comment and not at all unusual. However, it is difficult to believe that children are, in fact, so punctual. Mrs. Murphy goes on to note that she has trained her children to stay in their beds and read books. Even the three year old is expected to follow this pattern. The children wait until Mrs. Murphy has finished her own toilet, at which time they come into the kitchen and color until their favorite television program comes on at 6:55.

The morning routine is highly scheduled and lacks spontaneity. After giving the children their breakfast, Mrs. Murphy goes back to bed for another 45 minutes and arises again at about 7:45 to get Barbara dressed for school. Barbara rides the bus to school and is out the door by 8:30, at which time Mrs. Murphy makes the children's beds. Mrs. Murphy likes the Montessori school both because Barbara can improve her intellectual skills such as her "photographic memory" and because the sisters who run the school keep tight control over the children's activities. Mrs. Murphy is especially pleased when Barbara comes home with a poem she has memorized. The two boys continue to watch television until 10:30. During this time, Mrs. Murphy goes down to the basement to start the washing machine and dry mops the floor. Sometimes, during this time, she vacuums or does the dishes. From her account, it would appear that she is a neat housekeeper.

Often during the early morning, the two boys go downstairs and spend time with their grandmother, while their mother does her housework. By 10:30, Mrs. Murphy has finished her work and is ready to get the children dressed. At that time, as frequently during the day, she tells her children stories. She says that the reason for this is that her children are very bright. This is important to note for Mrs. Murphy's interest in telling stories stems less from a desire to be with her children or to have a good time with them than from a desire to increase their intellectual capacity.

It is only in this connection that Mrs. Murphy is able to admit to her worry about her youngest son whom she describes as somewhat slow. Ralph, now three years old, was born with an ear infection that greatly impaired his hearing during his first two years. At this time the hearing problem was corrected, but Ralph acquired a speech problem that has made it difficult for anyone but his mother to understand him. Mrs. Murphy notes that she has to act as his "interpreter" to others, so they can understand what he is saying. To improve his speech she has instituted a series of word drills with Ralph each morning. However, she feels that these sessions have not been very helpful.

Besides his speech difficulties, Ralph has been suffering from severe separation anxieties, dating from the time of his hospitalization, when he was alone in the hospital for several weeks. Ralph cannot stand to have his mother leave him. This problem has become more serious since Mrs. Murphy accompanied her husband to New York a few weeks ago:

For the past four weeks he has been miserable and now he's got to the point of crying when I go out the door. Which he wasn't before, but now he's really underfoot every minute, right on top of you. If you're walking, you take him with you. I stand up and say,

"Come, walk with me." Sometimes I might scream at him, "Go away" you know, "leave me alone for a couple of minutes, go take a book or toy. I try not to scream at him too much but . . . you will in the course of a day, especially if I'm on the phone."

Mrs. Murphy realizes that all children go through such a phase, but worries that with Ralph it is taking too long. She notes, in this regard, that Ralph is the only one of her three children who still carries his blanket around with him. At the same time, Mrs. Murphy has greater difficulty recognizing her own contribution to Ralph's difficulties. Consistent with her attitudes regarding separation, Mrs. Murphy manages to bind Ralph to her and to prevent his own developing individuation by insisting that only she can understand what he is saying and that she must intervene between him and the external world. Ralph's difficulties in hearing and his subsequent hospitalization only intensify conflict regarding separation for both mother and child.

As is true of his sister, William attends a highly structured and intellectually oriented nursery school. After he is picked up for school, Mrs. Murphy returns to her housework. Sometimes, Mrs. Murphy is able to talk Ralph into visiting his grandmother so she can continue with her chores. If the morning has gone smoothly, and Mrs. Murphy notes that she usually sees that it does, she takes out some time before lunch to make calls for her husband or to watch a television program with guests whose appearance she has helped to arrange. Barbara is returned from the Montessori school at about 11:50, and, as soon as she returns, Mrs. Murphy drops everything to prepare lunch.

Mrs. Murphy seldom eats lunch, but she sits with Ralph and Barbara while they eat their soup, sandwich, and jello. Generally, the children watch television during lunch. "Mister Rogers" is on then, and, since it is an educational program, Mrs. Murphy believes that the children should see it as often as possible. The television also leaves Mrs. Murphy free to make additional telephone calls for her husband during lunch. As her children finish eating, they wander off to their rooms to play with their blocks and look at their books. If it is a nice day, they are allowed to go out into the backyard for a half hour, while Mrs. Murphy finishes her calls. Frequently, she irons while making these calls. Thus, she is really never available to her children during the meal hour. On rare occasions, she does her shopping between lunchtime and 2:30, when William returns from nursery school. William's bus stops directly in front of the door, and Mrs. Murphy is grateful that he needs only to get off the bus and cross the yard into the backyard to get home. She notes that "I thank God a thousand times that we are in a suburban area; the bus stops right in front of the door so that all he has to do is to get off and walk right into the yard." Once more, we observe the distinction Mrs. Murphy makes between the private and safe backyard and the unpredictable and dangerous outside world.

William comes in and changes into his play clothes and then comes into the kitchen, where his mother has fixed his lunch. Ralph and Barbara, who have been playing outside or in their rooms, sometimes come into the kitchen at this time and watch a children's television program with William. When the program is over, Mrs. Murphy sends all three children out to the backyard and then tries to spend an hour working on various materials that her husband will need for an upcoming show. Sometimes, she helps collate scripts, while, other times, she may underline parts or copy notes her husband has made about "blocking" or describing the action on stage. She also likes to take a few minutes to admire her swan collection.

When the children go out to play, five-year-old William is expected to take the responsibility for Ralph. He has no other assigned chores. Barbara is encouraged to help dry mop the kitchen after supper, although Mrs. Murphy does not demand that she do so: she feels that her children are still much too young for such responsibilities.

The children are expected to play in different areas at different times of the day. In the morning, they play in or near their own rooms, while in the afternoon they play on the sun porch. After 4:00, as the sun sets, the children come back into the house and go into the front porch, where they have several toy trucks, a paint set, and modeling clay. In part, Mrs. Murphy wants them on the sun porch so that she can keep track of them while she is preparing supper. She says that since the hall is so long she can not hear what is going on if they are in their bedrooms when she is in the kitchen. The children almost always have a hamburger for supper, together with a glass of milk and some fruit. Sometimes, especially on days when the weather is bad, Mrs. Murphy will spend a few minutes reading a story to the children before she begins supper; more often, she leaves them to their own play while she prepares their meal.

Supper is on the table at 4:45, and the children are expected to finish dinner by 5:15. As was true of breakfast and lunch, supper is eaten in front of the television set. There has been no real effort to teach the children manners. What effort there has been comes from the few times when Mrs. Pescatore has fed the children. When the children mess with their food, it is taken away from them. However, if they can show they will eat properly, it is returned. Ralph is often sent to his room when he messes with his food during supper; if he comes back and promises to eat, Mrs. Murphy allows him to continue with his meal. Talking is permitted during supper time: "I mean, I will answer questions; they will ask questions." Mrs. Murphy notes that while the children are good eaters, they may sometimes balk at eating. In that case, she turns off the television and plays a game in which she tries to trick them into eating. For example, she will ask a riddle like "what's green that you walk on" and if the children give wrong answers, they have to take a bite.

Generally, Mrs. Murphy eats supper with the children. Sometimes, when she is going out with her husband, she only sits with the children while they eat. Less often, she keeps her children company while they eat and waits until they have gone to bed to prepare her own meal, which she eats as she reads the newspaper. She washes the pots and pans while she is cooking and cleans off the table and washes the dishes as soon as she and the children have finished with supper. She says she does not mind the dishes, although sometimes, when she is in a hurry, she uses paper plates and cups.

Dinner is over by 5:15, and at 5:55 the children begin baths. Exactly 12 hours to the minute from the time they arise, Mrs. Murphy has scheduled the children to prepare for bedtime. By 6:30, the baths are over and the children are in pajamas and ready for bed. While the children are taking baths, Mrs. Murphy walks back and forth from the kitchen, where she is finishing the dishes, and her own bedroom, where she may be changing her clothes prior to going out for the evening with her husband. The bathroom is cleaned between 6:30 and 6:45, and, if her husband is coming home prior to going out, he may play with the children between 6:30 and 7:00. At the same time, since her husband is frequently in a "bad mood" when he comes home, she warns the children against bothering him too much. On the weekend, if Mr. Murphy does not go to work on Saturday, he helps out with the children and gives them their baths. At 7:00 the children "hit the bed and are asleep almost at once." Mrs. Murphy comments that there is absolutely no problem about bedtime, because she has trained them in this ever since they were infants. It is only recently that the bed hour was pushed up to 7:00; until the past few months, the children had gone to bed between 6:00 and 6:30. The children always know it is time to go to bed, because they watch the same children's television program every night and go to bed when it is just halfway over. She notes that bedtime has been easier since she raised the bed hour from 6:00 to 7:00. On one occasion, Ralph balked for a few nights about going to bed. Mrs. Murphy's solution to this dilemma was simple: she grabbed hold of the door to his room and held it tightly to be sure he could not come out. After a while, Ralph realized that he could not escape and went back to bed.

This struggle with Ralph concerning his bed hour is quite typical of the problems Mrs. Murphy encounters with discipline and helps us to understand the basis of her extreme score on the attitude factor concerning the modification of the child's destructive impulses. Such an extreme score is earned by mothers who are either overly permissive or overly restrictive, for this factor measures attitudes regarding *appropriateness* of discipline. While she believes that the child's aggressive impulses will have only destructive results, with the exception of her struggle with Ralph regarding bedtime, Mrs. Murphy refuses to use any direct physical punishment with her children. She believes in trying to talk them into doing as she wishes and says that "there is no use trying to use force." When the children refuse to listen to her reasons or willfully disobey her, she becomes angry and screams at them, but feels that she has no way of following through except by relying on the kind of extreme measures her own mother had used when she was a child.

The discipline problem has become more difficult since two of the children have started school. These two school-aged children are increasingly unwilling to follow Mrs. Murphy's commands and have begun to "talk back" to her. Mrs. Murphy readily agrees with her mother's assessment that she "hollers" too much at the children without being able to have them do as she wishes. In explaining why Mrs. Murphy says that she has such painful memories of her own childhood that it is very difficult for her to use physical punishment, unless she has become so angry that she feels she has lost control of her own feelings. Mrs. Murphy is determined that her own children will not have to suffer as she did. However, in this effort to spare her children from the difficulties of her own childhood, she has created a problem with her own children that is likely to become even more serious as they grow up. Since her husband is so often unavailable, she must carry the burden of childrearing herself. In addition, her mother's rigid control of the children makes the conflict between the generations in this regard even more obvious. As long as Mrs. Murphy's discipline practices are based largely on the principle of doing things differently from the way her mother had done them, she is likely to have continued difficulty with her children and, increasingly, to feel unable to modify their aggression in socially approved ways.

After the children are in the bed, Mrs. Murphy sits down to read the evening papers. When her husband is home, she prepares dinner for the two of them, which is usually after the children have gone to bed. One night each week, Mrs. Murphy goes out to play bingo with her church group. She also enjoys ironing and may spend an hour or two ironing in the evening while she watches television. Less frequently, Mrs. Murphy and her husband spend the evening planning for some new play he is working on.

Mrs. Murphy leaves little time for herself in her schedule and does not express a need either to have time to herself or to "get away" from the house and tend to her own errands. In contrast with other mothers in the study, Mrs. Murphy is not very interested in shopping, errands, or in "going downtown." Those few chores for which she is responsible are either accomplished within the immediate neighborhood or on occasional Saturday shopping trips when she takes the children to the supermarket.

For many women, the weekly trip to the beauty shop is an eagerly anticipated event, for it means the possibility of getting out the house and having time to oneself. Mrs. Murphy has arranged for the beauty shop to come to her, so that even this part of her life can be managed within the confines of the gray house on Bridge Street. Mrs. Murphy's maternal aunt is a registered hairdresser and comes to her mother's apartment every Friday morning to do her mother's mother's hair, her mother's hair, Mrs. Murphy's hair, and, if Barbara should be at home, Barbara's hair as well. The only time Mrs. Murphy leaves the neighborhood is when she goes to the theater with her husband or when she is required to meet him at the airport.

Not only is Mrs. Murphy concerned about staying close to the self-contained world of her house and yard, but also she wants her children to stay within the confines of this world. We have already noted that she is pleased that the school bus stops directly in front of the house. In addition, she prefers that the children play in their own backyard rather than elsewhere around the neighborhood. Indeed, outside the daily bus trip, Saturday marketing trips are the only occasion her two older children have for exploring the outside world.

Such a contained life means that Mrs. Murphy and her children are together most of the time. It will be recalled that, of all the mothers in the study, Mrs. Murphy shows the least adaptive attitudes regarding this issue of separation, although on this factor her attitudes are quite similar to those of Mrs. Russo. In

Mrs. Murphy's description of her daily activities, we see a confirmation in behavior of these attitudes. It is not just that she is an overprotective mother who cannot separate her own needs from those of her children, but that, in addition, she is a woman who feels safer around the house than in the outside world and who values privacy and the possibility of a self-contained life. Her childrearing attitudes are but one more reflection of Mrs. Murphy's constriction as a person in which her need for privacy and security are among the most salient features of her personality.

We can only speculate on the effects of these values on her children's personalities. Certainly, with Mr. Murphy away so much of the time, Mrs. Murphy and her three children are forced on each other. Not only do they lose the possibility of exploring the world around them, but also her children are likely to become mere extensions of Mrs. Murphy herself. This can be seen in William's collection of glass and ceramic animals. Since elementary school demands more effective participation in the universal standards of adult society than nursery school, it is possible that the children will find it more difficult to separate from their mother when they have to go off to school, and that they will feel less effective than their contemporaries who have been given greater freedom in exploring the world around them. Since their mother does so much for them, the two boys are especially likely to react to school in a passive manner and to be unable to tolerate frustration. Barbara is likely to fare somewhat better, but, in all likelihood, will be a constricted and somewhat moody woman.

THE TWO GENERATIONS TOGETHER: VICISSITUDES OF INTERGENERATIONAL CONFLICT

Physical proximity and frequent contact between the two generations have not fostered a satisfying relationship between Mrs. Pescatore and Mrs. Murphy. Mrs. Pescatore's feelings about her son-in-law are a constant source of tension within the family, as is her criticism of Mrs. Murphy's more permissive childrearing practices. Since she has many opportunities to observe her daughter with her grandchildren, Mrs. Pescatore is continually reminded of the differences between the way she reared her children and the way her daughter is rearing her own children. As she notes:

> When you don't see them you don't hear . . . being so close today I see things that bother me a little more than they would have if she was far away. It isn't that I would be happier, now that I think of it, because if she was away from me I'd feel it because the children were born here and . . . they're in here more than they're in their own home, but it would be better because I wouldn't hear and see all those things . . .

This is a problem for Mrs. Murphy, as well as for Mrs. Pescatore. Mrs. Murphy is aware of the extent to which her mother is critical of her more "permissive" orientation to childrearing and correctly perceives her mother's complaints about how she is rearing her children. While Mrs. Murphy recognizes that there are some respects in which her values are congruent with those of her mother, such as in teaching respect for property and in being a "good listener" to others, she is concerned that her children not develop her mother's stereotyped attitudes toward minority groups.

Mrs. Murphy attempts consciously to be more lenient and less intrusive than she feels her mother was. She purposely allows her children to dress as they wish, except on Sunday, and allows them to express their preference for the clothes she purchases for them. As she says, "Clothes are clothes and why should everything be just so." In a similar way, while her mother had insisted on a perfectly balanced diet, Mrs. Murphy is very critical of this and feels that such a regime takes away all the fun from eating. Mrs. Murphy's slight rebellion against her mother's meticulous housekeeping poses a problem between her mother and her daughter, for Mrs. Pescatore has taken a special interest in Barbara and has attempted to instill in her granddaughter a concern with order. Mrs. Murphy notes:

> You know how precise she is . . . everything has to be so, and she's got our little girl to be just like that. The clothes have got to be put in just the right place, lying down just so, and heaven forbid that there should be a hole in the sock. My mother is a fanatic about that sort of thing and the little girl has picked it up from her.

The children refer to Mrs. Pescatore as "Ma," and it is true that they spend a great deal of time each day with their grandmother. Ralph and William usually go down to see her after breakfast, but there has usually been some contact between the two generations even before this visit. Generally, one woman calls the other, even before breakfast. Each is horrified at the suggestion that they might use the telephone to call. Rather, they shout back and forth up and down the stairs. Typically, Mrs. Pescatore prefers for Mrs. Murphy to come downstairs. She is especially careful to avoid coming up to the Murphy's apartment if Mr. Murphy is still at home. However, even when she is borrowing something from her daughter, she prefers for Mrs. Murphy to bring it down to her.

If they have not already seen each other in the morning, Mrs. Murphy and her mother meet to do the laundry. They take turns doing the wash and putting it out on the line. Doing the laundry frequently provokes quarrels, because Mrs. Pescatore does not like the manner in which Mrs. Murphy hangs the clothes out on the line. She complains that Mrs. Murphy is careless and that the clothes do not dry properly:

> I'll say, "Why don't you pull in the clothes." She turns to me and says, "Later on." They may be there a day or two . . . well, I suffer . . . if they're down here I pull them in but if they're upstairs in her place, you know, she says, I can wait. I have to have them in right away whereas she's different that way.

Mrs. Pescatore sees this problem with the laundry as a specific instance of a more general problem with her daughter, that of her seeming indifference to what she's doing:

When I go upstairs and see something, I'll say, "Why don't you wash this floor; why do you wait till the end of the week?" "If it's dirty, do it then," or the children spill and I'll say, "Teach those little kids; you're too easy with them," which she *is* easy with them. Then again, it may be a bad day today, so I'll say, why don't you put their rubbers on, or put their boots on? She doesn't, and all she'll say is "they don't need it." See, I'll say, put her hat on; it's windy today and she'll say, "Oh, they don't need it."

Mrs. Murphy's response to her mother's nagging is to insist that life is too short to spend it hanging out clothes or doing the floors.

Later in the morning, when Mrs. Murphy is trying to get both Ralph and William dressed, Mrs. Pescatore comes upstairs to help with the children. Mrs. Pescatore helped even more when the children were infants. In fact, Mrs. Murphy did not take care of the children as infants for the first three or four months. Before the two generations began to quarrel so much about Mr. Murphy and his work, Mrs. Pescatore typically made supper for the entire extended family. She is renowned for her soups and still serves soup on Monday nights to Mrs. Murphy and her children.

In the afternoon, Mrs. Pescatore may entertain all three children for short periods of time. In addition, she helps to supervise bath times, especially if Mr. Pescatore is late getting home from work. While neither generation was willing to admit that the whole family had supper together, Mrs. Pescatore did acknowledge that she frequently prepared supper for her daughter and brought it upstairs to her. The whole family loves Mrs. Pescatore's raviolis and her sausage and broccoli casserole.

The question of babysitting is one more area of tension between Mrs. Murphy and her mother. Mrs. Pescatore is unwilling to baby-sit at night, because she is critical of Mr. Murphy's work and hours. If she were to baby-sit at night, she would know the exact hour when the Murphys returned. Even more important, from Mrs. Pescatore's vantage point, she would appear to be giving tacit approval of his vocation and schedule. Even the request for Mrs. Pescatore to baby-sit during the day is made hesitantly. As Mrs. Murphy comments:

In part it depends what I'm going out for. If it's for my own real pleasure I feel guilty. If it's, ah . . . something that I have to do, well then I don't mind too much asking her. I feel that I'm tying her up, sometimes she seems to get so tired.

Mrs. Pescatore says that she generally baby-sits in preference to doing what she had planned to do during the day. For example, if she were planning to make one of her very infrequent trips to the city and her daughter asked her to baby-sit, Mrs. Pescatore would be willing to change her plans, especially if Mrs. Murphy had said that it was important that she go out. Finally, it should be noted that in spite of Mrs. Pescatore's principles about babysitting when the Murphys go out together, when Mr. Murphy recently invited his wife to accompany him on a trip to New York, Mrs. Pescatore took care of the children throughout this long weekend. The willingness with which she baby-sits is in marked contrast with Mrs. Limpari (Chapter 3), who regarded Mrs. McGorty's request as much more of a burden, or Mrs. Giorgio (Chapter 5), who also shares a residence with her daughter, and who also resents demands for babysitting.

Since the children spend such a large part of the day with her, Mrs. Pescatore has little hesitation about disciplining them when they misbehave. She acknowledges that she would hesitate far more if it were her daughter-in-law's rather than her daughter's children. One time recently, when both she and her daughter were in the backyard, William swung with his bat and narrowly missed Ralph. Her daughter said, "Now, William, you know you shouldn't do that." Mrs. Pescatore, outraged at what William had done, gave him a swat. She then turned to her daughter and said, "Why didn't you do that?" According to her account, her daughter said: "Ma, you do it this way, we do it that way; you brought yours up one way, and I'm going to bring them up my way." Mrs. Pescatore says she does not like her daughter's attitude, but she recognizes that there is little she can do.

Mrs. Pescatore worries that her daughter's leniency will have bad effects on the children and that some day they will start talking back to her; she says she already begins to see signs of this. More and more often, Mrs. Murphy engages in shouting matches with the children, because she feels the only way of disciplining the children is to talk them out of what they are doing. In Mrs. Pescatore's opinion, she could more effectively control them by means of corporal punishment. Mrs. Pescatore also objects to the fact that when her daughter asks the children to get something, the children tell her to get it herself. If they were to do this when they were with Mrs. Pescatore, she says they would receive a good hard swat.

Mrs. Murphy acknowledges the conflict with her mother regarding childcare, but believes that her firm stance usually settles the issue. As she talked, the emotion in her voice suggested that her feelings may be far stronger than she can admit. She described one recent incident when her children were sitting in the sun porch and playing with their Play-Doh factory, a machine that stamps out little models made out of a substance similar to clay. Mrs. Murphy's mother came up to talk with her while she was preparing supper and saw the Play-Doh all over the floor. She came over to the children and said, "Don't do it that way, you shouldn't have to do that." According to Mrs. Murphy, she told her mother, "Ma, stop picking at me, stop finding fault; you're always finding fault." Then, in a trembling voice, she told of her mother's answer: "I raised you and you're all right, you know." Mrs. Murphy then replied, "Well, I'm doing it, I'm sorry, you know, but you raised your kids one way and I'm doing it another." Mrs. Murphy's mother turned on her heels and stomped out, slamming the door behind her.

The other frequent conflict between mother and daughter concerning the children is the noise they make. Since her mother's apartment is directly below hers, her children's running can be heard quite audibly. Such noise often causes Mrs. Pescatore to come up and complain about the children and their behavior. These conflicts between the two generations, day after day, have taken their toll in emotional energy. Mrs. Murphy says that she has largely given up even arguing with her mother. "What's the use," she sighs, "Ma will only go on that way." Finally, in desperation, she screams at her mother, "Ma, stop picking at me, stop finding fault; you're always finding fault."

As we have mentioned, Mrs. Pescatore is also very critical of Mrs. Murphy's weight and frequently comments about her size and the kind of clothing she wears. Such comments anger Mrs. Murphy; when Mrs. Pescatore tells her to put on a girdle and a better kind of dress, Mrs. Murphy says that she will not and stomps off.

However, it is regarding Mr. Murphy that the most bitter conflict takes place. Mrs. Pescatore is reluctant to come upstairs when he is home, for she and her son-in-law have frequent arguments. She would have preferred Mr. Murphy to continue his earlier work as a cosmetics salesman in a big downtown department store and especially resents how he neglects Mrs. Murphy by his frequent absences. Beyond this neglect, Mrs. Pescatore believes that Mr. Murphy is extremely self-centered and that he always thinks of himself first. Since these same concerns trouble Mrs. Murphy herself, she is extremely sensitive to her mother's criticisms and attempts to rationalize them. For example, she says, in considering her mother's criticisms of her husband:

Theater is . . . any person who is interested in the theater is gonna . . . their self has to come first . . . everybody comes second . . . ah, fine, some women accept this, some women don't but, ah, (tears come to her eyes, her voice trembles) I started with him; I have the children, ah . . . to look out for; he's going to make it, he's making it already, and I'm going to be with him when he gets there . . .

As a result of this conflict between Mrs. Murphy and her mother regarding her childrearing, her body, and her marriage, the two generations have become increasingly distant in the past few years. Mrs. Pescatore feels that things between them are not as good as when her daughter was first married and would come down to eat supper with the Pescatores. Mrs. Pescatore also says that when the children were younger she could be a real help to her daughter. At that time she had offered financial aid and made sure that the children were well cared for. But of the situation now, she says:

. . . they're getting a little older and rougher and, not all the time, but more often, they're beginning to get on my nerves. They've got big and have a mind of their own, and I'll say now don't go downstairs and yet they'll go downstairs . . . I can no longer get them to mind me as well.

It is clear that Mrs. Pescatore resents the burden of trying to help care for grandchildren who fail to mind her. In addition, as the children grow older, differences in the childrearing practices of mother and grandmother become increasingly obvious. As the children show some initiative Mrs. Pescatore becomes increasingly restrictive. Naturally, the grandmother's disapproval of her grandchildren's behavior exacerbates the mother-daughter relationship. Mrs. Murphy, too, feels that there has been a deterioration in her relationship with her mother:

I think we still have a deep closeness though we don't have a surface closeness any-more. I think we're drawing apart. Then, I never was that close with a sisterly way, you know; she's my mother and that was it. We seemed to get a bit closer I think, not when I first got married, the second or third year of marriage when I had gone back to where I lived . . . I could go to her for anything or she could go to me for anything.

Both generations feel that their relationship, as it presently exists, is not very stable or satisfying. As the children grow up and differences between mother and daughter become increasingly evident, there is likely to be even more conflict. However, since there is little evidence that Mr. Murphy is able to provide the security for which Mrs. Murphy searches, apart from the gray frame house on Bridge Street, it is likely that in spite of her growing differences with her mother a secure but unhappy life in Woodland Park is preferable to the uncertain life in the outside world.

While, at first, Mrs. Murphy's relationship with her mother may appear to exemplify the generation gap, similarities in their personalities are far more im-portant than differences. Both mother and grandmother feel anxious and insecure, and each has been able to adapt to the stress of marriage and childrearing only by relying on the safety and certainty provided by their protected environment. While Mrs. Murphy has some capacity for forming meaningful relationships, she chooses to limit her circle of friends to one or two longtime acquaintances. Rather than feeling closed in by her house, critical mother, and disobedient children, she prefers to remain at home and limit her errands to those that are essential and which can be done with the least effort. Mrs. Murphy's fascination with her col-lection of white ceramic swans is not unlike her mother's interest in her collection of mundane and clichéd romantic religious art. In sum, Mrs. Murphy has internal-ized her mother's personality constriction as a means for achieving an adaptation to the external world. While her present life provides security, it offers little glamour. Indeed, Mrs. Murphy has traded an interest in a life of excitement for the possibility of a more certain but possibly less satisfying life upstairs in Wood-land Park.

CONCLUSION

While both Mrs. Pescatore and Mrs. Murphy are able to realize some advantages in sharing a common residence, conflicts between the two generations are so in-tense that the overall effect of living together has a disruptive impact on both generations. Of course, the conflicts between Mrs. Pescatore and her daughter began long before her daughter's marriage or her decision to return home to Woodland Park and rear her children in her parents' house. However, as Mrs. Murphy's children grow older, there is more tension between mother and grand-mother regarding acceptable childcare practices, and both mother and grandmoth-er appear less able to resolve their conflicts.

Mrs. Pescatore is a rigid, anxious woman who, in general, is unable to view a situation from a perspective other than her own. Thus, she only adds to the discomfort her daughter feels. This difficult situation is exacerbated by the fact that Mrs. Murphy has never been able to separate from her mother and establish her own identity. Mrs. Murphy still looks to her mother for guidance and security, while resenting the fact that her mother acts on the basis of her own needs rather than in terms of what is best for her daughter.

Considering the intense and ambivalent feelings between these two women, as well as the difficulties Mrs. Murphy faces in her relationships with her husband and children, the coming years are likely to be difficult ones for her. For Mrs. Murphy, Woodland Park offers security, not only at the cost of excitement and glamour, but also at the cost of increasing family disruption and of painful personal struggle.

CHAPTER 7

Dimensions of Family Organization in Three-Generation Families

The four families we have discussed in the present study were selected according to specific criteria: sharing a common residence or living apart and more or less adaptive attitudes regarding the MAS dimension of appropriate closeness. Even though selected in a particular manner, these four families show some similarities: all four families are Catholic, and all are predominantly Italian. Within the Italian-American community, ethnic ties remain important, and each of the families in this study has had to resolve this issue of the family's place in the ethnic community. All four families are matrilocal; in each instance, the married daughter, her husband, and their young children returned to live in the same community or same household as the wife's own parents. While in each instance the husband's family also resides in the area, it is clear that the significance of remaining in this geographic area is the possibility provided for closeness with the wife's family. This is consistent with observations reported by Fischer and Fischer (1963) regarding a New England community very much like those described in the present study that in most families a clearly stated goal is to minimize the physical distance between the wife-mother's residence and that of her own parents.

Two of the four husbands in the second generation were of Irish descent, the third was of mixed Hungarian-Irish descent, while the fourth was of middle European descent. Common to the husband's family in each of these cases was the emotional distance and lack of family traditions that contrasted sharply with the greater closeness and interpersonal involvement present in the wife's family. Particularly for the three families in which the husband was of Irish descent, the greater closeness offered by the wife's family was a salient factor in the husband's decision to propose marriage and, subsequently, to maintain a close tie with the wife's parents.

A complex bond was established in each of these four families between the married daughter and her own mother. In each instance, the daughter sought greater closeness and dependency than was comfortable for her own mother. The grandmothers in these families, finally freed from the task of childcare, wanted greater autonomy than their daughters could accept. It was nice to visit with their daughters, but, even when the two generations shared a common residence, they were unwilling to make regular babysitting arrangements or to assume significant

234

responsibilities within the daughter's household. This conflict between the daughter's dependency and her mother's wish for freedom and autonomy was clear in each of the four modified extended families and represented a major unresolved psychological issue within each of these four families.

Particularly among the two families in which the mother expressed adaptive attitudes regarding appropriate closeness, a part of the continuing conflict between the two generations regarding this issue stems from the fact that the mothers in these two families expected their daughters to be self-reliant and independent, while, at the same time, abdicating a part of the role as housekeeper and mother. During their childhood, both Mrs. McGorty (Chapter 3) and Mrs. Czaja (Chapter 5) were expected to look after younger brothers and sisters, while their mothers tended to their own interests. The more Mrs. McGorty and Mrs. Czaja demonstrated their own independence and competence, the less contact they were able to have with their mothers. On the other hand, it was only through demonstration of such self-reliance and competence that they were able to earn their mothers' admiration.

Each of these two women grew up somewhat resentful of this expectation on the mother's part for independence and self-reliance, and each has retaliated in subtle and passive ways. For Mrs. McGorty, this retaliation has been expressed through the refusal to practice law, to marry a man of high social status, and to become the autonomous professional woman that her mother had hoped she would become. In addition, her Saturday trips to Tower Point that are greeted by her own mother with such mixed feelings satisfy not only Mrs. McGorty's desire for greater closeness and contact with her mother, but also her wish for retaliation at having had to become so independent at such a young age, since she is aware that such visits disrupt her mother's plans.

In a similar way, Mrs. Czaja decided that someone needed to care for her elderly, widowed mother and insisted on returning home, in spite of the fact that her mother is terrified of losing her own autonomy. While her mother enjoys having her daughter and her family when she can control the amount of intergenerational contact, she is quite clear in her feeling that the amount of closeness she is forced to have with her daughter as a result of sharing her household with Mrs. Czaja is more contact, less carefully controlled, than she would like. For each of the grandmothers in these two families in which the daughters express adaptive attitudes regarding appropriate closeness, the extent of the daughter's demands for closeness and contact between the generations is a source of frustration for their mothers, and the more the mothers attempt to control the amount of contact, the more persistent their daughters become in obtaining such contact. Of course, in the other two families, where the daughters express maladaptive attitudes regarding the issue of appropriate closeness, the mother-daughter symbiosis is of such intensity that neither generation can express the clear wish for greater physical and emotional distance.

In each of the four families, the relationship between the mother and her own mother influenced the manner in which issues of separation and autonomy were handled with the third generation. In the two families in which the mother's attitudes toward the issue of appropriate closeness and separation are less adaptive, conflict regarding this issue is already developing between the mother and her own children; this important psychological issue within the family is being communicated to the third generation.

In discussing these four families from this comparative perspective, we shift our attention from the specific processes within these families and consider the implications of our findings in terms of the larger problem of conceptualizing family structure and process. Having arrived at some understanding of the meaning of the three generational tie for each of these modified extended families and having observed the manner in which the issue of closeness and separation is expressed within each of these families, it is possible to examine these families from the framework of some common dimensions. In this manner, we can compare and contrast cases that otherwise remain as discrete instances and which do not lend themselves to cross-case generalizations.

The problem of the dimensions to be used in studying families is itself problematic. As Handel (1965) has observed, while there are numerous clinical reports illustrating aspects of psychological processes within the family (Bettelheim and Sylvester, 1950; Henry and Warson, 1951; T. Parsons, 1955; Wynne et al., 1958; Vogel and Bell, 1960; Lidz, 1963; Lidz, Fleck, and Cornelison, 1965; Spiegel, 1971), there has been much less systematic study of those basic dimensions of family structure and process that may be used in studying what Handel (1967b) has termed the "psychological interior" of the family. Hess and Handel (1959), Rainwater, Coleman, and Handel (1959), and Handel (1967b) have devoted considerable attention to this problem. Ackerman (1958), Senn and Hartford (1968), and Grunebaum (1970) have outlined several dimensions of family structure and process, although their discussions are oriented primarily toward the treatment of psychopathology. The formulations of these several authors have been summarized in terms of eight dimensions of family organization:

    I.   Definition of family boundaries.
    II.   Establishment of role boundaries within the family.
    III.   Locus of family operations.
    IV.   Patterns of family closeness and separation.
    V.   Definition of unacceptable behavior and basis for sanctions.
    VI.   Expression and control of affect and impulses.
    VII.   Establishment of family identity and achievement of family goals.
    VIII.   Family problem-solving techniques.

These eight issues, described in Table 1 in terms of the specific aspects of family structure or process they consider, may be used in studying family relationships either among significant subsystems within the family, such as the mother and her own mother, or among the family as a whole.

This framework can be applied in studies such as the present one in organizing case material according to more general dimensions and also, in appropriate instances, can be used to make quantitative ratings. We have presented the results from the four case studies in terms of these dimensions of family organization, considering each three-generation modified extended family as one unit for purposes of cross-case comparison.

Table 1. Dimensions of Family Organization

I. Definition of family boundaries
- A. Family structure
  1. Nuclear
  2. Modified extended
  3. Extended
- B. Degree of consensus regarding family structure
  1. Are members in accord about who constitutes the family unit?
  2. What kind of discrepancies exist between husband and wife, parents and children?
- C. Degree of contact with relatives outside the defined family type; to what extent and in what manner are more distant relatives drawn into the family?

II. Establishment of role boundaries within the family
- A. Parent and child. What differences are emphasized as relevant to generations? How are parents and children expected to act differently or to have different goals and expectations?
  1. How rigidly are these generational differences maintained?
  2. How early in the childcare process are these differences emphasized?
  Д1103To what extent 05are theese differences accepted by both parent and children?
- B. Male and female. What differences are emphasized as sex-role appropriate, and how are these differences observed in action?
  1. How rigidly are these sex-role or gender distinctions maintained?
  2. How early in the childcare process are these differences emphasized?
  3. To what extent are these differences accepted by both parent and child and by the male and female parents and offspring?
- C. Old and young. Are there distinctions in terms of actions appropriate for the older and younger generation or in terms of older and younger children, and how are these distinctions observed in action?
  1. How rigidly are these age differences maintained?
  2. How early in the childcare process are these differences emphasized?
  3. To what extent are these distinctions shared by both generations and/or between older and younger children?
- D. Intrafamily role organization. How do family members resolve problems between roles as worker, parent and homemaker, and community participant?
  1. Parent oriented—Emphasis on parents' marriage as most significant role. Separate activities by parents, use of babysitting, few shared parent-child activities.
  2. Child oriented—Emphasis on family as socialization unit. Activities planned around parent-child family unit and parents' needs subservient to those of children.
  3. Community oriented—Emphasis on extrafamilial activities and work over either parent-child or marital unit. Typically, husband-father places greatest em-

phasis on work role or on civic-social obligations. Wife-mother may also place greatest emphasis on civic-social obligations that add to prestige in community.

III. Locus of family operations

    A. To what extent are family members able to use community services and agencies or, at least, are informed on how to use these services?

    B. How safe do family members feel in planning activities that are some distance from the familial residence?

    C. How widely have family members traveled?

        1. What do family members regard as the extent of their neighborhood?

        2. What do family members regard as the extent of their community?

        3. What is the range of the world that family members conceive of as within the scope of usual activities? To what extent are family members "provincial?"

    D. What kinds of involvements and investments have family members established outside the family and circle of relatives? Are members confined largely to the circle of near or distant relatives, or is there visiting in the wider community? Visiting with friends?

    E. What kinds of participation do family members demonstrate in various formal and voluntary organizations? How much participation is there in voluntary organizations?

    F. What is the role of work within the family?

        1. To what extent is the family income adequate for necessities and luxuries?

        2. Does the father or other family members working enjoy the work?

        3. How difficult and time consuming is the work?

        4. To what extent is work an excuse to move away from the family or to avoid others in the family?

        5. To what extent is the factor of economic nesessity used as a screen for compulsive working?

        6. How is work valued—as income, income as well as intrinsic satisfactions, or primarily in terms of intrinsic satisfactions?

        7. To what extent does work interfere in the performance of other role tasks within the family?

IV. Closeness and separation

    A. Where are the family members and the family as a whole located on the axis of inappropriate versus appropriate closeness?

        1. What possibilities exist either for withdrawal from the family or for overinvolvement and for the development of symbiotic attachments within the family, even to such an extent that extrafamilial relationships are excluded?

        2. What kinds of satisfactions are derived from being together as a family unit?

            a. To what extent do family members welcome or avoid the possibility of working as a unit?

            b. How effectively does the family work together as a unit?

    B. What kind of tolerance exists in the family for the possibility of maintaining attitudes and values that diverge from the rest of the family.

    C. What kind of balance is shown between the use of kin or nonfamily members in solution of problems?

        1. Are there some problems for whose solution family members are most appropriate or most useful?

        2. Are there some problems for whose solution nonfamily members are most appropriate or most useful?

3. Is there some association between the type of problem and the choice of family or nonfamily member selected?

V. Definition of unacceptable behavior and basis for sanctions
 A. What kinds of behavior are defined as unacceptable within the family?
 B. How consistent is this definition of unacceptable behavior with definitions generally prevalent in the culture?
 C. How are sanctions imposed and explained to other family members?
  1. Compliance and external constraints: "Because it's the law," "Because the neighbors will see."
  2. Identification: "It will please mommy," "Daddy says so, do like Daddy."
  3. Internalization: "It's the right way to act," "What do you think is the best way?"

VI. Expression and control of affect and impulses
 A. Expression and modulation of sexual impulses
  1. How do the parents handle their own expression of sexual impulses; to what extent do they modulate this expression?
  2. How do the parents handle the children's expression of sexual impulses; to what extent can they modulate these impulses versus either suppression of these impulses or permissive encouragement of uncontrolled expression? Can members express appropriate affection?
  3. What defenses are used in dealing with conflicts regarding sexuality?
 B. Expression and modulation of aggressive impulses
  1. How do the parents handle their own expression of aggressive impulses; to what extent can they modulate this expression?
  2. How do the parents handle the children's expression of aggressive impulses; to what extent can they modulate these impulses versus either complete suppression or unbridled encouragement of uncontrolled expression? Can members express appropriate anger?
  3. What is the view of the children regarding the manner in which aggressive impulses are expressed within the family?
  4. What defenses are used in dealing with conflicts regarding aggression?
 C. What is the general affective tone of the family?
  1. How much spontaneity is evidenced in the expression of feelings?
  2. How much restriction and dulling of emotional expression is evidenced? How colorless or drab are the family members?

VII. Establishment of family identity and achievement of family goals
 A. To what extent do there exist traditions that were present prior to the establishment of the family unit?
  1. How strongly are these traditions felt and expressed?
  2. What contributions come from maternal and paternal families?
  3. What kinds of conflicts are generated from the attempt to live up to these traditions or from the attempt to escape from these traditions?
  4. How strongly do the parents feel about the transmission of these traditions to their children?
   a. What modes of action obtain in the transmission of family traditions?
   b. What kind of hold do these traditions have for the children?
   c. To what extent do the children rebel against traditions?
 B. What is the nature of the relationship each parent perceives of having with his or her own parents?
  1. To what extent is there still conflict between these two generations, regardless of whether the parent's own parents are living?
  2. What does each parent perceive as his or her own place in the family of origin?

3. What changes are each parent attempting to make in the care of his or her own children that mark a departure from the manner in which they were reared?
    a. How much ambivalence is there about the care each parent received from his or her own parent?
    b. To what extent are the changes or lack of changes consciously worked through as opposed to preconscious forces?
4. In what ways are the parents' own conflicts with their own parents worked out in a different way or to a different extent with the children?

C. What are the major themes[a] the family members express?
1. To what extent are these themes conscious and overt or preconscious and not clearly specified?
2. To what extent are parents and children involved in different ways in working out these family themes?
3. To what extent is an apparent rebellion against a family theme actually an acceptance of this theme?

D. What kinds of family secrets have been maintained?
1. Are there incidents in the family history about which members feel ashamed, embarrassed, or guilty?
2. To what extent is the family secret expressed or discussed, at least within the family circle?
3. To what extent are family secrets visible only in a symbolic manner?
4. To what extent can modes of thinking, perceiving, and acting be explained in terms of these more or less shared family secrets?

VIII. Family problem-solving techniques
A. What do family members identify as the primary problem or problems that exist within the family?
B. What are the primary modes of defense used in dealing with these problems? To what extent are these defenses shared family defenses?
C. To what extent do these problems and the defenses used in dealing with them prevent the continued successful adaptation and maturation of family members? How pathognomonic are these problems?
D. How effectively can family members communicate with each other regarding these problems and their resolution? To what extent are there longstanding and unresolved misunderstandings?
E. To what extent can the family involve the larger community in the resolution of these problems? Can the family seek help from others if such help is required?

---

[a]Hess and Handel (1959) define *family themes* as critical issues of family interaction as defined by family members that represent unresolved psychological issues within the family. These themes represent a unifying elaboration of family activity and are acted out to a different degree and in a different manner by different family members, depending on their own character structure. This concept is similar to the "Unity Thema" of which Murray and Associates (1938) have spoken and is to be differentiated from the concept of problem as described in Issue VIII. The family theme is a unifying construct that serves to explain the family and its actions. "Problem," as used in Issue VIII, refers specifically to aspects of conflict which are fairly overt within the family and which may originate from these family themes, but which require some more or less adaptive solution if the family is to continue functioning as a unit.

DEFINITION OF FAMILY BOUNDARIES

Limpari-McGorty

This modified extended family consists of Mr. and Mrs. Limpari who live with their second youngest son in an apartment in Tower Point; Mr. and Mrs. Limpari's youngest son, who is married, has several children and lives across the fire escape in an adjoining building. The couple also has two daughters; one is married, has several children, and lives in California; the other, Mrs. McGorty, is married, has three young daughters, and lives in a Bethany suburb. The Limparis have the most frequent contact with the two boys. In fact, until recently, they did not have a bathroom of their own and shared a bathroom with their son living in the adjoining building. The second youngest son, who lives at home, has some responsibility for home repairs and for helping his mother around the apartment as needed. Mrs. Limpari has three brothers and a sister, and her husband has one brother, all of whom live in the greater Bethany area and are included in the celebration of major religious holidays but whom the Limparis see only infrequently in between holidays.

The McGortys typically have Saturday lunch with Mrs. Limpari, and Mrs. McGorty talks with her mother on the telephone at least daily between these weekend visits. Mrs. McGorty also visits occasionally with her married brother and his family. Relations are strained between Mrs. McGorty and her husband's family, and contact with Mr. McGorty's family is confined to an occasional Thanksgiving, Christmas, or Easter dinner. Mr. McGorty has one sister (she is married and has young children) and one cousin, both of whom are occasional visitors at the McGortys. However, these relatives on Mr. McGorty's side of the family are regarded as more "distant," in spite of the close blood tie between Mr. McGorty and his sister. This preference for visiting with his wife's family rather than with his own is consistent with Mr. McGorty's initial enthusiasm for marrying into an Italian-American family; at least one reason for marrying his wife was to gain the close family ties he had missed while growing up.

Scardoni-Russo

The Scardonis and the Russos comprise an unusually close modified extended family in which help and resources are frequently exchanged between the generations. Mrs. Scardoni helps Mrs. Russo cook and provides information about housekeeping. Mrs. Russo helps her mother with errands and marketing and sets her hair. In addition, through her daily telephone calls, she provides regular communication with Mr. Butoni (her brother) and his family. Mrs. Russo's company is important, for Mrs. Scardoni has few friends of her own and without her daughter would lead an even more confined and lonely existence. Mr. Scardoni was responsible for finding work for Mr. Russo; Mr. Scardoni continues to support Mr. Russo and help him along through his connections with the building trades.

The grandparental generation consists of Mr. and Mrs. Scardoni, the parental generation of Mrs. Russo, her husband, Mr. Butoni, and Mr. Butoni's wife. The child generation consists of the Russos' daughter, Charlotte, and two children in Mr. Butoni's family. Members of the family have reached consensus about who comprises this three-generation family, although Mrs. Russo and her stepfather have a tense relationship and Mr. Butoni does not want his stepfather to be a part of the family.

Shadow members of the family include Mrs. Scardoni's first husband who died while their young children were very young, Mr. Scardoni's first wife, and Mr. Russo's parents and sisters and brothers whom she seldom sees. The Russos hardly ever visit with Mr. Russo's parents and complain that his parents are unable to celebrate holidays successfully. However, on most Sundays and holidays, Mr. and Mrs. Scardoni have her son and daughter and their families out for the day. More distant relatives are never mentioned; the family is quite isolated from these relatives, as well as from Mrs. Scardoni's own sisters and brothers. Mrs. Scardoni feels these relatives have little to offer her, and she is quite competitive with them.

Giorgio-Czaja

While the Czajas and Mrs. Giorgio formerly were representatives of the modified extended family, since they have begun sharing a common household, they have become an extended family. Each family member has assigned tasks within this three-generation household, with the exception of Peter (the Czajas' son), who is still too young to be able to help with the chores. This extended family has clearly defined boundaries—everyone living in the house—that includes Mrs. Giorgio, Mrs. Czaja, Mr. Czaja, Peter, and the Czajas' baby who will be born in three months.

The Giorgios had little contact with friends or with relatives outside the immediate family. Mrs. Giorgio's family lived some distance away and was not inclined to come for a visit. The Giorgios were so involved with Dr. Giorgio's work as a physician that they found little opportunity to visit with Mrs. Giorgio's family. Mrs. Giorgio has maintained contact with one sister who spent some time with her in the difficult weeks following her husband's death. She occasionally speaks to this sister over the telephone and, less often, corresponds with another sister who lives in another New England state.

The Czajas maintain contact with both sides of the family. They have been to visit Mrs. Giorgio's sisters and have also been to the home of another and more distant relative of Mrs. Giorgio who was a partner in the family business. Obligations are felt toward Mr. Czaja's family, and occasional visits are made. Mrs. Czaja maintains close contact with her sister who also lives in the area. She finds less in common with her older brother whom she regards as "taking her mother for a ride." She complains that her mother sends him too large an allowance and that her brother has no desire to make an independent life for himself. She occasionally writes to her two sisters in California, but has not visited them.

Finally, it should be noted that while both Mr. and Mrs. Czaja's immediate family lives within the Bethany metropolitan area, there has not been one single time since the couple was married when the two sides of the family have gathered together to share a meal or to celebrate a holiday. Mrs. Giorgio feels that Mr. Czaja's family is beneath her social position and has little interest in getting to know his family. Mr. Czaja has little desire to bring his own family into the extended family unit and prefers instead to adopt his wife's family as his own.

Pescatore-Murphy

This three-generation family is closely linked by the clearly delineated patterns of mutual aid and assistance that characterize the modified extended family. Since the two generations share a common dwelling, there is daily contact both by telephone and in person. Mrs. Pescatore provides some meals for her daughter's family, financial assistance, babysitting, help with childcare when the children were infants, and help with daily chores. The fact that, on a typical day, Mrs. Pescatore and her daughter meet some 8 to 10 times, attests to the extent of their mutual involvement. Indeed, there are few other relatives with whom the Pescatores have any contact beside their daughter and her family: their two sons, both of whom are single; Mrs. Pescatore's mother who lives in a nursing home in an adjacent suburb; Mrs. Pescatore's cousin whom she has known since earliest childhood; and Mrs. Pescatore's maternal aunt. Mrs. Pescatore visits with her cousin, mother, and aunt at least weekly and sometimes more often.

The Murphys have only occasional contact with Mr. Murphy's parents or Mrs. Murphy's brothers. Mr. Murphy occasionally stops by his parents' house on the weekend, and, recently, when Mr. Murphy's mother was in the hospital for surgery, both Mr. and Mrs. Murphy called her daily. At the time of their marriage, Mr. and Mrs. Murphy agreed that they would align themselves with Mrs. Murphy's parents in preference to her husband's family. For Mr. Murphy, his wife's parents initially offered emotional involvement that was not possible within his own family. However, after his wife and his mother began to experience interpersonal conflict and he and his wife's mother began to quarrel, Mr. Murphy began to feel torn and, ultimately, ended up taking his mother's side in her quarrels with his wife. At the present time, he feels that his wife does not recognize her mother-in-law as a family member with legitimate demands and, generally, has refused to accede to her husband's wishes.

Conclusion

While each of these four families relies on some one or two relatives beyond the three-generation grandmother-mother-child family for assistance, relatives are less important for these families who are rather self-contained. Both the psychological issue of closeness and separation and the extent of tangible and emotional support that the two generations offer each other enhance this intrafamilial closeness. Only Mrs. Pescatore's mother is still alive, and the regular hairdressing appointments and occasional Sunday visits provide opportunities for the four generations of women (including Mrs. Murphy's daughter) in this family to assemble. Mrs. Scardoni has little use for the relatives in her parental family, and Mrs. Limpari sees her own family only at infrequent intervals. Mrs. Giorgio is the only grandmother to visit with more distant members of her own family who, ironically, live farther away than the less-often visited relatives of the other three grandmothers.

Although Mr. and Mrs. Murphy are presently not in agreement over the role of Mr. Murphy's parental family, in the past Mr. Murphy's own family was less important as a source of tangible and affectional resources. In the other three families, there is agreement that the wife's family constitutes the salient relatives. The extent to which the husbands in this study have adopted their wives' families as their own suggests that this may be an important factor in the decision to marry. At least a part of the tension about the mother-in-law in American society may be created by the husband's erotic and affectional interest in his wife's mother; at least some men marry their wives to receive, through the closeness afforded by the wife's family, the attention and affection missing in their own family during childhood. Location of residence makes little difference, since, in general, there was as intense contact between those families in which the mother and grandmother lived apart as in those families where they shared a common residence.

ESTABLISHMENT OF ROLE BOUNDARIES WITHIN THE FAMILY

Limpari-McGorty

Role boundaries, especially generational boundaries, were quite distinct within the Limpari household. Beginning at about the time they entered grammar school, the children were expected to understand and follow their parents' instructions, and disobedience was punished. The typical Tower Point first- or second-generation Italian-American family is patriarchal. However, while Mr. Limpari's word is respected; on several occasions, he has yielded to his wife.

The fact that Mrs. Limpari has worked continuously for more than 25 years has meant that Mr. Limpari has been forced to share the instrumental role within the family with his wife. Nor is the social network as loose as is typically found in Tower Point. Although he has his own friends, Mr. Limpari spends much time with members of Mrs. Limpari's family, and, since his retirement, Mr. Limpari has helped around the house and has accepted responsibility for some household chores.

Not only is the kinship network less tightly knit, and role segregation less complete than in typical Tower Point families, but also the Limparis maintained a more child-oriented family. This was due in large part to the fact that Mrs. Limpari had higher educational aspirations for her children than was typical in

Tower Point. Mrs. McGorty describes numerous occasions during her youth when her parents took her wishes into consideration in making family plans. Since Mrs. McGorty's marriage, Mrs. Limpari has become more self-centered and has been much less willing to make personal sacrifices for her daughter than during Mrs. McGorty's high school and college years. For example, Mrs. Limpari is not willing to change plans she and her husband have made to help her daughter out by babysitting.

The issue of confusion in sex-role boundaries was somewhat of a problem for Mrs. Limpari, but even more so for Mrs. McGorty. While Mrs. Limpari's husband had a firm conception of what was appropriate behavior for men and women, Mrs. McGorty's husband is much less concerned with this issue and tends to accept many tasks such as feeding, diapering, and bathing his young daughters that many men would not be willing to perform. The fact that Mrs. McGorty has much more education than her husband also tends to blur expectations of appropriate sex-role behavior within the family.

The McGortys are primarily child-centered. Just as was true of her mother, Mrs. McGorty is educationally ambitious for her children and has organized her day around the necessity of transporting her children to and from their private schools. A considerable part of the family budget is spent on schooling, and Mrs. McGorty and her husband plan few activities apart from the children.

Scardoni-Russo

Generational distinctions are less important than sex-role distinctions for this family. Mrs. Scardoni considers it proper that she give her daughter advice about childrearing and that her daughter come to her with her problems. While she discusses most of her problems with her daughter, she does not consider it appropriate that she discuss with her daughter her problems concerning her relationship with her husband.

Very clear sex-role distinctions are maintained by Mrs. Scardoni and her husband. In many ways, the couple's marriage is typical of first- and second-generation Italian-American marriages. Husband and wife each have their own friends, and the couple has tightly knit social networks and relatively segregated roles. While Mr. Scardoni is visiting with his friends in Tower Point, his wife visits with her son and daughter. Mrs. Scardoni has little acquaintance with her husband's friends. The Russos have a much more loosely knit social network, with the few friends they have being friends of both husband and wife. Although Mr. Russo still does not feel very comfortable with his brother-in-law, the two families frequently go places together, especially if they are visiting Mrs. Russo's mother.

Although Mr. Scardoni does gardening and work on the outside of the house, he does not like helping with the housework and regards the inside of the house as his wife's domain. Mr. Russo has a much-less stereotyped concept of the man's role in the family and readily helps around the house, doing the more difficult jobs. On weekends, he often baby-sits so that his wife may have some time to herself. While the Russos generally have a more companionate marriage than the Scardonis, Mr. and Mrs. Scardoni decide together on major household expenses and work together on paying the bills. This arrangement may be due, in part, to the fact that the Scardonis married later in life. Since Mrs. Scardoni had handled her own affairs for many years, she would have been less willing to have her husband take over control of the purse. In addition, Mrs. Scardoni's first husband had spent most of his paycheck on alcohol and "numbers" games, and Mrs. Scardoni was not eager to repeat this problem of not having enough money to run the household.

Since Mr. Scardoni has alimony to pay, he cannot let his wife handle the family purse strings, so that financial decisions are joint. On the other hand, Mr. Russo is very dutiful about bringing home his paycheck for his wife. He then receives a small amount for carfare and other incidentals.

Just as men are expected to work, women are expected to keep house and care for children. If they work, women are expected to learn traditional tasks. For this reason, Mrs. Scardoni worked as a cleaning woman at various times while the children were young. Mrs. Scardoni's daughter learned the trade of hairdressing, although she has only occasionally worked at this trade. During the time that her children were adolescents, Mrs. Scardoni considered it appropriate for her son to come and go as he pleased, but she expected her daughter to be in by about midnight and was concerned that neighbors might talk about her if she were home too late, a problem that would make little difference for a boy.

Since Mrs. Scardoni reared her children by herself, there was no distinction between occupational, marital, and parental roles; Mrs. Scardoni's orientation was entirely a child-centered one. The family symbiosis contributes to the exclusively child-oriented role organization within the Russo family, for there is almost no emphasis either on Mr. Russo's occupation or involvement in the wider community beyond the family.

Giorgio-Czaja

Mrs. Giorgio conceives of much more strongly demarcated boundaries between generations than is true of the Czajas. She feels that children should do as they are told, should not talk back to their elders, and should demonstrate deference to those who are older than themselves. In her relationship with Mrs. Czaja, Mrs. Giorgio recognizes that her authority has its limits. While she would like her daughter to be more attentive to housekeeping, she recognizes that there is little she can do. She would also like to be able to influence Mrs. Czaja's childcare practices to a greater extent than she is able to at the present time. She herself expected her children to be obedient, even as toddlers. Mrs. Giorgio's concern about protecting her own autonomy limits the extent of her willingness to tell her daughter how she feels, for such advice might mean that she would become entangled in a relationship that would impose a further burden on her. For this reason, while she has strong opinions, Mrs. Giorgio tends to observe events without direct intervention.

Mrs. Czaja expects much less in the way of obedience from her son Peter. While, on occasion, she gives him a spanking if he "talks back," she recognizes that he might have a strong feeling about some aspect of his care which should be told to his mother. In Mrs. Czaja's view, generational differences do not mean that children's rights should be compromised; Mr. Czaja concurs with his wife's views.

While Mrs. Czaja's mother expected that her son would be more aggressive than her daughters, she placed less emphasis on sex-role differences than did other mothers in the study. In part, this may be attributed to her somewhat higher level of educational attainment, as well as to her own husband's occupation as a physician. She was always impressed by her husband's sensitivity to other people's suffering. She saw nothing strange in a man assuming the role of caring for people. Concurrently, she believed that girls should not be limited to the role of housewife and encouraged the development of strong achievement motivation in her daughters. She herself greatly valued her own skills as a medical secretary and encouraged her daughters, particularly Mrs. Czaja, to pursue professional careers.

Mrs. Czaja and her husband also place little emphasis on sex-role differences. Mr. Czaja helps with housekeeping and, most evenings, washes the dinner dishes. In addition, he often helps his wife with major tasks such as washing the windows or waxing the kitchen floor. When Mr. Czaja's wife goes to her printmaking class, he is perfectly willing to give Peter his bath and to get him ready for bed. Peter is still too young to determine how much his parents will expect him to act in accordance with cultural expectations of sex-role appropriate behavior. It should be noted that Peter's mother was willing to provide him with a doll that he carries around the house during the day and sleeps with at night.

During the time when their children were young, the Giorgios could be characterized as a community-oriented family in which the primary concern was Dr. Giorgio's occupation and the family's image in the community. While her husband was, according to the accounts of several family members, much less concerned with social status, Dr. Giorgio's reputation within the community was of some importance to him. According to the reports of other family members, Dr. Giorgio enjoyed being consulted on various civic- and church-related projects and quite willingly gave his time to patients unable to afford medical care. At least a part of the doctor's reason for providing this care was that it enhanced his role as a generous person who cared about others. The Czajas, on the other hand, may be characterized as a child-oriented family. Both parents are involved in Peter's upbringing, and Mr. Czaja is relatively more involved in childcare than is true of fathers in child-oriented families.

Pescatore-Murphy

Generation boundaries were rigidly enforced in the Pescatore family. Mrs. Pescatore's children were expected to obey her commands without questioning. Her belief in the necessity of rigid control of behavior can be seen quite clearly in her reaction to her grandchildren's occasional disobedience and their tendency to talk back to their mother. Mrs. Murphy is either unwilling or unable to maintain firm control with her children. While she attempts discipline by reasoning with her children, she acknowledges that she is unable to control their behavior when they become unruly.

The distinction between male and female is fairly carefully maintained within the first generation, although Mr. Pescatore has occasionally been willing to help wash dishes. Typically, he was at work during those hours that the children were home from school and, because of his work schedule, was not expected to help around the house. Within the second generation, Mr. Murphy is unwilling to help out around the house and has his own friends and interests separate from those of his wife. The fact that Mr. Murphy is seldom at home only increases the role differentiation between husband and wife.

Mrs. Murphy has not, in general, emphasized gender distinctions with her own children. She focuses her educational aspirations on Barbara, her middle child and only daughter. She feels that her oldest child, William, as a boy, will be better able to get along in the public schools. She has been careful to separate her two boys from her girl in bedroom arrangements and feels that such an arrangement is important.

Mr. Murphy shows no greater deference to the boys than to Barbara, and, during the few minutes when he might be at home during the day, he does not play different games or in any way act differently toward the boys than he does toward Barbara. Generally, he roughhouses with all his children or reads them a story. The children seem, from Mrs. Murphy's account, to pay little attention to gender differences. While William is expected to watch out for the other two, this is largely because of his role as the oldest child.

The Pescatores were an atypical family in terms of intrafamily role organization, but somewhat more parent- than child-oriented. When Mr. Pescatore was home, plans were made that were convenient for the parents, and the children were expected to fit in with these plans. Intrafamilial role organization within the second generation is also complex. Mr. Murphy is almost entirely community-oriented, with his work occupying most of his time. Mr. Murphy's wife is child-oriented when he is away, but parent-centered whenever he is home, planning family activities in such a way that she can spend as much time as possible with her husband. At the same time, these joint activities center primarily around Mr. Murphy's work, and, when husband and wife go out together, it is primarily to attend some work-related event.

Conclusion

Among the four modified extended families in this study, generational distinctions were much less important than sex-role distinctions. Although each of the four sets of grandparents felt that children should respect their elders, only Mrs. Giorgio and Mrs. Pescatore had strong feelings about this issue, and it was expressed primarily in terms of the greater leniency that their daughters allowed their children compared to what they had allowed their daughters as children. This issue of generational boundaries was not very salient for the four sets of parents. Perhaps because their children are still young, generational distinctions are not sharply maintained. However, Mrs. Murphy feels unable to set limits and is disturbed by her children's willingness to talk back to her. Mrs. Russo is also concerned primarily about the issue of discipline, and she finds it difficult to get her daughter to do as she asks. On the other hand, Mrs. Czaja believes that it is important for Peter to be able to express his wishes to his parents and that, as he grows up, he should have a say in family affairs.

Partially because his wife also works and shares the instrumental role, Mr. Limpari is less concerned than other men in the grandparent generation about sex-role distinctions. He is willing to help with minor household chores, and, although he visits each evening with his own friends, he and his wife sometimes visit together with old friends and close relatives. Both Mr. Pescatore and Dr. Giorgio were at work much of the time their children were young, and neither engaged in much social life outside the house. Mr. Scardoni is not willing to help around the house, and, as is typical of men in working-class families (Suttles, 1968; Rainwater, Coleman, and Handel, 1959), he regards the inside of the house as the woman's world. Indeed, he is the most concerned about this issue of the four grandfathers.

Among the parents, only one family strongly emphasizes sex-role distinctions. Mr. Murphy is willing to play with his children, but is unwilling to help in child-care. When he is home, he expects his wife to tend to his needs. Mrs. Murphy shares her husband's concept of what is appropriate behavior for men and women and places greater emphasis on issues such as modesty training than other women in the parent generation. At the same time, Mrs. Murphy's aspirations for her children's education are centered primarily on her only daughter and middle child, whom she sees as like herself. Mr. Russo shares some of Mr. Murphy's concept of appropriate behavior for men and women. At the same time, although he regards housework as the woman's responsibility, he is willing to help with childcare.

To a greater degree than Mr. Murphy or Mr. Russo, both Mr. McGorty and Mr. Czaja help with the housework and childcare. Among the four parental families, traditional sex-role distinctions are most blurred in the McGorty household; Mr. McGorty does not have the same level of educational attainment as his wife, nor is he as ambitious. He has relatively little interest either in his wife's condominium project or his work as a clerk. He willingly helps with all aspects, both of housework and childcare, when he comes home from work. Because he is home so much of the time, Mr. Czaja is in a better position than other fathers in this study to help with childcare: the main household chore he handles is doing the dishes.

With the exception of Mrs. McGorty's project, none of the women in the parental generation work. However, both Mrs. Murphy and Mrs. Czaja like to help their husbands, and both women have found ways of remaining at home and yet of contributing to their husbands' work. Mrs. Czaja helps mount and wrap prints and paintings, while Mrs. Murphy makes most of her husband's appointments. Again, with the exception of Mrs. McGorty, none of the women in the parental generation have any activities or interests outside the household and hold to quite traditional definitions of the wife-mother role.

While all the families in the parent generation, with the exception of the Murphys, are child-oriented, only one of the families in the grandparental generation, the Limparis, was child-oriented. Since Mrs. Scardoni reared her children by herself, she had no choice but to be child-oriented. However, since her marriage to Mr. Scardoni, she is quite parent-centered, and the couple has interests appropriate to a postparental family. While their children were young, the Giorgios were community-centered and much interested in status. The Pescatores were largely parent-centered, with their needs as parents taking precedence whenever Mr. Pescatore was at home.

Overall, while concern with sex-role boundaries is evident, particularly for the grandparental generation, the issue of role boundaries is not one that very much concerns these four families. The parental generation emerges as largely child-oriented, with the wife-mother and husband-father roles somewhat differentiated, but with a good deal of overlap, particularly in the area of childcare.

LOCUS OF FAMILY OPERATIONS

Limpari-McGorty

Mrs. Limpari, because of her leadership role within the community, is more attuned to the availability of community services than many Tower Point residents. As a lawyer, Mrs. McGorty is uniquely prepared to deal with official agencies and describes, with obvious pleasure, her success in locating the appropriate community official or agency. She was able to obtain scholarship aid for her oldest daughter and to locate the very best schools in the community. She takes pride in her success in dealing with numerous community agencies regarding her condominium project.

Mrs. Limpari has a more limited sense of community than is true for her daughter. Tower Point is an unusually self-contained community, and the residents seldom have to venture far beyond the community's clearly defined boundaries. Mrs. Limpari does not look forward to her occasional visits to her daughter's suburban home and even shows some reluctance about shopping trips to the supermarket located outside the community. Even Mrs. Limpari's work is nearby, allowing her to be able to walk to and from her job and even to return home for her coffee break.

Neither generation has ventured beyond Bethany and southern New England. Mrs. McGorty's married sister lives in California, but no member of the family has gone to visit her. All other close relatives, with the exception of Mrs. McGorty, live within the confines of Tower Point. There is frequent visiting back and forth, particularly between Mrs. Limpari and her relatives. Mr. Limpari has a circle of close friends in the community with whom he plays cards almost every evening, but he is less likely to visit relatives.

The issue of visiting between the McGortys and the Limparis is one of the central issues in the family and the complex feelings that these visits engender has already been described (Chapter 3). The McGortys frequently entertain their friends at home, but are much less likely to entertain relatives. Rather, they return to Tower Point when visiting relatives. They also prefer to have their friends come over to their house rather than to visit at their friends' houses. Mrs. McGorty was unable to say why it was that she and her husband so seldom visited at their friends' houses. Like her own parents, Mrs. McGorty does have a rather limited concept of space. She travels some distance each day while driving her older daughter to school and picking up her younger daughter's classmates. However, outside this daily routine, she seems to prefer places she knows well and where she has previously been. The only reference the McGortys made to places outside South Tuxton and Tower Point was to vacation visits with some friends who have a home on Cape Cod.

Finally, it should be noted that, while Mrs. Limpari has assumed a leadership role in Tower Point, Mrs. McGorty and her family are quite uninvolved in their community. They feel isolated and out of touch with community processes, but express little desire to become more involved. While Mrs. McGorty does vote in the national elections, she says she finds local elections uninteresting; she does feel that this might change if she were living in Tower Point and felt more involved in community issues.

Work does not seem to be a very conflictful issue within either family except as it alters the ways in which family members view sex-role distinctions. Mr. Limpari enjoyed his work as a construction foreman and was quite successful. After his retirement last year, Mr. Limpari experienced some difficulty adjusting to his new-found leisure. He found himself frequently returning to his old job and talking to his fellow workers. However, especially during the past few months, he has been able to keep himself busier working around the house and becoming more involved in family affairs. Mr. Limpari's wife is nearing the age where she can retire with full benefits, but insists she will continue to work until her boss throws her out. Since she is an extremely skilled seamstress, she is likely to be able to continue for an indefinite time. In Chapter 3 we saw the importance of work for Mrs. Limpari; in the light of this discussion it is understandable that she would want to continue working.

In contrast with her mother, Mrs. McGorty derived very little satisfaction from her work as a lawyer. Perhaps the intensity of the competition she felt with her male colleagues was painful for her. Certainly, as soon as she was married she gave up her profession and resumed it only after her first marriage ended in divorce. While Mrs. McGorty is quite active in developing her condominium project, there is little likelihood that she will resume working. Nor is there any evidence that Mr. McGorty enjoys his work. Mr. McGorty is a solid and responsible worker who does not complain about his job but derives little pleasure from it.

Money is realistically valued among both generations. While there have been times when money was extremely tight for the Limparis, the attitude they have is that one should work hard and be grateful for what he or she has been able to earn; there is little feeling of financial deprivation. Financial issues have been less difficult for the McGortys. While money must be carefully budgeted, and there are always debts to be paid, there has never been a time when they were unable to make purchases they really desired.

Scardoni-Russo

Both generations of this family are quite isolated from the community. The most frequently used community agency is the hospital. Husbands and wives of both generations have all been hospitalized at some point in their lives. Other than hospitals the only community service the Scardonis have familiarized themselves with is the legal system. Beyond these occasional contacts with hospitals and courts, neither generation has had much contact with community agencies or institutions. Neither generation has ever traveled outside New England, with the exception of the Scardonis' honeymoon at Niagara Falls.

Although they watch the news on television, neither grandparents nor parents subscribe to newspapers or magazines. Both Mrs. Scardoni and Mrs. Russo occasionally purchase ladies' magazines to read the recipes and columns on family health.

Visiting, except between mother and daughter, is limited, and neither mother nor grandmother has close friends outside the family. Mrs. Russo's one good friend is a relative. In summary, Mrs. Russo's and Mrs. Scardoni's physical environment is very restricted. Mrs. Russo walks her daughter down to the square several times a week to do errands. While there she cashes her husband's paycheck at the supermarket, pays her bills by money order, and takes home the rest for her household expenses and her husband's allowance. The family has no checking account and acknowledges, with sadness, that they have not been able to save very much.

Neither generation of this modified extended family is involved in either voluntary or formal organizations. Both Mr. Scardoni and Mr. Russo are union members in good standing, but neither attends union social functions or even votes in union elections. Since Charlotte is not yet in school, even this contact with the larger community is missing.

Both Mr. Scardoni and Mr. Russo are good and steady workers, and each needs to work to support his family. Before the Russos were married, Mr. Russo had a very erratic work history, but in exchange for obtaining his in-laws' consent to marry, his prospective father-in-law obtained a job for him that he has kept ever since. Both men derive considerable satisfaction from their work but are not ambitious. Only Mrs. Russo's brother has moved from a blue-collar to a white-collar occupation. As a customer engineer for a small firm that manufactures office machines and small business computers, Mr. Butoni's work is highly technical and provides a good and steady income.

While all the men in this family work hard, by the time they have finished paying the usual household bills, income tax, union fees, and life and health insurance premiums, there is little left for savings. Given the variety of skills within the family, there is relatively little expense for household services. Mr. Scardoni is a good mason, plumber, and electrician, and Mr. Butoni, who used to be an auto mechanic, spends many of his Sundays at his parents' house repairing the family's cars. Mrs. Russo does her mother's and sister-in-law's hair, and cuts the men's hair as well.

Both Mr. Scardoni and Mr. Russo work regular hours, leaving for work very early in the morning and returning by midafternoon. Further evidence of their relatively satisfied attitude toward their work comes from the fact that each man is usually cheerful on coming home after work: neither Mrs. Scardoni nor Mrs. Russo complains that her husband is tired and cross when he comes home. Given these regular working hours and job satisfaction, work does not interfere for either man in fulfilling his role as husband and father.

Giorgio-Czaja

The Czajas and Giorgios are, of all the families in the study, the most creative in their use of community services and in their willingness to travel beyond the boundaries of their community. By their frequent trips to and from their Italian homeland and business and pleasure excursions within the United States, Mrs. Giorgio's parents clearly fostered in their child a love for travel. Mrs. Giorgio, at 64, is still interested in visiting places she has never seen. A cosmopolitan woman, she is almost as comfortable in Venice or San Francisco as she is in Bethany and has her favorite hotels and shops in each city. The Czajas also have traveled widely through New England, and Mrs. Czaja had been to Europe as a teenager. While they have not left the United States since their marriage, they have talked frequently of vacationing in Europe when their children are older.

Although neither generation has many personal friends, Dr. Giorgio, being an influential doctor, had contact with numerous agencies, including hospitals, universities, and voluntary associations such as the county medical society. Dr. Giorgio's son-in-law continues the tradition by teaching at a local college. Mrs. Czaja takes advantage of adult education classes offered by several universities in the Boston area, as well as classes at a local center for adult education.

The family places much less emphasis on visiting with friends, neighbors, and family than on an essentially impersonal involvement in the greater community. While Mrs. Giorgio occasionally talks on the telephone, she seldom ventures out with friends and, even less often, visits at a friend's house. Mrs. Czaja visits with several neighbors whose children play with Peter. She also has a few friends, including her sister, in a nearby community and visits with other friends after her printmaking class or when she goes shopping. In summary, the Czajas have relatively few friends and, partially from deference to Mrs. Giorgio, seldom ask friends over to the house. In general, the Czajas seem to derive more pleasure and companionship from family rather than from outsiders.

Work has been a central locus of family operations for three generations, beginning with Mrs. Giorgio's parents. Dr. Giorgio also loved his work, and, like his in-laws, he gained social status from his occupation. While Dr. Giorgio's work brought in a good income, he made less money than is typical for a physician because he donated so much of his time to patients who were unable to pay. Dr. Giorgio's work also, like his wife's parents' work, meant that he spent very little time with his family. Indeed, the only way Mrs. Giorgio could visit with her husband was to accompany him on his house calls. Work was valued primarily in terms of how much satisfaction it provided and, for Mrs. Giorgio, above all else, how much it contributed to the family's prestige in the community.

Work has some of the same meanings for Mr. Czaja as it did for Dr. Giorgio. It is valued primarily in terms of the inherent satisfaction it provides and for the extent that it can bring Mr. and Mrs. Czaja together. Mrs. Czaja feels that her interest in and knowledge about her husband's work will mean that they will have a closer relationship. Like her father, Mrs. Czaja's husband is frequently at home but less frequently involved with the family. Mrs. Czaja attempts to make important contact with her husband through participating in his work as her mother did in her father's work. Through becoming important in the process of getting the work done, she has both a chance to experience, vicariously, some of her husband's satisfactions with work and also a chance to build her relationship with her husband and to become more important to him. Mrs. Czaja worries, however, that her husband works too hard and that his desire to spend long hours isolated in his studio, while working on a painting, will interfere with his ability to provide the love and attention she and her children need. She is somewhat less concerned with the fact that her husband's preoccupation with his work means that they have little time to spend with friends.

Pescatore-Murphy

By choice, and consistent with community values, neither generation has extensive contact with the community. Rather, each has devoted some effort to remaining self-sufficient. When necessary, each generation can use community resources. While the children were growing up, the Pescatores took them to a variety of museums and historical sites and traveled almost exclusively by public transportation. Mrs. Murphy sends two of her children to school and has arranged for various public and private transportation services. Mr. Murphy has extensive contact with the wider community through his role in the theater, and, as a result of working with him, Mrs. Murphy has learned a good deal about the community and its services.

Particularly with Mrs. Murphy, a distinction has to be made between participation in the world outside the home in the interest of establishing a better relationship with her husband and helping him in his work, and her actual use of community services and resources in her own daily life. Mrs. Murphy arranges for actors and various theatrical performances and spends much time on the telephone. However, beyond this telephone work for her husband, she has almost no contact with others and prefers to stay at home where she feels more secure.

Outside her brief stay in New York when she was in business college and subsequent business trips with her husband, Mrs. Murphy has never traveled. In fact, she considers a day trip to the city a fairly important occasion. Essentially, Mrs. Murphy's world ends at the bottom of the hill where she takes her dry cleaning on Monday mornings. Outside brief trips to the "square" to pay utility bills or occasional trips to the market, her preference is to stay at home. Her subjective definition of her community as the neighborhood in which she lives is, of course, in striking contrast with her husband who commutes with regularity between New York and Bethany and who has numerous obligations all over the greater Bethany area.

Mrs. Murphy has made few friends outside the immediate family and does not have extensive contacts with the neighbors. She has no "girl friends" with whom she goes shopping or whom she telephones. The daily contacts she has are limited to her mother and her children. Even though she has a relative living next door, she hardly ever visits with this relative and prefers that her children not play with her relative's children who are about the same age as her own children.

This pattern of relationships reflects Mrs. Murphy's mother's own friendship pattern. Mrs. Pescatore, too, has only limited contacts with persons other than her daughter. While she talks with her own mother over the telephone each day, since she is in a nursing home, Mrs. Pescatore does not like visiting with her. She sees both her mother and her sister at the Friday morning beauty get-together and sees a cousin twice a week on a regular basis, as she has for the past 20 years. Clearly Mrs. Pescatore's entire circle of relationships is limited to her kinfolk.

Mr. Pescatore has enjoyed his work, but has also used it to avoid closer emotional involvement with his family. The income he makes has always been sufficient to provide for the family's needs, and he has derived considerable self-esteem from his promotion to foreman of his shop. At the same time, Mr. Pescatore's work schedule made it difficult for him to participate in family life and chores.

Work has served as a major source of conflict between Mr. Murphy and his wife and represents a continual source of family disruption. Not only is he gone for a larger part of the week than he is home, but also, while he works long hours, he brings in less income than is necessary for the family's present standard of living. While he says that his work provides him with creative satisfaction, Mr. Murphy's mood of continual frustration and irritation suggests that work is also a source of conflict for him. Mrs. Murphy makes allowances both for the less-than-adequate income and for his frequent bad moods by emphasizing the creative and difficult nature of his work, but does recognize that things are not going well for her husband.

Conclusion

With the exception of Mrs. Giorgio who visits her children both across the United States and in Europe, the families in this study stay very close to home. While Mrs. Limpari has a married daughter in California, she has never visited with her daughter and regards trips from Tower Point as dangerous. This view of the world outside the neighborhood as threatening is expressed even more clearly by both generations of the Pescatore-Murphy and Scardoni-Russo families. While Mr. Murphy is fairly cosmopolitan, neither Mrs. Murphy nor her own parents make use of resources outside their immediate community. Mrs. Murphy attends theater with her husband, but, except when she is with her husband, she does not venture beyond the shopping area near her house. Except for her trips out to her mother's house, Mrs. Russo goes no farther than her neighborhood shopping center. Mr. and Mrs. Czaja have traveled farther than other members of the parent generation, but even they have never traveled outside New England.

Just as the view that these four families have of space is quite limited, they are largely isolated from community resources. Mrs. McGorty and Mrs. Czaja make the most creative use of resources. Mrs. McGorty, because of her legal training, her construction project, and her involvement with her children's education, knows a good deal about her community and is able to use a variety of community resources. She knows whom to call in city government to have street repairs made, how to deal with federal agencies such as the Internal Revenue Service and what educational resources are available in the greater Bethany area. Mrs. Czaja is familiar with institutions of higher education and makes use of adult education facilities. The Scardonis and Russos have very low contact with community resources beyond the medical center. Mrs. Giorgio also has contact with medical facilities, for she volunteers at the hospital where her husband was formerly on the staff. In addition, she is able to use public transportation, a skill other grandmothers in this study do not have.

Work is a salient issue only for Mr. Murphy and Mr. Czaja, both of whom are involved with the arts. Among the men in the grandparent generation, only Dr. Giorgio was deeply involved with his work. Mr. Limpari is semiretired, and Mr. Pescatore is nearing retirement. Retirement is likely to be a source of conflict for all three of the men in the grandfather generation who have few other interests to occupy their time. Mr. Pescatore formerly raised poultry as a source of extra income, but was discouraged by his wife from continuing with his hobby. While they are steady and regular workers, neither Mr. McGorty nor Mr. Russo is much involved in their work.

At the present time, money is not a serious problem for any of the four families in this study. Indeed, of the four grandparent families, only Mrs. Scardoni suffered severe economic privation during the time she was rearing her family. With steady employment and carefully planned household budgets, all the parental and grandparental families are able to realize their immediate material needs and to maintain a life-style consistent with their rather prosaic orientation to their social environment.

FAMILY CLOSENESS AND SEPARATION ACROSS THE GENERATIONS

Limpari-McGorty

Both generations in this family have strong feelings regarding issues of closeness and separation. While both Mrs. Limpari and Mrs. McGorty express attitudes regarding this issue that are adaptive for their own generation, they have not been able to entirely resolve their own conflicting feelings. The weekly visits of the McGortys to Tower Point create residual feelings of disappointment for them and irritation on the part of the Limpari family. While there is considerable difference of opinion regarding the amount of freedom and individuality permitted within the family, it appears that Mrs. Limpari has encouraged greater separateness and individuality than her children wished. On the other hand, the children seem to have sensed their mother's mixed feelings regarding separation, a fact that may explain why three of the four children are either living with or near their parents or are planning to return.

Mrs. McGorty believes much less than her mother in separation between mothers and their grown children and hopes that her daughters will reside near her after they are married. While this belief is a reflection of her disappointment over her mother's discouragement of a closer bond between her mother and herself, Mrs. McGorty's own attitudes toward this issue may change greatly by the time her daughters are grown.

Scardoni-Russo

The issue of closeness is central for this three-generation family. The mother-grandmother pair was selected for intensive study precisely because of their attitudes concerning this issue of separation. Relationships between grandmother, mother, and daughter are so intense and binding that they preclude relationships outside the family. For both grandmother and mother, this symbiosis has a long history and is understood in terms of the resentment and hostility that each feels toward the role of wife and mother, in relation to her own unmet childhood needs.

Within such an overprotective and binding relationship, Mrs. Scardoni and Mrs. Russo are in agreement about what they expect from each other as adults. Although they do not live together, they call each other several times each day. They also get together several times each week for periods of time ranging from a few hours to the entire day.

While her fantasy productions show that Mrs. Russo feels trapped by her relationship with her mother in which she has to achieve perfection in order to win her mother's love and admiration, Mrs. Russo's more conscious description of her relationship with her mother indicates that she also looks forward to contact with her mother. Indeed, there are many times when Mrs. Russo wishes she could be a child and live with her mother instead of having to function more independently as an adult. This dependent involvement with her mother is generally handled in a realistic manner, and Mrs. Russo helps her mother with shopping and errands at those times when she visits.

Mrs. Scardoni is quite clear about what is permitted in the family and supervises even the most minute details of her daughter's life. For example, she talks with her daughter almost every week about the necessity of making out a budget and of putting aside some savings. She also criticizes her daughter for being thin and urges her to eat more. This nagging infuriates Mrs. Russo. Mrs. Scardoni also frequently asks about her son-in-law's health and wants to know what he is doing.

Mrs. Scardoni has no ties other than those with her children and their families. She quarrels with her own brothers and sisters, and, because of the social isolation she experienced both during her own childhood and during the years when her children were growing up, she has no friends outside the family. Mrs. Russo's two closest friends, her brother and a cousin, are both family members. Neither the Butonis nor the Russos list any friends who are not also relatives.

Mr. Butoni, while a hardworking and successful man who enjoys his wife and children, directs most of his energy toward strengthening family bonds and increasing feelings of closeness. He values his close and dependent relationship with his mother whose advice he seeks on major problems in his life. He welcomed the possibility of sharing a house with the Russos and looks forward to his almost nightly visits with his sister, as well as to weekend outings with the Russos at Mrs. Scardoni's house. He has always had a special concern for his sister's and mother's welfare and felt very much like the "man" of the family. It is for this reason that Mr. Butoni particularly resents Mr. Scardoni whom he regards as an intruder on the family.

Mr. Russo is also a dependent and compliant man with few friends or interests outside the family. The free time he has is spent helping his wife around the house or entertaining his daughter. He, too, looks forward to the Sunday outings with the Scardonis and sees his father-in-law at work almost daily. Mr. Russo's involvement with the family and his isolation from the larger society further intensifies his wife's symbiotic relationship with her mother. Only Mr. Scardoni has interests outside the family, and, since he is not very well accepted either by Mrs. Scardoni's children or their spouses, his outside interests do not have much impact on the close tie between Mrs. Scardoni, her children, and their families.

Giorgio-Czaja

Mrs. Giorgio's emphasis on separateness is highly overdetermined and is associated primarily with her belief that she will be exploited unless she exaggerates her own individuality. Mrs. Czaja uses her emphasis on separateness and uniqueness as a way of attracting her mother's interest in her. Mrs. Giorgio's fear of being trapped in emotional relationships leads her to be less involved in family celebrations and cultural and national holidays than other grandmothers in the study.

Largely as a result of the difference between Mrs. Giorgio and the Czajas regarding the value of closeness, there is continuous conflict in the family over this issue. Although Mrs. Giorgio sometimes grumbles about how her daughter does not share in the work, and although Mrs. Czaja sometimes complains that her mother refuses to help in washing the dishes, this informal division of labor appears to be effective. Mother and daughter have considerable difficulty reaching a degree of emotional separation that is comfortable for each, although this difficulty does not appear with regard to attitudinal issues. For example, the family shows considerable latitude in political, cultural, and religious views. Mrs. Giorgio typically votes Republican in state elections and sometimes in national elections as well. Mrs. Giorgio's daughter and son-in-law are determined Democrats, and, in the past, Mrs. Czaja has worked for the League of Women Voters. While political views are sometimes discussed, there is agreement on disagreement. Considerable differences in views are also tolerated in matters of religion. Mrs. Giorgio is fairly conservative in her views, but she accepts the fact that Mr. Czaja does not attend church except at Christmas and Easter. She believes that going to church does not necessarily make one religious and has not attempted to convert her son-in-law. Mrs. Giorgio respects the views of others and feels that religious, political, and social beliefs are private matters. On the other hand, Mrs. Czaja, while expressing more liberal attitudes, attempts much more than her mother to convert others to her beliefs.

Pescatore-Murphy

Across the two generations, this family has been largely unable to resolve the issue of appropriate versus inappropriate closeness. Both mother and daughter are involved in a complex relationship that excludes even the possibility of most extrafamilial relationships. As we have seen, Mrs. Pescatore depends on her daughter and her children for important emotional satisfactions and has little else of importance in her life beyond her daughter and her family. At the same time, she is both intrusive and uses her relationship with her daughter and her grandchildren chiefly to satisfy her own needs.

Mrs. Murphy also depends on her mother, both for help with daily chores and for advice in dealing with her own personal conflicts. Rather than having chosen to work together from a sense of common purpose or rational selection of the best means to some agreed-on ends, these two women need and use each other in ways ultimately destructive for each. Mrs. Pescatore has very little capacity to tolerate opinions that diverge from her own, but until Mrs. Murphy's children were old enough to develop relationships with their grandmother, Mrs. Murphy was able to hold contrary attitudes without undue disruption of the relationship. In the past few years, while there have been some times when differences of opinion have threatened to disrupt their relationship, one or the other woman usually backs away before creating a critical confrontation. Typically, it is Mrs. Pescatore who stalks off, but then it is relatively easier for her to do so than for Mrs. Murphy who must tend to her children.

Conclusion

Conflict regarding this issue of separation-closeness is the major unresolved psychological issue for each of the mothers and grandmothers in this study, regardless of their attitudes toward this issue with the third generation. With the exception of Mrs. Scardoni who would have liked to have even more contact with her daughter, the grandmothers in this study actively discouraged their daughters' demands for greater closeness and dependency. In her own way, each of these grandmothers expressed the feeling that her daughter did not realize that she had other interests besides babysitting and tending her daughter's needs. Mrs. Limpari and Mrs. Giorgio expressed this feeling with greatest intensity. Mrs. Limpari works every weekday and looks forward to the weekends. However, she is obliged to entertain Mrs. McGorty and her family almost every Saturday. Mrs. Giorgio has errands and other interests in the city and values her freedom to come and go as she pleases. Mrs. Pescatore tires of her daughter's demands for help, for she has her own household to manage and her husband's needs to consider.

In different ways, each of the daughters expresses conflict regarding the area of separation and resentment that their mothers do not spend more time with them and provide greater support. Mrs. McGorty expends a large part of her waking energy on a condominium project which will enable her to move back to Tower Point in a way that will win her mother's approval. Mrs. Murphy lives downstairs from her mother, and, while she becomes frantic when her mother criticizes her life-style, marriage, and childrearing practices, she also desperately needs her mother's advice, care, and approval. Mrs. Czaja continues to feel, as an adult, that her mother has not given her enough succorance and continues to hope that she will be able to receive the care and attention she felt she had missed as a child. However, the more Mrs. Czaja demands attention, the more her mother flees from her daughter's emotional demands. The fact that the conflict is so clear in this three-generation family may be due to the fact that Mrs. Giorgio is the only grandmother to be widowed and to actually share her household with her daughter.

While Mrs. Russo does not actually live with her own mother, she maintains close telephone communication and visits with her twice each week. Mrs. Russo is unable to make independent decisions without consulting her mother and depends on her mother for help even in marketing. It is an irony that it is the development of much the same childhood symbiotic relationship between Mrs. Russo and her daughter which prevents Mrs. Russo from being able to ask her mother to baby-sit for her. Since Mrs. Russo is unable to be apart from her daughter without worrying that some accident might befall her daughter, she cannot trust even her own mother to care for her daughter in her absence. Perhaps because she has never had the opportunity, Mrs. Scardoni is the only one of the four grandmothers to express the wish that she might have greater responsibility for her granddaughter's welfare.

Consistent with our previous quantitative findings, issues of closeness and separation represent the major psychological theme within these three-generation modified extended families, and, even when mother and grandmother do not share a common residence, this family theme stands out in both the psychological data and interviews. Achieving appropriate psychological distance from one's own mother is as much an issue for the women in this study as achieving such distance from one's children.

DEFINITION OF UNACCEPTABLE BEHAVIOR AND BASIS OF SANCTIONS

Limpari-McGorty

There is little concern in either the Limpari or the McGorty family regarding control of unacceptable behavior. Conventional standards of conduct are clearly understood, accepted, and internalized by both generations. Mrs. Limpari is quite interested in the question of moral values and has been involved in fostering the new ecumenical spirit in her parish by arranging visits between her church and various Protestant churches in the area. She has also attended several Yoga classes and expresses interest in Eastern religions. Other members of the family speak of her as having good principles. Mrs. McGorty is much less involved in these issues, but attempts to teach her children what she believes is the right way to act in order that "they will be able to feel from inside how they should behave." Since Mrs. McGorty's divorce from her first husband, she has been excommunicated from the Catholic church. She and her husband have attended several different Protestant churches in their community but have not felt that they belong. At the present time, they do not attend church.

Scardoni-Russo

As a family, the Scardonis and the Russos are quite conformist. Mrs. Scardoni wants nothing more than to be regarded as a part of the community, and Mrs. Russo shows much the same concern. Mrs. Russo closely watches and tries to imitate her neighbors' behavior. Given this grandmother's and mother's concern with conforming to their social environment, as well as Mrs. Russo's internal preoccupations with cleanliness, tidiness, and being responsible, there is little behavioral deviance allowed within either adult generation, although Mrs. Russo's daughter, Charlotte, is often in trouble because of her uncontrolled behavior in public. Mrs. Russo confesses to having had a period of rebellion during adolescence when she went against her mother's advice and stayed out too late. There is some indication that Mrs. Russo and her husband had sexual relations prior to marriage, and, although neither ever went out with anyone else, both regard this as improper conduct. The basis for proper behavior is that of "identification" or acting so as to please one's parents. This is seen quite clearly in the case of Mrs. Russo who tries to fulfill her mother's expectations of what a good wife and mother might be in order to win her mother's love and attention.

Within the family, family members are supposed to be warm, spontaneous, and demonstrative and to discuss readily their feelings with each other. Mrs. Russo's brother is considered an ideal family member because of this warmth. Indeed, the dimension of warmth-coldness is a central one to use in describing the salient personality attributes of other family members in both the grandparental and parental generations. Mrs. Russo is considered less of an ideal family member because she is more cold and reserved, and both her mother and her brother have talked with her about this "problem" in being a part of the family. While nonnegative sanctions are applied for failure to comply with expectations of other family members, Mrs. Russo's mother and brother hope that Mrs. Russo will become less reserved and less distant as she grows older.

Giorgio-Czaja

Mrs. Giorgio places great emphasis on the concept of respect for one's elders. Naturally, then, it upsets her when Mrs. Czaja allows Peter to be rude, for she punished her own children for similar behavior. However, Mrs. Giorgio recognizes that she does not have this degree of authority with Peter and that, for the moment, she has to live with his talking back to his parents.

Overall, for the Czajas, dicipline is not a terribly salient issue. Mrs. Czaja would prefer that Peter eat when she sets his food out for him, but she does not insist on this and permits him to refuse what is offered. She insists that Peter is still too young to be expected to "obey" but says also that on rare occasions she has been forced to spank him. Typically, this sanction has been applied when he "acts like a spoiled brat." Mrs. Czaja exemplifies in socialization research what is considered as a "permissive" rather than a "restrictive" mother. Where Peter is expected to comply with a request, the reasons advanced are explained to him in some detail, and he is expected to comply because it is the right thing to do rather than because it would please his parents or because failure to comply would result in punishment. Standards are taught through internalization rather than through compliance or identification.

Pescatore-Murphy

Behavior that is defined as most unacceptable for both generations largely concerns Mrs. Murphy's children. While Mr. Pescatore is uninvolved with his daughter's family and does not even mind the racket overhead each morning, Mrs. Pescatore becomes upset when the children make too much noise. Beyond the inconvenience, it is another reminder of the differences in control techniques of Mrs. Pescatore and her daughter. But this is one area in which her daughter stands firm. Mrs. Murphy recalls all too clearly the repressive measures used by her own mother and is determined to avoid them with her children.

Mrs. Pescatore also expects that her daughter and son-in-law will act in accordance with her own value system in which hard work and a regular life are very important. Since her son-in-law's life is so contrary to these values, she finds it difficult to accept his behavior and, having criticized him severely in the past, now avoids all contact with him. She also values order and cleanliness and is greatly disturbed at what she feels to be her daughter's lack of punctuality regarding household chores. She attempts to pressure her daughter into following her own wishes, and, when her daughter is unwilling to do so, arguments develop between them.

While her mother's values are the old-fashioned ones so characteristic of her generation, Mrs. Murphy is much less clear regarding what she views as unacceptable behavior. Since she greatly values privacy, she finds behavior that flaunts this value to be unacceptable. With regard to her children, she expects that they will do as she asks, within very broad limits. For Mrs. Murphy, compliance is to be achieved through internalization. She herself observes that there is "no use in trying to get the children to obey your commands, as was true with my mother. They have to think that it is right." For Mrs. Pescatore, both external constraints and identification were invoked as the rationale for sanctions. Mrs. Pescatore was much concerned with what other persons would think of the family and, in addition, felt that her commands should be obeyed simply because she said that they should be obeyed.

Conclusion

All four families in this study are much concerned with proper codes of conduct and do not condone antisocial or asocial behavior. Locus of sanctions is very much along social class and generational lines. The Scardoni-Russo family, the one completely working-class family in the study, relies on identification, as do all the three other grandparental families. However, Mrs. McGorty, Mrs. Murphy, and Mrs. Czaja all believe that children can only learn what is correct through fostering autonomous moral standards; rigid discipline and corporal punishment fail to achieve their purposes. To some extent, all four mothers are "permissive" in their attitudes toward misbehavior, and each of the parental families permits or actually encourages their children to express their views. Discipline is achieved primarily by reasoning and explanation rather than by punishment. At the same time, both Mrs. Murphy and Mrs. Russo feel at a loss in being able to control their children who could be considered, at least to some degree, to be "spoiled."

Sanctions are applied by parents against children almost entirely for disobedience. In general, the parents in this study are more tolerant of their children's misbehavior than their parents were of them. Mrs. Russo, Mrs. Murphy, and Mrs. Czaja all acknowledge a period of rebelliousness in late adolescence or early adulthood that was treated by their parents with censure and criticism. In all three cases, the daughters were too old for their parents to apply any more extreme sanctions.

The four grandparental families in this study all show awareness of the norm that they are not to interfere in their daughters' lives, and attempts to comment and criticize are recognized by both generations as somewhat outside the bounds of what is legitimate behavior on the part of the grandparental generation. However, these grandparents do continue to attempt to influence their daughters' behavior. This is seen most clearly in the case of Mrs. Pescatore who frankly admonishes Mrs. Murphy for her life-style. Mrs. Giorgio is somewhat critical of the degree of permissiveness Mrs. Czaja shows with Peter. At the same time, she admits that she is overstepping her bounds and acknowledges that her daughter's childcare practices are basically not her concern.

Of the four grandmothers, Mrs. Limpari is the most tolerant of her daughter's life-style and childrearing methods. Earlier in her life, when Mrs. McGorty sought a divorce from her first husband, her mother was quite sympathetic and even encouraging, although, as a woman of considerable prestige within her parish, her daughter's decision might lead to considerable embarrassment for her.

EXPRESSION AND CONTROL OF AFFECT AND IMPULSES

Limpari-McGorty

Neither the Limpari nor the McGorty family shows any significant problem regarding impulse control. Like many Italian families, the Limparis are quite expressive. When Mr. and Mrs. Limpari become excited or angry, they raise their voice, gesticulate, and speak in rapid Italian. Mrs. McGorty says that she can never remember a serious fight between her parents, although occasionally they raised their voices. Mrs. Limpari believes that men are inherently unfaithful, but does not mention any specific time her husband sought the affections of another woman.

Mrs. McGorty's first husband was described as an impulsive and disturbed person; he was abusive several times. However, since her marriage to Mr. McGorty, there have been few instances of conflict between them. Mrs. McGorty feels that Mr. McGorty has a "wonderful" disposition, and she is unable to remember a time when there was any conflict between them. Indeed, both Mrs. McGorty and her husband deny the presence of angry feelings. In general, the affective tone in the McGorty household is much more restricted than that of the Limpari household.

Scardoni-Russo

For both generations, the preferred means of control of both sexual and aggressive impulses is that of overcontrol. Mrs. Scardoni harbors considerable unconscious resentment against her daughter, since she perceives the maternal role as requiring inordinate self-sacrifice. To be a good mother, one must totally disregard one's own needs: feelings of resentment were replaced by their opposite. Rather than admit to her wish that something would happen to her children so that she would be freed from the maternal role, Mrs. Scardoni became zealously overprotective and worried continually about what might happen to them. Since she sees the world as a dangerous place, the children could easily fall victim to such hazards as a car that was out of control, a stray piece of glass that would cut a gash requiring major surgery, or a life-threatening illness.

Expression of anger has the same dangerous implications for Mrs. Russo as it does for her mother. Just as is true of her mother, Mrs. Russo is very overprotective. Just as was true of her mother, she worries about her daughter's health, particularly whether she is getting sufficient nourishment. Mrs. Russo's wish to starve her daughter has been replaced by its opposite: fear that her daughter does not get enough to eat and might starve. She also complains of nervousness and tension that is expressed in compulsive scheduling and fastidiousness and can be understood in terms of her emotional overcontrol.

Expression of sexuality is also a source of conflict for both generations. Mrs. Scardoni has experienced much difficulty with menopause and fears that she will no longer be considered an appealing and attractive woman by her husband: menopause is but one more example of how worthless she is. Prior to marriage, Mrs. Russo had been involved in a long-standing and apparently satisfying relationship with her prospective husband. Indeed, they had known each other for more than nine years at the time they got married. Since that time, Mrs. Russo's personality has become more and more restricted, and her satisfaction from life increasingly less rewarding. Feeling burdened by the responsibilities of adulthood, and resentful of what is expected of her, she can avoid loss of control only by constriction of her personality.

Accompanying this denial of impulse life, there has been a change in Mrs. Russo's attitude toward sexuality. She complains that she now derives little pleasure from sexual relations and that this has become one more area of her life where she complies with what is expected of her, in this instance by her husband.

This issue of the socialization of impulse expression has taken on new intensity as Mrs. Russo struggles to toilet train her two-and-a-half-year-old daughter. On the one hand, she feels that rigid impulse control is important and that to have Charlotte well trained would be a positive reflection of the success of her own inner controls. On the other hand, given Mrs. Russo's wish to express what she regards as unacceptable impulses, it would be less threatening to her own psychic equilibrium to act out this wish through discouraging her daughter's habit training than to express these aggressive impulses herself.

Finally, given her hostility toward her daughter, Mrs. Russo fears the intensity of her feelings with regard to Charlotte's habit training and has been unable to achieve her goal of helping her daughter achieve bowel and bladder control. Because of her tremendous ambivalence regarding this issue in her daughter's socialization, Charlotte is put on the toilet, after which a struggle ensues between mother and daughter about staying on the toilet. When Charlotte begins to cry, Mrs. Russo relents and gives her an additional day's reprieve. Each day that the battle is postponed, the issue of habit training becomes more explosive for both mother and daughter.

Spontaneous affect is expressed by Mrs. Scardoni who is a somewhat less constricted person than her daughter. Indeed, both Mrs. Scardoni and Mrs. Russo's brother complain about how Mrs. Russo is dull, lacking in affection, and colorless. Mr. Butoni greets his mother by tackling and wrestling with her, kissing her, and giving her big bear hugs. While this greeting is also a safe and ritualized way of expressing his own hostility, there is real and positive affection between mother and son. Mrs. Russo has a hard time expressing any real feelings to any-one, and her brother is particularly sensitive to this problem. At the same time, while it is permissible to express positive feelings, anger is less well tolerated. Mrs. Russo does not feel safe expressing anger toward her mother, for she also fears the loss of her mother's love and, as soon as the moment of greatest intensi-ty of anger is past, she calls her mother to once more make peace. Although Mrs. Russo and her mother nag each other, there are very few actual arguments of the kind that took place concerning the issue of who would call first in the morning. It is considered better for members of the family to contain their anger and avoid any public disagreements.

Giorgio-Czaja

No particular problem in the control of affect and impulse was observed for either generation. Mrs. Giorgio had a distant and proper relationship with her husband: for most of the time they were married, they had separate bedrooms and bath-rooms. Mrs. Czaja reports that her mother expresses very "old fashioned" atti-tudes about sex and that she does not believe women should admit to any enjoyment of sexual relations. A woman with such traditional attitudes toward sexuality must be troubled by her daughters' progressive sexual behavior. Three of the four girls lived with their future husbands for some time prior to marriage. Even Mrs. Giorgio's son escaped her mold. It is well known that he had had a series of girl friends who lived with him.

Mrs. Czaja admits to having been quite "wild" for a period of time before she returned home to care for her father. She says that she never discussed this time in her life with her mother, but she is sure her mother would not approve. Satis-factions that Mrs. Czaja could obtain from being at home and helping her mother were obviously far greater than those she could obtain by sexual promiscuity or working as a waitress, and she had little difficulty giving up this "wild" life when her father became ill. Mrs. Czaja does admit to feeling somewhat ashamed of her behavior during those few years when she was out on her own and worried about what her parents might think of her behavior.

There is little evidence that family members are conflicted in their expression of anger. Mrs. Giorgio and her daughter occasionally shout at each other, and, on rare occasions, one or the other will slam a door. Usually, after such explosions, mother and daughter can sit down and make up and are able to resolve differences that started the tiff. Mrs. Giorgio is concerned that Mrs. Czaja does not take a more definite stance when Peter hits her in a fit of anger. Mrs. Czaja assures her mother that she will do so when he is older, but believes that at three and a half, he is not yet capable of exercising such self-control.

The ease with which Mrs. Giorgio and her daughter can express their anger is consistent with the view that the expression and control of affect in this extended family is not a serious problem, although Mrs. Czaja does show some difficulty in controlling her feelings when she becomes excited. In contrast to other mothers in this study, Mrs. Czaja's problem is more that of being unable to maintain control of organized thought processes under stress than of exercising overcontrol. A good illustration of Mrs. Czaja's emotional reactions to stress is seen in her poorly articulated responses to Rorschach blots with bright colors or with emotionally laden content. Mrs. Czaja has similar reactions when discussion of her family leads to arousal of intense feelings. Thus, we see that while Mrs. Giorgio's preferred defenses are those of projection, reaction-formation, and withdrawal, Mrs. Czaja relies primarily on denial and regression as defenses against internal conflicts.

Pescatore-Murphy

It is unthinkable for Mrs. Pescatore that either sexual or aggressive impulses should be expressed or even recognized. Mrs. Pescatore deals with her own conflicts in this regard both by rigid denial and by externalization. Children who show aggression toward their parents should, of course, be severely punished. Aggression toward peers is tolerated as long as it does not involve the family's good name. As we have already noted, Mrs. Pescatore's attitudes toward the expression of impulses in behavior are very stereotyped.

Mrs. Murphy can accept her children's expression of aggression in their play, but expects that her children will not show aggression toward her. On the other hand, when the children do begin to argue, she is at a loss about how to deal with their anger. According to her account, she is too permissive with them, but is haunted by memories of her mother's almost cruel punishment when she was young. In sum, while her parents are unable to permit any display of anger, Mrs. Murphy has difficulty controlling such feelings in either her children or herself.

Mrs. Murphy often becomes angry when her mother criticizes her, and, after an initial period in which she attempts to hold back her anger, she explodes. Mrs. Pescatore then explodes as well, and a major quarrel develops. Mrs. Murphy experiences the same problem with regard to her husband. She becomes resentful, but is unable to directly express her anger until it becomes so overwhelming that she feels unable to contain it, at which point she explodes at her mother and then suffers feelings of overwhelming guilt.

There are little data concerning the expression of affection in the family. Mrs. Pescatore was totally unwilling to discuss her sexual relationship with her husband, beyond alluding to the fact that it was not satisfactory. There is some indication that Mr. Murphy has had extramarital affairs.

In neither family is there any evidence that affect may be expressed flexibly or spontaneously. The only real affect shown by either Mrs. Pescatore or her daughter concerned anger and resentment. When anger was shown, it was in the context of lack of control rather than of modulation. For Mrs. Pescatore, it was her son-in-law's behavior and her daughter's failure to obey her commands that provoked her anger. For Mrs. Murphy, it was her mother's intrusiveness and her husband's lack of consideration that provoked her anger. Neither mother nor grandmother felt comfortable expressing positive feelings or affection for any family member.

Conclusion

The denial most grandmothers and mothers show in dealing with the expression of either sexual or aggressive impulses is consistent with other data from this study suggesting that these women avoid extreme or upsetting events in their lives. Of the women in the grandmother generation, Mrs. Scardoni is the only one who can admit to her sexual conflicts, but even she is unable to acknowledge her anger or resentment, a source of her maternal overprotectiveness. Mrs. Limpari seems the least defended of the four mothers against impulse expression and most comfortable with her feelings.

Among the women in the mother generation, the capacity for intense feelings is one that is very important for Mrs. Czaja. Particularly open about admitting her sexual desires, Mrs. Czaja expresses a "liberated" attitude toward sexuality. The other three mothers are largely unable to acknowledge strong feelings or wishes of any sort. Both Mrs. Murphy and Mrs. Russo are overprotective toward their children, an indication of the intensity of their anger toward the maternal role. Mrs. Murphy also harbors anger and resentment toward her husband for his frequent absences. However, as is true also of Mrs. McGorty and Mrs. Czaja, it is necessary for these women to deny the intensity of their resentment toward childcare, for these feelings are regarded as "bad" in American culture. In no other basic relationship within the family is the expression of negative feelings perceived as so dangerous. This study highlights the extent to which both working- and middle-class women feel it is necessary to deny these negative feelings about childcare, as well as the degree of guilt that occurs when such feelings do emerge.

ESTABLISHMENT OF FAMILY IDENTITY AND ACHIEVEMENT OF FAMILY GOALS

Limpari-McGorty

The significant cultural tradition in both the McGorty and the Limpari families is that of southern Italy. Both Mrs. McGorty and Mrs. Limpari are renowned for their Italian cooking; each speaks quite fluent Italian. Mr. McGorty has very little involvement in the Irish tradition in which he was reared and greatly enjoys being a part of his wife's modified extended Italian family. Mr. McGorty looks to his wife as the source of the unifying tradition with the family. Mrs. McGorty's own children are still too young to make any conscious decision about what this tradition means to them.

As we have seen, relationships between the women in this family are quite complex. The conflict between Mrs. Limpari and Mrs. McGorty regarding the issue of separation and closeness is the major source of tension and the primary theme of unresolved psychological issues that concern this family. While the daughter, Mrs. McGorty, wants to achieve a greater sense of closeness with her mother, Mrs. Limpari perceives this bid for greater closeness as a threat to her own hard-won sense of separateness and autonomy. Mrs. Limpari was never able to resolve her conflicting feelings toward her own mother who died just this past year. She felt that her mother had been too controlling and was determined that her daughter should have a greater sense of separateness. As a result of this insistence on her daughter's development of self-reliance, stemming from her own inner conflicts, Mrs. Limpari had much the same impact on her daughter as her own restrictive mother had had on her. Mrs. McGorty reacted to the manner in which she was reared by using opportunities for separateness and autonomy as a means of obtaining her mother's approval, in order that her mother might then provide greater support and attention.

While her mother struggled to rear Mrs. McGorty differently from how she had been reared, Mrs. McGorty does not see a great need to rear her daughters differently from the way in which she had been reared. The major change she plans is to require less of her children in the way of chores and household responsibilities and feels that the amount of responsibility her mother expected of her prevented her from forming friendships with others her own age.

Scardoni-Russo

Just as was true with the issue of closeness, the issue of family identity is an important one for this tightly knit Italian-American family. Largely cut off from ties with other families from the same heritage, the Scardonis and Russos have been quite culturally isolated. Mrs. Scardoni has always lived in marginal areas where she knew few of her neighbors and lacked even the social bond that is provided by church membership. There were few traditions inherited from either Mrs. Scardoni's mother's or father's family, and her first husband's suicide meant that she was further isolated at a time when she was most in need of help and support. Feeling this lack of tradition, Mrs. Scardoni has tried to create an artificial tradition and to acquire the trappings of the core of New England culture without actually having become a part of it.

Once more, as in so many areas of her life, Mrs. Russo has adopted her mother's ways. She, too, is very sensitive to her social environment and tries as much as possible to be a typical Dorset resident, with all that this implies in terms of social conformity. Since Mrs. Russo's husband's family is also a socially isolated and fragmented family, he can add relatively little toward the development of family traditions. Even Mr. Scardoni is in a difficult position. Since he left his first wife, an act considered sinful by the church, he, too, has been cut off from the traditions in which he was reared. With the exception of Mrs. Butoni, none of the family members attend church, and, with the exception of Mr. Scardoni, who visits Tower Point with some regularity, none of these family members has any significant contact with the Italian-American community. Since Mr. Scardoni's divorce and remarriage, many of his old acquaintances in Tower Point shun him, and even he feels somewhat remote from the community in which he grew up.

One of the most striking characteristics of this family is the extent to which Mrs. Russo is rearing her own daughter in the same manner in which she herself was reared. Just as was true of her mother, Charlotte has developed an eating disturbance, and much of the time that Mrs. Russo spends with her daughter each day is occupied trying to get Charlotte to eat and being sure she is satisfied. Indeed, this conflict regarding nurturance emerges as a basic theme or unresolved issue in the family's interaction.

For Mrs. Russo, as for her mother, the maternal role leads to feelings of resentment she dare not express and emerges in its opposite form as an exaggerated concern with the child's health and welfare. This conflict is internalized by the next generation as a feeling of lack of self-worth and a desire to be better in order to gain food and care in a less ambivalent manner. Mrs. Russo's frantic calls to her mother and then to her doctor, in order to be sure that Charlotte is in good health, are strikingly similar to her mother's trips with Mrs. Russo to the drugstore, where milk was supplied as a form of medicine. The fact that this conflict is unconscious only lends greater power to its perpetuation within the family, for neither grandmother nor mother shows awareness of her own role in the transmission of this conflict to the next generation.

Since this conflict is largely unconscious, Mrs. Russo has made little effort to change the manner she is rearing her daughter from how she was reared. Indeed, she looks to her mother for advice in even the most minute aspects of childcare, and Mrs. Scardoni is more than happy to be able to supply such advice. As Mrs. Russo observed, in discussing the differences between the way she was reared and how she is rearing her daughter:

> Other than my mother letting me get away with too much when I was in high school, I can't think of anything I would do differently . . . I look to my mother for advice when I have a problem, and try to do things the way she does them. I can't think of any way in which I do things differently than she did . . .

Such conformity to her mother's ways of doing things means that Mrs. Russo has no difficulty in obtaining solutions to problems in rearing her daughter that have already been worked out during her own childhood. At the same time, Mrs. Russo sacrifices the growth that comes from finding new solutions and working problems through on her own. As in other aspects of her relationship with her mother, Mrs. Russo's dependency and desire to please her mother is achieved at the cost of her own autonomy. While Mrs. Russo feels some discomfort in the close and binding relationship she has with her mother, her fear of managing life on her own is so great that it is impossible for her to give up the closeness she struggles so hard to maintain.

Giorgio-Czaja

Family traditions are important for Mrs. Giorgio and the Czajas, but are less strongly emphasized than for the Pescatores and Murphys or Scardonis and Russos. Mrs. Giorgio recalls with some pride the status accorded her family and is concerned with the preservation of this status. Most of Mrs. Giorgio's feelings concern her father's side of the family. There is little mention of Mrs. Giorgio's mother's side of the family. While her own marriage was consistent with her family's social standing, Mrs. Giorgio regrets somewhat that her daughters have not married as well as she would have preferred. The daughter who married a medical student married out of the Catholic faith and, to make matters even worse, married the son of an Eastern European Jewish immigrant. Mrs. Giorgio's other three daughters made religiously acceptable marriages but to men of somewhat lower social status. While Mrs. Giorgio does not involve herself in serious conflict with her daughters regarding their choices of mates, her daughters are, nonetheless, aware of her feelings.

Like her mother, Mrs. Czaja accepts the family traditions and enjoys her Italian-American Catholic heritage. Mrs. Czaja's husband has explicitly rejected his family and its traditions that he views as destructive and as providing little satisfaction, but he greatly enjoys life with his wife's family. In fact, the Czajas really wish to strengthen the ties of family heritage and tradition rather than to discard them or separate from them.

The family theme in this three-generation family of Mrs. Giorgio, Mr. and Mrs. Czaja, and the couple's young son, Peter, is that of conflict about the issue of acceptance. For Mrs. Giorgio, acceptance is seen primarily in terms of social status, although she is also concerned that others will accept her need for independence and freedom of movement. For Mrs. Czaja, acceptance is defined as a need for others to accept her flamboyant gestures and somewhat idiosyncratic manner of speech and dress, and, of even greater importance, for her mother to accept her need to be dependent. For Mr. Czaja, the theme of acceptance is expressed primarily in terms of his need to be accepted by Mrs. Giorgio as part of the Italian-American tradition that he had hoped to make his own through his marriage to Mrs. Czaja.

Pescatore-Murphy

Both Mr. and Mrs. Pescatore's families are a part of the south Italian Catholic tradition. Although there is a plethora of religious art in their home, participation in religious observances is minimal. Outside some minimal obligations to the church, the Pescatores are isolated from this tradition. They have few contacts with other members of their parish and are uninvolved in community affairs. The Pescatores' life is focused on their house and yard that offer privacy and security. When the children were younger, the Pescatores had big Sunday dinners for relatives, but even these dinners have ceased long since. While she says that she values family closeness, Mrs. Pescatore's actions belie this statement.

Mrs. Murphy feels little need either to break away from the family religious and cultural traditions or to become more than superficially involved. She sends her daughter to a Catholic Montessori school, but plans to send her boys to public school. She occasionally goes to Mass, but feels little obligation to do so each week. She does miss the big parties held for the relatives and the Sunday dinners, but has little desire to carry on this tradition. Mrs. Murphy's husband has accepted his wife's religious and cultural traditions. However, while he, too, was reared a Catholic, he seldom goes to Mass and is only minimally involved in the church. Indeed, as is often true of men of Irish extraction who marry into Italian families, the greater closeness offered by his wife's Italian tradition was something he valued in getting married to her.

Mr. Murphy continues to see his mother and father, although there is considerable conflict between the generations. In fact, Mrs. Murphy wishes that her husband would see his parents less often than he does. She feels that they are a bad influence and that his mother, in particular, keeps him tied to her apron strings.

Mrs. Murphy's relationship with her mother is clearly both intense and conflicted. In the main, this conflict is evoked by differences between the generations regarding care of the children. Mrs. Pescatore's uncanny ability to trouble her daughter about precisely those aspects of Mr. Murphy that are of concern to her daughter further intensifies this conflict. The only area in which Mrs. Murphy is consciously trying to alter the way in which she was reared is that regarding the children. But since her permissiveness stems more from her own needs than from those of her children, Mrs. Murphy finds herself confronting frequent paradoxes as she tries to rear her children according to this more permissive philosophy that she does not feel comfortable with. She is forced either to react with harshness or to become involved in quarrels with them in which she is more of a peer than a parent. Mrs. Murphy's own ambivalence about her mother and the way in which she was reared clearly presents a problem in rearing her own children.

The most essential family secrets concern Mr. Murphy, his relationship with his own parents, his relationship with his wife, and his work. Mrs. Pescatore does not realize that Mr. Murphy's father is an alcoholic and that he was in and out of hospitals for many years. Mr. Murphy's possible extramarital affairs are a secret he keeps from his wife. Mrs. Murphy has reason to suspect such affairs but has not been able to confirm these suspicions. Finally, there is the matter of Mrs. Murphy's brother whom, she said, had been hospitalized for a nervous breakdown. The large number of family secrets will increasingly add to conflict within this family in the coming years. These secrets are not discussed within the family, nor are they represented in any symbolic manner except in the nuances of Mrs. Pescatore's comments to her daughter about her husband.

For both generations, family themes concern privacy and security and, in the case of Mrs. Murphy, the conflict between security and glamour. Given the number of family secrets and the value system of the community that emphasizes privacy and discretion, it is understandable why there is such a good fit between family needs and the community values. In a more tightly knit community such as Tower Point, it would be far more difficult to hide such family secrets. Security concerns both financial security, as seen in the question of whether Mr. Murphy can provide for his family, and also concerns the ability to be well taken care of, as in Mrs. Murphy's feeling that she was neglected by her own mother whose childrearing attitudes and practices were focused more around her own needs than those of her children. Of course, Mrs. Murphy herself is enacting this same problem in her overly permissive attitudes toward her children. Glamour is, of course, represented by Mr. Murphy's work in the theater, which satisfies Mrs. Murphy's own need for excitement, but also intensifies her need for security.

Conclusion

Family traditions are important in all four of these modified extended families. Common to all members of the grandparent generation is their Italian-American tradition and their Catholic religious heritage. While only Mrs. Pescatore was born in Italy (the three other grandmothers are second generation), all the grandparents except Mrs. Scardoni have some involvement with Italian culture and, with her present marriage, even Mrs. Scardoni has become more involved in her Italian heritage. While she shuns the church and celebrates July 4, Mrs. Scardoni also has big Christmas and Easter celebrations in the Italian-American tradition.

Family celebrations are particularly important for the parent generation. Of the four husbands, distance and tension characterizes relationships between three of these four husbands and their own families. Both Mr. Russo and Mr. Murphy maintain close contact with their parents, although, for Mr. Murphy, this is a source of conflict with his wife. Husbands in the other two families are not even from the same tradition as that of their wives. In the case of the two men from entirely Irish backgrounds, Mr. Murphy and Mr. McGorty, there were few family celebrations. In addition, serious social pathology was present in the parental families of both Mr. Murphy and Mr. Czaja, intensifying the desire of these two husbands for close family ties.

While preservation of ethnic traditions is important to both husband and wife in the parental generation, religion plays a less central role. While Mrs. Murphy, Mrs. Czaja, and Mrs. Russo attend church regularly, none of these three women express the degree of involvement in the church that characterizes the grandmothers (with the exception of Mrs. Scardoni, who shuns the church). While none of the men in the parent generation attend Mass regularly, Mr. Russo and Mr. Czaja would prefer that their wives show more devotion to the church than they do. This interest in the family's ethnic and religious traditions is consistent with our earlier observations that an important reason for marrying for each of the four men in the parent generation was the greater sense of attachment and identity that his wife's family provided.

A major family theme for each of these four modified extended families is the attainment of connectedness between generations. In none of the four families has this psychological issue in the family been resolved. In the case of the Scardonis and Russos, the family theme is expressed to such an extent that even the most minor family discussions on Mrs. Russo's part involve her mother's consideration. For her mother, other than her husband, Mrs. Scardoni's entire life is focused around the two-family house where her son and daughter and their families live. In the other three families, there continues to be intergenerational tension regarding the issues of closeness and connectedness. The dependence of the husbands in these four families on the cultural traditions of their wives only intensifies the wish on the part of the parents to maintain close contact with the wife's family and makes the attainment of separateness an even more complex psychological issue within the family.

FAMILY PROBLEM-SOLVING TECHNIQUES

Limpari-McGorty

The conflict that is evident between Mrs. McGorty and her mother regarding the issue of separation and closeness is not so intense that it disrupts the family's functioning or requires intervention. Indeed, there is little overt discussion of this issue within the family. While Mrs. Limpari clearly recognizes her daughter's feelings, she is determined to preserve her own separateness and autonomy. Family members suppress all discussion of this problem, even when it surfaces during the McGorty's disruptive Saturday visits. This modified extended family is not one in which conflicts are openly discussed. But because this family has fewer disruptive family problems, the fact that the family members fail to discuss their problems does not lead to any serious consequences.

Scardoni-Russo

The primary problem within this family is that of achieving closeness while still preserving some autonomy and individual initiative. For Mr. Russo, who is somewhat less involved in this conflict than his wife, mother, and brother-in-law, this has been less of a problem. While he enjoys visiting his mother-in-law on Sundays and holidays, Mr. Russo does not feel obligated to join his wife when she goes next door to visit her brother and sister-in-law. Since he is at work during the day, he does not spend the hours during the week that his wife spends with her mother. For this reason, the problem of closeness for Mr. Russo is much less central. Mrs. Russo denies any anger she has toward her mother, and, in her mind, she reworks hatred into love and admiration. This search for closeness and determination to continue the mother-daughter symbiosis is at the cost of her own emotional development and leads to the additional problem of continuing the symbiosis into the next generation.

Mrs. Russo's daughter is already sensitive to this issue and successfully manipulates her mother into giving up any of her own interests or activities in order to spend all her time with her. Since the underlying conflict is unconscious and since the fear of loss of love is so great that it prevents any reexamination of Mrs. Russo's relationship with her mother, this problem is likely to have lasting effects on her daughter's own emotional development.

Just as Mrs. Russo is unwilling to examine her own feelings, Mrs. Scardoni also finds the mother-daughter symbiosis to be too satisfying to change. In the case of Mrs. Scardoni, her own unrecognized hostility toward the maternal role provides an important motive for continuing this relationship in its present form.

Mrs. Scardoni, too, denies the intensity of her own anger and substitutes solicitous overconcern for the destructive fantasies that elicit so much guilt and anxiety.

Giorgio-Czaja

Conflict regarding acceptance of Mrs. Czaja by her mother emerges not only as an important component of the family theme, but also as the one problem this family seems unable to resolve. It is true that Mrs. Giorgio has some disagreements with her daughter about the ways in which Mrs. Czaja is too lenient with Peter or how she neglects her household chores. It is also true that Mrs. Giorgio wishes Mr. Czaja mowed the lawn more often. However, these are minor problems that are frequently discussed, and family members strive to achieve some resolution of them. Some compromise is nearly always possible, although there may be a good deal of shouting before the various parties in the dispute sit down to discuss their differences. However, considering, as an example, the panic Mrs. Giorgio feels when she believes that her daughter or son-in-law is making demands on her time which prevent her from being able to go out window-shopping or on any other personal business, it seems unlikely that these three family members will ever be able to resolve the conflict regarding acceptance. The sacrifice required of Mrs. Giorgio would threaten the very foundations of her own personality and would be perceived by her as a catastrophic situation. On the other hand, Mrs. Czaja sees very little chance of gaining the acceptance of her need to be dependent on her mother as long as Mrs. Giorgio insists so strongly on going her own way.

No member of the family regards this three-generation household as a permanent unit. Mrs. Giorgio announces with a tone of finality that her daughter and son-in-law are really moving out at the end of the year, and the Czajas, while not explicitly agreeing with Mrs. Giorgio, do talk about the position Mr. Czaja has been offered at that college in northern New England. Given how the family theme of acceptance is expressed, there is no solution except for the Czajas to find the acceptance for which they search in their own immediate household and for Mrs. Giorgio to be permitted once more to gain sole occupancy of the corner house in Somerset.

Pescatore-Murphy

Mrs. Pescatore sees her daughter's "misguided" ways of rearing her children and her son-in-law's "irresponsibility and immaturity" as major family problems. Mrs. Murphy sees her mother's continued overinvolvement in her own life and that of her children as well as her husband's failure to give her the support and consideration she requires as major family problems. In dealing with these concerns, mother and daughter frequently quarrel but fail to reach a satisfactory solution. Any attempt to suppress negative feelings or to transform negative into positive feelings is doomed to failure because both mother and daughter blame the other, and each attributes her own feelings to the other. Since family problems have not been resolved, they greatly interfere in family functioning.

Mrs. Murphy is ambivalent, both about her mother and her husband. While she wishes that she could move away from her mother and start life on her own, she is afraid that such a life would offer little security. She admires her husband's work, which provides her with some satisfactions. Yet she resents his aloofness, his self-involvement, and his inability to care for her or their children. These problems lead to misunderstandings, resentment, and, ultimately, to frustration, since there seems to be no way in which they can be resolved.

Both Mrs. Murphy and her mother are aware of the conflict between them; yet they are unable to resolve this conflict that is likely to intensify as Mrs. Pescatore grows older and becomes even less flexible. In addition, as her children start school and require more evenhanded guidance, Mrs. Murphy is going to experience even greater difficulty in controlling them. This development will only intensify Mrs. Murphy's anxiety and concern.

CONCLUSION

There is little evidence that any of the four families in this study are able to resolve the major problem that confronts them. In the case of the Giorgio-Czaja family, the problem may solve itself, if Mr. Czaja does indeed decide to accept the teaching job he has been offered. As is true of the Limpari-McGorty family, denial of the problem of closeness and separation is the prominent defense used by family members. For these two families, the problem is also relatively less serious, for it interferes much less in the capacity of family members to attain a comfortable interdependence between generations.

Among the Pescatore-Murphy and Scardoni-Russo families, the problem of separation-individuation and the means used for coping with this problem are much less successful. Mrs. Pescatore and Mrs. Murphy each attempt to blame the other for the problems that arise between them, and, when this fails, each withdraws, feeling wounded and victimized by the other. For Mrs. Scardoni and Mrs. Russo, the most primitive defenses are used, not just in the service of the conflict between them, but with the goal of preserving the mother-daughter symbiosis that has already seriously impaired Mrs. Russo's capacity to function as an autonomous person and appears to be interfering in the emotional development of her daughter as well. The more serious the conflict within the family regarding this issue of connectedness, the more significant is the failure to resolve this conflict in a way that fosters both the psychological development of individual family members, as well as the adaptive capacity of the family as a whole.

Chapter 8

Ethnicity and Intergenerational Continuities in Family Life

As both the introductory comments and the discussion of the four multigeneration families have suggested, the family continues to function as the basic institution of socialization in contemporary society. Across the life cycle, including adulthood, the parental family remains an important influence in the socialization of offspring into new roles. For example, a woman's primary source of information about mothering is her own mother; women continue to seek their mothers' advice as their own children move through infancy and childhood.

Socialization occurs within the context of a particular culture that determines the range of permissible solutions for both interpersonal and intrapsychic conflicts. For example, among all four Italian-American families discussed in the present study, it is believed more desirable to express feelings than to inhibit them. Alcoholism is not a solution family members use as a means for adapting to conflict: drinking is regarded as a way of facilitating sociability rather than as a way of inhibiting negative and disruptive feelings. This value is well portrayed in the photograph contained in Gans' (1962) study of an Italian-American community showing Gans and his informants grouped together with their arms around one another and their glasses held high. Chronic alcoholism in Italian-American culture is looked on with disfavor. Indeed, Mrs. McGorty (Chapter 3), a devout Catholic, sought to dissolve her first marriage because her husband was an alcoholic.

Both the content of mental life and the actual interactions between family members are shaped by culture, which T. Parsons (1951) defined as follows:

Patterned or ordered systems of symbols which are objects of the orientation of action, internalized components of the individual actors and institutionalized patterns of social systems . . . it is a set of abstractions from the *concrete* phenomena of social action processes. (1951, p. 327)

As T. Parsons emphasizes in his definition, culture is differentiated from actual social relations occurring between persons. Culture is abstracted from social action in the sense that it is composed of the symbols persons use in determining acceptable patterns of behavior and is more generalizable than norms, which refer to patterns of regularized reciprocity associated with particular role relationships.

Culture consists of symbols, values, and beliefs regarding the self and others, the external social world, events of nature, and events of history. For example, the belief that social institutions beyond the nuclear family are sources of potential threat to family interests is characteristic of southern Italian culture (Banfield, 1958; Silverman, 1968; Cronin, 1970). The world outside the family is regarded with suspicion. Such beliefs are transmitted across the generations among southern Italian families and govern the range of permissible relations with other institutions. For example, considering the extent to which southern Italians distrust institutions beyond the family, it is not surprising that public health officials would encounter hostility and suspicion when trying to influence the nutrition and sanitation practices of these southern Italian families. Culture represents symbols and other abstractions from behavior. These symbols are organized into institutions such as the family, including kinship, education, and religion. Clearly, these institutions both support and are supported by ongoing patterned relations between persons that comprise social systems. Culture represents the basis of concrete social action or what is more commonly called a ''way of life'' and includes those interwoven constructs that hold society together.

This distinction between society and culture becomes important in the present chapter, since it is possible for a society to have several cultures or subcultures. As M. G. Smith (1960) has observed, ''Culture and society are not always coterminous or independent'' (p. 767). In the case of American society, it is clear that several subcultures overlap to some extent within a society sharing a common administrative unity. The life-style of a New England family farmer is distinctly different from that of the California aerospace engineer, and the life-style of either of these two persons is distinctly different from that of Mr. Limpari in Tower Point (Chapter 3).

The present chapter considers the importance of culture in determining the way of life and extent of intergenerational continuity among the four families in the present study. While, as we suggested in Chapter 1, social status is associated with the extent of intergenerational contact (persons from working-class families have a greater degree of such contact), aspects of the common culture shared by these four families are also noteworthy. All four of these mothers are of Italian-American descent and show continuing devotion to the Catholic church. In addition, all mothers are married to Catholic men who are of mixed Irish and Italian or Hungarian descent. These intermarriages provide an opportunity to study a larger range of responses to this common cultural background. Among the grandmother generation, some women, like Mrs. Limpari, have remained in close proximity to background and traditions, while others, such as Mrs. Scardoni, show a greater degree of conflict regarding their cultural heritage. Among the mothers, with the exception of Mrs. Murphy, there is considerable sympathy with heritage and traditions, reminiscent of the pattern described most clearly by Hansen (1952) regarding the return of the third generation to traditions rejected by the second generation. Clearly, the experience of immigration to America and of contact with other cultures has affected the ways in which these families interpret their southern Italian heritage.

CULTURE, ETHNICITY, AND IMMIGRATION

In recent years, there has been a dramatic upsurge of interest among social scientists in the problem of ethnicity as a factor influencing social life. In part, this interest stems from the "social" conflicts of the past decade, together with increasing self-criticism of prejudice and discrimination among those who perceive themselves as the majority in American society. However, to a large extent, this increased interest in ethnicity results from changes in our understanding of the process of acculturation. There is growing realization that social evolution does not proceed from the assimilation of one cultural group by another, but by the development of cultural pluralism in which an immigrant group, while showing some degree of assimilation and accommodation to a host culture in secondary relations, still shows marked cultural differences in face-to-face or primary group relations (Gordon, 1961, 1964; Newman, 1973). Before considering the process by which persons become acculturated, it is important to clarify the concept of ethnicity and its relationship to culture.

Ethnicity differs from culture in the sense that it is culture made aware of itself. Southern Italians are not likely to be aware that their values differ from those of persons living in central or northern Italy. They are only aware of certain values that they and others within the community share in common, such as that all persons outside the immediate family are to be distrusted or viewed with suspicion; there is little awareness of alternatives perspectives. However, having immigrated to America, these immigrants become aware of another way of life, different from their own, and most likely in opposition to it (Greeley, 1971). For example, considering orientations toward time, there is an obvious contrast between the American emphasis on planning for the future and the southern Italian emphasis on enjoyment of the present.

Encountering American culture, where a future orientation is vital to success in education and work, the southern Italians discovered differences between their values and those of the host country. The effects of this value conflict have been noted by Covello (1944) who describes the dilemma facing the Italian child entering the American school system. Unaware of the value his adopted culture placed on planning for the future, the Italian-American school child was expected to accept the idea of preparing himself or herself in a variety of subjects designed only to insure acquisition of knowledge relevant to more advanced courses that, in turn, would insure success in college. No mention was ever made of how this schooling would prepare the child for later work. When the family asked what relevance this curriculum had to the present, school officials were unable to supply a satisfactory answer. Needless to say, the idea of a college education was totally irrelevant to the family's present economic status. Since the educational system seemed largely irrelevant to the present predicament of the school child and his or her family, truancy among Italian-American school children was accordingly quite high, and children preferred to work rather than to spend long hours engaged in tasks that, at best, could promise rewards in the distant future.

Only when confronted with values that differed greatly from their own did members of the Italian immigrant group become aware of cultural differences. As we have suggested, it is this subjective awareness of one's traditions as unique or different that is most characteristic of ethnicity. As Weber has noted, ethnic groups may be viewed as follows:

Those human groups that entertain a subjective belief in their common descent because of memories of colonization and migration; this belief must be important for the propagation of group formation; conversely, it does not matter whether or not an objective blood relationship exists. Ethnic membership (*Gemeinsamkeit*) differs from the kinship group precisely by being a presumed identity, not a group with concrete social action, like the latter. (1968, p. 389)

Weber's view is one that emphasizes culture or symbol systems, abstracted from behavior and providing particular orientations for behavior, together with the sense of ethnic identity (Devereux, 1975), which leads to a feeling of community or *Gemeinschaft* (Tonnies, 1887).

More recent formulations of the concept of ethnicity are generally consistent with Weber's classic definition (Barth, 1969; Schermerhorn, 1970; Kolm, 1971; Greeley and McGready, 1974; Gordon, 1978). Based on these more recent formulations, and, in keeping with the orientation of the present study, we may define ethnicity as follows:

A relatively homogeneous set of values, customs, and other symbols abstracted from behavior, which is continued in a distinctive form through particular socialization practices in a society which is historically and culturally separate from that in which these values and other folk-customs had originally developed.

This definition emphasizes both the cultural basis of ethnicity and also the role ethnicity has in providing for the apparent continuity of traditional beliefs in a historically and culturally separate society. It is important to recognize that the ethnic traditions of a particular people are not assumed to be necessarily related to the customs of the "native land." For example, the extended family structure of the Italian-American is of far greater importance in daily life than was true in southern Italy. It is largely as a result of "chain migration" (McDonald and Mc-Donald, 1962), in which members of a southern Italian village emigrated and then facilitated emigration of fellow townsmen, that the family system developed in a different manner in the United States from that of southern Italy. With immigration and subsequent experiences in the "New World," customs and beliefs emerged that were different both from those of the homeland and also those of other culturally distinct groups in American society.

From this cultural perspective, ethnicity is based on meaning systems that provide answers for fundamental human dilemmas (C. Kluckhohn, 1951) in different ways, depending on past customs, as well as those of the country of immigration. Cultural groups differ in the nature of the solutions that are proposed for such common dilemmas as the relationship between man and nature or man and his fellows. These solutions are transmitted across generations and, as T. Parsons

(1951) notes, become the orientation of action, internalized components of individual actors (p. 327). Such meaning systems lead to the development of particular "modal" personality types (Inkeles and Levinson, 1954; Inkeles, 1961) or ethnic personality (Devereux, 1975), such as the methodically rational capitalist practicing "this worldly" asceticism as dictated by the teachings of the Christian ethic (Weber, 1905). In contrast to ethnic identity or a shared sense of peoplehood (Francis, 1947; Weber, 1968), ethnic personality represents *observed* differences in behavior (including the verbal behavior comprising responses to psychological measures) that differentiate cultural groups. Transmitted through both preadult and adult socialization (LeVine, 1973; Greeley, 1974; Greeley and McCready, 1974), ethnic personality is further enhanced by residential propinquity.[1]

From a psychological perspective, the beliefs and customs comprising ethnicity have an adjustive function, alleviating anxiety and providing a supportive meaning system in times of personal crisis. The effect of immigration is that accepted solutions for basic human dilemmas, previously presumed to be universal, are discovered to be but alternatives, often not even normative solutions. Such value conflict leads to what Wallace (1956) has described as "mazeway disintegration" or the lack of certainty regarding the most appropriate solutions for basic human dilemmas. A sense of personal crisis or impaired adjustment results (Hallowell, 1955), leading to confusion or uncertainty regarding appropriate modes of action. For example, during the past several decades, there has been much discussion of the finding, reported in numerous studies and reviewed by Sauna (1969), Struening, Rabkin, and Peck (1969), and Cohler and Lieberman (1978), that immigrant groups are, more likely than their counterparts, equated for social status in the old world or the new, to show impaired mental health. The literature suggests that this increased "risk" is accounted for by pressures accompanying immigration rather than by enduring problems of adjustment and impaired mental health

[1]Darroch and Marston (1971) have identified two contrasting explanations for the propensity shown by immigrants and their descendants to live in ethnically distinct neighborhoods (Lieberson, 1963; Heiss, 1966). Yancey, Ericksen, and Juliana (1976) claim that ethnicity is a pseudophenomenon, arising as a result of residential segregation defined in terms of social status. However, as Darroch and Marston's (1971) study has shown, together with that of Breton (1964), and others, homogeneity of such neighborhoods along other than ethnic lines is to be questioned. Guest and Weed (1976) suggest that although ethnic neighborhoods do demonstrate lower social status, ethnic "segregation" would continue even if such differences in social status were eliminated. Most recently, Bleda (1979), in a study of data from several American cities, has shown that characteristics associated with ethnicity account for more variance than those associated with social status, although significant variance can be attributed to social status. Patterns of chain migration and the adjustive function served by living together with others sharing a similar set of value orientations during the difficult period of adaptation to a new culture are important determinants of the propensity to live together with others of the same ethnic group. Such shared living arrangements facilitate employment of newcomers in jobs similar in social status to those already settled, and such employment often tends to be in occupations where literacy and other valued skills are not required. Cultural differences and occupational stratification tend to support each other, creating the link often observed between low social status and residence in a segregated (inner city) ethnic community. Structural as well as cultural perspectives are clearly important in understanding the determinant of such ethnic communities.

among these immigrants (Sluzki, 1979). Indeed, persons choosing to emigrate are generally more aspiring and novelty seeking than those who remain behind (Cohler and Lieberman, 1978).

Following immigration, particular patterns of beliefs and customs develop in response to mazeway disintegration, but these elements of ethnicity often represent stereotyped and distorted versions of the original culture. Considering the powerful psychological functions served by continued participation in the ethnic group, it is not surprising that these ethnic traditions are preserved for generations after immigration and remain a powerful factor in understanding subsequent adjustment to American society (Glazer and Moynihan, 1970; Gordon, 1978). These traditions continue to promote adjustment across these successive generations, providing assurance that familiar patterns of ''face-to-face'' relations will be preserved across the life cycle and that enduring and diffuse socioemotional supports will be available for members of the ethnic group as they venture out beyond the confines of the community they have symbolically defined as ''safe'' into the world of secondary relations at school and work (Suttles, 1968). Such traditional ethnic beliefs and traditions continue to be available during times of personal crisis.

In sum, the concept of ethnicity involves the assumption of (1) some shared values expressed through the development of particular institutions in the original society, (2) a defined historical period during which these institutions developed in a culturally different society, (3) increasing articulation of these beliefs and traditions in the new society in response to pressure for conformity to the normative patterns of this new society, and (4) awareness by most members of the ethnic group that these beliefs and customs belong to them and are different from the beliefs and customs of other groups. Ethnicity provides both an identity and a means for achieving adjustment in a new society in which older values and customs, once normative, have become one of many cultural variants, resulting in a feeling of mazeway disintegration.

ETHNIC PATTERNS AND FAMILY LIFE: THE CASE OF THE ITALIAN-AMERICAN FAMILY

Some Characteristics of Italian Immigration to the United States

The basis for ethnicity is the emigration of persons from their traditional home to a new society. While such immigration need not be across clearly defined national borders, in contemporary society, with rather homogeneous nation-states, this is the typical pattern immigration takes (Barth, 1969), such as in European migration to America. In studying ethnicity in the United States, it is necessary to consider history, as well as culture, for, depending on the period of time being discussed, patterns of immigration and settlement have been quite varied. Hansen (1940) has suggested that there were three separate phases of immigration in the years between 1815 and 1917 when the first restrictive legislation was passed that seriously curtailed the influx of new immigrants, particularly immigrants from working-class origins in Southern and Eastern Europe.

The first period of immigration, beginning in the 1830s and continuing until about 1860, reached its zenith between the years 1847 and 1854. This was a period of predominantly English and Irish immigration, spurred on by the Irish famine from 1846 to 1848. These northern European immigrants were primarily skilled agricultural workers and found a ready labor market in rural America during these years of the great Westward expansion. A second period of immigration took place between 1860 and 1890 and was marked by the influx of German and Scandinavian groups (Hansen, 1940). However, beginning in about 1870, with Italian unification, and the development of ties between the Italian south and the outside world, increasing numbers of Italians began to emigrate to America. In the years before 1880, the majority of these emigrants landed in Argentina or Brazil [for many immigrants at this time had no knowledge of America and no understanding about their final destination, which depended on the whims of the shipping lines and the port of debarkation (Dore, 1969)].

The third period of migration, which concerns us particularly in the present instance, occurred from 1890 to 1914, and consisted almost entirely of immigrants from Southern and Eastern Europe. During the decade from 1871 to 1880, only 50,000 Italians emigrated to the United States. However, during the two decades from 1881 to 1901, more than two million Italians, almost all of whom lived south of the Po River, emigrated to the United States (L. G. Brown, 1933).

As Dore (1969) notes, several political and economic factors contributed to the the decision to emigrate. The south had long been an impoverished area in Italy. Indeed, some Sicilians trace their economic misery back to the ancient Greeks who they claim plundered the land and stripped the hillsides of timber for warships. This stripping caused land erosion and led to centuries of poor agricultural conditions.

Although feudalism ended in northern Italy with the Renaissance, communication and transportation were so difficult in southern Italy that feudal estates continued until the first part of the nineteenth century when, in 1806, Napoleon placed his brother Joseph on the Neapolitan throne and instituted administrative reform. Although serfdom was abolished, most of the landowners were nonresident, which made it difficult to redistribute the land.

Many in the south had hoped that national unification in 1870 would finally bring southern Italy into closer contact with the rest of the country, making possible economic aid and providing technology for economic development. However, while northern products were imported into the south, the very backward industry of the south could not compete with industry in northern Italy (Lopreato, 1970). In addition, substantial new taxes were levied on southerners, both to pay back debts incurred during the war of unification and to finance economic development; the absentee southern landowners were largely free of such tax burdens. Since many southerners felt that their life had not markedly improved, they were eager to emigrate (McDonald, 1956). Although the very first immigrants from Italy had come from the more prosperous north, nearly all immigrants during the years of heavy emigration from Italy to the United States were from the impoverished agricultural south. According to the Italian government's official figures, nearly half of these immigrants were either from Naples or Sicily (Lopreato, 1970).

Covello (1944) describes the social system of the southern Italian community as comprised of four classes: the *giornalieri,* or day laborers, the *contadini,* or peasants, the *mastro* group of artisans, and finally, the *galantuomini,* or *Dons,* the landed gentry, professionals, priests, and government officials. The overwhelming majority of the emigrants came from the ranks of the *contadini.* Indeed, the social class origins of three of the four families in the present study is that of the *contadino* (Dr. and Mrs. Giorgio's families were both from the artisan class).

It has been suggested that only those members of southern Italian society who were unable to eke out a living were willing to emigrate. Briggs (1972, 1974) is probably correct in his assertion that few members of the day laborer class emigrated. However, if the three families in the present study are at all representative of southern Italian immigrants, the *contadini* were not as well educated as Briggs maintains. While they may have been somewhat more successful than villagers who chose not to emigrate, these immigrants were untutored in the complexities of late nineteenth- and early twentieth-century urban civilization awaiting them on the other side of the Atlantic.

Once in America, south Italian culture came into contact with that of America, as shaped primarily by two early migrations of northern Europeans, which combined with the culture of the original New England and southern colonies which had diffused westward over the Allegheny mountains. Although there were many variations, the set of beliefs that, following Weber (1905), have been called the "Protestant ethic" formed the basis of "core American" culture. According to Weber, the essence of this ethos is the belief that visible worldly success, manifested by devotion to one's wordly calling is the best sign of devotion to God and success in winning a satisfactory afterlife.

Asceticism, which demanded the foreswearance of present gratifications in favor of rewards in the future and a planned, rational, future-oriented and methodical life, was intrinsic to success both in the present life and hereafter. In contrast, the Italian immigrant saw work as having little intrinsic reward and believed very much in living in the present, obtaining whatever satisfaction life has to offer while it was available. The core American cultural system came into clear and irrevocable conflict with that of southern Italian culture.

The problem of culture change due to immigration is a complex one that has sparked considerable debate among social scientists. As Spiro (1955) observed, much of this debate has focused on the bahavioral or social structural consequences of contact between peoples with different cultures leading to concern with issues of intergroup relations amid majority-minority group relations rather than with the problem of cultural change itself. Once members of a culture become immigrants, their culture changes as a result of contact with a new culture. In the case of the Italian emigrants, once they had arrived in New York and other eastern and midwestern cities, where they made their homes, their own culture was irrevocably affected by the Protestant ethic that characterized American culture.

Debate about the fate of immigrant culture has centered on three different perspectives on the accommodation of ethnic groups to American culture: Anglo conformity, the melting pot, and cultural pluralism. During the first or northern migrations to the United States, until about 1880, it was believed that immigrant groups would achieve conformity with the Protestant-Anglo culture. However, even as early as the Irish immigration, there was some awareness that acculturation did not mean simply assimilation. The Irish were the first immigrant group whose religion, Catholicism, differed from that of most Americans, and fear of Papism and the power of the Catholic church was clearly visible in the Know-Nothing political party of the 1850s. However, it took the "new" immigration following the Civil War to crystallize sentiment against foreigners who followed a different religion and spoke a different language. During the period between the Civil War and World War I, there was increasing pressure to force assimilation of immigrant groups into the mainstream of American life. With the onset of World War I, particular concern was expressed regarding the presence of German-Americans whose loyalty to the American idea was challenged. As a result, Americanization programs were stressed in the schools, with the goal of achieving "100% Americanization." The history of this movement has been well documented (Higham, 1955; Gordon, 1964).

Intellectuals of this time, prior to World War I, were distressed by the jingoism implicit in the concept of conformity to the core American culture. Taking their cue from a much-earlier remark of Crevecoeur (1782) that in America "individuals of all nations are melted into one new race of man (p. 39)," these intellectuals rallied around a young playwright, Israel Zangwill, whose play, *The Melting Pot,* crystallized a new ideology. As one of the characters in this play predicts in the last act:

There she lies, the great Melting-Pot—listen! Can't you hear the roaring and the bubbling. There gapes her mouth—the harbour where a thousand mammoth feeders come from the ends of the world to pour in their human freight. Ah, what a stirring and a seething . . . how the great Alchemist melts and fuses them with his purging flame! Here shall they all unite to build the Republic of Man and the Kingdom of God . . . what is the glory of Rome and Jerusalem where all nations and races come to worship and look back, compared with the glory of America, where all races and nations come to labor and look forward. (1909, pp. 198-199)

This powerful rhetoric shaped thinking about acculturation and assimilation for nearly half a century. While idealistic, and consonant with the American belief in the equality of opportunity, this view of the melting pot did not fit with the facts. Groups of persons differing in cultural background, either because of family relations, national origins, or some combination, lived in segregated communities (Handlin, 1959; Lieberson, 1963) and maintained endogenous marriage patterns (M. Barron, 1946; Kennedy, 1944, 1952).

The experience of settlement of immigrant groups in America during the first half of the twentieth century showed how problematic was this melting pot theory. Already, before World War I, Horace Kallen (1915), a philosopher, had suggested that American society was constructed of many different ethnic groups, each of which should be encouraged to develop the perfection proper to it. This theme was taken up with renewed vigor first by Jane Addams in her work at Hull House in Chicago and later by Louis Adamic in his 1944 novel, *A Nation of Nations*. At the same time, social science theory was finally "catching up" with the rapid social changes of the twentieth century.

Sociological and ethnographic inquiry led social scientists to begin thinking in terms of social and cultural pluralism which, following M. G. Smith (1960), Barth (1969), and LeVine and Campbell (1972), may be defined as follows:

> Groups differentiated according to social structure, or culture sharing a common territory and, most typically, living under a common government.

Stated in its most elementary terms, cultural pluralism recognizes that two or more groups comprising a polity agree to differ. Although there is diversity across the population in terms of such basic institutions as religion, family, and kinship, these groups accept a common government and have no fixed territorial boundaries. Barth and his colleagues have described pluralistic societies both in Scandinavia and Africa, where ethnic groups live according to quite different customs within the same territory. Suttles (1968) describes a similar situation within an American urban community where Italian-Americans, Blacks, Puerto-Ricans, and Mexicans share a common neighborhood that has many of the characteristics of a segmentary system (Fortes and Evans-Pritchard, 1940). Foremost among these characteristics is that of corporate responsibility, with all groups joining in the definition of both the social system and location of the community, and in the preservation of the segmentation that has become a shared norm.

Perhaps the most influential contemporary statement of cultural pluralism as applied to American ethnic groups is that of Glazer (1952) and Glazer and Moynihan (1970) in their classic study *Beyond the Melting Pot*. Glazer and Moynihan start with the assumption that the very culture of immigrant groups is changed as a result of immigration. From the outset, these groups make some accommodation to American culture, which is designed to preserve their traditional culture most successfully while permitting the accommodations necessary to succeed in America; the importance of the ethnic group is that it provides for continuity in primary group relations and also fosters the development of a viable interest group.

Gordon (1961, 1964, 1978) has attempted to resolve the ambiguity inherent in the concept of ethnic assimilation by positing two processes in assimilation, acculturation or cultural assimilation, and assimilation into institutional structures, including primary group attachments. Gordon makes the same assumption as the Anglo-conformists that the goal of the immigrant group is that of assimilation. As we will see, third and succeeding generations, feel somewhat isolated from their cultural heritage, may actually seek to reestablish the ethnic ties to the "old country" that the second generation had attempted to dissolve (Hansen, 1952).

As a result of his concern with the issue of discrimination in American life, Gordon (1978) tends to neglect the possibility that ethnic groups do not wish complete structural assimilation. As Newman (1973) observes, in discussing Gordon's work, it is probably correct that once structural assimilation has been achieved, there will be complete acculturation. The question is whether such assimilation is possible in American society or indeed whether it should take place. Glazer and Moynihan (1970) argue that it is unlikely that ethnic or cultural differences based on factors such as common national heritage or religion will ever disappear from American life. A similar argument has been made by Kennedy (1944, 1952), Herberg (1955), Lenski (1961), and, more recently, by Abramson (1973) that religion still represents a major source of cultural diversity in American society.

There is a parallel between Gordon's views and those of both the Anglo-conformity and the melting pot theorists. Gordon assumes that the only direction of influence is that of the host culture on newer ethnic groups, without realizing that the host culture may well absorb customs of the ethnic group. The theories of Barth, Suttles, Glazer and Moynihan, and Newman suppose that social tension rather than amalgamation are more appropriate within our diverse society. As Suttles has demonstrated on the basis of his fieldwork, it is possible for groups with differing cultural traditions to achieve ordered segmentation and to exist in a state of tension or balance without conflict. Newman, citing Simmel's (1898) discussion of this problem, believes that multiple, crisscrossing cleavages serve to cement a society and make possible the delicate homeostasis which preserves diversity.

In the preceding discussion, we have considered the impact of immigration on cultural patterns of the immigrants' original culture. Differences as a result of religion overlap and reinforce differences due to ethnic origins. The importance of religion in fostering cultural diversity was first described in detail by Kennedy (1944, 1952). In a study of religious affiliations in New Haven, Connecticut, Kennedy reported that marriage patterns over a 70-year period among the five largest ethnic groups in the community varied according to religious preference, with Catholics (Irish, Italian, and Polish), Protestants (British, German, and Scandinavian) and Jews marrying within their own religion. Of particular interest for the present study, Italian-Americans were especially unwilling to marry outside their religion and more unwilling in this regard than the Irish-Americans. Ten years later (Kennedy, 1952), there was a shift toward greater intermarriage among religious groups, although Italian women were still particularly unwilling to marry outside the Catholic religion and felt it important to marry within their own ethnic group.

Similar conclusions were reported by M. Barron (1946) in a study of another New England community, with Italians increasing their rate of marriage within their own ethnic group between 1929 and 1940. Also of significance for the present study, (where, it will be recalled, the three second generation non-Italian husbands were at least part Irish,) when Italian women in M. Barron's study did marry outside their ethnic group and within the ranks of Catholics, both in 1929 and 1940 there was a clear preference for marriage to Irish men. A review of other studies published at about the same time reveals this same preference across a variety of communities in the northeastern United States for Italian women to marry Irish men in preference to those from other Catholic ethnic groups (M. Barron, 1946, p. 206). This factor is particularly surprising in view of the antagonism that had earlier marked relations between the Italians and the Catholic church which was largely dominated by the Irish at the time of the Italian emigration (Nelli, 1970a, 1970b; Russo, 1970; O'Brien, 1972).

More recent reports are consistent with earlier findings regarding the importance of religion, together with ethnicity, as factors determining major cultural distinctions in American life. Herberg (1955) argued that religion had essentially supplanted ethnicity as the major source of cultural diversity in American society, a viewpoint echoed some years later first by Lenski (1961) in his study of Detroit and then by Glazer and Moynihan in the first edition (1963) of their study of New York City (although both of these reports recognized the importance of the Negroes as a potential source of influence in urban politics).

The major recent source of data regarding this issue derives from Abramson's (1973) important study, based on national survey data, of marriage in Catholic America. Abramson's data suggest that the more recent the arrival of ethnic groups in American society, the higher the rate of religious endogamy. Indeed, the Italians, in 1964, maintained a rate of ethnic endogamy in marriage considerably higher than that of all Catholic groups combined and more consistent than that of Catholic groups as a whole, across the two generations. On the other hand, Abramson's study raises some puzzling questions about marriage among Italian-Americans. Alone among the Catholic groups studied, the more religious the respondent's parents and the more extensive the respondent's Catholic education, the more likely the respondent was to marry outside the Italian ethnic group.

This reversal of findings, with exposure to religion overcoming the effects of ethnic origins, unexplained in Abramson's account, may reflect the fact that a religious education enabled the respondent to become more cosmopolitan and to overcome the tremendously strong ethnic ties that existed independent of religion. In a sense, the respondent could see that there were other groups in the community besides Italian-Americans and a Catholic church generally perceived as Irish, and it may well be that the parents of respondents in the Italian group who attended church more frequently were themselves more cosmopolitan and more willing to permit intermarriage with other Catholics.

Social status has little effect in determining religious behavior within the several ethnic groups, independent of generation in the United States. Abramson's study does show clearly that most Italian-Americans remain Catholic through marriage to other Catholics, preferably those of Irish descent. At the same time, as we see in discussing Italian culture in America, the Italian-American's definition of Catholicism is itself unique.

On the basis of all available evidence, it is clear that "Old World" institutions are maintained, in an altered form, in the "New World." By providing a sense of identity, a secure base from which to venture out into the more formal institutions of work and education, and ready-made solution for such life crises or transitions as marriage, advent of parenthood, and illness and death, these institutions promote the successful adaptation of members of the ethnic community. However, to understand the manner in which these institutions have changed as a result of immigration, it is first necessary to appreciate aspects of these institutions as they existed in the Old World, and then to understand the impact on these institutions of unique patterns of immigration to the new country. To appreciate the structure of Italian-American culture in Bethany, it is important to understand south Italian culture, together with the impact of immigration to America, as this altered southern Italian culture.

Social Organization and the Family in Southern Italy and the United States

The area of Italy known as the "south" may be defined as the provinces south of the Po River (Campania, Abruzzi, Pulia, Basilicata, and Calabria, and the islands of Sardinia and Sicily). The further south one travels, the more characteristically southern is the culture. This southern Italian culture has been a favorite subject of study among economists (Schachter, 1965; Galtung, 1971), anthropologists (Chapman, 1935; Whyte, 1944; Moss and Cappannari, 1954, 1960a, 1960b; Moss and Thompson, 1959; Cancian, 1966; Boissevain, 1966; Silverman, 1968; Cronin, 1970), sociologists (Lopreato, 1967, 1970; Muraskin, 1974), and political scientists (Banfield, 1958). Much of this interest in the peoples of southern Italy arises from the fact that in spite of determined efforts by the Italian government to raise the standard of living in southern Italy and Sicily the people of this region remain entangled in the same poverty and social conflict that has marked this region since antiquity (Schooler, 1976). It should be noted, however, that Lopreato (1967) has provided some evidence of change in the direction of economic development in the past decade.

Mistrust, Fatalism, and the Origins of Amoral Familism in Southern Italy

The peasants refer to their land as the source of "La Miseria" (Friedman, 1953) or misery. There is little question that this has long been an impoverished area and that problems of geography, history, and social organization have combined to shape a world view emphasizing that which is least noble in relations with one another and least optimistic regarding the possibility of improving one's life.

Although Italy as a whole is a rugged land, problems of terrain are much worse in the south than in the north. Lopreato (1967), summarizing the literature on the geography of the south, notes that the percentage of soil that is clay and loam is far greater in the south and that the rainfall is two-fifths less than in the north.

There are no major rivers in the south, and the hilly land is subject to easy erosion. To make matters worse, what rainfall there is occurs chiefly in the winter months when there is little land under cultivation.

The combination of insufficient rainfall, constant heat whose intensity is magnified by the hot, dry winds that blow across the Mediterranean from the African deserts, scarcity of water, and centuries' old erosion that makes it impossible to hold moisture in the ground have all taken their toll on the land. Finally, to compound these difficulties, the major agricultural crop consists of wheat and other grains that do not grow well on these hot rocky hillsides.

Problems of geography have been compounded by problems of history. Partially because transportation and communication are so difficult in the mountainous south, feudalism continued well into the nineteenth century. Most of the land was owned either by the church or by wealthy, absent landlords, members of the Neapolitan Court, where their influence was successful in preventing redistribution of the land. Even the land reforms instituted under the brief period of Napoleon's reign had little effect on land ownership. Until well into the nineteenth century, there were only two classes of persons: the absent landowners (represented by the *gabelleto,* land agents who leased and supervised the work) and the agricultural workers who suffered under the harsh regime of the ''boss.''

During the Napoleonic reign, in 1806, rights of pasturing were given to the people, but title to the land was preserved for any landowner making significant improvements. After 1815 and the Bourbon restoration, the requirement was largely ignored that such improvements needed to be demonstrated in order to retain title to the land, and wide-scale abuses by large landowners were common. Even when the church lands were auctioned, the circumstances of the auction were such that impoverished agricultural workers could not afford the land. The effect of all attempts at redistribution of the land during the first two-thirds of the nineteenth century was to consolidate the holdings of the large landowners at the expense of the agricultural workers. Where there was some land redistribution, former serfs were generally offered narrow strips of poor land on several separate estates often many miles distant over mountainous roads. Realizing the impossibility of working these small properties, many of the small farmers sold out to the estates, leaving a class of landless agricultural workers.

Those peasants who did retain their land, even if the plots were widely scattered, became differentiated from those who remained landless and became itinerant workers. Although the life-styles of these two peasant groups were not very different, it was considered a disgrace for a *contadino* to marry a *giornaliero*.

Like the *giornaliero,* the *contadino* led a seminomadic life during the agricultural season, moving from estate to estate to supplement the meager living he could obtain from his own land. He did at least have some land, farm implements, and perhaps a few domestic animals that provided some prestige in the community. However, as Covello (1944) notes, ownership was also a burden, since taxes were heavy. Some landowning peasants paid more each year in taxes than they earned from the land.

No matter how wealthy, members of the two peasant classes were separated by a wide social gulf from the higher social classes in southern Italian society. Covello (1944) describes a four-class system, with the two peasant classes at the bottom, a class of artisans and small shopkeepers who enjoyed a considerably better standard of living as substantial members of the community, and a class of *galantuomini*, including the landed gentry, the professionals, schoolteachers, and clergy. On the basis of empirical study of a southern Italian community, Lopreato (1961, 1967) found a six-class system. The two lower peasant classes were similar to those described by Covello. However, Lopreato describes a transitional class of new artisans between the artisans and peasants, comprised of persons who have left the land entirely within the past decade. Members of this class are upwardly mobile. It is probable that this class did not exist until the end of World War II (after the time of Covello's observational study) and was given big impetus by the provision of help from relatives who had immigrated to America.

Lopreato concurs with Covello's description of the artisan class, but differentiates two upper classes: the less prestigious class is characterized by recent arrival from the artisan class and is comprised of first-generation university-educated persons who are upwardly mobile (including government officials) or schoolteachers and minor government officials, even without university degrees; members of the highest class, *signori* or gentlemen, may be less educated than members of the next lower class, but they can trace their origins back to the old estate owners. Members of this first class have traditionally been the large nonresident landowners and continue to control most of the land surrounding the town.

This brief review of the social structure of the Italian community supports Pitkin's (1959) conclusion, based on the ethnographic study of a southern Italian community, that there has been little social change in the more than 100 years since unification and supposed significant land reform. With the exception of two transitional classes, one from the ranks of the peasants and one from the ranks of the artisans, the southern Italian social structure has remained relatively resistant to change. Major political events such as the national unification of 1870 brought about even greater problems. Throughout the latter part of the nineteenth century and up to the very recent past, the "southern problem" has continued to vex Italian politics. Southern Italians believe that they have had to bear an unnecessarily large part of the economic burden of modernization. Prior to national unification there was hardly any tax, but, in the succeeding years, southern Italians were expected to pay a proportionately greater share than northern Italians of the tax, much of which went into foreign adventures. In addition, changes in trade policy that led to the protectionist policies of the late nineteenth century made goods from southern Italy less competitive with goods from the north which cost less to produce and transport to market.

The continued absence of the gentry from the land, and this group's control of provincial politics, also affected economic development, increasing corruption and placing an even greater share of the economic burden on the peasant classes. Peasant organizations that had begun to develop before World War II were abolished by fascism. The power of the peasants was so diminished that they were not even permitted to migrate to the north, where there were more jobs. The history of postwar southern Italy has been a repeat of the previous century. Little progress has been made in developing industry in the south, and the education of the peasants in modern agricultural techniques has been painfully slow. In part, this problem in educating the small farmer is the result of the lack of attachment that the peasant farmer feels toward the land. Since land was precious and since there was no defined acreage that could be considered the family farm, the typical relationship between the peasant and his land (Redfield, 1956) has never developed in southern Italy. There was no one farm with defined boundaries that the peasant could view as his own and toward which he could develop a reverential, sentimental attachment. Furthermore, when land ownership did occur, land parcels were so small and so spread apart that there was little use in having a large extended family to help till the land.

The typical arrangement among European peasantry was for a man and his family to cultivate a defined family farm, typically over the course of many generations.The family lived on the farm and maintained the family dwelling units and whatever outbuildings were necessary to house stock and store corn and grain. Given such an arrangement, there was an advantage in having a large extended family to share the chores, and considerable cooperation was necessary between farmers in order to purchase equipment and supplies that several farmers could share. With no family farm, and with tillable acreage at a premium, farm workers lived in small agrotowns (Boissevain, 1966) of tightly clustered stone buildings that served as both a dwelling for the nuclear family and as a stable for stock; from this agrotown, workers could go forth to cultivate their lands.

The agrotown was not an urban center, but rather a concentration of agricultural workers living on a rocky hillside, surrounded by the estates of wealthy landowners. As Covello (1944) notes, land was so scarce that it was often impossible even to have a garden, and houses were shoved as close together as possible to conserve valuable land. With a dense concentration of workers and their immediate family, tension in these agrotowns was often great. Banfield (1958) has well stated the dominant value of these people:

> Maximize the material short-run advantage of the nuclear family; assume that others will do likewise. (p. 83)

This world view, which Banfield terms "amoral familism," presumes that affairs, both public and private, are governed by one's hope for material gain and by the desire to advance oneself at the expense of others. It should be noted that since the publication of Banfield's classic study there has been considerable discussion of whether this view of the southern Italian agricultural workers is the cause or the result of life circumstances (Cancian, 1966; Muraskin, 1974). For the present purposes, it is pointless to take a stand on either side of this controversy. Suffice it to say that whatever the cause-and-effect relationship between values and behavior, Banfield's description of life in a southern Italian agrotown is consistent with other reports in the literature (Chapman, 1935; Covello, 1944; Friedman, 1953; Silverman, 1968, 1975; Cornelison, 1969, 1976; Cronin, 1970) both by those writing prior to his study and even those such as Silverman who disagree with the conclusions he makes from his observations.

An essential consequence of amoral familism is that relatives beyond the nuclear family cannot be counted on for assistance or advice. First, since all necessary labor can be accomplished by the nuclear family, there is little need for cooperation with an extended family unit. Second, since everyone attempts to maximize his own personal gain, there is little reason to trust the counsel of others. It is presumed that the only interest is personal gain at someone else's expense. Members of the family are highly suspicious of relatives; indeed, the culture of southern Italy is characterized by pervasive mistrust of others. Lopreato (1967) quotes a peasant informant:

Italy is a stinking place. We are all like cats and dogs, constantly at each other's throats. I don't know why, but one can't trust even the Lord God himself. If you don't look after your own things 24 hours a day, people will spit on you, steal everything you have, and then will say you did it to them. (p. 66)

The sole relationship between the nuclear and extended family is that of *honore* and generally occurs only in the context of marriage. Since any stain on the reputation of one family member is a stain on the reputation of all, the extended family through the father's line must concur on the marriage choice of all young men within the family (Cronin, 1970). An essential part of the world view of southern Italians is that men are essentially evil and seek to take advantage of unwary young women. At the same time, it is also acknowledged that women have strong sexual desires and that, unless carefully supervised, they are likely to engage in trysts with the men of the community. It is a task of the entire family to protect the virginity of the young woman until marriage. Therefore, young women are expected to remain at home throughout adolescence, avoiding public places, where their presence would be a source of gossip. Consistent with the Saracen influence on southern Italian culture, young women going about in daylight are expected to cover their faces and to wear long skirts covering their ankles.

Social control is swift and harsh. The concept of the *"Mafiosi,"* or a corporate family group acting to avenge the honor of one of its members, is commonplace in southern Italy (Boissevain, 1966; Cronin, 1970; Ianni, 1972) and acts with a unity quite rare in this nonfamilial society. Honor is avenged by the gun, and a young man who even flirts with an eligible girl or a married woman takes his life in his hands.

At the time of marriage, the young man's parents visit as many of the father's relatives as possible, discussing the forthcoming marriage and seeking the approval of the young man's choice. Family members make inquiry throughout the town, determining the reputation both of the young woman and her family. The process by which the decision comes back from the extended kin group is, however, haphazard, and, as Cronin (1970) observes, there is little systematic attempt to poll the extended family. The task of providing consent is complicated by the fact that while wishing to preserve the honor of the family everyone is concerned about safeguarding the autonomy of individual nuclear family units. Therefore, while there is strong social pressure to follow the wishes of the larger family group, there is still some latitude available to the parents of the young man in making the final decision. It is possible for the parents to decide in favor of the young woman, even in the face of negative opinion from the extended family, especially when it is believed that the decision of family members might have been motivated by jealousy or maliciousness.

Even after marriage, husbands and wives continue to be suspicious of each other. There are numerous accounts in ethnographic studies of southern Italy in which one or the other member of the couple heard rumors that led to a violent confrontation. The place of the wife is clearly in the home, and, even when she ventures out to market, she must be highly circumspect, keeping her face hidden and not stopping to talk to anyone. However, a woman also has the right to expect proper behavior from her husband. Even though he is expected to go to the town square after supper to gossip with his cronies, the man is not expected to participate in any sexual intimacies outside marriage (Moss and Thompson, 1959).

Several authors have noted that the stereotype of the dominant husband and submissive wife in the southern Italian family is largely inaccurate (Covello, 1944; Barzini, 1964; A. Parsons, 1969c; Cronin, 1970; Cornelisen, 1976). While men are the unquestioned source of authority within the home, wives are expected to intercede between their husband and their children and can press not only their children's cases, but also their own. A husband is expected to take his wife's viewpoint into consideration when making the final decision, and the husband who does not sometimes yield to his wife's wishes is considered to be acting badly (Moss and Thompson, 1959). As A. Parsons (1969b, 1969c) notes, much of the importance given to the Madonna in Italian Catholicism is a reflection of the family structure in which the powerful and effective mother intercedes on behalf of her children before a stern but caring father.

Socialization of young children leads quite early to the development of the sense of mistrust so pervasive in south Italian culture. Children are taught that the world outside the house is dangerous and that they must be suspicious of the motives of everyone outside the immediate family. As Cronin (1970) observes, in discussing the socialization practices of these families:

> Children just out of infancy learn that the world away from home is a dangerous place filled with strange unspecified "types" who will teach one "bad" things. Security and safety are to be found only at home with one's own—i miei (mine). The home is not necessarily a pleasant place, but the other world is made so unpleasant that any other alternative is preferable. (p. 94)

Before age six, children are regarded as cute and innocent. They are encouraged to play freely and to express their needs without constraint. However, beginning at about age five, they are expected to become income-producing members of the family. Typically, children attend school in the morning and have chores to do in the afternoon. For the school-age child, the period of earlier freedom gives way to that of heavy responsibility. Little girls stay with their mothers and learn domestic chores, while little boys go off to the fields with their fathers. Such responsibility serves to keep the children off the streets and out of danger. At the same time, children are kept at their chores by reason of parental discipline.

Children learn early in life that control is external and harsh and that failure to attend to rigidly specified social norms has direct and powerful implications. Furthermore, they learn that the focus of all their concerns is the family unit. Almost every waking hour, outside the time spent at school or the market, is spent with other family members. Individuation is discouraged, and the child's identity becomes fused with that of other family members.

The brutal poverty that characterizes the Italian south, combined with centuries of maltreatment, had led to a sense of fatalism. The misery in which the southern Italian lives is so all-encompassing that there is little desire to live for the future (Friedman, 1953). Banfield (1958) reports that 64% of his respondents in southern Italy provided endings for thematic apperceptive stories that were characterized by calamity and misfortune, as compared with 24% of northern Italian respondents. Success is viewed as either due to good luck or crafty manipulations at the expense of some unfortunate other. As Banfield observes, in discussing this fatalism:

> The idea that one's welfare depends crucially upon conditions beyond one's control—upon luck or the caprice of a saint—and that one can at best only improve upon good fortune, not create it—this idea must certainly be a check on initiative. Its influence on economic life is obvious: one who lives in so capricious a world is not likely to save and invest in the expectation of ultimate gain. (p. 109)

Much of this fatalism and mistrust of the world is reflected in the particular orientation of the south Italian toward Catholicism. As is true of other Latin countries, southern Italians have maintained a folk religion, and to it they have grafted elements of Catholic dogma (Covello, 1944; Moss and Cappannari, 1954, 1960a; Banfield, 1958). Most characteristic of the southern Italians' religious orientation is their preoccupation with the uncanny and the occult. Superstition and sorcery are prevalent components of religion. Many of these components of folk religion come together in the cult of the Madonna, who is viewed as a magical source of all good fortune. Covello (1944) suggests that this cult was borrowed from the Greeks, while Moss and Cappannari (1954) suggest that it infused from central Europe. However, as A. Parsons (1969b, 1969c) notes, it is consistent with the organization of the nuclear family in which the mother intercedes on behalf of the children with the authoritarian father.

The Madonna, as worshipped by the southern Italian, bears little resemblance to the Virgin Mary of official church doctrine. Each village has its special Madonna, a saint who intercedes with the heavenly Father on behalf of His earthly children. The Madonna is worshipped for her power rather than for her grace, as is more usual in Catholic dogma. The clergy's attempts to educate southern Italians in the correct interpretation of the Madonna have met with failure. In some communities, the power of the Madonna in working necessary miracles has been supplemented by that of lesser local saints.

Consistent with the suspiciousness with which outsiders are regarded, southern Italians have little use for the clergy, whose desire to be of help is regarded with suspicion: there is no reason why any person outside the family should wish to help. In addition, to confess one's sins and to reveal one's weakness can only lead to increased vulnerability and to the possibility that one can be taken advantage of by another (Moss and Thompson, 1959). Women are much more likely to attend Mass than men and to take an active role in parish affairs, but this participation is dictated by the extent to which the parish priest accedes to the wishes of his parishioners that folk elements of religion be preserved. The southern Italian is as suspicious of the church and of attempts by Rome to govern local affairs as he is of government officials.

It is useful to summarize this discussion of southern Italian culture in terms of the value orientations outlined by F. Kluckhohn and Strodtbeck (1961). Value orientations are ways of conceptualizing the major tenets of the value system of a particular culture, or, as C. Kluckhohn (1951) has commented;

A value orientation may be defined as a generalized and organized conception, influencing behavior, of nature, man's place in it, of man's relation to man, and of the desirable and nondesirable, as they relate to man-environment and interhuman relations. (p. 409)

Spiegel (1971) has noted that the classification of values in terms of value orientation presumes that (1) there are a limited number of solutions to common human problems, (2) solutions to these problems are not limitless or random, and (3) all possible solutions can be found as variants within any one culture, with a particular solution being preferred by most persons.

Four value orientations have been viewed as worth particular consideration: (1) the relation of man to nature (man-nature orientation), (2) the temporal focus of human life (time orientation), (3) the modality of human activity (activity orientation), and (4) the relationship of man to his fellows (relational orientation). Within each value orientation, there are solutions that are more and less preferable, and these solutions can be rank ordered within any one value orientation for any one culture. Application of this paradigm to the cultures of the American Southwest (Vogt and Albert, 1966) and to Mexican-American and Japanese-American ethnic groups in San Francisco (Clark, 1973) has demonstrated the utility of this paradigm in describing cultural differences. In the present study, this same approach can be useful in discussing changes observed between southern Italian culture and that of Italians in America.

In southern Italy, the orientation to nature is clearly that of subjugation rather than harmony or mastery. Viewing their inhospitable climate and geography as dominant factors in their life, southern Italians have resigned themselves to living within the economic confines these factors necessitate. They rely primarily on folk religion to provide solutions to problems viewed as beyond their control. While they attempt to grow grain that cannot be grown in hot and dry climates, this attempt arises more from sheer necessity than from a desire to attain control over nature.

The temporal focus of southern Italians is clearly that of the present rather than the past or the future. Given "La Miseria," there is no hope for the future, which will be as bleak as the past. For the same reason, there is no reason to dwell on the past, since it was never a time of particular glory and achievement. The only use made of the past is to explain current difficulties. Southen Italians view their task as to live in and for the present and to seek satisfaction in the here and now.

The modality of human activity most characteristic of southern Italian culture is that of being rather than being-in-becoming (emphasis on development of the person) or doing and accomplishment. The being orientation emphasizes the spontaneous, immediate expression of needs. It is expected that one should express present needs in the most direct possible manner, without concern for future accomplishment. Tension discharge is of greater value than the delay of immediate gratification for the sake of future accomplishment or achievement.

The greatest difficulty in fitting the value orientation paradigm to southern Italian culture is precisely in the area where the greatest controversy has developed regarding this cultural system. Spiegel (1971) suggests that the relation of man to his fellows is collateral, with emphasis on proximity to relatives rather than either individualistic, or lineal, emphasizing worship of ancestors. Although there is a sense in which there are collateral family ties, the concept of amoral familism works against the cooperation of the family as a corporate group. As we have seen, since family members are suspicious of the motives of all others beyond the nuclear family, collaterality can extend no further than the nuclear family.

The only time collateral relations become important is when a young man is about to marry: a young man's marriage threatens the honor that is viewed as characterizing the entire patrilineal kinship group. Once honor has been preserved, members of the extended family feel little obligation to attend the wedding or to attend baptisms or funerals. When the family's honor has been violated, strong pressure is exerted by the extended family to seek revenge, but, unless the act leading to loss of honor was highly visible in the community, it is unlikely that family members will take action on their own, with the exception of the aggrieved party.

Overall, the collateral solution is preferred when considering the nuclear family, with its emphasis on close, binding relationships, but individualistic when considering the relationship between the nuclear family and other units. For example, while each child in the family has a godparent, there is a separate godparent for each child, creating bonds to an extended family unique to that particular family member (Moss and Cappannari, 1960b).

Further, because contact with relatives beyond the immediate nuclear family would expose family secrets and increase the vulnerability of family members to sorcery, members of the nuclear family are strongly discouraged from having any contact with relatives. Secrecy is vital for protection and self-preservation.

The lineal solution in ordering man's relations with his fellows is the least likely of the three possible solutions to be chosen by the southern Italian. Since a person has worth only as long as he or she contributes to the economic well-being of the family, aged persons are treated with lack of respect. An aged person becomes a drain on meager family resources, taking but not giving. Sole authority is vested in those members of the family with the greatest control of resources, a position that could be predicted on the basis of the southern Italian's orientation toward time (present time emphasized) and activity (being emphasized).

Immigration and the Fate of Amoral Familism in the United States

The image of southern Italian culture that emerges from this review of observational, ethnographic, and survey studies of southern Italian society over the past century suggests numerous reasons why the Italian peasant would have wished to emigrate. It was, however, still a difficult decision to begin life anew in a strange land. Emigration was complicated by restrictions imposed by large estate owners as the emigration movement swelled. Between 1870 and 1886, fearing the depletion of their labor supply, these landowners tried to pressure the government to enact restrictive emigration laws. After attempts at Italian expansion into Ethiopia were thwarted in 1887, the government realized that emigration could be an attractive alternative in dealing with population pressures. In addition, the profits from transporting emigrants led the merchants and shipbuilders to abandon their traditional coalition with the landowners, adding to the impetus for the liberalized emigration laws of 1888 (Dore, 1969).

While the decision to emigrate was difficult, as Handlin (1951) has noted, the southern Italian peasant was not confronted with the temptation to remain in the Old Country, which faced northern European peasants. Lacking historical ties to particular farms on which forefathers were buried and lacking the ties of a close-knit extended family, southern Italians had little reason to remain in Italy. The southern Italian peasant was simply not the traditionalistic, sentimental familistic person described by Handlin. As Vecoli (1964) has observed, in his critique of Handlin's thesis:

> The idealized peasant village which Handlin depicts in *The Uprooted* did not exist in the southern Italy of the late 19th century. Handlin's village was a harmonious social entity in which the individual derived his identity . . . the ethos of his village was one of solidarity, communality, and neighborliness. The typical south Italian peasant, however, did not live in a small village, but in a "rural city" with a population of thousands or even tens of thousands. (p. 404)

This discussion of south Italian culture has emphasized the extent to which the peasant felt alienated both from the land and from fellow villagers. No group of persons could be in a better position to emigrate than the impoverished class of *contadini* who were largely isolated from greater social participation and who despaired of any improvements in living conditions. It has been suggested (Briggs, 1972, 1974) that only those more affluent peasants who were upwardly mobile had shown the desire to emigrate. It is more accurate to suggest that large numbers of persons in the two peasant classes emigrated, but that about half of these persons actually returned to Italy (Yans-McLaughlin, 1977). It is likely that those who remained in America were at least somewhat more willing to take the chance of starting life in the new country and may have been somewhat more adventurous than those who returned.

Certainly, those who emigrated were drawn from the two lowest peasant classes, attracted by the posters that found their way to even the smallest Italian village (Dore, 1969). Some members of the peasant classes tended, in the beginning, to migrate to South America rather than the United States, because of the shipping routes. Somewhat later, as the first immigrants arrived in the United States, some of them were hired as agents or *Padroni* (bosses), returning to Italy to obtain additional indentured labor. The peasants, used to working for bosses in the form of agents or *gabelleta* who represented absent landlords, were willing to accept this indenture in return for securing passage (McDonald and McDonald, 1962). In the period after 1890, when indenture was discouraged by both American and Italian officials, most emigration was facilitated by arrangements made by friends and relatives already in the United States who paid for passage and provided housing for the immigrants.

Immigration had a profound effect on traditional south Italian culture. While mistrust and individualism had characterized interpersonal relations in the Italian provinces, immigration fostered a sense of cooperation and joint participation. As McDonald (1956) and McDonald and McDonald (1962, 1964) have noted and as has been so clearly shown in Bianco's (1974) comparative study of an Italian and a southern Italian ethnic community in the United States, a frequent emigration pattern was for a group of young men in a village to journey together to America, settle, arrange for housing and jobs, and then to return and bring their families. An alternative pattern was that in which one member of the town would settle in America, write to those left behind of his or her new life, and encourage them to come also. The fact that southern Italian peasants lived together in agrotowns both facilitated communication about emigration and provided the basic social structure for this chain migration. In other parts of Europe, where peasants lived in scattered farm settlements, there was less possibility of such communication. In addition, having been town dwellers for centuries, southern Italians became urban dwellers in the United States with fewer serious social consequences than was true for other peasant groups (Tomasi, 1972). Adjustment to living in large cities where there was a ready demand for work was not an alien experience for southern Italians. Used to living in crowded quarters, southern Italians were willing to settle for cramped quarters in tenement sections (Lieberson, 1963; Ward, 1971; Golab, 1973; Varbero, 1973).

The effect first of the *padrone* system and then of the chain migration of families was that persons from the same agrotowns in southern Italy moved as a group to the same city, neighborhood, block, and, frequently, the same apartment building in the United States. As Glazer and Moynihan (1970) have noted, the Italian conception of home was expanded in the United States to mean neighborhood. In

Chapter 3 we described this living pattern in discussing Mrs. Limpari's life in Tower Point. It is worth noting that even after several generations, it is common for descendants of the original immigrants to maintain these living arrangements.

Settlement along the lines of the family's original town in southern Italy perpetuated, as social distance, the geographic distance that had characterized relations between these communities in Italy (McDonald and McDonald, 1962). For example, Lalli (1969) reports that marriage within an urban neighborhood in the United States was supposed to be endogamous, and it was not considered proper for descendants of one agrotown to intermarry with the descendants of another such agrotown living around the corner in the United States. Here, again, we see that the neighborhood had become an extension of the safety provided by the nuclear family; as a result of migration, the suspicion characterizing relations between townspeople in southern Italy had been displaced to relations between descendants of different southern Italian communities now residing in separate and, often, adjoining neighborhoods.

Most of the jobs available for men were in construction (Ianni, 1957), while the women and children worked mainly in textile factories, doing piecework. Since there was a great need for labor in the United States and since the earlier *padrone* tradition had already established the practice of obtaining jobs in advance for prospective immigrants, those who migrated later continued this practice of obtaining jobs for their townspeople. This practice sanctioned by United States' immigration officials (McDonald and McDonald, 1962) further cemented ties between persons from the same village.

At the same time that these townspeople became more interdependent in the United States, the suspiciousness that characterized interpersonal relations in Italy began to break down, resulting in greater distinction between members of the same ethnic group and community in south Italy who could be trusted and persons who were not of Italian background and who must be regarded with suspicion (O'Brien, 1972). The practice of obtaining jobs through family ties continues to the present, as we have seen in Chapter 4 in the case of Mr. Scardoni and Mr. Russo, and demonstrates once more the inadequacy of the belief that employment in our highly mobile society is based on achieved rather than ascribed characteristics.

Since children were regarded as income-producing members of the family, it was common to continue child-labor practices in the United States. Attempts to change this practice were often unsuccessful, as were attempts by school authorities to get the children into public school (Covello, 1944; Yans-McLaughlin, 1977). First, parents could ill afford the loss of income represented by the child's full-time attendance at school. Second, given the value on present-time orientation and on being rather than being-in-becoming, emphasis on preparing and sacrificing in the present for the future was meaningless to the southern Italian immigrant.

Third, given the concern of the immigrants with the status of unmarried daughters, the most certain way of overseeing the daughter's activity when her mother was at work all day was for her daughter to work alongside her. Yans-McLaughlin (1977), in explaining the large Italian community in Buffalo, New York, notes that picking grapes in the nearby vineyards satisfied the need to keep the family together doing labor much like that they had performed in Italy and preserved the stability of the family unit at the same time that it permitted continued supervision of unmarried daughters.

Given this concern with the behavior of their children, most Italian immigrants would not let their daughters go to work as domestic servants. Indeed, it is uncommon to find members of the Italian ethnic group represented among household employees in the United States. It was not considered proper for an unmarried girl to be in the same household as an unmarried or strange man. On the other hand, many immigrants took in boarders, especially if they had been responsible for convincing members of their agrotown to emigrate. Frequently, the immigrant remained with the family until he or she had secured housing and a job. During this time, there was always danger that intimacies would develop between the newcomer and unmarried girls in the family. As we have seen, in discussing Mrs. Scardoni's childhood, the presence of boarders in the home was a constant source of conflict and was considered a questionable means of providing extra income for the family.

Perhaps the best way of gaining perspective on the role of immigration in changing south Italian culture into Italian-American ethnicity is to examine the impact of immigration on the family itself. Of course, the most striking change was that the nuclear family was no longer the self-contained isolated unit that it had been in southern Italy. The necessity for cooperation in the new land, fostered by patterns of chain migration, brought about a dramatic change in family organization. For the first time, a truly extended family developed, based on patterns of mutal aid and assistance across generations among relatives. As the identity of the individual nuclear unit was merged with that of the larger family group (a process aided by the close proximity of the residential unit), the identity of family members became that of the larger kinship unit. Many of these changes have been documented in recent reviews of the Italian-American family (Femminella and Quadagno, 1976). In contrast with earlier observations (Campisi, 1948), these more recent discussions point to the extent to which these first-generation changes in family structure were preserved over succeeding generations.

Many of the changes in the family attributed to immigration were actually features of the family in Italy that had been insufficiently recognized. For example, Campisi points to the diminution in the father's authority in the family. However, the present review of the southern Italian family in Italy and the United States suggested that the father was much less the undisputed autocrat than might at first appear. Nor is it true that immigration destroyed an extended family form present in the Old World (Handlin, 1951). As has been repeatedly emphasized in this discussion, quite the opposite is true. In contrast with other peasant groups, such as Irish working-class families that had lived as an extended family on the same land for countless centuries, immigration fostered rather than destroyed the extended family structure. For example, A. Parsons (1969c) reports that immigrant families tend to have *more* children than their counterparts who remain in southern Italy. Furthermore, with the passage of generations, as Italian-Americans become used to this new form of family organization, participation in the extended family increases rather than decreases (Palisi, 1966). Such findings are consistent with the view proposed in the present instance that, in contrast with other European peasant groups that were originally part of extended kinship groups working a common farm, the adjustment of the southern Italian family to the United States did not lead to significant family disorganization. In contrast with these other immigrant groups who suffered true disruption on leaving the homeland, the southern Italian emigrants realized greater stability and more extensive intergenerational contact than was true among those who remained in southern Italy.

In other respects, Italian-American socialization patterns in the United States resembled those of the southern Italian family. In the first generation, the *padrone* or other sponsor took the role of the godparent who was present at baptism. In subsequent generations, this practice of godparenthood has been maintained. The mother's role in the family has been to provide stability and security, although major decisions were reserved for the husband-father who otherwise remained aloof from more mundane decisions (Gambino, 1974).

The husband-father had his friends with whom he would play cards in the evening at the neighborhood coffee house. In this respect, the man's role in the household was similar to that of the father in the Italian family. Husband and wife had clearly different roles in the family, with different responsibilities and different circles of friends outside the family. As we have seen with the four families in the present study, even after several generations, the husband-father still maintains a separate circle of friends and, like Mr. Scardoni, will drive in from a distant suburb several nights a week to spend time with his companions. The wife-mother spends most of her free time with her own mother and her extended family. In this respect, the woman's pattern of leisure differs from that of the southern Italian family, where the wife-mother has little free time and does not believe in talking about intimate matters with relatives.

The pattern of husband-wife relations described in the literature (Gans, 1962) and confirmed in the present study is much like that described by Bott (1971) for an English working-class group. Husband and wife have separate household duties and separate friends. While there is some change in this pattern of conjugal relations in third- and fourth-generation families, the pattern is much like that described by first- and second-generation families, particularly among those Italian-Americans who remain within the ranks of the working class.

Several studies have suggested that young children are socialized to rely on external norms of conduct, much like socialization practices in Italy (Whyte, 1943; Gans, 1962; Suttles, 1968). Parents view children as a source of prestige and believe that children should serve the best interests of the family. This belief corresponds to the importance of the nuclear family unit in Italy, and, as is true in southern Italy, children are encouraged to remain attached to the family, which is seen as the source of nurturance and support; separation and individuation is discouraged.

Within this adult-centered family, children are expected to remain quiet and unobtrusive. Boys are given greater freedom to play about the neighborhood than girls, who are expected to begin helping their mothers from about age seven. Gans (1962) notes that the gulf between the world of parents and that of children is nearly as great as that between parents themselves. Since the family is no longer involved in heavy labor, children in second- and third-generation families have greater freedom and parents are not expected to have to supervise children's activities so long as the children remain out of trouble. However, punishment is sure and swift when the child's misdeeds come to his or her parents' attention.

Gans (1962) describes the childcare practices of Italian-American parents as impulsive, with an emphasis on teaching a child how to act in public and with little concern for the child's perception of his or her parents' motives. Parents are not very concerned with the development of the child's character and have little conception of what they want for the child in the future. The result of this attitude toward childcare is that the child develops a pragmatic outlook on the world, realizing that outward appearance is all important, a characteristic Schooler (1976) interprets as consistent with the feudal tradition, so important in southern Italian society until the past few decades.

The role of the peer group is much more important for the Italian-American child than for his or her counterpart in Italy, although A. Parsons (1969c) reports that the peer group is an important socialization agent among Italian children living in the city. The peer group is especially important for adolescent boys, since it enables them to shift their allegiance from the family to the larger community. Boys are permitted to achieve a far greater measure of independence than girls, who are expected to remain at home with their mothers, as discussed in greater detail in Chapter 1, and typical more generally of working-class American culture (Rubin, 1976).

Given these differences in socialization practices between Italian and Italian-American families, some shift in value orientation would be expected. The greatest shift in value orientation would be expected in relations with others. Since Strodtbeck (1958), Femminella (1968), Femminella and Quadagno (1976), and Spiegel (1971) all have discussed Italian-American culture within the framework of the Kluckhohn-Strodtbeck (1961) paradigm of value orientations, it is possible to compare the value orientations of Italian-Americans both with those of southern Italians, as well as with other ethnic groups in American culture whose value orientations have been contrasted with those of Italian-Americans.

Considering the first of these value orientations, that of the relation of man to nature, Strodtbeck (1958) maintains that the Italian-American family preserved the emphasis on subjugation to nature as the preferred solution. Certainly, the Italian-American family has preserved the folk elements in Catholicism that emphasize magical solutions rather than mastery over a natural world perceived of as superior to man. O'Brien (1972) describes a conflict between the Chicago archdiocese and a group of suburban parishioners who had brought their revered Madonna from their Italian village when they immigrated to the United States. The bishop was appalled when the parishioners built a special chapel for their Madonna, adjoining the Catholic church, and went first to Mass and then to worship before their Madonna. However, it should be noted that the American clergy has always been Irish and intolerant of Italian Catholics who are both mystical in their attitude toward Catholicism and embittered at the extent to which the Irish church has prevented members of the Italian community from true participation (Vecoli, 1964; Russo, 1970).

Suffice it to say that for whatever reason, Italian-Americans have continued to practice Catholicism in a manner consistent with subjugation to nature. Femminella (1968) reports that, using his procedure for scoring the Kluckhohn-Strodtbeck value orientation measure, he does not find much difference across first-, second-, and third-generation Italian-Americans in this component of value orientation, but, across the three generations, there is a clear lack of preference for mastery over nature, the preferred American solution.

Considering the second of the value orientations, the temporal focus of human activity, Italian-Americans have maintained their preference for living in the present rather than the future or past. Zborowski (1969) notes that when they feel pain Italians are concerned almost entirely with the sensation of pain and its sedation in contrast, for example, with the Jews, who worry about the diagnostic significance of the pain. Strodtbeck (1958) notes that although Italian-American parents are aware of the American emphasis on future accomplishment, they take a very present-oriented attitude toward achievement. Spiegel (1971) also notes the preference of Italian-Americans for living in the present, although noting a greater awareness of the meaning of the future than is true among southern Italians.

Singer and Opler (1956b) provide empirical evidence that this preference for present time is reflected in behavior. In studies of time estimation with groups if Irish-American and Italian-American schizophrenics, the Irish-Americans showed a greater capacity to inhibit responses before answering and provided estimates of time intervals significantly greater than those provided by Italian-American respondents. Femminella's empirical study of value orientations also suggest that, independent of generation in the United States, present time was selected by Italian-American respondents in preference to either past or future.

With regard to the third of these value orientations, modality of activities, the preference of south Italians and Italian-Americans for the being over the being-in-becoming or doing orientation is reported in all research except that of Femminella (1968), who reports a clear preference for the doing orientation among all generations, including the first or immigrant generation of Italian-Americans, and Danesino and Layman (1969) who find that Italian-American college students are more achievement oriented than Irish-American students. Comparing the parents of Italian- and Jewish-American boys, Strodtbeck (1958) reports a highly significant difference in the direction of greater emphasis among the Jewish parents on doing and achievement; a finding consistent with Spiegel's (1971) observational data regarding the Italian-American family. Tsushima (1968) reports that, equating the groups on social status, Italian-American patients are far more willing than Irish-American patients to express their hostility and tension prior to major surgery. Similar findings regarding the ease of expression of angry feelings have been reported by Stein (1971), comparing emotionally disturbed and well Irish-American and Italian American boys. Stein reports that the Italian-American boys, whether disturbed or well, are more exhibitionistic and impulsive than Irish-American boys. Such findings are consistent with the view of the being alternative as emphasizing immediate expression of emotions, together with an inability to bear tension over time.

The most obvious shift in value orientations when comparing southern Italians with Italian-Americans is in the greater importance among the Italian-Americans that is placed on collateral relationships. As indicated in discussing this value orientation among southern Italians, the concept of amoral familism emphasizes the suspicion with which the extended family is to be viewed. On immigrating to the United States, there was a dramatic shift in the emphasis placed on relations with the extended family. On immigration, Italian-Americans came to value extended family relations to a greater extent and tended to view ties with other family members and members of the Italian community as sources of support and assistance in contrast to the rest of American society, which was viewed with the same hostility shown in southern Italy to members of one's own extended family and to other members of one's community. This preference expressed for collateral over lineal and individualistic solutions to the dilemma of relations with others has been found empirically across all three generations in Femminella's (1968) study of Italian-Americans and is clearly emphasized in observational studies of Italian-American communities such as those of Gans (1962) and O'Brien (1972).

The impact of differences in preference for collateral and lineal solutions regarding relations with others is nicely demonstrated in a case report by Pinderhughes (1974) on the reaction of hospital staff to relations among family members of patients facing kidney transplants. Following immigration, Irish-Americans have moved from a lineal to an individualistic orientation toward family relations quite different from that of the Italian-Americans, who had emphasized collateral relations. Irish spouses married to Italians were particularly irate that, since visiting was limited, time had to be shared with relatives. In this context Pinderhughes observes the following:

Italian people . . . maintained strong bonds to extended family members along with bonds to the marital family, while the Irish people . . . . placed far greater emphasis on bonds to the marital family. Thus, family bonds for the Italians tended to be conducted in parallel, and for the Irish in series. When the Irish mates told their spouses "You aren't children anymore, you now have a family of your own" they revealed their belief that dependent affiliative attachments to parents and siblings were permissible in childhood but were to be overcome by adults. The Italians viewed strong interdependent family attachments as desirable for adults as well as for children. (p. 172)

In Pinderhughes' study, Irish Americans believed in maximizing relations between husband and wife, thereby avoiding dependence on the extended family, while Italian-American couples believed that affectionate support from the extended family was critical in helping the patient to a full recovery. Emphasis on individuation was of greatest importance for Irish patients and their spouses, while dependent and symbiotic ties and lack of differentiation of body boundaries characterized Italian patients and their spouses.

ETHNICITY AND INTERGENERATIONAL TIES AMONG FOUR BETHANY FAMILIES

This review of the Italian family in Italy and the United States indicates that close and reciprocal intergenerational relations are a phenomenon largely unknown in southern Italian culture. In particular, differential patterns of socialization for boys and for girls in the United States accentuate the close tie between women in the family in the manner suggested by discussions of socialization into the female sex role (Komarovsky, 1950; Chodorow, 1978). Class and ethnicity combine to reinforce a strong bond in the working class Italian-American family, presenting a particular problem for the women. The expectation that collateral relations are more important than individualistic relations is not constant across the life cycle. As we have seen in the case of the four families described in this book, grandmothers tend to be wary of acceding to their daughters' wishes for assistance. It is perhaps most useful to demonstrate this contribution of the cultural perspective to the understanding of intergenerational relations by considering the four families in somewhat greater detail.

In reviewing these families from the perspective of ethnicity, both the intensity of the family's involvement in the Italian-American culture and the family's preferred solution to the several value orientations delineated by (Kluckhohn and Strodtbeck, 1961) must be considered. While it is not possible to specify the rankings of preferred solutions, it is possible to determine the extent to which these families deviate from the modal solution for each value orientation reported more generally among Italian-American families.

From the perspective of ethnicity, among the most salient characteristics of these four families is that at least one member of the grandparental generation is the first generation in the United States (Mr. Limpari, Mrs. Limpari, Mrs. Pescatore, Dr. Giorgio, and Mr. Scardoni). All grandparents immigrated during the period between 1910 and 1920 when they were children. They were immigrants at the end of the period of high immigration, just prior to the enactment of the quota laws in the United States. While all immigrant grandparents remember their childhood in Italy, only Dr. Giorgio has ever returned to his native land (his wife is the only grandmother to visit Italy). Those grandparents born in the United States were all of the second generation, but only one, Mrs. Scardoni, shows the interest in assimilation described in the literature; she has struck out for a life largely independent of the Italian-American community. Ironically, in spite of her earlier interest in achieving a Yankee identity, she has married a man, born in Italy, who continues to drive from the suburbs to Tower Point several times a week to visit with his old friends.

Finally, it should be noted that all grandparents, with the exception of Dr. Giorgio and Mrs. Scardoni, were brought up in Tower Point and moved out to a suburban community with a concentration of Italian-American families. This pattern of settlement is consistent with that reported in the literature. Although seen most clearly in the Limparis' present living arrangements, all grandparents resided initially in the same neighborhood as that of their townspeople from southern

Italy. Mrs. Limpari observes that there is one woman living in her building whose parents quarreled with her parents in Italy. The animosity between the two families has continued unabated in the New Country, and perhaps because of her present-time orientation, she does not consider it unusual that this family quarrel has been perpetuated over several generations in two countries.

There is considerable variation across the four families in the extent to which persons subjectively feel themselves to be "Italian." If ethnic identification is measured by awareness of the history of the "Old Country," use of the Italian language in the home and with friends, preference for Italian food, and effort to preserve Italian holidays, the Limparis and Mrs. Pescatore show the greatest ethnic identity. Of course, the Limparis are the only grandparental generation family in which both husband and wife have emigrated from Italy. They are also the only family to settle permanently in Tower Point. Mrs. Limpari's ethnic identity is among the highest of the women in the study, as shown by her involvement in the church and various Italian American civic groups. She cooks only Italian food, and Italian is spoken almost exclusively in the home. She continues to celebrate holidays as they were celebrated in southern Italy and receives considerable encouragment in the perpetuating of Italian customs from her daughter who is quite different from the second-generation immigrants described in the literature.

Mrs. McGorty prefers to speak Italian with her mother and has considerable knowledge of Italian history. She is very much concerned that her children receive a cultural education that includes an appreciation of their Italian heritage. Mrs. McGorty prefers to cook Italian foods and uses her need to seek information about recipes from her mother as an excuse for her daily telephone calls. Rather than rebelling against her heritage as is believed to be typical in the second generation, because of her close relationship with her mother, Mrs. McGorty clings tenaciously to it.

Mrs. Pescatore shows the second strongest ethnic identity among the four grandmothers. Not only does she cook entirely Italian foods, but also she speaks fluent Italian, which she finds easier to use than English. Since she, too, was an immigrant, Italian was her first language, and she complains that she still has difficulty "thinking in English." Mrs. Pescatore devotes most of her time and effort to family affairs and lives outside Tower Point; she has relatively less contact with other members of her ethnic group than Mrs. Limpari. As we have already seen, she has relatively few friends beyond the extended family, although she does make frequent trips to Tower Point for groceries.

It should be noted that Mrs. Pescatore uses her strong ethnic identification in quite a different manner from Mrs. Limpari. A strong ethnic identification increases Mrs. Limpari's participation in the numerous Tower Point civic and religious organizations of which she is a part. It was not uncommon during our visits with Mrs. Limpari for her to lean her head from her apartment and call out in animated Italian either to a passerby on the street or to a neighbor in the adjoining apartment building. One senses about Mrs. Limpari's life an intense involvement in her community. Mrs. Pescatore uses her ethnic identification as a way of further isolating herself from the community. Other than her frequent conversations with Mrs. Murphy and her children, typically shouted up and down the back stairs, there are few contacts with neighbors. Indeed, Mrs. Pescatore hardly knows the family living on the third floor, beyond their name and the fact that they pay their rent on time. Mrs. Pescatore's life is spent largely behind the safety of her high picket fence. The fact that her English is less clear than that of Mrs. Limpari, also an immigrant, futher reflects her isolation from American society. While both grandmothers distinguish between the safe and familiar and the foreign and dangerous, a far greater part of Mrs. Pescatore's world is viewed as dangerous than is true for Mrs. Limpari, and Mrs. Pescatore's life is largely devoid of ties to persons other than family members.

Mrs. Murphy is ranked second of the four mothers in terms of her ethnic identity. While she cooks in the same way as her mother, Mrs. Murphy understands Italian less well and has less knowledge of Italian history and customs than is true for Mrs. McGorty. It is not that she has rebelled against her traditions, it is just that she follows them without thinking about them, "because that's the way it has always been." For Mrs. Murphy, as for her mother, ethnicity is used in the service of isolating the extended family from the outside world that, as is true for her mother, is of little interest.

Mrs. Giorgio has only moderate interest in her ethnic traditions. While she is pleased that her husband was so prominent in the Italian-American community she herself has little interest in continuing her husband's civic work. In part, Mrs. Giorgio's diffidence may stem from her higher standing in the community status structure. Both Mrs. Giorgio's own family and her husband's had considerably higher standing in the Italian community from which they emigrated than was true among other families in this study, and her world view is somewhat different from that of the other three grandmothers. Mrs. Czaja is intrigued with her southern Italian origins, but while she enjoys the expressive traditions of Italian culture and believes in following Italian holidays, she cannot understand Italian very well and speaks to her mother in English.

Mrs. Scardoni is the least involved of the four grandmothers in her ethnic heritage. Mrs. Scardoni's chaotic early life and lack of contact with others during a childhood marked by poverty did not permit her to become involved with the Italian-American community. Indeed, of the four grandmothers, Mrs. Scardoni is the only one who has always lived outside Tower Point. Only with her marriage to Mr. Scardoni, several years ago, was she in a position to become involved with her ethnic heritage. On the other hand, she does cook almost entirely Italian foods and both understands and speaks Italian.

Since Mrs. Scardoni's identification with colonial New England culture was largely defensive, designed to provide a personal identity in a world viewed as fragmented both in time and space, her adaptation has been somewhat impaired. However, as she has grown older, Mrs. Scardoni has been able to achieve greater perspective on her traumatic earlier life and has begun to accept and rely on her own genuine ethnic heritage as a new basis for her identity. We can speculate that Mrs. Scardoni's second marriage, to a man with enduring ties to the Tower Point Italian-American community, represents a positive step in this consolidation of her own identity. For the first time in her life Mrs. Scardoni is able to integrate her own past experiences into her present life. For this reason, it is likely that Mrs. Scardoni's Italian American ethnic identity will become increasingly salient in the next few years and that, accompanying this shift, Mrs. Scardoni will show a more successful adaptation.

Mrs. Russo is somewhat more identified with her ethnic heritage than is her mother, largely as a result of her husband's ethnic identity. It is interesting that both mother and daughter in this family became involved with their cultural tradition through marriage. Mr. Russo's family is quite closely identified with the Tower Point community that also serves to cement the bonds between Mr. Russo and Mr. Scardoni who is a friend of the Russo family. In a way parallel to the situation with the Pescatore-Murphy family, the mother-daughter tie is so intense and important that there is little interest on the part of either mother or daughter in aspects of life beyond their close relationship.

Religion plays a much less important role than ethnic traditions in shaping the world view of these families. We have seen that Catholicism in southern Italy was heavily influenced by folk religion and that suspicion of outsiders was combined with a belief in magic and sorcery in sharply limiting the influence of dogma on the ordinary life of south Italian residents. Coming to the United States, these immigrants found the church still to be alien. Relations with the clergy had never been very cordial in Italy, and, unless a priest was willing to accept aspects of folk religion, he had little influence on lives of the villagers. Given this centuries-old hostility to the clergy, few Italian priests had any desire to immigrate to the New World.

This disinterest in the immigration of the southern Italian church was in marked contrast with that of Irish-Americans who arrived in the New World together with their priests. By the time of the Italian immigration, the Catholic church in America was clearly an Irish church. Italian immigrants found themselves excluded from Catholicism in America and also found good reason to distrust the American clergy to even a greater extent than the clergy in southern Italy. The American church did not understand the Italian immigrants' fascination with magic, their concern with the Madonna and the saints, and their insistence on the perpetuation of local religious customs in the New World. For these reasons, Catholicism has had little impact on the Italian-American, as can be seen quite clearly from the present study.

The fact that divorce has occurred in two of the four families means that attitudes toward religion in these families may be somewhat discrepant from that of Italian-American families in general. Both Mrs. McGorty and Mrs. Scardoni have been excommunicated (although Mrs. McGorty has been permitted to retain some ties to the church). Mrs. Limpari, Mrs. Pescatore, and Mrs. Giorgio regularly attend Mass and express devotion to the church. While they believe that their children should marry Catholics, they show a relaxed attitude which is quite different from that of their Irish Catholic sons-in-law. Mr. Murphy avoids church or attends a Greek Orthodox service, while Mr. Czaja (only part Irish) does not attend church at all. Mr. Russo drives his wife to Mass, but, in the manner described by A. Parsons (1969b), believes that church is the woman's world and feels more comfortable having coffee with "the boys" while his wife attends Mass. Mrs. Murphy attends church regulary with her mother and other members of her mother's family, but more from a sense of obligation to her mother than to the church.

Of the three grandmothers who do attend church, Mrs. Limpari is clearly the most involved, but then her experience with the church in America is somewhat unusual. Prior to the Italian immigration to the United States, Portuguese fishermen had been living along the New England coast where the climate had suited them and where they could continue their vocation as fisherman. Much less rigid in their approach to Catholicism than the Irish, the parish church in Tower Point had been adandoned by the Irish who started a new church of their own. The Italians were welcomed in the parish and were soon able to install an Italian American priest and to continue with their southern Italian folk religion that the small Portuguese community found acceptable.

Mrs. Limpari was a part of the immigrant group that had originally "settled" this Tower Point parish, and she feels it to be important to continue the religious customs she and her fellow immigrants had helped to establish. In addition, because of her involvement in Tower Point civic affairs, she provides an important link between the community and the church and recognizes the importance of remaining active in church affairs.

While Mrs. Giorgio and Mrs. Pescatore attend Mass, they do so from a sense both of devotion and of tradition. Mrs. Pescatore is the most involved of the three churchgoing grandmothers in the dogma of the church, and she was the only one of the three grandmothers who prominently displayed religious art in her house. However, as we have noted, this devotion has not been transmitted to her daughter. Indeed, with the exception of Mrs. Russo, mothers in these families have maintained little interest in Catholicism, and, as we have noted, Mrs. Russo's interest derives primarily from her husband's family rather than from her own. Based on our intensive study of these four families, it would appear that religion will come to play an even less important role in the lives of Italian-Americans. While religious endogamy is maintained, it is important primarily because it is a part of the known and safe world rather than because of dogma itself.

The grandmothers in the present study strongly believed that their daughters should marry men from Catholic families. At the same time, it is also important that the men be from the right social class. In this sense, class emerges as a determinant of mate selection to almost the same extent as religious affiliation. For example, Mrs. Limpari's principal objection to Mr. McGorty was that his educational background was inferior to that of her daughter. In keeping with her image of her family's standing in the community, Mrs. Giorgio considers it appropriate that Mr. Czaja be a college graduate and a professional. The one consolation Mrs. Pescatore takes from her daughter's marriage to Mr. Murphy is that he is intelligent, but she also worries that "he may be too smart and too much different from the rest of us in his views about the world." Consistent with the literature, when the daughters married outside their own ethnic group, all three married men partially or totally Irish.

Turning from institutional participation to major value orientations, we find that families who are predominantly working class correspond more exactly than middle–class families to the value orientations described for Italian-Americans. At the same time, this discussion of the value orientations of the four families must be somewhat tentative, since preferred solutions have to be inferred from the interview and test data, and the rank order of alternative solutions is difficult to determine.

The least satisfactory results are obtained when considering the orientation to nature. Since all families in this study are urban, there was relatively little consideration of problems related to the control of nature. We do know that the construction project planned by Mrs. McGorty and her mother involves numerous technical problems and that neither generation views these problems as serious obstacles in completing the project. Indeed, Mrs. McGorty takes pride in her work with the architect to overcome this problem, showing her belief in the capacity to master nature. Dr. Giorgio also showed his thinking about the capacity to master nature in his belief in the healing power of modern medicine. Dr. Giorgio's wife also subscribes to this belief.

Mrs. Pescatore reveals some belief in subjugation to nature, when, in referring to her garden, she explained her powerlessness against the forest that bounded her property. As much as she would try to have a lawn and garden, she could not stop the forest from encroaching and reclaiming the land. Both Mr. Scardoni and Mr. Russo express feelings of resignation to the power of nature, for, given the seasonal aspects of their work, their earning power is largely determined by nature; when the weather is bad, they suffer the loss of their paycheck.

Across the four families, time orientation reflects both the impact of immigration to America on the southern Italian preference for the present over the past and the future, as well as the impact of their present social position in American society. Two of the grandmothers show a preference for the present over the future and the past that is quite consistent with southern Italian and Italian-American ideals. Mrs. Pescatore expresses this belief most dramatically when she says, in talking about her problems with her son-in-law, Mr. Murphy, that "there's no use worrying about the future. I try to take each day as it comes." Mrs. Giorgio also lives very much in the present and does not like to make plans more than a day in advance; one of the problems she has in visiting her friends is that she is totally unwilling to commit herself ahead of time to these arrangements. Mrs. Giorgio's need to preserve her autonomy fits well with her value on the importance of living in the present. In addition, she both needs and enjoys the daily schedule she has arranged for herself and that remains constant over weeks and months. She becomes quite upset when her plans must be changed.

Once again, with Mrs. Scardoni we see how personality interacts with culture in supporting individual adaptation. Mrs. Scardoni is the one grandmother who shows a clear preference for the past over both present and future. We believe that this emphasis on the past represents an attempt to provide a sense of order and continuity in a life that is otherwise so disjointed and fragmented.

Mrs. Limpari shows a preference for the future over both the present and the past, a choice particularly ironic, since, on the basis of the fact that she has the strongest overall ethnic indentification with Italian American culture of the four grandmothers, it would be expected that she would show the classic Italian and Italian-American preference for the present over both past and future. While somewhat uncomfortable about the fact that she will be living so close to her daughter, Mrs. Limpari looks forward to the completion of the condominium project. Indeed Mrs. Limpari's purchase of the property on which the building is being constructed was predicated on the belief many years ago, that land would rise in value and that she could look forward in the future to substantial profit. Mrs. Limpari has always saved a part of her own and her husband's earnings and has recently remodeled her own apartment. Mrs. McGorty notes that even in the old days her parents' apartment was the most modern in the building and that neighbors were surprised at the extent to which Mrs. Limpari carefully planned for future changes to the apartment. She describes her mother as a women of "vision" who was always forward-thinking, ahead of the times.

With the exception of Mrs. Russo, all the daughters express a preference for the future over both the present and the past. Mrs. Russo prefers the present over the past and the future in the manner that would be expected both among Italian-Americans and blue-collar families more generally in American society. Mrs. McGorty is the most clearly future oriented, consistent with her many projects, as well as with her concern for the quality of her children's education as preparation for future success in college and, ultimately, a career in business or the professions. As is true of these other middle-class women, Mrs. Czaja also prefers the future over both the present and the past. She is particularly concerned with her husband's artistic career and looks forward to the possibility that his work will obtain national recognition. She maintains that her present living arrangements with her mother are only temporary and talks of moving to a neighboring state where her husband has been offered a job.

Considering the third of these value orientations, that of orientation to activity, it is apparent that there is considerable variation both within and across generations. While Mrs. Scardoni prefers the being solution over being-in-becoming or doing, both Mrs. Limpari and Mrs. Giorgio show a preference for doing over being over being-in-becoming. Mrs. Limpari's interest in her construction project is but one sign of her commitment to a doing orientation. Mrs. Limpari was much interested in her daughter's education and eventual success in the legal profession, which, as we have already suggested, represented a vicarious resolution of her feelings regarding her own passivity as a woman. It is important for Mrs. Limpari to have numerous projects, and this concern with doing and activity has been communicated to Mrs. McGorty who also clearly values doing over being-in-becoming over being.

Mrs. Giorgio reveals the same preference for activity shown by Mrs. Limpari, although her volunteer services to the hospital, where her deceased husband was on the staff, and her round of shopping has a much more mechanical and passive quality. Mrs. Giorgio is particularly concerned with her son's career as a physician and with his ability to graduate from medical school. Her son's failure to succeed in the prestigious medical school attended by her husband was a real disappointment to Mrs. Giorgio.

While the views expressed by Mrs. Limpari and Mrs. Giorgio are consistent with a preference for doing over being and being-in-becoming, Mrs. Pescatore prefers the being-in-becoming over the being and doing orientations toward activity. In part, this stems from the fact that her grandchildren are among the oldest of the grandchildren in these four families. Mrs. Pescatore has a greater time perspective in which to compare her grandchildren's development. However, a more important factor determining this unusual preference for being-in-becoming arises from the problems she has in achieving appropriate emotional distance from her daughter and her daughter's family; not only is she preoccupied with her grandchildren's development, but also she has an opportunity to maintain a constant vigil. She spends a far greater number of hours each day with her grandchildren than is true for the other three grandmothers in the study and invests a greater degree of concern in childcare. Indeed, she is the only grandmother in the study to express concern with her grandchildren's "emotional" development and the only grandmother to describe how her grandchildren had changed over time.

Three of the four mothers stress doing as a preferred solution over being or being-in-becoming in resolving the problem of orientation to activity. Not only does this solution differ from that of their own mothers, but also variation within the mother generation can be understood largely in terms of social status differences, a finding which parallels that reported for orientation to time. The one working class mother, Mrs. Russo, believes in a being orientation and is little concerned about what her daughter might achieve in the world.

On the other hand, all three middle–class mothers are much concerned about their children's achievements. Mrs. McGorty demonstrates the greatest concern with this value orientation, and Mrs. McGorty's preference for the doing solution is seen in terms of the effort she expends and the extent of the sacrifices she makes so that her children will have the best preparation for future success. Mrs. Murphy places similar emphasis on achievement, although she expresses somewhat more conflict about learning and aspiration for the future. She demands achievement from her children at school, while providing little in the way of a home atmosphere in which achievement can be realized. Mrs. Czaja is also concerned with achievement, but doing is a more clearly preferred alternative for her than for the other two middle class women. Because of her own and her husband's interests in art, she is more concerned with the intrinsic satisfaction to be gained from artistic achievement. The close tie between doing and being is explained less by Mrs. Czaja's ethnic background than by her involvement in the world of art. Mrs. Czaja's father was very much involved in achievement and hoped that his son would show the same concern and become a famous physician. Much conflict was generated within the family when Mrs. Czaja's brother did not do well enough in college to be admitted to an American medical school.

Of the four value orientations, the one that most clearly reflects the effect of ethnicity rather than simply social status is the relational orientation. We have suggested that, as a result of the particular pattern of immigration, Italian-Americans developed a preference for extended or collateral family ties rather than lineal or individualistic relations. Authority was less central an issue in family relations than the extent to which families were of help to each other. The degree of reciprocity and closeness is the single most salient characteristic of Italian American families in this study. All members of both the grandmother and mother generations express a strong belief in the importance of extended family ties and of mutual aid and assistance.

While, as we have suggested throughout this book, collateral ties are of greater importance in relations between family members in American society than has often been recognized, they are particularly accentuated within members of these Italian-American families. This degree of emphasis on collateral relations and its importance for family members is shown by the fact that in the three families in which daughters married men who were not from Italian-American backgrounds, the major motive for each of the men marrying into the family was to experience the greater closeness and involvement demonstrated in these families. All three men had come from families organized either on lineal (authority of elders) or individualistic lines, with little mutual sharing and participation. These three men found satisfaction of their need for participation within the Italian-American extended family.

Of the three men marrying into these Italian-American families, Mr. Murphy feels most ambivalent about his ties to his in-laws and his own family, a problem that stems from his conflict with his mother-in-law regarding his life-style. One of the results of living in families organized according to a collateral principle is that there is little value on privacy and little opportunity for deviance. The family culture emphasizes the extent to which the business of one family member is the business of all. Secrets are difficult to keep, and it is hard to maintain a life-style which differs in significant ways from that of other family members. As in cooperative cultures, where sharing and mutual cooperation are the rule (Mead, 1935), the demand for conformity is much greater than in less cooperative cultures, and it is this demand for conformity that has been so problematic for Mr. Murphy in his relationship with other members of his wife's family.

CONCLUSION

Neither the individual personality of family members nor the social organization of the family as a unit can be understood apart from such cultural factors as ethnic origins. In a study in which all the members of the grandparental generation are first- or second-generation Italian Americans, the role of ethnicity becomes particularly important. Old World traditions are remembered with particular intensity, and patterns of behavior of both daughters and grandchildren are evaluated both in terms of the culture in which the grandparents were brought up and the subsequent modification of Old World culture as a result of immigration to the United States.

While the amoral familism of southern Italy has been replaced in the United States by close ties which characterize relations between members of the extended family, the pervasive suspicion that characterized relations between family members has been displaced into the world beyond the family and the immediate neighborhood comprised of immigrants from the same Italian agrotown. All family members, of both the grandparental and parental generation, are suspicious of outsiders. Mrs. Limpari seldom ventures beyond Tower Point; Mr. Limpari was extremely upset with the idea that his daughter would attend high school and college outside the known boundaries of the family's tightly knit community. Mrs. McGorty is suspicious of her neighbors, feeling that they do not share her values or understand her way of life. Mrs. Pescatore and Mrs. Murphy share this suspicion of the outside world and seldom venture far from home, where their backyard is sealed off from the rest of the world by a high fence.

Unlike Mrs. McGorty who has made plans to return to a neighborhood she believes to be safer and more familiar, Mrs. Pescatore and Mrs. Murphy have retreated behind the anonymity of their fence. Mrs. Scardoni and Mrs. Russo also show this fear and suspicion of the world beyond family and neighborhood, with neither grandmother nor mother venturing very far from home. Mrs. Scardoni leads a very isolated life, unable to move beyond the confines of her house. Mrs. Russo feels safe only going as far as the nearby shopping center, a sentiment she shares with Mrs. Murphy. The effect of amoral familism transplanted to the United States is a marked constriction on the use of space and a strengthening of the difference between "we" and "they" to such an extent that there is little contact between members of these tightly knit Italian American families and the outside world. Only Mrs. Giorgio and Mrs. Czaja have been able to transcend the bounds of their community. Mrs. Czaja was the only daughter to attend college away from home. Both mother nor daughter use mass transportation and take advantage of the many cultural opportunities available to them in the Bethany area.

Within these four families, Italian American ethnic patterns are being maintained and strengthened across the generations. There is little of the second-generation rebellion against long-standing Old World traditions described in the literature. Ethnic traditions are important because they reinforce family solidarity and maintain the primacy of the family over other institutions. These ethnic traditions that have influenced the development of the modified extended family in American society have influenced the development of family ties based on closeness, cooperation, and the need for affectional interdependence. At the same time, bonds based on interdependency may lead to conflict, as well as cohesion, particularly among the grandmothers in this study. Among these middle-aged women, the Italian-American ethnic tradition, with its emphasis on the importance of extended family ties, conflicts with an age-related phenomenon present in American society emphasizing the importance of increased concern with self (Neugarten, 1973).

CHAPTER 9

In Review: Socialization, Psychodynamics, and Intergenerational Relations

This discussion of the lives of women in four multigeneration urban families has illustrated the importance of the modified extended family in contemporary industrialized society. These women continue to have frequent contact across generations as a part of a complex set of interdependent relationships that characterize relations between parents and offspring, not just in childhood but across the life cycle. This relationship fosters forward socialization or the transmission of values and particular skills from the older to the younger generation and reverse socialization or influence exerted by the younger on the older generation. The relationship between women of two and three generations preserves and strengthens the emotional ties between them formed early in the life of the younger generation. At the same time such emotional ties become the means by which these generations of women may continue to remain involved in a relationship marked by incomplete psychological differentiation. This continuing relationship has important consequences for the adult psychological development of both mother and daughter, as well as for continuing socialization across these generations that is so essential in providing for orderly continuity in social life.

The concept of generation has three quite different definitions in the social science literature (Troll, 1970; Bengtson and Black, 1973; Troll and Bengtson, 1979). The first refers solely to separate age groups within the family. For example, the generation of middle-aged persons is simply the second oldest of the three generations in a family that includes grandparents and young offspring. It is a description of a rank within a lineage. Within each society the age interval between family generations is a function of fertility rates, age at marriage, and other demographic factors. While a period of about 25 years between generations is characteristic of American families, in other societies, where marriage takes place at an earlier age, the interval between generations is shorter, and a larger number of generations is possible within the typical family. Even in the United States, it is not uncommon to find four-generation family units, with persons in their sixties taking care of their older parents (Hagestad, 1979; Troll, Miller, and Atchley, 1979).

A second definition of generation refers to the developmental stage within the family life cycle. In the present study, we have been concerned with adult daughters, their older mothers, and their young children. Implicit in this discussion is
316

the significance for members of each generation of their own developmental place within the life cycle. Changes in personality, as well as in the social roles characteristic of particular developmental periods, mean that mothers of young children understand themselves and their social surround in quite different ways from their own mothers. Indeed, each generation has a different understanding of the role of mother.

A third definition of generation refers to a particular historically defined cohort (Mannheim, 1952; Cain, 1964, 1967; Riley, Johnson, and Foner, 1972; Neugarten and Hagestad, 1976). A group of persons who experience a major social or economic event such as the Great Depression at roughly the same age are uniquely affected by that event (Elder, 1974, 1978). The subsequent reactions of those within this group to both the social surround and their own inner experiences will be different from groups who precede or follow. Elder's (1974) study of adults who were children during the Great Depression shows that these persons have become particularly responsible adults, preoccupied with the issues of economic and social stability. The depression shaped their attitudes toward family life and their concerns with providing for self and others in ways that are different from other age cohorts. This distinct outlook inevitably shapes the manner these persons respond to a variety of developmental issues or tasks associated with the passage through adulthood.

These three different definitions of generation must be considered in our discussion of the four families described in this study. It is often difficult to determine whether differences reported for the four families, across the generations, are simply due to age stratum, developmental differences, cohort differences, or some complex interaction between these factors in determining responses across adulthood to the issue of childcare. It is important to consider these three quite different meanings of the concept of generation in reviewing each of the three major areas of findings from the present study: (1) nature and extent of contact across generations, (2) impact of intergenerational relations on the psychological development of mothers and grandmothers, and (3) the transmission of family themes across generations. In this concluding chapter, each of these three areas of findings are discussed in greater detail in terms of the three contrasting perspectives on the concept of generation.

LIVING ARRANGEMENTS AND PATTERNS OF CONTACT WITHIN FAMILIES

A review of previous studies of patterns of contact between members of families across generations has pointed to the discrepancy between earlier theories of family life in the city which maintained that urban life disrupted continuing family ties and to the reality of frequent contact noted in both survey research and detailed ethnographic studies. While fewer than 10% of American households contain members of all three generations, it is characteristic of older persons to have at least one adult son or daughter living within an hour's drive

(Shanas, 1968, 1979; Adams, 1968; Rosenberg, 1970). Consistent with the proximity of living arrangements, both cross-national studies (Shanas et al., 1968; Shanas, 1973) and survey studies of American families (Harris and Associates, 1975; Hill 1970) report contact between adults and their parents at least weekly in greater than three-fourths of all families surveyed. However, as Troll, Miller, and Atchley (1979) observe in summarizing the literature, the visiting lineage within the family is nearly always that of the women. As noted in Chapter 1 of this book, there is clearly an asymmetry in American families, with a tilt to matrilocality.

This use of the term ''generation'' relies principally on rank or age stratum. Associated with old age, at least within American society, are such roles as grandparent, retiree, and widow. From a developmental perspective, the implications of patterns of visiting and exchange of resources has a quite different impact on late middle-aged and older grandmothers from that generally understood regarding the role of grandparent in American society. It should also be noted that patterns of contact are considered here in terms of particular generational cohorts. In each of the four grandparental families, there is at least one spouse who was born in Italy and immigrated to the United States. In each of the four other families, the grandparent was born in an ethnically stratified community of immigrant parents.

The understanding each of these grandparents has of family life, and of patterns of contact across generations, is shaped by their experiences as part of a cohort of older persons within a particular ethnic group, who, at about the same age, were required to accommodate to American society. For example, the men in these families make greater distinction between appropriate roles for men and for women than is characteristic of American society. This leads to even greater emphasis during the parental years on the enactment of appropriate sex roles for men and for women as discussed in Chapter 1, than is found more generally regarding the parental imperative (Gutmann, 1975) and may further intensify the mother-daughter bond among the ethnic families discussed in the present study.

Within these four families, the pattern of contact between Mrs. McGorty and Mrs. Limpari (Chapter 3) is most characteristic of intergenerational relations as reported in other studies of American families. As described earlier, weekly visits to Tower Point are supplemented by daily telephone calls, with Mrs. McGorty typically initiating contact. However, the present detailed study of this mother-grandmother relationship has considered not only patterns of contact, but also the psychological significance for each generation of such contact, an issue not generally discussed in the literature on intergenerational relations. For example, while Mrs. McGorty looks forward with eager anticipation to telephone calls and visits, her mother often feels this contact to be burdensome. Mrs. Limpari complains that her daughter calls her at inconvenient times and chooses Saturdays for visits when Mrs. Limpari herself would like to be visiting her friends. Although Mrs. Limpari places much of the responsibility for the complaints on her son, explaining that since he still lives at home such visits interfere with his privacy, it is clear that Mrs. Limpari does not look forward to having to prepare Saturday dinners for Mrs. McGorty and her family.

Mrs. Russo, who also lives apart from her mother and at about the same distance as that between Mrs. McGorty and Mrs. Limpari, also calls her mother first each day. However, as is true of nearly all aspects of the relationship between Mrs. Russo and Mrs. Scardoni in Chapter 4, the nature of the contact between the generations and also how the contact is initiated are much more complex than for Mrs. McGorty and Mrs. Limpari. Mrs. Russo has expended considerable effort in arranging for her mother to be the one to call her, most recently developing a signal that she uses in the morning for her mother to call her back. Since both Mrs. Russo and her brother live in adjoining households at some distance from their mother, Mrs. Russo does "kinkeeping" both for her own household and also for Mr. Butoni. Mr. Butoni's wife, in turn, is busy with the kin-keeping for her own lineage. Carrying out this kin-keeping for two households gives Mrs. Russo added legitimacy in the frequency with which she contacts her mother. This exchange of information by telephone is supplemented by Mrs. Russo's frequent telephoned requests for assistance. In addition to this contact by telephone, the mother and daughter visit in person several times each week. Mrs. Russo and her young daughter visit her mother in Winterfield at least weekly, while Mrs. Scardoni visits with both her daughter and her son several times a week.

The two families in the present study who have shared a common household with the wife's mother are somewhat atypical in terms of permanent living arrangements in American families. Indeed, in the case of the Cazjas and Mrs. Giorgio (Chapter 5), this is viewed as a temporary arrangement. However, it is not uncommon for the two generations to live together temporarily for at least some time after the marriage of the second generation. Within these families in which the two generations of adults share a common residence, contact between them is not without tension. For example, Mrs. Giorgio continues to harbor resentment regarding the necessity of sharing a household with her daughter and her daughter's family.

Only in the case of the families of Mrs. Pescatore and Mrs. Murphy (Chapter 6) is there evidence of a long-term arrangement, with the two families living in separate households within the same dwelling. This family is most like the extended family characteristic of self-contained societies described in the anthropological literature, with specific tasks delegated to individual family members, including shared responsibility for the care of Mrs. Pescatore's mother. However, such complete interdependence between the generations in this family is at the cost of greater involvement with the urban community. Life is organized largely behind the picket fence that separates family from community.

Contact between generations facilitates exchange of help and assistance across generations in addition to satisfaction of affectional needs. Most often, mothers look to their own mothers for assistance in babysitting, but other functions are also served by frequent contact, including assistance in helping the mother learn to prepare traditional ethnic foods, in the case of Mrs. Limpari and Mrs.

McGorty, assistance in shopping, in the case of the Pescatore and Giorgio families. Once again, it is clear how urban life facilitates both continuing contact across the generations within the family and exchange of resources, including finding employment for family members. This is most clearly seen in the case of the Scardonis and Russos, where Mr. Scardoni was able to find his son-in-law a job in the same firm in which he was employed.

Consistent with findings from previous research, most of the exchange of resources is in the direction from the older to the younger generation. Sussman's earlier research (1953, 1954, 1965) had suggested that this pattern appeared to shift when the older generation reached late middle age and offspring began to provide more for their older parents than was provided by their parents for them. On the other hand, findings from the study reported by Hill (1970), and the national survey study of L. Harris and associates (1975) suggest that exchange of resources is mutual, and even that there is some tilt toward continued greater giving than receiving, even among families in which the parental generation was aged 80 and greater. What these previous studies do not document is the personal cost involved in such exchange of resources: Mrs. Limpari and Mrs. Giorgio both express considerable resentment about the demand that their daughters make on their own time. Mrs. Giorgio believes that a part of the problem arises from her daughter's failure to recognize that she has an active and satisfying life that is disrupted when she has to help her daughter. Mrs. Scardoni and Mrs. Pescatore are more willing to provide help, but also complain at times of the burdens involved in caring for their daughters and their daughters' families.

The study of these four multigeneration families provides evidence to support previous findings from survey studies regarding the high rate of contact across generations in contemporary American families, as well as of the high rate of exchange of assistance and support. Such contact and exchange seem to be facilitated by the urban situation; life in the city makes it easier for families to remain in geographic proximity and for family members to visit with each other. Particularly within the Italian-American ethnic group, the social structure that was partially determined by the pattern of chain migration from an urban environment in southern Italy to one in the United States, family members take advantage of the bonds forged by the ethnic community to continue family traditions, to obtain work for each other, and to provide a broad range of services that have a rather large cash equivalent.

It is not certain whether this pattern of resource exchange is unique to the present generation of urban families, particularly those in working-class ethnic communities or is more generally characteristic of intergenerational relations in contemporary society. Clearly, among Italian-Americans, members of an ethnic group familiar with life in an urban setting in the Old World, adaptation to life in the city after immigration has not been as difficult as within those ethnic groups where immigrants had previously lived apart from each other on separate farms. Settling into urban neighborhoods in which the traditions of particular villages in southern Italy could be continued, these urban villagers (Gans, 1962) have developed dense social networks and complex forms of exchange of resources and assistance across generations. Over time, if these urban villages should dissolve, and family members begin to move farther apart from each other, it is possible that this pattern will not be maintained. On the other hand, there is evidence from a sufficiently large number of studies, carried out in sufficiently diverse areas of the country, with sufficiently diverse groups of multigeneration families, that the pattern of contact reported among the families in the present study is not limited to a particular cohort, but many reflect rank or age stratum in American families more generally.

THE PSYCHOLOGICAL IMPACT OF GENERATIONAL RELATIONS

As interesting as these findings are regarding patterns of contact across the generations in the modified extended family, such findings provide little understanding of the psychological response among members of either generation, not only regarding offers of assistance, but also acceptance of such help. Both the extent of contact between the generations and the exchange of support and services have significant psychological consequences among members of each generation. These consequences have to be understood in terms of reciprocal socialization across the life cycle, as well as in terms of the shifting meaning of this intergenerational contact for family members as they move from young adulthood to middle age and then to old age. These psychological consequences must be discussed separately for adult daughters and for their own late middle-aged mothers.

The Mother Generation

In describing the telephone contact between Mrs. Russo and Mrs. Scardoni, it was clear that much of the concern Mrs. Russo expressed regarding household routine and childcare, and much of the information she seeks from her mother, has another meaning for her as well: that of affectional dependence. Indeed, consistently, across all four families, it was clear that affectional and informational dependence were both present in the adult daughters' relationships with their older mothers. Mrs. McGorty enjoyed her weekly visits to Tower Point, particularly the care she received from her mother who cooked a large meal for the family. Exchange of recipes, discussion of their joint business venture, and review of family news all served as a "carrier" for the satisfaction of dependency needs and the preservation of a close relationship. Mrs. Russo's visits with her mother were even more complex; although her mother assisted her with her grocery shopping, Mrs. Russo's mother was also very critical of her diet and weight. However, Mrs. Russo also relied on her mother's implicit criticisms as a form of substitute for absent inner regulation, so that a variety of complex needs were satisfied. Similar patterns of simultaneous satisfaction of affectional and informational dependency needs may also be observed within those families where the generations shared a common household.

Each of the four mothers in this study appears to be involved in a dependent relationship with her own mother. This continuing dependence in adulthood is a function of at least three separate aspects of preadult and adult socialization, together with the nature of the mother's present role "portfolio." First, the present, dependent orientation observed among these mothers is the outcome of a complex normative socialization process in which women are taught a relational and dependent role from early childhood across the first half of life. Second, the increasing role complementarity of the mother and her own mother means that the two generations have increasingly similar interests and concerns. Under such circumstances, daughters look to their own mothers for information and assistance, for the mother's mother is an ideal role model. A lifelong dependent relationship means that the daughter is uniquely receptive to the mother's socialization into such adult roles as wife and mother.

Third, the nature of the role strain and overload created as a result of the assumption of the maternal role (Bernard, 1975; Grunebaum et al., 1975; G. Brown and Harris, 1978) often propels mothers of young children to seek help from others. As a result of a lifelong relationship, enhanced by role complementarity, the mother's own mother is the most often selected and most significant source of assistance. The unique aspects of the mother-daughter relationship in particular families affects the daughter's own perception of this advice and assistance in particular ways, but often with marked ambivalence that appears characteristic of the relationship between young adult women and their own middle-aged mothers in contemporary society.

Those two mothers showing a more successful adult adjustment (Mrs. McGorty and Mrs. Cazja) are more comfortable with this undifferentiated and interdependent tie than those two mothers (Mrs. Russo and Mrs. Murphy) showing a less successful adjustment. These two better-adjusted women appear to be less ambivalent about their relationships with their own mothers and more comfortable seeking to maintain a dependent tie. They appear better able to use what Mahler, Pine, and Bergman (1975) have termed "emotional refueling" or what Kohut (1971, 1977) has referred to as a "self-object." For example, Mrs. McGorty has a quite straightforward interest in returning to live in Tower Point and, as a result, obtaining increased physical proximity and emotional closeness with her mother. In a similar manner, Mrs. Cazja has enjoyed her stay with her mother and the opportunity provided as an adult for her to obtain some of the feelings of satisfaction from a close relationship with her mother that she believes had eluded her during childhood. It is interesting to note that each of these women maintaining "mature dependence"(Fairbairn, 1941, 1951), in which they feel relatively comfortable seeking to preserve an interdependent and undifferentiated relationship with their own mother, also showed scores on the MAS on the factor of appropriate closeness which are believed to reflect a more adaptive resolution of the issue of separation-individuation in caring for one's own children.

In contrast with Mrs. McGorty and Mrs. Czaja, neither Mrs. Murphy nor Mrs. Russo shows this degree of comfort in their relationships with their own mothers. In the case of these two women, each of whom was selected for the study on the basis of her markedly less adaptive scores regarding the MAS issue of separation-individuation, conflict between the generations is pervasive and takes its toll on both mother and adult daughter. Much of the conflict between Mrs. Pescatore and Mrs. Murphy concerns Mrs. Murphy's childcare practices that her mother believes are too lenient and inconsistent. Mrs. Pescatore is critical of just about every other aspect of Mrs. Murphy's life as well, including her marriage, her housekeeping, and even her figure. Certainly, the fact that Mrs. Pescatore and Mrs. Murphy share a common residence may further increase the conflict between them, but similar conflict can also be observed in the relationship between Mrs. Scardoni and Mrs. Russo, where the mother's criticisms of her daughter's housekeeping and childcare characterize many of their telephone conversations as well. Mrs. Russo continues to search for her mother's approval, but her mother can only respond critically. This conflict is particularly intense regarding Charlotte's eating and strikes a resonant chord for Mrs. Russo whose own concerns about nourishment and autonomously initiated activity are so central to her anorectic-like response as an adult.

This finding regarding the intensity of the need for comfort, and the maintenance of an undifferentiated relationship among daughters during the time that their children are young, is one of the most important to emerge from this study. Even within those families where the mother has fostered greater sense of separateness and autonomy in her daughter, as a result of preadult socialization, the daughter's search for emotional refueling and emotional security remains the predominant factor in her own life, overshadowing her relationship with her husband and her children (Kerr, 1958).

While the wives in these four families maintain generally satisfying relationships with their husbands, it is clear that intimacy between husbands and wives is of less importance than the satisfactions the wives seek from the continuing close ties with their own mothers. At the same time, these ties between the generations of the wives' families do not appear to strain the marriages, because the husbands in these families are also so much involved with their wives' families and support maintenance of close ties between their wives and their own mothers. These husbands had sought marriages that would provide such extended family support, just as their wives had sought husbands who would support their own continuing relationships with their mothers.

Three of the four husbands explicitly commented, that having grown up in a family where there were few such strong ties between family members, they had enjoyed participating in the day-to-day life within their wives families. This is seen most clearly with Mr. McGorty who had grown up in an Irish-American family in which there was little sense of closeness and reciprocity across generations. Mr. Czaja expressed similar feelings and clearly enjoyed the satisfaction provided by life in a larger and more closely knit family than that in which he had grown up. Mr. Russo had experienced a particularly chaotic and deprived childhood and spoke of how important his in-laws have been in providing a greater sense of stability in his life than he had achieved before marrying into this family. Mr. Murphy appreciates the stability provided by life in a modified extended household, even though he is much less a part of his wife's family than is true among the three other husbands. In part, this is because of his continuing close relationship with his own mother, unusual for the husbands in this study, and also because of his frequent trips away from home.

The comments of these husbands fit well with the observation made by J. Fischer and A. Fischer (1963) that it appears to be desirable in American families to live near the wife's parents. Husbands appear to enjoy continuing participation in the wife's family, which contributes to this matrilocal "tilt." Indeed, each of the husbands in this study appeared to marry not only a wife, but also the wife's family, and to find a source of support and assistance that may have been missing in his own parental family. This satisfaction is complementary to that which his wife desires; the husband's search for support and affection within his wife's family both encourages and supports his wife's own wish to continue the dependent tie with her own mother.

The Grandmother Generation

In spite of the fact that two of the four daughters (Mrs. McGorty and Mrs. Czaja) feel quite comfortable in their relatively undifferentiated and dependent position within the larger family unit, three of the four grandmothers—Mrs. Limpari, Mrs. Scardoni and Mrs. Giorgio—feel quite uncomfortable with their daughters' expression of this wish for continued care as an adult. Indeed, in the case of Mrs. McGorty, and also of Mrs. Czaja, if the mother's mother had been willing and able to accept the undifferentiated and dependent relationship the daughter has sought to maintain, there would have been very little conflict between the two generations. However, largely as a result of continuing psychological development in late middle age, even these two mothers feel some degree of discomfort regarding their relationships with their adult daughters. This discomfort is a result of earlier socialization as determined by the mothers' own personalities, their adult daughters' responses to past and present socialization efforts, and the very different stage of psychological development of the women in these two generations.

Having first socialized her daughter into a relationship in which dependency was the desirable and appropriate mode of getting along together, the late-middle-aged woman now becomes frightened by the intensity of her daughter's continuing demand for emotional refueling and denies the validity of her daughter's demands, seeking refuge in increased emotional distance. Beneath the norm of reciprocity and mutual obligation that is supposed to characterize intergenerational relations among adults in these modified extended families, we have found a complex and often painful relationship between young married women with their own children and their own mothers. Intense, developmentally determined conflicts between mother and grandmother lead the mother to feel resentment and disappointment and lead the grandmother to feel frustrated and annoyed, even within those families where there is no accompanying psychopathology apparent within either generation.

For example, Mrs. Limpari had communicated to Mrs. McGorty the importance of autonomy, in part as a way of overcomimg her fear of her passivity as a woman. As an adult, Mrs. McGorty uses the adaptive skills she learned through her education in the service of trying to return home and live with her own mother, a goal that disturbs her mother. Mrs. Limpari does not understand why her daughter is so insistent on returning from the suburbs to her family home in Tower Point, while Mrs. McGorty is confused at the lack of enthusiasm her mother shows in providing the emotional refueling she seeks. Mrs. Czaja wisely surmised that the only possible way of returning home to obtain emotional security was to come on a "temporary" basis. Since the move was not permanent, Mrs. Czaja's mother would not feel that her own need for autonomy would be compromised; therefore, her mother would more willingly tolerate her demand for maternal care.

In contrast with Mrs. Scardoni and Mrs. Pescatore, each of whom had fostered a symbiotic tie between daughter and self since early childhood, Mrs. Limpari and Mrs. Giorgio had fostered a sense of greater autonomy. In the case of Mrs. Limpari, this emphasis on autonomy stemmed from her struggle with her own mother, while, in the case of Mrs. Giorgio, this emphasis on autonomy stemmed from the mother's own difficulties in accepting the caretaking role. Particularly in the case of Mrs. Limpari and her daughter, and Mrs. Giorgio and her daughter, the outcome in terms of the mother-daughter relationship is somewhat paradoxical. On the one hand, each of these adult daughters clearly believes in fostering a sense of appropriate closeness with their own children, as shown by the scores on the relevant factor of the MAS. Each of these women is effective in her personal life, but each is also concerned with continued dependence on her mother to a greater extent than would be expected on the basis of the mother's own concerns and goals for her daughter.

This increased concern with the issue of dependency is in part a result of unresolved conflicts within the grandmother herself that were enacted anew in the course of rearing her daughter. In the case of Mrs. Limpari, this early emphasis on autonomy was a result of the conflict she had faced as the only daughter in an immigrant family in which distinctive aspects of southern Italian family organization were continued in the New World. In the case of Mrs. Giorgio, this emphasis on autonomy resulted from her own difficulties in achieving closeness and in accepting a nurturant and caretaking role. Because the issue of autonomy was stressed primarily as a result of the grandmother's own needs rather than as a result of her daughter's needs, this emphasis on autonomy has had a quite different outcome than either grandmother would have expected.

At the same time, it should be noted that even though Mrs. McGorty and Mrs. Czaja rely more on their own mothers than either of these grandmothers believes to be desirable, each of these women has a relatively good adult adjustment which is in striking contrast with that of Mrs. Russo and Mrs. Murphy, each of whom shows problems in maintaining a satisfactory adult adjustment. In contrast with Mrs. Limpari and Mrs. Giorgio, each of whom was, for quite different reasons, particularly concerned with the development of autonomy, both Mrs. Pescatore and Mrs. Scardoni were determined to extend the mother-daughter symbiosis. This determination played a part in the accentuation of normatively and situationally determined dependence of the adult daughter on her own mother that has resulted in particularly difficult intergenerational relations in these two modified extended families, characterized by feelings of personal distress on the part of both mother and grandmother.

Mrs. Pescatore and Mrs. Scardoni were themselves particularly suspicious about the world outside the family, the extension in America of amoral familism (Banfield, 1958), which characterizes the world view of southern Italians; each woman communicated this suspiciousness to her daughter. In each case, fledgling adolescent attempts at developing greater autonomy were compromised, and each of the daughters became enmeshed in a sustained and unsatisfying relationship with her own mother. Mrs. Scardoni appears to have communicated her own identity confusion to her daughter; in this family, the demand for merger replaced expectations of separateness, and the effect has been the same: neither mother nor daughter in either of these two families feels comfortable, together or apart, and much of this conflict appears to have been communicated to the third generation, transmitting this family conflict to yet another generation.

Developmental and normative factors, including the quality of continuing inter-dependent ties in adulthood, are of particular importance in understanding the origins of expectations among women in the mother generation that their own mothers will provide the support and assistance which they seek. Cultural, social, developmental, and psychodynamic factors are also important in understanding the responses of women in the grandmother generation to such responses for as-sistance among their young adult daughters.

At the cultural level, we find an orientation of these grandmothers toward fami-ly ties that is consistent with their ethnic background. We have suggested that the development of extended family ties among Italian-Americans has been a very recent phenomenon, largely due to immigration patterns based on chain migration from southern Italy to the United States. The collateral solution to the problem of relations with others now predominates over the individualistic solution more characteristic of southern Italian culture. Still, there is some concern regarding this solution to the problem of family ties. For example, in Mrs. Limpari's dis-cussion of her family, it is clear that she is not sure whether it is advisable to maintain continuing family contact. Mrs. Limpari feels that the problems her son is having in becoming an adult should not be of concern to her daughter who has married and now has her own family. Mrs. Limpari is somewhat suspicious of Mrs. McGorty's motives in being concerned about her brother's success in find-ing a job and in his relationship with his girl friend. This suspicion is not unlike that of southern Italian families who are certain that others wish to know about family problems in order to take advantage of such problems for their own mate-rial advancement (Banfield, 1958; Cronin, 1970). It is possible that first- and second-generation Italian-Americans feel a greater degree of conflict regarding such extended family ties than would be found among ethnic groups in America where the extended family had been a more viable form of social organization in the Old World. Finally, it is important to note that this experience of American society on the part of Italian immigrants and their immediate descendants was characteristic of this cohort of persons who left Europe during the first decade of the twentieth century as a part of the Great Migration that Handlin (1951, 1961) has so vividly described.

The second of these levels of analysis of the grandmother's response to her adult daughter concerns social context and focuses particularly on the conflict inherent in the role of grandparent. It should be noted that this is one role determined almost completely by the actions of others (Neugarten and Weinstein, 1964). Many persons in their forties who become grandparents complain that being assigned to this role makes them feel particularly old, since it is one typically perceived as being associated with old age. Second, as Rosow (1967) has so well noted, the rights and responsibilities of this role are largely determined by the younger generation. Most grandparents feel that they cannot arrange directly to visit with their grandchildren, but must first seek permission of the child's parents who, in turn, often attempt to limit grandparental access to the children. Either the parents feel that the grandparents will spoil the children, or, more likely, they fear that visiting may provide the grandparents an opportunity to criticize their childrearing practices.

Following Rosow's (1976) concept of grandparenthood as a tenuous role, Hagestad (1979) has suggested that there are few structurally given guidelines for how grandparents are to act in this newly created role. Further, Hagestad notes that, as the life span is ever further extended, and the fourth and fifth generations continue to be involved in family life, there are both grandparental and great-grandparental roles within the family and few clear normative prescriptions regarding appropriate modes of behavior of these older generations within the family. Hess and Waring (1978) have suggested that the grandparental role is anomic. Hagestad (1979) suggests that greater affluence in American society as a whole means that the definition of the grandparental role largely in economic terms is no longer viable, depriving grandparents of what was once a central aspect of their function for their adult offspring and their grandchildren.

Much of this role ambiguity is seen in visiting patterns across generations. There is repeated evidence from the present study that these problems inherent in the grandparental role are a concern to both generations, and also that the grandparental generation is, in fact, highly critical of the manner in which their offspring are being reared. All four grandmothers are united in the concern that their grandchildren are being reared in a more lenient manner than they reared their own children. Once again, this view of childrearing represents a complex generational phenomenon in which both developmental and cohort effects are involved.

The tension that exists regarding visiting is reflected in other studies such as that by Hill (1970) who report on a low frequency of visiting between grandparents and their grandchildren as contrasted with that between grandparents and their own adult offspring. In addition to this relative lack of contact, grandparents also feel relatively uninvolved with their grandchildren (Cumming and Henry, 1961). Neugarten and Weinstein (1964) and Wood and Robertson (1976) suggest that older grandparents are particularly distant from their grandchildren. It is interesting to note that at age 64 Mrs. Giorgio is the oldest of the four grandmothers and also the grandmother most distant from her grandchildren. Taken as a whole, the grandparental role does not appear to be one that is particularly a source of satisfaction for older persons (Rosow, 1976; Bernard, 1975; Lopata, 1973; Hess and Waring, 1978). It is amorphously defined, ascribed, and replete with tension involved in negotiating a complex relationship mediated by the parental generation (E. Johnson and Bursk, 1977). Older grandparents feel even more distant from their grandchildren than younger ones, but, overall, this is not a comfortable role for the older family member. This discomfort has to be understood in terms of the third level of explanation that has to do with the developmental place in the life course (A. Brown, 1974).

Previous research concerning the impact of aging on personality (Neugarten and Associates, 1964) has shown that, accompanying the transition to late middle age, both men and women show increased "interiority" that is reflected in "measurable increases in inward orientation, and measurable decreases in cathexses for outer-world events" (Neugarten, 1973, p. 321). Cohler and Lieberman (1979) have reviewed the empirical literature supporting such increased interiority with age and note that this interiority is expressed by men principally as increased passivity and need for oral satisfaction, while it is expressed by women principally as increased egocentrism and aggression. Among both men and women, as Cohler and Lieberman note, there is evidence of increased introversion, together with increased preoccupation with satisfaction of personal needs. A similar formulation by Gutmann (1975) has already been reviewed in Chapter 1. Gutmann argues that it is parenthood that organizes the life cycle; with the advent of the "empty nest," both men and women shift away from their earlier instrumental and expressive roles.

With their children now adults, older parents become freed from this stereotyped definition of the roles of men and women required by the parental imperative (Gutmann, 1975). Women are now freed from their roles as housewives and mothers and are able to devote greater time and energy to the task of satisfying their own needs. Consistent with this formulation, Cohler and Lieberman (in press) report that among older women within the Italian-American and Polish-American ethnic groups, where women are highly embedded in complex social networks, there is a significant negative relationship between nature and the extent of social commitments and self-reports, both of morale and of extent of perceived psychological and psychophysiological symptoms.

Continued demands by others for grandparental help and assistance, such as represented by the insistence of Mrs. McGorty that her mother care for her during her trips to Tower Point or that Mrs. Giorgio give up her free time and window-shopping for babysitting, are greeted with little enthusiasm by the grandparent, as done by these two grandmothers in the cases cited here. Unfortunately, the daughter's need for help and assistance is intensified as a result of her assumption of the parental role at just about the time when her own mother is increasingly preoccupied with her own aging. The older woman has even less tolerance than before for her daughter's need for inner sustainment. Once again this concern seemed to be expressed most clearly by Mrs. Giorgio, who was still grieving over her husband's death, and by Mrs. Limpari, whose husband had recently retired. These two women had been forced to confront their own aging in ways not yet true for Mrs. Pescatore and, especially, for Mrs. Scardoni, who sees herself in some ways as a young bride.

Findings from the present study, as well as tentative findings from Low's (1978) investigation, suggest that the nature of the mother-daughter tie shifts across adulthood. This developmental process has not been studied in detail. As Chodorow (1978) has suggested, little girls are taught to be mothers rather than women and are encouraged in the maintenance of an undifferentiated relationship. This early socialization leads to conflict between mother and daughter during adolescence and young adulthood, but seems to be resolved with increasing role complementarity as the young adult daughter becomes a wife and then a mother.

Much of the popular literature concerning conflict in the mother-daughter relationship refers to the period of early adulthood before the daughter becomes a mother herself. With the advent of motherhood, some of the daughter's earlier conflict about her relatively undifferentiated relationship with her mother is resolved, and the daughter comes to seek more comfortably that dependency in adulthood for which she had been prepared by earlier socialization. However, depending on the nature of her mother's own pre-adult and adult development, this bid for dependence, with which the daughter now feels comfortable, may increase the discomfort her mother feels. With the termination of direct responsibility for childcare, and the resolution of the parental imperative, there is a marked change in the mother's own definition of her role within the family toward increased interiority that creates conflict anew with her daughter. A new imbalance is created that must be resolved between mother and daughter for their relationship to continue across adulthood.

A critically important effect of this realization of increased self-assertiveness among late-middle-aged women may be the achievement of increased psychic autonomy from their own mothers, whether alive or not (Neugarten and Gutmann, 1958). Low (1978) reports that the intensity of the identification of the women in her study with their own mothers diminished greatly after age 40. Once again, it would appear that the timing of the mother's increased need for affectional dependence and for the preservation of an undifferentiated relationship takes place just as her own mother, freed from the parental imperative, begins the painful task, perhaps for the first time in her life, of achieving psychic autonomy from her own mother.

It is an irony that women are socialized from earliest childhood into a nondifferentiated relationship in which the boundary between self and mother remains unclear; with the increasing role complementarity possible in adulthood, and the chance to finally realize the fruit of this earlier socialization into dependency, these older mothers who had earlier socialized their daughters into this culturally approved relational mode now themselves move beyond this relational mode and thus frustrate the daughter's realization of the goal of true adult closeness.

A fourth level of explanation of the grandmother's response to her adult daughter, not unrelated to the other three, has to do with individual differences in personality. For example, both Mrs. Scardoni and, to a lesser extent, Mrs. Pescatore show a need to maintain a symbiosis across generations. The conflicts these grandmothers express, both in interview materials and also on the projective tests, are consistent with their lifelong conflicts regarding these issues. Mrs. Pescatore and Mrs. Murphy are locked into a relationship in which identity and self have merged across the two generations. While feeling frantic about the degree of intrusion in her life shown by her mother, Mrs. Murphy nevertheless continues to seek out her mother; she is unable either to live with her or apart from her. This conflict has taken its toll on Mrs. Murphy's capacity to adapt to the many problems in her life. A defensive and unhappy woman, Mrs. Murphy sees no alternative to her present distress. This conclusion applies with perhaps even greater emphasis to the relationship between Mrs. Scardoni and Mrs. Russo. Mrs. Russo is the most seriously disturbed of the four mothers in this study. She has been so much a part of her own mother that boundaries between mother and daughter have become merged and confused. Even though the two generations live apart, the extent to which her own mother lives within her as an archaic image (Kernberg, 1976) is so great that she might as well be physically present. Of course, the intensity of Mrs. Russo's mother's intrapsychic existence is maintained by frequent visits and telephone calls.

All four of these levels of explanation of the discomfort shown by the late middle-aged woman with the grandparental role and with the relationship with her adult daughter must be qualified in terms of the concept of generation as a cohort. It is clear that the grandmothers in the present study have not viewed the role of grandparent in a manner consistent with stereotyped views of grandparenthood. This response may be determined, at least in part, by unique historical experiences affecting so many women of this generation, including the immigration from the Old World to the New World, two world wars and a major period of economic upheaval during the Great Depression, and then the period of rapid technological development of the past three decades. It is clear that these women regard both the grandparental role and their role as the mother's mother with considerable ambivalence and that perceived conflict between their own developmentally determined needs and those of their daughters continues to inspire tension in the relationship between these two generations of adult women.

Findings from the present study have supported other discussions of the development of adult sex roles in contemporary society which suggest that women are usually socialized from earliest childhood into a dependent, relational mode in which there is incomplete differentiation between self and mother. In contrast with the socialization of men, who are expected to develop an instrumental and task-oriented modality as adults, the early socialization into a relational mode, combined with the demands on the adult woman as wife, mother, and kin-keeper, can foster a symbiotic relationship between a woman and her own mother characterized by ambivalence and personal discomfort across the first half of life. In addition, such conflict may be transmitted to the next generation, leading to the perpetuation of this conflict. There is some very tentative evidence to suggest that with the advent of middle age and the end of the parental imperative women are finally able to resolve this earlier dependent mode and to achieve a more differentiated perspective from their own mothers.

The success of this midlife transition in achieving increased differentiation, and the degree of personal comfort experienced by the mother of young children during the adult years, is influenced, at least to some degree, by the nature of her own mother's reactions to this issue. Where the mother's mother feels relatively comfortable with a relational mode, it need not evoke feelings of distress. In those cases where the mother's mother places undue emphasis on self-reliance in her daughter's preadult socialization, the daughter's adult dependence need is likely to become intensified. Where the mother attempts to foster a symbiosis across the generations, the daughter is likely to be impaired in her own personal adjustment and development of the capacity for intimacy and nurturance during adulthood.

Finally, it is important to note the distinction already made in the Introduction to the present study between interdependence and dependence. "Interdependence" refers to the fact of high rates of interaction across generations and accompanying exchanges of resources and services that take place across the generations in American society. This interdependence contributes to the maintenance of the multigeneration family as a "unity of interacting personalities" (Burgess, 1926). In contrast, "dependence" refers to a psychological characteristic in which, particularly among women during the first half of the life cycle, there is a psychological representation of one's own mother as a source of soothing and support. This psychological representation is the result of a particular mode of socialization from earliest childhood in which, while little boys are encouraged to become instrumental and independent, little girls are encouraged to maintain an undifferentiated tie with their mothers. Assumption of adult roles, particularly that of parent, accentuates such differences in relations with others resulting from earlier socialization (Gutmann, 1975) and leads to enhanced wishes among mothers of young children for the continuation of this earlier soothing and supportive tie to their own mothers.

CONCLUSION

Three distinct findings emerge from this study of the relationship between mothers of young children and their own late middle-aged mothers living in modified extended urban families:

1. From earliest childhood, the daughter in contemporary society is usually socialized into an undifferentiated and interdependent relationship with her own mother that continues into adulthood as the daughter becomes a mother herself. This relationship, which becomes the model for the daughter's relational mode as an adult, is further supported in adulthood by the increasing complementarity of

the role portfolio of the two generations, including the convergence of interests and sentiments of the older mother and her adult daughter.

2. As a result of the developmental changes in personality across adulthood, which, in part at least, may be cohort related, the request by the adult daughter for continued support and assistance and, in particular, for intensification of the mother-daughter relationship is responded to by the late middle-aged mother with great discomfort. Increasingly concerned with the issue of interiority (Neugarten, 1973), understood as the developmental task of achieving increased inner harmony as she reaches old age, this older mother is increasingly preoccupied with the psychological consequences of her own aging at just the time her daughter is expressing the desire for increased contact and additional assistance in performing the roles of housewife and mother. It is possible that, with the developmental shift from middle to old age, women finally are able to realize differentiation from their own mothers. Consistent with this change in the older woman's perception of her relationship with her own mother, she also finds it difficult to continue with her daughter that undifferentiated relationship which had characterized their relationship since the time the adult daughter was a toddler. Problems inherent in the role of grandparent further increase the sense of discomfort the mother's mother reports, particularly the demands on her time for baby-sitting when the children are young and for physical and emotional support of her daughter, as her daughter struggles to resolve the strain and overload she may experience in her roles as housewife, wife, daughter, and mother.

3. The issue of interdependence, often incorrectly termed dependence, emerges as a particularly salient theme within the multigeneration adult family. In contrast with the myth of the American nuclear family as isolated from extended kinship ties, not only is there continuing interaction among parents and their adult offspring, but also there is interdependence across the generations both at the level of social relations and at the level of psychological representations of salient relationships within the family. To date, family theory has had great difficulty dealing with this fact of this continuing closeness observed within the multigeneration family. Although "network therapy" has become accepted as a clinical modality (Speck and Rueveni, 1969), all too often both investigator and therapist still believe that the goal both of development across the life cycle and the therapeutic process should be in the direction of increased "independence" and autonomy of the nuclear family unit. Such emphasis on autonomy fails to consider the "invisible loyalties" (Boszormenyi-Nagy and Spark, 1973) that bind families together.

As a result of this failure to explicitly recognize the continuation of such interdependence across the life cycle, adults may come to believe that it is inappropriate to maintain such close family ties. Continued involvement in the multigeneration family provides an important source of ego strength, identity, and sense of personal congruence all of which foster adjustment. Interdependence across generations only becomes a source of conflict among family members when it is so intense that a true merger of self and others occurs (Stierlin, Levi, and Savard, 1971, 1973). While such distortions of interdependence, and accompanying psychopathology may occur, this psychopathology does not mean that interdependence among family members is inherently destructive or that it necessarily reflects family psychopathology.

Where psychopathology does occur, it is most likely to be found in the relationship between young adult women and their own middle-aged mothers. Because of the manner in which a woman is socialized into a continuing tie to her mother, the mother's failure to recognize and accept the importance of this tie and then to feel comfortable with the daughter's continuing use of this relationship as a psychological function across childhood, adolescence, and adulthood may lead the daughter to experience personal distress. However, even in such situations, the therapeutic task is one of correcting the imbalance in the relationship, helping each generation to accept the significance of this continuing tie between them rather than to foster an artificial autonomy that is inconsistent with the reality of intergenerational relations in contemporary urban society.

In conclusion, some comment should be made regarding the two dimensions used in selecting these four families for intensive study. This study was sparked by initial findings suggesting that for both mother and grandmother attitudes regarding appropriate closeness with one's own children were associated with residence—that is, whether the two women lived together or apart. While this initial finding did not permit any assumptions about causality it did suggest that among multigeneration families living together there may be factors associated with the continuing relationship between mother and grandmother which would lead the generations to decide to live together and that these factors might explain both choice of residence and attitudes toward childcare.

On the basis of this more detailed study of families living together and apart, it is clear that problems in resolving the issue of an appropriate degree of closeness between the mother of young children and her children is reflected in a similar conflict between the mother and her own mother. While all four mothers showed some wish to maintain a relatively undifferentiated relationship, in those two families in which the mother's attitudes reflected less adaptive attitudes regarding the issue of appropriate closeness, the conflict and discomfort in the relationship between the generations was particularly striking. Among those families in which attitudes toward the resolution of this issue were more adaptive, the mother felt a far greater degree of comfort in seeking to maintain an undifferentiated relationship with her own mother.

All four of the women in the mother generation expressed this wish to maintain close ties with their own mothers. What differentiated these four women, all mothers of young children, was the degree of conflict and discomfort engendered by this wish. Among the women in the grandmother generation, however, none appeared to be comfortable about accepting her daughter's wish for such a close relationship. Within those two families in which the grandmother and her adult daughter were involved in a struggle regarding this issue, the daughter's attitudes toward the issue of appropriate closeness with the child were less adaptive than in those two families in which there was less conflict in the relationship between the two women. The mother's attitudes toward childcare are the outcome of a complex socialization process that includes not only such social context factors as ethnicity and social status, but also the nature of the continuing relationship between the mother and her own mother. This adult relationship is determined by the personality and by present and previous life experiences of the women within each generation. These findings should be qualified in view of the fact that mothers participating in the study with their own mothers were found to be more dependent on their mothers than in a previous group (peers) who had not been recruited together with their mothers.

Residence appears to be less significant than continuing socialization in affecting the relationship between the generations. The decision to share a common residence appears to be determined principally by such situational factors as the nature of the husband's career and the health of the older generation. In those two families sharing a common residence, this arrangement was understood as temporary in one instance, while, in the other, it appeared to be relatively permanent. However, in neither case did residence appear to affect the quality of the relationship between the mother and her adult daughter in ways markedly different from the quality of the relationship that would be present if the women in the two generations had lived apart from each other. In fact, the most prevalent conflict was found within one multigeneration family in which the two generations lived apart at some distance from each other.

Family relations across the generations in our urban society involve more than frequent visits and exchange of resources and assistance. Such patterns of exchange take place among relatives who are persons with unique personalities and life histories. Personality, culture, and society must simultaneously be considered in understanding the nature of the complexities that exist between the generations in the family. This book has pointed to the relationship between adult women who are mothers of young children and their own mothers as the most central and complex relationship within the multigeneration family, and has pointed to the importance of the mother's continuing relationship with her own mother as a primary adult socialization determinant into such roles as that of wife and mother.

Our discussion of personality development and social relations among adult women in two generations, and the young children of the second-generation adult women, presents a genuine dilemma. On the one hand, findings based both on the intensive study of these four families and on those of other investigators support the conclusion that persons in contemporary families are much more a part of closely knit social groups than has traditionally been understood either by social scientists or by those, particularly mental health professionals, who read what social scientists write. Throughout life, people continue to remain attached to or dependent both on their own parents and on their offspring to a far greater extent than has been considered "ideal" by many psychological theorists. On the other hand, as this book shows, many adult women may not have become fully differentiated or psychologically separate from their own mothers. This statement sounds at first pejorative—a most unfortunate conclusion for two men to make—particularly since we have tried to avoid making any judgment regarding the significance for adjustment of this flexible differentiation that characterizes the mode of relationship between women and their relatives. Clearly, it is time to re-examine traditional views of the supposed ideal mode of adult interpersonal relationships and to recognize the degree of interdependence that is far more characteristic of adult relationships than the "autonomy" described by theorists such as Goldfarb (1965).

Part of the predicament may arise from those approaches to the study of personality development that tend to understand adult lives primarily in terms of childhood wishes and actions without considering the importance of personality development and change across the life cycle. As the contributions to the recent three-volume series on the psychoanalytic study of personality development show (Greenspan and Pollock, 1980), a life course perspective significantly changes our understanding of the relationship between perceived past, experienced present, and anticipated future in the study of adult lives. Another part of the predicament arises from the fact that the language of everyday life is much less constricted than the language of personality theory. Words like "love," "caring," "devotion," "loyalty," and "trust" abound in everyday characterizations of adult relationships. Caring for older parents or serving as a mentor for younger colleagues is a common experience of middle-aged adults, and devotion in these tasks is spoken of with respect (Levinson, 1977). We admire those who courageously deal with difficult family situations, using sound judgment and showing devoted concern. Such concern and caring are much more signs of maturity than the independent autonomy recommended as the ideal mode of adult relationships by some mental health professionals and students of adult personality.

Viewed from this commonsense perspective on adult lives, devotion and mutal caring are far more appropriate as a mode of relating to other family members, and close friends as well, than determined autonomy (Boszormenyi-Nagy and Spark, 1973). The findings from the present study suggest that the important dimension in the study of adult relationships within the family is not that of closeness versus distance from others, but the extent to which adults are able to adapt to situations and events calling for either a more autonomous or a more caring response. It is important to consider anew the very concepts of differentiation and separation used in studies of adult relationships. Just as women learn from earliest childhood to be particularly responsive to cues from others, they are also taught to respond in an active, intuitive, and empathic manner to the needs of others. The capacity to respond in this way represents a competence of particular importance for both family and social order (J. Grunebaum, 1980). While the dimension of field-independence versus field-dependence has been used to describe the cognitive style associated with such sensitivity to context, the term "environmentally sensitive" versus "environmentally oblivious" might provide a better way of describing this dimension and sounds quite different.

However, it is important to note that there is no way of avoiding discussion of the problem of values in social science investigations. The mothers, grandmothers, and daughters in this study act in ways they believe to be right and appropriate in the social context in which they lead their lives. In the same manner, social scientists value particular kinds of adult relationships. Given the degree of mobility that characterizes upper-middle-class life, and academic life in particular, some of the value placed on the importance of autonomous adult relationships may be more a reflection of a particular life-style than of the life-styles of most families in the community. Studies such as the present one focus attention on modes of relating to others, and on the psychological significance of such relationships, characteristic of family members in the largest number of families, where loyalty and interdependence are to be more valued than autonomy and independence.

Family theory, in particular, should attend more to the development of such loyalty among adults, should value relatedness more and individuality less. In this regard, we will have a greater sense of the chain of being that unites the generations going back to the unknown past and forward to the unanticipated future. We will hopefully have a greater sense of the things that hold us together rather than those which separate us from each other and from the rest of the delicate fabric of life on this planet. Perhaps women have been more attuned to these transcendent issues of continuity and context than have men.

CHAPTER 10

Four Years Later

Four years have intervened between the time of the first visit with the families portrayed in this study and the publication of this book. In the meantime, there have been rapid changes in post-Vietnam American society. Not only has inflation taken its toll, but also increasing numbers of women with young children have entered the labor force. It is believed that the women's movement has contributed to an increased interest among mothers in beginning or returning to work. To determine the impact of such social changes on these four families, as well as to evaluate the success of short-term predictions about relations across the generations, each family was seen again. Mothers and grandmothers were interviewed, and, in some instances, interviews were also arranged with husbands and with children in the third generation.

While noting that discrimination against women still exists in the workplace, Robey (1975) and Houston-Stein and Higgins-Trenk (1978) both maintain that working-class women are increasingly sensitive to this discrimination and are actively working to change conditions in the workplace, even foregoing the traditional roles of wives and mothers to achieve occupationally. However, an earlier study (Social Research, Inc., 1972) reported that the only change found in a national survey study was that, as a result of the women's movement, fewer working-class women were willing to spend as much time cooking and increasingly preferred to use convenience foods. Rubin (1976) reports that working-class women in her study were largely uninterested in the issues of women's rights and work discrimination and were much more concerned with their more traditional roles as wives, housewives, and mothers; Rubin's respondents appeared to view work as a necessity rather than as a pleasure.

While more than half of married women with children of school age are now in the labor force, at least on a part-time basis (Hoffman and Nye, 1974), it is not clear that the proportion of working-class women in the labor force has changed over time (Sawhill, 1974). Among such women, employment supplements family income and makes possible some discretionary purchases (Sweet, 1973) rather than simply being a means of realizing an intrinsic need for accomplishment. Even more important, such work may be a woman's only opportunity to have her own spending money. Such part-time employment provides a feeling of independence and security in today's world, just as it has in times past. Such work appears to be available for women; Rainwater (1979) notes that only 8% of married women with children who wanted to work at least part-time were unable to find work.

To determine the views of women in these four families regarding work and to determine the impact of larger social changes on these four families, each mother and grandmother was contacted individually regarding an additional interview. Each family agreed to take part in this phase of the study, and appointments were subsequently arranged. The four families are discussed in the same order as presented earlier in this book.

MRS. LIMPARI—MRS. MCGORTY

The past several years have not been kind to Mrs. Limpari. Mrs. Limpari's husband has been forced to take early retirement because of the discovery of a spreading malignancy; Mr. Limpari's chemotherapy has required constant care from Mrs. Limpari and some change in her own schedule. Partially as a result of the emotional strain she has felt, Mrs. Limpari has also developed a variety of physical symptoms; one physician has even suggested that she may have suffered a very mild stroke. Such problems have prompted Mrs. Limpari's family to rally around her. Although her youngest son has moved out of the apartment, taking an apartment in an adjoining community, her other son and his family, who live next door, have assumed increased responsibility for the care of the older couple. Mrs. McGorty now spends much of the weekend with her mother and father. Having moved to another suburb approximately the same distance from Tower Point as her previous residence, she has several times invited her mother and father to spend the weekend in her new home. In spite of illness, the Limparis have not chosen to remodel their apartment and still must climb over the fire escape to use the toilet facilities in their son's apartment.

Over the past several years, Mrs. Limpari has remained active in the community. Partially as a result of her husband's illness, she has become increasingly concerned with the problems of older persons and has worked toward the provision by the city of increased social and medical services. In addition, working through her parish, she has developed a self-help group through which older members of the community can provide support for each other. At the same time, Mrs. Limpari has been working to develop more satisfactory day-care arrangements for children of working mothers in Tower Point. Once again, she turned to the parish priest for help and has led a campaign for a complete licensed facility through the church that will serve hot breakfasts and lunches. At the time of the most recent contact with Mrs. Limpari, the center had been open for several months and has received enthusiastic support from the community.

It has come as a surprise to Mrs. Limpari to discover that she is financially secure. In addition to her own and her husband's Social Security benefits, she has decided to gather her financial resources together. She had taken her money, which she used to hoard in her mattress, and put it in a more lucrative money market account. Since earlier contacts, Mrs. Limpari has purchased yet an additional parking lot so that she now owns a considerable amount of real estate in one of the most rapidly developing areas of the city. The condominium project with Mrs. McGorty has not fared as well. The project had been planned just as the state first enacted laws permitting such condominium ownership; Mrs. McGorty believes that this project may have even been the first to take advantage of the new laws. However, since the project was financed with Federal Housing Administrations funds, there was concern in the community that other low-income groups besides the Italian Americans would be permitted to move into the building. In a city beset with racial tensions over the past several years, such a possibility has caused considerable distress.

Mrs. Limpari has used her money to provide herself with luxuries that, a few years ago, she would not have permitted herself. Two years ago, she and her husband realized their life's dream of returning to Italy and visiting with relatives. Last year, they took a cruise to the Caribbean and spent much of the winter in Florida. This year, if Mr. Limpari's health permits, they again plan to spend much of the winter in Florida. Such travel is striking for this couple, particularly in view of Mr. Limpari's suspicion of the world beyond Tower Point. In part, Mr. Limpari's illness has made him ever more dependent on his wife, and Mr. Limpari accedes from the desire to please her. In part, he has found the warm climate during the winter helpful for his arthritis. Mrs. Limpari's only regret is that they did not travel before, but she recognizes, with some amusement, that she had always believed they were too poor to move beyond Tower Point.

It is clear that Mrs. Limpari has continued as an active, successful, and significant figure in her community. She attributes this success to hard work over nearly half a century. Commenting on the women's movement she observes:

I guess some of them would say I ought to support them. One of them from City Hall, a college girl, wanted to write about me. But I don't go for it. A woman's place is at home, caring for her family. You know, I only worked to help make ends meet—times were very tough when the children were little, and my husband got laid off sometimes from his job. Also, I liked to be able to have some of my own money and to do with it as I wanted to. But I don't see it as a big issue. You wake up in the morning and go to work to help support the famly. It's just what's always been done.

In a very nonself-conscious manner, Mrs. Limpari has achieved economic success and respect from the community. At the same time, such success has been achieved while maintaining a very traditional view of the roles of men and women in society.

Much of Mrs. Limpari's attitude toward relations between men and women can be summarized in her description of a younger couple she worked with in peer counseling provided by the parish for couples with marital problems. The wife had complained that her husband demanded sexual intimacies every night. In discussing this problem with the wife, who felt bothered by her husband's demands to such an extent that she wanted a separation, Mrs. Limpari reports that this was her advice:

I says it wasn't a hell of a lot that he wanted. I says, waste five minutes of your time and satisfy him and then you're through. I said all you have to do is give him five or ten minutes of your time, then the rest of the 24 hours he's at peace with you . . . don't let him beg all the time and deny him; give it to him and then forget about it.

Mrs. Limpari reports that this advice saved the marriage. Clearly, like many women of her generation-or age-cohort, women are not expected to enjoy sex. However, as she perceives the woman's role in the family, there is an implicit exchange process in which women have to put up with some inconveniences but receive security that is more than an acceptable reward for such inconveniences.

Relations between Mrs. Limpari and her children have continued to be generally positive over the past few years. She acknowledges that she feels more comfortable with her daughters than with her sons and feels particularly close to Mrs. McGorty. Mrs. McGorty's other daughter still lives in California and only occasionally returns East to visit the family. While Mrs. McGorty's search for greater affection and support from her mother was an issue at the time for the original study, this issue has diminished in intensity over the past four years. In part, as the condominium project has been dropped, it has become less likely that Mrs. McGorty would move back to Tower Point and interfere in her mother's daily round. In part, as a result of both her own and her husband's illnesses, Mrs. Limpari has had to depend more on her daughter, which brings the two generations into increased contact and satisfies Mrs. McGorty's desire for such involvement. Having Mrs. McGorty's daughters available to help her with her community projects has also fostered increased contact between the generations.

The issue of Mr. Limpari's own limited mobility and his increasing need for skilled nursing care has been the major point of disagreement between Mrs. Limpari and Mrs. McGorty. While her daughter feels strongly that Mr. Limpari should be placed in a nursing home, Mrs. Limpari insists that she is able to care for him and believes that he and she will both be happier and more comfortable if he is permitted to remain at home. Mrs. Limpari readily admits that her interest in creating additional services for older residents of Tower Point stems from her own experiences in caring for her husband and her wish to be able to keep him at home.

Just as at the time of the original study, Mrs. Limpari continues to feel caught between her own developmentally determined need for increased time for herself and her wish to serve her family and her community. The problem is that there is conflict between a developmentally determined need for increased interiority, which leads to the wish to have more time for herself, and a long-standing need to be active in the community as a way of resolving a fundamental conflict between activity and passivity. Further, such community effort fosters Mrs. Limpari's concept of herself as an effective woman and is hard to relinquish without loss of self-esteem. One way Mrs. Limpari appears to have dealt with this tension between caring for self and serving the community is to tolerate greater personal comfort. As Gutmann (1975) has suggested, increased receptivity and sensuousness accompany the shift from middle to old age. Being able to take a cruise or to spend time in Florida to escape the harsh winter represents a way of providing such increased personal comfort in ways that would have been unacceptable to her when she was younger.

As she approaches middle age, Mrs. McGorty looks strikingly like her mother and describes a pattern of daily activity and community concerns that sound very much like those of her mother. The extent of this involvement was apparent in the difficulty experienced arranging a time to talk with her. The condominium project has been replaced by numerous other activities. Over the past few years, Mrs. McGorty has resumed work part time as an attorney. However, she has also returned to school for an advanced degree in education in order to run the private school her daughters attend and has also begun a catering service. Mrs. McGorty's story about the catering service provides a particularly apt description of this competent woman. Hearing of her culinary skills, a neighbor had approached her about preparing foods for the party his company was planning. The catering was such a success that Mrs. McGorty decided to go in business for herself. She figured that since she must prepare dinner for her family she could combine catering with her usual meal preparation. She merely cooks extra amounts of whatever is planned for her family on a given evening and then provides the food for that evening's clients before she completes the meal for her own family.

Mrs. McGorty's pursuit of the education degree resulted from a controversy that developed at the school her daughters were attending. The director of the school had been dismissed, and, knowing of her administrative skills, the parents asked her if she would be willing to run the school on an interim basis while a new director was recruited. Still later, the McGortys decided to move to a more prosperous neighborhood; after her daughters changed to public schools, Mrs. McGorty also decided to work for the public schools in the new community. In the meantime, she continued to serve as a bus driver for the school in her old neighborhood. However, this did finally prove to be too much work. Mr. McGorty had reached the age when he could retire from the civil service at nearly full pension. The McGortys decided that the best solution would be for Mr. McGorty to retire and take over the bus route, while his wife pursued her careers as teacher, lawyer, and caterer. Such efforts have meant considerable additional income, and the family has been able to take summer vacations, as well as to move to a prosperous suburb.

In commenting on this change in their lives, Mrs. McGorty notes:

We have sort of come full circle to what women's lib is all about, that we have come to reverse roles and he is now the parent who stays home, and we think it is important that someone is home for the children.

This role reversal in the family was accomplished largely by accident rather than as a deliberate decision based on a specific ideology. Indeed, Mrs. McGorty says she pays little attention to the women's movement, even though she has several friends who are active in it. Mrs. McGorty's own orientation is essentially child centered, and much of her motivation to work has been to insure her children's education. In discussing her views regarding the women's movement, Mrs. McGorty observes:

> How each woman thinks is how she should react. If you're not happy taking care of babies and home . . . if you're not happy with what you're doing, then you can't do a good job unless you're happy.

At the same time, she feels it not best for women to have careers at the expense of their children, using paid helpers in the home. Central to her concern about such helpers is that the children will be "spoiled" and not grow up to be hardworking and conscientious adults.

In her involvement in many community activities, Mrs. McGorty demonstrates her continued identification with her mother's own coping techniques. As is true of her mother, she becomes anxious when she feels that her activities might be circumscribed, but rearranges the environment in such a way that she can continue to be effective. A few years ago, when her husband was still working, problems arose in arranging for childcare during the afternoon before she could get home from work. To resolve this problem, Mrs. McGorty developed an after-school play program for the neighborhood that she then developed further into a community center. Finally, she led a building program that resulted in a modest community center fully staffed for a variety of activities, including after-school play, senior citizen activities, and even Lamaze classes for expectant parents.

As is true of her mother, Mrs. McGorty's marriage is to a man somewhat less active than she. Mr. McGorty was happy to be able to retire early from his job with the civil service and enjoys staying at home and caring for the children. In the past year, he has been discovered to have hypertension and is grateful now that he does not have to work. In the manner typical for her, Mrs. McGorty has researched possible medications and is in the process of organizing a self-help group for other patients and, in collaboration with a physician, has been developing a biofeedback manual for the treatment of this disorder.

Mrs. McGorty's oldest daughter looks very much like her mother and grandmother. A heavy-set youngster with close cropped hair, she has selected for herself a set of after-school activities that keep her busy all week long. A grade ahead of herself in school, she has become active in an organization started by the young people in her school to promote integrated education. In describing this daughter, Mrs. McGorty observes:

> [She] really likes things to run smoothly, but that's of course because of the way she was brought up. She loves to be challenged and is very competitive and loves to get an A or A + and loves to study . . . she's the kind of kid who goes to the bathroom with a book and she sits in the bus with a book—we don't go to the supermarket but that she drags a book with her.

The two younger girls maintain a less ambitious but still busy schedule. The girls spend much time talking about what they will be when they grow up, with the oldest daughter, now in junior high school, planning on becoming a physician. The younger girls have settled on careers as teachers, but Mrs. McGorty notes that their career plans shift nearly everyday. All three girls assume that careers properly have a place in a woman's life, a reflection of their identification with their mother's values. Mrs. McGorty herself places much emphasis on the importance of both having a career and being a homemaker. She is very concerned about the way her children use their time in her absence and makes sure that she is home in the evenings and on the weekends to spend time with them. In addition, the family takes frequent holidays together, such as a long weekend at the beach. Mrs. McGorty says that her children come first with her, even before her husband and her career.

In her conscientious and methodical attitude toward life, Mrs. McGorty has been successful not only for herself, but also for her daughters. Indeed, much of Mrs. McGorty's activity is in the service of caring for the next generation. At the same time, such an orderly life, marked by achievement, provides little opportunity for spontaneity, particularly with her husband. Mrs. McGorty's relationship with her husband is much like that of Mrs. Limpari with her husband, except lacking in the clear affection the Limparis feel toward each other. In the case of both generations, active and successful women married somewhat more passive men who received some satisfaction from the caretaking provided by their wives. In the case of each generation, the husband's illness prompted further restructuring of the environment with benefit to the larger community. However, in Mrs. McGorty's life, this illness has not brought the couple closer together, although the family unit is a close-knit one.

Mrs. McGorty feels her life is much like what she would hope for. Although she views opportunities largely as due to good fortune, she recognizes her achievements and takes pride in them. In coping with problems by restructuring the environment, she is truly her mother's daughter. Mrs. Limpari's mother is pleased that, at least, Mrs. McGorty is using the intellectual skills she had worked so hard to be sure her daughter obtained and speaks with admiration of Mrs. McGorty's accomplishments, just as Mrs. McGorty recognizes, with pride, her mother's unusual achievements.

This modified extended family clearly shows a set of responses across generations that have continued into the third generation. Not only in physical appearance, but also in salient attitudes and values, and in personality organization as well, Mrs. Limpari and Mrs. McGorty and the latter's own three daughters show particular consistency in their outlook on the world and in salient means for resolving conflicts.

MRS. SCARDONI-MRS. RUSSO

At the time of the original study, the relationship between these two women was among the most ambivalent of these four families. Four years later, the two women's relationship remains ambivalent. In the interim, Mrs. Russo has moved to another neighborhood and no longer lives next door to her brother. As a result of this move and increased reluctance on the part of Mrs. Scardoni's husband to drive her to visit her daughter, mother and daughter see each other somewhat less often.

Some indication of the tension between mother and daughter was apparent from the very first contact with this family. Mrs. Russo readily agreed to talk about the past four years, but warned that her mother had an unlisted telephone number and refused to talk to anyone beside herself and her brother. However, a note to Mrs. Scardoni brought a cordial response and a suggested time for the meeting. The Scardoni house looked much the same as it had four years before, except that the neighborhood had become much more built up and now looked like a reasonably prosperous suburb. Mrs. Scardoni had aged perceptibly in the intervening years and had also gained additional weight. At the time of the interview, Mrs. Scardoni's husband was home from work with the flu. He had been established on the couch in the living room, so that Mrs. Scardoni could check on him as she did her housework. Mrs. Scardoni noted that two years previously he had come down with pneumonia and had nearly died; since that time she had watched her husband's health very carefully as, indeed, she watched her own health and that of her daughter.

Mrs. Scardoni is preoccupied with issues of health and illness at this point in her life. Female complaints head the list of such problems, although she also reports having had a coronary in the past four years and a minor foot operation that led to complications. Such concern with her body can be understood in view of the depression she openly acknowledges. She notes that if every little detail of the day does not go right, she becomes terribly upset; in the same way, she is concerned that everything around her be absolutely clean. She says that she had always had these concerns, but that over the past few years they have become much more intense. While Mrs. Scardoni is aware of her increased concern with cleanliness, she is less aware of her increased suspiciousness of everyone around her. She complains that her neighbors purposely do things to annoy her: for example, her next door neighbor leaves his trash barrel too close to her driveway on the day of trash collection in order that she will have to move it.

This suspiciousness, somewhat troubling in her relations with the neighbors, provides a source of overt conflict in her relations with her family. Mrs. Scardoni is harsh in her accusations of Mr. Russo and his family. Indeed, Mrs. Scardoni's insulting remarks have caused such a problem that she is no longer able to attend holiday festivities with Mr. Russo's family, even though the two families have long known each other. Mr. Russo tries to avoid fights with his mother-in-law, but every contact leads to renewed conflict. Mrs. Scardoni's major complaint is that her son-in-law "leeches" off her daughter and that he could not take care of himself on his own, although Mr. Russo has advanced to the rank of foreman in a different branch of the same construction company in which her husband is now also a foreman.

Four years ago, it was clear that Mrs. Scardoni was very suspicious of men and feared their power. Many of the struggles she has with her son-in-law, as well as with her husband, reflect that continuing concern. Mrs. Scardoni believes that if women do not protect themselves, men will take advantage of them personally and sexually. She has resolved this concern for herself by taking complete responsibility for all family financial matters. She notes, for example, that her husband does not even know the date on which the mortgage is due. When she was sick, she says, he began to worry about his lack of familiarity with such financial matters, but Mrs. Scardoni has been reluctant to inform him and has managed to keep control of the money in sickness and health. She observes that she taught Mrs. Russo how to manage men and money and notes with approval that Mrs. Russo has managed to maintain equally great control over finances in her family.

Fearful of men, and of their power to control her life, Mrs. Scardoni nevertheless has not considered the women's movement in terms of her own life. When asked her views, she at first did not understand what she was being asked: she said that she did not read newspapers. When the issue was clarified, she still did not have any opinion regarding the issue of women and work. She said she guessed that those who were protesting the place of women in society must be "hippies" or "reds." She commented that most women of her generation were forced to work, at least part time, for otherwise there would be nothing to eat. She thought it would be a great luxury to have a choice whether to work or not.

It is clear that Mrs. Scardoni is so preoccupied by personal concerns that she has little interest in larger social issues. She herself noted that she was so concerned with her own health and that of her husband that she had little time for anything else. At the same time, she said that she does feel cut off from others and feels isolated from her family, even though Mrs. Russo visits with her at least weekly and speaks over the telphone with her at least daily. However, since her son and daughter now live about an hour's drive in opposite directions, she visits less often with each of her children and grandchildren.

Mrs. Scardoni is acutely concerned with her own aging. This concern, already evident four years ago, has become even greater over the past four years. This terror of growing old, which partially accounts for her hypochondriasis, has received some support from the fact that neither she nor her husband is able to take care of the house as well as before. Managing such chores as shoveling snow has become a problem. During last year's very snowy winter, her son and son-in-law took turns with the shoveling and home repairs. However, her son, Mr. Butoni, feels that more of this responsibility should be taken by Mr. Russo, since he has his own elderly in-laws to care for.

Mrs. Scardoni's suspiciousness of others, together with her continuing harsh criticism of her son and daughter and their families, has increased the degree of tension between the generations. Caring for her two grandchildren, on those few occasions when she has been asked to sit for them, has been a particular source of conflict. She invariably feels resentful and angry. Not only do her grandchildren disturb her routine, but also they make demands for care she finds difficult to meet. Her view is in sharp contrast to her previous preferences regarding this issue. As she says:

I don't have much strength and they always want me to do for them. When they're around, I get tired and begin to hurt.

She comments that after she has baby-sat for one of her grandchildren she feels exhausted and often gets sick. As a result, she has discouraged her son and daughter from asking for such help. In addition, she feels that her grandchildren are badly behaved and resents the freedom their parents permit them, viewing this freedom as a sign of parental irresponsibility.

Criticisms by grandparents of the freedom provided grandchildren, and of the more lenient childrearing techniques practiced by their children in rearing their own children, were voiced by each of the grandmothers, both at the time of the initial study and four years later. Reflected in these criticisms is a difference in childrearing attitudes due to generation, cohort, and age. Specific childrearing advice provided for these grandparents when they were rearing their own children stressed the importance of discipline (Stendler, 1950; Wolfenstein, 1953). The impact of the harsh economic circumstances of the depression experienced by each of these grandparents during the time their children were growing up served as a specific historical circumstance that affected their attitude of conservatism and restraint (Elder, 1974). The effects of aging itself, which evokes increased rigidity and more conventional attitudes (Chown, 1968; Botwinick, 1973), together with the effects of being the oldest generation in social position, leading to increased expectation of respect and deference for authority, further strengthens this more traditional orientation of the grandmothers in this study toward childrearing. Further, as grandparents, access to grandchildren is determined almost entirely by the parents' preferences (Rosow, 1967). Such factors, taken together with increased interiority which results in decreased investment in social relations (Neugarten, 1973; Gutmann, 1975), further intensifies the diffidence so many of the grandmothers in this study show toward caring for their grandchildren, and which has increased over the four years since previous contacts with these families.

Mrs. Scardoni's harsh attacks on her daughter's childrearing practices, and her reluctance to help take care of her granddaughter, together with her continuing conflict with her son-in-law, all reflect her own very tenuous adjustment, as well as problems, seen more generally in each of these four families, inherent in being a grandparent.

Among these four grandmothers, Mrs. Scardoni is the most socially isolated and the most personally troubled. While Mrs. Limpari has suffered more serious physical illnesses, none of the other three grandmothers has shown the degree of emotional upset shown by Mrs. Scardoni. While Mrs. Pescatore and Mrs. Giorgio each have experienced some discomfort in developing close ties with others, they currently experience less direct conflict with other family members. On the other hand, none of these other grandmothers had experienced the degree of chaos and deprivation in earlier life that Mrs. Scardoni has experienced. There is some evidence in Mrs. Scardoni's current adjustment that these earlier events have affected her ability to successfully adapt to aging.

Mrs. Scardoni's forceful personality, together with her malevolent view of the world, has had a direct impact on her daughter's own personality and adjustment, which is even more striking now than four years previously. During these past four years, Mrs. Russo has become increasingly afraid of her mother's "powers" over her, believing that her mother is in possession of the "evil eye." The idea of the evil eye is a part of the folklore of southern Italian culture connected with the suspiciousness that characterizes human relations more generally within this peasant society (Banfield, 1958; Cancian, 1966; Cornelisen, 1969, 1976). In a world in which there is chronic scarcity, and in which personal advantage is believed to be envied by others to such an extent that such advantage might be destroyed (as has been suggested in Chapter 8), emphasis is place not only on maximization of personal gain at the expense of others, represented by Banfield's concept of amortal familism, but also on the belief that others' envy can destroy such personal advantage through black magic (Moss and Cappannari, 1960a). The evil tongue spreads reports of such good fortune, while the evil eye actually can undo it.

In southern Italian society, any person presumed to have power over another is also presumed capable of using the evil eye to bring about personal misfortune. Detection of the evil eye is typically through observation of a drop of oil placed in a cup of water. If the oil spreads, then the evil eye is present (Moss and Cappannari, 1960a; Bianco, 1974). At that point, making the sign of the cross in the center of the forehead is supposed to protect against the most potent effects of the evil eye. Of course, such a test tends to err in the direction of detecting the presence of the evil eye.

Given the power Mrs. Russo believes her mother to have over her, as seen in her discussion of their relationship four years ago, it is not surprising that she should attribute the source of this evil eye to her mother. As she herself observed, only someone with great power can have the evil eye, and who else but her mother could have such great power! Mrs. Russo also reported that, over the course of the past few years, she has had several severe headaches; she believes that these headaches are evidence of the evil eye at work. The only way of getting rid of these headaches is to make the sign of the cross, after which they do disappear.

Mrs. Russo not only believes her mother to be the source of the evil eye, but also the source of a protection against it. She showed a necklace her mother had given her when she was much younger, but that she had just begun wearing, and which her mother had always assured her would protect against some of the most potent effects of the evil eye.

From a psychological perspective, the evil eye represents a projective identification, as formulated by Klein (1952, 1957b) and elaborated by Segal (1973) and, most recently, by Ogden (1979), in which unacceptable retaliatory wishes are viewed as having their source in the other. The effect of this projective identification is to get rid of any unacceptable wishes by making the other the repository for them (Cohler, 1977). In this sense, the evil eye represents the repository of Mrs. Russo's unacceptable, frightening, destructive wishes toward her mother, in her mother, which then has the effect of preserving, intact, the continuing mother-daughter symbiosis.

It is possible that the decision to move to a new home had contributed to the development of the belief in the evil eye over the past four years. Previously, the

Russos and the Butonis had lived together in a two-family duplex. Mrs. Russo and her brother had remained very close, much to the dismay of her husband, who often felt excluded from their relationship. During these years, Mrs. Russo also saw more of her mother than after her recent move. The fact that she and her brother lived at the same address made it possible for her mother to visit with them both at the same time rather than alternating her visits. Further, because their house was on a route convenient for Mr. Scardoni in his frequent visits to his own former neighborhood meant that there was increased likelihood that Mrs. Scardoni would drop by on a frequent basis.

Such contact may have been comforting for Mrs. Russo, who, in addition, could be reassured that her own destructive wishes had not harmed her mother. A concern of this sort may also have been a partial motivation for Mrs. Russo's frequent telephone calls many times each day. With less frequent contact such reassurance may not have been so easy to obtain, leading to the necessity of finding another solution for resolving these unacceptable feelings, through attribution of them to her mother.

Mr. Russo's discomfort with the closeness between Mrs. Russo and her brother must have played some part in his desire to move, for Mrs. Russo commented that her husband had exerted much pressure on her to move, even though their previous home had been large enough for the three of them. At the present time, Mrs. Russo and brother still speak on the telephone at least daily; Mr. Russo remains resentful of this close contact, but Mrs. Russo notes that his family is so very different from her own. Mrs. Russo's husband puts her before his own family, while she views her mother and stepfather and her husband and her daughter all as important for her (in that order).

In other respects, Mrs. Russo feels that the marriage has grown over the past four years. The house in which she and her family are now living was one Mr. Russo built as a part of a larger housing development created by his employer. Both husband and wife are talented and have worked together to decorate the house in an elaborate manner that could never have been possible if they had been required to use a decorator and other contractors. Having gotten married so young, even though they had known each other for a long time before getting married, Mrs. Russo says that when she was first married, it was like playing house. She feels that there is now greater intimacy between her husband and herself.

The only topic that husband and wife disagree on is Mr. Russo's relationship with Mrs. Russo's mother. Mr. Russo is hurt by Mrs. Scardoni's continual attacks on him and feels that she stands in the way of his relationship with his wife. Mrs. Russo acknowledges that her husband's complaints are legitimate and that her mother acts "insane" around her husband. At the same time, she feels both loyal to her mother and frightened of what her mother might do if she took her husband's side. The intensity of Mrs. Russo's conflicting loyalties undoubtedly contributes to her frequent and severe headaches.

Mrs. Russo talks over the telephone with her mother at least once a day, just as she did four years previous. She also visits with her mother once a week and still does her weekly shopping while visiting with her mother. At the same time, she readily acknowledges the conflict between them. Mrs. Scardoni is still concerned about her daughter's weight and, as Mrs. Russo has developed headaches over the course of the past four years, also about this new symptom. Mrs. Russo says that her mother focuses on her body in just the same way that she focuses on her own body. Indeed, it seems to her that her mother sometimes does not distinguish between them, and that scares her.

According to Mrs. Russo, there is nothing wrong with her mother other than a touch of arthritis and that she becomes dramatic and regards herself as having life-threatening illnesses. What is clear is that mother and daughter discuss intimate details of their life with each other. Even though Mrs. Russo does not want to, she becomes involved in such intimate discussions that lead her to feel increasingly angry with her mother and frightened of the power her mother has to make her do things she does not want to do. For example, she may be determined that she is not going to visit her mother anymore, but when she is done on the telephone, she feels herself mysteriously pulled in the direction of driving to her mother's house. When together, mother and daughter spend much time arguing. According to Mrs. Russo, she raises her voice and her mother raises her voice until they are screaming so loud that the whole neighborhood can hear them. Mrs. Russo is terribly worried about her stepfather's health; she fears that if anything happens to him, then she would have to have her mother live with her, and that would be intolerable. Even at the present time, she cannot have her mother visit in her house, for her mother begins a complete housecleaning, accompanied by abusive criticisms of Mrs. Russo's housekeeping.

Since Mrs. Russo does not work, now that Charlotte is gone for increasing amounts of time during the day, she finds herself with free time. A "house-proud" woman (Cooper and McNeill, 1968) who is remarkably efficient in her schedule, Mrs. Russo has her housework done early in the day. Further, since her husband helps with the chores, Mrs. Russo's housework is not terribly demanding. Although she knows she has a flair for decorating, Mrs. Russo feels that it is not right for a woman to work. In talking about the women's movement she says:

> I think first a woman, her duty is taking care of her home . . . I could never go out to work knowing that I have all this to do . . . to face all this work in the house. I have to get everything done, do what I have to do.

At one point, she did actually explore the possibility of a job, but then became worried that Charlotte would suffer and that there would be no one to take care of her if she became ill.

Conflict regarding the issue of appropriate closeness, so apparent in Mrs. Russo's expressed childrearing attitudes four years earlier, appears to have continued to the present time, although Mrs. Russo finds it much less difficult now than in the past to take care of her daughter. At the time of previous contact with this family, Charlotte was a "terrible two" and had temper tantrums that evoked feelings of terror in Mrs. Russo, whose own tenuous impulse control was threatened by her daughter's outbursts. Four years later, Charlotte is a subdued but pretty six

six-year-old who is compliant and well behaved. Although liked by her teacher and her classmates, she appears to have lost the zest that was earlier apparent.

Mrs. Russo is pleased that her daughter is doing well in school and that she is so well behaved; like her mother, Charlotte appears to have few strong likes and dislikes and shows a "low-keyed" demeanor (Mahler, Pine, and Bergman, 1975) which suggests that she is on the way to becoming depressed like her mother, struggling to keep tight hold of her own tensions. The family conflict reflected by the evil eye seems to have taken its toll on Charlotte as well, and she has become involved in the tangled web of conflict linking the generations within this family.

After a four-year interval, the adjustment of both grandmother and mother appears still to be quite brittle. These two women in the adult generations within the family have maintained a symbiotic realtionship based on shared concern with issues of sufficiency and basic trust, together with commitment to the primitive defenses of projection and splitting. Each of these women expresses her basic concern regarding integrity of the self through hypochondriacal preoccupation with bodily functioning. This concern with the cohesiveness of the self appears to have been communicated to Mrs. Russo's daughter, who shows a relationship with her mother marked by a symbiotic tie similar to that between mother and grandmother, with accompanying low-keyedness. The pep which was apparent at age two has been replaced by a kind of lethargic compliance at age six, suggesting that Charlotte may have joined her mother and grandmother in the continuation of serious conflicts into the third generation. As each generation of women continues to exercise power over the psychological development of the next, the evil eye continues its domination within this multigeneration family.

MRS. GIORGIO—MRS. CZAJA

Since the earlier contact with Mrs. Giorgio and Mrs. Czaja, Mrs. Czaja and her husband and their two children have moved to another city, and Mrs. Czaja's youngest sister and her husband and children now share Mrs. Giorgio's house with her. Mrs. Giorgio is the least changed of the four grandmothers in this study. She still maintains an active schedule as a volunteer and still avoids what she feels are intrusive attempts by her children to interfere in her life in their misguided attempt to be of help to her. Mrs. Giorgio is one of two grandmothers whose offspring continue to share a common household with her. In contrast with Mrs. Pescatore, who offers the accommodation upstairs from her in an attempt to help her children with housing and who seeks some emotional benefits from this continuing contact, Mrs. Giorgio is explicitly resentful of the fact that her children insist on living with her. A widow for nearly 20 years, she feels that she is well able to manage her life. However, Mrs. Giorgio's children worry that at age 70 their mother simply cannot manage to live alone as well as she did 20 or even 10 years ago. Mrs. Giorgio has a rather large house and several valuable furnishings, including room-sized Oriental rugs, but lives in a neighborhood where the crime rate has been increasing.

Mrs. Giorgio takes pride in the fact that she looks much younger than her stated age. She prefers active sportswear to the shift dresses selected by other grandmothers in the study. She still volunteers at the same hospital where her husband served on the medical staff for nearly his entire career. In addition, she is active in church affairs and has worked toward the extension of parish social services for less-priviledged ethnic groups. She is quite explicit in her criticism of the church for failing to keep pace with contemporary social changes and, although she herself would not feel comfortable, believes particularly that the church must change its attitudes toward birth control. In other respects, she is a conservative woman; Mrs. Giorgio's children complain that she is the only Republican in the family.

When asked directly about her feelings toward women and work, women's liberation, and related issues, Mrs. Giorgio demurred. She noted that she herself had always worked, but that she had been forced to help her husband in his practice. She felt that it was each woman's decision whether to work or not, but, like other grandmothers in the study, was critical of the tendency of contemporary women to neglect their responsibilities at home to take on responsibilities outside the home.

Other than one minor operation a few years ago, Mrs. Giorgio's health has been good. While she could not acknowledge it, her comments suggested that it is terribly important for her to feel that she is able to continue to get about and thus to avoid dealing with her own aging. Her daughters are critical of her clothing and her use of makeup, believing that she should dress and act her age to a greater extent. Mrs. Giorgio's daughters are also critical of her continued refusal to be of help in family emergencies and of the emotional distance she still maintains from them. When her daughters were young, Mrs. Giorgio was often unavailable, since she served as her husband's receptionist in his office attached to the house. Now that she has more time, she has filled that time with activities she finds personally satisfying. She says that she does not want to be burdened with her children's demands and that she thoroughly dislikes keeping house; during the years the children lived at home, Mrs. Giorgio had a housekeeper, although she always tended to the cooking.

A part of the concern Mrs. Giorgio shows in "keeping busy" is her need to fend off the depression she has felt almost continually since her husband's death. Four years ago, it was clear that this woman had not yet succeeded in dealing with the loss she had felt when her husband died. This same issue seems to have continued into the present. There is a sense in which her volunteering at the hospital, of which her husband was so much a part that a new wing was named after him, represents an attempt to keep his memory alive. A part of the pressure she feels to volunteer, together with the panic engendered when she feels that her children's demands might keep her from her appointed rounds at the hospital, results from having been left alone when her husband died. Volunteering, as a kind of restitution for her anger, appears to be an important factor in Mrs. Giorgio's present adjustment. What is so often perceived by her children as a cold refusal to be of help is, as felt by Mrs. Giorgio, vitally necessary to maintain her adjustment. Although this same issue was present four years ago, it was less obvious than at the present when Mrs. Giorgio maintains her daily schedule in an increasingly rigid manner.

Because her daughter has moved away from Somerset to another city, visits between Mrs. Giorgio and Mrs. Czaja are infrequent. Mrs. Czaja complains that her mother seldom visits her, while she, in turn, tries to visit her mother every few months. In addition, Mrs. Czaja calls her mother several times every week. This frequent long-distance calling represents an attempt to ease the burden on Mrs. Czaja's youngest sister who is currently living with Mrs. Giorgio and, at least from the perspective of her children, has been helping to "look after her." Mrs. Giorgio claims that she is quite willing to visit, and even enjoys the seven-hour bus ride, but that she is too busy to be able to take the time off. Indeed, she is even too busy to find time to purchase birthday and Christmas presents for her grandchildren. Mrs. Giorgio acknowledges that her children do get hurt by her refusal to purchase gifts, but claims that all the children already have sufficient toys. When she does find time and has the inclination, she sends small gifts of money for birthdays, but she claims that there are too many grandchildren with too many birthdays to be able to keep them all straight.

There are relatively few other areas of conflict between Mrs. Giorgio and her children. Because she avoids contact, little overt disagreement is likely. The major source of disagreement is with the youngest daughter, now living in her household, who, she feels, married too young and without her explicit consent.

A somewhat distant, formal woman, Mrs. Giorgio reveals little warmth or charm. As in the past, she has continued to maintain emotional distance from her children and continues to be greatly concerned with her own autonomy. From her children's perspective, she appears to be self-centered and withholding, unwilling to help them in times of need, and apparently disinterested in her grandchildren. It is clear that, as presented, Mrs. Giorgio's lack of interest in her family and in being a grandparent is at variance with the stereotyped picture of grandparenthood. On the other hand, at least some of her lack of interest is a result of her own psychological struggle, dealing with her own unresolved mourning of her husband. It is Mrs. Giorgio's lack of involvement, rather than the overinvolvement so characteristic of some other multigeneration families in the study, that is a major source of conflict within the family.

Mrs. Czaja, an outspoken, articulate, colorful woman, was quite explicit in her frustration with her mother. For her, it is her mother's lack of interest in the children's birthdays and in Christmas that is most difficult. According to Mrs. Czaja, last year she called her mother to discuss Christmas plans. Mrs. Giorgio was not interested in a large holiday gathering, so the Czajas did not come to celebrate with her. Mrs. Giorgio did send some gifts, but charged these gifts to Mrs. Czaja's account with a large national retail chain. What was most galling was that, according to her daughter, Mrs. Giorgio is a very wealthy woman. Having made a series of shrewd investments, both with her husband and after his death, Mrs. Giorgio was well able to afford these gifts that she charged to her daughter.

While Mrs. Giorgio attributes her daughter's decision to move out to a new job Mr. Czaja was offered in another city, and while job pressures were certainly a major factor, Mrs. Czaja notes that they moved because it had become impossible to share a household with her mother. First Mrs. Giorgio made clear her dissatisfaction that Mrs. Czaja had not married a physician like Dr. Giorgio. Second, Mrs. Giorgio had no tolerance for the disarray three small children can cause in a house. When the children tracked mud across the floor, Mrs. Giorgio exploded, and, when they turned on the television while Mrs. Giorgio was reading a book, she became harsh in her criticism. According to Mrs. Czaja, the tension was so great that they had to find another place to live. When a job offer materialized, the family jumped at the chance to move away.

At the present time, Mr. Czaja teaches creative arts in a college in the Northeast, several hours' drive from Somerset. Living out in the country, the Czajas and their two children, a boy, now eight, and a girl, age five, enjoy a simpler life than when they lived in the city. Mrs. Czaja has moved several times on account of her husband's work and has never been able to develop firm roots. Trained as a teacher, she has not found time to work since her children were born. In addition, she is not sure that she could easily return to teaching, since she now has a picture of what life is like for children in the hours when they are not in school and worries about how her children would feel if she were not available to them at such times. She notes that she has particular empathy for what life is like for children and recalls only too well her own childhood and her own unhappiness that her mother was so often unavailable.

Largely as a result of these childhood memories, Mrs. Czaja finds it difficult to think of herself going to work and leaving her young children at home. As she says:

I like being at home. I enjoy my TV, and puttering around the house. It's ridiculous, but I fold clothes, do things around the house, look after the goats and rabbits. Our kids are very important to us, and my husband's career is very important too. I think it would jeopardize everything if I had a job . . .

She adds that people should be encouraged to do "their own thing" and that there is no reason why a woman should not work, if she is able to juggle family and work, but that work right now is not for her. It is likely that her recent experiences with her mother and her mother's work still affect her own attitudes. She notes, for example, that she would never volunteer, especially if it would "tie her down" and prevent her from doing other things such as being available to her husband and children. Little can be said about the children in this family; the Czaja children were the only children who were not visited in this follow-up study. Mrs. Czaja reports no particular difficulties in caring for them or few problems they have presented in their development thus far.

Mrs. Czaja worries about the lack of stability connected with her husband's job. She and he have discussed several times whether he should give up teaching in order that he could have more time for his own creative work. On the other hand, he has been a successful and popular instructor and enjoys his teaching.

Mrs. Czaja has little interest in the academic community at the college. She says her best friends are "regular people," such as drugstore clerks. She recalls her own past and says that she grew up in a working-class community and never realized that her own family was different in any way till she went away to college. Even now, she prefers friends who are like people she grew up with. However, with two young children to care for, she says she does not have a lot of extra time. Once again, she emphasizes that she does not regret the fact that she does not have more time for herself. Such comments suggest that Mrs. Czaja is quite consciously trying to be a different kind of mother than she recalls her own mother as having been and that her recent experiences living with her mother have added to this determination to do things differently.

Mrs. Czaja feels sad that her mother has such little interest in coming to visit or in being more a part of the family and complains that her mother is not very sentimental. While sarcastic about her mother's lack of interest in her own life, and her children's, she can also freely admit to her disappointments in the regard. Partially as a result of this conflict with her mother, partially as a result of her concern with her husband's career, and partially as a result of the same lifelong feeling of not having received enough, so clearly evident four years previously, Mrs. Czaja appears somewhat pessimistic. However, she herself is aware of this depressed mood:

> I get quite "down" sometimes. I went to four years of college and worked for four years to fold socks . . . but I think everyone has his bad days (laughs) . . .

Mr. Czaja has also experienced a good deal of pessimism over the past four years. In part, this has been related to his job and the conflict he feels between teaching and personal creative activity. However, during the past four years, Mr. Czaja's chronically mentally ill father has taken a turn for the worse; Mr. Czaja has been forced to place his father in a public hospital, since he could not afford private care and realized that his father's condition would only deteriorate further. The Czajas have talked with each other at great length about this problem, and Mr. Czaja even sought psychological help, but felt that this help was not useful and left treatment after just a few visits.

In spite of reasonably comfortable lives, and despite enjoying certain material advantages and good health, there is a degree of gloom, together with a continuing feeling of lack of sufficiency and support, that both Mr. and Mrs. Czaja reflect. Children of parents who, they feel, neglected them either emotionally or physically, they have tried to insure that their own children will not experience the same feelings of insufficiency. Mrs. Czaja is somewhat wistful in her observation that after years of schooling and work she is mending socks, while Mr. Czaja is concerned that he be able to support his family and yet feels that this responsibility affects his own freedom to carry forward with his artistic interests. In this sense, the perception these parents have of their own experiences affects how they have faced the developmental task of parenthood and adds to the purposeful lack of consistency in important family themes across the generations.

Partially related to their more clearly middle-class orientation, the Czajas are better able than the three other parental couples to articulate the manner in which experiences of present and childhood relations within their own parental families affect their present adjustment and their continuing relationships with both their parents and their children. Perhaps because their children are younger than those in the other families, and were not seen at the time of the present contact, it is less clear what the future holds for this family. With several brothers and sisters, Mrs. Czaja will have much help in caring for her older mother. Mr. Czaja has made the necessary decision regarding his father's care. Even though he could visit his father, Mr. Czaja finds that seeing his father's deteriorated condition is too painful, and he elected not to see him again. Memories of the past rather than overt family strife represent a major problem to be resolved by each parent. Making peace with memories can be at least as difficult as resolving real family crises, with an equally unpredictable outcome (Pollock, 1981).

MRS. PRESCATORE-MRS. MURPHY

Over the past four years, there have been several life changes that have had important effects on the adjustment of members of each generation in this family. From Mrs. Pescatore's perspective, things are a good deal better than previously. Feeling particularly burdened by the intensity of her relationship with her daughter, Mrs. Murphy, including Mrs. Murphy's own struggles with her marriage and her children, Mrs. Pescatore began to develop what her doctor later termed "psychosomatic symptoms." It was he who first suggested that she ought to get out of the house and find something for herself. As a result, she found a downtown clerical job and reports that for nearly the first time in her life she looks forward to getting up in the morning.

At the same time, Mrs. Pescatore does continue to worry about Mrs. Murphy and the grandchildren. Three years ago, Mrs. Murphy and her husband separated. Since that time, Mrs. Murphy has made ever more insistent demands on her mother for assistance and support. Mrs. Pescatore is better able now than four years ago to express her annoyance with her daughter. At the same time, she notes, there is reason for concern. The oldest boy does well in school but has few friends. The middle child, and only girl, has frequent temper tantrums and continually quarrels with her mother. This child's schoolwork is not good, and her attention span is quite limited. As a result, the school has suggested that Mrs. Murphy seek treatment for her. The youngest boy is also having difficulties. While his schoolwork is satisfactory, he is quite shy and not at all interested in sports, games, or other activities of boys his age. He has few friends and spends much time around the house; he has had a severe fear of going to school and is being seen by a guidance counselor.

Shortly after the original study, Mrs. Pescatore suggested to her daughter that she move out of the house and into a place of her own. Mrs. Pescatore says that she asked her daughter to leave because the youngest son had married and needed a place to live. Since he had very little money, Mrs. Pescatore wanted to help him out and felt that the best she could do was to provide housing. She does not believe that feelings about her relationship with her daughter played any part in this suggestion that Mrs. Murphy move. Mrs. Murphy felt that the move was a good idea, since she hoped it would force her husband to take greater responsibility for the support of the family. However, shortly after the move, her husband announced that he was moving to the West Coast to pursue his career in television. As a result, Mrs. Murphy has had to rear her three children by herself, supporting them through part-time work, together with financial help from her parents. After a series of disastrous moves, the Pescatores finally bought a house for Mrs. Murphy on the same street on which they are living; it is only a few minutes' walk from one house to the other. In fact, Mrs. Pescatore walks right by her daughter's house on the way to catch the bus to work and feels some uncertainty about whether she should stop by to visit.

In addition to her concern about her daughter and her grandchildren, Mrs. Pescatore also has to consider Mr. Pescatore who has also had a number of difficulties over the past several years. Partially as a result of Mrs. Murphy's problems, and partially as a result of his own aging and impending retirement from work, Mr. Pescatore has developed a serious depresssion. He complains of feeling lethargic, unable to get up in the morning, and of being unable to concentrate. Mrs. Pescatore feels he ought to see a doctor, but he has refused to seek help for his problem. Mr. Pescatore's only interests at this point are television and occasional trips to Sunday morning flea markets. His problems have been made worse by technological changes in his workplace that have made his skills obsolete. Mr. Pescatore particularly resents the fact that young workers just beginning on the job know more than he does and are able to work more efficiently with the tools.

For Mrs. Pescatore, work has become a refuge from problems at home. Increasingly, she has joined her co-workers for social events in the evenings and on weekends. This past summer she even joined a charter flight to Europe, the first time she had returned to Italy since she came to the United States as a child. These changes in Mrs. Pescatore's life are quite striking in view of her attitude toward the world outside her neighborhood as intrinsically dangerous. While her husband still maintains this view, and has refused to attend social events with her co-workers and even refused to accompany her on her charter flight, Mrs. Pescatore has received great pleasure from her travels and new schedule.

Such striking changes in Mrs. Pescatore's life cannot be understood within a paradigm of personality development which maintains that there is little additional development across adulthood. On the other hand, a developmental perspective on adult personality such as that proposed by Gutmann (1975) would explain many of these changes: Gutmann suggests that accompanying the shift toward old age women become increasingly executive and instrumental in their interests and increasingly concerned with obtaining satisfaction for themselves rather than simply for providing for others. Mrs. Pescatore's increased instrumental orientation can clearly be seen in her interest in work, which is even more striking, since it comes at a time when her husband is considering early retirement and a shift to a more expressive and succorant orientation believed to be characteristic of aging in men (Gutmann, 1975). Her travels and increased sociability on her own, without specifically considering her family's needs, are also a reflection of this new instrumental and, increasingly, self- rather than other-centered orientation.

In her relationship with her daughter and grandchildren, Mrs. Pescatore does show the same concern with issues of separation and individuation apparent in earlier talks with her. In particular, she remains concerned that unless she oversees their activities her grandchildren are likely to be hurt while playing or going to school (perhaps a reflection of her own maternal overprotectiveness). For this reason, she checks with her daughter at least once each day to be sure the children are all right. As she notes:

> I'm afraid all the time. I worry about them all the time. They're going different places. Even in broad daylight, I say to my daughter to be careful . . . You can't be too careful or watch close enough . . .

In expressing this concern, there is still some sentiment that the world beyond the neighborhood is dangerous, but now this concern is focused much more on the grandchildren than on herself and her own life.

Mrs. Pescatore does find the role of grandmother to be somewhat less burdensome than in the years when her daughter and the children were living in the same house. She prefers to take one of the children with her when going to the market or to a movie. That way, she notes, she can get to know the children better and, in addition, not have to become involved when they quarrel among themselves. It is also common for one or more of the grandchildren to come over on the weekend to watch television or help around the house. Since the two generations live so close, such visiting can be impromptu. However, when Mrs. Pescatore's son's eldest child, now nearly four, comes downstairs to visit at a time when her daughter's children are also there, chaos and quarreling may develop. At such times, Mrs. Pescatore is able to send one or another child home. Most visiting takes place at the Pescatores rather than at Mrs. Murphy's own house. In part, this is because Mr. Pescatore finds it difficult to mobilize himself on the weekends and, in part, because there is so much more space in the grandparents' house. Mrs. Pescatore is quite adamant that she will not baby-sit. Recently, Mrs. Murphy has become involved in the school-busing controversy in her community; as a result, she is frequently out at night. Mrs. Pescatore insists that it is her daughter's responsibility to provide babysitters at such times. She does not want to be burdened by such demands, particularly since, in the past few years, she has made new friends and often goes out herself in the evening. Mrs. Murphy complains that Mrs. Pescatore likes the children for amusement, but scarcely ever takes responsibility for their care.

In other respects, there is still considerable tension between Mrs. Pescatore and Mrs. Murphy. Mrs. Pescatore is continually critical of her daughter's childrearing, in ways similar to her criticisms of several years previously. The somewhat increased physical distance between these two women has eased some of the tensions in their relationship; the separation has meant that Mrs. Murphy is less involved in a social and intellectual world which Mrs. Pescatore finds confusing and unsettling. Finally, Mrs. Pescatore's clear statement to her daughter that she will no longer baby-sit, combined with the fact that Mrs. Murphy is no longer able simply to send her children downstairs, means that Mrs. Murphy has been forced to make more enduring arrangements for sitters, which has reduced her need to seek her mother's assistance.

Mrs. Pescatore has taken little notice of significant social issues, including that of the place of women in society. Still a cautious woman, she does not approve of current fashions and beliefs. She is still critical of persons whom she terms "hippies," those who go against the values that are important to her. The women's movement is viewed by her as an extension of such hippie values, and she sees little connection between women's issues and changes in her own life. She is critical of her daughter's husband as a person who holds such different values and connects such issues as changes in women's roles with the kind of crowd with whom her son-in-law associates. As is true of many women in her generation, she views the woman's role as one demanding much sacrifice, particularly when there are young children at home, with the wife and mother responsible for traditional household tasks. She asks, rhetorically, yet with some hint of weariness in her voice, whether it has not always been that way, that women struggle to keep the family going, sometimes even working full time in addition.

Easily depleted by the needs of others, particularly those of her daughter and her grandchildren, Mrs. Pescatore has, nonetheless, found ways of spending time with other family members that do not exhaust her, but will provide her with some satisfaction in her roles as mother and grandmother. As she has rearranged her life to obtain greater satisfaction for herself, many of her earlier physical symptoms have disappeared. While lacking the financial security of the other grandmothers in this study, particularly Mrs. Limpari and Mrs. Giorgio, she has sufficient means to enjoy a modest life. Having been able to extend the boundaries of her previous life and to put aside some of the burdens that have weighed on her, Mrs. Pescatore seems better adjusted to the circumstances of her life now than she had appeared on previous visits.

If life has been somewhat less difficult for Mrs. Pescatore during the past four years, it has been somewhat more difficult for Mrs. Murphy. The breakup of Mrs. Murphy's marriage was particularly difficult, and this separation, combined with a series of unfortunate moves, has made life more difficult for her. Mrs. Murphy does not view the move she had to make as related in any way to problems in her relationship with her mother, nor does she appear to harbor resentment toward her mother for being forced to move out the house. Rather, she justifies this move as having been necessary to encourage her husband to take increased responsibility for the family. Mrs. Murphy is not very clear about the circumstances associated with the separation. As she explains it, Mr. Murphy was having a difficult time making ends meet and had experienced a series of disappointments in finding work in the technical aspects of theater. Believing that he would have an easier time finding work in California, he decided to move. Mrs.

Murphy did not want to leave her home and family and decided she would not join him. The result was that the couple drifted apart, without any clear understanding about the future.

To make ends meet, Mrs. Murphy began with a variety of part-time jobs. Both to help her out and as a vehicle for their own investments, the Pescatores purchased the home in which Mrs. Murphy now lives. As a result of her many contacts in the community, Mrs. Murphy has been able to secure an important position in the city administration, where she runs a human services program that has been regarded as highly successful. However, much of the work for this program must be done at night, requiring Mrs. Murphy to be away from home quite frequently in the evening. Since her mother will not baby-sit, Mrs. Murphy has been forced to make a series of elaborate arrangements for sitters that continues to be a source of conflict between herself and her three children.

During the past several years, Mrs. Murphy has also assumed important leadership positions in her neighborhood, representing a very vocal segment of the community opposed to forced school integration. Mrs. Murphy's articulate statements on behalf of her position, together with her organizational skill, have earned her visibility within her community, and there have been numerous suggestions that she run for elective office. Mrs. Murphy acknowledges that she finds such suggestions to be tempting and has formed an enthusiastic group of volunteers to help her if she decides to make such an effort.

Even though she has been active in community affairs and has taken on a significant city job, Mrs. Murphy does not feel any allegiance with the women's movement. She regards work as a necessity forced on her as a result of her husband's problems in supporting a family. Further, she attributes much of her own present success to luck, even though it is clear that she is a highly effective political organizer. She finds working with the budget to be the most challenging and satisfying aspect of her work and observes that in contrast to people who can be unfaithful, figures always tell the truth. At the same time, she observes that, if a woman is lucky enough to have a husband who can support her, it is better that she stay home and take care of the children.

This latter observation is somewhat ironic in view of the apparent difficulty Mrs. Murphy has encountered caring for her children. The children complain that she is as unavailable to them as she perceives her own mother as having been to her and also that she is as rigid and unyielding. Mrs. Murphy expects the children to follow a tight schedule based largely on her own. The children appear full of smoldering rebellion, and there are times of marked strife between Mrs. Murphy and Barbara, now in second grade. Indeed, such a battle was taking place on the morning of the most recent visit when Barbara had apparently thrown her plate and glass in a temper tantrum. Both Mrs. Pescatore and Mrs. Murphy have commented on this problem with Barbara's temper tantrums, and Mrs. Murphy acknowledged that, on the basis of suggestions by Barbara's teachers, she had talked over Barbara's situation with a psychiatrist friend. According to Mrs. Murphy, many of Barbara's problems stem from the fact that she has grown up in a household with so many boys and without a father.

The youngest boy has continued to show a severe school phobia and has been seen by a guidance counselor on a regular basis. The appearance of this school phobia would be expected on the basis of observations of Mrs. Murphy's relationship with Ralph made some four years previous, as well as on the basis of her attitudes toward the issue of appropriate closeness on the MAS. The oldest child has also been expected to provide much of the supervision for his younger sister and brother. Mrs. Murphy says all her hopes are placed on William who, she believes, might become a lawyer. Currently, William is interested in singing and says that he would like to be an opera singer like Caruso.

Watching Mrs. Murphy with her children and hearing her tell of her life with them, it is clear that she has very mixed feelings regarding the maternal role, which reflect both feelings of suffering engendered by having to give to the children and her continuing difficulty in establishing satisfying relationships more generally. As she says, in talking about the maternal role:

> There's really no joy in motherhood. Motherhood is a chore and it's a constant working, morning, noon, and night, of preaching to them, and showing them right and wrong.

She also complains that she is so uncertain what is best to do in rearing her children. She says that she sees one way of rearing them, but that others, particularly her mother, see another way. Caught between such conflicting alternatives, she feels unable to make any decisions at all.

Care of the children serves as the basis for considerable conflict between Mrs. Murphy and her mother. Mrs. Murphy acknowledges that her mother does not approve of the way she is bringing the children up. Mrs. Pescatore still maintains that Mrs. Murphy permits the children too much "back talk." Mrs. Pescatore also complains that her daughter is away from home too often, particularly in the evening, and that the babysitters, generally high school girls in the neighborhood, are not sufficiently reliable or mature. When confronted by her mother regarding this issue, she has challenged her mother to help with childcare so that she would not need to use teenagers as babysitters.

In some respects, Mrs. Murphy has improved her circumstances over the past four years. Since she no longer shares a house with her parents, she is able to avoid much of the daily contact that provided an opportunity for conflict with her mother. The separation from Mr. Murphy has meant that the stimulus for much of this controversy has disappeared. Most suprising, and not expected on the basis of earlier contacts with Mrs. Murphy, has been the way she has been able to rely on those traditional values that had been such an important source of security for her, as well as for her mother, as a means for providing the sense of excitement she had sought earlier in her adult life, but had foregone when it conflicted with her concern regarding issues of safety and certainty. Mrs. Murphy's demonstrated effectiveness working both on her own behalf and that of her community has been an important source of self-esteem, although she still feels particularly vulnerable to her mother's criticisms. At the same time, Mrs. Murphy appears to be a rather lonely woman, with few satisfying, intimate relationships. As her children grow up, the vicissitudes of the family struggle across the generations will begin to appear in the third generation. Indeed, two of Mrs. Murphy's three children show some difficulty at home or in school and either need or have received professional help.

CONCLUSION

Additional information gathered from members of these four multigeneration families after four years shows considerable continuity of personality and adjustment over time, together with surprising changes, the result of personal initiative, courage, and hard work. Perhaps the greatest change has been shown by Mrs. Pescatore, who has both taken on a new career and has begun, for the first time in many years, to explore the world beyond the security of her own house and yard. It is interesting to note that those grandparents most concerned with this issue of security, particularly Mrs. Pescatore and Mrs. Limpari, have traveled the most extensively over the past four years. Mrs. Limpari's willingness to organize her assets and to use some of her accumulated savings for the comfort of her husband and herself is also notable.

None of these four grandparental families face the severe economic pressures so often associated with aging. Indeed, both Mrs. Limpari and Mrs. Giorgio seem to have made particularly good investments. The Pescatores have enough surplus to purchase a home for Mrs. Murphy, and the Scardonis live a comfortable but frugal life. Two of the four grandmothers have had some serious illness during the past four years, and two of the three living grandfathers have also had some serious illness, but only Mr. Limpari has actually retired over the past four years.

Within the mother generation, both families living with the wife's mother have moved out. Problems in the relationship between the generations directly affected the Czajas' decision to move and may also have influenced Mrs. Pescatore's request that her daughter move. However, three of the four families report continuing and frequent personal contact, so that even moderate geographic distance has not altered the close mutually supportive relations between the generations. The greatest changes over the past four years within the parental generation was the Murphys' separation and Mrs. Murphy's subsequent return to work. However, even four years previously it was clear that this couple had serious marital problems. Mr. McGorty has retired to help his wife around the house; this unusually early retirement can be understood in terms of the relationship among husband and wife, where, by mutual agreement and comparable with their personalities, Mrs. McGorty has been the more instrumental and assertive member.

It is interesting to note that, within those two families (the Murphys and Russos) in which, four years previously, the mother had shown less adaptive attitudes regarding the issue of attaining appropriate closeness, the present relationship between mother and children is still a particularly ambivalent one. Mrs. Murphy and her children seem to be engaged in a continuing conflict regarding continuity of their care. The children are rebellious, and Mrs. Murphy's daughter, in particular, appears to be having problems both at home and at school. Mrs. Murphy is explicit in her recognition that she obtains little satisfaction from childcare, a sentiment echoed by Mrs. Russo as well. In contrast with Mrs. Murphy's daughter, who is rebellious, Mrs. Russo's daughter is unusually compliant and appears to be somewhat depressed. Levy (1943) suggested that maternal overprotectiveness, such as is reflected in conflict regarding issues of separation and closeness in the mother-child relationship, arises from the hostility the mother feels regarding childcare. The wish to be apart from the child takes the reverse form in the expressed attitude favoring undue closeness and fear of separation. Ambivalent feelings regarding the maternal role may lead to oversolicitousness in the mother's fear that, magically, her destructive wishes will be realized. It is certainly the case that these two mothers have expressed very ambivalent feelings regarding the maternal role. Early attitudes toward the issue of separation and appropriate closeness, such as measured by the MAS, may have some value in predicting subsequent maternal adjustment.

While based on only a very small number of women in each generation, findings from this interim contact suggest that the women's movement has had little impact on either working-class or middle-class mothers and grandmothers. Three of the four grandmothers have had to work as an economic necessity. Even in the case of Mrs. Pescatore, who has begun to work over the past four years, the decision to work had little impact on her prevailing attitudes toward the woman's role in society. None of the four women in the mother generation report being at all influenced by the women's movement. While varying in the degree of satisfaction they report with their roles as housewives, wives, and mothers, none of the four mothers believe that a change is required in the role of women within society and each subscribes to the traditional (expressive) feminine role of housewife and mother so characteristic of the parental phase of the life cycle (T. Parsons, 1955; Gutmann, 1975).

In her interview study of a small number of working-class women, Rubin (1976) reports a finding similar to that of the present study regarding the women's movement. A similar finding also emerges from the earlier survey research study of housewives (Social Research, Inc., 1972). While it has been claimed that social innovations "trickle down" from the middle to the working class, even the middle-class women in this study maintain that the women's movement has had little influence on their lives. It is not difficult to understand that the grandmothers would pay little attention to such possibilities for social change. Historical circumstances shaping rather conservative political and social views among this particular cohort of older women, combined with the impact of aging itself on political attitudes, together with generation in the life cycle, all contribute to the unwillingness of these women to examine their roles in society or to embrace social change. The lack of interest in the women's movement shown by the women in the mother generation is more surprising. It is likely that the impact of the parental imperative (Gutmann, 1975) is so powerful as to exclude the possibility of reconsideration of their adult roles by women who are already parents. Indeed, much of the emphasis of the women's movement has been on the development of alternatives to these traditional roles among young women just completing their education who are in a quite different phase of the personal and family life cycle from the women in the mother generation in this study.

Finally, with regard to the central concern of the study—the relationship between mothers of young children and their own mothers—the past four years seem to have brought about few changes. Mrs. Russo is more explicitly concerned with the impact of her lifelong overly close and conflicted relationship with her mother, while Mrs. Czaja has become increasingly aware of the impact on her own morale of her mother's continuing interpersonal distance. Positive change in Mrs. McGorty's relationship with her mother has occurred largely as a result of her mother's increased need to accept her daughter's bid for closeness resulting from her own and Mr. Limpari's illnesses. Conflict between Mrs. Pescatore and Mrs. Murphy has been lessened only because the two generations no longer share a common household and because, as a result of work schedules, they no longer spend as much time together. Such changes appear to be largely the result of external circumstances rather than of intrinsic changes resulting from continuing personality development in either generation across adulthood.

Regardless of the quality of the actual relationship between women in the two generations it is clear that each of the four mothers sought to maintain a relatively close and intimate relationship with her own mother, while each of the four grandmothers, at a very different stage in her own adult psychological development, has expressed some discomfort regarding this close psychological tie. Mrs. Czaja has found it difficult to share a household with her mother, but is also hurt by her mother's continuing lack of interest in being with her. Mrs. McGorty has managed to obtain much of the closeness she had sought earlier, while Mrs. Murphy continues to hope for increased closeness with her mother and Mrs. Russo struggles to preserve a very intimate relationship by defending against primitive destructive wishes that would otherwise threaten the continuity of the symbiosis. Mrs. Limpari has largely resigned herself to greater dependence on her daughter, while Mrs. Giorgio and Mrs. Scardoni are too greatly concerned about their own aging to be able to acknowledge their daughters' concerns. Mrs. Pescatore attempts increased closeness, but then becomes increasingly anxious and protects herself from this closeness by stinging criticism.

This continuing psychological struggle between the two generations of adult women in these four families has had an impact on the adjustment of the daughters in the third generation. Daughters in those families in which the relationship between mother and grandmother is characterized by greatest overt strife and continuing closeness and intimacy (Scardoni-Russo and Pescatore-Murphy) themselves show greater difficulty in personal adjustment. Daughters in those families in which there has been less strife and more comfortable and continuing interdependence across the generations with the ability to tolerate personal differences and disagreements (Limpari-McGorty and Giorgio-Czaja) show better personal adjustment. Particularly striking is the extent that Mrs. McGorty's oldest daughter has continued the competence and community concern characteristic of both her mother and grandmother. Such findings point to the importance of the nature of continuing relations across the generations of adults within the family on the adjustment of succeeding generations.

While a review of the four families in this study after a period of four years has led to few changes in the picture that had previously emerged regarding the adult development and present adjustment of either mother or grandmother, it is equally clear that time does not stand still and that as a result of external life events and individual decisions and initiatives there may well be important psychological changes in either generation, as well as among the children in the third generation. While continuity of both personal adjustment and social relations appears to have been most characteristic of these families over time, there is a danger in social science research that insufficient allowance will be made for the possibility of change. It is still true that more is known about factors accounting for continuity in personality and adjustment than those accounting for change. Continuing studies of multigeneration families over a period of many years can do much to enrich the understanding of human development across the life cycle.

REFERENCES

Abramson, H. *Ethnic Diversity in Catholic America*. New York: Wiley-Interscience, 1973.

Abraham, K. A short study of the development of libido, viewed in the light of the mental disorders (1924), In Abraham, K., *Selected Papers on Psychoanalysis*. New York: Basic Books, 1960, 418–502.

Abrahams, J., & Varon, E. *Maternal Dependency and Schizophrenia: Mothers and Daughters in a Therapeutic Group*. New York: International Universities Press, 1953.

Ackerman, N. *The Psychodynamics of Family Life*. New York: Basic Books, 1958.

Ackerman, N., & Franklin, P. Family dynamics and the reversibility of delusional formation: A case study in family therapy. In Boszormenyi-Nagy I. & J. Framo, (Eds.), *Intensive Family Therapy: Theoretical and Practical Aspects*. New York: Harper-Hoeber, 1965, 245–287.

Adamic, L. *A Nation of Nations*. New York: Harper Brothers, 1944.

Adams, B. *Kinship in an Urban Setting*. Chicago: Markham Publishing Co., 1968.

Adams, B. Isolation, function and beyond: American kinship in the 1960's. *Journal of Marriage and the Family,* 1970, 32, 575–597.

Addams, J. *Twenty Years at Hull House*. New York: Macmillan, 1914.

Adorno, T.. Frenkel-Brunswick, E., Levinson, D. & Sanford, R. N. *The Authoritarian Personality*. New York: Harper & Row, 1950.

Ainsworth, M. Patterns of attachment behavior shown by the infant in interaction with his mother. *Merrill-Palmer Quarterly,* 1964, 10, 51–58.

Ainsworth, M. Object relations, dependency, and attachment: A theoretical review of the mother-infant relationship, *Child Development,* 1969, 40, 969–1025.

Ainsworth, M. The development of infant-mother attachment, In B. Caldwell, & H. Ricciuti (Eds.), *Review of Child Development Research*. Chicago: University of Chicago Press, 1973, 1–93.

Albrecht, R. The relationships of older parents with their children. *Marriage and Family Living,* 1954a, 16, 32–35.

Albrecht, R. The parental responsibilities of grandparents. *Marriage and Family Living,* 1954b, 16, 201–204.

Aldous, J. Intergenerational visiting patterns: Variation in boundary maintenance as an explanation. *Family Process,* 1967, 6, 235–251.

Aldous, J., & Hill, R. Social.cohesion, lineage type, and intergenerational transmission. *Social Forces,* 1965, 43, 471–482.

Allport, G. W. *Personality: A Psychological Interpretation*. New York: Holt, Rinehart & Winston, 1937.

Allport, G. W. The general and the unique in psychological science. *Journal of Personality,* 1962, 30, 405–422.

Anderson, W. *Rural Family Participation and the Family Life Cycle*. Ithaca, N. Y.: Cornell University Agricultural Experiment Station, 1953, Memoir Number 314.

Angel, K. The role of the internal object and external object in object relationships, separtion anxiety, object constancy and symbiosis. *International Journal of Psychoanalysis*, 1972, 53, 541–546.

Angres, S. Intergenerational Relations and Value Consensus between Young Adults and Their Parents. Unpublished doctoral dissertation, University of Chicago, 1974.

Anspach, D. & Rosenberg, G. Working-class matricentricity. *Journal of Marriage and the Family*, 1972, 34, 437–442.

Anthony, E. J. The reactions of parents to adolescents and to their behavior. In E Anthony & T. Benedek. (Eds.), *Parenthood: Its Psychology and Psychopathology*. Boston: Little, Brown, 1970, 307–324.

Anthony, E. J. Folie a Deux: A developmental failure in the process of separation-individuation, In J. McDevitt, & C. Settlage (Eds.), *Separation-Individuation: Essays in Honor of Margret Mahler*. New York: International Universities Press, 1971, 253–273.

Apple, D. The social structure of grandparenthood, *American Anthropologist*, 1956, 58, 656–663.

Arensberg, C. *The Irish Countryman: An Anthropological Study* (1937). Gloucester, Mass: *Peter Smith*, 1959.

Arensberg, C., & Kimball, S. *Family and Community in Ireland* (2nd ed.). Cambridge, Mass.: Harvard University Press, 1968.

Aristotle, Nicomachean ethics. Translated by W. D. Ross, In R. McKeon (Ed.), *The Basic Works of Aristotle*. New York: Random House, 1941, 935–1126.

Arnold, D. Dimensional sampling: An approach for studying a small number of cases. *American Sociologist*, 1970, 5, 147–150.

Aronfreed, J. *Conduct and Conscience: The Socialization of Internalized Control over Behavior*. New York: Academic Press, 1969a.

Aronfreed, J. The concept of internalization. In D. Goslin (Ed.), *Handbook of Socialization Theory and Research*. Chicago: Rand McNally, 1969b, 263–324.

Atkinson, J. W., & McClelland, D. C. The projective expression of needs. II. The effect of different intensities of the hunger drive on thematic apperception. *Journal of Experimental Psychology*, 1948, 38, 643–658.

Axelrad, S., & Maury, L. Identification as a mechanism of adaption. In G. Wilbur & W. Muensterberger (Eds.), *Psychoanalysis and Culture*. New York: International Universities Press, 1961, 168–184.

Balint, D. *Primary Love and Psychoanalytic Technique*. New York: Liveright, 1965.

Bandura, A., & Walters, R. *Social Learning Theory and Personality Development*. New York: Holt, Rinehart & Winston, 1963.

Bane, M. J. *Here to Stay: American Families in the Twentieth Century*. New York: Basic Books, 1976.

Banfield, E. *The Moral Basis of a Backward Society*. New York: Free Press, 1958.

Barrabee, P., & Von Mering, O. Ethnic variations in mental stress in families with psychotic children. *Social Problems*, 1953, 1, 48–53.

Barron, F. A case study of a residual, In A. Burton, & R. Harris, (Eds.), *Clinical Studies of Personality*. New York: Harper and Brothers, 1955, 668–693.

Barron, M. *People Who Intermarry: Intermarriage in a New England Industrial Community*. Syracuse, N.Y.: Syracuse University Press, 1946.

Barth, F. Introduction, In F. Barth, (Ed.), *Ethnic Groups and Boundaries: The Social Organization of Culture Difference*. Boston: Little, Brown, 1969, 9–38.

Barzini, L. *The Italians*. New York: Atheneum, 1964.

Basch, M. Developmental psychology and explanatory theory in psychoanalysis. *Annual of Psychoanalysis*, 1977, 5, 229–263.

Beals, R. Urbanism, urbanization, and acculturation. *American Anthropologist*, 1951, 53, 1–10.

Behrens, M. Childbearing and the character structure of the mother. *Child Development*, 1954, 25, 225–238.

Bell, N. Extended family relations of disturbed and well families. *Family Process*, 1962, 1, 175–193.

Beloff, H. The structure and origin of the anal character. *Genetic Psychology Monographs*, 1957, 55, 141–172.

Benedek, T. Parenthood as a developmental phase: A contribution to the libido theory. *Journal of the American Psychoanalytic Association*, 1959, 7, 389–417.

Benedek, T. Parenthood during the life-cycle. In E. Anthony & T. Benedek, (Eds.), *Parenthood: Its Psychology and Psychopathology*. Boston: Little, Brown, 1970, 185–206.

Benedek, T. Discussion: Parenthood as a developmental phase. In T. Benedek, *Psychoanalytic Investigations: Selected Papers*. Chicago: Quadrangle Press, 1973, 401–407.

Bender, E., & Kagiwada, G. Hansen's law of "Third-Generation Return" and the study of American religio-ethnic groups. *Phylon*, 1968, 29, 360–370.

Bengtson, V. The generation gap: A review and typology of social psychological perspectives. *Youth and Society*, 1970, 2, 7–32.

Bengtson, V. Inter-age perceptions and the generation gap. *Gerontologist*, 1971, 11, 86–89.

Bengtson, V. Family solidarity and psychological well-being in three generations. Paper presented as the symposium on life-span models of adjustment, Annual Meeting of the American Psychological Association, Honolulu, 1972.

Bengtson, V., & Black, K. D. Intergenerational relations and continuities in socialization. In P. Baltes, & K. W. Schaie, (Eds.), *Life Span Developmental Psychology: Personality and Socialization*. New York: Academic Press, 1973, 207 –234.

Bengtson, V., & Kuypers, J. Generational differences and the developmental stake, *Aging and Human Development*, 1971, 2, 249–260.

Beres, D. Vicissitudes of superego function and superego precursors in childhood. *Psychoanalytic Study of the Child*, 1958, 13, 324–351.

Berkowitz, L. *Aggression: A Social Psychological Analysis*. New York: McGraw-Hill, 1962.

Bernard, J. *Women, Wives, Mothers*. Chicago: Aldine, 1975.

Bernardo, F., Kinship interaction and communication among space-age migrants. *Journal of Marriage and the Family*, 1967, 29, 541–554.

Bettelheim, B. *Truants from Life.* New York: Free Press, 1955.

Bettelheim, B. The problem of generations. *Daedalus,* 1962, 91, 68–96.

Bettelheim, B. *The Empty Fortress.* New York: Free Press, 1967.

Bettelheim, B., & Sylvester, E. Parental occupations and childrens' symptoms. *American Journal of Orthopsychiatry,* 1950, 785–795.

Bianco, C. *The Two Rosetos.* Bloomington: Indiana University Press, 1974.

Bibring, G. Some considerations of the psychological process in pregnancy. *Psychoanalytic Study of the Child,* 1959, 14, 113–121.

Bibring, G., Dwyer, T., Huntington, D., Valenstein, A., A study of the psychological processes of pregnancy and the earliest mother-child relationship. *Psychoanalytic Study of the Child,* 1961, 16, 9–72.

Bild, B. Young Adult-Parent Relationships and Consensus. Unpublished doctoral dissertation, University of Chicago, 1974.

Bleda, S. Socioeconomic, demographic, and cultural bases of ethnic residential segregation. *Ethnicity,* 1979, 6, 147–167.

Block, J., Haan, N., & Smith, M. B. Socialization correlates of student activism. *Journal of Social Issues,* 1969, 29, 143–177.

Blood, R., & Wolfe, D. *Husbands and Wives: The Dynamics of Married Living.* New York: Free Press, 1960.

Blos, P., The second individuation process of adolescence. *Psychoanalytic Study of the Child,* 1967, 12, 162–186.

Blum, G. A study of the psychoanalytic theory of psychosexual development. *Genetic Psychology Monographs,* 1949, 39, 3 –99.

Blum, G. *The Blacky Pictures.* New York: Psychological Corporation, 1950.

Blum, G. A guide for the research use of the Blacky pictures. *Journal of Projective Techniques,* 1962, 26, 3–29.

Blum, H. Reconstruction in a case of post-partum depression. *Psychoanalytic Study of the Child,* 1978, 33, 335–362.

Blumberg, L., & Bell, R. Urban migration and kinship ties. *Social Problems,* 1959, 6, 328–340.

Boissevain, J. Poverty and politics in a Sicilian agro-town. *International Archives of Ethnography,* 1966, 1, 198–236.

Borke, H. A family over three generations: The transmission of interacting and relating patterns. *Journal of Marriage and the Family,* 1967, 29, 638–655.

Borke, H. Continuity and change in the transmission of adaptive patterns over two generations. *Marriage and Family Living,* 1963, 25, 294–301.

Boszormenyi-Nagy, I., & Spark, G. *Invisible Loyalties: Reciprocity in Intergenerational Family Therapy.* New York: Harper & Row, 1973.

Botwinick, J. *Aging and Behavior: A Comparative Integration of Research Findings.* New York: Springer, 1973.

Bott, E. *Family and Social Network* (2nd ed.). London: Travistock Publications, 1971.

Bowlby, J. *Attachment and Loss. Volume I: Attachment* New York: Basic Books, 1969.

Bowlby, J. *Attachment and Loss. Volume II: Separation, Anxiety, and Anger* New York: Basic Books, 1973.

Boyd, R. The valued grandparent: A changing social role, In W. Donahue (Ed.), *Living in the Multigeneration Family*. Ann Arbor, Mich.: Institute of Gerontology, 1969, 90–106.

Breton, R. Institutional completeness of ethnic communities and the personal relations of immigrants. *American Journal of Sociology*, 1964, 70, 193–205.

Briggs, J., Italians in Italy and America: A Study of Change Within Continuity for Immigrants to Three American Cities, 1720–1930. Unpublished doctoral dissertation, University of Minnesota, 1972.

Briggs, J. Family structure, education and mobility: A cross-generational approach. *Division Generator, American Educational Research Association* 1974, 4, 3–8.

Brim, O., Jr. Socialization through the life cycle. In O. Brim, Jr. & S. Wheeler, *Socialization after Childhood: Two Essays*. New York: Wiley, 1966, 1–50.

Bronfenbrenner, U. Socialization and social class through time and space, In E. Maccoby, T. Newcomb & E. Hartley (Eds.), *Readings in Social Psychology* New York: Holt, Rinehart & Winston, 1958a, 400–425.

Bronfenbrenner, U. The study of indentification through interpersonal processes. In T. Taguri & L. Petruillo E. K. *Person Perception and Interpersonal Behavior* Stanford, Calif.: Stanford University Press, 1958b, 110–130.

Bronfenbrenner, U. Freudian theories of identification and their derivatives. *Child Development* 1960, 31, 15–40.

Brown, A. Satisfying relationships for the elderly and their patterns of disengagement. *Gerontologist*, 1974, 14, 258–262.

Brown, G., & Harris, T. *Social Origins of Depression: A Study of Psychiatric Disorder in Women*. New York: Free Press, 1978.

Brown, L. *Immigration*. New York: Longmans, Green and Company, 1933.

Bruch, H. Family transactions in eating disorders. *Comprehensive Psychiatry*, 1971, 12, 238–248.

Bruch, H. *Eating Disorders: Obesity, Anorexia Nervosa and the Person Within*. New York: Basic Books, 1973.

Burgess, E. The family as a unity of interacting personalities. *Family*, 1926, 7, 3–9.

Cain, L. Life–course and social structure. In R. E. Faris (Ed.), *Handbook of Modern Sociology*. Chicago: Rand McNally, 1964, 272–309.

Cain, L. Age status and generational phenomena: The new old people in contemporary America. *Gerontologist*, 1967, 7, 83–92.

Caldwell, B. The effects of infant care. In M. Hoffman & L. Hoffman (Eds.), *Review of Child Development Research*, Vol. 2. New York: Russell-Sage Foundation, 1964, 9–88.

Caldwell, B. The fourth dimension in early child education. In R. O. Hess & R. Bear, (Eds.), *Early Education*. Chicago: Aldine, 1968, 71–82.

Campbell, A., Converse, P., & Rodgers, W. *The Quality of American Life*. New York: Russell Sage Foundation, 1976.

Campbell, D.,& Fiske, D. Convergent and discriminant validation by the multi-method-multitrait matrix. *Psychological Bulletin*, 1959, 36, 81–105.

Campisi, P. Ethnic family patterns: The Italian family of the United States. *American Journal of Sociology*, 1948, 53, 443–449.

Cancian, F. The southern Italian peasant: World view and political behavior. *Anthropoligical Quarterly,* 1966, 28, 1–18.

Caudill, W. & Doi, L. T. Interrelations of psychiatry, culture, and emotions in Japan. In I. Galdston (Ed.) *Man's Image in Medicine and Anthropology.* New York: International Universities Press, 1963, 374–421.

Caudill, W., & Plath, W. Who sleeps by whom? Parent-child involvement in urban Japanese families. *Psychiatry,* 1969, 32, 12–43.

Caudill, W. & L. Frost, A comparison of maternal care and infant behavior in Japanese-American, American, and Japanese families. In W. Lebra (Ed.), *Youth, Socialization, and Mental Health.* Honolulu: University Press of Hawaii, 1974, 3–15.

Caudill, W., & Weinstein, H. Maternal care and infant behavior in Japanese and American urban middle class families. In R. Hill & Konig R. (Eds.) *Families in East and West: Socialization Process and Kinship Ties.* The Hague: Mouton, 1970, 39–71.

Chapman, C. *Milocca: A Sicilian Village* (1935). Cambridge Mass.: Schenkman Publishing Co.; 1971.

Child, I. *Italian or American? The Second Generation in Conflict.* New Haven: Yale University Press, 1943.

Chodorow, N. Being and doing: A cross-cultural examination of the socialization of males and females. In V. Gornick & B. Moran (Eds.), *Woman in Sexist Society: Studies in Power and Powerlessness.* New York: Basic Books, 1971, 173–197.

Chodorow, N. *The Reproduction of mothering: Psychoanalysis and the Sociology of Gender.* Berkeley: University of California Press, 1978.

Choldin, H. Kinship networks in immigration. *International Migration Review,* 1973, 8, 163–175.

Chown, S. M. Personality and aging. In K. W. Schaie (Ed.), *Theory and Methods of Research on Aging.* Morgantown: West Virginia Library, 1968, 134–157.

Clark, M. Changing value systems and intergenerational conflict: American subcultural comparisons. Paper read at International Gerontological Congress, Washington, D.C., 1969.

Clark, M. Personal communication, 1973.

Clarke, A. H. The dominant matriarch syndrome. *British Journal of Psychiatry,* 1967, 113, 1069–1071.

Cleveland, E., & Longaker, W. Neurotic patterns in the family. In A. Leighton A. (Ed.), *Explorations in Social Psychiatry.* New York: Basic Books, 1957, 167–195.

Cohler, B. Character, mental illness and mothering. In H. Grunebaum, H. J. Weiss, B. Cohler, C. Hartman, & D. Gallant, *Mentally Ill Mothers and Their Children.* Chicago: University of Chicago Press, 1975, 234–512.

Cohler, B. The significance of the therapist's feelings in the residential treatment of anorexia nervosa. In S. Feinstein & P. Giovacchini (Eds.), *Adolescent Psychiatry,* 1977, 5, 352–384.

Cohler, B., Grunebaum, H., Weiss, J., Gallant, D., & Abernethy, V. Social relations, stress, and psychiatric hospitalization among mothers of young children. *Social Psychiatry,* 1974, 9, 7–12.

Cohler, B., Gallant, D., Grunebaum, H., Weiss, J., & Gamer, E. Child care attitudes and the development of the young children of mentally ill and well mothers. *Psychological Reports*, 1980, 46, 31–46.

Cohler, B., Grunebaum, H., Weiss, J., Gallant, D., & Hartman, C. Child care attitudes and adaptation to the maternal role among mentally ill and well mothers. *American Journal of Orthopsychiatry*, 1976, 46, 123–134.

Cohler, B., Grunebaum, H., Weiss, J., Hartman, C., & Gallant, D. Life-stress and psychopathology among mothers of young children. *American Journal of Orthopsychiatry*, 1975, 45, 58–73.

Cohler, B., Grunebaum, H., Weiss, J., Robbins, D., Shader, R., Gallant, D., Hartman, C. Social role performance and psychopathology among recently hospitalized and non-hospitalized mothers. II: Correlates with life-stress and self-reported psychopathology. *Journal of Nervous and Mental Disease*, 1974, 159, 81–90.

Cohler, B., & Lieberman, M. Ethnicity and Personal adaptation. *International Journal of Group Tensions*, 1978, 7, 20–41.

Cohler, B., & Lieberman, M. Personality development across the second-half of life: Findings from a study of Irish, Italian and Polish-American men and women. In D. Gelfand & A. Kutznik (Eds.), *Ethnicity and aging*. New York: Springer, 1979, 227–245.

Cohler, B., & Lieberman, M. *Social relations and mental health among three European ethnic groups*. Research on Aging, 1981, 3, In Press.

Cohler, B., Weiss, J., & Grunebaum, H. Childcare attitudes and emotional disturbance among mothers of young children. *Genetic Psychology Monographs*, 1970, 82, 3–47.

Cohler, B., Weiss, J., & Grunebaum, H. "Short-form" content scales for the MMPI. *Journal of Personality Assessment*, 1974, 38, 663–672.

Cohler, B., Woolsey, S., Weiss, J., & Grunebaum, H. Childrearing attitudes among mothers volunteering and revolunteering for a psychological study. *Psychological Reports*, 1968, 23, 603–612.

Colarusso, C., & Nemiroff, R. Some observations and hypotheses about the psychoanalytic theory of adult development. *International Journal of Psychoanalysis*, 1979, 60, 59–71.

Collingwood, R. G. *The Idea of History* (1946). New York: Oxford University Press, 1976.

Cooper, J., & McNeill, J. A study of housebound housewives and their interaction with their children. *Journal of Child Psychology and Psychiatry*, 1968, 9, 173–188.

Cornelisen, A. *Torregreca: Life Death and Miracles*. Boston: Little Brown, 1969.

Cornelisen, A. *Women of the Shadows*. Boston: Little Brown, 1976.

Couch, A. & Keniston, K. Yeasayers and naysayers: Agreeing response set as a personality variable. *Journal of Abnormal and Social Psychology*, 1960, 60, 151–174.

Covello, L. *The Social Background of the Italo-American School Child* (1944). Totowa, N. J.: Rowman and Littlefield, 1972.

Cox, R. *Youth into Maturity: A Study of Men and Women in the First Years after College*. New York: Mental Health Materials Center, 1970.

Crevecouer, J. *Letters from an American Farmer* (1782). New York: Dutton, 1957.

Cronbach, L. J. Processes affecting scores on "understanding of others" and "assumed similarity." *Psychological Bulletin,* 1955, 52, 177–193.

Cronbach, L., & Meehl, P. Construct validity in psychological tests. *Psychological Bulletin,* 1955, 52, 281–302.

Cronin, C. *The Sting of Change: Sicilians in Sicily and Australia.* Chicago: University of Chicago Press, 1970.

Cumming, E., & Henry, W. *Growing Old.* New York: Basic Books, 1961.

D'Andrade, R. Sex differences and cultural institutions. In E. Maccoby (Ed.), *The Development of Sex Differences.* Stanford, Calif.: Stanford University Press, 1966, 173–203.

Danesino, A., & Layman, W. Contrasting personality patterns of high and low achievers among college students of Italian and Irish descent. *Journal of Psychology,* 1969, 72, 71–83.

Darroch, A. G., & Marston, W. G. The social class basis of ethnic residental segregation: The Canadian case. *American Journal of Sociology,* 1971, 77, 491–510.

Davidson, P., & Costello, C. *N-1: Experimental Studies of Single Cases.* New York: Van Nostrand Insight Books, 1969.

Davis, A. *Social Class Influences on Learning.* Cambridge, Mass.: Harvard University Press, 1955.

Decarie, T. *Intelligence and Affectivity in Early Childhood.* New York: International Universities Press, 1965.

Dell, P., & Applebaum, A. Trigenerational enmeshment: Unresolved ties of single parents to family of origin. *American Journal of Orthopsychiatry,* 1977, 47, 52–59.

Demos, J., *A Little Community: Family Life in Plymouth Colony.* New York: Oxford University Press, 1970.

Deutsch, F. A footnote to Freud's "Fragment of an analysis of a case of hysteria," *Psychoanalytic Quarterly,* 1957, 26, 159–167.

Deutsch, H. *The Psychology of Women,* Vols. 1 and 2. New York: Grune and Stratton, 1945.

Deutsch, H. An introduction to the discussion of the psychological problems of pregnancy. In M. Senn (Ed.), *Problems of Early Infancy,* Second Conference, New York: Macy Foundation, 1948.

Deutscher, I. The quality of post-parental life: Definitions of the situation. *Journal of Marriage and the Family,* 1964, 26, 52–59.

Devereux, G. Ethnic identity: Its logical functions and its dysfunctions. In G. DeVos & L. Romanucci-Ross (Eds.), *Ethnic Identity: Cultural Continuities and Change.* Palo Alto, Calif.: Mayfield, 1975, 5–41.

Diamond, M. A critical review of the ontogeny of human sexual behavior. *Quarterly Review of Biology,* 1965, 40, 147–175.

Doi, L. T. Amae: A key concept for understanding Japanese personality structure. In R. Smith, & R. Beardsley, (Eds.), *Japanese Culture: Its development and Characteristics.* New York: Viking Fund Publications in Anthropology-Werner-Gren Foundation, 1962, 132–139.

Doi, L. T. Some thoughts on helplessness and the desire to be loved. *Psychiatry,* 1963, 26, 266–272.

Doi, L. T. *The Anatomy of Dependence*. Tokyo: Kodansha International, 1973.

Dore, G. Some social and historical aspects of Italian emigration to America. *Journal of Social History*, 1969, 2, 95–122.

DuBrin, A. J. The Rorschach "eyes" hypothesis and paranoid schizophrenia. *Journal of Clinical Psychology*, 1962, 18, 468–471.

Dunham, H. W. *Community and Schizophrenia*. Detroit, Mich.: Wayne State University Press, 1965.

Dyer, W. The interlocking of work and family social systems among lower occupational families. *Social Forces*, 1956, 34, 230–233.

Edwards, C. Cultural values and role decisions. *Journal of Counseling Psychology*, 1969, 16, 36–40.

Ehrensing, R., & Weitzman, E. The mother-daughter relationship in anorexia nervosa. *Psychosomatic Medicine*, 1970, 32, 201–208.

Ehrenwald, J. Neurosis in the family: A study of psychiatric epidemiology. *Archives of General Psychiatry*, 1960, 3, 232–241.

Eisenstadt, S. N. From Generation to Generation: Age Groups and Social Structure. New York: Free Press, 1956.

Elder, G. *Children of the Great Depression: Social Change in Life Experience*. Chicago: University of Chicago Press, 1974.

Elder, G. Family history and the life-course. In T. Hareven (Ed.), *Transitions: The Family and the Life-Course in Historical Perspective*. New York: Academic Press, 1978, 17–64.

Elles, G. A family pattern of distress. In P. Lomas (Ed.), *The Predicament of the Family*. Neich York: International Universities Press, 1967, 57–89.

Emmerich W. Parental identification in young children. *Genetic Psychology Monographs*, 1958, 60, 257–308.

Erikson, E. *Childhood and Society* (rev. edition). New York: Norton Press, 1963.

Erikson, E. Identity and the life-cycle: Selected papers, *Psychological Issues*, 1959, 1, Monograph number 1. New York: International Universities Press, 1959.

Erikson, E. *Identity: Youth and Crisis* (1952). New York: Norton, 1968.

Erikson, E. Psychosocial identity. In D. Sills (Ed.), *International Encyclopedia of the Social Sciences*. New York: Free Press, 1967, 61–65.

Erikson, E. *Young Man Luther*. New York: Norton, 1958.

Eron, L. Responses of women to the Thematic Apperception Test. *Journal of Consulting Psychology*, 1953, 17, 269–282.

Evans, J. *Three Men*. New York: Knopf, 1954.

Fairbairn, W. R. D. A revised psychopathology of the psychoses and psychoneuroses (1941). In W. R. D. Fairbairn, *Psychoanalytic Studies of the Personality*. London: Tavistock Publications, 1952, 28–58.

Fairbairn, W. R. D. A synopsis of the author's views regarding the structure of personality (1951). In W. R. D. Fairbairn, *Psychoanalytic Studies of the Personality*. London: Tavistock Publications, 1952, 162–179.

Fantl, B., & Schiro, J. Cultural variables in the behavior patterns and symptom formation of fifteen Irish and fifteen Italian female schizophrenics. *International Journal of Social Psychiatry*, 1959, 4, 245–253.

Farber, B. Types of family organization: Child-oriented, home-oriented, and parent-oriented, In A. Rose (Ed.), *Human Behavior and Social Process*. Boston: Houghton Mifflin, 1962, 285–306.

Farber, B. *Kinship and Class: A Midwestern Study*. New York: Basic Books, 1971.

Faris, R. Interaction of generations and family stability. *American Sociological Review*, 1947, 12, 159–165.

Farris, R. L., & Dunham, H. W. *Mental Disorders in Urban Areas*. Chicago: University of Chicago Press, 1939.

Femminella, F. The impact of Italian migration and American Catholicism. *American Catholic Sociological Review*, 1961, 22, 233–241.

Femminella, F. Ethnicity and Ego-Identity. Unpublished doctoral dissertation, New York University, 1968.

Femminella, F. The Italian-American family. In M. Barash & A. Scourby (Eds.), *Marriage and the Family: A Comparative Analysis of Contemporary Problems*. New York: Random House, 1970, 127–143.

Femminella, F., & Quadagno, J. The Italian-American family. In C. Mindel & R. Habenstein (Eds.), *Ethnic Families in America*. New York: Elsevier, 1976, 61–88.

Ferreira, A. J. Family myth and homeostasis. *Archives of General Psychiatry*, 1963, 9, 457–463.

Ferreira, A. J. Family myth, *Psychiatric Research Reports*, 1967, 21, 85–90.

Firestone, H. A Comparative Study of Reformation and Recidivism among Italian and Polish Adult Male Criminal Offenders. Unpublished doctoral dissertation, University of Chicago, 1964.

Firth, R. *Two Studies of Kinship in London*. London: University of London Press, 1956.

Firth, R., Hubert, J., & Forge, A. *Families and Their Relatives: Kinship in a Middle Class Sector of London*. New York: Humanities Press, 1970.

Fischer, J., & Fischer, A. The New Englanders of Orchard Town. In B. Whiting (Ed.), *Six Cultures: Studies of Childrearing*. New York: Wiley, 1963, 869–1010.

Fisher, S., & Fisher, R. A projective test analysis of ethnic subculture themes in families. *Journal of Projective Techniques*, 1960, 24, 366–369.

Fisher, S., & Mendell, D. The communication of neurotic patterns over two and three generations. *Psychiatry*, 1956, 19, 41–56.

Fiske, D. The limits for the conventional science of personality. *Journal of Personality*, 1974, 42, 2–11.

Fiske, D. *Strategies for Personality Research*. San Francisco: Jossey-Bass, 1978.

Flacks, R. The liberated generation: An exploration of the roots of student protest. *Journal of Social Issues*, 1967, 23, 52–75.

Fortes, M., & Evans-Pritchard, E. *African Political Systems*. London: Oxford University Press, 1940.

Francis, E. K. The nature of the ethnic group. *American Journal of Sociology*, 1947, 52, 393–400.

Freeman, L. *Who is Sylvia?* New York: Arbor House, 1979.

Freud, A. *Normality and Psychopathology in Childhood*. New York: International Universities Press, 1965.

Freud, S. Fragment of an analysis of a case of hysteria (1905b). In S. Freud *Standard Edition*, Vol. 7, 7–124.

Freud, S. Three essays on the theory of sexuality (1905a). *Standard Edition*, Vol. 7, 125–243.

Freud, S. Totem and taboo (1912–13). *Standard Edition of the Complete Psychological Works of Sigmund Freud*, Vol. 13, 1–164.

Freud, S. *The Complete Introductory Lectures on Psychoanalysis* (1917, 1932). New York: Norton, 1966.

Freud, S. Mourning and melancholia (1917). *Standard Edition*, Vol. 14, 243–260.

Freud, S. *Group psychology and the analysis of the ego* (1921). *Standard Edition*, Vol. 18, 69–145.

Freud, S. *The ego and the id* (1923). *Standard Edition*, Vol. 19, 12–68.

Freud, S. Inhibitions, symptoms and anxiety (1926). *Standard Edition*, Vol. 20, 87–178.

Freud, S. Splitting of the ego in the defensive processes (1938a). *Standard Edition*, Vol. 23, 271–278.

Freud, S. An outline of psychoanalysis (1938b). *Standard Edition*, Vol. 23, 144–208.

Friday, N. *My Mother/Myself*. New York: Delacorte, 1977.

Fried, E., & Stern, K. The situation of the aged within the family. *American Journal of Orthopsychiatry*, 1948, 18, 31–54.

Fried, M. *The World of the Urban Working Class*. Cambridge: Harvard University Press, 1973.

Friedman, F. The world of "La Miseria." *Partisan Review*, 1953, 20, 218–231.

Furstenberg, F. Industrialization and the American family: A look backward. *American Sociological Review*, 1966, 31, 326–337.

Gage, B. L., & Cronbach, L. J. Conceptual and methodological problems in interpersonal perception. *Psychological Review*, 1955, 62, 411–422.

Galtung, J. *Members of Two Worlds: A Development Study of Three Villages in Southern Italy*. New York: Columbia University Press, 1971.

Gambino, R. *Blood of My Blood*. New York: Doubleday, 1974.

Gans, H. *The Urban Villagers: Group and Class in the Life of Italian-Americans*. New York: Free Press, 1962.

Gardiner, P. *Theories of History*. New York: Free Press, 1959.

Giovacchini, P. Effects of adaptive and disruptive aspects of early object relationships upon later parental functioning. In E. Anthony & T. Benedek (Eds.), *Parenthood: Its Psychology and Psychopathology*. Boston: Little, Brown, 1970, 525–537.

Glaser, D. Dynamics of ethnic identification. *American Sociological Review*, 1958, 23, 31–40.

Glazer, N. America's ethnic pattern. *Commentary*, 1952, 15, 401–408.

Glazer, N. Ethnic groups in America: From national culture to ideology. In M. Berger, T. Abel, & C. Page (Eds.), *Freedom and Control in Modern Society:* New York: Van Nostrand, 1954, 158–173.

Glazer, N., & Moynihan, D. *Beyond the Melting Pot: The Negroes, Puerto Ricans, Jews, Italians, and Irish of New York City* (1963) (Revised Edition) Cambridge Mass. MIT Press, 1970.

Glick, *P. American Families*. New York: Wily, 1957.

Gloye, E., & Zimmerman, I. MMPI item changes by college students under ideal-self response. *Journal of Projective Techniques and Personality Assessment,* 1967, 31, 63–69.

Golab, C. The immigrant and the city: Poles, Italians and Jews in Philadelphia, 1870–1920. In A. Davis & M. Haller (Eds.), *The Peoples of Philadelphia.* Philadelphia: Temple University Press, 1973, 203–230.

Goldfarb, A. Psychodynamics and the three generation family. In Shanas, E., & Streib, G. (Eds.), Social Structure and the Family: Generational Relations. Englewood-Cliffs, N.J.: Printice- Hall, 1965, 10–45.

Goode, W. J., *World Revolution and Family Patterns.* New York: Free Press, 1963.

Goodrich, W. Toward a taxonomy of marriage. In J. Marmor (Ed.), *Handbook of Psychoanalysis.* New York: Basic Books, 1968, 407–423.

Gordon, M. Assimilation in America: Theory and reality. *Daedalus,* 1961, 90, 263–285.

Gordon, M. *Assimilation in American Life: The Role of Race, Religion and National Origins.* New York: Oxford University Press, 1964.

Gordon, M. *Human Nature, Class and Ethnicity.* New York: Oxford University Press, 1978.

Gottheil, E., Paredes, A., & Exline, R. Parental schemata in emotionally disturbed women. *Journal of Abnormal Psychology,* 1968, 73, 416–419.

Gottesman, I. Heritability of personality: A demonstration. *Psychological Monographs,* 1963, 77, Whole Number 572.

Gove, W. & Tudor, J. Adult sex roles and mental illness. *American Journal of Sociology,* 1972, 78, 812–835.

Gray, R., & Smith, T. Effect of employment on sex differences in attitudes toward the parental family. *Journal of Marriage and the Family,* 1960, 22, 36–38.

Gray, S., & Klaus, R. The assessment of parental identification. *Genetic Psychology Monographs,* 1956, 54, 87–114.

Greeley, A. Ethnicity as an influence on behavior. In O. Feinstein, *Ethnic Groups in the City.* Lexington, Mass.: D.C. Heath-Lexington Books, 1971, 3–16.

Greeley, A. *That Most Distressful Nation: The Taming of the American Irish.* Chicago: Quadrangle Books, 1972.

Greeley, A. *Ethnicity in the United States.* New York, Wiley, 1974.

Greeley, A., & McCready, W. Does ethnicity matter. *Ethnicity,* 1974, 1, 89–108.

Green, A. A Re-examination of the marginal man concept. *Social Forces,* 1947, 26, 167–627.

Greenfield, S. Industrialization and the family in sociological theory. *American Journal of Sociology,* 1967, 67, 312–322.

Greenson, R. The struggle against indentification. *Journal of the American Psychoanalytic Association,* 1954a, 2, 200–217.

Greenson, R. Problems of identification. *Journal of the American Psycholanalytic Association,* 1954b, 2, 197–199.

Greenspan, S., & Pollock, G. (Eds.) *The Course of Life: Psychoanalytic Contributions toward Understanding Personality Development.* Washington, D.C.: U.S. Government Printing Office, 1980.

Grummon, D., & Jones, E. Changes over client-centered therapy evaluated in psychoanalytically based thematic apperception test scales. In C. Rogers C. & R. Dymond (Eds.) *Psychotherapy and Personality Change*. Chicago: University of Chicago Press, 1954, 121–144.

Grunebaum, H. The family In H. Grunebaum (Ed.) *The Practice of Community Mental Health*. Boston: Little, Brown, 1970, 57–78.

Guest, A., & Weed, J. Ethnic residential segregation: Patterns of change. *American Journal of Sociology*, 1976, 81, 1088–78.

Gutmann, D. Parenthood: A key to comparative study of the life cycle. In N. Datan & L. Ginsberg (Eds.), *Life-Span Developmental Psychology: Normative Crises*. New York: Academic Press, 1975, 167–184.

Grunebaum, H., Weiss, J., Cohler, B., Hartman, C., & Gallant, D. *Mentally Ill Mothers and Their Children*. Chicago. University of Chicago Press, 1975.

Grunebaum, H., Children at risk for psychosis and their families: Approaches to Prevention. In M. McMillan & S. Henao (Eds.) *Child Psychiatry: Treatment and Research*. New York: Brunner-Mazel, 1977, 172–189

Grunebaum, J., Clinical issues related to the stereotyping of women as mothers, Unpublished Manuscript, Cambridge, Mass., 1980

Hader, M. The importance of grandparents in family life. *Family Process*, 1965, 4, 228–240.

Hagestad, G. *Middle Aged Women and Their Children: Exploring Changes in a Role Relationship*. Unpublished doctoral dissertation, University of Minnesota, 1974.

Hagestad, G. Problems and promises in the social psychology of intergenerational relations. Paper presented to Workshop on Stability and Change in the Family, Committee on Aging, National Research Council, Annapolis, Maryland, 1979.

Hagstrom, W., & Hadden, J. Sentiment and kinship terminology in American society. *Journal of Marriage and the Family, 1965, 27, 324–332*.

Haller, A. O. The urban family, *American Journal of Sociology*, 1961, 66, 621–622.

Hallowell, A. The self and its behavioral environment. In A. Hallowell, *Culture and Experience*. Philadelphia: University of Pennsylvania Press, 1955, 75–110.

Hammer, S. *Daughters and Mothers*. New York: Quadrangle Press, 1975. .

Handel, G. Psychological study of whole families. *Psychological Bulletin*, 1965, 19–41, 63.

Handel, G. The analysis of correlative meaning, in Handel, G. (Ed.) *The Psychosocial Interior of the Family*. Chicago: Aldine Press, 1967, 104–130.

Handel, G. (Ed.) *The Psychosocial Interior of the Family*. Chicago: Aldine, 1967b.

Handlin, O. *The Uprooted (1951* Second Edition). Boston: Little Brown-Atlantic Monthly Press, 1973.

Handlin, O. *Race and Nationality in American Life*. New York: Doubleday Anchor Books, 1957.

Handlin, O. (Ed.) *Immigration as a Factor in American History*. Englewood Cliffs N.J.: Prentice-Hall, 1959.

Handlin, O. Historical perspectives on the American ethnic group, *Daedalus*, 1961, 90, 220–233.

Handlin, O. *Boston's Immigrants. A Study in Acculturation* (1959). New York: Atheneum Books, 1972.

Hansen, M. *The Immigrant in American History*. Cambridge, Mass.: Harvard University Press, 1940.

Hansen, M. The third generation in America: A classic essay in immigrant history. *Commentary*, 1952, 14, 492–500.

Hareven, T., & Langenbach, R. *Amoskeag: Life and Work in an American Factory Town*. New York: Pantheon Books, 1978.

Harkins, E. Effects of empty nest transition on self-report of psychological and physical well being. *Journal of Marriage and the Family*, 1978, 40, 549–556.

Harris, I. *Normal Children and Mothers*. New York: The Free Press, 1959.

Harris, L. and Associates, *The Myth and Reality of Aging in America*. Washington, D.C.: National Council on the Aging, 1975.

Hartmann, H. *Ego Psychology and the Problem of Adaptation* (1939). Translated by David Rapaport. New York: International Universities Press, 1958.

Hartmann, H., & Lowenstein, R. Notes on the superego. *Psychoanalytic Study of the Child*, 1962, 16, 42–81.

Hatch, D., & Hatch, M. An unhappy family: Some observations on the relationship between the Calvinist ethic and interpersonal relations over four generations. *Marriage and Family Living*, 1962, 24, 213–233.

Havighurst, R., Neugarten, B., & Tobin S. Disengagement and patterns of aging. In B. Neugarten (Ed.), *Middle Age and Aging*. Chicago: University of Chicago Press, 1968, 161–172.

Hawkinson, W. Wish, expectancy, and practice in the interaction of generations. In A. Rose & W. Peterson (Eds.), *Older People and Their Social World*. Philadelphia. F. A. Davis, 1965, 181–190.

Heilbrun, A. B. The measurement of identification. *Child Development*, 1965, 36, 111–127.

Heimann, P. Certain functions of introjection and projection in early infancy. In M. Klein, P. Heimann, S. Isaacs, & J. Riviere, (Eds.) *Developments in Psychoanalysis*. London: Hogarth Press, 1952, 122–168.

Heiss, J. Residential segregation and the assimilation of Italians in an Australian city. *International Migration*, 1966, 4, 165–171.

Hempel, C. Operationism, observation and scientific terms. In A. Danto & S. Morgenbesser (Eds.), *Philosophy of Science*. New York: Meridian Books, 1960, 101–120.

Hendrick, I. Early development of the ego: Identification in infancy. *Psychoanalytic Quarterly*, 1951, 20, 44–51.

Henry, J. Family structure and the transmission of neurotic behavior. *American Journal of Orthopsychiatry*, 1951, 21, 800–818.

Henry, J., & Warson, S. Family structure and psychic development. *American Journal of Orthopsychiatry*, 1951, 21, 59–73.

Herberg, W. *Protestant-Catholic-Jew: An Essay in Religious Sociology*. New York: Random House, 1955.

Hess, R., & Handel, G. Patterns of aggression in parents and their children. *Journal of Genetic Psychology*, 1956, 89, 199–212.

Hess, R., & Handel, G. *Family Worlds*. Chicago: University of Chicago Press, 1959.

Hess, R., & Shipman, V. Early experience and socialization of cognitive modes in children. *Child Development*, 1965, 36, 860–886.

Hess, R., & Shipman, V. Cognitive elements in maternal behavior. In J. Hill (Ed.), *Minnesota Symposium on Child Development*. Minneapolis: University of Minnesota Press, 1967, 57–81.

Hess, R. D., & Shipman, V. Maternal influences upon learning: The cognitive environments of urban pre-school children. In R. Hess & R. M. Baer (Eds.), *Early Education*. Chicago: Aldine, 1968, 91–104.

Hess, B., & Waring, J. Changing patterns of aging and family bonds in later life. *Family Coordinator*, 1978, 27, 303–314.

Hetherington, E., & Brackbill, Y. Etiology and covariation of obstinacy, orderliness and parsimony in young children. *Child Development*, 1963, 34, 919–943.

Higham, J. *Strangers in the Land: Patterns of American Nativism 1860–1925* (1955). New York: Atheneum, 1963.

Hilgard, J., & Fisk, F. Disruption of adult ego identity as related to childhood loss of a mother through hospitalization for psychosis. *Journal of Nervous and Mental Disease*, 1960, 131, 47–57.

Hilgard, R. Anniversary reactions in parents precipitated by children. *Psychiatry*, 1953, 16, 13–80.

Hilgard, R. Anniversaries in mental illness. *Psychiatry*, 1959, 22, 113–121.

Hill, R., & Rodgers, R. The developmental approach. In H. Christensen (Ed.) *Handbook of Marriage and the Family*. Chicago. Rand McNally, 1964, 171–214.

Hill, R. *Family Development in Three Generations*. Cambridge, Mass.: Schenkman Publishing Co., 1970.

Hochschild, A. Disengagement theory: A critique and a proposal. *American Sociological Review*, 1975, 40, 553–569.

Hoffman, L., & Nye, L. *Working Mothers*. San Francisco: Jossey-Bass, 1974.

Hoffman, M. An interview technique for obtaining descriptions of parent–child interaction. *Merrill-Palmer Quarterly*, Fall, 1954, 76–83.

Holt, R. A method for assessing primary process manifestations and their content in Rorschach responses. In M. Rickers-Ovsiankina (Ed.), *Rorschach Psychology* (Rev. Ed.). Huntington, N.Y.: Robert E. Krieger Publishing Co., 1977, 375–420.

Holt, R. R. Clinical judgment as a disciplined inquiry. *Journal of Nervous and Mental Disease*, 1961, 133, 369–381.

Holt, R. R. Individuality and generalization in the psychology of personality. *Journal of Personality*, 1962, 30, 377–404.

Houston-Stein, A., & Higgins-Trenk, A. Development of females from childhood through adulthood: Career and feminine role orientations. In P. Baltes (Ed.), *Life-Span Development and Behavior*, Vol. 1. New York: Academic Press, 1978, 257–297.

Hurvitz, N. Marital strain in the blue-collar family. In A. Shostak & W. Gomberg (Eds.), *Blue-Collar World: Studies of the American Worker*. Englewood Cliffs, N.J.: Prentice-Hall, 1964, 92–109.

Ianni, F. Residential and occupational mobility as indices of the acculturation of an ethnic group. *Social Forces*, 1957, 36, 65–72.

Ianni, F. *A Family Business: Kinship and Social Control in Organized Crime*. New York: Russell-Sage Foundation, 1972.

Inkeles, A. Personality and social structure. In R. Merton, L. Broom & L. S. Cottrell (Eds.), *Sociology Today: Problems and Prospects*. New York: Basic Books, 1961, 249–276.

Inkeles, A. & Levinson, D. National character: The study of modal personality and socio-cultural systems. In G. Lindzey (Ed.), *Handbook of Social Psychology* (1st ed.), Vol. 2. Reading, Mass.: Addison-Wesley, 1954, 249–276.

Isaacs, H. Basic group identity: The Idols of the tribe. *Ethnicity*, 1974, 1, 15–42.

Isaacs, K. Relatability: A proposed construct and an approach to its validity. Unpublished doctoral dissertation, University of Chicago, 1956.

Isaacs, S. The nature and function of fantasy. In M. Klein, P. Heimann, S. Isaacs & J. Riviere (Eds.), *Developments in Psychoanalysis*. London: Hogarth Press, 1952, 67–121.

Jacobson, E. The self and the object world: Vicissitudes of their infantile cathexses and their influence on ideational and affective development. *Psychoanalytic Study of the Child*, 1954a, 9, 75–127.

Jacobson, E. Contribution to the metapsychology of psychotic identifications. *Journal of the American Psychoanalytic Association*, 1954b, 2, 239–262.

Jacobson, E. *The Self and the Object World*. New York: International Universities Press, 1964.

Jaher, F. *Oscar Handlin's The Uprooted: A Critical Commentary*. New York: American R.D.M. Corporation, 1966.

John, E. Mental Health and the Principle of Least Effort. Unpublished doctoral dissertation, University of Chicago, 1953.

Johnson, E. & Bursk, B. Relationships between the elderly and their adult children. *The Gerontologist*, 1977, 17, 90–96.

Johnson, M. Fathers, mothers and sex typing. *Sociological Inquiry*, 1975, 45, 15–26.

Jones, E. & Gerard, H. *Foundations of Social Psychology*. New York: Wiley, 1967.

Josslyn, I. The family as a psychological unit. *Social Casework*, 1953, 336–343.

Kadushin, P., Cutler, C., Waxenberg, S. & Sager, C. The family story technique and intrafamily analysis. *Journal of Projective Techniques and Personality Assessment*, 1971, 35, 438–450.

Kagan, J. The concept of identification. *Psychological Review*, 1958, 58, 357–364.

Kahana, B. & Kahana, E. Grandparenthood from the perspective of the developing grandchild. *Developmental Psychology*, 1970, 3, 98–105.

Kahana, E. & Kahana, B. Theoretical and research perspectives on grandparenthood. *Aging and Human Development*, 1971, 2, 261–268.

Kakar, S. *The Inner World*: A Psychoanalytic Study of Childhood and Society in India: Delhi: Oxford University Press, 1978

Kalish, R. & Knudtson, F. Attachment versus disengagement: A life-span conceptualization. *Human Development*, 1976, 19, 171–181.

Kallen, H. Democracy versus the melting pot. *The Nation*, 1915, 219.

Kanner, L. Early infantile autism. *Journal of Pediatrics*, 1944, 25, 211–217.

Kanter, R. *Work and family in the United States: A critical review and agenda for research and policy*. New York: Russell Sage Foundation, 1977.

Kanter, R. Families, family processes, and economic life: Toward systematic analysis of social historical research. In J. Demos & S. Boocock (Eds.), *Turning Points: Historical and Sociological Essays on the Family*. Chicago: University of Chicago Press, 1978, 316–340.

Kardiner, A. *The Individual and His Society*. New York: Columbia University Press, 1945.

Katz, D. & Stotland, E. A preliminary statement to a theory of attitude formation and change. In S. Koch (Ed.), *Psychology: A Study of a Science*, Vol. 3. New York: McGraw-Hill, 1959, 423–475.

Kell, L. & Aldous, J. Trends in childcare over three generations. *Marriage and Family Living*, 1960, 22, 176–177.

Kelman, H. Compliance, identification, and internalization: Three processes in attitude change. *Journal of Conflict Resolution*, 1958, 2, 51–60.

Keniston, K. An American Ishmael. In K. Keniston, *The Uncommitted*. New York: Harcourt, Brace, 1960, 23–55.

Keniston, K. *Young Radicals: Notes on Committed Youth*. New York: Harcourt, Brace and World, 1968.

Kennedy, R. Single or triple melting pot? Intermarriage trends in New Haven, 1870–1940. *American Journal of Sociology*, 1944, 49, 331–339.

Kennedy, R. Single or triple melting pot? Intermarriage in New Haven, 1870–1950. *American Journal of Sociology*, 1952, 58, 56–59.

Kerckhoff, A. Nuclear and extended family relationships: A normative and behavorial analysis. In E. Shanas & G. Streib (Eds.), *Social Structure and the Family: Generational Relations*. Englewood Cliffs, N.J.: Prentice-Hall, 1965, 93–112.

Kernberg, O. Structural derivatives of object relations, *International Journal of Psychoanalysis*, 1966, 47, 236–253.

Kernberg, O. *Object Relations Theory and Classical Psychoanalysis*. New York: Aronson, 1976.

Kerr, M. *The People of Ship Street*. London: Routledge and Kegan Paul, 1958.

Kitano, H. Inter and intragenerational differences in maternal attitudes towards childrearing. *Journal of Social Psychology*, 1964, 63, 215–220.

Klein, M. *Contributions to Psychoanalysis 1921–1945*. London: Hogarth Press, 1950.

Klein, M. Notes on some schizoid mechanisms. In M. Klein, P. Heimann, S. Isaacs & J. Riviere (Eds.), *Developments in Psychoanalysis*. London: Hogarth Press, 1952a, 292–320.

Klein, M. Some theoretical conclusions regarding the emotional life of the infant. In M. Klein, P. Heimann S. Isaacs, & J. Riviere (Eds.), *Developments in Psychoanalysis*. London: Hogarth Press, 1952b, 237–270.

Klein, M. Some theoretical considerations regarding the emotional life of the infant. In M. Klein, P. Heimann S. Isaacs & J. Riviere (Eds.), *Developments in Psychoanalysis*. London: Hogarth Press, 1952c, 198–236.

Klein, M. *Envy and Gratitude: A Study of Unconscious Sources*. London: Tavistock Publications, 1957.

Klein, M. *The Psychoanalysis of Children* (1937). New York: Grove Press, 1960.

Kluckhohn, C. Values and value orientations. In T. Parsons & E. Shils (Eds.), *Toward a General Theory of Action*. Cambridge, Mass.: Harvard University Press, 1951, 388–433.

Kluckhohn, F. & Strodtbeck, F. *Variations in Value Orientations*. Evanston, Ill., and New York: Harper & Row, 1961.

Knight, R. Introjection, projection, and identification. *Psychoanalytic Quarterly,* 1940, 9, 334–341.

Koenig, S. Second and third generation Americans. In F. Brown & J. Roucek (Eds.), *One America*. Englewood Cliffs, N.J.: Prentice-Hall, 1945, 471–485.

Koff, R. H. A definition of identification: A review of the literature. *International Journal of Psychoanalysis,* 1961, 42, 362–370.

Kohn, M. *Class and Conformity: A Study in Values*. Homewood, Ill.: Dorsey Press, 1969.

Kohut, H. *The Analysis of the Self*. New York: International Universities Press, 1971 (Monograph Number 4, Monograph Series of the Psychoanalytic Study of the Child).

Kohut, H. *The Restoration of the Self*. New York: International Universities Press, 1977.

Kohut, H. & Wolf, E. The disorders of the self and their treatment: An outline. *International Journal of Psychoanalysis,* 1978, 59, 413–425.

Koller, M. Studies of three generation households. *Marriage and Family Living,* 1954, 16, 205–206.

Koller, M. *Families: A Multigenerational Approach*. New York: McGraw-Hill, 1974.

Kolm, R. Ethnicity in society and community. In O. Feinstein (Ed.), *Ethnic Groups in the City: Culture, Institutions and Power*. Lexington, Mass.: D. C. Heath-Lexington Books, 1971, 57–77.

Komarovsky, M. *Blue-Collar Marriage*. New York: Random House, 1962.

Komarovsky, M. Continuities in family research: A case study. *American Journal of Sociology,* 1956, 62, 466–469.

Komarovsky, M. Functional analysis of sex roles. *American Sociological Review,* 1950, 15, 508–516.

Kosa, J., Rachiele, L. & Schomer, C. Sharing the home with relatives. *Marriage and Family Living,* 1960, 22, 129–131.

Kramer, S. & Masur, J. *Jewish Grandmothers*. Boston: Beacon Press, 1976.

Krause, C. Urbanization without breakdown: Italian, Jewish and Slavic immigrant women in Pittsburgh, 1900–1945. *Journal of Urban History,* 1978, 4, 291–306.

Krause, C. *Grandmothers, Mothers and Daughters: A Report of Findings of Women, Ethnicity and Mental Health*. New York: Institute on Pluralism and Group Identity and the American Jewish Committee, 1979.

LaBarre, M., Jessner, L. & Ussery, L. The significance of grandmothers in the psychopathology of children. *American Journal of Orthopsychiatry,* 1960, 30, 175–185.

Lalli, M. The Italian-American family: Assimilation and change. *Family Coordinator,* 1969, 18, 44–48.

Langman, L. Generational identification and value transmission. Paper presented at annual meeting, Eastern Sociological Society, New York, April 1973.

Lanham, B. Aspects of child care in Japan: Preliminary report, In D. Haring (Ed.), *Personal Character and Cultural Milieu* (3rd ed.). Syracuse, N.Y.: Syracuse University Press, 1956, 565–583.

Laslett, B. Family membership, past and present. *Social Problems,* 1978, 25, 476–487.

Laslett, P. Characteristics of the Western family considered over time. *Journal of Family History,* 1977, 2, 89–115.

Laslett, P. & Wall, R. *Household and Family in Past Time.* New York: Cambridge University Press, 1972.

Laumann, E. *Bonds of Pluralism: The Form and Substance of Urban Social Networks.* New York: Wiley-Interscience, 1973.

Laurie, E. Sex and stage differences in perceptions of marital and family relationships. *Journal of Marriage and the Family,* 1974, 36, 260–268.

Lazerwitz, B. & Rowitz, L. The three-generation hypothesis. *American Journal of Sociology,* 1964, 69, 529–538.

Lazowick, L. On the nature of identification. *Journal of Abnormal and Social Psychology,* 1955, 51, 175–183.

Leichter, H. & Mitchell, W. *Kinship and Casework.* New York: Russell Sage Foundation, 1967.

Lenski, G. *The Religious Factor.* New York: Doubleday, 1961.

Leowald, H. Identification, separation, mourning and the superego. *Psychoanalytic Quarterly,* 1962, 31, 483–504.

Lerner, R. & Spanier, G. *Child influences on marital and family interaction: A life-span perspective.* New York: Academic Press, 1978a.

Lerner, R. & Spanier, G. A dynamic interactional view of child and family development. In R. Lerner & G. Spanier (Eds.), *Child Influences on Marital and Family Interaction: A Life-Span Perspective.* New York: Academic Press, 1978b, 1–22.

LeVine, R. & Campbell, D. *Ethnocentrism: Theories of Conflict, Ethnic Attitudes and Group Behavior.* New York: Wiley, 1972.

LeVine, R. *Culture, Behavior and Personality.* Chicago: Aldine, 1973.

Levinson, D. *Seasons of a Man's Life.* New York: Knopf, 1977.

Levy, D. *Maternal Overprotection.* New York: Columbia University Press, 1943.

Levy, K. Simultaneous analysis of a mother and her adolescent daughter. *Psychoanalytic Study of the Child,* 1960, 15, 378–391.

Lewin, K. Conceptual representation and the measurement of psychological forces. In K. Lewin, *Contributions to Psychological Theory.* Durham, N.C.: University of North Carolina Press, 1938.

Lewis, A. & Landis, B. Symbiotic pairings in adults. *Contemporary Psychoanalysis,* 1979, 230–251.

Lichtenberg, J. The development of the sense of self. *Journal of the American Psychoanalytic Association,* 1975, 23, 453–484.

Lidz, T. *The Family and Human Adaptation.* New York: International Universities Press, 1963.

Lidz, T., Fleck, S. & Cornelison, A. *Schizophrenia and the Family.* New York: International Universities Press, 1965.

Lieberson, S. *Ethnic Patterns in American Cities.* New York: Free Press, 1963.

Littman, R. A., Moore, R. & Pierce-Jones, J. Social class differences in childrearing: A third community for comparison with Chicago and Newton. *American Sociological Review,* 1957, 22, 694–704.

Litwak, E. Occupational mobility and extended family cohesion. *American Sociological Review,* 1960a, 25, 9–21.

Litwak, E. Geographical mobility and extended family cohesion. *American Sociological Review,* 1960b, 25, 385–394.

Litwak, E. Extended kin relations in an industrial democratic society. In E. Shanas & G. Streib (Eds.), *Social Structure and the Family: Generational Relations.* Englewood-Cliffs, N.J.: Prentice-Hall, 1965, 290–325.

Loevinger, J. The meaning and measurement of ego development. *American Psychologist,* 1966, 21, 195–206.

Loevinger, J. Measuring ego-development by sentence completions. *Proceedings of the 76th Annual Meetings, American Psychological Association, San Francisco, 1968.* Washington, D.C.: American Psychological Association, 1968, 748.

Loevinger, J., Wessler, R., & Redmore, C. *Measuring Ego Development,* 2 vols. San Francisco: Jossey-Bass, 1970.

Lofland, L. The "thereness" of women: A selective review of urban sociology. In M. Millman, & R. Kanter (Eds.), *Another voice: Feminist Perspectives on Social Life and Social Science.* New York: Anchor Press/Doubleday, 1975, 145–170.

Lolli, G., Serianni, G., & Luzzatto-Fegiz, P. *Alcohol in Italian Culture.* New York: Free Press, 1958.

Lopata, H. *Occupation: Housewife.* New York: Oxford University Press, 1971.

Lopata, H. *Widowhood in an American City.* Cambridge, Mass.: Schenkman Publishing Co., 1973.

Lopata, H. Contributions of extended families to the support systems of metropolitan areas' widows: Limitations of the modified kin network. *Journal of Marriage and the Family,* 1978, 40, 355–364.

Lopreato, J. Social stratification and mobility in a south Italian town, *American Sociological Review,* 1961, 26, 585–596.

Lopreato, J. *Peasants No More: Social Class and Social Change in an Underdeveloped Society.* Scranton, Pa.: Chandler Publishing Company, 1967.

Lopreato, J. *Italian Americans.* New York: Random House, 1970.

LoSciuto, L., & Karlin, R. Correlates of the generation gap. *Journal of Psychology,* 1972, 81, 253-262.

Low, N. The relationship of adult daughters to their mothers. Paper presented at the annual meetings, Massachusetts Psychological Association, Boston, May 1978.

Lowenthal, M. & Chiriboga, D. Transition to the empty nest: Crisis, challenge, or relief? *Archives of General Psychiatry,* 1972, 26, 8–14.

Lyketsos, G. C. On the formation of mother-daughter symbotic relationship patterns in schizophrenia. *Psychiatry,* 1959, 22, 161–166.

Lynn, D. A note on sex differences in the development of masculine and feminine identification. *Psychological Review,* 1959, 66, 126–135.

Lynn, D. Sex-role and parental identification. *Child Development,* 1962, 33, 555–564.

McClelland, D. *Personality*. New York: Dryden Press, 1951.

McClelland, D. Wanted: A new self-image for women. In R. Lifton (Ed.), *The Woman in America*. Cambridge, Mass.: Houghton Mifflin, 1965, 175–191.

McClelland, D., & Atkinson, J. The projective expression of needs. I. The effect of different intensities of the hunger drive on perception. *Journal of Psychology*, 1948, 25, 205–232.

McDonald, J. S. Italy's rural social structure and emigration. *Occidente*, 1956, 12, 437–455.

McDonald, J., & McDonald, L. Chain migration, ethnic neighborhood formation, and social networks. *Milbank Memorial Fund Quarterly*, 1964, 42, 82–97.

McDonald, J. & McDonald, L. Urbanization, ethnic groups, and social segmentation. *Social Research*, 1962, 29, 433–438.

McGahey, C., & Sporakowski, M. Intergenerational attitudes toward childbearing and childrearing. *Journal of Home Economics*, 1972, 64, 27–31.

McGuire, M. *Reconstructions in Psychoanalysis*. New York: Appleton-Century-Crofts, 1971.

McLaughlin, V. Like the Fingers of the Hand: The Family and Community Life of First-Generation Italian-Americans in Buffalo, New York, 1880–1930. Unpublished doctoral dissertation, State University of New York at Buffalo, 1970.

Maccoby, E. (Ed.) *The Development of Sex Differences*. Stanford, Calif.: Stanford University Press, 1966.

Mahler, M. On child psychosis and schizophrenia. Autistic and symbiotic infantile psychoses. *Psychoanalytic Study of the Child*, 1952, 7, 286–305.

Mahler, M. Autism and symbiosis: Two extreme disturbances of identity. *International Journal of Psychoanalysis*, 1958, 39, 77–83.

Mahler, M. Thoughts about development and individuation. *Psychoanalytic Study of the Child*, 1963, 18, 307–323.

Mahler, M. On the significance of the normal separation-individuation phase: With reference to research in symbiotic child psychosis. In M. Schur (Ed.), *Drives, Affects, Behavior: Essays in Memory of Marie Bonaparte*. New York: International Universities Press, 1965, 161–169.

Mahler, M. *On Human Symbiosis and the Vicissitudes of Individuation, Volume I: Infantile Psychosis*. New York: International Universities Press, 1968.

Mahler, M. On the first three phases of the separation-individuation process. *International Journal of Psychoanalysis*, 1972a, 53, 333–338.

Mahler, M. Rapprochement subphase of the separation-individuation process. *Psychoanalytic Quarterly*, 1972b, 41, 487–506.

Mahler, M., & Furer, M. Certain aspects of the separation-individuation phase. *Psychoanalytic Quarterly*, 1963, 32, 1–14.

Mahler, M., & La Perriere, K. Mother-child interaction during separation-individuation. *Psychoanalytic Quarterly*, 1965, 34, 483–498.

Mahler, M., Pine, F., & Bergman, A. *The Psychological Birth of the Human Infant*. New York: Basic Books, 1975.

Mancini, J. Family relationships and morale among people sixty-five years of age and older. *American Journal of Orthopsychiatry*, 1979, 49, 292–300.

Mannheim, K. The problem of generations. In K. Mannheim (Ed.), *Essays on the Sociology of Knowledge*. London: Routledge and Kegan Paul, 1952, 276–322.

Mayman, M. Manual for scoring Rorschach form level. Mimeographed. Ann Arbor, Mich.: Psychological Clinic, 1968.

Mead, M. *Sex and Temperament in Three Primitive Societies*. New York: Morrow, 1935.

Mednick, S., & Schaeffer, J. Mothers' retrospective reports in childrearing research. *American Journal of Orthopsychiatry*, 1963, 33, 457–461.

Meissner, W. W. Internalization and object relations. *Journal of the American Psychoanalytic Association*, 1979, 27, 345–360.

Meissner, W. W. Notes on identification. I. Origins in Freud. *Psychoanalytic Quarterly*, 1970, 39, 563–589.

Meisner, W. W. Notes on identification. II. Clarification of related concepts. *Psychoanalytic Quarterly*, 1971, 40, 277–302.

Meissner, W. W. Notes on identification. III. The concept of identification. *Psychoanalytic Quarterly*, 1972, 41, 224–260.

Meissner, W. W. Identification and learning. *Psychoanalytic Quarterly*, 1973, 42, 788–816.

Mendell, D., Cleveland, S., & Fisher, S. A five generation family theme. *Family Process*, 1968, 7, 126–132.

Mendell, D., & Fisher, S. An approach to neurotic behavior in terms of a three generation family model. *Journal of Nervous and Mental Disease*, 1956, 123, 171–180.

Mendell, D., & Fisher S. A multi-generation approach to treatment of psychopathology. *Journal of Nervous and Mental Disease*, 1958, 126, 523–529.

Michigan, University of. *A Social Profile of Detroit, 1956*. Ann Arbor: Department of Sociology and Survey Research Center, 1957.

Middlemore, M. *The Nursing Couple*. London: Hamish-Hamilton Medical Books, 1941.

Miller, A., & Cohler, B. Identification and development. *Bulletin of the Chicago Society for Adolescent Psychiatry*, 1971, 1, 1–7.

Miller, A., Pollock, G., Bernstein, H., & Robbins, F. An approach to the concept of identification. *Bulletin of the Menninger Clinic*, 1968, 32, 239–252.

Miller, D., & Swanson, G. *The Changing American Parent*. New York: Wiley, 1958.

Miller, N., & Dollard, J. *Social Learning Theory and Imitation*. New Haven: Yale University Press, 1941.

Miller, S., & Riessman, F. The working class subculture: A new view. *Social Problems*, 1961, 9, 86–97.

Minturn, L., & Lambert, W. *Mothers of Six Cultures: Antecedents of Childrearing*. New York: Wiley, 1964.

Mintz, N., & Schwartz, D. Urban ecology and psychosis: Community factors in the incidence of schizophrenia and manic-depression among Italians in greater Boston. *International Journal of Social Psychiatry*, 1964, 10, 101–118.

Mischel, W. Toward a cognitive social learning reconceptualization of personality. *Psychological Review*, 1973, 80, 252–283.

Mischel, W. On the future of personality measurement. *American Psychologist*, 1977, 32, 246–254.

Modell, A. *Object Love and Reality*. New York: International Universities Press, 1968.

Monahan, T. The number of children in American families and the sharing of households. *Marriage and Family Living*, 1956, 18, 201–204.

Mortimer, J., & Simmons, R. Adult socialization. *Annual Review of Sociology*, 1978, 4, 421–454.

Moss, L., & Cappannari, S. The Black Madonna: An example of culture borrowing. *Scientific Monthly*, June 1954, 319–324.

Moss, L., & Cappannari, S. Folklore and medicine in an Italian village. *Journal of American Folklore*, 1960a, 73, 95–102.

Moss, L., & Cappannari, S. Patterns of kinship, comparagio, and community in a south Italian village. *Anthropological Quarterly*, 1960b, 33, 24–32.

Moss, L., & Thompson, W. The south Italian family: Literature and observation. *Human Organization*, 1959, 18, 35–41.

Mowerer, O. H. *Learning Theory and Personality Dynamics*. New York: Ronald Press, 1950.

Muraskin, W. The moral basis of a backward sociologist: Edward Banfield, the Italians and the Italian-Americans. *American Journal of Sociology*, 1974, 6, 1484–1496.

Murphey, E., Silber, E., Coelho, G., Hamburg, D., & Greenberg, I. Development of autonomy and parent-child interaction in late adolescence. *American Journal of Orthopsychiatry*, 1963, 33, 643–652.

Murray, H. *The Thematic Apperception Technique*. Cambridge, Mass.: Harvard University Press, 1943.

Murray H. An American Icarus, In A. Burton & R. Harris (Eds.), *Clinical Studies of Personality*. New York: Harper Brothers, 1955, 615–641.

Murray, H., and Associates. *Explorations in Personality* (1938). New York: Science Editions, 1961.

Myers, J. Assimilation to the ecological and social systems of a community. *American Sociological Review*, 1950, 15, 367–372.

Myers, J., & Bean, L. *A Decade Later: A Follow Up of Social-Class and Mental Illness*. New York: Wiley, 1968.

Myerson, A. Mental disorders in urban areas: A review. *American Journal of Psychiatry*, 1941, 96, 995–997.

Naegele, K. Some problems in the study of hostility and aggression in middle-class American families. In N. Bell & E. Vogel (Eds.), *A Modern Introduction to the Family*. New York: Free Press, 1960, 417–428.

Nagel, E. *The Structure of Science*. New York: Harcourt Brace and World, 1961.

Napier, A. The marriage of families: Cross-generational complementarity. *Family Process*, 1971, 10, 373–395.

Neisser, E. Mothers and daughters: A lifelong relationship (rev. ed.). New York: Harper & Row, 1973.

Nelli, H. *Italians in Chicago, 1880–1930: A Study in Ethnic Mobility*. New York: Oxford University Press, 1970a.

Nelli, H. Italians in urban America. In S. Tomasi & M. Engel (Eds.), *The Italian Experience in the United States*. Staten Island, N.Y.: Center for Migration Studies, 1970b, 77–107.

Neugarten, B. Dynamics of transition of middle age to old age: Adaptation and the life cycle. *Journal of Geriatric Psychiatry,* 1970, 4, 71–87.

Neugarten, B. Comments on the experience of separation-individuation in infancy and its reverberations through the course of life: maturity, senescence, and its sociological implications, Presented at annual meetings, *the American Psychoanalytic Association,* New York, 1972.

Neugarten, B. Personality change in late life: A developmental perspective. In C. Eisdorfer & M. P. Lawton (Eds.), *The Psychology of Adult Development and Aging.* Washington, D.C.: American Psychological Association, 1973, 311–335.

Neugarten, B. Personality and aging. In J. Birren & W. Schaie (Eds.), *Handbook of the Psychology of Aging.* New York: Van Nostrand-Reinhold, 1977, 626–649.

Neugarten, B. Time, age, and the life cycle. *American Journal of Psychiatry,* 1979, 136, 887–894.

Neugarten, B., and Associates. *Personality in Middle and Late Life.* New York: Atherton, 1964.

Neugarten, B., & Datan, N. Sociological perspectives on the life cycle. In P. Baltes & K. Schaie (Eds.), *Life-Span Developmental Psychology: Personality and Socialization.* New York: Academic Press, 1973, 53–69.

Neugarten, B., & Datan, N. The middle years. In S. Arieti (Ed.), *The American Handbook of Psychiatry* (rev. ed.), Vol. 5. New York: Basic Books, 1974, 592–608.

Neugarten, B., & Gutmann, D. *Age-sex roles and personality in middle age:* A thematic apperception study. *Psychological Monographs,* 1958, 72 whole number 470.

Neugarten, B., & Hagestad, G. Age and the life-course. In R. Binstock & E. Shanas (Eds.), *Handbook of Aging and the Social Sciences.* New York: Van Nostrand-Reinhold, 1976, 35–57.

Neugarten, B., & Weinstein, K. The changing American grandparent. *Journal of Marriage and the Family,* 1964, 26, 197–205.

Neugarten, B., Wood, V., Kraines, R., & Loomis, B. Women's attitudes toward the menopause. *Human Development (Vita Humana),* 1963, 6, 140–151.

Newcomb, T., & Svehla, G. Intra-family relationships in attitude. *Sociometry,* 1937, 1, 200.

Newman, W. *American Pluralism: A Study of Minority Groups and Social Theory.* New York: Harper & Row, 1973.

Novey, S. The meaning of the concept of mental representation of objects. *Psychoanalytic Quarterly,* 1958, 27, 57–79.

Novey, S. *The Second Look: The Reconstruction of Personal History in Psychoanalysis.* Baltimore: Johns Hopkins University Press, 1968.

Nye, L., & Hoffman L. (Eds.), *The Employed Mother in America.* Chicago: Rand McNally, 1963.

O'Brien, T. Attitudes of Suburban Italian-Americans Toward the Roman Catholic Church, Formal Education, and the Parochial School. Unpublished doctoral dissertation, University of Chicago, 1972.

Ogburn, W. F. The changing function of the family. In R. Winch & R. McGinnis (Eds.), *Selected Readings in Marriage and the Family.* New York: Holt, Rinehart, & Winston, 1953, 74–78.

Ogden, T. On projective identification. *International Journal of Psychoanalysis,* 1979, 60, 357–373.

Opler, M. Cultural differences in mental disorders: An Italian and Irish contrast in the schizophrenias-U.S.A. In M. Opler (Ed.), *Culture and Mental Health.* New York: Macmillan, 1959, 425–44.

Opler, M., & Singer, J. Ethnic differences in behavior and psychopathology: Italian and Irish. *International Journal of Social Psychiatry,* 1956, 2, 11–22.

Orne, M. On the social psychology of the psychological experiment: With particular reference to demand characteristics and their implications. *American Psychologist,* 1962, 17, 776–783.

Ornstein, P. Introduction: The evolution of Heinz Kohut's psychoanalytic psychology of the self. In P. Ornstein (Ed.), *The Search for the Self: Selected Writings of Heinz Kohut: 1950 –1978* (2 volumes). New York: International Universities Press, 1978, 1–106.

Palazzoli, M. The families of patients with anorexia nervosa. In E. Anthony & C. Koupernic (Eds.), *The Child in His Family.* New York: Wiley, 1970, 319–332.

Palazzoli, M. Anorexia nervosa. In S. Arieti (Ed.), *World Biennial of Psychiatry,* Vol. 1. New York: Basic Books, 1971, 197–218.

Palisi, B. Ethnic generation and family structure. *Journal of Marriage and the Family,* 1966, 28, 49–50.

Panel. The experience of separation-individuation in infancy and its reverberations through the course of life. I. Infancy and childhood. *Journal of the American Psychoanalytic Association,* 1972c, 21, 135–154.

Panel. The experience of separation-individuation in infancy and its reverberations through the course of life. 2. Adolescence and maturity. *Journal of the American Psychoanalytic Association,* 1972b, 21, 155–167.

Panel. The experience of separation-individuation in infancy and its reverberations through the course of life: Maturity, senescence, and sociological implications. *Journal of the American Psychoanalytic Association,* 1972c, 21, 633–645.

Parens, H., & Saul, L. *Dependence in Man: A Psychoanalytic Study.* New York: International Universities Press, 1971.

Park, R., Burgess, E., & McKenzie, R. *The City* (1925). Chicago: University of Chicago Press, 1967.

Park, R., & Miller, H. *Old World Traits Transplanted.* New York: Harper & Row, 1921.

Parker, B. *A Mingled Yarn: Chronicle of a Troubled Family.* New Haven: Yale University Press, 1972.

Parsons, A. *Belief, Magic, and Anomie: Essays in Psychosocial Anthropology.* New York: Free Press, 1969a.

Parsons, A. Is the Oedipus complex universal? The Jones-Malinowski debate revisited. In A. Parsons, *Belief, Magic, and Anomie, Essays in Psychosocial Anthropology.* New York: Free Press, 1969b, 3–66.

Parsons, A. Paternal and maternal authority in the Neopolitan family. In A Parsons, *Belief, Magic, and Anomie, Essays in Psychosocial Anthropology.* New York: Free Press, 1969c, 67–97.

Parsons, T. The social structure of the family. In R. Anshen (Ed.), *The Family: Its Function and Destiny*. New York: Harper & Row, 1949, 190.

Parsons, T. *The Social System*. New York: Free Press, 1951.

Parsons, T. The superego and the theory of social systems. *Psychiatry,* 1952, 15, 15–26.

Parsons, T. Family structure and the socialization of the child. In T. Parsons & F. Bales, *Family, Socialization and Interaction Processes*. New York: Free Press, 1955, 35–131.

Parsons, T. Social structure and the development of personality. *Psychiatry,* 1958, 21, 332–340.

Paterson, J. Marketing and the working class family. In A. Shostak & W. Gomberg (Eds.), *Blue-Collar World: Studies of the American Worker*. Englewood Cliffs, N.J.: Prentice-Hall, 1964, 76 –80.

Pavenstedt, E. A study of immature mothers and their children. In G. Caplan (Ed.), *Prevention of Mental Disorders in Children*. New York: Basic Books, 1961, 192–217.

Pearlin, L. *Class, Context and Family Relations: A Cross-National Study*. Boston: Little, Brown, 1971.

Pearlin, L., & Kohn, M. Social class, occupation, and parental values: A cross-national study. *American Sociological Review,* 1966, 31, 466–479.

Piaget, J. *The Construction of Reality in the Child*. New York: Basic Books, 1954.

Piedmont, E. An Investigation of the Influence of Ethnic Grouping Differences in the Development of Schizophrenia. Unpublished doctoral dissertation, University of Buffalo, 1962.

Pinderhughes, C. Ego development and cultural differences. *American Journal of Psychiatry,* 1974, 131, 171–175.

Pine, F., & Furer, M. Studies of the separation-individuation phase: A methodological overview. *Psychoanalytic Study of the Child,* 1963, 18, 325–342.

Pisani, L. F. *The Italian in America*. New York: Exposition Press, 1957.

Pitkin, D. Land tenure and family organization in an Italian village. *Human Organization,* 1959, 18, 169–173.

Pollock, G. On symbiosis and symbiotic neurosis. *International Journal of Psychoanalysis,* 1964, 45, 1–30.

Radloff, L. Sex differences in mental health: The effects of marital and occupational status. *Sex Roles,* 1975, 3, 249–265.

Rainwater, L. Mothers' contributions to the family money economy in Europe and the United States. *Journal of Family History,* 1979, 4, 198–211.

Rainwater, L., Coleman, R., & Handel, G. *Workingman's Wife*. New York: Oceana Publications, 1959.

Rainwater, L., & Handel, G. Changing family roles in the working class. In A. Shostak & W. Gombert (Eds.), *Blue Collar World: Studies of the American Worker*. Englewood Cliffs, N.J.: Prentice-Hall, 1964, 70–76.

Rangell, L. The return of the repressed "Oedipus." *Bulletin of the Menninger Clinic,* 1955, 19, 9–15.

Rapaport, D. A theoretical analysis of the superego concept (1957). In M. Gill (Ed.), *The Collected Papers of David Rapaport*. New York: Basic Books, 1967a, 685–709.

Rapaport, D. Some metapsychological considerations concerning activity and passivity. (1961) In M. Gill (Ed.), *The Collected Papers of David Rapaport.* New York: Basic Books, 1967b, 530 –568.

Rapaport, D., Gill, M., & Schafer, R. *Diagnostic Projective Testing* (rev. ed.). Edited by Robert R. Holt. New York: International Universities Press, 1968.

Rappaport, E. The grandparent syndrome. *Psychoanalytic Quarterly,* 1958, 27, 518–538.

Rebelsky, F., & Hanks, C. Fathers' verbal interaction with infants in the first three months of life. *Child Development,* 1971, 42, 63–68.

Redfield, R. *Peasant Society and Culture.* Chicago: University of Chicago Press, 1956.

Reich, A. Narcissistic object-choice in women. *Journal of the American Psychoanalytic Association,* 1953, 1, 22–44.

Reich, A. Early identifications as archaic elements in the superego. *Journal of the American Psychoanalytic Association,* 1954, 2, 218–238.

Reiss, P. The extended kinship system: Correlates of an attitude on frequency of interaction. *Journal of Marriage and the Family,* 1962, 24, 333–339.

Rheingold, J. *The Fear of Being a Woman: A Theory of Maternal Destructiveness.* New York: Grune and Stratton, 1964.

Richman, N. Depression in mothers in preschool children. *Journal of Child Psychology and Psychiatry,* 1976, 17, 75–78.

Ricoeur, P. *Freud and Philosophy: An Essay on Interpretation.* New Haven: Yale University Press, 1970.

Ricoeur, P. The question of proof in Freud's psychoanalytic writings. *Journal of the American Psychoanalytic Association,* 1977, 25, 835–872.

Riley, A. Irish Americans. In F. Brown (Ed.), *One America. Englewood-Cliffs, N. J.:* Prentice-Hall, 1945, 43–51.

Riley, M., Johnson, M. & Foner, A., (Eds.) *Aging and Society: Vol. 3. A Sociology of Age Stratification.* New York: Russel Sage Foundation, 1972.

Ripley, H. Depression and life-span epidemiology. In G. Usdin (Ed.), *Depression: Clinical, Biological and Psychological Perspectives.* New York: Brunner/Mazel, 1977, 1–27.

Robbins, L. C. The accuracy of parental recall of aspects of child development and of childrearing practices. *Journal of Abnormal and Social Psychology,* 1963, 66, 261–270.

Roberts, B., & Myers, J. Religion, national origin, immigration, and mental illness. *American Journal of Psychiatry,* 1954, 110, 759–764.

Robertson, J. Grandmotherhood: A study of role conceptions. *Journal of Marriage and the Family,* 1977, 39, 165–174.

Robey, P. Sociology and women in working class jobs. In M. Millman & R. Kanter (Eds.), *Another Voice: Feminist Perspectives on Social Life and Social Science.* New York: Doubleday/Anchor, 1975, 203–239.

Robins, A. Family relations of the aging in three-generation households. In C. Tibbitts & W. Donahue (Eds.), *Social and Psychological Aspects of Aging.* New York: Columbia University Press, 1962, 464–474.

Robins, L., & Tomanec, M. Closeness to blood relatives outside the immediate family. *Marriage and Family Living,* 1962, 24, 340–346.

Roff, M. Intra-family resemblances in personality characteristics. *Journal of Psychology,* 1950, 30, 199–227.

Rogler, L., & Hollingshead, A. *Trapped: Families and Schizophrenia.* New York: Wiley, 1965.

Rose, A. The prevalence of mental disorders in Italy. *International Journal of Social Psychiatry,* 1964, 10, 87–100.

Rosen, J., & Neugarten, B. Ego functions in the middle and later years: A thematic apperception study. In B. Neugarten and Associates, *Personality in Middle and Late Life.* New York: Atherton, 1964, 90–101.

Rosenberg, G. *The Worker Grows Old: Poverty and Isolation in the City.* San Francisco: Jossey-Bass, 1970.

Rosenberg, G., & Anspach, D. *Working Class Kinship.* Lexington, Mass.: D.C. Heath-Lexington Books, 1973.

Rosenfeld, S. Sex differences in depression: Do women always have higher rates? *Journal of Health and Social Behavior,* 1980, 21, 33–42.

Rosensweig, S., & Isham, A. C. Complementary Thematic Apperception Test patterns in close kin. *American Journal of Orthopsychiatry,* 1947, 17, 129–142.

Rosow, I. *Social Integration of the Aged.* New York: Free Press, 1967.

Rosow, I. *Socialization to Old Age.* Berkeley: University of California Press, 1976.

Rossi, A. Transition to parenthood. *Journal of Marriage and the Family,* 1968, 30, 26–39.

Rotter, J. *Social Learning Theory and Clinical Psychology.* Englewood Cliffs, N.J.: Prentice-Hall, 1954.

Rubin, L. *Worlds of Pain: Life in the Working-Class Family.* New York: Basic Books, 1976.

Rubin, L. *Women of a Certain Age: The Midlife Search for Self.* New York: Harper & Row, 1979.

Rudolph, S., & Rudolph, L. Rajput adulthood: Reflections on the Amar Singh diary. In E. Erikson (Ed.), *Adulthood.* New York: Norton, 1978, 149–172.

Russo, N. Three generations of Italians in New York City: The religious acculturation. In S. Tomasi & M. Engel (Eds.), *The Italian Experience in the United States.* Staten Island, N.Y.: Center for Migration Studies, 1970, 195–213.

Ryder, N. The cohort as a concept in the study of social change. *American Sociological Review,* 1965, 30, 843–861.

Sampson, H., Messinger, S., & Towne, R. *Schizophrenic Women: Studies in Marital Crisis.* New York: Atherton and Prentice-Hall, 1964.

Sander, L. Issues in early mother-child interaction. *Journal of the American Academy of Child Psychiatry,* 1964, 3, 211–263.

Sander, L. The longitudinal course of early mother-child interaction: Cross-case comparison in a sample of mother-child pairs. In B. Foss (Ed.), *Determinants of Infant Behavior.* London: Methuen, 1969, 189–228.

Sander, L. Infant and caretaking environment: Investigation and conceptualization of adaptive behavior in a system of increasing complexity. In E. J. Anthony (Ed.), *Explorations in Child Psychiatry.* New York: Plenum Press, 1975, 129–166.

Sandler, J. On the concept of the superego. *Psychoanalytic Study of the Child,* 1960, 15, 128–162.

Sandler, J., & Rosenblatt, B. The concept of the representational world. *Psychoanalytic Study of the Child,* 1962, 17, 128–145.

Sanford, N. The dynamics of identification. *Psychological Review,* 1955, 62, 106–117.

Sarnoff, I. Psychoanalytic theory and social attitudes. *Public Opinion Quarterly,* 1960, 24, 251–279.

Sauna, V. Immigration, migration and mental illness: A review of the literature with special emphasis on schizophrenia. In E. Brody (Ed.), *Behavior in New Environments: Adaptation of Migrant Populations.* Beverly Hills, Calif.: Sage, 1969, 291–352.

Sawhill, I. A Perspective on Women and Work in America. In J. O'Toole (Ed.), *Work and the Quality of Life: Resource Papers for Work in America.* Cambridge, Mass.: M.I.T. Press, 1974, 98–105.

Schachter, G. *The Italian South: Economic Development in Mediterranean Europe.* New York: Random House, 1965.

Schafer, R. The loving and beloved superego in Freud's structural theory. *Psychoanalytic Study of the Child,* 1960, 15, 163–188.

Schafer, R. *A New Language for Psychoanalysis.* New Haven: Yale University Press, 1976.

Schafer, R. Action: Its place in psychoanalytic interpretation and theory. In Chicago Institute for Psychoanalysis, *The Annual of Psychoanalysis,* Vol. 1. New York: Quadrangle Books, 1973, 159–196.

Schafer, R. *Aspects of Internalization.* New York: International Universities Press, 1968.

Schafer, R. Internalization: Process or fantasy? *Psychoanalytic Study of the Child,* 1972a, 27, 411–436.

Schafer, R. Self and identity concepts and the experience of separation-individuation in adolescence. Paper presented at annual meetings, American Psychoanalytic Association, New York, 1972b.

Schaffer, D. Addenda to an annotated bibliography of the Blacky Test (1949–1967). *Journal of Projective Techniques and Personality Assessment,* 1968, 32, 550–555.

Schaie, K. W. A reinterpretation of age-related changes in cognitive structure and functioning. In L. Goulet & P. Baltes (Eds.), *Life-Span Developmental Psychology.* New York: Academic Press, 1970, 485–507.

Schecter, D. Identification and individuation. *Journal of the American Psychoanalytic Association,* 1968, 16, 48–80.

Schermerhorn, R. A. *Comparative Ethnic Relations: A Framework for Theory and Research.* New York: Random House, 1970.

Schneider, D. *American Kinship: A Cultural Account.* Englewood Cliffs, N.J.: Prentice-Hall, 1968.

Schooler, C. Serfdom's legacy: An ethnic continuum. *American Journal of Sociology,* 1976, 81, 1265–1285.

Sears, R., Maccoby, E., & Levin, H. *Patterns of Childrearing.* Evanston, Ill. and New York. Harper & Row, 1957.

Sears, R. R. Identification as a form of behavior development. In D. Harris (Ed.), *The Concept of Development*. Minneapolis: University of Minnesota Press, 1957, 149–161.

Sears, R. R. Whiting, J. M. W., Nowlis, V., & Sears, P. Some childrearing antecedents of aggression and dependency in young children. *Genetic Psychology Monographs,* 1953, 47, 135–234.

Segal, H. *Introduction to the Work of Melanie Klein* (rev. ed.). New York: Basic Books, 1973.

Senn, M. Fads and facts as the bases of childcare practices. *Children,* 1957, 4, 43–47.

Senn, M., & Hartford, C. *The First Born: Eight American Families*. Cambridge, Mass.: Harvard University Press, 1968.

Settlage, C. Discussion of Mahler's paper on the first three sub-phases of the separation-individuation process. Annual meetings of the American Psychoanalytic Association, New York, 1971.

Seward, R. *The American Family: A Demographic History*. Beverly Hills, Calif.: Sage, 1978.

Sewell, W. H. Some recent developments in socialization theory and research. *Annals of the American Academy of Political and Social Science,* 1963, 349, 163–181.

Shanas, E. *Family Relationships of Older People*. New York: Health Information Foundation Research, Series Number 20, 1961a.

Shanas, E. Living arrangements of older people in the United States. *Gerontologist,* 1961b, 1, 27–29.

Shanas, E. Townsend, P., Wedderburn, D., Friis, H., Milhoj, P., & Stehouwer, J. *Old People in Three Industrial Societies*. Chicago: Atherton-Aldine, 1968.

Shanas, E. Family-kin networks and aging in cross-cultural perspective. *Journal of Marriage and the Family,* 1973, 35, 505–511.

Shanas, E. Social myth as hypothesis: The case of the family realities of old people. *The Gerontologist*, 1979, 19, 3–9.

Shanas, E., & Streib, G. (Eds.). *Social Structure and the Family: Generational Relations*. Englewood-Cliffs, N.J.: Prentice-Hall, 1965.

Shannon, W. *The American Irish*. New York: Collier-Macmillan, 1963.

Shapiro, D. *Neurotic Styles*. New York: Basic Books, 1965.

Shapiro, D. A. Symbiosis in adulthood. *American Journal of Psychiatry,* 1972, 129, 65–68.

Sheehy, G. *Passages: Predictable Crisis of Adult Life*. New York: Dutton, 1976.

Sherwood, M. *The Logic of Explanation In Psychoanalysis*. New York: Academic Press, 1969.

Shibutani, T., & Kwan, K. *Ethnic Stratification: A Comparative Approach*. New York: Collier-Macmillan, 1964.

Shweder, R. How relevant is an individual difference theory of personality? *Journal of Personality,* 1975, 43, 455–484.

Siassi, I., Crocetti, G., & Spiro, H. Loneliness and dissatisfaction in a blue collar population. *Archives of General Psychiatry,* 1974, 30, 261–265.

Sigel, I., Hoffman, M., Dreyer, A., & Torgoff, I. Influence techniques used by parents to modify the behavior of children: A case presentation. *American Journal of Orthopsychiatry*, 1957, 27, 356–364.

Sigel, I., Hoffman, M., Dreyer, A., & Torgoff, I. Toward a theory of influence techniques. *Merrill-Palmer Quarterly*, Fall, 1954, 4–17.

Silverman, S. Agricultural organization, social structure and values in Italy: Amoral familism reconsidered. *American Anthropologist*, 1968, 70, 1–20.

Silverman, S. *Three bells of civilization: The life of an Italian hill town.* New York: Columbia University Press, 1975.

Simmel, G. The persistence of social groups. *American Journal of Sociology*, 1898, 3, 662–698.

Simmel, G. Conflict. In K. Wolff & R. Bendix (Eds.), *Conflict and the Web of Group Affiliations.* New York: Free Press, 1955.

Singer, J., & Opler, M. Ethnic differences in behavior and psychopathology. *International Journal of Social Psychiatry*, 1956a, 2, 11–23.

Singer, J., & Opler, M. Contrasting patterns of fantasy and motility in Irish and Italian schizophrenics. *Journal of Abnormal and Social Psychology*, 1956b, 53, 42–47.

Singer, M., & Wynne, L. Differentiating characteristics of parents of childhood schizophrenics, childhood neurotics, and young adult schizophrenics. *American Journal of Psychiatry*, 1963, 120, 234–243.

Singer, M., & Wynne, L. Principles for scoring communication defects and deviances in parents of schizophrenics: Rorschach and TAT scoring manuals. *Psychiatry*, 1966, 29, 260–288.

Singer, M., & Wynne, L. Thought disorder and family relations of schizophrenics: III. Methodology using projective techniques. *Archives of General Psychiatry*, 1965a, 12, 187–200.

Singer, M., & Wynne, L. Thought disorder and family relations of schizophrenics: IV. Results and Implications. *Archives of General Psychiatry*, 1965b, 12, 201–212.

Sluzki, C. Migration and family conflict. *Family Process*, 1979, 18, 379–390.

Smith, D. Life course, norms, and the family system of older Americans in 1900. *Journal of Family History*, 1979, 4, 285–298.

Smith, H. Family interaction patterns of the aged: A review. In A. Rose & W. Peterson (Eds.), *Older People and Their Social World: The Sub-Culture of Aging.* Philadelphia: F. A. Davis, 1965, 143–161.

Smith, M. B., Bruner, J., & White, R. W. *Opinions and Personality.* New York: Wiley, 1956.

Smith, M. G. Social and cultural pluralism. *Annals of the New York Academy of Sciences*, 83, Art-5, 1960.

Smith, W., Jr. Family plans for later years. *Journal of Marriage and the Family*, 1954, 16, 36–40.

Smith, W., Britton, J., & Britton, J. *Relationships within Three-Generation Families.* University Park: Pennsylvania State University College of Home Economics, 1958.

Social Research, Inc. *Changing Perception of Food in Modern Life: A Study of Trends in the Thinking of American Homemakers.* Chicago: Social Research, Inc., 1972.

Sours, J. A. Anorexia nervosa: Nosology, diagnosis, developmental patterns, and power control dynamics. In G. Caplan & S. Lebovici (Eds.), *Adolescence: Psychosocial Perspectives*. New York: Basic Books, 1969, 185–212.

Spark, G. Grandparents and intergenerational family therapy. *Family Process,* 1974, 13, 225–237.

Spark, G., & Brody, E. The aged are family members. *Family Process,* 1970, 9, 195–210.

Speck, R., & Rueveni, U. Network therapy—a developing concept. *Family Process,* 1969, 8, 182–191.

Spence, D., & Lonner, T. The "empty nest": A transition within motherhood. *Family Coordinator,* 1971, 20, 369–375.

Sperling, M. The clinical effects of parental neurosis on the child. In E. Anthony & T. Benedek (Eds.), *Parenthood: Its Psychology and Psychopathology*. Boston: Little, Brown, 1970, 539–569.

Spiegel, J. The resolution of role conflict within the family. In M. Greenblatt, D. Levinson, & R. Williams (Eds.), *The Patient and the Mental Hospital*. New York: Free Press, 1957, 545–564.

Spiegel, J. *Transactions: The Interplay between Individual, Family and Society*. New York: Science House, 1971.

Spiro, M. The acculturation of American ethnic groups. *American Anthropologist,* 1955, 57, 1241–1252.

Spitz, R. On the genesis of the superego. *Psychoanalytic Study of the Child,* 1958, 13, 375–404.

Sprince, M. The development of a preoedipal partnership between an adolescent girl and her mother. *Psychoanalytic Study of the Child,* 1962, 17, 418–450.

Srole, L., Langer, T., Michael, S., Opler, M., & Rennie, T. *Mental Health in the Metropolis: The Midtown Study,* Vol. 1. New York: McGraw-Hill, 1962.

Staples, R., & Smith, J. Attitudes of grandmothers and mothers towards childrearing practices. *Child Development,* 1954, 25, 91–97.

Stehouwer, J. Relations between generations and the three-generation household in Denmark. In E. Shanas & G. Streib (Eds.), *Social Structure and the Family: Generational Relationships*. Englewood Cliffs, N.J.: Prentice-Hall, 1965, 142–162.

Stein, M. Vidich, A. J., & White, D. M. *Identity and Anxiety: Survival of the Person in Mass Society*. New York: Free Press, 1960.

Stein, R. *Disturbed Youth and Ethnic Family Patterns*. Albany, N.Y.: State University of New York Press, 1971.

Stendler, C. B. Sixty years of child training practices. *Journal of Pediatrics,* 1950, 36, 122–134.

Stern, D. *The First Relationship; Mother and Infant*. Cambridge, Mass.: Harvard University Press, 1977.

Stern, G. *People in Context*. New York: Wiley, 1970.

Sternbach, T., & Tursky, B. Ethnic differences among housewives in psychophysical and skin potential responses to electric shock. *Psychophysiology,* 1965, 1, 241–246.

Stierlin, H. Interpersonal aspects of internalizations. *International Journal of Psychoanalysis,* 1973, 54, 203–213.

Stierlin, H. *Separating Parents and Adolescents*. New York: Quadrangle Books, 1974.

Stierlin, H., Levi, D., & Savard, R. Centrifugal versus centripetal separation in adolescence: Two patterns and some of their implications. In S. Feinstein & P. Giovacchini (Eds.), *Adolescent Psychiatry, Volume II: Developmental and Clinical Studies*. New York: Basic Books, 1973, 211–239.

Stierlin, H., Levi, L. D., & Savard, R. Parental perceptions of separating children. *Family Process*, 1971, 10, 411–427.

Stierlin, H., & Ravenscroft, K. Varieties of adolescent "separation conflicts." *British Journal of Medical Psychology*, 1972, 45, 299–313.

Stinnett, N., Collins, J., & Montgomery, J. Marital need satisfaction of older husbands and wives. *Journal of Marriage and the Family*, 1970, 23, 428–434.

Stolz, L. *Influences on Parent Behavior*. Palo Alto, Calif.: Stanford University Press, 1967.

Streib, G., & Thompson, W. The older person in a family context. In C. Tibbitts (Ed.), *Handbook of Social Gerontology*. Chicago: University of Chicago Press, 1960, 447–488.

Strodtbeck, F. Family interaction, values, and achievement. In D. McClelland, A. Baldwin, U. Bronfenbrenner, & F. Strodtbeck (Eds.), *Talent and Society: New Perspectives in the Identification of Talent*. Princeton, N.J.: Van Nostrand, 1958, 259–268.

Struening, E., Rabkin, J., & Peck, H. Migration and ethnic membership in relation to social problems. In E. Brody (Ed.), *Behavior in New Environments: Adaptation of Migrant Populations*. Beverly Hills, Calif.: Sage, 1969, 217–247.

Stryker, S. The adjustment of married offspring to their parents. *American Sociological Review*, 1955, 20, 149–154.

Sussman, M. The help pattern in the middle class family. *American Sociological Review*, 1953, 18, 22–28.

Sussman, M. Family continuity: Selective factors which affect relationships between families at generational levels. *Marriage and Family Living*, 1954, 16, 112–120.

Sussman, M. Activity patterns of post-parental couples and their relationship to family continuity. *Marriage and Family Living*, 1955, 18, 338–341.

Sussman, M. The isolated nuclear family: Fact or fiction. *Social Problems*, 1959, 6, 333–340.

Sussman, M. Intergenerational family relationships and social role changes in middle age. *Journal of Gerontology*, 1960, 15, 71–75.

Sussman, M. Relationships of adult children with their parents in the United States. In E. Shanas & G. Streib (Eds.), *Social Structure and the Family: Generational Relations*. Englewood Cliffs, N.J.: Prentice-Hall, 1965, 62–92.

Sussman, M. The urban kin network in the formulation of family theory. In R. Hill & R. Konig (Eds.), *Families in East and West: Socialization Processes and Kinship Ties*. The Hague: Mouton, 1970, 481–503.

Sussman, M., & Burchinal, L. Kin family network: Unheralded structure in current conceptualizations of family functioning. *Marriage and Family Living*, 1962a, 24, 231–240.

Sussman, M., & Burchinal, L. Parental aid to married children: Implications for family functioning. *Marriage and Family Living*, 1962b, 24, 320–332.

Suttles, G. *The Social Order of the Slums: Ethnicity and Territory in the Inner City.* Chicago: University of Chicago Press, 1968.

Sweet, J. *Women in the Labor Force.* New York: Seminar Press, 1973.

Sweetser, D. Asymmetry in intergenerational family relationships. *Social Forces,* 1963, 41, 346–352.

Sweetser, D. Mother-daughter ties between generations in industrial societies. *Family Process,* 1964, 3, 332–343.

Sweetser, D. The effect of industrialization on intergenerational solidarity. *Rural Sociology,* 1966, 31, 156–170.

Tallman, I. Working-class wives in suburbia: Fulfillment or crisis. *Journal of Marriage and the Family,* 1969, 31, 65–72.

Tallman, I., & Morgner, R. Life-style differences among urban and suburban blue-collar families. *Social Forces,* 1969, 48, 334–348.

Taulbee, E., & Stenmark, D. The Blacky Pictures Test: A comprehensive annotated and indexed bibliography (1949–1967). *Journal of Projective Techniques,* 1968, 32, 105–137.

Thernstrom, S. *The Other Bostonians: Poverty and Progress in the American Metropolis, 1880–1970.* Cambridge, Mass.: Harvard University Press, 1973.

Thigpen, C. H., & Cleckley, H. A case of multiple personality. *Journal of Abnormal and Social Psychology,* 1954, 49, 135–151.

Thomas, J. L. The new immigration and cultural pluralism. *American Catholic Sociological Review,* 1954, 15, 310–322.

Thomas, J. L. *The American Catholic Family.* Englewood Cliffs, N.J.: Prentice-Hall, 1956.

Thomas, L. Family correlates of student political activism. *Developmental Psychology,* 1971, 4, 206–214.

Thompson, B. Cultural ties as determinants of immigrant settlement in urban areas: A case study of an Italian neighborhood in Worchester, Massachusetts, 1875–1922. Unpublished doctoral dissertation, Clark University, 1971.

Tolpin, M., & Kohut, H. The disorders of the self: The psychopathology of the first years of life. Paper presented to the Chicago Psychoanalytic Society, May 1979.

Tomasi, L. *The Italian-American Family.* Staten Island, N.Y.: Center for Migration Studies, 1972.

Tonnies, F. *Community and Society (1887).* New York: Harper Torchbooks, 1957.

Townsend, P. *The Family Life of Old People: An Inquiry in East London.* London: Routledge and Kegan Paul, 1957.

Troll, L. Issues in the study of generations. International Journal of *Aging and Human Development,* 1970, 7, 199–218.

Troll, L. The family of later life: A decade review. *Journal of Marriage and the Family,* 1971, 33, 263–290.

Troll, L., & Bengtson, V. Generations in the family. In W. Burr, B. Hill, F. I. Nye, & I. L. Reiss (Eds.), *Contemporary Theories about the Family: Volume I: Research Based Theories.* New York: Free Press, 1979, 127–161.

Troll, L., Miller, S., & Atchley, R. *Families in Later Life.* Belmont, Calif.: Wadsworth Publishing Co., 1979.

Troll, L., & Smith, J. Attachment through the life-span: Some questions about dyadic bonds among adults. *Human Development,* 1976, 19, 156–170.

Tsushima, W. Responses of Irish and Italian patients of two social classes under preoperative stress. *Journal of Personality and Social Psychology,* 1968, 8, 43–48.

Tulkin, S., & Cohler, B. Childrearing attitudes and mother-child interaction in the first year of life. *Merrill-Palmer Quarterly,* 1973, 19, 95–106.

Uzoka, A. The myth of the nuclear family: Historical background and clinical implications. *American Psychologist,* 1979, 34, 1095–1106.

Vaillant, G. *Adaptation to Life.* Boston: Little, Brown, 1977.

Varbero, R. Philadelphia's south Italians in the 1920s. In A. Davis & M. Haller (Eds.), *The Peoples of Philadelphia.* Philadelphia: Temple University Press, 1973, 255–275.

Vecoli, R. *Contadini* in Chicago: A critique of *The Uprooted. Journal of American History,* 1964, 51 405–417.

Vecoli, R. European Americans: From immigrants to ethnics. In W. Cartwright & R. Watson, (Eds.), *The Reinterpretation of American History.* Washington, D.C.: National Council for the Social Studies, 1973, 81–112.

Vecoli, R. Prelates and peasants: Italian immigrants and the Catholic church. *Journal of Social History,* 1969, 2, 217–268.

Vogel, E., & Vogel, S. Family security, personal immaturity, and emotional health in a Japanese sample. *Marriage and Family Living,* 1961, 23, 161–166.

Vogel, E., & Bell, N. The emotionally disturbed child as the family scapegoat. In N. Bell & E. Vogel, (Eds.), *A Modern Introduction to the Family.* New York: Free Press, 1960, 382–397.

Vogt, E., & Albert, E. *People of Rimrock: A Study of Values in Five Cultures.* Cambridge, Mass.: Harvard University Press, 1966.

Vollmer, H. The grandmother: A problem in childrearing. *American Journal of Orthopsychiatry,* 1937, 7, 378 –382.

Von Mises, R. *Positivism.* Cambridge, Mass.: Harvard University Press, 1951.

Wallin, P. Sex differences in attitudes to "in-laws." *American Journal of Sociology,* 1954, 50, 466–469.

Wallace, A. Revitalization movements. *American Anthropologist,* 1956, 58, 264–281.

Wallace, A., & Fogelson, R. The identity struggle. In M. Boszormenyi-Nagy, & J. Framo (Eds.), *Intensive Family Therapy.* New York: Harper & Row, 1965.

Ward, D. *Cities and Immigrants: A Geography of Change in Nineteenth-Century America* New York: Oxford University Press, 1971.

Ware, C. The breakdown of ethnic solidarity: The case of the Italian in Greenwich Village. In H. Stein, & C. Cloward (Eds.), *Social Perspectives on Behavior.* New York: Free Press, 1958, 114–138.

Warner, W. L., & Srole, L. *The Social Systems of American Ethnic Groups.* New Haven: Yale University Press, 1945.

Warner, W. L. *The Living and the Dead: Symbolic Life of Americans.* New Haven: Yale University Press, 1959.

Weber, M. Bureaucracy. In H. Girth, & C. W. Mills (Eds.), *From Max Weber: Essays in Sociology.* New York: Oxford University Press, 1958b, 196–244.

Weber, M. *The Protestant Ethic and the Spirit of Capitalism, (1905).* Translated by Talcott Parsons. New York: Charles Scribner, 1958a.

Weber, M. Ethnic groups. In M. Weber (Eds.), *Economy and Society.* Edited by Roth Guenther and Claus Wittick. New York: Bedminster Press, 1968, 385–398.

Weinstein, F., & Platt, G. *Psychoanalytic Sociology.* Baltimore: Johns Hopkins University Press, 1973.

Weiss, J. L., Grunebaum, H., & Schell, R. Psychotic mothers and their young children. II: Psychological studies of mothers caring for their infants in a psychiatric hospital. *Archives of General Psychiatry,* 1964, 2, 90–98.

Weiss, R., & Samelson, N. Social roles of American women: Their contribution to a sense of usefulness and importance. *Marriage and Family Living,* 1958, 20, 358–366.

Weissman, M., & Klerman, G. Sex differences in the epidemiology of depression. *Archives of General Psychiatry,* 1977, 34, 98–111.

Weissman, M., & Meyers, J. Affective disorders in a US urban community. *Archives of General Psychiatry, 1978, 35, 1304–1311.*

Weissman, M., Paykel, E., & Klerman, G. The depressed woman as a mother. *Social Psychiatry,* 1972, 7, 98–108.

Wenar, C. The reliability of mothers' histories. *Child Development,* 1961, 32, 491–500.

Wessman, A., & Ricks, D. *Mood and Personality.* New York: Wiley, 1966.

White, M. Social class, childrearing practices, and infant behavior. *American Sociological Review,* 1957, 22, 704–712.

White, R. W. Ego and reality in psychoanalytic theory. *Psychological Issues,* 1963, 3, Monograph Number 11.

White, R. W. *Lives in Progress* (rev. ed.). New York: Holt, Rinehart & Winston, 1966.

Whiting, B. (Ed.) *Six Cultures: Studies of Childrearing.* New York: Wiley, 1963.

Whiting, J., & Child, I. *Child Training and Personality.* New Haven: Yale University Press, 1953.

Whiting, J., Child, I., & Lambert, W. *Field Guide for a Study of Socialization.* New York: Wiley, 1966.

Whyte, W. *Street Corner Society.* Chicago: University of Chicago Press, 1943.

Whyte, W. Sicilian peasant society. *American Anthropologist,* 1944, 46, 65–74.

Wilmott, P., & Young, M. *Family and Class in a London Suburb.* London: Routledge and Kegan Paul, 1960.

Winch, R. Some observations on extended familism in the United States. In R. Winch, & L. Goodman (Eds.), *Selected Studies in Marriage and the Family. (3rd ed.).* New York: Holt, Rinehart & Winston, 1968, 127–138.

Winch, R., & Blumberg, R. Societal complexity and familial organization. In R. Winch, & L. Goodman (Eds.), *Selected Studies in Marriage and the Family* (3rd ed.). New York: Holt, Rinehart & Winston, 1968, 70–92.

Winch, R., & Greer, S. Urbanism, ethnicity and extended familism. *Journal of Marriage and the Family, 1968, 30, 40–45.*

Winch, R., Greer, S., & Blumberg, R. Ethnicity and extended familism in an upper-middle-class suburb. *American Sociological Review,* 1967, 32, 265–272.

Winnicott, D. W. Psychiatric disorders in terms of infantile maturational processes (1963). In D. W. Winnicott (Ed.), *The Maturational Processes and the Facilitating Environment*. New York: International Universities Press, 1965b, 230–242.

Winnicott, D. W. The theory of the parent-infant relationship (1960). In D. W. Winnicott (Ed.), *The Maturational Processes and the Facilitating Environment*. New York: International Universities Press, 1965a, 37–55.

Wirth, L. Urbanism as a way of life. *American Journal of Sociology*, 1938, 1–24, 40.

Wirth, L. The problem of minority groups. In R. Linton (Ed.), *Science of Man in the World Crisis*. New York: Columbia University Press, 1954, 347–372.

Wittke, C. *The Irish in America*. Baton Rouge: Louisiana State University Press, 1956.

Wolfenstein, M. Trends in infant care. *American Journal of Orthopsychiatry*, 1953, 23, 120–130.

Wolff, P. Observations on the early development of smiling. In B. Foss (Ed.), *Determinants of Infant Behavior*. New York: Wiley, 1963, 113–134.

Wolff, P. The causes, controls, and organization of behavior. *Psychological Issues*, 1966, 5, Whole Number 17.

Wood, V., & Robertson, J. Grandparenthood: A significant role to older individuals: Fact or fancy? Paper presented at annual meeting, Gerontological Society, Houston, 1970.

Wood, V., & Robertson, J. The significance of grandparenthood. In J. Gubrium (Ed.), *Time, Roles, and Self in Old Age*. New York: Human Sciences Press, 1976, 278–357.

Woods, R., Glavin, K., & Kettle, C. Mother-daughter comparison on selected aspects of childrearing in a high socioeconomic group. *Child Development*, 1960, 31, 121–128.

Wyatt, F. A psychologist looks at history. *Journal of Social Issues*, 1962, 26, 66–77.

Wyatt, F. The reconstruction of the individual and the collective past. In R. White (Ed.), *The Study of Lives: Essays in Honor of Henry Murray*. New York: Atherton, 1963, 305–320.

Wyatt, F., & Wilcox, S. B. Sir Henry Clinton: A psychological exploration in history. *William and Mary Quarterly*, 1959, 16, 3–26.

Wynne, L., Ryckoff, I., Day, J., & Hirsch, S. Pseudo-mutuality in the family relations of schizophrenics. *Psychiatry*, 21, 1958, 205–220.

Wynne, L., & Singer, M. Thought disorder and family relations of schizophrenics; I. A research strategy. *Archives of General Psychiatry*, 1963a, 9, 191–198.

Wynne, L., & Singer, M. Thought disorder and family relations of schizophrenics: II. A classification of forms of thinking. *Archives of General Psychiatry*, 1963b, 9, 199–206.

Yancey, W., Ericksen, E., & Juliana, R. Emergent ethnicity: A review and formulation. *American Sociological Review*, 1976, 41, 391–403.

Yans-McLaughlin, V. *Family and Community: Italian Immigrants in Buffalo, 1880–1930 (1971)*. Ithaca, N.Y.: Cornell University Press, 1977.

Yarrow, L., & Yarrow, M. Personality continuity and change in the family context. In P. Worchel, & D. Byrne (Eds.), *Personality Change*. New York: Wiley, 1964, 489–523.

Yarrow, M., Campbell, J., & Burton, R. *Childrearing: An Inquiry into Research and Methods*. San Francisco: Jossey-Bass, 1968.

Young, M., & Geertz, H. Old age in London and San Francisco: Some families compared. *British Journal of Sociology,* 1961, 12, 124–141.

Young, M., & Wilmott, P. *Family and Kinship in East London.* London: Routledge and Kegan Paul, 1957.

Zangwill, I. *The Melting Pot.* New York: Macmillan, 1909.

Zelen, S. Rorschach patterns in three generations of a family. In W. Klopfer (Ed.), *Developments in the Rorschach Technique,* Vol. 3. New York: Harper & Row, 1971, 143–205.

Zborowski, M. *People in Pain.* San Francisco: Jossey-Bass, 1969.

Zinberg, N., & Kaufman, I. *Normal Psychology of the Aging Process.* New York: International Universities Press, 1963.

Zuccino, A. The three-generation rural family in Italy. In E. Burgess (Ed.), *Aging in Western Societies.* Chicago: University of Chicago: University of Chicago Press, 1960, 439–440.

Appendix A

Pictures for the Interpersonal Apperception Technique

APPENDIX B

Mother Interview

As we may have told you before, we are interested in learning more about how families get along together, and we are especially interested in those everyday problems which arise in taking care of children. I would appreciate it if, in describing how things go in your family, you could be as specific as possible. In this way, we can get a better picture of what actually takes place.

1. To begin with, we'd like to get a picture of your family. How many children do you have?

    a. What are their names?

    b. How old are they?

2. Does anyone else live in your household beside you, your husband, and your children?

    a. Where do your own parents live now?

    (Be sure to determine if parents live in an adjoining household, either next door or share a duplex)

        (1) (If parents live apart from the mother) about how far is it from your house to their house? How long does it take to drive there?

3. Now, I'd like to talk with you about a typical day in your household. Was yesterday a fairly typical day for you? (If not, find a recent day which was fairly typical.)

    a. Now, I'd like for you to tell me *everything* that took place yesterday in your household from the time you awoke until the time you went to bed. As we go on, there may be some things which I'll want to talk about with you in greater detail.

    b. Let's start with the morning. How does the day begin in your household? What happens after you awaken?

        1. Who gets up first?

        2. What chores are there to be done in the morning?

            a. What specific chores do you have to do?

            b. Your husband?

            c. Any of your children?

        3. What kinds of time pressures are there to get off to school or work?

4. Who makes breakfast?

5. What do the children do while breakfast is being made?

6. What does your husband do while breakfast is being made?

7. (If someone else like maternal grandmother lives in household) What does _____ do while breakfast is being made?

8. How does your husband get to work?

9. (If mother has school-aged children) How do the children get to school? Who sees them off?

10. Is there any other important part of your routine in the morning that we haven't talked about yet?

c. What do you do after the children go off to school and/or your husband goes off to work? What is it like for you after the day has gotten underway?

1. Can you tell me how it feels after your husband has gone off to work?

2. How do you go about the morning chores? What do you do first?

3. What kinds of housework do you have? Are there certain things which you have to do, but not everyday?

    a. How long does it take you to do your housework?

    b. What parts of the housework do you like the least?

    c. What part of the housework do you most look forward to?

    d. What kind of help do you have in doing these chores?

4. (If m.g.m. lives in household or adjoining household) Does your mother ever help with the chores?

5. What do you do for a break in the morning from your work? What do you do when you have time free in the morning?

6. What does your baby do in the morning?

    a. What kind of a schedule does he/she have?

    b. Does he/she nap? For how long?

    c. How do you manage to do your work and look after the baby?

    d. What happens when the baby cries while you are doing the housework?

7. (If mother-grandmother in household or adjoining residence) Does your mother ever help with the baby in the morning? How were arrangements made for her to help out with P.?

d. How do things go at lunchtime?

1. Who is around at lunchtime?

2. (If mother-grandmother in household or nearby) Does your mother help out with the lunch?

3. Does the baby eat lunch with you?

a. How about fixing the baby's lunch and that of the other children? How do you arrange to get everyone's lunch fixed?

4. (If there are school-aged children) Do the children come home for lunch? Do they go back to school after lunch?

a. What time do they get home for lunch?

b. How do they get home?

c. How do they get back to school after lunch? What happens when it is raining outside?

5. How about cleaning up from lunch? Do you get any help with this?

6. Is your husband ever home at lunchtime? In what ways does he help you at this time?

e. What happens after lunchtime? How do you find time for yourself?

1. Do you ever have time for a nap?

2. What other forms of relaxation do you have at this time during the day?

3. How do you arrange to see your friends during the day?

4. Who helps care for the children when you wish to go out for the afternoon? How do you arrange for this?

5. Do you ever have people over for the afternoon?

a. How do you arrange for the care of the children at these times?

6. How about errands? What kinds of errands do you have to do?

a. How do you manage both errands and taking care of the children?

b. How does it go when the children come with you to the store?

7. What kinds of difficulties do you have arranging time to do things for yourself?

f. (If mother has school-aged children) What happens when the children come home from school? What sort of things do they do then?

1. How about when the children want to go off with their chums after school? What arrangements do you make with them?

2. How do the children seek your permission?

3. Do their playmates ever come to your house? How does this work out?

a. How do you feel about their going into the kitchen?

b. What happens if they are playing and bring their play into other rooms of the house?

c. In what ways do these activities interfere with what you are trying to do?

d. Do the children have some friends you'd rather not have them invite over? Why? What do you do about this?

g. (If mother-grandmother lives in household, adjoining or within a short drive) In what ways does your mother help out with the children during the day? Does she ever come to baby-sit? How about if you want to go out during the day? Can she come over to sit at such times? How do you feel about her taking care of the children at such times?

h. (If mother has school-aged children) Do the children have chores in the afternoon?

    1. What happens if the children don't do their chores? What do you do then?

    2. Do the children get paid for their chores? Do they get any sort of allowance?

    3. How do they feel about doing the chores? Who is responsible for seeing that the chores get done?

i. What other things do the children do in the afternoon?

    1. What sorts of things do you and they do together?

        a. What is your favorite thing to do with them in the afternoon?

        b. What sorts of things would you rather not do with them?

        c. How does this differ, depending on whether it is summertime or wintertime?

        d. What sorts of things that the children do in the afternoon most upset you?

j. (If the mother has both older and younger children) What responsibilities have the older children for caring for their younger brothers and sisters?

    1. What happens when the older children wish to go out with their friends and not care for their younger brother (sister)?

k. What time does your husband come home from work?

    1. What is the first thing he does when he comes in the door?

    2. What is his mood usually like at this time?

    3. How does this make you feel? When he's cross? When he's cheerful?

    4. Does your husband help out with the children at this time?

    5. What does your husband most like to do when he comes home? What would you most like for him to do?

    6. What do the children do when your husband comes home? How do they react?

l. What time do you have supper?

    1. Do you try to finish up with the children before dinner? How do you manage to both tend to the children and get dinner?

2. (If mother has both a baby and older children) How do you manage to care for the baby at this time? Do you try to get the baby fed into bed before you start supper?

3. (If mother-grandmother in household or adjoining) Does your mother help at this time?

    a. In what ways does she help with the baby at this time?

    b. Does she help prepare the dinner?

    c. How about the older children, does she help with them?

    d. Does she have particular dishes that she makes which you like? How about dishes she makes which you don't like?

4. Who teaches the children table manners at dinner?

    a. What kinds of table manners do you expect?

    b. What happens if one of the chidren refuses to "eat properly?" What do you do then?

5. If the children do not like what has been prepared, what happens then?

    a. Are they ever forced to finish their plates?

    b. Do you force them to take taste-bites?

m. After dinner, who cleans up? In what ways do you get help at this time?

n. What happens after dinner in your household?

    1. What do you do at this time?

    2. What does your husband do at this time?

    3. What do your children do now?

    4. If mother-grandmother in household) What does your mother do at this time?

o. What time do the children go to bed? Who gets them to bed?

    1. What happens if they refuse to go to bed?

    2. What happens when they want to get up, get a drink of water, etc., after you have put them to bed?

    3. How do you let the children know it is time for bed?

    4. (If mother has school-aged children) What happens if _____ hasn't finished his school work and bedtime comes?

    5. What does your husband do to help get the children in bed? Who is more firm about the bedtime regime?

p. What do you do after the children are in bed?

    1. What kinds of chores remain to be done at this time?

    2. What forms of relaxation do you have in the evening?

q. What happens when you want to go out for the evening alone, with your friends? Who baby-sits at this time?

r.   What about when you and your husband want to go out at night? Who baby-sits then?

   1.   Why do you choose a particular sitter?

   2.   What is the sitter supposed to do about it if the children wake up? If they won't stay in bed?

   3.   What happens when the children fuss and cry when left with the babysitter?

      a.   Do you ever cancel your plans rather than go out?

      b.   Do you call in during the evening? Do you worry about the children at such times?

      c.   Some mothers feel guilty about going out and leaving the children with a babysitter. In what ways do you feel guilty about going out and leaving the children with a babysitter?

   4.   (If mother-grandmother in household, adjoining residence, or nearby)

      a.   Does your mother ever sit for you in the evening?

      b.   What problems does this raise? Different from when other people baby-sit for you?

4. We've talked a good deal about how things go in your family. Now, before we finish, I'd like to talk with you about yourself and some of your own feelings.

(If mother and grandmother *share a common household* or *live adjacent*)

   a.   How did you and your mother decide to share a common household (or live next door to each other)?

   b.   When did this take place?

   c.   How did your husband feel about this decision?

   d.   How do your mother and husband get along together? Can you tell me about a recent disagreement that they had? How was this disagreement resolved?

   e.   How about you? What kinds of disagreements do you have with your mother? Can you tell me about one such disagreement? How was it settled? How do these disagreements differ from those you had, say, about the time you got married?

   f.   How does it make you feel living with (next door to) your own mother? What special problems does it create for you? For your family? What advantages do you see from living next door to your mother?

   g.   What kinds of disagreements do you and your mother have regarding the care of the children? How do you settle these disagreements? Can you tell me about one such time recently?

   h.   How frequently do you see your mother? (If mother lives adjoining) How often do you see your mother? Who usually makes the first contact? Any special time during the day? How? Telephone or in person? How frequently do you contact her? How frequently does she contact you? What kinds of things do you do together during the day? What kinds of things does she like to do that you don't like to do? How about things you like to do which she does not? Has your pattern of visiting and talking with each other changed over the years? Do you think you have become more or less close to each other as you have grown and had children of your own? How would you compare your relationship with your own mother with that which you have with your mother-in-law?

a.   How often do you see your mother-in-law? What sorts of things do you do when you are together?

b.   In what ways is it easier to get along with your mother-in-law than with your mother?

c.   In what ways is it more difficult to get along with your mother-in-law than with your mother?

i.   How do your children get along with your mother? What special problems do they have getting along with her? What special problems do they cause her? What kinds of disagreements do your children and your mother get into? How are they resolved?

j.   As you look back over the years, and your own childhood, how would you compare the ways in which you are raising your children with the ways in which your mother raised you? What specific similarities do you see? What differences do you see?

(1) Are the differences you see the result of conscious decisions to do things differently from your mother? How did this come about?

k.   Are there things which your mother does with the children which you would rather she not do? Are there some things which she doesn't do which you would like for her to do?

l.   How about you? In what ways could your mother be of more help to you than she is? What kind of advice do you ask her about caring for the children?

m.   How about with your husband? Are there ways in which he could be of more help to you than he is?

1.   What particular kinds of disagreements do you have with your husband? Can you describe one time recently when you had a disagreement?

2.   How about in terms of raising children? Are there ways in which you and your husband disagree on how children are to be raised? How do you settle these disagreements?

n.   Are there some other things about how things are going now in your family which we should know in order to get the best picture of what things are like in your household?

(If mother and grandmother *live apart*)

a.   How close to each other do you and your mother live? Was there ever a time when you lived closer to each other? Did you ever share a common house or apartment? When?

b.   How do your husband and mother get along together? Can you tell me about a recent disagreement that they had? How was this disagreement resolved?

c.   How about you? What kinds of disagreements do you have with your mother? Can you describe one recent disagreement for me? How was it resolved? How do these disagreements differ from those you had, say, about the time you got married?

d.   How do you feel living as far from your mother as you do? What special problems does this create for you? What advantages do you see from living as far apart as you do?

e.   What kinds of disagreements do you and your mother have regarding the care of the children? How do you settle these disagreements? Can you tell me about one time recently when you had a disagreement about this? How was it resolved?

f.   How frequently do you talk with your mother over the telephone? Who usually calls first? Any special time during the day?

g.   How about visiting with each other? How frequently do you visit with each other? Who usually arranges such visits?

Do you go to her house? Does she come to your house? Any special time during the day? How long does it take to get from your house to hers? Can you walk there? What sorts of things do you do when you get together? What sorts of things do you talk about? Are there some things which she likes to do which you don't like to do? Are there some things which you like to do which she does not? Has your pattern of visiting changed over the years? Do you think you have gotten more or less close to each other as you have grown and had children of your own?

h.   How do your children get along with your mother? What special problems do they have getting along with her? What special problems do they cause her? What kinds of disagreements do your children and your mother get into? How are they resolved?

How would you compare your relationship with your own mother with that which you have with your mother-in-law?

a.   How often do you see your mother-in-law? What sorts of things do you do when you are together?

b.   In what ways is it easier to get along with your mother-in-law than with your mother?

c.   In what ways is it more difficult to get along with your mother-in-law than with your mother?

i.   As you look back over the years, and your own childhood, how would you compare the ways in which you are raising your children with the ways in which your mother raised you? What specific similarities do you see? What differences do you see?

    1.   Are the differences you see the result of conscious decisions to do things differently from your mother? How did this come about?

j.   Are there things which your mother does with the children which you would rather she not do? Are there some things which she doesn't do which you would like for her to do?

k.   How about you? In what ways could your mother be of more help to you than she is? What kind of advice do you ask your mother about caring for children?

l.   How about your husband? Are there ways in which he could be of more help to you than he is?

    1.   What particular kinds of disagreements do you have with your husband? Can you describe a time recently when you had a disagreement. How was it resolved?

    2.   How about in terms of raising children? Are there ways in which you and your husband disagree about how the children are to be raised? How do you settle these disagreements?

m.   Are there some other things going on in your family which we should know about in order to have the best picture of how things go in your household?

5. Finally, I'd like to ask a bit about your family cultural traditions.

a.   Are you and your mother of the same religion? Same cultural group? (If not) how did this come about? What kinds of tensions does it create in the family?

b.   How about you and your husband? Are you of the same religious tradition? How has this worked out in raising your children? (If different traditions) what kinds of problems has this created? What solutions have you tried? How about in terms of cultural background? What differences are these? What problems has this created in bringing up your children?

APPENDIX C

Grandmother Interview

As we may have told you before, we are interested in how families get along together and in how different members of the family understand what happens. Grandmothers, since they have raised their own children, and watch another generation growing up, are in an especially good position to see what is going on in a family. We have some questions to ask you about how things have changed since your own family grew up. I would appreciate it if you could be as specific as possible in answering our questions, in order that we may be sure to understand things as you see them.

1. To begin with, how many children do you have?

    a. How old are they?

    b. Which ones are married?

    c. Where do they live? How far away?

2. Who else lives in your household at this time?

    a. (If mother and grandmother do not share common or adjacent households) How long does it take to get from your house to Mrs. X's household? How frequently do you visit? How do you usually get there?

    b. (If mother and grandmother share common or adjacent residence) Can you tell me how it developed that you and Mrs. X decided to live next door (upstairs/downstairs) or together?

3. How often do you and Mrs. X see each other?

    a. (If mother and grandmother live in same household) When during the day do you see each other? What sorts of things do you do together?

    b. If mother and grandmother live in adjoining residence) What arrangements have you and Mrs. X made to see each other during the day? How do you contact each other? Does she call and come to see you, or do you come to see her? How frequently do you call each other? How frequently do you see each other?

    c. (If mother and grandmother live apart) How often each week do you speak with each other on the phone? How often each week do you see each other? Who usually arranges these contacts? How do you get together— does she come to your house or do you go to her house? Are there any particular occasions when you are more likely to visit with each other?

4. Now I'd like to talk with you about a typical day in your household. Was yesterday a typical day? (If not, find a recent day which was typical.)

a. I'd like you to describe for me what a typical day is like for you. (Try and get grandmother's description of what she did the preceding day. If she works, the time she leaves the house and comes home. We are interested here mainly in her contacts with her own daughter, and not in her life apart from the family.)

b. (If grandmother and mother share a common household) I'm especially interested in how you see your place in the household, what sorts of things you must do during the day and how the day goes for you.

1. What time do you wake up in the morning? Who is up in the morning when you get up? What specific chores do you have in the morning? How was it decided that these were things you would do?

2. How about in getting the breakfast? What do you do at this time?

3. How about when Mr. X is off to work (and/or the children are off to school)? Wht do you do at these times?

4. In what ways do you help with the morning housework? What do you do around the house in the morning?

5. What about relaxation in the morning? What do you do when you want a few minutes to yourself?

6. How about lunchtime? What happens in the household at lunchtime. Do you help with preparation of the lunch? Do you have particular responsibilities at this time?

7. After lunch, what do you like to do? Do you and Mrs. X ever do anything together at this time?

8. (If school-aged children in the house) How about when the children come home from school in the afternoon? Do you have to look after them at these times?

q. What about when Mrs. X goes off to shop or run errands? Do you usually go with her? What do you do at home at these times?

10. How about when Mrs. X goes off with friends during the day? What arrangements do you and she make at these times?

11. What happens at suppertime in the household? What does everyone do at this time? Do you help prepare supper? Do the dishes?

12. How about in getting the children ready for bed? What do you do at these times?

13. After the children are in bed, the dishes done, what do you do in the evening?

14. In what ways do you wish you had more privacy or more time to yourself in the evenings or during the day? What have you done about this? How do you manage to see your own friends? What arrangements

do you make? Do your own friends ever come by to see you during the day?

c.   (If mother and grandmother live in adjoining residences) I'm especially interested in what contact you and Mrs. X have during the day and in the things you do together or for each other. (If grandmother has children below age 12, use the mother typical day schedule.) Was yesterday a typical day? (If not, find a recent day which was typical.)

  1.   When did you and Mrs. X first have contact with each other? By phone? In person? Who contacts whom? Who usually contacts the other first?

  2.   Do you and Mrs. X have any particular things which you do together each day? What sorts of things are they?

  3.   What other times yesterday did you see or talk to Mrs. X?

  4.   What sorts of problems arise from living so close to each other? Do you have any particular chores or responsibilities to help Mrs. X? How about leading separate lives? In what ways is it difficult to lead your own lives? How do you manage to avoid seeing each other when you wish to do so?

  5.   What advantages come from living as close to each other as you do?

c.   (If mother and grandmother live apart from each other) I'm especially interested in what contact you and Mrs. X have during the day and in the things you do together or the ways in which you help each other during the day. Was yesterday a typical day for you? (If not, find a typical recent day.)

  1.   When did you and Mrs. X first have contact with each other yesterday? By phone? In person? Who contacted whom? Who usually makes the first contact?

  2.   Do you and Mrs. X have any particular things which you do together? What?

  3.   Are there any particular duties such as babysitting which you help with? How frequently? How is this arranged?

  4.   What kinds of difficulties are there in not living closer to each other than you do? Was there ever a time when you did live closer to each other than now? (Get detailed picture of mother-grandmother relationship at that time, using either b. or c. above.)

  5.   What kinds of difficulties are there in not living closer to each other than you do?

5. We've talked quite a bit about what happens in your household during the course of a typical day and about how frequently you see and talk with each other. Now I'd like to talk with you about some things related more closely to yourself and how you and Mrs. X's family get along together.

a. How do you and Mr. X get along together? What kinds of disagreements have you had? Can you give me an example of one time recently when this happened? How was it resolved?

b. How about you and Mrs. X? What kinds of disagreements have you two had? Can you describe one such disagreement recently? How was it resolved? How have things between you changed as Mrs. X has had a family of her own? What kinds of disagreements do you have now that you didn't have before? What kinds of disagreements you used to have no longer happen?

c. What happens when your daughter asks you to baby-sit for her and you have other plans? What do you say to her at such times?

d. What about when she's busy and you need her help? What does she say to you?

e. As you look back over the way in which you raised Mrs. X, and the way she is raising her own children, what differences do you see between the way in which you raised your children and the way in which she is raising her own children?

    1. What special kinds of difficulties did you have rearing Mrs. X which you didn't have raising your other children? In what ways was she easier to raise than your other children?

    2. In what ways has Mrs. X grown up to be different from what you had hoped or expected?

f. What kinds of things which Mrs. X does with her children would you prefer that she not do? What sorts of things doesn't she do which you would prefer that she do?

    1. Do you ever talk with Mrs. X about the way in whch she is raising her children? Does she ever come to talk with you about the difficulties she is having with her children? What sorts of things about the way she is raising her children do you talk over together?

g. How would you compare the way in which your mother raised you with the way in which you raised your own children?

    1. In what ways did your mother discipline the children different from the ways in which you disciplined the chidren?

    2. How about in terms of manners and social freedoms, what kinds of differences were there?

    3. How about in terms of what you expected your children to be like around the house? Did your own mother expect children to behave any differently from the way in which you expected children to behave?

h. What was (is) your husband like? Can you describe him for me?

    1. What kinds of things did (do) you like to do together?

    2. In what ways did (does) he help with chores around the house?

3. In what ways did you and he disagree on the ways in which Mrs. X was to be raised? In what ways did you agree?

4. In what ways did he fail to understand you and your problems? What kinds of disagreements did you have with him?

5. What differences did you and your husband have in your expectations of what Mrs. X and the other children would be like when they were grown up?

i.   Finally, I'd like to ask you a bit about your family cultural traditions.

1. Are you and Mrs. X from the same religion or national group? (If not)

   a.   How did this difference come about?

   b.   What kinds of tensions has it created in the family?

2. How about your son-in-law? Is he from the same religious background or cultural tradition as your family? (If not)

   a.   What kinds of tensions has this caused in the family?

   b.   How have these problems been settled?

j.   Are there any other things we should know in order to understand how your family gets along? Are there any questions you would like to ask me about the interview and our study?

Appendix D

Questionnaire for Mothers (Form DD)

The following statements represent matters of interest and concern to mothers. Not all mothers feel the same way about them. Read each statement carefully and circle the number at the left which most closely reflects YOUR degree of agreement or disagreement. Try to answer all statements without skipping items or looking back.

1	2	3	4	5	6
Strongly agree	Moderately agree	Slightly agree	Slightly disagree	Moderately disagree	Strongly disagree

(Circle one)

1 2 3 4 5 6   (1)   When the baby is born he (she) already has a personality of his (her) own.

1 2 3 4 5 6   (2)   Holding and caressing a baby when he (she) cries is good for him (her).

1 2 3 4 5 6   (3)   A newborn baby doesn't cry unless something is wrong.

1 2 3 4 5 6   (4)   Ships, snails and puppy dog tails, that's what little boys are made of.

1 2 3 4 5 6   (5)   Newborn babies are fragile and delicate and must be handled extremely carefully.

1 2 3 4 5 6   (6)   A mother just naturally knows when to pick up a crying baby.

1 2 3 4 5 6   (7)   It is worth a great deal of effort on the mother's part to provide surprises for her child.

1 2 3 4 5 6   (8)   Taking care of a baby is much more work than pleasure.

1 2 3 4 5 6   (9)   A mother doesn't really think of her baby as a person until it begins to smile and recognize people.

1 2 3 4 5 6   (10)   Babies wish that their mothers would stop fussing over them too much.

427

1	2	3	4	5	6
Strongly agree	Moderately agree	Slightly agree	Slightly disagree	Moderately disagree	Strongly disagree

(Circle one)

1 2 3 4 5 6   (11)   It is a terribly frustrating task to care for a newborn infant, because he (she) can't let you know what he (she) needs.

1 2 3 4 5 6   (12)   It is upsetting to a mother when her infant leaves half the formula in his (her) bottle.

1 2 3 4 5 6   (13)   A mother's carelessness, even for a moment, can easily cause an infant to die.

1 2 3 4 5 6   (14)   A neat, well-ordered home is one of the most important things a narent can provide a child in growing up.

1 2 3 4 5 6   (15)   Mother ᴊoy breast feeding much more than bottle feedinɡ.

1 2 3 4 5 6   (16)   A mother and her five month old child should be able to understand each other fairly well.

1 2 3 4 5 6   (17)   Parents often over-estimate the importance of encouraging children's curiosity about the world around them.

1 2 3 4 5 6   (18)   A child never gets angry with his (her) mother.

1 2 3 4 5 6   (19)   A woman wants her mother nearby when she is giving birth.

1 2 3 4 5 6   (20)   A three month old baby can't really tell you what he (she) is thinking by a smile.

1 2 3 4 5 6   (21)   Infants should be kept on a regular feeding schedule and should be fed only at certain times.

1 2 3 4 5 6   (22)   When a child cries, his (her) parents should comfort him (her).

1 2 3 4 5 6   (23)   Mothers are better than fathers at raising girls.

1 2 3 4 5 6   (24)   Infants under five months of age are not well able to occupy themselves, and they like frequent adult attention.

1 2 3 4 5 6   (25)   Bodily changes in pregnancy make a woman feel very unattractive.

1 2 3 4 5 6   (26)   If a baby seldom smiles or coos it's because his (her) mother doesn't play with him (her) enough.

1	2	3	4	5	6
Strongly agree	Moderately agree	Slightly agree	Slightly disagree	Moderately disagree	Strongly disagree

(Circle one)

1 2 3 4 5 6 (27) Babies are more difficult to take care of when they are very young than when they are older.

1 2 3 4 5 6 (28) New mothers may feel a little uncomfortable the first time they wash their baby's genitals.

1 2 3 4 5 6 (29) The questions children ask often seem to be ridiculous.

1 2 3 4 5 6 (30) Babies prefer to be cared for by their mothers rather than by their fathers.

1 2 3 4 5 6 (31) One big trouble about having babies is that you can't do the things you liked to do before the baby was born.

1 2 3 4 5 6 (32) Too long feeding at the breast is apt to make the baby too dependent on the mother.

1 2 3 4 5 6 (33) Opinions of neighbors, relatives, and friends should be ignored in raising your own children.

1 2 3 4 5 6 (34) Nowadays a little girl should be allowed to do the same things her brother does.

1 2 3 4 5 6 (35) In deciding when the baby is really ready to give up the bottle, a mother's judgment should be more important than what the baby seems to want.

1 2 3 4 5 6 (36) The pleasure of one or both partners is the main reason for sexual intercourse.

1 2 3 4 5 6 (37) Mothers have no difficulties in bringing up children.

1 2 3 4 5 6 (38) Mothers don't like it when babies grab the spoon while being fed.

1 2 3 4 5 6 (39) Newborn babies are much more like each other than they are different from each other.

1 2 3 4 5 6 (40) It is foolish for a mother to lie awake at night worrying about whether or not her infant is breathing.

1 2 3 4 5 6 (41) A mother's milk can be bad for her infant.

1 2 3 4 5 6 (42) Babies are frequently so demanding that their mothers have no time for anything else.

1 2 3 4 5 6 (43) The best person to help you be a mother is your own mother.

1	2	3	4	5	6
Strongly agree	Moderately agree	Slightly agree	Slightly disagree	Moderately disagree	Strongly disagree

(Circle one)

1 2 3 4 5 6   (44)   Most of the time small babies don't even understand it when their mothers smile at them.

1 2 3 4 5 6   (45)   Children should always be polite and courteous to their parents.

1 2 3 4 5 6   (46)   The six-month-old baby can tell you exactly what he (she) wants if you watch and listen.

1 2 3 4 5 6   (47)   Regardless of their age, babies sometimes seem to be lonely and unhappy.

1 2 3 4 5 6   (48)   Pediatricians could be much more useful in helping mothers to bring up their children.

1 2 3 4 5 6   (49)   A mother is especially glad to let someone else hold her baby, but she is secretly pleased when the baby shows that it prefers her.

1 2 3 4 5 6   (50)   A seven-month-old baby should be picked up when he (she) cries.

1 2 3 4 5 6   (51)   Preventing a child from sucking his (her) thumb when he (she) wants may be bad for the child.

1 2 3 4 5 6   (52)   It's a healthy sign of growing up when a child can defy his (her) parents' commands.

1 2 3 4 5 6   (53)   Naturally, a child is born with the feeling that his (her) feces and urine are dirty and unpleasant.

1 2 3 4 5 6   (54)   Feeding at the breast is more satisfying for a child than feeding from the bottle.

1 2 3 4 5 6   (55)   Children are people, and their right to disagree with their parents should be respected.

1 2 3 4 5 6   (56)   If a mother plays very much with her seven-month-old baby he (she) will want her to be around all the time.

1 2 3 4 5 6   (57)   A woman's body can never look quite the same once she has given birth to a child.

1 2 3 4 5 6   (58)   If a young boy is to develop into the right kind of man, he should begin while he is still quite young to learn what men do.

1	2	3	4	5	6
Strongly agree	Moderately agree	Slightly agree	Slightly disagree	Moderately disagree	Strongly disagree

(Circle one)

1 2 3 4 5 6   (59)   Doctors should pay a lot more attention to the mother's feelings during labor and childbirth than they do.

1 2 3 4 5 6   (60)   Mothers would prefer that their little babies not squirm and wiggle so much.

1 2 3 4 5 6   (61)   Sugar and spice and everything nice, that's what little girls are made of.

1 2 3 4 5 6   (62)   A child should not be permitted to cry.

1 2 3 4 5 6   (63)   If you want to know how good a mother any woman will be, find out how good her own mother was.

1 2 3 4 5 6   (64)   Parents are never embarrassed by what their children say in public.

1 2 3 4 5 6   (65)   Babies are only sad on a few occasions; mostly they giggle and seem happy.

1 2 3 4 5 6   (66)   A mother gets physical pleasure out of holding, hugging, and kissing her child.

1 2 3 4 5 6   (67)   A child must get his (her) anger out of his (her) system, even if his (her) mother happens to be the victim.

1 2 3 4 5 6   (68)   It is better that babies do not use the cup until they themselves are ready to do so.

1 2 3 4 5 6   (69)   It is perfectly all right for a three or four year old to take a bath or shower with his (her) parents.

1 2 3 4 5 6   (70)   Babies need love and attention, but not nearly as much as most mothers give them.

1 2 3 4 5 6   (71)   Fathers don't know so very much about small babies, so its better to leave things to the mother.

1 2 3 4 5 6   (72)   Even the best mother feels some disgust when cleaning up the mess in her infant's diapers.

1 2 3 4 5 6   (73)   Even though a seven-month-old baby can do some things for himself (herself) it is better for the mother to do them until she is sure.

1 2 3 4 5 6   (74)   Mothers have a special knack for raising boys.

1	2	3	4	5	6
Strongly agree	Moderately agree	Slightly agree	Slightly disagree	Moderately disagree	Strongly disagree

(Circle one)

1 2 3 4 5 6   (75)   Parents should ignore their child's crying when it is just for attention.

1 2 3 4 5 6   (76)   A mother should breast feed her baby only if she can.

1 2 3 4 5 6   (77)   It is often better for a mother to suffer than to frustrate her young child.

1 2 3 4 5 6   (78)   Sexual intercourse should be at the suggestion of the man.

1 2 3 4 5 6   (79)   Thumb sucking should be curbed by the use of medicine or gloves.

1 2 3 4 5 6   (80)   If a young girl is to develop into the right kind of woman, she should begin while she is still quite young to learn what women do.

1 2 3 4 5 6   (81)   A mother has to make great sacrifices for her child.

1 2 3 4 5 6   (82)   A one-year-old child doesn't really feel his (her) mother is "with him (her)" if she is doing something else at the same time.

1 2 3 4 5 6   (83)   A child should be weaned as early as possible, even though he (she) may protest somewhat.

1 2 3 4 5 6   (84)   Young children should be allowed to see other members of the household in the nude.

1 2 3 4 5 6   (85)   Good mothers keep a tight hold on their child's expression of angry feelings.

1 2 3 4 5 6   (86)   Children never lie to their mothers.

1 2 3 4 5 6   (87)   A mother has more pride in herself than a childless woman.

1 2 3 4 5 6   (88)   It is wrong to tell young children that the stork brought them.

1 2 3 4 5 6   (89)   While it is well to take the baby's feelings into account, he (she) should learn to use the cup even if he (she) doesn't like it at first.

1 2 3 4 5 6   (90)   Most ten-month-old babies are too young to enjoy being with other babies of the same age.

1	2	3	4	5	6
Strongly agree	Moderately agree	Slightly agree	Slightly disagree	Moderately disagree	Strongly disagree

(Circle one)

1 2 3 4 5 6   (91)   Little boys and little girls are both mischievous, but a mother has to be more firm with her little boy than with her little girl.

1 2 3 4 5 6   (92)   A one-year-old child enjoys playing games with his (her) parents but cannot be expected to begin them himself (herself).

1 2 3 4 5 6   (93)   If parents are ready to go out for the evening and their year-old baby reacts by crying and screaming, it is best for them to cancel their plans.

1 2 3 4 5 6   (94)   One of the worst things a mother can do is to insist that the child obey her every command.

1 2 3 4 5 6   (95)   Little boys can be expected to cry just as much as little girls.

1 2 3 4 5 6   (96)   A child is only as curious about the world as his (her) parents encourage him (her) to be.

1 2 3 4 5 6   (97)   Mothers who are pregnant should volunteer information about sex to their children.

1 2 3 4 5 6   (98)   A child should be punished for breaking his (her) own toys in a fit of anger.

1 2 3 4 5 6   (99)   dMost of the time a one-year-old hates to let his (her) mother out of his (her) sight.

1 2 3 4 5 6   (100)   Children seem to ask questions about things which should not concern them.

1 2 3 4 5 6   (101)   There is some kind of a bond between mothers and their young sons which fathers may even be a little jealous of.

1 2 3 4 5 6   (102)   The more permissive a mother is, the better it is for her baby.

1 2 3 4 5 6   (103)   Giving an eighteen-month old things which he (she) is allowed to break encourages destructive tendencies and makes for later problems.

1 2 3 4 5 6   (104)   A woman needs her mother nearby when she is giving birth.

1	2	3	4	5	6
Strongly agree	Moderately agree	Slightly agree	Slightly disagree	Moderately disagree	Strongly disagree

(Circle one)

1 2 3 4 5 6   (105)   It is never too early to start teaching a child to obey commands.

1 2 3 4 5 6   (106)   Children cannot be expected to begin controlling their tempers before they are one year old.

1 2 3 4 5 6   (107)   A child should be fed when he (she) is hungry.

1 2 3 4 5 6   (108)   A typical one-year-old baby is likely to get upset when he (she) is left with a babysitter.

1 2 3 4 5 6   (109)   Children should be more considerate of their mothers, since their mothers do so much for them.

1 2 3 4 5 6   (110)   No matter what their parents request, children often shake their heads "no".

1 2 3 4 5 6   (111)   Parents always tell the truth to their children.

1 2 3 4 5 6   (112)   At the age of twelve to eighteen months a child should be put to bed at a fixed hour even if he (she) protests to show that he (she) is not sleepy.

1 2 3 4 5 6   (113)   Mothers have a special knack for raising girls.

1 2 3 4 5 6   (114)   A child should be permitted to say "I hate you" to his (her) parents.

1 2 3 4 5 6   (115)   When an eighteen-month old begins to destroy things around the house, it is well to let him (her) express the same feelings with things he (she) is allowed to break.

1 2 3 4 5 6   (116)   A fifteen-month-old child should decide for himself (herself) when he (she) is ready to begin using the toilet.

1 2 3 4 5 6   (117)   Generally a one-year-old child should not feel frightened when he (she) sees new faces.

1 2 3 4 5 6   (118)   "Spare the rod and spoil the child" is old-fashioned foolishness.

1 2 3 4 5 6   (119)   Everything a mother does for a child is done with the child's best interests in mind.

1 2 3 4 5 6   (120)   Little boys do not like their mothers to be tender and show fondness towards them as much as little girls do.

1	2	3	4	5	6
Strongly agree	Moderately agree	Slightly agree	Slightly disagree	Moderately disagree	Strongly disagree

(Circle one)

1 2 3 4 5 6   (121)   Parents should encourage a child to use his (her) imagination, even if it leads to fantastic ideas.

1 2 3 4 5 6   (122)   Parents cannot make children learn anything unless they want to.

1 2 3 4 5 6   (123)   It is his mother's own fault if her son acts like a sissy and "hangs on her apron strings."

1 2 3 4 5 6   (124)   A mother can easily understand how a child gets great pleasure out of taking things apart and knocking things down.

1 2 3 4 5 6   (125)   A child enjoys exploring new things, but what is known and familiar to him (her) is much more important if he (she) is to feel secure.

1 2 3 4 5 6   (126)   Babies act like they are the most important people in the household and are always demanding things.

1 2 3 4 5 6   (127)   A mother needs to be clever in learning how to discourage her four year old from asking questions about sex until he (she) is old enough.

1 2 3 4 5 6   (128)   The ability to be a good mother is mainly an innate or inborn quality.

1 2 3 4 5 6   (129)   Children should be permitted to argue with their parents.

1 2 3 4 5 6   (130)   Even though a three or four year old boy might like to play with dolls, he should be encouraged to do other things instead.

1 2 3 4 5 6   (131)   A stubborn child should be taught early that his (her) parents' will is stronger than his (hers).

1 2 3 4 5 6   (132)   It is reasonable for a mother to be disturbed when she sees a child playing with his or her genitals.

1 2 3 4 5 6   (133)   Menstruation is an important reminder of a woman's femininity and her ability to bear children.

1 2 3 4 5 6   (134)   Children should be encouraged to express their anger as well as their more pleasant feelings.

1 2 3 4 5 6   (135)   Little boys are naturally tougher than little girls.

1	2	3	4	5	6
Strongly agree	Moderately agree	Slightly agree	Slightly disagree	Moderately disagree	Strongly disagree

(Circle one)

1 2 3 4 5 6   (136)   Mothers never worry about what their children will turn into when they grow up.

1 2 3 4 5 6   (137)   It is very hard to know where to stop once you allow a child of twenty-one months to get away with destructive behavior.

1 2 3 4 5 6   (138)   Husbands could do a great deal more to be of help to their wives during the early months of motherhood.

1 2 3 4 5 6   (139)   The earlier the child is put on the potty, the easier it is to train him (her).

1 2 3 4 5 6   (140)   If you give a child an inch, he (she) will take a mile.

1 2 3 4 5 6   (141)   Parents prefer quiet children to active ones.

1 2 3 4 5 6   (142)   It is a good idea to dress a baby boy in blue and a baby girl in pink.

1 2 3 4 5 6   (143)   A mother should take action the very first time her child disobeys her.

1 2 3 4 5 6   (144)   Even when they are young, some little children seem to be too "sexy".

1 2 3 4 5 6   (145)   Although she realizes that boys must be boys, it scares the living daylights out of a mother to think of what they might do.

1 2 3 4 5 6   (146)   A child of two should not have temper tantrums.

1 2 3 4 5 6   (147)   A child is never too young to have a pet.

1 2 3 4 5 6   (148)   Feeling a baby kicking and moving inside you is a wonderful sign of new life.

1 2 3 4 5 6   (149)   When a child doesn't like certain foods, his (her) mother should stop feeding them to him (her).

1 2 3 4 5 6   (150)   Children should be permitted to play in sand and mud if they wish to.

1 2 3 4 5 6   (151)   If three-year-olds have toys they can take apart, they are likely to think they can do the same with valuable things in the house.

1	2	3	4	5	6
Strongly agree	Moderately agree	Slightly agree	Slightly disagree	Moderately disagree	Strongly disagree

(Circle one)

1 2 3 4 5 6   (152)   When you come right down to it, the main reason for sexual relations is bringing children into the world.

1 2 3 4 5 6   (153)   It is embarrassing to a mother to have her child oppose her when friends or neighbors are present.

1 2 3 4 5 6   (154)   Children should not be allowed to refuse parental requests and commands.

1 2 3 4 5 6   (155)   Mothers should do everything they can to discourage their young sons from playing with dolls.

1 2 3 4 5 6   (156)   A two-year-old should be permitted to play with his (her) bowel movements.

1 2 3 4 5 6   (157)   Parents should be careful not to make any distinctions between what they expect of their little girls and their little boys.

1 2 3 4 5 6   (158)   It is unreasonable for parents to become very angry when their two-year-old repeatedly opens drawers and spills the contents on the floor.

1 2 3 4 5 6   (159)   During childbirth a mother's health is often seriously damaged.

1 2 3 4 5 6   (160)   A mother should never back down once she has told her child not to do something.

1 2 3 4 5 6   (161)   Mothers have every right to get angry at children who are always trying to find out if they mean what they say.

1 2 3 4 5 6   (162)   It is quite understandable that a woman should not want to have sexual relations while she is pregnant.

1 2 3 4 5 6   (163)   If a child makes occasioal slips after he (she) has been toilet trained, his (her) slips should be ignored.

1 2 3 4 5 6   (164)   When a mother limits a child's expression of angry feelings, she does it for his (her) own good.

1 2 3 4 5 6   (165)   It is perfectly all right to allow children to touch their genitals.

1 2 3 4 5 6   (166)   Children should be raised so that everyone in the neighborhood feels they are good children.

1	2	3	4	5	6
Strongly agree	Moderately agree	Slightly agree	Slightly disagree	Moderately disagree	Strongly disagree

(Circle one)

1 2 3 4 5 6 (167) A child should be permitted to express his (her) opinions freely.

1 2 3 4 5 6 (168) Mothers never get angry with their children.

1 2 3 4 5 6 (169) Menstruation is rightly called ''the curse''.

1 2 3 4 5 6 (170) When a two-year-old refuses to do what his (her) parents ask, he (she) should not be allowed to get away with it.

1 2 3 4 5 6 (171) Boys should be taught to be independent at an earlier age than girls.

1 2 3 4 5 6 (172) The pain of childbirth is so great that a woman sometimes wonders if it's worthwhile.

1 2 3 4 5 6 (173) There is nothing to worry about if a two-year-old has temper tantrums.

1 2 3 4 5 6 (174) The child who shows his (her) anger frequently is badly brought up.

1 2 3 4 5 6 (175) Children of two-and-a-half should be made to eat their food for the sake of their health, even if they protest strongly.

1 2 3 4 5 6 (176) Hospitals send mothers home too soon after the child is born.

1 2 3 4 5 6 (177) A good child does not disobey his (her) mother's orders.

1 2 3 4 5 6 (178) A child should be permitted to talk about his (her) bowel movements and urination whenever he (she) wishes.

1 2 3 4 5 6 (179) Nowadays there is hardly any point in getting a little girl dressed up.

1 2 3 4 5 6 (180) Three-year-old children have a right to their own opinions and ought to express them even if their parents disagree.

1 2 3 4 5 6 (181) Being able to watch while she gives birth is one of the most thrilling experiences of a mother's life.

1	2	3	4	5	6
Strongly agree	Moderately agree	Slightly agree	Slightly disagree	Moderately disagree	Strongly disagree

(Circle one)

1 2 3 4 5 6   (182)   It is unfair for a mother to expect different things from a little girl than she does from a little boy.

1 2 3 4 5 6   (183)   A mother has a right to feel angry when her child stands right in front of her and breaks his (her) own toys.

1 2 3 4 5 6   (184)   Once parents have decided on a rule, children should follow it without any back-talk.

1 2 3 4 5 6   (185)   By the time children are four, they are getting a little old for imaginary friends or make-believe games.

1 2 3 4 5 6   (186)   Husbands do not usually give their wives enough support or help during pregnancy.

1 2 3 4 5 6   (187)   It is important that boys learn to act likes boys and girls learn to act like girls, but a mother does not need to be concerned about this when her children are only three years old.

1 2 3 4 5 6   (188)   When one thinks of how often she was told "no" as a child, its easier to let children have their own ways.

1 2 3 4 5 6   (189)   A three-year-old should not be told how babies are made.

1 2 3 4 5 6   (190)   A woman wants to be able to call on her mother for help when she returns from the hospital with her newborn baby.

1 2 3 4 5 6   (191)   It is better for a three-year-old to be imaginative than realistic.

1 2 3 4 5 6   (192)   A child should be permitted in the bathroom even if one of his (her) parents is in there.

1 2 3 4 5 6   (193)   When a child accidentally breaks a valuable object, he (she) should not be punished.

1 2 3 4 5 6   (194)   A mother must be sure that her little girl is dressed to look like a girl.

1 2 3 4 5 6   (195)   It is only natural for a child of three years to be interested in the physical differences between men and women.

1	2	3	4	5	6
Strongly agree	Moderately agree	Slightly agree	Slightly disagree	Moderately disagree	Strongly disagree

(Circle one)

1 2 3 4 5 6   (196)   Mothers never demand that their children will do as they are asked.

1 2 3 4 5 6   (197)   Although a three year old boy may find it hard to ask, he needs as much tenderness as a girl of the same age.

1 2 3 4 5 6   (198)   It is reasonable for a mother to worry when her daughter and her husband become very affectionate with each other.

1 2 3 4 5 6   (199)   A child should obey and like it.

1 2 3 4 5 6   (200)   It is better to take a child off bottle feeding late than early.

1 2 3 4 5 6   (201)   A three or four year old boy is entitled to as much love as a girl of the same age, but he may not need it as much.

1 2 3 4 5 6   (202)   Often a child's anger toward his (her) mother is justified.

1 2 3 4 5 6   (203)   A mother should resist the temptation to take her yound children with her wherever she feels like it.

1 2 3 4 5 6   (204)   A father should not bathe his four-year-old daughter.

1 2 3 4 5 6   (205)   The child who is always quiet and peaceful is the best kind of child to have.

1 2 3 4 5 6   (206)   A child under three is still too young to be curious about where babies come from.

1 2 3 4 5 6   (207)   If her three-year-old girls act like a tomboy and has little interest in girlish things, a mother should do something about it.

1 2 3 4 5 6   (208)   Human conception should be accurately explained to children.

1 2 3 4 5 6   (209)   Children take great delight in annoying parents by pushing the rules to the limit.

1 2 3 4 5 6   (210)   It is sometimes difficult for a mother to know whether or not her child is angry.

1 2 3 4 5 6   (211)   Mothers worry that young children who play with their genitals will be harmed by this play.

1	2	3	4	5	6
Strongly agree	Moderately agree	Slightly agree	Slightly disagree	Moderately disagree	Strongly disagree

(Circle one)

1 2 3 4 5 6   (212)   When three-year-olds want to help you with what you're doing, you should encourage them because that's how they learn.

1 2 3 4 5 6   (213)   When children disobey their mother, it is probably because too much is being asked of them.

1 2 3 4 5 6   (214)   Little boys can be expected to cry just as much as little girls.

1 2 3 4 5 6   (215)   If a mother changes her mind after telling her child to do something, she need not feel quilty about backing down.

1 2 3 4 5 6   (216)   There are many things a three-year-old girl should not do that are all right for a boy.

1 2 3 4 5 6   (217)   Young children seem to ask far too many questions.

1 2 3 4 5 6   (218)   Children are likely to get into something and break it if mothers don't keep their eyes on them every moment.

1 2 3 4 5 6   (219)   A child's curiosity about sex should be curbed if he (she) is to grow into a satisfactory adult.

1 2 3 4 5 6   (220)   Fathers are better than mothers at raising boys.

1 2 3 4 5 6   (221)   It is often easier to let a child do what he (she) shouldn't than to say "no".

1 2 3 4 5 6   (222)   A woman never feels so good physically and mentally as she does when she is pregnant.

1 2 3 4 5 6   (223)   Even though a three-year-old girl may like to play with flashlights, tools, and bugs, she should be encouraged to do other things instead.

1 2 3 4 5 6   (224)   A child's objections often make more sense than his (her) mother's rules.

1 2 3 4 5 6   (225)   When children are being destructive they are expressing anger at their mother.

1 2 3 4 5 6   (226)   What you read in books about a boy being afraid of having his penis cut off is just nonsense.

1 2 3 4 5 6   (227)   There are times in the lives of three-year-olds when they need to be with people other than their mothers.

1	2	3	4	5	6
Strongly agree	Moderately agree	Slightly agree	Slightly disagree	Moderately disagree	Strongly disagree

(Circle one)

1 2 3 4 5 6   (228)   A woman's life is really not complete unless she has a child.

1 2 3 4 5 6   (229)   No matter how hurried parents might be, they always take time to listen to their child's complaints and requests.

1 2 3 4 5 6   (230)   The child of three who spends his (her) time playing happily at home is better off than the one who is always out with playmates.

1 2 3 4 5 6   (231)   It's a waste of time teaching little boys of three how to act like men and teaching little girls of three how to act like women because they're still too young to learn.

1 2 3 4 5 6   (232)   One of the sacrifices a mother must make is to let her young children have their own way even when she thinks they are wrong.

1 2 3 4 5 6   (233)   By the time a boy is three or four years old he should be taught to be "a little man".

Author Index

Subject Index